Adobe Photoshop™
Handbook

PHOTOSHOP 3 EDITION

Adobe Photoshop™
Handbook

PHOTOSHOP 3 EDITION

Mark Siprut

RANDOM HOUSE
ELECTRONIC PUBLISHING

New York   Toronto   London   Sydney   Auckland

To my wife, Anna, for her inspiration, support, and friendship

Contents
at a Glance

Contents

C H A P T E R   2

Setting Up Your System   21

CHAPTER   3

Configuring Photoshop   *51*

CHAPTER 4

Input   103

CHAPTER 5

Tools and Palettes   145

CHAPTER 6

Image Selection and Masking   209

CHAPTER 9

Filters and Plug-ins   359

CHAPTER 10

Compositing   *431*

CHAPTER 11

Output   *475*

CHAPTER 12

Multimedia   521

CHAPTER 13

Case Studies   549

Foreword

February 1995 marks the fifth anniversary of the introduction of Adobe Photoshop. Over the course of five years, Adobe Photoshop has become the hub of desktop imaging, enabling an explosion of desktop color publishing with continuous-tone images.

Adobe Systems has gone to great lengths to keep Adobe Photoshop on the leading edge of image editing. However, the success of Adobe Photoshop cannot be attributed to the product alone. Adobe Photoshop has given rise to, and in turn, has been supported by scores of companies and products, including software and hardware developers and training providers. The *Adobe Photoshop Handbook* is exactly such a product.

Like Adobe Photoshop, the *Adobe Photoshop Handbook* broke new ground when introduced by leading Photoshop experts David Biedney and Bert Monroy in 1991. With the 2.5 Edition update, the baton was passed to Mark Siprut, who made a great reference guide even better. With this new Version 3 edition of the *Adobe Photoshop Handbook*, Mark Siprut continues to demonstrate his mastery of desktop color and of Adobe Photoshop 3 in particular.

The *Adobe Photoshop Handbook* serves as an excellent reference guide, with full chapters dedicated to fundamentals such as input, color correction, filters, and mask generation.

If you are new to Adobe Photoshop and the world of desktop color publishing, you will find the *Adobe Photoshop Handbook* a great learning complement to the documentation tutorials provided with the product. More experienced users of Adobe Photoshop will find invaluable the in-depth case studies and the Color Gallery featuring the works of some of the world's leading Photoshop artists.

Great software is like a living being. Each new version is merely a snapshot of an ongoing development process that refines and distills the thinking of a team of creative individuals pursuing a common objective. The *Adobe Photoshop Handbook*, Photoshop 3 edition echoes this dedication to excellence and continued refinement that will benefit all of our users as they strive to get the most out of Adobe Photoshop 3.

Bryan Lamkin
Senior Product Marketing Manager
Adobe Systems Incorporated

Preface

I wrote the *Adobe Photoshop Handbook* with the Photoshop artist in mind. The book provides the kind of practical advice and techniques that you usually learn only through real-life experience and years of trial and error. This is the third edition in the Handbook series; the books have become progressively more dense as Adobe Photoshop has become more complex. Listen to what artists are saying about Photoshop version 3:

> Version 3.0 is a radical departure from 2.5. The layers will revolutionize the way commercial illustrations are done, because they give the artist freedom to experiment at no risk. You don't have to save 10-15 copies because the client may want to make changes—you save one version with 15 different layers.
> —Wendy Grossman, Illustrator

> Photoshop 3.0 is an example of a better interface. In 2.5 I would have to jump through hoops to do what I can in 3.0 with ease. Now that hoop jumping time and energy can be expended into the artistic process.
> —Greg Vander Houwen, Photographer

> Photoshop 3.0 is definitely a step beyond 2.5. There are almost too many choices. Many fine artists are still daunted by technology. The technical tool is not transparent; the learning curve is definitely there. Computer artists, unless they have a technical background, will run into many stumbling blocks. But if something is meaningful, it's worth the time and effort it takes. With 3.0 my work has taken another leap forward. I'm doing my best work ever.
> —Diane Fenster, Fine Artist

> The development of each new version of Photoshop really seems to be in step with my needs as I develop as an artist
> —Adam Cohen, Illustrator

You can learn almost any program by methodically plowing through each and every command in sequence, but in Photoshop the tendency is to play with the features, creating "happy accidents." Many of the techniques described in the following chapters were discovered this way, and I encourage you to explore (as long as you keep backups of your master graphics files!). Advises photographer Stephen Johnson, "Get a good scan, and then let your heart be the motivator for the work, not the tools. Be very critical of your own work."

For those of you just starting out with Photoshop, this book contains discussions and techniques that will help you in your quest to produce quality work. If you have already spent some time in the Photoshop universe, you'll appreciate the expert perspectives and more advanced techniques found throughout the chapters.

This book is not, however, a replacement for the *Adobe Photoshop User Guide* included with the program, which describes functional aspects of Photoshop in technical detail. Rather, the goal of this book is to share useful techniques and tips, and to provide creative suggestions for using the feature-rich program. This book will compliment and augment the *User Guide*, explaining how Photoshop's features work together and how the program can be incorporated into the larger picture of visual communication.

I am continually amazed at the depth and complexity of Adobe Photoshop. I constantly discover new subtleties within the program as I explore it (and remember, I work with Photoshop almost full time!). So don't be overwhelmed. Dig in and enjoy!

Book Organization

Although this book is structured for random access, you may want to read it sequentially the first time around, especially if you are new to Photoshop. You should also keep the *Adobe Photoshop User Guide* handy for further reference.

Through the Photoshop Handbook you will discover the many arenas in which Photoshop can be applied: photography, print production, multimedia, video, illustration, fine arts, and more. Depending on your job, some of the program features may be more useful than others. For example, different filters may be appropriate for special animation effects but not for corporate newsletter production.

Topics discussed and demystified in this book include an overview of Photoshop, its uses, and its main features in Chapter 1, "Welcome to Photoshop;" essential system issues and tips for Macintosh *and* Windows users in Chapter 2, "Setting Up Your System;" calibrating your system in Chapter 3, "Configuring Photoshop;" getting a good scan and working with

Photo CDs and digital cameras in Chapter 4, "Input;" the myriad of controls available with the tools and palettes in Chapter 5, "Tools and Palettes;" layers and channels in Chapter 6, "Image Selection and Masking;" manipulating and editing images in Chapter 7, "Image Processing;" color theory and control in Chapter 8, "Color;" creative uses of filters in Chapter 9, "Filters and Plug-ins;" combining images and effects using layers, channels, and calculations in Chapter 10, "Compositing;" how to output images using color digital printers, offset lithography, and video in Chapter 11, "Output;" and preparing images for interactive on-screen presentations in Chapter 12, "Multimedia." The book concludes with case studies from more than 30 talented artists who use Photoshop.

This Book is for Macintosh and Windows Users

Previous versions of the *Adobe Photoshop Handbook* were written for the Macintosh only. For the most part, Photoshop 3.0 functions identically on both the Macintosh and IBM-compatible personal computers running under the Microsoft Windows operating system. This book now serves both platforms. Information specific to Photoshop for Windows has been integrated into each chapter. Wherever possible I point out where the Macintosh and Windows systems differ, so watch for notes and warnings.

Although this book uses Macintosh keyboard instructions, these are easily translated for those of you using the Windows version. Two global assumptions about the keyboard instructions can be made for the Windows user: where you see the Command key mentioned, substitute the Ctrl key, and for the Option key substitute your Alt key.

Acknowledgments

Many people helped with the Photoshop 3 revision of the *Adobe Photoshop Handbook*, contributing artwork and tips, locating facts, and chatting about Photoshop over the phone and on-line. I would like to thank the following:

Special thanks to Michael Roney, a patient and understanding editor.

More special thanks to Anna Stump for copy editing, creative suggestions, and moral support.

Bill Niffenegger created this book's stunning cover art and provided creative and technical advice.

Steve Werner contributed to Chapter 4, "Input," Chapter 8, "Color," and Chapter 11, "Output." Werner is Manager of Training and Development for Rapid Graphics of San Francisco, California. He has taught graphic arts software and electronic prepress at Platt College in San Diego and Universities of California at Los Angeles and San Diego Extension programs.

Steve Shubitz contributed the Windows guidelines to this book. Shubitz is President of Published Perfection!, a La Jolla, California electronic publishing and consulting company providing production, training, and integration for the Windows and Macintosh platforms. Shubitz is a faculty member at The Advertising Arts College where he teaches Desktop Publishing. He has written numerous magazine articles about publishing in Windows and has co-authored three books on desktop publishing.

Andrew Rodney, a photographer and digital artist, contributed to Chapter 9, "Filters and Plug-Ins." Rodney is Vice President of PhotoFX, a chain of hybrid imaging centers based in Santa Fe, New Mexico, which provides digital imaging services and training to both consumers and professionals. He has taught electronic imaging at Winona School of Photography, The Scitex Color Center and The Santa Fe Photographic Workshops. His work has been featured in Photographic Magazine, Camera and Darkroom, Shooters Rag and Photo District News.

Chris Swetlin, a commercial artist working in video and multimedia, contributed to Chapter 12, "Multimedia." Swetlin is the co-owner, with Gary McDaniel, of Mediaweave, a multimedia development company in Fremont, California.

Sandra Alvez, a computer graphic artist at Scripps Research Institute in La Jolla, California, contributed to Chapter 6, "Image Selection and Masking."

Matt Brown, of Adaptive Solutions in Sunnyvale, California, provided a technical review of the book and contributed to Chapter 6, "Image Selection and Masking," and Chapter 10, "Compositing." Brown is the Technical Marketing Manager for the PowerShop 64 Image Processing Accelerator for Photoshop on the Macintosh.

Kai Krause of HSC Software in Santa Barbara, California contributed his Chops to Chapter 10, "Compositing."

Rita Amladi, John Leddy, Brian Lamkin, Tracy Wright, and Sonya Schaefer at Adobe Systems Inc. provided invaluable assistance.

Sybil and Emil Ihrig of VersaTech Associates in Prescott, Arizona provided invaluable professional expertise on the book layout and production.

Charles Levine, vice president and publisher, Random House Reference and Electronic Publishing, provided valuable assistance in coordinating book production.

Additional technical advice and support came from Gerry Yeager of Nelson Photography, San Diego; Bruce Powell and Sharon Powell of Synergy, San Diego; Jeff Raby of TX Unlimited in San Francisco; Ralph L. Mittman of Commercial Press in San Diego; Dan Ziagos, Multimedia Training Consultant at Pacific Bell in San Ramon, California; Kristin Keyes, Susan Kitchens and Julie Sigwart of HSC Software; Gary Dailey and David Methven of DayStar; Chi Huang of Radius; Bart Wilson of PhotoFX in Santa Fe; Keri Walker at Apple Computer Inc.; Linnea Dayton; Jim Abbott, Joe Runde, Lisa Gardner, Marilyn Berwind, Terry McArdle, and Paul McAfee of Kodak; Carol McClendon of Waterside Productions; Kim Haas and Michelle Hassan of McLaen Public Relations; Melkan Khosrovian of Microtek, Inc.; Cindy Czyrak of Image Bank; Sheila Dye of Strata Inc.; Barry Weiss of Adaptive Solutions; Jan Sanborn at Pixar; Tim Gill and Elizabeth Jones of Quark, Inc.; Steve Guttman of Fractal Design, Inc.; Eve Elberg; and Lior Saar of Xaos Tools.

Special thanks to the talented artists who contributed their images to the book: Joseph Bellacera, Eric Benson, Alan Brown, Dan Burkholder, Craig Carlson, Nino Cocchiarella, Adam Cohen, Hagit Cohen, Tom Cross,

Margaret Evans, Sarah Everding, Nick Fain, Diane Fenster, Ed Foster, Charly Franklin, Craig Freeman, Wendy Grossman, Francois Guerin, David Herrold, Emil Ihrig, Stephen Johnson, Sanjay Kothari, Dorothy Simpson Krause, Ellen Land-Weber, John Lund, Gary McDaniel, Hiroshi Miyazaki, Bert Monroy, Rick Nease, Bill Niffenegger, Merrill Nix, Greg Notzelman, Jean-Francois Podevin, Guy Powers, Andrew Rodney, Mike Roney, Philip Rostron, Larry Scher, Jeff Schewe, Sharon Steuer, Anna Stump, Rob Sturtz, Chris Swetlin, Cher Threinen-Pendarvis, Terry Toyama, Joseph Tracy, Ellen Van Going, Varden Studios, Greg Vander Houwen, and Lanny Webb.

Photo CD images were scanned by ZZYX in Los Angeles, California, thanks to Bob Goldstein.

Stock photography images were provided on CD ROM by CD Folios Sky, Cloud Gallery from Mary and Michael, CMDC Stock Photos, Comstock Digital Photography from Comstock, Inc., Digital Photographics from Husom & Rose Photographics, Digital Stock Inc., D'pix Folio from D'pix, Inc., Fresco from Xaos Tools Inc., The Image Bank, Classic Textures from Pixar, PhotoDisc Inc., and PhotoSphere.

Of course, Photoshop couldn't be thoroughly explored without the necessary hardware and software, including the following products, which were made available by their manufacturers: Radius SuperMac PressView 21•T monitor, and the Thunder II GX•1360 accelerated video card; DayStar Digital Charger accelerator, Turbo 040 processor upgrade, Power Pro 601 Power PC upgrade, and Colorimeter 24 Precision Display Callibrator; Microtek 45T Film Scanner and 35T Film Scanner; Wacom ArtZ ADB Digitizing Tablet from Wacom Technology Corp; and Fujitsu Dynamo 128 Mb Magneto Optical drive from Fujitsu Computer Products of America.

The following companies also provided assistance: Adobe Corporation, Alias Research Inc., Alien Skin Software, Andromeda Software, Inc., Apple Inc., Applied Graphics Technologies, Calgari, Electronics for Imaging, DayStar Digital, Equilibrium Technologies, Delta Tao Software, Inc., Eastman Kodak Co., Fifth Generation Systems, Focoltone Ltd., Fractal Design Corporation, Gryphon Software, HSC Software, Imspace Systems, InSoftware, Leaf Systems Inc., Light Source, Macromedia, Mainstay, Micro Frontier, Newspaper Association of America, Pantone Inc., Pixar, Pre-Press Technology, Quark, Inc., Ray Dream Inc., Savitar, Second Glance Software, S. H. Pierce and Co., Silicon Wizards Inc., Solutions, Inc., Specular International, Strata, Symantec Corp., Total Integration, Inc., Toyo Ink Co., Trumatch Inc., Ultimatte Corp., VideoFusion, Vision Software Inc., Vividus Corp., and Xaos Tools.

Thanks to the School of Art, Design and Art History at San Diego State University for support. And thanks to Maile Sakamoto for brightening this book with her smile.

Last but not least, thanks to David Biedny and Bert Monroy for their initial vision and continuing support.

Mark Siprut
San Diego, California

1

Welcome to Photoshop

Since its release in 1990, Adobe Photoshop has revolutionized the world of computer graphics and image manipulation, bringing the capabilities of million-dollar color publishing systems such as Scitex and Quantel PaintBox down to the level of the personal computer. Photoshop maintains all the essential power of the older dedicated systems, while adding sets of modular, creative tools that exceed anything that has come before—at any price (Figure 1–1).

Photoshop's deep feature set and extensible architecture have made it an indispensable tool for anyone working in digital imaging and production. With the release of version 3 for Macintosh and Windows, Photoshop has become even more powerful and useful. Its system of modular palettes allows users to customize its interface for personal needs and working styles. Its support of 24 Alpha channels and powerful masking tools is augmented with the capability of supporting up to 99 possible independent image layers and a background, allowing vastly greater flexibility for experimentation and the creation of composite images. Its extensible "plug-in" architecture supports 48 native Photoshop special effects and production filters, and literally hundreds more from third-party manufacturers. Its multiple color modes, color correction and separation capabilities, file format support, and links to high-end systems continue to delight production specialists.

This introductory chapter provides an overview of Photoshop's position in the computer graphics world, its applications, and its main features.

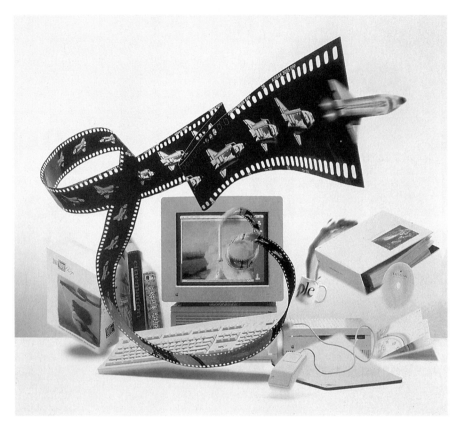

Figure 1–1
Photographer John Lund
demonstrates the power
of Photoshop.
(© John Lund)

MACINTOSH AND PC

This book has been written for both Macintosh users and PC users running Microsoft Windows. Information specific to Photoshop for Windows has been integrated into each chapter. Where ever possible we have pointed out where the Macintosh and Windows systems differ. Most of the screenshots were captured from a Macintosh computer, but where they differ for Windows, we have tried to present both. Watch for notes and warnings.

For the most part, Photoshop now functions virtually identically on all platforms, so whatever the platform you work on, this book is for you.

Although this book uses Macintosh keyboard instructions, these are easily translated for those of you using the Windows version of Photoshop. Two global assumptions about the keyboard instructions can be made for the Windows user: Where you see the Command key mentioned, substitute the Ctrl key; and for the Option key, substitute the Alt key.

Who Uses Photoshop?

The audience for Photoshop is a large one. In only a few years, this program has become the standard image editing, image compositing, image finishing, and prepress production program for photographers, designers, illustrators, fine artists, multimedia producers, printers, and other professionals from a broad range of disciplines.

Photographers

With the advent of digital photographs and cameras, large image libraries on CD-ROM, and the general demand in the graphics industry for images on disc, most photographers have reason to use Photoshop. A great many photographers, both amateur and professional, already consider the program indispensable to their work. Photoshop is an electronic darkroom. All the procedures that a photographer goes through to make a finished photograph can be done in Photoshop: tonal adjustment, contrast control, color balance, sharpening, scaling, cropping, etc. Special effects and image compositing previously created in the darkroom, requiring hours of valuable time and costly film and chemicals, can now be done in minutes at moderate cost using Photoshop. The program interface encourages creative experimentation that is expensive and imprecise in the darkroom.

Fine and Commercial Artists

Photoshop's extensive array of tools and special effects offer artists more flexibility than they have ever experienced with any other medium. Fine artists can experiment and explore without wasting canvas and paper, and commercial artists can make as many changes as clients demand. Drawing and painting from scratch with a digitizing tablet and pressure-sensitive stylus simulates the artist's traditional tools. Filters can encourage endless hours of experimentation to create striking and exotic visual fantasies. Photographs can be manipulated to create special effects never before possible with a microcomputer. Many artists are now making lithographs, monoprints, photographs, and digital fine art prints from images created in Photoshop.

Multimedia Artists and Producers

Multimedia producers can use Photoshop in a variety of ways. They can perform frame-by-frame and global manipulation on digital video and animation frames imported into Photoshop. These movies can then be combined in presentations to be played on other computers or output to videotape. Photoshop can also be used to create screen interface designs, buttons, and backgrounds. The ATM-based anti-aliased text is unequaled for smooth onscreen type for use in animated presentations, and Photoshop works well with such multimedia programs as Macromedia Director, Adobe Premiere, Kodak Arrange–It and Create–It Photo CD software, Vividus Cinemation, and VideoFusion Quick Flix.

Print Publishers and Corporate Communicators

Print publishers have found Photoshop to be an invaluable production tool for enhancing, correcting, manipulating, and preparing for press both grayscale and color images. For the prepress world, Photoshop boasts sophisticated color correction and tonal adjustment and separation capabilities. It can communicate with the high-end systems via Pixar, Targa, and Scitex CT formats, which are directly supported as an output option. Other production features include CMYK preview and support for seven color edit modes and 33 graphics file formats.

Service Bureaus

Photoshop allows service bureaus to offer services far beyond their typesetting roots. One major service is creating color separations, providing the film for printers. This has always been a costly process; using Photoshop, a service bureau can now handle it at a fraction of the traditional cost.

Advertising

Photoshop is now used in the advertising industry to create full-color comprehensives. Traditionally, "comps" have been produced by hand using pencils, markers, or airbrush at an enormous cost in time, money, and legibility. High-end systems were employed for better results, but at an even higher cost. Photoshop puts the capability to create comps in the hands of the art director, designer, and the board artist. The production department therefore has more control over the final production phases, thus reducing costly and time-consuming redos.

Scientific and Medical Applications

Many of the image-processing features in Photoshop (such as the convolution, high-pass, and sharpening filters, multichannel mathematics, and the ability to read raw multiple-channel data files from sources such as satellite data) appeal to professionals working in various scientific endeavors, from a doctor making a diagnosis to a scientist publishing a new theory.

Manufacturing

Technical drawings and product photographs can be created and manipulated in Photoshop for manuals and visual aids in manufacturing, production and presentation.

The Digital Revolution

As a descendant of both desktop paint programs and high-end electronic prepress systems, Adobe Photoshop occupies a unique place in the world of graphics and imagery. At the dawn of the 1980s—not that long ago—graphics, fine arts, and printing were still in the analog era. The tools of the trade were paint and brush, X-Acto knife and hot wax, and camera lens and enlarger. We are now witnessing a digital revolution in the tools and technology of art and communication.

But what about the images these new tools are used to produce? How are artists reacting to pixels versus pigment? When the graphics world started going digital with the release of the Macintosh personal computer in 1984, image makers were justifiably concerned mainly with the process and with technology. Those bells and whistles are still exciting, but today artists are increasingly aware that technology in itself is not an end. Digital image makers realize that they are contributing to a new aesthetic. They are using Photoshop as a tool to help them realize their personal artistic vision, decrying images that simply show off what technology can do. Content is at the forefront of discussion.

Following are several examples of how artists from different fields are reacting to Photoshop and digital imaging in general:

ILLUSTRATION

Adam Cohen is an illustrator (Figure 1–2):

> I was an airbrush artist before I began using the computer. What a nightmare: The masking was tedious, frustrating, and time consuming. With Photoshop I can complete a piece in two days that used to take me one month.

Figure 1–2   "Urban Landscape" by Adam Cohen (© Adam Cohen)

Figure 1–3
"Cowboy Walking by
Tent" by Dan Burkholder
(© Dan Burkpholder)

PHOTOGRAPHY

Dan Burkholder is a fine arts photographer (Figure 1–3):

> I'm certain the first time a progressive cave artist picked up a piece of charcoal instead of the accepted/standard rock or natural chalk, he was met with looks of doubt and disbelief. "That isn't real petroglyphy!" Today I'm constantly approached by fellow photographers—invariably ones currently enamored with infrared film or hand-colored black-and-white prints—who plead the current version of that prehistoric whine: "That isn't real photography." What a crock!
>
> In these early stages of digital imaging we'll see some good work, and lots of mediocre work. Walk past any music store in a mall and you're likely to see an electronic organ that is wondrously easy to play. In fact, with only two fingers you can be playing the base and rhythm in no time at all. Does this make you a musician? Of course not. It makes you (or it would make me anyway) a lay person standing before a great deal of good electronics. Digital photography is following exactly the same path.

Figure 1–4
"Hope in Sight,"
an editorial
illustration, addresses the
small yet significant
gains that handicapped
people have made
in society.
(© Rick Nease, *The
Toledo Blade*)

EDITORIAL ILLUSTRATION

Rick Nease is a newspaper editorial art editor for *The Toledo Blade* (Figure 1–4):

> Because of the nature of newspaper work, speed is of the essence. Photoshop allows me to create beautiful, full color illustrations in a fraction of the time it takes to create them conventionally.

COMPREHENSIVES

Rob Sturtz is a comp artist (Figure 1–5):

> Up until the early '60s, artists drew with pastels, color pencils, and/or pen & ink wash. Around this time, markers were introduced. A limited color palette and only one nib size hampered their wide acceptance, but by the mid '60s, as more colors and forms of markers appeared, artists had to make the transition from pastels to markers. Adapt or die.
>
> A current revolution/transition is occurring now with computers and the artist. Early drawing programs and color printers could not compete visually with a marker comp. But now, with programs like Adobe Photoshop and incredible color printers, that has changed. Computer comps will become the standard. Adapt or die.

Figure 1–5
Concept board comp art
for Connecticut
Marketing Associates
by Rob Sturtz
(© Rob Sturtz)

Changes in the Printing Industry

To prepare for printing in the past, a prepress department had to shoot black and white images as half tone screens to strip into the film which had been photographed from the layout pasted up by hand. Color images had to go to a color separation house to be separated to film for stripping into the final film composite. Now images can be scanned, prepared in Photoshop, placed into page layout programs with type, and other graphics and color separated electronically. These radical technological changes have caused job roles to shift throughout the graphics industry.

Ethics, Copyright, and Responsibilities of the Artist

Because Photoshop is such a powerful tool, artists have a great deal of personal responsibility when using it. "Borrowing," appropriating, or scanning someone else's image, whether photographic or painted, famous or obscure, to use in your own work without permission is against the laws of copyrights and good ethics. Even images in the public domain may belong to a collection or be published in a book, and permission to use them must be granted.

Photoshop can be used as a creation tool (drawing and painting from scratch), a manipulation tool (compositing, applying filters to scanned or otherwise input images), or as a retouching and finishing tool (color balance, tonal adjustments, sharpening, cropping, photographic restoration). Creating from scratch is obviously safe in terms of copyrights. Manipulating your own image is fine. Respectful retouching, adjusting tones, or color balance of someone else's image with permission is fine. Manipulating someone else's image for editorial comment or parody is risky, but you may get away with it if you are doing fine art, not for profit or publication.

Consider the following:

- Almost every photograph, illustration, melody, or piece of text belongs to the person or company who created or owns it.
- Whether or not you feel appropriation is ethical and valid as an art form, if you use an appropriated image commercially, or if you cause someone else to lose money because you have appropriated their image, think twice.
- If you want to use someone else's image, you must have the permission or the right to use it. Even stock photos purchased on CDs have usage parameters.
- Obtaining permission to use an image does not, however, give you permission to change it. Even something as minor as cropping an image without permission may cause problems.

When using someone's image with permission, follow these guidelines (unless you have specific permission to manipulate the image):

- Use it only for the specific purpose for which you have permission.
- Do not crop.
- Scale in proportion—hold the Shift key down when scaling or make sure that Proportions is checked in the Image Size dialog. Otherwise you will stretch an image out of its proper shape.
- Do not radically change the tone or colors.
- Do not combine it with other images.
- Do not place text over an image.
- Give credit to the artist/photographer.

Beyond copyright law, artists using Photoshop should treat their own original images with respect. A manipulated image used in an advertising campaign or the *National Enquirer* can be taken with a grain of salt by the public, but that same image published in a major newspaper or magazine may cause the public to lose trust. For example, *Time* magazine recently caused an uproar because it used an image of O.J. Simpson on its cover that had been digitally darkened and made more sinister by an artist.

Landscape photographer Stephen Johnson states, "With regard to photojournalism, documentary, or traditional landscape photography, the point is not to assault the integrity of the image but, by careful finishing (just like in the darkroom), to make it the most striking and beautiful image possible."

Photoshop Main Features

RAM: Working in Real Time

There's an old computer adage many of you might be familiar with: "You can never have enough processing speed or RAM." RAM is random access memory, a temporary storage space that holds your current work. Those of you who work with large color files are all to aware of the time required to apply certain effects to color images. However, this speed issue has become less of a problem with Photoshop's optimized code, System 7's and Window's 32-bit addressing schemes, larger SIMMs chips (which allow you to easily install more RAM in your machine), Photoshop and third-party software solutions, and the availability of accelerator cards featuring powerful, dedicated processors.

It is not unusual now to operate with at least 20 to 30 megabytes of RAM, regardless of your platform. Accelerated 24-bit video cards and add-on DSP (digital signal processor) accelerator cards, such as the Radius/SuperMac Thunder II GX, the Daystar Charger boards, and the Radius PhotoEngine, which are specific to Photoshop functions, can increase speed even further. Some cards claim to accelerate operations by as much as 3600 times.

You can also effectively increase productivity and performance by using Photoshop's Quick Edit feature (available from the Acquire submenu under the File menu), which allows you to work only a portion of the overall image, or by using a third-party application such as FITS Imaging's Live Picture, distributed in the United States by HSC Software. Live Picture allows users to assemble and edit multiple-megabyte images in real time using a resolution-independent mathematical representation of the bitmapped image.

Support for Multiple Open Documents

Photoshop was one of the first high-resolution Macintosh graphics programs to support multiple open documents (Figure 1–6). Full editing functions (cut, copy, and paste) are supported between documents. Colors and palettes selected and open in one document apply to all other open documents. This is great for using the colors in one image as a palette for another.

Cross-Platform Flexibility

Photoshop 2.5 provided an almost identical set of tools for Macintosh, Windows, Silicon Graphics, and Sun Microsystems. Starting with Version 3, however, Adobe took compatibility one step further by optimizing Photoshop's code to run native on the Power Macintosh, and in 32-bit mode under Windows NT. Photoshop also supports Windows 3.1 and Windows for Workgroups on the PC platform. Now, you can rest assured that you can work with the same files under different operating environments, and that you will also be able to upgrade your hardware platform while maintaining optimum performance with Photoshop.

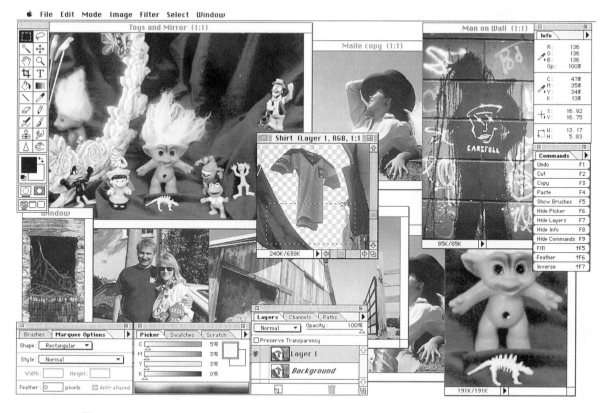

Figure 1–6   Photoshop supports full editing capabilities in multiple open documents.

NOTE: Beginning with version 2.5, Photoshop has been written in the C++ programming language, which is easily translated among major computing platforms, such as Macintosh, Windows, Silicon Graphics, and Sun Microsystems. This has provided an easier path for Photoshop's growth and addition of features. This enhanced "open architecture" has allowed an explosion of third-party plug-ins to augment many functions and tools even beyond the Acquire, Export, and Filters menus. See Chapter 9, "Filters and Plug-ins," for details on these amazing new tools.

Wide Variety of Image-Processing Features

Despite the powerful capabilities of such Macintosh and PC paint, image-editing and image-composition applications as Fractal Design Painter, PixelPaint Professional, Micrografx Picture Publisher, Corel PhotoPaint, Aldus PhotoStyler, Specular Collage, and Live Picture, the image manipulation and enhancement features found in Photoshop stand alone in the desktop graphics world. The variety of filters, image processing tools, and controls for every aspect of an image can be almost overwhelming (Figure 1–7). Many Image controls, such as the Color Balance, Brightness and Contrast, Posterization,

Figure 1–7
An image with a wide variety of filters and curves applied: Special effects previously created in the darkroom, requiring valuable time and costly materials, can now be done in minutes at moderate cost using Photoshop. (© Mark Siprut)

and Hue/Saturation, work in "real-time" on 8- and 24-bit displays. As you change the settings, the screen display responds by displaying the changes instantaneously. Refer to Chapter 7, "Image Processing," for details.

No Screen Redraw

A unique feature of Photoshop is that you can open menus and access the program's tools while the screen is being redrawn without having to wait for the redraw to finish. When working with large, high-resolution images, this time savings can be quite substantial.

DirectSet Entries on Real-Time Color Controllers

Many of the currently available 24-bit color display boards, such as those in the Radius, SuperMac, and RasterOps lines, offer hardware support for DirectSetEntries. Color and brightness changes therefore occur in real time. Photoshop's color correction and processing controls also work in real time with these display boards, allowing you to see changes on the screen interactively with the controls. As you drag a color correction slider, the screen is updated instantly.

Virtual Memory

Although the more RAM the better, Photoshop doesn't totally rely on RAM memory in order to work with large images. By using a hard disk to "emulate" RAM memory, you can manipulate images much larger than the available RAM in your computer.

TIP: Photoshop likes hard-disk space. Lots of it! Make sure that you have at least three to five times the size of the document in free space on your hard disk. The more space you can spare, the better.

Virtual memory is built into Apple's Macintosh System 7 and Microsoft Windows 3.1 and above.

TIP: If you are working in Macintosh System 7, turn off Virtual Memory when working in Photoshop. If you are Running Photoshop under Windows, leave Virtual Memory on.

Although Photoshop uses your startup hard disk as its default scratch disk, its virtual memory can take advantage of multiple hard disks or drive partitions. In the Preferences dialog, select your largest hard disk or partition as the primary scratch disk and another hard disk or partition as your secondary scratch disk. When the primary scratch disk is completely utilized for virtual memory, Photoshop switches to the secondary scratch disk to prevent out-of-memory errors. See Chapter 2, "Setting Up Your System," for how to specify virtual memory and scratch disks.

Variable Resolution

Photoshop can import graphics files scanned or created at almost any resolution. Unlike most color bitmap programs, which are limited to the resolution of the display, Photoshop's tools work at all resolutions. Photoshop can also handle any resolution output format, ensuring compatibility with output devices. The only limitation is the amount of memory that the user's hardware can handle.

Anti-Aliasing

Anti-aliasing is a technique used to enhance the "softness" of hard edges by minimizing the pixel contrast. Harsh edges can be made to appear very smooth on the screen by the use of lighter and darker shades of an object's color. Essentially, the edges of an object are blended with the background to simulate a smooth transition between the foreground and background objects. Anti-aliasing is built into all of Photoshop's tools (with the exception of the Pencil tool), including type, and can be applied to the edges of selections (Figure 1–8).

Virtual 24-Bit Working Environment

When you work in Photoshop, all operations are calculated and output in 24 bit. The smoothness of 24-bit color on a monitor, displaying up to 16.7 million colors, will be most apparent in subtle value changes such as skin tones, sky, and pastel colors. On an 8-bit monitor, displaying up to 256 colors or tones, these same tones will appear dithered or posterized (unless you are working in black and white). The first time you use the Paintbrush,

Figure 1–8
The mask on the left was selected with anti-aliasing on; the one on the right without anti-aliasing.

Airbrush, or Line tool on a 24-bit monitor, you'll be amazed at the smoothness in the edges of the strokes.

Crazy Eights: Working in 8-Bit?

Even if you are working on an 8-bit (256 color) system, you can still edit images with a greater bit depth. Obviously, this limits the amount of color displayed, though Photoshop will nevertheless edit all the pixels in the image: The image will be displayed in a dithered pattern, which randomly scatters the pixels to make the best use of the colors available. Working in 8 bit is fine for grayscale images because all you need is 256 tones anyway.

It's All Black and White

On the Macintosh platform you can work with Photoshop on a screen which only displays black-and-white or grayscale images. Color images can be manipulated with Photoshop on a black-and-white or grayscale monitor just as if you were working on a color monitor. Although you can't see what you're doing in color, you can read the color data in the Info palette. Photoshop also happens to be a superb image manipulation program for grayscale images, and works quite efficiently on Macintosh systems with monochrome displays. (Photoshop needs a minimum of 8-bit color to run under Windows.) See Chapter 3, "Configuring Photoshop," for details on the program's many display formats and modes.

Filters

With roots in photography, the filters in Photoshop offer an overwhelming range of image-enhancement and manipulation tools. Some are subtle and essential to normal production tasks and others alter images dramatically for creative effects.

One of the most interesting of the native filters to ship with Photoshop is Lighting Effects (new with version 3), which can lend entirely new perspectives to images. Lighting Effects lets you position lighting sources on any side of an image, and choose light style, type, color, intensity, and texture, in a range of possible combinations. Other filters new with version 3 include Dust & Scratches, which allows you to remove these blemishes from scanned images, Mezzotint, the whimsical Clouds, and, most notably, Filter Factory, which actually lets you create new Photoshop filters. See Chapter 9, "Filters," for details.

Extension with Plug-Ins

Photoshop's open architecture allows the use of software extensions called plug-ins, which enhance a wide range of program features: filters, exporting to unique file formats and various printers, acquiring from scanners and digital cameras, saving to unique file formats, editing portions of images, and numerous processing functions. Photoshop 3 shipped with 48 native plug-ins, and third-party software publishers offer literally hundreds more. When placed in the Plug-ins folder/directory, or in a location specified in the Preferences dialog, plug-ins generally appear in the Acquire, Export, and Filter menus (Figure 1–9).

TIP: Check out the PhotoMatic plug-in from DayStar. It allows you to record repetitive tasks in Photoshop as scripts that can be saved for later use.

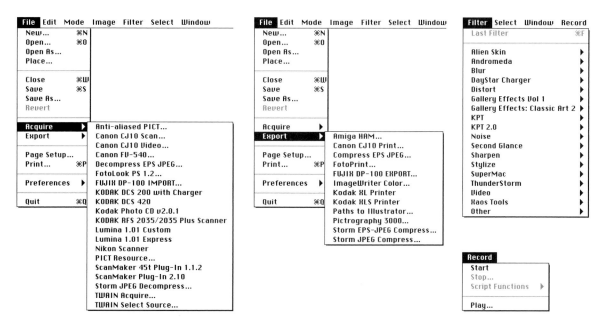

Figure 1–9   Most plug-in filters appear in Photoshop's Filters, Acquire and Export menus.

Image Selection and Masking

Photoshop offers a wide variety of tools and methods of selecting areas in an image, saving the selections, and moving them to other parts of the same image or to other images. Utilizing its anti-aliasing and feathering controls, selections can have crisp, defined edges or very soft ethereal edges. Selections can be combined or subtracted from each other. A selection can be saved as a Channel or Path for use at later time. Precise paths can be drawn with the Pen tool and converted to selections. Paths can be saved with an image to act as mask in order to silhouette the image in another program.

Layers, Masks, and Channels

One of the major limitations of bitmap "paint" and image editing programs has been the difficulty (or impossibility) of maintaining multiple image layers, or levels, normally associated with illustration and object-oriented design software. Adobe Photoshop now supports up to 99 image layers that can be edited independently. This feature is a great leap forward for Photoshop, allowing free experimentation with effects and treatments without altering the overall image. Obviously, it's also a great tool for compositing images.

In addition to these "layers," Photoshop also supports up to 24 *alpha channels* that can be added to an image in order to edit and store selections called *masks* (Figure 1–10). These channels have their roots in the world of video. The next time that you watch television, take note (especially during commercials) of graphics or titles that appear to be suspended over live video, either as opaque or transparent images. This is accomplished with video alpha channels—live masks that are implemented in the hardware of the special-effects devices used in video production. The alpha channels in Photoshop are essentially the same, except that they're made to work with still images.

TIP: Channels and Layers aren't free; they occupy memory. Every Channel and Layer added to a document increases its file size. Make sure you have enough RAM and hard-disk space available before you create a monster that you can't save anywhere.

Figure 1–10
An image
with its channel
being used as a mask in
order to paste in the sky
(© Mark Siprut)

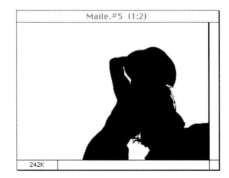

A Channel is analogous to a plate for an individual color in the printing process (Figure 1–11). Normally, when working with a 24-bit color image (which takes up 3 of the 24 channels for the red, green, and blue components), you can have up to 21 channels saved along with the image file. The channels can be loaded as selections into the main image on any Layer or they can store component elements. You can process any of the channels independently, with most of the program's tools and filters. You can work with any Channel while working with any Layer.

NOTE: While working with 24-bit color images, each channel contains 8 bits of information. Channels are not color; they only contain grayscale information. When you copy something into a channel, Photoshop automatically strips color hue information from the pasted image.

See Chapter 6, "Image Selection and Masking," and Chapter 10, "Compositing," for more information on using layers, masks, channels, and Calculate commands.

Figure 1–11
The Channels of an image can be viewed and manipulated independently of each other.

Sophisticated Color Tools

Photoshop gives you absolute control over color in an image, and boasts a variety of sophisticated color tools.

REMAPPING TO ANY COLOR PALETTE

One of the biggest challenges facing multimedia artists and animators is to get the most out of the limitation of 256 colors on the screen at any one time. Photoshop can convert a 24-bit color image into a 256-color image (8-bit) with the highest possible onscreen quality. It can make optimum use of the standard system palette, or create a custom palette based on the colors it finds in the original color file. Users can choose from multiple dithering schemes, or convert to less than 256 colors. (If you want the best-possible quality in displaying a color image on a 4-bit, 16-color graphics cards, Photoshop can do it.) See Chapter 8, "Color," for details on putting these features to work.

COLOR CORRECTION CONTROL

Photoshop not only features the standard brightness and contrast tools found in grayscale programs, but also lets you control each individual color component in an image in ways you've always wanted (and, in some ways, never imagined). All color correction and enhancements features can be applied to entire images or to specific portions. Photoshop also features a Gamut Warning alarm and CMYK Preview, which can be used together with these selective color correction tools to apply ink to individual color plates in precise values. See Chapter 8, "Color," for information on color correction and manipulation controls.

COLOR SEPARATIONS

Photoshop can fully color-separate a color image, breaking it down into its four primary components—cyan, magenta, yellow, and black—which a printer then uses to create four-color-process printing plates. While most programs with this capability separate the file only at printing time, Photoshop does the separation in software, and displays the separated channels and the composite on the screen (Figure 1–11). This allows you to preview the effects of the separation process and manipulate the individual plates before sending them to the output device. Using the Desktop Color Separation (DCS) format, you can export images to other programs like Adobe Illustrator, Macromedia FreeHand, Adobe PageMaker, or QuarkXPress to be separated on pages with full text and illustration art in place. See Chapter 11, "Output," for information on color separation issues.

DUOTONES

In addition to producing process color separations, Photoshop can make spot color separations of black-and-white images as duotones (two colors), tritones (three colors), and quadtones (four colors). Pantone, Trumatch, and other spot separation models are supported for making color choices. See Figures C–2, C–3, and C–4 in the Color Section and Chapter 8, "Color," for more on duotones.

Variety of File Formats

Photoshop can open and save more file formats than most other graphics packages. Besides allowing you to work with almost all of the graphics formats found in the Macintosh and Windows world, Photoshop also supports formats found in higher-end environments, such as Pixar, Scitex CT, and Targa, opening a plethora of possibilities in terms of output options and integration with high-end prepress systems. Many of the limitations of the clipboard and scrapbook in converting different graphic-image file formats have been resolved in Photoshop. See Chapter 3, "Configuring Photoshop," for a look at using the program with different file formats. Refer to Appendix A for explanations of formats supported by Photoshop.

Dynamic Data Sharing

Photoshop supports the Mac's Publish and Subscribe feature, which lets you share data dynamically among different applications. For example, a Photoshop image placed in a QuarkXPress document always automatically updates to reflect any changes made to the Photoshop file. See Chapter 3, "Configuring Photoshop," for details on creating dynamic links with other applications.

Compatibility with Object-Oriented Programs

Photoshop can import object-oriented PICT files generated in most vector programs and Postscript files from Adobe Illustrator for raster file (bitmapped) processing with filters and other tools. You can also export paths created in Photoshop back to Illustrator. See Chapter 11, "Output," for details on using Adobe Illustrator and Photoshop together.

Summary

As you can see, there are numerous reasons why Photoshop has become the graphics standard it is today. Its power and flexibility are truly unmatched. Because this program is so complex, it takes perseverance and patience to master it. Refer to the Photoshop User Guide and this book to help you navigate and explore. Remember that Photoshop is just a tool—use it ethically to achieve your creative goals.

The next two chapters will show you how to best configure Photoshop and your computer system for the kind of work you want to do, with special attention given to choosing hardware peripherals and configuring Photoshop preferences.

C H A P T E R

2

Setting Up Your System

Photoshop will only work as well as the computer system on which it's running—and Photoshop is a very hungry application in terms of processing power, storage requirements, and hardware support. You may be one of the millions of users already publishing in an office or corporate communications department with hardware more than adequate for Microsoft Word, Microsoft Excel, Adobe Persuasion, Adobe Illustrator, CorelDRAW!, and Adobe PageMaker. But that's no guarantee that you have enough horsepower for Photoshop. If you already use an earlier version of the program, but your hardware is barely powerful enough, sit down, count to ten, and accept that Photoshop 3 requires even more muscle. (Of course, your specific system requirements will vary according to personal Photoshop needs and your plans for the future.)

This chapter describes what you need for a smoothly running Photoshop system, and makes specific suggestions as to the numerous hardware options available. It looks at the idiosyncrasies of the Macintosh and Windows in relationship to Photoshop, and discusses the tools and technologies for input, display, and accelerated performance.

System Requirements

Have you seen someone using Photoshop throw a fit because applying a filter took 120 seconds? How much of a difference is two minutes going to make in your life? It could make a big difference if your job requires you to apply that filter 30 times a day. That adds up to 60 minutes per day! Five hours per week! One hundred fifty . . . well, you get the idea. The point is that having the fastest machine possible can result in some astonishing time savings. The faster your machine, the faster Photoshop will work.

If the following hardware recommendations sound daunting, remember that prior to Photoshop, most image processing capabilities were available only on a $50,000 system.

TIP: Mount a mirror on the wall behind your computers so that you can easily see where to plug and unplug peripheral devices. This way you won't have to crawl over the all gear (Figure 2–1).

Macintosh

For Photoshop 3, Adobe recommends a minimum system configuration of an Apple Macintosh II computer with a 68020 or greater processor, Apple System Software 7 or greater, at least 6 Mb (megabytes) of application random access memory (RAM) —11 Mb on a Power Mac, and at least 20 Mb of free hard disk space. Application RAM is the memory left over after meeting the System's memory requirements. Now, let's get realistic. Saying you can run Photoshop with a setup like this is like saying you can get from New York to L.A. on foot. You can do it (especially if you work with low-resolution images) but it's going to take a heck of a long time. We realize that most of you aren't going to run Photoshop on Quadras or PowerMacs with 256 megabytes of RAM, 2 Gb of hard disk space, 21-inch color-calibrated, accelerated monitors, and DSP boards—although some might call that the "minimum" configuration!

To make the best use of Photoshop and to greatly reduce your waiting time, use the fastest Macintosh or Power Mac you can afford. For Photoshop to run effectively, use a 68040 or above processor with System 7.1.2 or greater, 20 Mb of RAM, a hard disk with at least 60 Mb of space, CD double

Figure 2–1
Mount a mirror on the wall behind your computers so that you can easily see where to plug and unplug peripheral devices.
(© Mark Siprut)

speed drive, and a 24-bit display. If you can't afford to rush out and buy the latest model, consider adding a CPU accelerator or Power PC upgrade to your machine. Accelerators are discussed in this chapter after the sections on displays and disk drives. You should also consider removable storage media such as a SyQuest, Bernoulli, or magneto-optical drive.

If you are a power user, you should also have a Power Macintosh with at least 56 Mb to 256 Mb of RAM, one big hard disk (at least one Gb) and tape backup.

Windows

Choosing and setting up a system to run the Windows version of Photoshop is far more complex than setting up a Macintosh system because of the wide choice of hardware, the lack of standards, and the archaic nature of DOS, which is required to run Windows 3.1 Fortunately, the highly competitive nature of the PC platform produces relatively inexpensive hardware that can run Photoshop.

Adobe recommends a minimum system of an Intel i386, i486, or Pentium processor, DOS 5.0, Windows 3.1 or Windows NT 3.5, 10 Mb of RAM (16Mb for Windows NT), at least 50 Mb of free hard disk space, and a 256 color VGA display.

For Photoshop to run all operations smoothly for a variety of image processing tasks, you really need at least a 486 class computer running at 66 MHz, 16 megabytes of memory, a 500 Mb hard drive, a CD double-speed drive, a 24 bit video card, and a multisync color monitor.

If you do a significant amount of work in Photoshop we suggest one of the new 66 or 90 MHz Pentium class 486 machines equipped with 32 Mb of memory, a one Gb SCSI (Small Computer System Interface) hard drive, and a 24 bit video card. Your video card should use the PCI (Peripheral Component Interconnect) or VESA (Video Electronics Standards Association) bus to dramatically speed up screen display.

If you spend most of your day in Photoshop, then expand this Pentium system with 64 Mb to 200 Mb of RAM, and a 21-inch multisync monitor.

WINDOWS TIP: If you're trying to launch Photoshop under Windows on a 10 Mb to 12 Mb machine and you get a "Not Enough RAM" message, it's because you don't have enough "free RAM" to run the program. You'll need to invest in additional RAM for your PC (see below), or try to "rem out" lots of items in the WIN.INI file. You could also reduce the amount of memory allocated to your disk cache (discussed later in this chapter).

These hardware recommendations are only half of the equation. Next you need to properly configure your system software for Photoshop.

Setting up a Mac for Photoshop

To optimize the performance of your Macintosh (using System 7 and above), open the Memory dialog in the Control Panels folder under the File menu (Figure 2–2). Set the System Disk Cache to the lowest number possible (32). Turn off Virtual Memory and turn on 32 bit addressing.

Photoshop is designed to use the 32-bit addressing capability of System 7 and higher. This capability means that a program can use more than 8 Mb of RAM. Macintosh models released earlier than the Macintosh IIci and IIfx do not recognize 32-bit addressing. To access more than 8 Mb of RAM by accessing 32 bit addressing on these older computers use MODE32 by Connectix Corporation (Figure 2–3). After installing it in your System folder, turn MODE32 on by choosing it in the Control Panels under the Apple Menu.

Setting up Windows for Photoshop

After Windows is properly installed you need to optimize its performance. Photoshop and Windows do a lot of disk thrashing (reading and writing) so you need at least a 2 Mb disk *cache*. A cache is software that reserves an area of memory to hold frequently used data and is much faster than accessing your hard disk. Windows includes a disk cache called SmartDrive and many other vendors offer suitable caches that will dramatically increase the performance of Windows and most Windows applications, including Photoshop.

Once your cache is properly installed the next step is to configure a *permanent swap file* (Figure 2–4). A permanent swap file is Microsoft terminology for virtual memory. It is a contiguous area of your hard disk that Windows

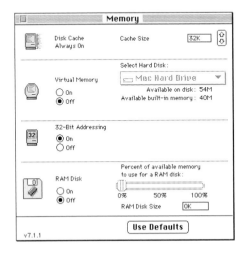

Figure 2–2
In the Memory control panel, set the System Disk Cache to 32K, turn off Virtual Memory and turn on 32-bit addressing.

Figure 2–3
Use MODE 32 to access more than 8 MB of RAM by recognizing 32 bit addressing on older Macs.

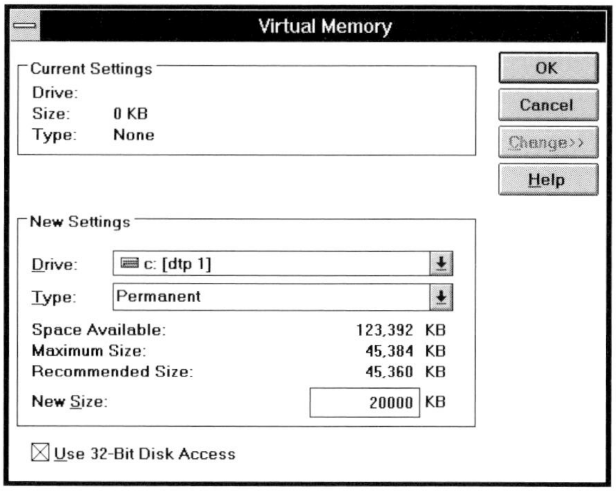

Figure 2–4
Setting up a Windows
permanent swap file and
32-bit file access

```
┌─────────────────────────────────────────────────────┐
│ �▢                Virtual Memory               │
├─────────────────────────────────────────────────────┤
│ ┌─Current Settings──────────────────┐   ┌────────┐  │
│ │ Drive:                            │   │   OK   │  │
│ │ Size:    0 KB                     │   └────────┘  │
│ │ Type:    None                     │   ┌────────┐  │
│ │                                   │   │ Cancel │  │
│ └───────────────────────────────────┘   └────────┘  │
│                                          ┌────────┐  │
│                                          │Change>>│  │
│                                          └────────┘  │
│                                          ┌────────┐  │
│                                          │  Help  │  │
│                                          └────────┘  │
│ ┌─New Settings──────────────────────────────────┐   │
│ │ Drive:   [▭ c: [dtp 1]              ] ▼       │   │
│ │                                               │   │
│ │ Type:    [Permanent                 ] ▼       │   │
│ │                                               │   │
│ │ Space Available:         123,392  KB          │   │
│ │ Maximum Size:             45,384  KB          │   │
│ │ Recommended Size:         45,360  KB          │   │
│ │ New Size:               [ 20000] KB           │   │
│ │                                               │   │
│ │ ☒ Use 32-Bit Disk Access                      │   │
│ └───────────────────────────────────────────────┘   │
└─────────────────────────────────────────────────────┘
```

and most applications, including Photoshop, use to store or swap parts of themselves when more memory is needed or when these applications are not being used. Please don't confuse this with a scratch disk which is a proprietary scheme only used by Photoshop which we will discuss later in this chapter and in Chapter 3, "Configuring Photoshop." Supported by most hard disks, a permanent swap file usually improves the performance of your system.

A permanent swap file may also be configured to use 32-bit file access, which can improve performance even more. Not all hard disks support a 32-bit permanent swap file, so back up your system before you enable this feature. If you enable this feature and your hard disk is not compatible, you may corrupt all your files. Most IDE hard disks support this feature while most SCSI hard disks do not. To enable your permanent swap file launch the Control Panel and double click on the 386 Enhanced icon. Select the fastest hard disk on your system to hold your swap file. Windows and most applications perform best with a 10 Mb permanent swap file. Photoshop *requires* a permanent swap file equal in size to the available RAM on your system before Windows loads. You might want to experiment on your system with various sizes of permanent swap files to determine the best one.

Fonts and Photoshop

Juggling fonts, especially if you have many of them, can be an art. Luckily, once you create type in Photoshop, it becomes part of the bitmap and the font is not needed to print the image. You do, however, need the font on the computer in order to properly print layouts created in vector and page layout programs.

Anti-Aliased Typefaces

When creating text in Photoshop, you can specify that the type appear on the screen with anti-aliasing. As mention in Chapter 1, anti-aliasing smoothes the jagged edges of shapes, and can make type appear sharper than it actually is (Figure 2–5).

With Photoshop, you need the PostScript and/or TrueType font on the computer in order to rasterize (convert to bitmap) type with anti-aliased edges. This is achieved by referencing the vector outline font resident on the computer. Common to both the Macintosh and Windows, Adobe Type Manager (ATM) and the TrueType both support rasterized type in Photoshop. ATM is a program that you install into your System folder on the Macintosh or into your Windows directory on your PC (Figure 2–6). TrueType support is always enabled on the Macintosh and may be turned on or off in Windows via the Fonts module of the Control Panel.

TIP: Beware that not all fonts have PostScript/vector outlines. There are hundreds of fonts available that are bitmap only, that will usually neither print with good quality nor anti-alias at any desired size in Photoshop. On the Mac, any font with a city name is a bitmapped font. On the Windows platform, most applications (including Photoshop) do not display bitmap font names like MS Sans Serif in your type menu.

Both PostScript and TrueType fonts use vector outlines, which eliminate the need to install point-specific bitmap printer fonts on your system. In spite of this identical feature there are some differences between the two formats. TrueType is a font technology and not a language. PostScript is a font technology and a page description language that provides device independence and supports EPS graphics created in vector illustration packages and print-to-disk (PRN) files across multiple platforms.

Only the TrueType font specification for Windows permits you to embed these fonts in your document using a supporting application like Microsoft Word for Windows 6. Embedding lets you to transfer the document and the TrueType font to a co-worker.

PostScript fonts are the standard in service bureau work because most of their clients work on the Macintosh platform. TrueType users are a very small segment of the population in the graphics world and PostScript fonts have been used since the dawn of desktop publishing. On the Windows platform TrueType has enjoyed wide acceptance since its introduction in 1992 and most office publishers use this format.

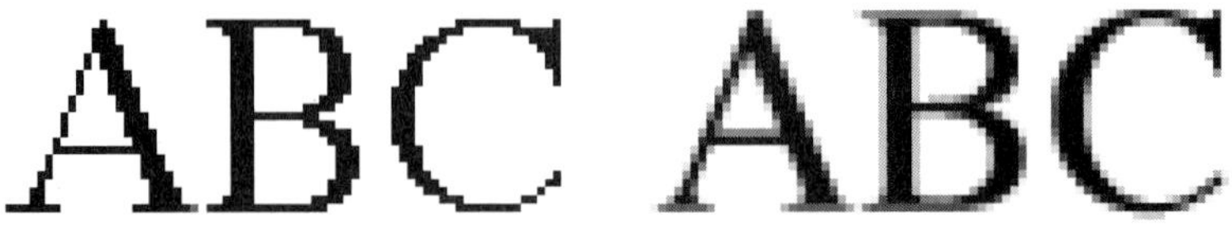

Figure 2–5
Bitmapped type on the left and anti-aliased type on the right

Photoshop supports type anti-aliasing through the following methods:

- Multiple font sizes are not necessary if TrueType fonts are being used.
- If you are using ATM (Adobe Type Manager), you can create smooth type of any size and color from PostScript fonts installed on your system. ATM is a program that allows you to have smooth, optimized screen representations of any PostScript font. When combined with Photoshop, these type faces are fully anti-aliased.

TIP: To get ATM to work with all of the 35 PostScript typefaces resident in most laser printers, such as Times, Helvetica, and Palatino, you need to purchase and install the Adobe Plus Pack on your system.

Fonts and Macintosh

Although not as refined looking as anti-aliased vector fonts, any bitmapped screen typeface with larger sizes installed in the system can be drawn on the screen with anti-aliased edges. For example, if you have a 24-point screen face installed in your system, you can create smooth 12–point text on the screen. Photoshop accomplishes this by using the larger installed sizes to create optimized versions of the smaller faces.

If you are running many fonts on your computer, use a font management utility such as Suitcase from Fifth Generation Software. A font manager allows you to store fonts in folders rather than in your System folder, which will help your computer run more efficiently (Figure 2–7).

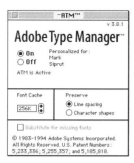

Figure 2–6
Turn on ATM and control its parameters by opening it in the Control Panels under the Apple menu.

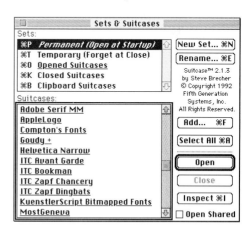

Figure 2–7
Load and unload fonts as needed with Suitcase.

CAUTION: There are situations in Photoshop when having too many fonts (120 or more) will cause menus to disappear. Try to use only the fonts you need when you go into Photoshop.

Fonts and Windows

Windows contains built in support for TrueType fonts just like Apple's System 7. If you wish to use PostScript fonts with Windows you need to install ATM (Adobe Type Manager) which is included with Photoshop. You can use both formats at the same time in Photoshop and most Windows applications; this strategy sometimes leads to confusion and problems in vector illustration programs and page layout software. For example, a typeface with the same menu name in each format may contain different kerning values or the letterforms may be slightly different. Because of these problems we suggest you standardize on one format and avoid mixing formats.

Windows is not yet robust enough to operate efficiently with 400 PostScript or TrueType fonts installed. In this case Windows and most Windows applications (including Photoshop) run significantly slower. To solve this problem you need font management software like Ares FontMinder (Figure 2–8), which permits you to easily and quickly install and remove TrueType or PostScript fonts which are grouped into font packs. Windows runs best on most systems with a maximum of 150 fonts installed.

WINDOWS TIP: If you have a PostScript and TrueType font installed on your system with an identical Windows menu name only one format will be available. Windows and most applications (including Photoshop) will use the TrueType font. This is another reason to standardize on either PostScript or TrueType fonts.

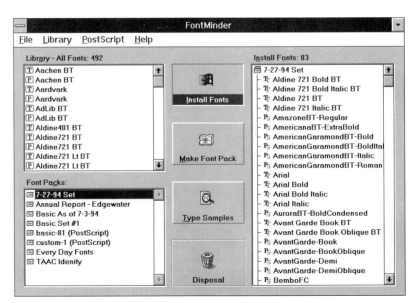

Figure 2–8
Ares FontMinder font management software for Windows

Memory

Having access to lots and lots of random access memory (RAM) is as important as having a fast computer. Photoshop requires RAM that is three to five times an image's file size to process that image. For example, if the image you are working on is 2 Mb in size, Photoshop will want to have available 6 to 10 Mb of free memory in order to function well. If you have a computer with 10 Mb of RAM installed, Photoshop can easily take most of that RAM, and more, just to work efficiently with a relatively small 2-Mb image. And that doesn't include RAM that needs to be used by the System!

Virtually Speaking

So what happens if you only have only 6 Mb of RAM available and you want to use Photoshop? Well, as we mentioned previously, Photoshop has a well designed method for using *virtual memory* which it calls a Scratch Disk. Virtual memory means that when Photoshop uses up all the RAM it has been allocated and still needs more, the program will temporarily use part of your empty hard space disk as a sort of "pseudo-RAM." The problem with using hard disk space as RAM is that accessing it is not nearly as efficient as accessing RAM (translation: it slows things down).

When running more than one hard disk, you can control which hard disks Photoshop uses for virtual memory. Choose the Scratch Disk submenu in Preferences under the File menu while running Photoshop (Figure 2–9). Assign hard disks as primary and secondary scratch disks.

RAMming it in

The best way to allow Photoshop to run faster, short of buying a new, faster computer, is to have as much RAM as you can afford. Since images can average 4 to 20 Mb or more in size, Photoshop can easily eat up 12 to 100 Mb of RAM! First, decide what you can afford and buy wisely. A few companies make special cards containing a number of extra slots in which RAM can be installed. For example, Power PC upgrade cards such as the DayStar PowerPro have extra slots for adding additional RAM to speed up performance.

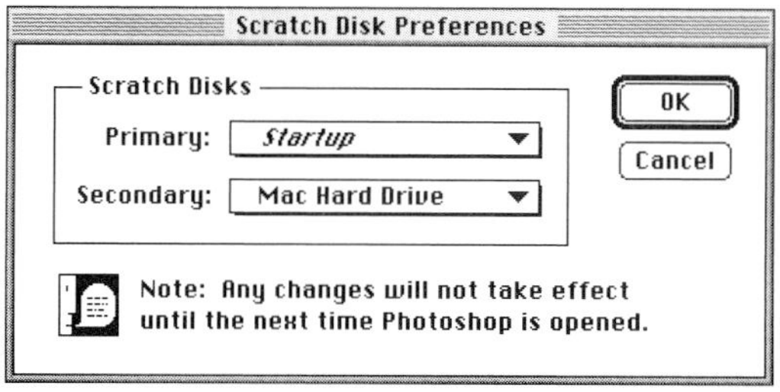

Figure 2–9
Assign hard disks as primary and secondary scratch disks in the Scratch disk Preferences dialog under the File menu in Photoshop.

Memory Sources

There are a number of sources for RAM, some substantially less expensive than others. Shop around for the best deal you can get from a reliable vendor. Some earlier Macintoshes, like the IIcx or older, cannot recognize more than 8 Mb of RAM without installing a special INIT, such as Mode 32 or the appropriate Apple System Enabler. Windows uses an extended memory scheme which allows users to add memory to the capacity of their hardware.

A consideration when purchasing a new computer is the maximum amount of RAM that can be installed. Find out the slot configuration to plan how to purchase SIMMS Chips (RAM). Some computers need to have SIMMS chips installed in pairs or groups of four, which won't allow for mixing and matching. For example, earlier Macs and many PCs have eight slots in two banks, and all chips in each bank must match. SIMMS chips can be purchased in one, four, eight, 16, or 32 megabyte configurations.

TIP: Check the maximum RAM that your computer motherboard can accommodate. There is a wide variety of options in this regard which range from 32 Mb to over 200 Mb. Don't purchase a machine that limits your options to expand the memory as your requirements change.

RAM Disks

RAM disks are created by setting aside a portion of available RAM to act as a temporary hard disk. This portion of memory can then be used to store files, which can be accessed much faster than would be possible from a physical storage device. With many applications, using a RAM disk is a real advantage. However, the performance advantages are not so clear with Photoshop.

When you launch Photoshop, it grabs as much RAM as possible for its processing environment, limited only by the amount of memory allocated to it (see the next section for details). Therefore, while a RAM disk will allow you to more rapidly open any files it contains, it doesn't accelerate Photoshop any more than by assigning RAM to the application itself, and will even subtract from the memory available for Photoshop's processing functions. It is also unsuitable for assignment as a scratch disk, since it will almost always be too small (compared to what would be available on physical media), and will force Photoshop to go to the secondary scratch disk almost immediately.

What's more, data stored in a RAM disk will disappear if your system is shut off or goes down before you have a chance to save the RAM disk to a physical drive.

Consider these factors before deciding to use a RAM disk with Photoshop, and if you do set one up, be careful. On the Mac, a RAM disk can be created with System 7.1 or above, or with third-party software.

Under Windows, you can also use third-party utilities or add the following line to your CONFIG.SYS file:

```
DEVICE=C:\WINDOWS\RAMDRIVE.SYS 2048 /E
```

(The 2048 represents the amount of RAM disk memory, in bytes.)

Allocating RAM/Macintosh

Check how much RAM you have installed in your system by selecting About This Macintosh... from the Apple menu while in the Finder (Figure 2–10). The total amount of installed RAM is shown in kilobytes (Kb) after the words "Total Memory." The current available RAM is shown after "Largest Unused Block." The lower portion shows how much memory currently running applications are using.

RAM is allocated to Photoshop, and other applications, by clicking on the program and then choosing the Get Info command under the Finder's File menu. The Get Info box has an area in the bottom-right corner that allows you to specify the amount of available RAM for the program to access (Figure 2–11). If you have 8 Mb (8,192 Kb) of RAM in your computer, might allow Photoshop to use up to 7 Mb (7,168 KB) or less, depending on how lean your System file is, how many INITs and Extensions you are running, and how many fonts you have installed. To be exact, the total amount of RAM minus the memory allocated to the System, less 500 Kb, equals the amount you can allocate to Photoshop, assuming that you will not run any other programs at the same time. If you want to run other applications along with Photoshop, add their memory

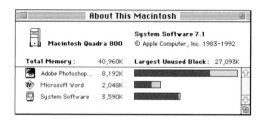

Figure 2–10
The About This Macintosh dialog displays the status of RAM on your computer.

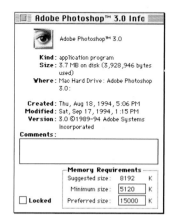

Figure 2–11
Allocate RAM to Photoshop in Get Info dialog box.

requirements to the equation. Enter the amount of RAM in Kb to allocate to Photoshop by typing in the amount in the Current size (Preferred size in System 7.1 or later) text field. Although one megabyte equals 1,024 kilobytes, it's easier to round off, so to allocate 7 Mb enter 7000.

Allocating RAM/Windows

In Windows you can determine how much memory is available to Photoshop by selecting About Program Manager from the Help menu in Program Manager (Figure 2–12). This dialog box will also give the size of your swap file. The bottom number is the sum of available RAM and the size of your swap file. You also see a percent free for System Resources which will be discussed next.

To configure your RAM in Photoshop select Preferences from the File menu and the Memory submenu (Figure 2–13). The Memory Preferences dialog box, unique to Windows, combines the Scratch Disk preference found on the Macintosh version with a Physical Memory Usage section. Any settings you change in this dialog box require you to restart Photoshop. The Scratch Disk preferences function exactly the same way as in the Macintosh version. Rather than use your Windows permanent swap file, they use a proprietary scratch disk that Photoshop creates and uses to store your images. It is not recommended that you point the Scratch Disk to a compressed drive. Compressed drives have caused problems, such as lost data and corrupted files, with Windows and many applications that use them.

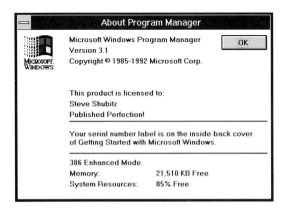

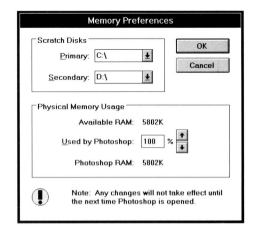

Figure 2–12
The About Program Manager dialog box which is displayed from the Help menu in Program Manager

Figure 2–13
Configuring the amount of RAM that Photoshop will use in the Memory Preferences dialog box

The Physical Memory Usage section is very important and may require some experimentation on your system. The Available RAM field indicates all the memory (RAM) available on your system which Photoshop may use *after* it's running. Photoshop computes the Available RAM field in the following manner: the total available RAM on your system *after* Windows is running minus a variable number (1 Mb to 6 Mb maximum), which is memory reserved for Windows and scanners. If you want Photoshop to use all the available RAM on your system, set the Used by Photoshop field to 100%. This setting provides maximum performance for Photoshop but limits the number and size of other Windows applications you can run at the same time.

If for some reason you anticipate running another application, change this field to 75% to automatically change the Photoshop RAM field which reflects the amount of memory that Photoshop *will* use on your system after it's running. Because of the System Resources limitation and the robust requirements of Photoshop it's unlikely that you will be able to run more than one other major application.

MANAGING SYSTEM RESOURCES IN WINDOWS

Photoshop for Windows uses a significant amount of System Resources. System Resources are a small 64 Kb segment or *heap* of memory that Windows and all Windows applications use. Each window, icon, dialog box, and palette also consume these resources. Once this tiny segment of memory is depleted or reduced to a low level (about 40%) Windows and all your applications become unstable, regardless of the amount of RAM or the size of the swap file installed on your system.

Sometimes Windows erroneously reports "Insufficient memory to run applications" when you have plenty of free RAM or you receive a GPF (General Protection Fault). When Windows first loads most systems have about 80 to 85 percent free system resources. This figure is displayed in the System Resources field at the bottom of the About Program Manager dialog box we mentioned earlier. Because of this archaic limitation in the present version of Windows we suggest you maximize available system resources on your system.

Eliminate any programs that automatically launch when Windows starts. If these are installed in your Start Up group, hold down the Shift key before you launch Windows to temporarily disable them. Third party shells, which replace the Windows Program Manager, can also consume large amounts of system resources, as can wallpaper and fancy screen savers.

Exercise caution and restraint when using another application while Photoshop is running. For example, launching CorelDRAW! 5 and displaying *alll* of its palettes (roll-ups in Corel lingo) is guaranteed to crash your systm or render it unstable.

Closing an application usually frees the system resources it consumed, but many large applications continue to "hold" system resources after they are closed down. Because of these issues we suggest you re-start Windows before any Photoshop session and then launch Photoshop first. If you decide to run another application, be selective in your use of palettes and close them when finished.

Storage

You can never have enough hard disk storage space, and your hard disk is never fast enough. Are you getting the message? First it's a fast computer and then it's oodles of RAM. Now you need a huge, quick hard disk, too? Well, sorry, but it's true. As mentioned above, if you are lucky enough to have enough RAM to enable Photoshop to contain your images while working on them, the capacity and speed of your hard drive become less important. But, if you're like most of us, Photoshop will be forced to use your hard disk for virtual memory. If you have a slow, low-capacity hard disk, you will be limiting not only Photoshop's speed, but the maximum size of the images you can work with. Most of us aren't throwing around 40-Mb files, so we can handle a little waiting in exchange for having money to pay the bills. But if you want Photoshop to work as fast as it can when using its virtual memory scheme, it will help to have a large, fast hard drive.

NOTE: If you normally work with file sizes of 10–20 Mb, you may want to invest less in memory (20 Mb or so) and put money into a dual-drive array. Arrays use two drives as one interactively, providing performance (for scratch space) at or near the speed of RAM.

Using the Hard Disk for Virtual Memory

Photoshop's scratch disk is a virtual memory scheme . You can select a primary and, if needed, secondary *scratch disk*. A scratch disk is what Photoshop calls the hard disk(s) it uses to hold data temporarily. This is a proprietary technique that is separate from your Windows permanent swap file or Apple's System Virtual Memory.

What can you do to speed up virtual memory, no matter the size and speed of your hard disk? Here are some tips.

TIP: A rule of thumb for RAM/Scratch space disks is that the total available Application size and Scratch space should equal four times the size of the file being edited in Photoshop 2.5.1 and five times the file size in Photoshop 3.0.

MACINTOSH

- Always reserve as much free space on your hard disk as you have allocated RAM to Adobe Photoshop. You may be stopped in your tracks with a Scratch Disk Full error if you have allocated more RAM to Photoshop than is available on your hard disk, even if you have enough actual RAM for the function.

- Set the System Disk Cache in the Memory control panel to the lowest number possible; 32 is a good start (Figure 2–2).

- Under System 7, also make sure you have Virtual Memory turned off in the Memory control panel (Figure 2–2).

- Defragment the drive used by Photoshop for your scratch disk with a hard disk utility like Norton Utilities' Speed Disk.

- Don't use a removable hard disk like SyQuest or Bernoulli as a scratch disk, because these types of disks get rougher treatment than fixed hard disks. As a result, they are a bit less reliable. Their speed also leaves something to be desired, especially in comparison to a good fixed hard disk.

WINDOWS

- Locate your Windows permanent swap file on the fastest hard drive available on your system and turn on the 32-bit file access. To enable 32-bit file access launch the Control Panel and double-click on the 386 Enhanced icon.

- Locate your Photoshop scratch disk on the fastest hard drive with the most free space, using the Memory Preferences submenu under the File menu in Photoshop.

- Defragment your hard disk on a regular basis using DOS's DEFRAG or SCANDISK, or a third-party utility such as PC-Kwik's WinMaster.

- Avoid assigning your swap file or your scratch disk to an external, removable cartridge system, which usually has slower performance than internal drives.

- Increase the memory parameter in the command that configures SmartDrive in your CONFIG.SYS file, or do the same with a third-party disk caching utility such as Super PC-Kwik. Keep in mind that the more memory you allocate for your drive cache, the slower virtual memory will run. It may take some trial and error to find the right balance.

Drive Types

Today there are a variety of media to use for storing data. All of the devices and technologies have their own peculiarities and features. These are briefly described below.

MAGNETIC

This is the kind of disk most people associate with their computers, either inside their Macintosh or PC, or as an external device. Magnetic disks use rapidly spinning platters of machined aluminum with a magnetic coating. Data is read from or written to the platters in millionths of a second by tiny heads attached to quickly moving arms. The speed of the platters and the speed with which the arms move across the platters generally determine a hard disk's speed in transferring data.

Magnetic hard disks are a relatively inexpensive, fast storage medium. Their cost per megabyte generally declines as you move to larger capacities, and the larger capacity disks are generally the fastest.

ARRAYS

Arrays are simply two or more magnetic hard disks attached via some controlling circuitry to act as one. Disk arrays, as they are sometimes called, are the fastest possible medium for storing large amounts of data. Disk arrays are expensive, but if you need speed look closely into this option.

OPTICAL

Optical drives use a laser to read and write data onto media similar to a Compact Disk. Optical drives, called WORM drives (write once, read many times), can store a large amount of data onto a super-stable, removable, CD-like platter. The drawbacks are that they are slow and, once you store something using a WORM drive, it's there for good and cannot be changed (although it can be retrieved as many times as you like). Use these drives to store data you want to keep for a long time, and which you will want read-only access to.

WORM drives have fallen out of fashion recently with the advent of new optical technology, which allows you to write and read from the same type of CD-like disk. These drives, called magneto-optical drives, are described below.

MAGNETO-OPTICAL

Magneto-optical drives are, as their name implies, a hybrid of magnetic and optical technology. They use disks that have tiny particles of metal embedded in them. The polarity of these particles can be altered by a laser, giving these drives the capability to store lots of data safely and to change it just like a magnetic hard disk. Magneto-optical drives are not as fast as magnetic disks, but have the added benefit of a removable medium and inexpensive disks. They come in $3^1/_2$ inch, which stores either 128 Mb or 230 Mb, and the $5^1/_2$ inch size, which stores 650 Mb or 1.3 Gb. In either size, the larger capacity drives can read and write the smaller capacity disks. For example the Fujitsu Dynamo 240 can also read and write 128 Mb disks.

SYQUEST

SyQuest removable drives have been universal among artists, designers and service bureaus. The original 44 Mb cartridges, although expensive in cost per megabyte, is still widely used. SyQuest drives are available in two sizes, $3^1/_2$ inch and $5^1/_4$ inch. The popular $5^1/_4$ inch 200 Mb SyQuest drive also reads and writes 88 Mb and 44 Mb disks. Beware that using a 44 Mb cartridge in a 200 Mb drive is much slower than using it in one made to work with only the 44 Mb size. In the smaller $3^1/_2$ inch size SyQuest, drives are available in the 105 Mb and 270 Mb formats. The 270 Mb drive is compatible with the 105 Mb disks.

BERNOULLI

Bernoulli is another standard removable drive. Its claim is more durability and stability than other removable media. The durable Bernoulli disks are less likely to get damaged when transporting because they are more resistant to shock. The drives come in 150 Mb and 90 Mb formats, the larger capacity drives are downward compatible.

TAPE

Magnetic tape drives can store lots of data on what looks like normal audio magnetic tapes. The various drive type can store from 2 to 10 Gb of data on a single tape. There are two basic formats, 8 mm Exabyte and 4 mm DAT. The Exabyte costs a bit more but is faster and more reliable. The benefit of using tape drive is that the tapes are very cheap, ranging from ten to twenty five dollars. The drawback is that a tape drive is REALLY slow. It is primarily used for back up—let it do its work at night while you are sleeping. Retrieving work from a tape is also painfully slow. Don't even think of using a tape drive for regular daily work.

CD-ROM

A technology which is going through an explosion now is the CD-ROM. CD-ROM stands for Compact Disk–Read Only Memory. These discs look just like regular audio CDs, and they can hold over 600 Mb of data. Unlike WORM drive disks, CD-ROMs require expensive hardware and software to store data and are, therefore, not widely used as a personal storage medium. Rather they are used to distribute large amounts of data inexpensively to people who own CD-ROM drives.

CD-ROMs also are versatile. They can be used to distribute stock photographs, typefaces, patterns, textures, multimedia presentations, and even software safely and economically. The most famous widespread is Kodak's Photo CD system. Anyone with color and/or black-and-white negatives or slides can send them to a processing lab to be scanned and stored on a special type of CD-ROM called a Photo CD. This medium is great if you don't have a scanner because you can unload time-consuming scanning onto someone else's system. Furthermore, the scan quality is excellent and should satisfy all but the most demanding applications.

Hardware allowing individual users to make their own CD-ROMs is also on the market and will certainly be an area to watch in the future as prices drop.

Small Computer System Interface (SCSI)

On the Macintosh, most external devices are connected through a SCSI interface. With SCSI, you can attach up to six devices to a single bus on a computer via a SCSI chain, such as a SyQuest drive, CD reader, external hard disk, a desktop scanner, and whatever else you need. SCSI is standard on the Macintosh, and most Macintosh users have been using it for years. However, it's a relatively new option for PC users. Most PCs sold today do not include true built-in SCSI support and until recently DOS and Windows did not directly support SCSI (Windows 95 includes a SCSI Manager).

SCSI FOR WINDOWS

SCSI, now a viable option on PCs, should be a benefit to PC users everywhere. Not only do SCSI devices operate significantly faster than those connected by parallel or serial interfaces, but large hard disks (1 Gb and over) are available only as SCSI devices.

You need two things to add SCSI to your PC: a SCSI card and the appropriate software. Many desktop scanners, SyQuest drives, and CD readers include their own proprietary cards (not a SCSI card) to install in a vacant slot in your PC. Unfortunately this procedure means a separate card for each SCSI device, which can use all your available slots and cause software problems when these devices are set up. With a SCSI card, you can create a single SCSI port into which you can connect a chain of SCSI devices.

Before you purchase a SCSI card make sure it includes a standard SCSI interface (most do); connect all your SCSI devices to this card. Recommendations include the Adaptec and Future Domain cards. If your PC has a PCI or VESA bus, purchase a SCSI card that works with these buses because all your peripherals will run significantly faster. Finally, ensure that your SCSI card supports the Advanced SCSI Peripheral Interface (ASPI). This is the de facto standard developed by Adaptec Corporation and supported by many vendors. The ASPI driver is included with your card and loaded in your CONFIG.SYS file. Many vendors also include CorelSCSI for Windows, discussed below.

Installing SCSI may cost you an extra $300, but your system will run faster. You will benefit from SCSI's easy expansion via the SCSI chain, and you'll have fewer software problems with DOS and Windows. If you work in a mixed environment (Windows and Macintosh) you can also move your SCSI peripherals from one machine to the other.

WINDOWS TIP: **If your SCSI card conforms to the ASPI standard, you might purchase CorelSCSI for Windows software. It provides an efficient way to connect and control your SCSI devices in Windows, and can allow you to replace many vendors' proprietary cards. CorelSCSI for Windows supports dozens of SCSI devices from various vendors, including CD readers, WORM drives, scanners, CD recorders, internal and external hard drives, flopticals, removable media like SyQuest and Bernoulli drives, and tape drives. *Always* get the latest drivers for whatever device you have—check with your vendor.**

GENERAL SCSI TIPS

Here are a few SCSI tips that should make your life easier.

- Terminate the last device in the SCSI chain.
- Purchase SCSI devices that support an external terminator. This permits you to add another device to your SCSI chain without having to remove an internal terminator from a hard drive by taking it apart. This also makes it much easier to switch devices in your chain.
- Purchase the shortest cable possible for all your devices. (The maximum length of all the external cables that connect your SCSI devices is 6 meters.)
- Spend the extra money for high-quality cables and terminators to connect your devices. Sometimes an inexpensive cable or terminator can cause problems. They may not work properly or may intermittently fail.

- Sometimes the order in which you turn on your external SCSI devices is very important. For example, if have a SyQuest drive connected to a Macintosh, the machine might not start properly unless you first turn on the drive, insert a cartridge, let the drive spin up to full speed, and then boot the computer.

- Finally, if you plan to purchase a storage device that supports removable media like the SyQuest or Bernoulli drives, conduct a survey of your local service bureaus or color houses to determine exactly which devices and media they support. You don't want to purchase a drive, only to find out that your service bureau has no way to use your cartridge.

Acceleration

If you can't afford to purchase a newer, faster computer, consider speeding up the one you already own. Computer acceleration is sort of like putting a Porsche engine in a Geo, or making spaghetti sauce with lobster.

CPU Acceleration

The most common type of acceleration is to replace the Central Processing Unit (CPU) with a newer, faster version. Apple offers upgrades for some computers in which all of the Mac's circuitry (motherboard) can be replaced. In some instances, a new case is included. Of course, plug-in accelerator boards are also available, including a line of PowerPC boards for older Macs. Apple upgrades tend to be expensive, however, and a number of third-party suppliers have stepped in to supply lower cost alternatives.

CPU accelerators for PC/Windows computers are a complex subject due to the wide variety of PC manufactures and lack of true standards. If you want to upgrade your present machine try calling the manufacturer first. Some CPUs are removable and can be replaced with a faster chip. For example, a PC that contains a removable 66 MHz 486 CPU can be replaced with a much faster 66 or 90 MHz Pentium chip.

Many PCs sold today do not contain a removable CPU, so your other option is to replace the entire motherboard, an easy way to significantly increase the performance of Photoshop and Windows. Be sure your existing peripherals, RAM chips, video cards, and SCSI adapters are compatible with your new motherboard. This may require some research, but swapping motherboards is often cheaper than purchasing a new machine.

THIRD-PARTY OPTIONS AVAILABLE

There are a number of companies that offer acceleration solutions for speeding up your Macintosh or PC. (These can make performance 100 times faster.) DayStar Digital, for example, has a complete line of user-installable cards and replacement CPU chips. Radius, RasterOps, Spectral Innovations, Applied Engineering, Tech Works, Storm, Newer Technology, and others provide a myriad of alternatives at widely differing prices. In some cases, a user can simply slide a small circuit board into the Processor Direct or NuBus slot of a Macintosh and end up with a substantial speed increase. Another solution is that the CPU chip itself be removed from the motherboard and replaced by a new one, such as putting a DayStar 40 MHz Turbo 040 accelerator on an older Macintosh (Figure 2–14). This is a bit more complicated than simply sliding in a board, but any evenhanded, patient user should be able to complete the task with little difficulty.

The ultimate acceleration on a Macintosh is to install a Power PC upgrade card such as the DayStar Power Pro 601, which comes in 80 MHz and 66 MHz models.

Check out computer magazines for advice when it comes to the specifics about CPU acceleration. The market is constantly changing and new products appear at a dizzying pace. Be aware of any compatibility issues with software you may own. As always, look before you leap.

Photoshop-Specific Acceleration

Photoshop users can now greatly increase the speed at which certain specific functions of Photoshop are accomplished. For example, companies like DayStar Digital, Radius, SuperMac, RasterOps, Newer Technology, Storm, and Spectral Innovations offer NuBus cards with specialized chips that will supposedly speed the application of some Photoshop filters by as much as 2000 percent!

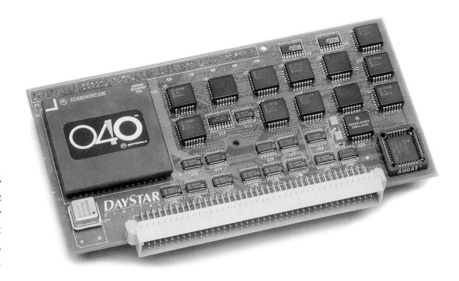

Figure 2–14
The DayStar 40 MHz
Turbo 040 accelerator
can turn a tired old Mac
into a fast,
productive machine.

ACCELERATION: HOW DOES IT WORK?

The above cards use custom-designed chips that can process specific instructions very quickly—more quickly than the main CPU. By using special software provided by the card makers, some processor-intensive tasks, like the application of the Unsharp Mask filter, can be handled by these special high-speed chips instead of by the main CPU. It's like having a separate engine for each wheel of your car.

The most common chip used for Photoshop-specific acceleration is called a Digital Signal Processor (DSP) chip. Used by the telephone company for years, these speed demons have made the jump to personal computers. DSP chips do a superior job of handling the kinds of calculations required for many of Photoshop's most complicated functions. Some boards even use two DSP chips that work together for the fastest possible results.

The other type of chip used is called a Reduced Instruction Set Computing (RISC) chip. An example is the RasterOps PhotoPro RISC-based acceleration board. These fast microprocessors are more efficient than today's generation of microprocessors because they require less internal code, or instruction, to get things done. RISC chips are easily programmable and have a potential impact across a wide variety of applications besides Photoshop.

An example of a Photoshop-specific acceleration board on the Macintosh is the DayStar Charger. It comes with specific software, Charger Suites Volume 1, which includes DayStar's filter interface, PowerPreview, and a library of Photoshop functions (Figure 2–15). Accelerated functions include Sharpen, Blur, Skew, Rotate, Resize, Find Edges, Feathering,

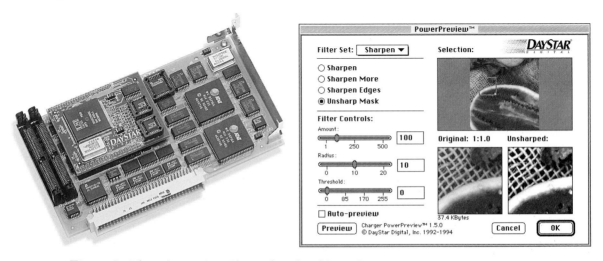

Figure 2–15   The DayStar Charger board and PowerPreview

Despeckle, and more. Other Charger Suites are available for accelerating Kodak CMS, Photo CD, Kodak DCS camera, and more.

The Radius Thunder line of cards offers Photoshop-specific DSP acceleration linked to an accelerated video card. A Thunder card speeds up image acquisition, image manipulation, image compression, and printing.

On the Windows platform, the PhotoDSP 400 by Storm Technology is available to speed up Photoshop. The PhotoDSP 400 uses an ISA (Industry Standard Architecture) DSP board and software that speed up certain functions in Photoshop like Image Resize, Rotate, Gaussian Blur, and Unsharp Mask.

HOOKS AND GRABS: THE SOFTWARE

Although many Photoshop-specific acceleration boards increase speed in a similar way or use similar types of chips, the software that accompanies the boards varies. Adobe has been very good about providing key portions of the Photoshop code to board vendors so that they can write the special software needed to accomplish the desired acceleration. This means that once you purchase a board, updates provided via software (hooks) are the only things that change. This leaves open the possibility that more software companies will allow these special hooks to be written for their programs so that they can take advantage of the sometimes incredible acceleration the cards offer.

Adobe has come up with a scheme in which software accompanying acceleration boards is given a special label—the Adobe Charged logo pictured at left—if written to conform to Adobe standards.

Displays

Since Photoshop is a program for working on images, you want to view them at the best possible quality. On a Macintosh you can run Photoshop with any monitor plus video card from 1-bit to 24 bits. You should really use at least 8-bit video (256 color or grayscale). Under Windows, Photoshop won't even start unless you are running an 8-bit monitor and video card. For working with grayscale images 8 bits is fine, because Photoshop can only handle 256 graytones. For a faithful display of all colors in your images, however, you really need 16- or 24-bit color capability. This requires both a monitor and video card that will display these colors.

24-Bit Color

Twenty-four-bit color, or photo-realistic color, makes available 16,772,216 colors to any of a monitor's pixels at any given time. Since the human eye can discern substantially less than 16.7 million colors, 24-bit color is more than adequate for displaying images at the highest quality. Photo-realistic color requires a fast and reliable 24-bit display card or a machine capable of 24-bit on-board video output. Twenty-four-bit display cards are available from a wide variety of manufacturers at an even wider variety of prices. Some Quadras and Power PCs, however, can run most small and medium-sized monitors at the 24-bit level without using a separate video card with 2 Mb of video RAM (VRAM) installed.

On the PC side, upgrade your graphics capability by installing a 24-bit video card that supports two to four Mb of VRAM. VRAM is more efficient than dynamic random access memory (DRAM), supported by many video cards. If you have a free PCI or VESA slot, purchase a video card that supports these buses for dramatically faster screen display. For example, the Graphics Pro Turbo by ATI Technologies is available in a 4 Mb configuration for PCI or VESA bus machines as well as the older and slower ISA (Industry Standard Architecture) bus.

COLOR IN THE FAST LANE

A number of very sophisticated 24-bit display cards and monitors are available for the Macintosh and Windows PCs. Some include specialized circuitry to speed up screen redraw, accelerate specific Photoshop functions and control color balance. For example the SuperMac PressView 21 T running on a SuperMac Thunder II GX 1360 video card is ideal for color correction and retouching (Figure 2–16). It has super high resolution and software controls for accurate and consistent color, offers viewing with multiple viewing resolutions, includes a colorimeter for calibrating the display, and supports color management systems. The Thunder II GX video card accelerates image processing functions in Photoshop and speeds up processing of CMYK images. This system is geared toward prepress professionals.

16-Bit Color

An alternative for those without a 24-bit system is to work in a color mode that can display of up to 32,768 colors per monitor pixel. This mode is called 16-bit color. Most people can't tell the difference between an image displayed on a monitor in 16-bit and 24-bit color, and many of the newer Macs support 16-bit color through their built-in video circuitry. For example, certain models in the Performa, Quadra, and Centris lines support 16-bit color on at least the smaller color displays.

8 Bits and Less

You can run Photoshop with an 8-bit display, but you will only have the capacity to show 256 colors or shades of gray. If you are working exclusively in black and white 8-bit display is all you need. Remember that PCs require at least an 8-bit display system for Photoshop to run.

Figure 2–16
The SuperMac
PressView 21 T from
Radius, geared for
prepress professionals, is
ideal for editing and
color-correcting
photorealistic 24 bit
images (© Radius).

On the Macintosh you can run Photoshop on monitors as low as 1-bit. Prior to the Mac II that's all we had: the Mac SE, Plus, and Classic. One-bit displays show black and white with no graytones. When running Photoshop on a 1-bit display you cannot accurately see what you are doing, which is no problem if you work by the numbers. Running a display at 2-bits produces four graytones or colors, and 4-bits produces 16 graytones or colors.

TIP: If you process lots of images, beef up an old Macintosh with RAM and a cheap 1 bit or 8 bit monitor and use it for cropping, resizing, changing modes, converting file formats, applying filters—any functions that do not require critical visual assessment.

Changing Monitor Bit Depth Characteristics

There are several reasons for changing bit depth. The lower your bit depth, the faster your screen will redraw. You may want to preview an image at lower bit depth. To switch Macintosh bit depth, choose Monitors in the Control Panels folder under the Apple menu (Figure 2–17). To change your bit depth in Windows launch Windows Setup (SETUP.EXE) located in your Windows directory (Figure 2–18). Next select Change System

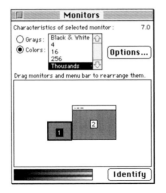

Figure 2–17
Choose Monitors in the
Control Panel under the
Apple menu to change
the bit depth of a
Macintosh monitor.

Figure 2–18
The Change System Settings dialog box in
Windows Setup. Select Change System Settings
from the Options menu to navigate to this dialog
box. Choose the appropriate video driver in the
Display field.

Settings from the Options menu. Don't forget to restart Windows after you change your bit depth. Some video cards also provide proprietary software to accomplish this task.

TIP: Color Switch from Ambrosia allows you to quickly change the bit depth of your monitor from the desktop on the Mac.

Monitors: Sizing Things Up

That brings us to monitor size. It can be safely said that when it comes to monitor or screen size, bigger is better. Although larger monitors are definitely more expensive, the time saved in scrolling images up and down and the comfort gained from not straining to see a dinky screen, makes the cost worth it. Nineteen-, 20- and 21-inch monitors are *de rigeur* for Photoshop pros. The range of choices in these and the popular 16- and 17-inch sizes are numerous; do your homework before deciding what's best for your needs—and pocketbook. Computer and digital graphics magazines run frequent tests of large monitors and display cards, and are a good source of information. But the ultimate decision rests with your eyes. Check out possible monitors in person. It's difficult to make a wise monitor choice sight unseen, especially if it's something you'll be looking at for hours on end.

TIP: If you are concerned about energy usage, buy an energy efficient monitor, a new development on the market. Make sure that it states it is Energy Star compliant.

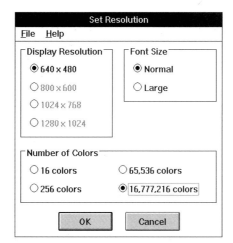

Figure 2–19
Use third-party software
to configure Windows
and Photoshop to the
maximum resolution
that supports
24-bit color. This
usually requires
restarting Windows.

Windows Display Glitches and Setup

Video display in Windows can be problematic because each Windows application may handle screen display in a slightly different way and many vendors' video drivers for Windows are buggy. For example, a given video card and its Windows drivers may work perfectly with Photoshop but cause problems in other applications. Seek advice from users who use similar software before purchasing a video card.

Perhaps you have a 24-bit video card installed in your system and some of your applications exhibit strange behavior, such as text that disappears, frequent crashes, strange artifacts on your screen, and art that does not display properly. These problems are often attributable to your video cards and Windows driver software. Contact your vendor and obtain the latest version, as most of these vendors routinely update there drivers to solve such problems.

All 24-bit video cards and most multisync color monitors sold today support at least one of three popular resolutions: 640 by 480, 800 by 600, or 1024 by 768. Configure your video card's Windows drivers to run at the maximum resolution that supports 24-bit color and your monitor's display capability (Figure 2–19). The higher the resolution, the more you see on your monitor. This reduces the number of times you must scroll your window to see other parts of your image and gives you more room to display all those floating palettes in Photoshop.

Mice and Graphics Tablets

Many digital artists find that the standard mouse is far from perfect for navigating the computer and for drawing images freehand. Numerous options are available, such mice variations, track balls, and pressure-sensitive tablets.

Mouse Options

Many companies produce variations on the mouse to suite different working styles. The shape and feel of the mouse can vary. Some have extra buttons, such as a left button that represents a single click and a right button that represents a double click.

Track Balls

Instead of rolling a mouse (with a ball underneath) around on a bad, you can use a large ball mounted on a holder with a button. It's like turning the mouse upside down.

Digitizing Tablets

Most artists prefer a digitizing tablet and pressure-sensitive stylus as an alternative to a mouse. There are many manufacturers of graphics tablets for both Macintosh and Windows, but some of them are designed for specific applications, such as engineering. The tablets that are of most interest to artists are those manufactured by Wacom, CalComp, and Kurta. The Wacom ArtZ is a popular model among artists.

Photoshop supports the use of pressure-sensitive digital tablets in many painting tools. Set the parameters in the Options palette for how the tablet's pen will affect the use of the tool:

TIP: Double-click on a tool's icon in the Toolbox to open the Options palette.

Pencil	to vary Size, Color, or Opacity
Airbrush	to vary Color or Pressure
Paintbrush	to vary Size, Color, or Opacity
Rubber stamp	to vary Size or Opacity
Smudge	to vary Size or Pressure
Blur/Sharpen	to vary Size or Pressure
Dodge/Burn	to vary Size or Exposure
Sponge	to vary Size or Pressure

For example, if you select the Size option for the Paintbrush tool (Figure 2–20), applying downward pressure to the pen against the tablet interactively increases the width of the brush. Reducing pressure reduces the brush width, simulating real paintbrush strokes.

Figure 2–20
Changing the pressure when drawing with the stylus on the pressure sensitive WACOM ArtZ tablet varies the size of the Pencil tool's stroke.

Tablets are available in a variety of sizes, resolutions, sampling rates, and pressure levels. A tablet can connect either to the ADB connector (used by the mouse) or to a serial port on the Macintosh, and to a serial port on most PCs. Most of the newer tablets on the Macintosh can connect to the ADB (keyboard/mouse) port. These tablets are usually easier to configure and less troublesome over time. Try out different tablets, and purchase one which matches your purposes. For example, you might not need the largest (and most expensive) tablet if you will only use it to trace small pieces of artwork. Large tablets also use up valuable physical desk space and can be cumbersome to use.

Introduction to Printers

What good is Photoshop if what you see on your screen can't be printed out in some fashion? While working in Photoshop is fun, having a print in your hands completes the circle.

There are a number of options available for producing hard copy with Photoshop, depending on your needs. They range from Dot Matrix printers (useful for adding a retro-computer flair to your prints) and color lasers (suitable for comprehensives), to dye-sublimation devices (for surprisingly good photo-quality digital images) and imagesetters and film recorders (for the highest-quality output for reproduction on press). These devices and options for using them are discussed in detail in Chapter 11, "Output."

Introduction to Calibration

Before you start working seriously in Photoshop you should calibrate your system to assure that the color and tonal qualities of the prescanned original, the display, and the final output all match as closely as possible. See Chapter 3, "Configuring Photoshop," for details on how to calibrate and tune up your computer system to ensure predictable results.

Summary

This chapter focused on the hardware and software you need for an efficiently functioning Photoshop system, including basic system requirements for Photoshop, and the external devices to accomplish your imaging goals.

- If you really want Photoshop to function quickly and smoothly with a minimum of hassle, set up a system with much more processing power, memory, RAM, and storage than Adobe's recommended "minimum."

- Properly configure your Windows permanent swap file and ensure that 32-bit file access is enabled if your disk supports it.

- In the Memory Control Panel on the Mac, Set the System Disk Cache to lowest number, turn off Virtual Memory and turn on 32 bit addressing.

- To maximize the performance of Photoshop for Windows, ensure that the Physical Memory Usage section is set to 100% in the Used by Photoshop field. This allocates all the available RAM on your system to Photoshop.

- Consider adding a video accelerator to your system if you work with large, high-resolution images.

- You can further tweak performance by installing a CPU accelerator board and function-specific accelerators for Photoshop.

- If time is money to you, acceleration boards are definitely worth it. A function such as an Unsharp Mask filter that takes over two minutes to apply to a 6-Mb image in Photoshop and may take less than ten seconds using an acceleration board!

- Windows users can now connect their external devices through a superior SCSI interface.

- When it comes to input devices, displays, and output devices, you have many choices. Choose the hardware that is best for your primary work. Think ahead, buy equipment that allows you to add as much RAM as you might need and that has an upgrade path.

The next chapter covers the configuration and operating issues *within* Photoshop itself, including menus, preferences, display modes, file formats, and calibration.

CHAPTER 3

Configuring Photoshop

Photoshop is full of menus, dialog boxes, and controls that give you an exhaustive selection of tools and features. Navigating through this maze can take some time and requires a certain degree of patience.

Chapter 2 explained how to get your computer ready for Photoshop. This chapter discusses setting up Photoshop for your particular working situation. You will also be introduced to some of the most important aspects of Photoshop, including program preferences, the display modes, calibration, and creating and saving files. Do not be overwhelmed by the sheer number of options in the program. If approached methodically, you will see that Photoshop is logically organized (Figure 3–1).

General Organization

If you are a beginner to Photoshop, your first impression may be that this is one of the most complicated graphics programs you have ever encountered. Most graphics programs are not quite this dense. You have to pay a price for power.

Some software, such as Microsoft Word, have Short/Full or Beginner/Expert modes. These modes toggle certain features that a beginner might find confusing or intimidating. Once the user is familiar with the basic operations of a program, the full or expert menus can be turned on to access all of the features of the software. Photoshop does not offer a similar set of modes; all of the program's features are always present, whether you need them or not. However,

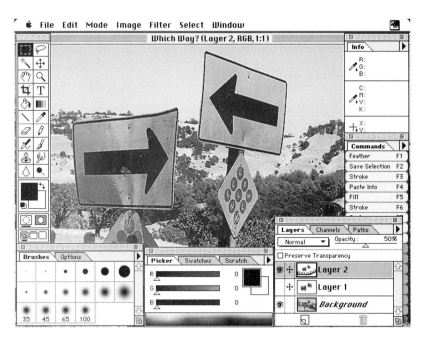

Figure 3–1
Photoshop's toolbox and
floating palettes in their
default positions.

after you spend some time with Photoshop you will find that it is more
straightforward than you might have imagined.

You access Photoshop's functions through:

- Menus and submenus, many of which open dialog boxes
- The toolbox
- Floating palettes, which also have pop-up menus, some of which also
  open dialog boxes
- Keyboard commands, some of which are built into the program and
  others which you can assign in the Commands palette

When painting, editing, manipulating, etc. on any document in
Photoshop you must always know where your work is taking place (layers
and channels) and where it is eventually going (output). Don't work with
your eyes closed. Aspects in Photoshop that deal with where your work is
taking place are:

- modes
- layers
- channels
- paths

Screen Display

Screen display can be managed in the Toolbox and opened automatically when Photoshop is launched. It can also be managed through the floating palettes, opened in the Palettes submenu under the Windows menu.

At the bottom of the toolbox are three small icons that control the screen display mode (shown at left). The default mode is the left-hand icon, displaying the menu bar and all open document windows. When you click on the middle icon, the current active document fills the screen and the menu bar remains visible. Clicking on the icon on the right makes the menu bar disappear, expanding the current active document to fill the whole screen.

TIP: You can temporarily make the Toolbox and any other open palette (window) invisible by pressing the Tab key on your keyboard, toggling the palettes on and off.

Assuming that you have enough memory, try working with more than one document open at a time. Open a new image by selecting New or Open under the File menu, or switch the active document by opening the Window menu and choose another open document from the list of open files at the bottom of the Window menu. Or simply click anywhere on the window of an open document and it will move to the front as an active document.

SCREEN DISPLAY FOR WINDOWS

Photoshop supports the Windows MDI (Multiple Document Interface) standard (Figure 3–2). You work in the program using Photoshop's own desktop which permits multiple images to be minimized (reduced to an icon) on this desktop by clicking the Minimize box (the box with the down arrow in the upper right corner of the image window.). This is an efficient way to free screen real estate to display your images or floating pallets. To view your minimized image double-click on the icon, which includes a thumbnail representation of your image and the file name, name of the selected layer, Mode, and magnification factor in the caption.

You can also maximize a window by clicking the Maximize box (the box with the up arrow in the right corner of the image window). Windows will enlarge your window to fill the entire Photoshop desktop. After your window is maximized, Windows will replace the maximize box with the Restore box (the box with the double arrow). If you click the Restore box, Windows will restore your window to its previous state. Each image displayed on your desktop contains the file name, name of the selected layer, Mode, and magnification factor in the title bar. You can double-click on this title bar to maximize the window.

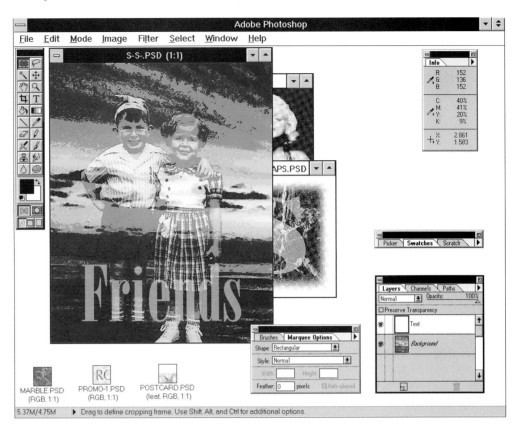

Figure 3–2   The Photoshop for Windows desktop showing images in a window, images reduced to an icon with a preview, palettes displayed open and rolled up, and the minimize and maximize boxes

---

The Menus

The menus always appear at the top of the screen. Press on a menu name to access the list of commands associated with it. Drag down to the desired name to activate the command (Figure 3–3).

- A triangle next to a name indicates that it has a submenu, so continue pressing the mouse to open the submenu. Continue pressing and drag down the submenu to the desired command.

- Three dots following a menu command indicate that a dialog box will open, requiring you to specify some parameters for the command. After entering the parameters or data, click the OK button to execute the command.

- When selected, some menu items have a check mark next to them indicating that they are currently active.

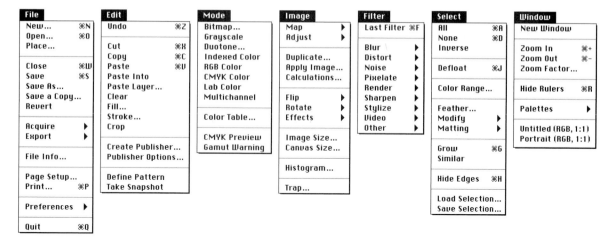

Figure 3–3   The menus in Photoshop (Macintosh version)

- Some menu commands toggle between two commands. For example, the Show Info command changes to the Hide Info command when the Info palette is open.
- The Windows version supports keyboard acceleration, which conforms to the Windows standard and is built into most Windows applications. This permits you to access all the menus in Photoshop by holding down the Alt key and pressing the underlined character in the menu name, the first character in the menu name. For example, to access the File menu hold down your Alt key and press F. Additionally, each menu option has one character which is underlined. For example to access Save As in the File menu hold down the Alt key and then press F and then V (Figure 3–4).

For a full discussion of the menus, see Chapters 5, 6, and 7.

FILE

File contains all the pertinent file functions (New, Open, Place, Save, Close, etc.), as well as menus (Acquire and Export) for any external drivers or plug-ins (such as third-party JPEG compression routines, scanner drivers, printers), preferences, and printing functions.

The Windows version has two additional menu options. The Open As command is used if the file extension is missing or incorrect but you know the correct file format or the file does not appear in the Open dialog box. The second menu option unique to Windows is the listing of the last four documents you worked on at the bottom of the File menu. This listing

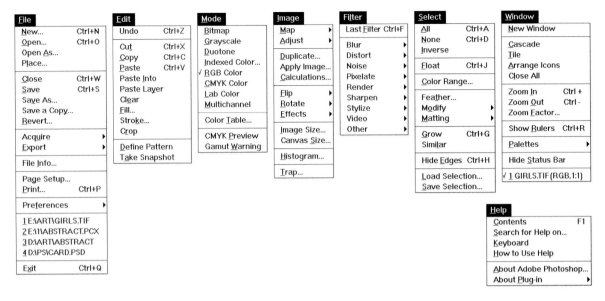

Figure 3–4   The Windows menus for Photoshop

includes the path to the document and saves time when searching for files to open. Choose the appropriate listing to open the file.

EDIT

Edit provides basic editing functions (Cut, Copy, and Paste); special paste modes for pasting into selections and onto layers; Fill, Stroke, and Crop commands; access to System 7 Publish and Subscribe on the Macintosh only; and controls for defining patterns and taking a snapshot.

MODE

The Mode menu includes access to the various display modes that allow you to view and process images in black-and-white, grayscale, duotone, additive color (red, green, and blue), subtractive color (cyan, magenta, yellow, and black), Lab color, and indexed color systems. From this menu you can also create multichannel images, create a CMYK preview of your image, and display out-of-gamut colors.

IMAGE

The Image menu controls image processing, tone control, color correction, multichannel effects, layer and channel compositing, dynamic effects (such as flipping, rotating, scaling, distorting), resizing and resampling, Histogram, and trapping.

FILTER

The Filter menu provides access to numerous filters for enhancing, sharpening, blurring, manipulating, and distorting images. Any plug-in filters installed will appear as additional menu commands under the Filter menu.

SELECT

The Select menu works with active selections or assists in making selections. Selections can be inversed, deselected, and duplicated. The edges of selections can be feathered, modified, matted, or hidden. Save selections as channels or load channels as selections. Included are commands to select the entire document, make selections based on a range of colors or similar colors within a selection, and grow an active selection beyond its current boundaries.

WINDOW

The Window menu creates new windows for a document, zoomed in and out, accesses rulers, and shows and hides the floating palettes. Currently open documents are displayed at the bottom of the menu.

   The Windows version contains a Status Bar option to display onscreen help. It describes the functions of the currently selected tool at the bottom of the Photoshop desktop. To turn this option off, select Hide Status Bar from the Window menu.

HELP (WINDOWS ONLY)

On-line help is available in this menu. Press F1 to open the Photoshop help file or select Search for Help from the Help menu.

Palettes

Palettes are interactive floating windows that you can move around the screen. The ten palettes are essential to interfacing with Photoshop's tools. In default mode they are Brushes and Options (grouped in one window), Picker, Swatches and Scratch (grouped in one window), Layers, Channels and Paths (grouped in one window), the Info palette, and the Commands palette.

   Start working with palettes in their default positions (Figure 3–1). At first palettes will seem to be in your way. Move them around the screen by dragging the Title Bar. Click on the Zoom box in the right side of the Title Bar or double-click on the palette tab to collapse or expand the palette and

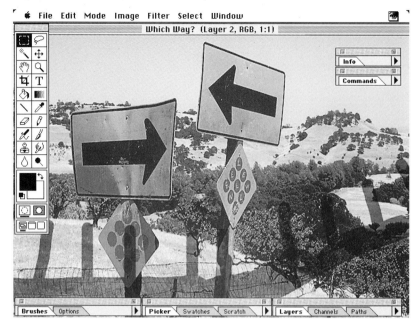

Figure 3–5
The Photoshop desktop
with all the floating
palettes collapsed
allowing more working
space. Collapse a palette
by clicking on the Zoom
box in the Title Bar or
double-clicking on the
palette's tab.

it will magically roll up and out of your way (Figure 3–5). After you get comfortable with palettes, you can shuffle them around to suit your needs.

TIP: **Keep the Options, Brushes, Layers, and Info palettes open at all times when painting, editing, or manipulating documents.**

See Chapter 5, "Tools and Palettes," for a discussion of palettes.

Display Modes

The display modes determine the color or tone description of a document. This description, referred to as a color model or color space, can be very simple, as in the case of the Bitmap mode, which has only black or white pixels, to a more complex color description such as the multichannel RGB or CMYK Color modes.

Use the different display modes for the following:

- Editing grayscale images
- Creating and manipulating duotones
- Working with color images and creating color separations
- Preparing images for optimized screen display for multimedia or video
- Creating and using masks with color and grayscale images
- Creating special effects with multiple channels
- Working with imported Photo CD images

Not all of the filters and image-processing features in Photoshop work with all of the display modes. For instance, if you want to process an imported 8-bit PICT file through most of Photoshop's special effects, you must convert the indexed image to RGB, manipulate the image, convert it back to indexed color, and then save it in PICT format for exporting. When working with grayscale images, the only features that will not work are those specifically relating to color.

NOTE: **Mode conversions change the data in your document. Don't change back and forth. Generally it's best to change in one direction only.**

Refer to Chapter 8, "Color," for more information on the display modes and mode conversions. The display modes available under the Mode menu include the following:

BITMAP

The Bitmap mode displays only black-and-white. Referred to as 1-bit display, all pixels are either black or white with no color or grayscale information. Use this mode for simple graphic images, and for creating dithered or pixelated effects and custom halftone screens.

GRAYSCALE

The Grayscale mode uses up to 256 shades of gray for each pixel in the image. Grayscale images can be obtained by scanning a black-and-white image, opening a Photo CD file created from a black-and-white negative, or converting a color image to Grayscale mode.

DUOTONE

Duotones, tritones, and quadtones are used in offset printing to increase the tonal range and to add color to black-and-white images. The monitor can display up to 256 shades of gray but the printing press can only reproduce about 50 tones of gray (or an ink color). By printing the same image two, three, or four times with different colors in register, the range of tones increases, rendering a richer, more saturated or colorful image.

INDEXED COLOR

The Indexed Color mode is used when you want to limit the number of colors used to display an image. Typical applications include on-screen presentations, multimedia, and animation. An indexed color image has a specific color look-up table, or fixed palette. In addition to making custom palettes, there are five default color palettes that can be used when converting to Indexed Color mode.

RGB COLOR

RGB (red-green-blue) Color mode is the normal Photoshop working mode. When you open a color scanned image into Photoshop (regardless of the file format), it is usually in the RGB display mode. RGB mode gives you access to all the capabilities of Photoshop's tools, commands, layers, channels, palettes, and filters. Each of the RGB channels can be viewed and edited separately. Since the monitor displays with RGB colors, the RGB Color mode offers the most synchronized display of pixel data.

CMYK COLOR

CMYK (cyan-magenta-yellow-black) Color mode is used for processing and creating four-color separations of a color image. The CMYK colors are the primary colors used in offset printing to create the full range of printable colors. An RGB image must be converted (color separated) to CMYK colors in order to have the image printed. Each of the CMYK channels can be viewed and edited separately.

LAB COLOR

The Lab Color mode is based on visual color perception using a standard created by the Commission Internationale de L'Éclairage (CIE). International standards for color measurements were established by this organization in 1931. Color values are defined mathematically so that they can exist independent of any device. The Lab color is an independent color space used by Photoshop to internally convert between color modes. In the Lab Color mode, values are separated from color information, allowing you to manipulate the tones without affecting colors or manipulate colors without affecting values.

MULTICHANNEL

The Multichannel mode is probably the most "generic" display mode in Photoshop. It consists of one to 24 grayscale channels that can be displayed individually or as a composite. When viewed as a composite each channel will appear in the color set in Channel Options (a hierarchical submenu in

Figure 3–6
Identify the target layer in the Layers palette on the Mac (left) by a solid gray panel and in Windows (right) by a solid white panel. The "eye" icon indicates visible layers.

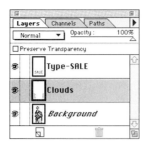

the Channel Palette). You can use the Multichannel mode to view duotone color plates in grayscale but not to save duotones. The Multichannel mode is also used as a transition to convert duotones to the Scitex CT file format.

Layers

Layers, a dynamic new feature in Photoshop 3, allows for the stacking of multiple layers (up to 99) in perfect register. These transparent layers liberate you to alter the pixel data when combining (pasting) images. A layered document appears as one flat layer, but in reality all layers maintain their position in a suspended space. The layers, analogues to sheets of acetate, can be edited and manipulated with any of Photoshop's tools and functions. Layer order can be easily changed by dragging layers to new positions in the Layers palette (Figure 3–6). In the Layers palette you can duplicate, merge, group, and move layers. You can also control how layers combine with each other with the modes (Figure C–1 in the Color section).

You can only paint, edit, or manipulate one layer (the target layer) at a time. The target layer is identified in the Layers palette by a solid gray panel on the Macintosh and a solid white panel in the Windows version. The "eye" icon indicates the current visible layer.

TIP: Keep the Layers palette open at all times. Beware that it is easy to accidentally alter one layer while viewing another layer.

Issues relating to layers and the Layers palette will come up throughout this book. For more information, refer to Chapter 5, "Tools and Palettes," Chapter 6, "Image Selection and Masking," and Chapter 10, "Compositing."

Channels

A color image in Photoshop is actually a combination of independent channels. The number of channels that contribute to the composite image depends on the color mode. For example, an image in RGB Color mode is composed of three channels: red, green, and blue. Since Photoshop can have up 24 channels in a document, the remaining channels are typically used to store selections which are then used as masks. Channels can be added to all of the modes except for the Bitmap mode.

Every pixel of a channel (8 bits) has a brightness value ranging between black (0) and white (255), and the values in between correspond to the grayscale spectrum of 256 tones. Each channel is actually a grayscale image with 256 tones. In the case of a color image, these values in each channel are assigned color values which combine to create millions of colors. For example, in RGB Color mode, the three 8-bit channels with 256 tones in each channel total 24 bits, yielding 16,777,216 colors. In CMYK Color mode the first four channels are reserved for cyan, magenta, yellow, and black.

NOTE: Every pixel of a color image on a 24-bit monitor consists of a mix of red, green, and blue values. A monitor displays with RGB colors regardless of mode. A pixel with a value of 0 for each of the RGB tones is black, while 255 for each of the RGB values results in a white pixel. A pixel with a red value of 255 and blue and green values of 0 is red, and values of 255 for both red and blue and 0 for green yield magenta. See Chapter 8, "Color," for more on color.

Channels can be viewed and edited independently of each other (see Figure 1–11). To view and manipulate individual channels or combinations of channels, use the Channels palette in the Window menu. The "eye" indicates which channel(s) you are viewing and a gray background (white in Windows) on a channel name indicates that you can edit the selected channel.

TIP: It is possible to view one channel and while editing another. But be careful—don't accidentally work in the wrong channel.

See Chapter 6, "Image Selection and Masking," and Chapter 10, "Compositing," for more information on using channels.

Paths

Photoshop contains a mini vector graphics component with a drawing tool, the Pen tool, similar to the pen tools in Adobe Illustrator and Macromedia FreeHand. The Pen tool and related controls are available in the Paths palette. Use it to draw precise shapes that can be converted to selections or saved as clipping paths to mask images placed in other programs. In addition to converting paths to selections, selections can be converted to paths. Paths can be named and saved in the Paths palette.

TIP: Paths use less memory than channels.

To learn more about paths, see Chapter 6, "Image Selection and Masking."

Document Management

Magnifying Image Elements

You can zoom into and out from an image by using the Zoom tool in the main toolbox. Click the magnifier on the image window to zoom in, and Option-click to zoom out. When zooming in, the magnifier icon will contain a "+" character and when zooming out it will contain a "−" character. If the character disappears from inside the Zoom tool, you are as far as you can go in that direction. The maximum magnification and reduction ratios are 16:1 (1600%) and 1:16. You can also magnify a specific portion of an image by dragging the Zoom tool over that portion.

Zoom controls are also located in the Window menu. You can use these commands instead of the Zoom tool, but it's usually easier to use the keyboard equivalents: Command "+" for magnification, Command "−" for reduction.

WINDOWS TIP: Remember, on a PC, substitute the Ctrl key for the Command key.

There are other keyboard shortcuts for zooming and scrolling: Command, Spacebar, and click with the mouse on the area to zoom in; Option, Command, Spacebar, and click on the area to zoom out; and hold the Spacebar and drag with the mouse to scroll (Hand Tool).

TIP: To zoom in on a particular area to the maximum magnification possible in the current window size, select the Zoom tool and then drag a rectangle on the desired area. Double-clicking on the Zoom tool will restore the 1:1 view of the image.

The current magnification ratio is displayed in the title bar of a document's window. As you zoom in and out of a document, the ratio is updated in the title bar (Figure 3–7). This ratio represents the relationship of the screen resolution to the image resolution. At a 1:1 view the resolution of the screen and the image are matched and Photoshop is using every pixel of the monitor to represent every pixel of recorded information in the image. A high-resolution image will appear very large at a 1:1 view and a low-resolution image will be small. Zooming in and out changes only the view of an image, not its size.

TIP: If you are working on a document and want to create multiple views of an image, choose the New Window command from the Windows menu to create multiple, simultaneously magnified views of a working document. When

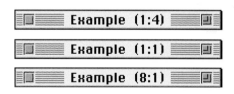

Figure 3–7
The title bars showing the zoom factor
of 1:4 (reduced to 25%), 1:1 (actual
size), and 8:1 (800% magnification)

Figure 3–8
The document size indicator
in the lower left of the
document window

you paint in one view, the other views are updated immediately after you
release the mouse button.

Document and Scratch Size Indicators

In the lower-left corner of a document window is a document size indicator
(Figure 3–8). The number to the left of the slash represents the amount of
RAM the active document is using. The value to the right of the slash is
the approximate size of the document when saved on disk.

By pressing on the triangle to the right of the document size indicator
and then selecting Scratch Sizes from the pop-up menu, you can also monitor the amount of virtual memory used by your open documents. In this
case, the number to the left of the slash refers to the amount of space in
kilobytes Photoshop is using for all open images. The value on the right is
the amount of RAM available to Photoshop. When the number on the left
is larger than the one on the right, Photoshop is using hard disk space (the
specified *scratch disk*) as virtual memory.

NOTE: Photoshop divides each image into tiles, which has a direct effect on
how Photoshop assigns memory for layers. If you add a full image on a layer
into an illustration and all the tiles of the new layer have data in them, the size
of your file could double. If you add a partial image to your illustration so that
only some of the layers' tiles contain data, Photoshop will add only the size of
the filled tiles to the size of the file.

Previewing Page Size

If you press and hold on the size indicator number, a Page Preview window
pops up and displays a dummy of a full page (as specified in the Page Setup
dialog). It shows a bounding box of the total area occupied by the document. Even if you have two separate elements on two extreme sides of the

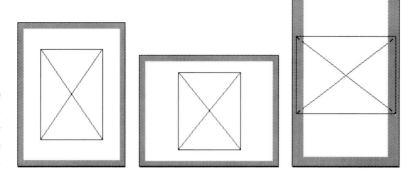

Figure 3–9
The Page Preview pop-up display appears by pressing on the document size indicator.

image, the bounding box is drawn based on the defined size of the document (Figure 3–9).

If your image is larger than the current page size, the bounding box will extend off the edge of the page and the image will print cropped. Photoshop cannot tile an image for multiple-page registered output, a capability found in many page layout programs. You must take Photoshop images into PosterWorks, Adobe PageMaker, QuarkXPress, or another program that has tiling capabilities.

Any parameters set in the Page Setup dialog box is displayed in the miniature page view, including crop and registration marks, calibration bars, negative output, and emulsion type (Figure 3–10).

Other Size Parameters

If you hold the Option key while pressing on the size indicator, the Page Preview display is replaced by a numerical readout that includes information on the resolution, size, and number of channels in the document (Figure 3–11).

The size of the image is displayed in both pixels and any other units selected in the Units dialog found in the Preferences command under the File menu.

If you hold the Command key while pressing on the size indicator, the Page Preview display is replaced by a numerical readout. This readout includes information on the size and number of the tiles into which Photoshop breaks your image to store in RAM and on the disk.

The size and resolution of the document can be controlled with the Image Size command under the Image menu. If you need some extra space to work with around an image, use the Canvas Size command, also under the Image menu. Image Size and Canvas Size are explained in Chapter 7, "Image Processing."

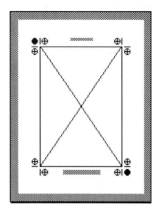

Figure 3–10
The Page Preview pop-up
displays crop marks,
registration marks, and
calibration bars, which are
set in the Page Setup
dialog box.

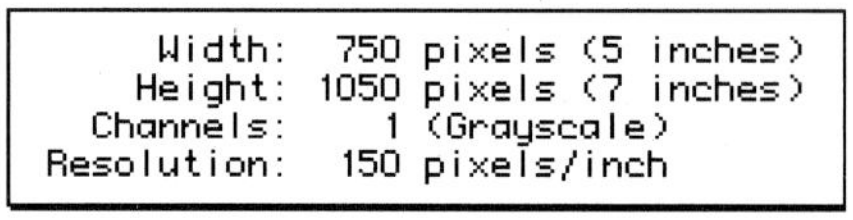

```
Width:    750 pixels (5 inches)
Height:  1050 pixels (7 inches)
Channels:    1 (Grayscale)
Resolution:  150 pixels/inch
```

Figure 3–11
A numerical readout appears if you
hold the Option key while pressing on
the document size indicator.

Rulers

You can activate Photoshop's onscreen rulers by choosing the Show Rulers command under the Window menu. The measurement units used in the rulers display are set with the Units submenu found in Preferences under the File menu. Set the units individually for the vertical and horizontal rulers in pixels, inches, centimeters, picas, or points (and in the case of the width, columns), as discussed in the next section, "Setting Preferences."

You can also change the ruler's origin points by dragging from the upper-left corner where the two rulers meet (Figure 3–12). This control works exactly as its equivalent in many other design programs. Press the pointer in this area, drag to the new desired zero origin location, and release the mouse button. Double-clicking on the upper-left corner where the two rulers meet will restore the origin point of the rulers.

Entering File Info

You can add specific instructions and comments to any image using the File Info dialog accessed under the File menu. Selecting either Caption, Keywords, Credits, Categories, or Origin from the pop-up menu brings up a set of data fields specific to each type of comment (Figure 3–13). This is very handy for your own record keeping, for processing images for clients in a work group, or for ensuring that photocredits stay with an image. You can search for keywords and captions in some image cataloging programs, such as Adobe Fetch.

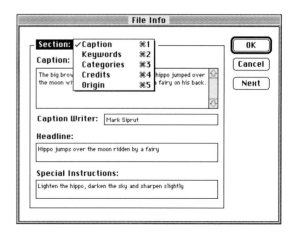

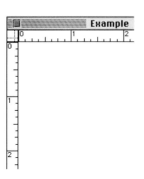

Figure 3–12
The Ruler's zero origin point can be repositioned by dragging from the upper-left corner of the rulers.

Figure 3–13
Enter data about an image in the File Info dialog box.

The Newspaper Association of America (NAA) and the International Press Telecommunications Council (IPTC) have developed an information standard for captioning transmitted text and graphics. This standard is supported in Photoshop with the File Info command.

Setting Preferences

Photoshop remembers a variety of settings by creating a Preferences file, stored in your Preferences folder/directory. In the File menu are the Preferences submenus (Figure 3–14). The Preferences settings control general display options, scratch disks for virtual memory, color separation setup information, calibration options, display options, tool options, ruler units, and more.

NOTE: Be aware that once you set or change any of the preferences, these settings affect all future documents that are opened in Photoshop. Some settings affect only the display of a document, some affect the output only, and some affect both.

TIP: If Photoshop exhibits strange behavior, like crashing when launched or failing to print properly, you can sometimes correct these problems by deleting your Preference file in the Macintosh or Windows version while Photoshop is

Figure 3–14
The Preferences sub-
menu in the Mac version
of Photoshop on the left
and the Windows
version on the right

closed. **Photoshop will create a new one the next time you open the program. The settings will return to the factory defaults.**

General

General Preferences has a variety of settings that affect how documents are viewed and manipulated (Figure 3–15).

COLOR PICKER

You have your choice of either the standard Apple Color Picker or the Photoshop Color Picker. In the Windows version the Color Picker list box lets you select the Windows color picker to specify your colors. The Apple and Windows Color Pickers allow you to select colors from the HSB or RGB color models.

The Photoshop Color Picker offers much more color selection control than does the Apple or Windows Color Picker. For example, the Photoshop Color Picker alerts you to colors that cannot be printed on a printing press. Choose colors from several systems: HSB (hue, saturation, and brightness), RGB (red, green, and blue), CMYK (cyan, magenta, yellow, and black), Lab (luminance and chroma), or Custom Color Palettes.

See Chapter 8, "Color," for more on selecting and using colors.

INTERPOLATION

Through interpolation Photoshop determines the color of pixels to be added or deleted when an image is resampled, rotated, or distorted. All the dynamic effects in Photoshop are tied into the interpolation settings, including resizing (both the interactive resizing controls and the Resize command in the Image menu), distortion, perspective, and rotation commands. The quality and speed performance of these features are directly affected by the interpolation mode selected in the Preferences dialog:

- **Nearest Neighbor** is the fastest interpolation method, but yields the lowest quality. If you distort or resize an image, the image will be recalculated with a large amount of distortion.

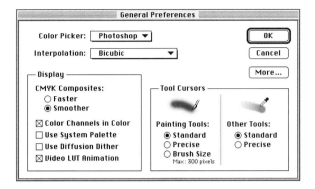 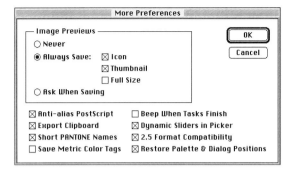

Figure 3–15 The General Preferences dialog box. Click on the More button for more preferences

- **Bilinear** is a medium-quality method, with the quality residing somewhere between nearest neighbor and bicubic.
- **Bicubic** is the slowest of the methods, but gives you the highest-quality results. This method is the default setting when you run the program.

Figure 3–16 demonstrates the differences in quality between the three interpolation modes with the Scale, Skew, Perspective, Distort, and Rotate commands applied.

DISPLAY

There are several options that control how documents are displayed on the monitor. These display options affect only what you see on the screen, not the output data.

- **CMYK Composites** When working in CMYK Color mode the computer has to temporarily convert the pixels of the image to the red, green, and blue primary colors of the monitor. With the Faster option selected, the screen is drawn almost as fast as it is in RGB Color mode. However, these colors and values will be less accurate than if you select the Smoother option. Smoother takes longer to redraw.
- **Color Channels in Color** When you view individual Lab, RGB, or CMYK channels on the screen, they can be viewed as shades of gray or in the actual color of the channel. For example, when looking at the channels of a 24-bit color image, you can view them in their actual colors of shades of red, green, or blue. Displaying in gray is appropriate for a yellow channel, which is difficult to see. Viewing channels without colors enabled also allows you to precisely evaluate the color saturation by looking at corresponding gray values.

Nearest Neighbor   *Bilinear*   *Bicubic*

Figure 3–16   These examples demonstrate Nearest Neighbor, Bilinear, and Bicubic interpolation methods. The Scale, Skew, Perspective, Distort, and Rotate commands were applied.

This setting will have no effect on your display if you use a grayscale monitor or black-and-white system.

- **Use System Palette** When working with Photoshop on a system with an 8-bit video display, you can force the display to use the standard Macintosh or Windows System palette. When working with multiple 24-bit Photoshop files, each time you select a different document window the colors in the other document windows will go crazy for a few moments because Photoshop is calculating an optimized 256-color palette to best represent the 24-bit data in the active document. The colors in the other open documents are remapped to the colors in the current active palette, resulting in a fun, but useless, color effects show. By activating Use System Palette, you are effectively forcing Photoshop to use the standard Apple/Windows 256-color default palette to represent all of the open documents. Although you will have a less accurate 8-bit representation of 24-bit data, all of the open windows will show consistent color.

Choose Use System Palette if you use an 8-bit video display and plan to work with multiple color files at one time. If you open files from any program that can create and save images with custom 256-color palettes, you will notice that as you click on each different window the colors in the other windows will redraw, usually with odd results. The custom color palette for the currently selected window overrides all other palettes. This redrawing becomes more noticeable depending on the number of documents open at once, and on the resolution of the images. If your open documents are high-resolution images, screen redraw might become quite a bother (the higher the resolution of an image, the longer it takes to redraw the image on the screen).

TIP: One way to check if a custom palette is being used by the foreground window is to look at the little colored apple used by the desk accessory menu. If its colors aren't the normal rainbow colors, a custom palette is in use.

- **Use Diffusion Dither** This option enhances color transitions in an image when using an 8-bit video display. Dithering gives the illusion of a color or value in between adjacent pixels by scattering or dispersing two different-colored pixels together.

  The Use System Palette and Use Diffusion Dither controls will have no effect if you are running Photoshop in 24-bit display mode with a 24-bit video card because many different 256-color palettes can be handled simultaneously without palette remapping.

- **Video LUT Animation** If Video LUT Animation is on with the preview button not selected while using the image-processing controls (the Map and Adjust commands), all open Photoshop documents will show changes in real-time. If the preview box is selected, the adjustments will show only in the active document.

  With Video LUT Animation off when using image-processing controls with the preview button deselected, open windows will not show changes as they are being made. If the preview box is selected, the adjustments will show only in the active document.

TOOL CURSORS

Each Photoshop tool is represented by a distinct icon that has a *hot spot* to determine where a selection or action begins. For detailed work, use the

Tool Cursors preferences to change a default cursor to cross hairs or to the brush size in the case of painting tools (Figure 5-33 shows the tools and their hot spots).

The **Painting Tools** options let you change the default cursors for the Gradient, Line, Eraser, Pencil, Airbursh, Paintbrush, Rubber stamp, Smudge, Sharpen/blur, and Dodge/burn/sponge tools.

The **Other Tools** options change the cursor for the Marquee, Lasso, Magic Wand, Cropping, Eyedropper, and Paint Bucket tools.

MORE BUTTON

Click on the More button to access more general preferences.

- **Image Previews (Macintosh only)** Image Previews lets you set defaults for file icons, Open dialog box thumbnails, and full-size 72 dpi previews required by some other applications that open Photoshop images.

  When running System 7, Image Previews shows thumbnail images of the documents as icons in folders on the desktop. These thumbnails are helpful for remembering what images look like without having to open them. The choices Never, Always Save, or Ask When Saving allow you to decide whether or not to include an image icon to represent your document on the desktop. With the Ask When Saving option on, you are given the option to save previews in the Save As dialog box when saving a document.

  NOTE: Saving previews uses more memory.

- **Anti-Alias Postscript** When placing or pasting a PostScript vector image (e.g., Adobe Illustrator) into Photoshop, Anti-Alias Postscript improves the quality of an image as it is rasterized. Because it takes more work, this function will slow down the operation.

- **Export Clipboard** By deselecting Export Clipboard the clipboard will be emptied when switching applications or when quitting Photoshop. If you want to copy and paste between programs, leave this button on.

  TIP: Every time you open a desk accessory in Photoshop or switch to another program, the clipboard is processed according to the selected clipboard export option. If you have a large image on the clipboard this conversion process makes you wait until the conversion is finished before proceeding. If you need to access a peripheral desk accessory while in Photoshop or want to work in another program, abandon "Export Clipboard." Leave it on it you want to copy and paste between programs.

- **Short Pantone Names** Use Short Pantone Names if you plan on exporting duotones, tritones, or quadtones to other programs with Pantone names for the colors (Figure 3–17). If you do not use Short Pantone Names the colors will not output on the corresponding plates when making separations in other programs because the names will not have the same spellings (unless you manually specify the spelling in each of the programs). See Chapter 8, "Color," for more on creating duotones, tritones, and quadtones, and see Chapter 11, "Output," for printing considerations.

- **Save Metric Color Tags** Photoshop version 3 enables you to save files with EFI Color metric color tags, assuring color consistency between Photoshop, QuarkXPress, and numerous output devices.

- **Beep When Tasks Finish** This reminder tells your computer to beep when an operation is completed. This is helpful when performing time-consuming tasks, allowing you to read, daydream, or work on your other computer.

- **Dynamic Sliders in Picker** Photoshop's Picker palette lets you edit the foreground and background colors using several different color models. This is accomplished by moving sliders representing different color components. By default these sliders change colors as you drag. Turning off this feature can improve performance. (See Chapter 5, "Tools and Palettes," for details on using the Picker palette.)

- **2.5 Format Compatibility** 2.5 Format Compatibility lets you determine whether or not Photoshop 3 opens version 2.5 files by double-clicking. The default setting for the 2.5 Format Compatibility check box is on. This means that when you save a file in Photoshop 3 format, a layerless version 2.5 compatible file is saved inside the file so it opens in 2.5. If you *only* use version 3 on the Macintosh or Windows platforms turn this option off to save disk space. These files are about 25 to 35 percent smaller and still contain your layers.

- **Restore Palette and Dialog Positions** Select this option if you want Photoshop to remember the position of all your open windows the next time you open the program; otherwise, only the default windows (toolbox and Brushes palette) will open.

Figure 3–17
Use the "Short Pantone Names" option to avoid costly output mistakes.

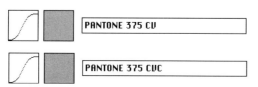

PANTONE 375 CU

PANTONE 375 CUC

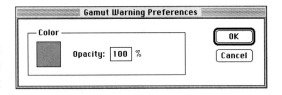

Figure 3–18
The Gamut Warning
dialog box

Gamut Warning

Photoshop by default identifies out-of-gamut colors by displaying them in gray. Use the Gamut Warning Preferences option to select a different color and opacity for the warning (Figure 3–18). Bright green or shocking pink usually does the trick!

Plug-ins

You can use the Plug-ins preference dialog to select a different folder or directory from which Photoshop will access plug-ins. Photoshop's default folder/directory is named Plug-ins on the Macintosh and PLUGINS on the PC. Photoshop can load plug-ins which are in folders inside the plug-in folder. It also supports aliases of plug-ins and folders on the Macintosh. You can use this feature to locate all your plug-ins in one folder and then make aliases of the ones you want to load and place these in your Photoshop plug-in folder.

TIP: Plug-ins that Photoshop loads at startup consume memory even if you never use them. Move infrequently used plug-ins to a new folder (directory) like "Removed plug-ins," which is located outside of the Plug-ins folder.

Scratch Disks (Macintosh Only)

In addition to RAM (random access memory), Photoshop uses a designated hard disk to temporarily store your document. This proprietary technique is called virtual memory. Please don't confuse this technique with the virtual memory built into System 7.

TIP: The process of using disk space for RAM, called virtual memory, is built into System 7. Virtual memory needs to be turned off in the Memory control panel for Photoshop's virtual memory to work correctly.

On the Mac, virtual memory is assigned in Photoshop's Scratch Disks preferences dialog box. It can be assigned to any hard disk attached to your computer. The default scratch disk for virtual memory is the startup disk, but any disk on your system can be used. You can even assign a secondary disk in case the primary one becomes overloaded. It's a good idea to use your fastest hard disk, leaving as much space free as possible (Figure 2–9).

Memory (Windows Only)

The Memory Preferences dialog box, unique to Windows, combines the Scratch Disk preference found on the Macintosh version of Photoshop with the Physical Memory Usage section which was discussed in Chapter 2 (Figure 2–13). Any settings you change in this dialog box require you to restart Photoshop. Within the Memory Preferences dialog box, the Scratch Disk preferences function the same way as in the Macintosh version. Rather than use your Windows permanent swap file, Photoshop uses a proprietary scratch disk which it creates and uses to store your images.

It is not recommended that you point the Scratch Disk to a compressed drive. Compressed drives have caused problems, such as lost data and corrupted files, with Windows and many applications that use them.

Transparency

When working with layers or a transparent image, transparent areas are indicated by a gray checkerboard pattern. The Transparency Preferences option allows you to vary the pattern, size, and color (Figure 3–19).

Units

You can specify ruler units in pixels, inches, centimeters, points, and picas. These units apply to any dialog box or window that uses measurements.

The Column size and gutter controls allow you to simulate multiple-column layouts within Photoshop to create comprehensive layouts without a page layout program. By setting a fixed column and gutter size that corresponds to the related settings in your page layout program, you can crop images so that the ratio of the cropped image matches the column specifications in the receiving page layout program (Figure 3–20).

Monitor Setup

The Monitor Setup dialog box balances several factors that affect how colors and values are viewed on the monitor (Figure 3–21). This dialog also affects the conversion of colors between modes. Monitor Setup should only be used as part of the calibration process (see the next section).

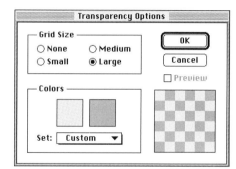

Figure 3–19
The Transparency
Options dialog box

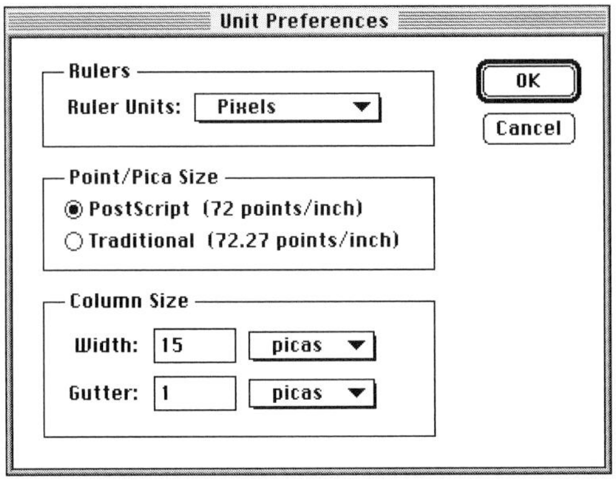

Figure 3–20
The Unit Preferences
dialog box

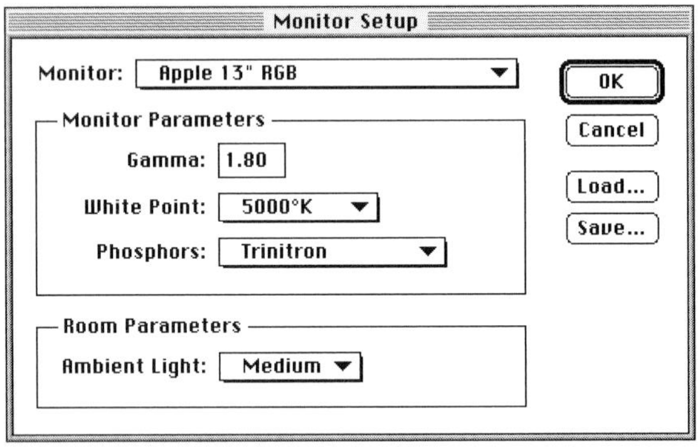

Figure 3–21
The Monitor Setup
dialog box in Preferences

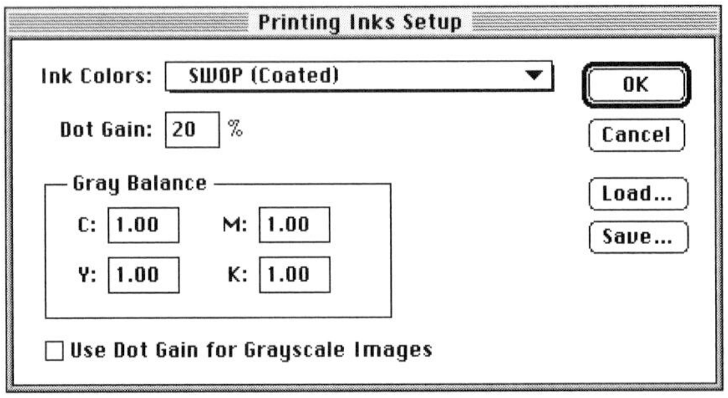

Figure 3–22
The Printing Inks Setup
dialog box
under Preferences

NOTE: Monitor Setup, Printing Inks Setup, and Separation Setup are part of the calibration process. See the next section for more information on calibration.

Printing Inks Setup

Printing Inks Setup affects the conversion to CMYK Color mode (Figure 3–22). Adjust the colors and values for printing to a CMYK postscript printer and outputting from other than the CMYK mode. See the next section on calibration for more information.

Separation Setup

The Separation Setup preference controls the amount of black generated in the black plate when converting to CMYK Color mode. This preference also affects the black generation when printing to a CMYK postscript printer if output from other than the CMYK mode.

The Separation Type buttons toggle the choices GCR (Gray Component Replacement) and UCR (Undercolor Removal). The black generation can be set to None, Light, Medium, or Maximum, or a custom setting.

Separation Tables

If you print images to a variety of output devices or different paper stocks, Separation Tables can be used to save and then load the settings made in Separation Setup and Printing Inks Setup.

TIP: Don't adjust Monitor Setup, Printing Inks Setup, or Separation Tables in the middle of a project. These settings are generally adjusted as part of the calibration process or after consultation with your printer and/or service bureau. See the following section on Calibration, Chapter 8, "Color," and Chapter 11, "Output," for more information.

Calibration

Any experience working with color images quickly exposes you to the difficulties and frustrations of getting color the way you want it. If you start with a color transparency or print and scan it on your desktop scanner, it will probably look different on the screen from the original. When you print the image on a digital color printer or printing press, the output colors may stray even farther from the original colors. And color output will probably vary according to each different kind of output device.

If you do serious work in Photoshop (and what work isn't?) you should calibrate your system to assure that the color and tonal qualities of the prescanned original, the display, and the final output all match each other as closely as possible. Calibration is a process to adjust equipment to a standard measurement in order to produce reliable consistent output. Equipment can be calibrated to a specific standard, as in the case of a printer calibrated to produce consistent gray values (linearized). Two or more pieces of equipment can also be calibrated to match each other as close as possible. A calibration process can be standardized to meet specific output devices and needs.

TIP: In addition to calibrating your system, you can use a color management system to establish profiles of all the devices in your system. The color management system will transform an image to the optimal profile of an output device. See the following section on Color Management for more information.

Calibrating your system has two parts. First, each element of your system—your room lighting, monitor, scanner, and printer—should, in itself, be consistent. You cannot trust what you see if your room lighting changes, your monitor displays color images differently as it warms up, or as your printer's output varies. Second, you should calibrate your whole system together, including off-site output devices. In particular, adjust your monitor to display color and tones that match your intended output. More than one output device might require different monitor settings for each device. Once you can obtain predictable results from your output devices, you should establish scanner settings or calibration to produce as good a digital reproduction of the original as possible.

Even if your system is exactly calibrated, you will never get a perfect match between any two components. Humans can see many more colors than can be recorded on film, so reality can't be matched by a photograph. A scanner cannot record all the colors that are on film or in a photographic print, so a photograph cannot be matched by a digitized image viewed on a monitor. And what you see on a monitor will not match exactly what gets printed, no matter how high-end the output device.

Remember that a monitor *uses projected light*, which is composed of the additive primary colors (red, green, and blue—RGB). Printed output *reflects light*, optically mixing the subtractive primary colors (cyan, yellow, and magenta, plus black—CMYK). For more information on color theory, see Chapter 8, "Color."

The complex issues of calibration in the production process are most critical when using Photoshop to separate a color image into four process colors (converting to CMYK Color mode). Your monitor calibration and the settings you make in Photoshop's Preferences significantly affect the display and printing of your image. For more information on color separations and printing, see Chapter 11, "Output."

Monitor calibration also affects all other work you do in Photoshop. Even if you purchase scans from a high-end drum scanner already separated into CMYK Color mode, monitor calibration affects the display of the image on the screen because the monitor displays with the RGB primary colors. The computer interprets the CMYK colors in the image for the RGB representation on the screen.

Calibration is important even if you work only with grayscale images. Most monitors are much brighter and bluer than output. Settings in Monitor Preferences for white point and gamma, which control how a monitor's output reflects the given input values, affect the brightness and contrast of grayscale images.

The bottom line is that you must calibrate your system to trust that what you see on your screen will have any relationship to what you eventually print.

The following discussion will help you get the monitor and printer components of your system working together. To optimize your scans to your calibrated system, see Chapter 4, "Input."

The Steps of Calibration: An Overview

1. Create an environment in which your images can be properly viewed.
2. Calibrate your monitor to consistently and predictably display images and to make your display more closely match your output.
3. Make sure that your output devices or proofing system is calibrated and producing consistent results.
4. Print an image that has an identifiable range of colors or tones like the *Olé No Moiré* (Mac) or TESTPICT.JPG (PC) image that comes with Photoshop. If your target is commercial printing, have your color service bureau or printer make a laminated proof from film separations.
5. Examine the proof, whether digital or laminated, and compare it to the same document open in Photoshop on the monitor. If necessary, make adjustments to the display with the Gamma utility (or third-party calibration software) or in Photoshop's Preferences.
6. Establish an input or scanning procedure that will produce a result closely matching your original.

Create a Color Environment

Before you calibrate your system, set up an environment in which to view and display color. Your color perception depends on the brightness and color of the room lighting, on any bright colors in the area of your monitor, and on the actual background color set on your monitor.

Ideally, view images in a room with neutral gray walls and controlled subdued lighting. Although you may not have a perfect environment for working with color (perhaps gray walls and subdued lighting drive you crazy), try to stabilize your work space as much as possible. A good start is to move your monitor away from windows and use window shades.

Depending on your system, set the background of your monitor to neutral gray:

- On the Mac, using system 7.1 or earlier, choose General Controls in the Control Panel under the Apple menu and set the desktop pattern to a solid neutral gray (Figure 3–23).
- On the Mac, using System 7.5, choose Desktop Patterns in the Control Panel under the Apple menu and set the desktop pattern to a solid neutral gray by choosing Pattern number 4 (Figure 3–24).
- On a PC under Windows, choose the neutral gray desktop pattern by launching the Windows Control Panel and double-clicking on the Color icon. Click the Color Palette button and select Desktop in the Screen Element drop-down list (Figure 3–25).

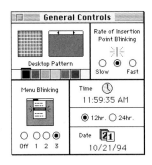

Figure 3–23
On the Mac, using System 7.1 or earlier. set the background of the monitor to neutral gray in the General Control Panel.

Figure 3–24
On the Mac, using System 7.5 set the background of the monitor to neutral gray in the Control Panel Desktop Patterns.

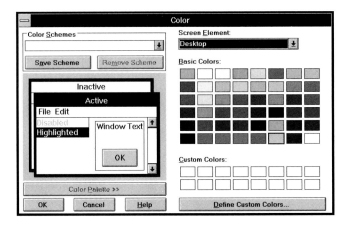

Figure 3–25
Change your Windows desktop color to a solid neutral gray via the Color Dialog box in the Windows Control Panel.

Finally, all the good work you do setting up your environment can be undone if someone mucks around with your monitor controls. Tape your monitor's brightness and contrast controls into position.

Monitor Calibration

Monitor calibration software achieves consistency and predictability of the colors a monitor displays. The software can adjust display colors, affecting brightness, contrast and gray balance. Monitor calibration can also help remove color cast and adjust the gamma, or brightness curve, to make the monitor resemble the effect of various paper stocks or to match the gamma of a slide film recorder or television screen (for video).

CAUTION: Do not trust the color on a monitor until it warms up. As a monitor warms up, its display color changes. Monitor color will also change as the monitor ages, which calls for checking and recalibrating.

There are two approaches to monitor calibration. Use one method but not both: the Gamma utility that comes with Photoshop or a Third-Party Calibrator. If you use Third-Party Calibration, turn off or remove Gamma.

GAMMA

Use the Gamma utility that comes with Photoshop to manually calibrate your monitor (Figure 3–26). On the Macintosh, the Gamma utility is a Control Panel device (under the Apple menu) that adjusts monitor display for all applications on the computer—not just Photoshop. Move the Gamma utility from the Photoshop folder to the Control Panel folder.

To access Gamma Calibration in the Windows version of Photoshop, select Preferences from the File menu and choose Monitor Setup from the submenu. Then click the Calibrate button in the Monitor Setup dialog box (Figure 3–27). These settings apply *only* to Photoshop and do not affect other Windows applications.

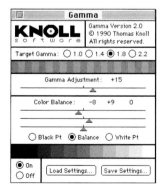

Figure 3–26
On the Mac, calibrate the monitor with the Gamma Control Panel device.

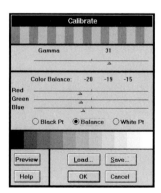

Figure 3–27
The Windows Calibrate dialog box, located in Photoshop under Preferences

The Gamma utility allows you to set precisely the gamma levels of any monitors you have attached to your computer for optimum screen brightness. Using this utility you can set the white and black points, the brightest white, and the darkest black the monitor can display. Adjustments can also remove color casts from your monitor display.

Gamma can also be used to calibrate monitors among various workstations so that there is consistent color representation from screen to screen. Refer to Chapter 2 in the Photoshop 3 *User Guide* for a full description of how to use Gamma utility on your platform.

THIRD-PARTY CALIBRATION

Another approach to calibrating your monitor is to use a third-party monitor calibration system. Examples of calibrators are the SuperMatch Display Calibrator and the DayStar Colorimeter 24.

A third-party monitor calibrator usually includes a suction cup sensor device or colorimeter that sticks on your screen. The device measures the light produced by your monitor's phosphors, adjusting the colors through software. The software then sends corrected signals back to the display. When used with a color management system, a monitor calibrator can write the color information to a profile to match the colors on your monitor to the colors produced by your output device.

The software interface on a monitor calibrator offers robust controls for viewing images to approximate viewing conditions of your final project. For example, a setting of 5000° Kelvin approximates the color of white under sunlight at noon and 4100° approximates the color of white under fluorescent light. Most uncalibrated monitors display white at 6500° or 9300°. By setting the white point on the monitor, all other colors get adjusted to their correct values. Other controls include gamma, brightness, and contrast settings. Settings can be saved for variable output devices as well as several display situations.

The Radius SuperMatch Display Calibrator (Figure 3–28) works with color management systems from Kodak, Agfa, Apple, and Electronics for Imaging to create profiles ensuring consistent color matching from scan to proof to final print.

The Colorimeter 24 (Figure 3–29) and its accompanying calibration software, ColorSet, works with DayStar's ColorMatch color management system to create custom profiles to ensure accurate color display from Photoshop.

Follow the instructions included with your calibrator to determine which of the following steps relate to your system. See the next section in this chapter for more information on Color Management.

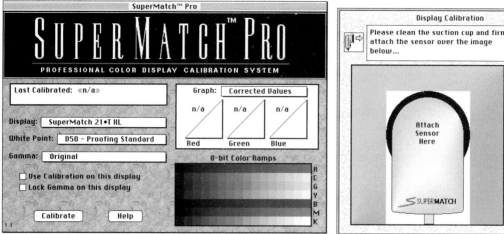

Figure 3–28   SuperMatch Display Calibrator from Radius will help you match your display to your printed output.

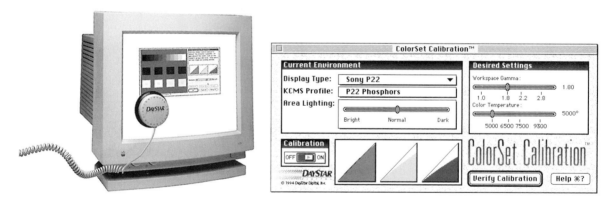

Figure 3–29   The DayStar Colorimeter 24 and ColorSet software will help you match your display to your printed output.

Monitor Setup Preferences

After you have calibrated your monitor, choose the Photoshop Monitor Setup submenu from Preferences under the File menu (Figure 3–21). Then choose your monitor from the Monitor pop-up menu and enter the Gamma value you entered in the Gamma utility or the value set by your third-party calibration software.

TIP: The Photoshop manual suggests a value of 1.8 to best match printed output. If your final output is slide film or video, you should set a higher gamma

value to match the gamma of the film recorder or television; try a Gamma value of 2.2 unless your service bureau recommends a different value.

Choose the White Point value established by your calibration software. If you use the Gamma utility, leave the default value at 6500K.

Next, choose the monitor type in the Phosphors pop-up menu. (If you don't see your monitor listed, you may need to set Custom values—get them from your monitor manufacturer.)

Finally, choose a setting for Ambient Light that models the lighting in the room.

- Choose Medium if room lighting is about as bright as your monitor.

- Choose High if room lighting is brighter than your monitor.

- Choose Low if room lighting is dimmer than your monitor.

TIP: The type and amount of room lighting can make a significant difference in the color you see. When viewing an image, always keep the room lighting consistent. Ideally, view prints under a white (5000° K) viewing lamp.

Printing Inks Preferences

Choose the target printer or press setup for your image. If you are printing to a printing press, press setup refers to different combinations of press and paper that produce different colors and tones. The way Photoshop outputs your image is dependent on settings that you make in the Printing Inks Setup submenu from Preferences under the File menu (Figure 3–22). Photoshop uses these settings when converting from RGB to CMYK (or converting from Lab to CMYK) and when displaying a CMYK image on a monitor.

The numerous printers and press set-ups require different settings for dot gain and gray balance. Dot gain is the growth of the halftone dot in the production process. Dot gain is explained in Chapter 11, "Output." Gray balance controls the strength of CMYK values to compensate for the color characteristics of different printers. If one particular color is stronger it can cause a color cast in an image. Gray balance is discussed in Chapter 8, "Color."

Choose the Ink Colors pop-up menu to display a long list of printers or printing press setups. The many options available offer a generic set of RGB to CMYK conversion tables.

If your images will be printed on an offset printing press, you should usually choose SWOP (Coated) as your target printer, which produces the closest match to a laminated proof and to printing on coated paper.

If your output is to a digital color printer, then choose your printer from the list. If your digital color printer is not on the list, choose another make or model of a similar type. Leave the Dot Gain values and Gray Balance values alone for now. You may adjust these after making the proof to tune in your calibration (described below). If you want the settings to affect the display of grayscale and duotone images, click the Use Dot Gain for Grayscale check box.

NOTE: Printing Inks Setup and Separation Setup only affect RGB to CMYK conversions. If you are outputting to an RGB printer, film recorder, video, or to other on screen presentations, any changes in Printing Inks Setup and Separation Setup do not apply.

Printing a Color Proof

The next step is to print an image to a digital printer or as process color separations and to make a laminated proof. For more information on printing separations and proofs, see Chapter 11, "Output."

Choose a CMYK image that has a an identifiable range of colors and swatches of the process colors and color mixes. In the Calibration folder on the Macintosh Adobe has provided a CMYK image called Olé No Moiré which is perfect for the job. In the Windows version this image is named TESTPICT.JPG and is located in the CALIBRAT directory (Figure 3–30).

For those of you targeting a printing press, take this image to your color service bureau and have them print film separations (if you don't have access to an imagesetter). Be sure that the image is printed with the Calibration Bar option checked in Page Setup. Then have a laminated proof made from the separated film.

Figure 3–30
Make a print of the Olé No Moiré image that comes with Photoshop to calibrate your system.

If your target output is an RGB printer, film recorder, video, or other on screen presentations, use an RGB image for your initial print. Several RGB images come with Photoshop.

Adjusting the Display to the Output

After you have printed a proof, adjust how the monitor and Photoshop display the image so that it matches the proof print as close as possible. The print should be viewed under white light (ideally under a 5000° K lamp) next to your monitor with the same document open in Photoshop. When viewing a CMYK color image, Photoshop uses a conversion table to display the CMYK image in RGB on the monitor—the same table used to convert RGB images to CMYK.

There are several ways to fine-tune the display of the image. You can adjust the monitor's display of RGB color with the Gamma utility or third-party calibration software. You can also adjust the dot gain and gray balance in the Printing Inks Setup preferences dialog box. Or you can get even more techno by adjusting specific colors in the Ink Colors dialog box, creating a custom conversion table.

NOTE: If you are using third-party calibration software, follow the directions with the application.

GAMMA

The simplest method of fine-tuning the display is to use the Gamma utility. Open the Gamma Control Panel Device with your calibration image on the screen. Position the proof print next to the monitor under a controlled white light source. Adjust the settings until you get as close a match as possible. This method changes how the computer displays the RGB data. It does not alter the CMYK to RGB conversion tables. Refer to Chapter 2 in the Photoshop User Guide for instructions on how to use Gamma.

If your work and output will be RGB only, use the Gamma utility and do not attempt to adjust settings in Printing Inks setup.

PRINTING INKS SETUP

Adjustments made in the Printing Inks Setup dialog box in Photoshop's Preference (under the File menu) change the actual RGB to CMYK conversion tables. If you are new to Photoshop and desktop color, you might want stick with adjusting the Gamma (above).

While viewing both the proof print next to the monitor with the document open in Photoshop, adjust the display of the image in the Printing

Inks Setup preferences dialog box. There are three different kinds of adjustments that can be made.

CAUTION: Changes made in Printing Inks Setup alters the RGB to CMYK conversion tables. Do not use this method unless you are experienced with the complex issues that relate to making color separations.

- You can adjust the Dot Gain value to more precisely reflect the actual dot gain for your printer or press setup. (See Dot Gain in Chapter 11, "Output.") Adjust the dot gain value by choosing larger or smaller numbers. If you enter a lower percentage, you'll make the screen image appear lighter. If you enter a higher percentage, the image will appear darker. Dot gain values less than 22 percent are not recommended.

- You can use the Gray Balance checkbox to compensate for color casts in an image by adjusting the gamma of individual channels. The procedure for doing this is described in the Photoshop manual.

- If you must make critical custom color adjustments to the conversion tables, choose Custom from the Ink Colors pop-up menu. The Ink Colors dialog box offers editable text fields for the CIE coordinates for each primary color and color mix (see Chapter 8, "Color," for more on CIE color). You can either match each color visually to the proof print by clicking on the color patch (opens the Color Picker) or you can take readings of the CMYK values on the color proof with a colorimeter or spectrophotometer and then enter the CIE Yxy coordinates for each color in the appropriate text field.

NOTE: The complexities of making accurate color separations can require using custom conversion tables or a color management system, since every proofing and printing situation offers variations in output.

For more information on color theory and mode conversions refer to Chapter 8, "Color," and for more on color separations and printing, refer to Chapter 11, "Output."

Optimizing Input

Once you can get predictable results through output, you should establish an input and scanning procedure to ensure images come into Photoshop with the optimal information for your output needs. For example, a scan intended for color separation would be inappropriate for output to a film recorder.

Optimize your scans by trial and error testing through your calibrated system or use automated scanner calibration software such as Ofoto from Light

Source Inc., Scanmatch from Savitar Inc., or Color Encore from Southwest Software. For more information on scanning, see Chapter 4, "Input."

Another option for managing scanned images so they correctly output in a variety of methods is to use a color management system. This system will establish profiles of your scanner (or other input source) and convert the data to the profile of any of your output devices.

Color Management Systems

A color management system (CMS) provides a communication link between different devices and applications by defining and translating the description of colors. Every device or application interprets or displays colors in a unique way which can be described by a device profile. A color management system translates device profiles of different devices and applications through an independent color space.

Think of device profiles and the conversion of one profile to another as color translators that work with color files as language translators work with different languages. The user specifies the input profile for the scanner, the monitor, and the output device. Since the CMS knows the characteristics of each device in the loop, it can translate from one device to another, providing an accurate color match.

If you don't use a color management system, to get predictable color you have to manually create calibration settings for every device and application. For example, you must establish a calibration setting for a digital printer and different setting for color separations. A CMS works behind the scenes to provide a common ground between all your hardware and software to ensure matching color.

For example, you might have a PhotoCD scan and want to output it to a Kodak XL-7700 printer. By identifying the input and output devices, the color management system optimizes the conversions so that the print and the original match.

Because a CMS matches the original to the output, be aware that if an original is off in some regard, the output also will be off. If the original is too green, the CMS will ensure that the output is also too green. This is another reason to start with the best-quality originals possible. If the CMS works with a calibrated monitor, corrections can be made in Photoshop and the corrected file should output within reason as it appears on screen. Since monitors have the capability to display far more colors than any other output, the CMS will display nonprintable colors as close as possible to printable colors, because the CMS has information about the specifics of the output device.

Some color management systems include Kodak Color Management System, DayStar ColorMatch, Electronic for Imaging's EFIColor Works, Agfa's FotoFlow, and Pantone/Light Source POCE. In addition, Apple provides a basic architecture for color calibration and matching called ColorSync, which is built into System 7.5.

TIP: Use only one color management system on your computer; two different CMSs could conflict with each other.

Kodak Color Management System

Adobe provides the Kodak Color Management System (KCMS) with Photoshop for both the Macintosh and Windows so users can work with PhotoCD images. KCMS works with Device Color Profiles (DCP) that mathematically describe the color gamut (color range) of each device. There are DCPs for scanners, monitors, and output devices available. The DCPs are interpreted by Precision Transforms (PTs) which have information on how the colors are mapped on each device and translated to the profiles of other devices.

Kodak also sells a product called Precision Input Color Characterization (PICC) that allows the user to create an input Precision Transfer for any scanner. This product works with the KCMS and ensures that slight differences in each input device are taken into account. The PICC software creates a precision transform (PT) from a scan of a target file (included with PICC).

DayStar ColorMatch

DayStar's ColorMatch software, based on a patented color separation technology from Kodak, which was initially used on high end CEPS workstations, provides a perceptual match of colors from scanner to monitor to print. ColorMatch runs on the Macintosh using the Kodak Color Management System (KCMS) as a basis, incorporating the same Device Color Profiles (DCPs) and Precision Transforms (PTs). ColorMatch comes with a basic set of profiles; other more specific profiles for scanners and output devices can be purchased from either Kodak or DayStar.

ColorMatch works best when the display is calibrated with ColorSet calibration software and ideally with the Colorimeter 24. Knowing the profile of your calibrated monitor, ColorMatch displays the color using a device-independent color space. This color model can be translated transparently to any device and between Photoshop and QuarkXPress without any color loss.

Installed as a plug-in, ColorMatch bypasses Photoshop's conversion tables by converting files using its own tables at the time the file is opened, saved, or printed. Under the Filter menu, choose Correct for Display to view a scanned image that has been opened in Photoshop with a KCMS profile. Choose the Color Match Preview filter to specify an output profile to display a soft proof, previewing colors as they appear in the gamut of the output device prior to printing the final output.

Color-corrected images can be saved in the ColorMatch TIFF file format, including special color tags readable by any program that can open a TIFF file. The most accurate monitor preview and print matches will occur when used with programs that support KCMS, such as QuarkXPress.

EfiColor Works

Electronics for Imaging (EFI) produces a product called EfiColor Works. A component of EfiColor Works is EfiColor for Adobe Photoshop, which uses an EFI proprietary color management system. The same EfiColor profiles are also used in Cachet, EFI's color correction and separation product, and EfiColor XTension for QuarkXPress 3.3.

Significant for Photoshop users are EfiColor's Separation Tables which replace the selections usually made in Monitor Setup, Printer Ink Setup, and Separation Setup. By choosing the digital color printer or press setup that matches your output, the separation table will convert the image to CMYK, taking into account the color gamut and dot gain for the digital printer or printing press.

EfiColor Works offers profiles for many scanners, monitors, and digital color printers, as well as profiles for offset printing.

Agfa FotoFlow

Agfa FotoFlow color management system consists of a suite of modules that include support for calibration, ColorSync, CIELab, QuarkXTension, TIFF files, out of gamut warning, and color tags.

FotoTune, the core module in the suite, includes scanner target images that you scan to develop profiles for input devices. FotoTune has a basic set of predefined input and output device Color Tags. Additional Color Tags are available free from Agfa or CompuServe.

PhotoTune color data can be saved as a separation table for use in Photoshop. PhotoTune can make CMYK to CMYK conversions, allowing you to print to different specifications. Also included is Pantone Calculator which allows you to enter a Pantone number and select an output device to calculate the closest CMYK values needed to reproduce the Pantone color.

PANTONE Open Color Environment

Pantone, a leader in establishing color standards long before desktop publishing, teamed up with Light Source to create a cross platform color management system, the PANTONE Open Color Environment (POCE). Although not supported by many applications at the time of this writing, POCE is available free and operates at the system level. POCE provides predictable color from scan to monitor to print on a PC under Windows or on a Macintosh using ColorSync. Access to POCE is made available through the Color Picker.

In addition to providing profiles and translations for standard RGB and CMYK colors, POCE ties into the PANTONE MATCHING SYSTEM (PMS) and the PANTONE PROCESS COLOR system, producing color matching for both spot and process colors.

Creating New Documents

When choosing the *New* command from the File menu, a dialog box appears to set the characteristics of the new document (Figure 3–31).

TIP: **If you have an image on the Macintosh or Windows clipboard, the dimensions and resolution will match the image so that the clipboard image can then be pasted directly into the new document (Holding down the Option key bypasses the clipboard information.)**

Specify the Image Size in the Height and Width text fields. By pressing on the Units pop-up menu to the right of the text fields, you can specify the measurement in units of pixels, inches, centimeters, points, or picas. The width units can also be specified in terms of columns. A new document can be opened in the Bitmap, Grayscale, RGB Color, CMYK Color, and Lab Color modes.

Resolution can be specified in pixels per inch or pixels per centimeter. Set the units by pressing on the pop-up menu to the right of the resolution value. It's important when you create a new image that you choose the proper resolution based on your final output. See "Correct Image Resolution" in Chapter 4, "Input."

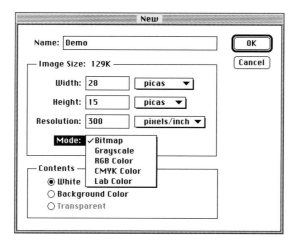

Figure 3–31
The New dialog box

TIP: You can change the resolution or size of an image at any time by selecting Image Size under the Image menu.

Also note that you can create a new file which begins with white or the background color to fill your working area. Either of those two options will create an opaque layer. The third option, Transparent, creates a transparent layer with no color values. If you choose this option, you must save in the Photoshop 3 format to save this information because this is the only format that can save layering. You can use the Save a Copy option (see below) to save it in a different format in which the layering information will be "flattened."

TIP: Sometimes you might wish to create a file exactly the same size as another one. To do this, with the New dialog box showing, select the image that you want to match in the Windows menu. The dimensions in the New dialog box will change to match the selected file.

Opening and Saving Documents

Opening Existing Documents

Photoshop, the "universal can opener," can open and save in a number of graphics formats. Most computer users will be familiar with many of the formats found in the format menu in the Open and Save As dialog boxes. Each format has specific uses, some very specialized.

Using the Open command in the File menu, Photoshop 3 can directly open the following different file formats. These include:

- Photoshop 3
- Photoshop 2.5
- Photoshop 2.0 (Macintosh only)
- Adobe Illustrator
- Amiga IFF
- BMP
- CompuServe GIF
- EPS (Encapsulated PostScript)
- EPS PICT Preview
- EPS TIFF Preview
- Filmstrip
- JPEG
- Kodak CMS Photo CD

- MacPaint
- PCX
- PICT File
- PICT Resource
- PIXAR
- PixelPaint
- RAW
- Scitex CT
- Targa
- TIFF

Refer to Appendix A for more detailed information about each file format.

Choose Open on the Macintosh. In the Open dialog box click on a document from the list and you'll see the file type and size. Click the Show Thumbnail button to see a preview. If you don't see the file you want or if a document won't open, choose Show All Files. All the formats which Photoshop recognizes by file type will appear.

In Windows chose Open As if you don't see a document that you want, if a document can't be opened, or if the file extension is missing or incorrect but you know the correct file format (Figure 3–32).

The Show All File option in the Open dialog box on the Macintosh and the Open As command on the PC can open file formats not normally used on your platform—for example, in Windows type .TIF for TIFF files or .TGA for Targa files to open images created on the Macintosh.

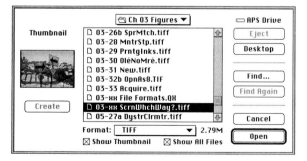 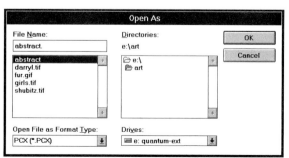

Figure 3–32   The Open dialog box for the Mac on the left and the Open As dialog box for Windows on the right

TIP: Adobe Illustrator files can be opened or placed into open documents. Photoshop rasterizes the mathematically defined vector graphics into pixels at the selected resolution. Upon selecting an Illustrator EPS file, the EPS Rasterizer dialog box will appear. Select the appropriate size, resolution, and mode. Normally you should select anti-aliased and constrain proportions. The opening of Adobe Illustrator files (as well as files from Aldus FreeHand and CorelDRAW!) is discussed in "Importing Images" in Chapter 4, "Input."

ACQUIRE PLUG-INS

Acquire Plug-in modules installed in the Plug-ins folder will appear as an Acquire submenu under the File menu. These plug-ins allow Photoshop to open images in other formats, open Photo CDs, import images into documents, access scanners directly, and download images from digital cameras (Figure 3–33). Refer to Chapter 4, "Input," for a discussion of Acquire plug-ins. The standard plug-ins that come with Photoshop 3 include the following:

- Anti-Aliased PICT (Macintosh)
- PICT Resources (Macintosh)
- Quick Edit files
- TWAIN images

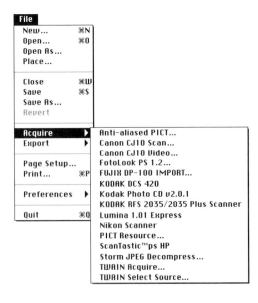

Figure 3–33
Acquire plug-ins appear
in the Acquire submenu
under the File menu.

PICT resources and Anti-Aliased PICT are modules only available on the Macintosh platform. Anti-Aliased PICT offers you the option of rasterizing vector PICT images at a specified resolution.

Quick Edit files provide a way to open a portion of a Photoshop image, make changes to it, and seamlessly resave it back into the original file.

TWAIN is an interface that is used for acquiring images digitized by scanners and framegrabbers, particularly in the PC world.

Compression

After you scan and begin working with an image, you usually want to store it in the most efficient way possible while also preserving quality. Compression allows you to make optimum use of your hard disk space, both for working with and archiving large images. There are various options for image compression for Photoshop images that fall into basic categories: lossy and lossless. Lossy compression causes a loss of image quality and detail each time an image is compressed and decompressed. Lossless compression never loses any image quality or detail after compression and decompression.

LOSSY COMPRESSION

The JPEG (Joint Photographic Expert Group) method for compressing images is based on the Discrete Cosine Transform (DCT) algorithm, which analyzes 8×8 or 16×16 pixel areas of an image (independent of resolution), and performs a sophisticated "averaging" of the values in the cell. This process reduces the image size dramatically.

The Lossy JPEG compression method allows you to specify the compression ratio in order to control the relationship of image quality to the degree of compression. The higher the compression factor, the more data that is stripped from the image, resulting in increasingly poorer quality in the final image.

In general, images meant for prepress are candidates for lower compression ratios; high-quality color separations require as much original information as possible. Images intended for video output are candidates for much higher compression ratios.

JPEG compression is supported directly within Photoshop in several ways. When you choose Open from the File menu, you can open a JPEG compressed file and Photoshop will automatically decompress it. When you choose Save from the File menu and select the JPEG format choice, you are presented with a dialog box (Figure 3–34) where you can choose a level of compression. "Maximum" will produce a larger file of higher quality and "Low" will produce a smaller of file of poorer quality.

There are many applications that perform JPEG compression. Theoretically Photoshop should open them all, but this will probably not

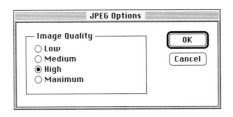

Figure 3–34
The Image Quality
options when saving a
JPEG file

be the case for some time. JPEG is not a single algorithm, but actually a set of methods which can be implemented in several ways (similar to the TIFF format in the first few years it was used, where different software wrote different "flavors" of TIFF). JPEG compression is also an option when saving PICT files. See PICT in Appendix A.

TIP: Be sure to do tests to determine the levels of compression that work best for your image. The level of compression possible may also vary with the image content. An image with an extreme amount of detail (a sailing ship with rigging, for example) might not be a good candidate for compression.

Saving in JPEG format makes the most sense when you are staying within Photoshop. Among the most popular graphic applications, only QuarkXPress and CorelDRAW! currently support the format for printing images. Beware that opening the image in these programs will be slower because the JPEG file must be decompressed.

Compressing and decompressing a JPEG file with software alone is slow because it requires much computation, depending on the speed of your computer's processor. If JPEG compression is important to you and you work on a Macintosh, you should consider buying a NuBus board with a DSP chip that does JPEG compression and decompression much faster. You can purchase a dedicated JPEG board, but a better choice is a multipurpose DSP board designed to speed up many Photoshop operations. These boards work with any Macintosh with a NuBus slot. Each product will have a software plug-in or plug-ins that replace certain filters in Photoshop. DSP cards, which are certified as "Adobe Charged," utilize Adobe's own algorithms for the filters, and produce effects identical to the Photoshop software. As of this writing, DSP cards with JPEG are not available in Windows.

Besides speed, another advantage of a DSP board is that the JPEG implementation is usually more accurate. With some JPEG software implementations, repeated image compression and decompression causes progressive quality loss. Graphic arts professionals report the best JPEG implementation is developed by Storm Technologies, an early pioneer in the JPEG arena. Their JPEG, running on DSPs from Radius, SuperMac, and DayStar, does not lose any more information after the second iteration;

other implementations, notably those built into Apple's QuickTime, will lose quality with successive compressions.

TIP: **Even with a good JPEG implementation, minimize the number of times you compress an image. Save in JPEG after you've done all of the desired manipulation and you want to save a final compressed version on disk.**

Another JPEG compression alternative available in Photoshop is a to save a JPEG compressed EPS file. The advantage of this method is that when you print to a PostScript Level 2 printer, the image will be decompressed as it is printed, reducing the amount of data sent over a network or serial cable to the printer. Unfortunately, there are some serious limitations in doing this:

- JPEG compressed EPS files will cause an error if sent to a PostScript Level 1 printer.
- In Windows, you can only send a JPEG compressed EPS file if you are using the Adobe printer driver.
- You can only send composite images to color printers. No application will color separate a JPEG encoded EPS file.

For more details about EPS files and JPEG compression, see the "How to Save Your EPS File" section in Chapter 11, "Output."

LOSSLESS COMPRESSION

There are several software products that can compress Photoshop images (as well as other files) using non-lossy (lossless) compression. On the Macintosh, the most popular are StuffIt Deluxe, DiskDoubler, Now Utilities, and Compact Pro. Each product does a serviceable job of compressing Photoshop files.

The de facto standard on the PC platform is PKZIP which is a shareware DOS application published by PKWare. You can avoid dealing with the DOS prompt by using WinZip. This shareware Windows application is available on most on-line services and bulletin boards. It features built in PKZIP support to compress your files and PKUNZIP to decompress your archives. It also supports the following less-popular compression schemes: .ARJ, .LZH, and .ARC. A .ZIP archive can also be created or decompressed on the Macintosh platform using a shareware application called ZipIt, also available on most on-line services and bulletin boards. ZIP archives are Binary files which do not require any translation when transported between the Macintosh and PC/Windows platforms. Photoshop's native files (.PSD) are about 25% smaller when compressed using PKZIP. Another feature in the latest versions of PKZIP and WinZIP is the ability to *span* disks. A single archive larger than the capacity of a 1.44 Mb floppy or SyQuest cartridge is safely broken into pieces onto separate media. When the disk or cartridge is transported to your service bureau or printer, PKUNZIP restores the archive to a single file on your hard disk.

Use Lossless compression if you or your service bureau has concerns about quality loss from JPEG lossy compression. The drawback is that Lossless compression ratios are much lower than those from lossy compression.

TIP: **If you are planning to send compressed files to an output provider always check ahead to make sure that they can decompress the files in the format that you're providing. Most compression software can write files as ".sea" files (self-extracting archives). If you do this, your recipient simply double-clicks on the file for the image to be decompressed.**

Saving

Photoshop was originally conceived as a file-format translation program and, as a result, it can save images in most of the formats you're likely to ever want or need. The Save As dialog box contains a pop-up menu of the output file formats (Figure 3–35).

TIP: **Each of the different display modes presents you with different options when saving a file. Some of the file formats in the Save As dialog aren't available, depending on the display mode you're in when you select the Save command. Photoshop knows what saving options will logically work based on the display mode. For example, to save a file in Scitex CT format, you need to be in RBG, CMYK or Grayscale display modes. If you're working on an image in Photoshop's normal RGB mode, you won't be able to save an image as a MacPaint file without first converting the display mode to Grayscale and then to Bitmap mode.**

After you choose the file format for output—and name the document—pressing the Save button will open a dialog that lists the options associated with the selected format.

TIP: **If an image doesn't fit on a floppy disk, Photoshop 3 cannot save the file on multiple disks. To split files, use Photoshop 2.5 or a compression program such as Stuffit or Disk Doubler.**

As a general rule, when working in Photoshop always try to use the native Photoshop 3 format for saving images, regardless of the mode you are working in or the platform you're working on. Only the Photoshop 3 format supports layers. It will also store any channels and paths you create in your image.

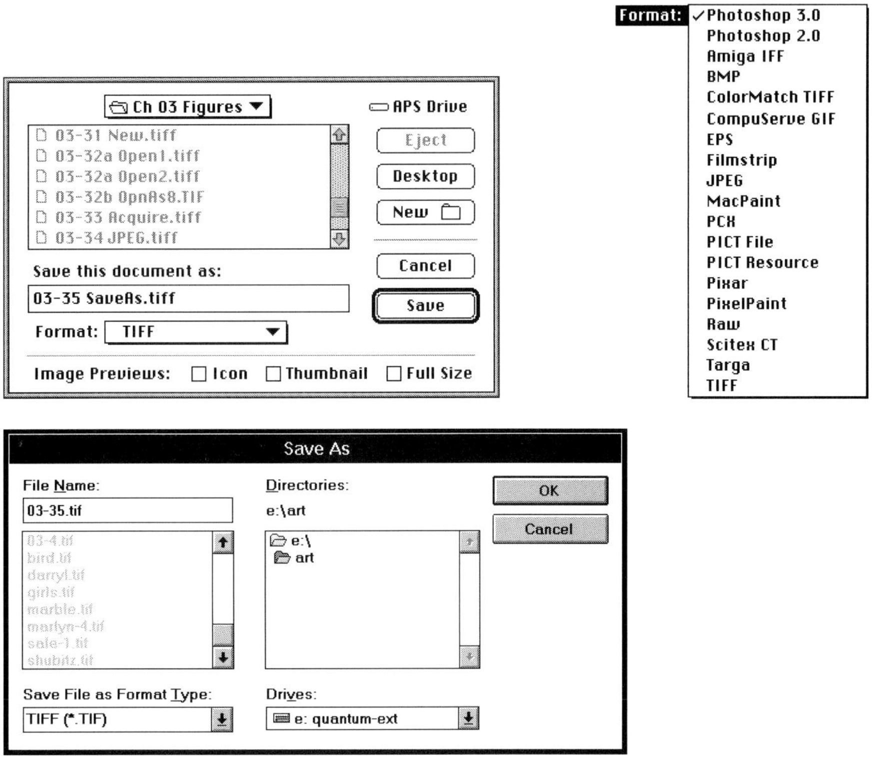

Figure 3–35
The Save As dialog box
for the Macintosh
(above) and for
Windows (below)

CAUTION: If you save in any format other than Photoshop 3, the layers in your image will be merged and flattened into one layer. Use the Save a Copy command (see below) to retain the original file while saving a flattened copy.

When you are saving images to be placed page layout programs (like QuarkXPress and PageMaker), the best format to save in is TIFF or EPS. These formats are widely recognized on both the Macintosh and Windows platforms. They can be reliably used for printing grayscale or color images, or for printing process or spot color separations. To learn more about these formats, which to use, and how to save them, see the "Preparing Images for Use in Other Applications" section in Chapter 11, "Output," and Appendix A.

SAVING AN IMAGE FOR ANOTHER PLATFORM

Transporting files between the PC/Windows and Macintosh platforms is significantly easier today than it was a few years ago. The best solution is to transport the Photoshop 3 native file format (.PSD extension in Windows) between the Macintosh and PC/Windows platforms. If both platforms don't use Photoshop, then use TIFF (.TIF in Windows) or EPS (.EPS). Be sure to save the name with a maximum of eight digits plus the correct three digit extension if the file is headed for a PC. Refer to Appendix A for a list of the correct file format extension.

SAVING A COPY

Ordinarily, when you choose Save As from the File menu, you are presented with a dialog box to save the file under a new name and file format. After the image is saved, the new image is the one which is left open and the image it was saved from is closed. You can save a copy of a file by choosing Save a Copy from the File menu. With this command, the original file is left open on the screen. This method is especially useful when you'd like to delete any unused channels, flatten your image (merge visible layers) or experiment on other versions of an image.

Summary

- Work in Photoshop's default settings until you get used to the program.
- Keep the Layers, Brushes, Options, Picker, and Info palettes open at all times. Pay attention to the target layer in the Layers palette and the brush parameters in the Brushes and Options palettes.
- Maintain an awareness of the size of your document. Don't let it get so big that it slows you down or that you can't save it anywhere.
- To speed up your work, set keyboard commands in the Commands palette for your most-used menu commands.
- Set your preferences to your specific output and project needs.
- Install plug-ins in the Plug-ins folder. Remove any unused plug-ins from the folder for more efficiency.
- Calibrate your system and use only one calibration system to avoid conflicts. For further output control, use a Color Management System.
- Although you can get close with calibration or a Color Management System, you will never get an exact match. The monitor projects light and the print reflects light. The monitor displays the image using RGB primary colors, while the print was created using CMYK colors.
- Mode conversions change the data in your document. Don't change back and forth. Generally its best to change in one direction only. Refer to Chapter 8, "Color," for more information on mode conversions.

- Save in Photoshop's native format until the final stage, at which time you should save in the file format appropriate to your output needs. Make sure that the receiving application can accept the file format that you save in.
- When saving a document for the PC, make sure to use only eight characters plus the correct three-character extension.

Now that you have Photoshop configured, the next chapter will discuss how to get images into Photoshop.

Chapter 4: Input

The range of input choices available to the Photoshop user is immense and growing constantly. This chapter will discuss a variety of input methods and devices that are useful for getting images into your computer. These can include:

- Scanners
- CD-ROMs, including Photo CD and digital stock photography
- On-line services
- Video
- Digital cameras

We'll also talk about the variety of files that can be imported into Photoshop by opening or using Acquire modules. We will discuss what you need to know about starting with a good original image, scanning skill, and quality, and how to select the correct resolution for your chosen output device—whether that be a black-and-white laser printer, a digital color printer, an imagesetter, or a film recorder.

Whatever method of input is used, there is one underlying concept in working with Photoshop, and that is the *pixel*. The pixel, which is short for picture element, is the atom from which a Photoshop image is composed.

Images in Photoshop are created from these tiny, square elements in a fixed grid. This fixed grid is often called a bitmap, and hence Photoshop images are often called *bitmapped* or *raster* images (Figure 4–1).

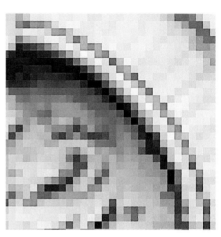

Figure 4–1
The enlarged detail of
the building shows that
raster images are made of
tiny square elements
called pixels.
(© Mark Siprut)

Pixels and Resolution

When inputting or digitizing images, you must define the resolution of the pixel grid in relation to the image size. This information can be defined at the time of the scan, when importing into Photoshop, or when creating a new document in Photoshop. (The resolution can be changed in Photoshop.)

When using scanners or other digitizers, choices in your device's software define the *scanning resolution*—the number of samples which the device takes from the source image. The scan will also define the *image resolution* in Photoshop, expressed as the number of pixels per inch or pixels per centimeter.

If you use Photo CD or stock photography images stored in the Photo CD format, you choose from one of five image resolutions which are stored on the CD-ROM. (With Pro Photo CD, you have a choice of six resolutions.)

With Photo CD images and certain file formats such as Targa, image resolution is defined by the number of pixels in each dimension. For example, the largest Photo CD format provides an image dimension of 2048 × 3072 pixels. The advantage of this method is that the number is not tied to a particular unit of measure. Photoshop will open these files at 72 ppi (the dimensions may be huge). You can then adjust to the size and output resolution you desire by choosing Image Size from the Image menu.

You can also control the resolution and size of an image when opening or placing vector graphics such as EPS or PICT files. (When you place anti-aliased PICTs, you get a height and width choice, but not a resolution box.)

You can create a new Photoshop document in which you can paint from scratch or paste images into by choosing New from the File menu. The dialog box will ask you to define the image resolution in pixels per inch or pixels per centimeter.

Calculating the appropriate resolution for your image will be discussed later in this chapter.

Figure 4–2
A 1-bit image has no
gray tones, only
black and white.
(© Mark Siprut, original
photograph courtesy
of PhotoDisc)

BIT DEPTH AND RESOLUTION

Resolution, as we have seen, refers to the number of pixels in an image in relation to its size. But there is another aspect of resolution which refers to the amount of information stored for each pixel, or the pixel's value. This is also called *bit depth*.

Depending on the capabilities of your scanner or image digitizer and the nature of the source image, you may import or create images in black-and-white (stored in Photoshop as Bitmap mode), grayscale (stored as Grayscale mode), or color (stored as RGB, Indexed, CMYK, or Lab mode).

Black-and-white images, sometimes called line art images, store the smallest amount of information. Each pixel has a value of either black or white (Figure 4–2). When stored on the computer, each pixel takes up one *bit* of information. A bit is the smallest unit of storage on a computer. Therefore, black-and-white images can also be called 1-bit images. One-bit images can be generated in Photoshop from the Bitmap mode.

Each pixel in a grayscale image, when imported from a scanner or Photo CD or created as a new document, usually represents one of 256 different values from white to black. On the computer it takes eight bits of storage to store 256 values, so a grayscale image can also be called an 8-bit image.

As discussed in the Chapter 2, "Setting Up Your System," color images are stored as 8-bits of information for each channel of color. For color images, the input will be in RGB mode if your source is a desktop scanner, so your image will be 24 bits per pixel (three channels times 8 bits). Photo

Figure 4–3   RGB color images are stored as 8 bits of information for each channel of color for a total of 24 bits per pixel. Each channel has 256 tones. (© Michael Roney)

CD images, which use the YCC format as a native color space, opened in either Lab or RGB mode and are also 24-bit (Figure 4–3). If you have purchased a drum scan from a color service bureau, it will probably already be converted to CMYK mode. A CMYK image has four channels, so it will contain 32 bits of information for each pixel (four channels times 8 bits).

Higher quality (and more expensive) scanners compensate for some natural tonal degradation by capturing more information than will actually be stored. They might capture 10, 12, or 16 bits of information per pixel for a grayscale scan (this would be 30, 36, or 48 bits for an RGB scan) to capture more tones. This is called expanding the scanner's *dynamic range*. In most cases, the scanner software then selects the 8 most accurate bits per channel to store.

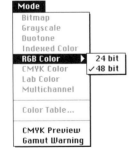

Photoshop can open a 48-bit file, which has 16 bits per channel in RGB. The only functions available, however, are Levels and Curves, which allow you to adjust the tones and color balance. To otherwise manipulate a 48-bit file, it must be converted to a 24-bit file by choosing RGB Color under the Mode menu. A pop-up menu like the one at left will appear; choose 24 bit.

WHEN TO GO FROM ANALOG TO DIGITAL

At some point during the input process the continuous tone information of your imported image must be converted from analog to digital bitmapped information. With the advent of digital cameras, this process becomes almost instantaneous. Digital cameras bypass the need for film, chemicals, processing time, and a separate scanning step. They are a good input choice if you know exactly how you will be using your image.

On the other hand, photographing with conventional cameras and film and then scanning or digitizing the images later is advantageous because very high resolution information can be stored in a small space — the film. When shooting with a digital camera you are limited to the resolution of the camera and the amount of digital storage you have, while film is relatively cheap. An image on film (analog) can be scanned later at just the resolution and format required.

Input Sources

If you use Photoshop, most likely you will employ a variety of input sources, depending on the type of work you are doing. Some of these input sources may be devices you use yourself, such as a desktop scanner. However, for critical high-quality work you may want to purchase scans captured on a drum scanner by a service bureau. You might also purchase or acquire images that have been digitized by someone else, such as from a CD-ROM disk or an online service. Below is a discussion of some of the essential criteria for selecting the best method of input for your needs.

Most of the hardware and software discussed in this chapter is available for Windows users. Vendors usually provide proprietary interface cards for your PC along with Windows applications and drivers. Wherever possible these devices should be connected to your PC using a SCSI card (see Chapter 2, "Setting Up Your System"). When we mention an input device that is only available for one platform we will point this out.

CAUTION: **When you scan or acquire images make sure that you have permission to use them. Images that have been published are often copyrighted (somebody owns the image). Likewise, images from Stock Photo agencies, CD-ROM collections, or online services may only be licensed to use for certain purposes. See Chapter 1, "Welcome to Photoshop," for a discussion of copyright issues.**

Scanners

It has been said that "eyes are the windows of the soul." These words also apply to the relationship between computers and scanners. Scanners open the eyes of the computer to a virtually unlimited world of continuous-tone artwork. The scanner market is now flooded with a wide range of offerings (in terms of both capability and price), which can be confusing to the prospective buyer. Photoshop is the ultimate scanned-image processor, and everyone from the fine artist to the corporate publisher will probably end up using a scanner in conjunction with Photoshop. There are some basic issues in selecting and using a scanner, based on final output requirements and budget factors.

HAND-HELD AND SHEET-FED SCANNERS

The least expensive scanners available are hand-held and sheet-fed scanners. You use a hand-held scanner by physically moving it across the image, a line at a time. Sheet-fed scanners digitize sheets of reflective copy by pushing or pulling them through a scanning mechanism. These inexpensive scanners are useful for capturing low-resolution images for placement only or for use in screen presentations.

FLATBED SCANNERS

Flatbed scanners are often favored for input because of their economy and flexibility. Scanner prices have dropped dramatically in recent years. Many can be purchased below $2000, some for under $1000 (Figure 4–4).

Flatbed scanners use CCDs (charged-coupled devices) as photoreceptors. A linear arrangement of CCD elements samples information from the source artwork. Common scanning resolutions for desktop scanners are 300, 400, or 600 CCD elements per inch, which is also called the scanner's *optical resolution*. Ideally you should scan at the optical resolution or at that number divided by a whole number. For example, if your scanner has an optical resolution of 600 pixels per inch (ppi), you should scan at 600, 300, 200, 150, 100, or 75 ppi. You can then resample your image down to the desired resolution in Photoshop, as discussed later in this chapter. If you scan at other resolutions, the flatbed scanner software must interpolate to the new scanning resolution. (Interpolation in Photoshop is discussed in Chapter 3, "Setup and Document Management.")

Flatbed scanners work like photocopiers. They are designed for handling reflective art, prints, and flat artwork, although attachments for scanning transparencies are available for some scanners. Images are placed face down on a glass. Light is reflected off the source image and captured by the line of CCD elements. A row of pixels is captured, and then a stepper motor moves the elements to capture the next row until the entire image is recorded.

NOTE: Flatbed scanners are designed for the lower dynamic ranges of reflective art. If your original images are on photographic film (anywhere between 35mm slides to 8 x 10 inches), you will not be able to use a standard flatbed scanner unless it has an option for scanning transparencies. Even then you may be disappointed with the quality. The scans may, however, be of sufficient quality for "for position only" (FPO) images or color comprehensives. **For better quality scans from film use a scanner designed specifically for film.**

Color flatbed scanners capture color information by passing the light through red, green, and blue filters. As mentioned above, scans from desktop scanners are opened in RGB mode in Photoshop.

There are several variables to consider when purchasing a flatbed scanner. One is resolution. Note the difference between the image resolution that the scanner's software can store (the pixels per inch choices available in the scanner's software interface) and the scanner's optical resolution. As discussed above, scanner software uses interpolation to achieve higher image resolution. If you will be regularly enlarging images for final film output or scanning line art, it's best to choose a scanner with a higher optical resolution.

Another important issue is the number of bits per pixel that the scanner captures. Flatbed scanners are susceptible to "noise." Sampling distortions take place and not all the bits of information captured are accurate. This may show up in an image as lack of detail, particularly in shadow areas, or as visible speckling. As mentioned earlier, most scanners capture 8 bits per pixel for black and white and 24 bit for color. Higher quality scanners capture tones and colors more accurately because they have a greater dynamic range (they scan more bits per pixel than actually are needed).

CAUTION: Three-pass scanners can create blurring not caused by one-pass scanners.

FILM SCANNERS

If you want to scan your own photographs from film, either negatives or positive transparencies, you might want to use a desktop film scanner. It is better to scan the original film than a print made from the film. A scanned print will not have the dynamic range that the film will produce when scanned.

Film scanners are typically in the $1,500–$20,000 price range, depending on the types of film accepted and the output resolution. Film scanners made by vendors such as Leaf Systems, Eastman Kodak, Pixelcraft, Microtek, Polaroid, and Nikon have higher-resolution photoreceptors than flatbed scanners—from 1,000 to 6,000 ppi.

On the high end, the Leafscan 45 features resolutions up to 5,000 ppi and 16 bits per color (48 bit RGB files). The Nikon LS-3510AF, Kodak RFS 2035 Plus (Figure 4–5) and Microtek 45T (Figure 4–6) are good models in the middle price range. For an economical 35mm slide scanner check out the Nikon CoolScan, Microtek ScanMaker 35T (Figure 4–7), and Polaroid SprintScan 35.

Figure 4–4
A Microtek flatbed scanner

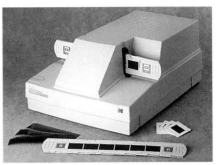

Figure 4–5
The Kodak RFS 2035 Plus film scanner

Figure 4–6
The Microtek 45T film scanner

Figure 4–7
The Microtek ScanMaker 35T
film scanner

TIP: **If you need to scan many slides, both the Nikon LS3510F and the Kodak
RFS 2035 Plus can be fitted with a stack loader to automate the scanning of up
to 100 slides at one time.**

DRUM SCANNERS

One of the realistic limitations of Photoshop is the quality of scanned
source files. While desktop scanners are typically useful for a variety of line
art, grayscale, or color printing applications, a project which requires the
highest quality might dictate the use of more expensive, professional scanners and output systems.

For critical prepress applications, use Photoshop with images scanned on
high-end drum scanners (Figure 4–8). These days color service bureaus are
competing with traditional color prepress houses in providing scans that

Figure 4–8
A Linotype-Hell
drum scanner

can be saved in formats such as TIFF and Scitex CT, which Photoshop can read directly.

Drum scanners use a different technology involving photomultiplier tubes (PMTs) to sample information. PMTs capture more information and a wider dynamic range of tones than can CCDs, particularly in shadow areas of an image. Drum scanners usually have a color computer built in which converts the RGB information to CMYK on the fly. They also usually apply sharpening as the image is being scanned; the same function you would apply in Photoshop using the Unsharp Mask filter.

More affordable drum scanners from Optronics (the ColorGetter), Screen (the DT-S1015 and DT-S1030), Howtek (the Scanmaster), and ScanView (the ScanMate) are appearing on the market in the $20,000–$60,000 price range. They will deliver prepress-quality source scans. Most have interfaces that work with Macintosh computers and PC's.

SCANNER SOFTWARE

Most desktop scanners today are provided with software plug-ins for Adobe Photoshop (Figure 4–9). You will have to inquire about the availability of a driver from the scanner manufacturer. After you install the plug-in the Plug-ins folder (the PLUGINS directory for Windows users) and reopen Photoshop, access the scanner software by choosing Acquire from the File menu and then selecting the scanner module from the Acquire submenu.

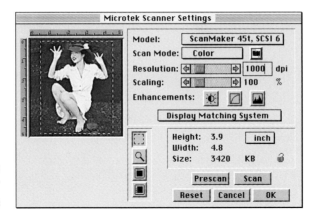

Figure 4–9
The Microtek 45T
scanner interface

Some scanners, particularly those with software for the Windows plat-form, use the TWAIN interface, which can also be accessed as an Acquire plug-in. Most scanners sold today for Windows include the necessary dri-vers, typically installed in your CONFIG.SYS and/or AUTOEXEC.BAT files in Windows. The scanner manufacturer must provide a Source Manager and TWAIN Data source for your scanner. When using your scan-ner for the first time only, choose Acquire from the File menu and TWAIN Select Source (Select TWAIN Source for Windows users) from the sub-menu, then choose your device. To use the scanner, choose Acquire under the File menu and then choose TWAIN Acquire (TWAIN for Windows users). If your scanner has neither a Photoshop plug-in nor a TWAIN interface, you can still use run the scanner's software as an independent application. In this case, you should save your digitized image in a compati-ble format like TIFF and then open it in Photoshop.

If your scanner does not have an Acquire plug-in, you can use scanner software from an another company. For example, ScanTastic from Second Glance Software can drive a Hewlett-Packard ScanJet IIc flatbed scanner from a Macintosh (Figure 4–10). This program will also work with popular scanner models from Apple, Epson, and UMAX. It provides control of reso-lution, bit depth, scaling, brightness and contrast, and transfer curves for each of the RGB channels. Scanned images automatically become an open Photoshop document without saving and then importing the scan.

Some software packages such as Ofoto from Light Source Computer Images Inc. offer calibration and automated control of the scanning opera-tion. Ofoto can be set up to scan for printing on specific output devices. By using its simple calibration process, it configures itself to match the original as close as possible (Figure 4–11). Other scanner-to-final-output calibration and color-control programs include Color Encore from Southwest Software and ScanMatch from Savitar Color Communication.

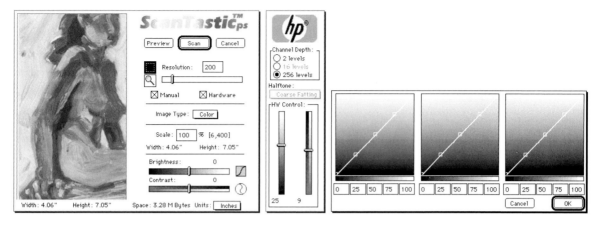

Figure 4–10   The ScanTastic Acquire module from Second Glance Software driving a Hewlett-Packard ScanJet IIc flatbed scanner (© Anna Stump)

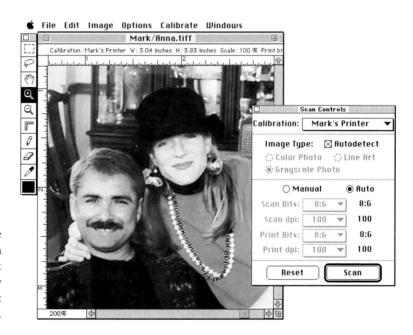

Figure 4–11
Ofoto's easy-to-use interface and calibration process allows you to set it up to automatically scan images for specific output devices.

CD-ROM, Digital Stock Images and Photo CD

A CD-ROM (Compact Disk Read Only Memory) can store and access large amounts of data (over 600 megabytes per disk) at relatively low cost. This makes it an excellent medium for storage of high-resolution color images, as well as multimedia, voices, music, and other data that requires huge amounts of storage space.

Every year since the technology was introduced in 1984, industry pundits predicted that "this is the year of CD-ROM," but use of the medium grew slowly. Recently, however, sales of CD-ROM drives for Macintosh and PC computers have taken off. They are now being widely used for software distribution, games, multimedia applications and storage of photographs.

For Photoshop users, two developments in this technology provide a potentially new source of images for input: *digital stock images* and *Photo CD*.

DIGITAL STOCK IMAGERY

CD-ROM technology is widely used for storing stock photographs in digital format. Traditionally, if you wanted photographs you either hired a photographer or licensed the use of a transparency from a stock photo agency. Although using stock photos was usually the lesser of the two in terms of expense, it did not come cheap. You paid a royalty fee of between $200 and $4,000 for use of an image, depending on the kind of publication and the size at which it would be printed. Then you had the image scanned by a color house for another $100 to $200.

Collections of photographs and illustrations on CD-ROMs are now being offered for as little as 40 cents per image (see Figure 4–12). Many of the collections first produced focused on nature scenes, textures, and backgrounds, with varying degrees of quality. Some collections are marred by poorly scanned, washed out, or dirty images. The least expensive images are relatively low resolution, suitable only for multimedia or laser-printing quality. Other collections, sometimes sold at considerably higher cost, provide carefully chosen, well-exposed and -scanned images which can be invaluable for high-quality projects. Most vendors' stock photography and Photo CDs may be used on both the Macintosh and Windows platforms.

CD-ROM stock collections vary from digital clip art to illustrations to specialty interests such as travel, sports, industrial photographs. Also available for a low cost are such images as simple icons, objects, symbols, skies, maps, animals, people, etc.

CAUTION: Carefully check the license agreement that comes with an image collection. You are not purchasing the images; you are being licensed to use the images in specific ways. For example, most licenses will not allow you to resell the images or to post them on a bulletin board. Other licenses may be more restrictive. Ask the vendor if you are not sure about the reproduction rights for your specific use.

Traditional stock photography agencies are now getting into the act by distributing their images on CD-ROMs. These agencies market to professional graphic artists who design books, magazines, and advertisements, and who have used their services before. Usage restrictions on these collections are much more severe. Comstock, one of the largest agencies, distributes a collection of low-resolution versions of their images on CD-ROM, but only for rough comps or for in-house publications. If you want to publish the image, you must still negotiate a royalty fee as before CD-ROM. Comstock will then supply you with the full-resolution image on a SyQuest cartridge or a transparency for scanning. Other agencies provide you a digital "key" which unlocks the high-resolution image you wish to purchase.

Accessing *digital stock photographs* on CDs in Photoshop requires the software for Macintosh or PC which comes with your CD-ROM drive. It consists of a CD-capable driver, such as Apple's CD-ROM drivers and QuickTime.

Stock photography and image library companies which take special care with their collections and offer high-quality images include Comstock, Image Bank, Artbeats, CD Folios, CMCD Inc., Digital Stock, Husom and Rose Photographics, PhotoDisc, Xaos Tools's, Pixar and D'pix. See Appendix C for a list of suppliers of digital stock images.

PHOTO CD

Kodak Photo CD is another of the driving forces behind the development of the CD-ROM market. Kodak Photo CDs use CD-ROMs to store and display images that are taken by conventional photographic methods. Photo CD uses a proprietary, compressed image format developed by Eastman Kodak called Image Pac.

Users take color negative, color transparency, or black-and-white negative film to their photofinisher, who is equipped with Kodak's Photo CD Imaging Workstation. This workstation can handle 35mm formats and write up to 100 images on one Photo CD Disc. Some photo processors also have Kodak's Pro Photo CD Master, a scanner that can scan as high as 4096×6144 pixels of resolution and can handle film up to a 4×5 inch format, a format commonly used by professional photographers. The Pro Photo CD Master disc can store between 25 and 100 images, depending on their file size. This format can accommodate electronically edited files, can include a watermark over an image, and can encrypt high-resolution images to impede unauthorized use.

Prints or slides are developed using normal processes, the film is scanned, color corrections are made based on the film type, and then the image data is written onto a Photo CD disk. Individual photographs from existing negatives or slides can also be put onto a Photo CD for a slightly higher price. The photofinisher will make an indexed color proofsheet print of the images on the disk for reference.

Prices vary. Generally, commercial film processors who use mass production methods will digitize each slide for as little as $1. Consumer processing labs use automatic settings when digitizing images for Photo CDs, which are averaged for viewing on monitors or television screens. Professionals usually do not want their scans corrected. If you are more concerned with

Comstock Encyclopedia of Stock Photography (© Comstock, Inc.)

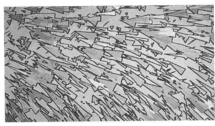 

Artist in Residence Fresco (© Xaos Tools)

Visual Symbols Sampler and Metaphorically Speaking (© CMCD, Inc.)

Figure 4–12
A diversity of imagery is available on CD-ROM. Be aware that usage rights vary. See Appendix B for a listing of stock imagery vendors.

Indigenous Peoples (© Digital Stock Professional)

Sky, Volume One (© CD Folios)

Digital Photographics (© Husom & Rose)

Retro Americana (© PhotoDisc)

© The Image Bank, Kaz Mori (left), Alex Stewart (right)

quality, go to a professional laboratory which will charge more but can give your slides more attention. In either case, the cost is considerably less than traditional scanning.

The Photo CD images can be viewed either on a Photo CD player, which can be connected to almost any television set, or read by a Photo CD-compatible CD-ROM drive connected to a computer, where the images can be used in programs like Photoshop.

Color images are stored in YCC, a device independent color space similar to Lab, in the following resolutions:

Base/16	128×192 pixels (thumbnail size)
Base/4	256×384 pixels
Base	512×768 pixels (closest to TV and monitor resolution)
4 Base	1024×1536 pixels (the proposed HDTV resolution)
16 Base	2048×3072 pixels (usable printing at 133 lpi at up to 8×10 inches)
64 Base	4096×6144 pixels (Pro Photo CD format)

In addition to the standard Photo CD and Pro Photo CD Master disc formats, Kodak offers several other products and systems that work with Photo CDs:

- The **Print Photo CD** system allows images scanned on high-end systems to be written to a CD-ROM in the Image Pack format. This format is designed to meet the needs of the color offset printing and publishing industry. These files can be stored in CMYK color mode at high resolution.

- The **Portfolio CD** format allows you to create your own interactive presentations combining photographs, graphics, sound, and text. The show is then recorded to a Photo CD disc. Many of the same service bureaus who image Photo CD can also image Portfolio CDs. This format can be used for multimedia presentations playable on computers or televisions such as interactive education, business presentations, information kiosks, and trade show displays. Kodak's Create-It presentation software allows you to create simple interactive presentations, and Arrange-It Portfolio layout software allows you to design more complicated multimedia presentations requiring sophisticated branching. Both programs output a script language that can be read at the service bureau by the Build-It program which assembles and writes the presentation to a CD. See Chapter 12 for more on Multimedia.

- The **Photo CD Catalog Disc** format is aimed at organizations that desire to store many images on a disc for wide distribution. Up to

4,400 images can be stored on one disc for playback on computers or televisions that read CDs.

A simple method of accessing Photo CD images is to use Kodak PhotoEdge or Photo CD Access Plus software. PhotoEdge will open Photo CD files and allow simple image editing, such as sharpen, adjust tones, rotate, and crop. PhotoEdge is useful to generate proofsheets of the images stored on a Photo CD. Photo CD Access Plus software can open Photo CD images, and translate and export them as PICT, EPS, TIFF, PCX, and BMP (DIB) file formats.

All of Kodak's Photo CD products except Create-it are available for the Windows platform.

PHOTOSHOP AND PHOTO CD

The two most common ways to open Photo CD files in Photoshop are to purchase an acquire plug-in from Kodak, or to use Photoshop's Open command, which makes use of Kodak's Color Management System (KCMS). KCMS will be installed automatically in your System Folder when you install Photoshop 3.0. This method uses Photoshop's Open dialog box and is available on both the Macintosh and PC.

To open a Photo CD image using the KCMS, simply choose Open under the File menu, and select the Photo CD image you want to open. A dialog box will appear (Figure 4–13). Choose the resolution from the pop-up menu. Click Source and choose a device profile for the three most common film types: negative, Ektachrome, and Kodachrome. Click Destination and choose from the various RGB, Lab, or CMYK profiles specific to your output needs from the pop-up menu. These profiles have been developed by Kodak

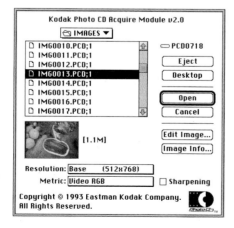
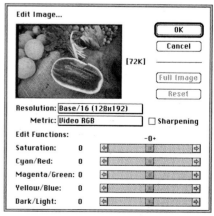

Figure 4–13
Kodak Photo CD
Acquire module
dialog box

to yield optimal results from your display, output device, or proofing method. Kodak sells specialized transforms for more specific output needs.

TIP: For optimal results using KCMS through the Open command, it is best to have your images scanned by a professional lab. Ask to have the images scanned with film terms off and to make no color corrections.

A faster choice is to use the Photo CD Acquire module available from Kodak, which you can place in your plug-ins folder or directory. Choose Acquire from the File menu and Kodak Photo CD from the submenu (Figure 4–14). This method is available for both Macintosh and Windows. You can view thumbnail previews of the images on the disk before opening them. There are also some simple tools for cropping, zooming, and rotating images, but it usually makes more sense to do these functions within Photoshop.

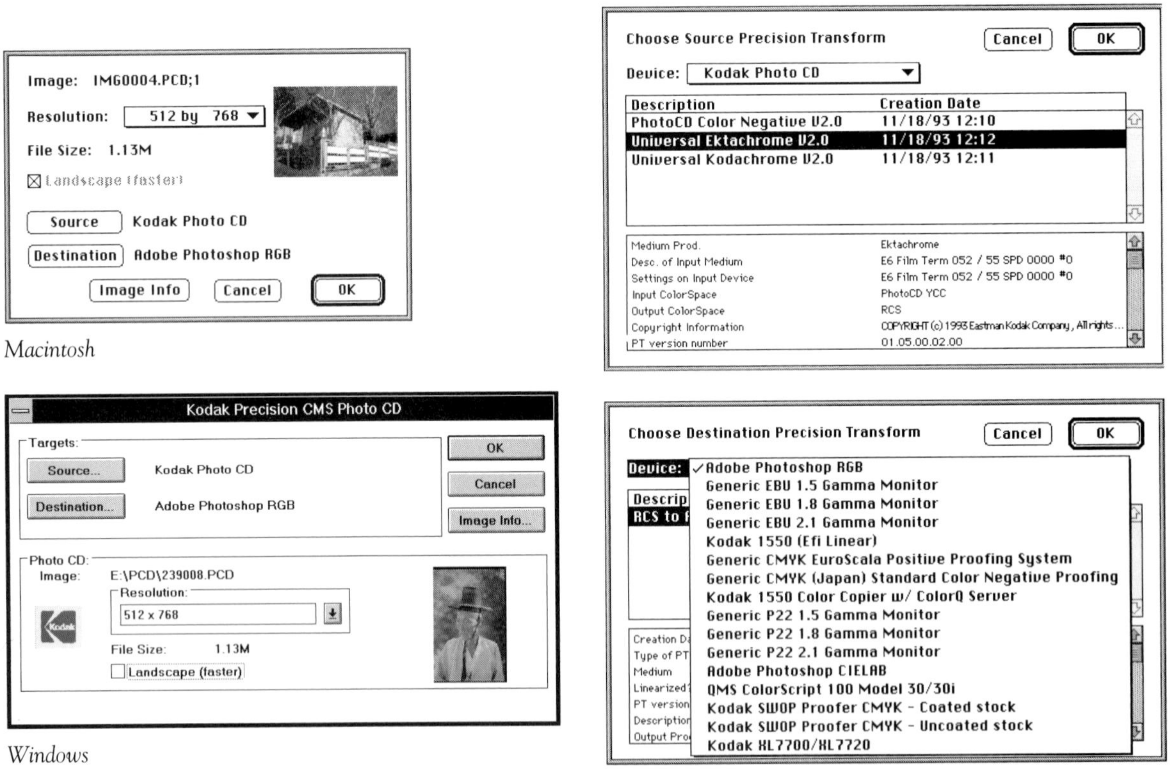

Macintosh

Windows

Figure 4–14   The Open dialog box to open a Photo CD image uses the Kodak Color Management System. Select the source and destination transforms. In the Windows version, note that the Image field contains the path to your file.

The Kodak Acquire module gives you options for opening the images in Video RGB, Photo CD YCC (which is not useful unless you want to do your own color mapping), grayscale, and several choices for RGB based on different gamma and white point settings. Normally you would choose a gamma and white point which matches your settings in Monitor Setup in Photoshop Preferences (see Chapter 3, "Configuring Photoshop"). You may also choose a different setting which will affect the tonal curve of your image; higher gamma settings generally produce a lighter image. There is no option to open in Lab or CMYK mode so you'll still need to convert your image to CMYK in Photoshop if you are preparing the image for color offset printing.

TIP: Whichever method you choose to open a CD-ROM, Acquire or Open, your images will open at 72 ppi resolution. Go to the Image Size command under the Image menu to change to the size (and resolution) that you will use for the image.

On-Line Technologies

Images have been available from on-line services like CompuServe for many years. In fact, Compuserve was the originator of the GIF format, which provides a platform-independent way to share images which are in Bitmap, Grayscale, and Indexed Color modes. (For more about the GIF format, see Appendix A.) But until recently most images available were low-quality, screen-resolution pictures. This is rapidly changing.

Stock photography has also become available from professional on-line image services: Kodak Picture Exchange, Comstock On-Line Access, Picture Network and PressLink. Images can also be accessed through other on-line services such as America Online, CompuServe, eWorld, and the Internet. These services attempt to speed the process of searching for and obtaining images for newspapers, magazines, and other industries that use stock photography. Accessing these services requires a modem, and you must pay sign-up and usage fees, plus the cost of images retrieved. You search for images using the provided software. For example, you could search for vertical format images with a sunset and then download possible thumbnail images to view. Place an order for your chosen images on-line for download or delivery. As with CD-ROM stock images, usage rules vary considerably. A listing of on-line services is found in Appendix C.

Video

Video digitizers were among the first input devices to hit the computer graphics world. Although scanners have replaced digitizers as the preferred method of input, the former are still quite popular for situations that specifically warrant their use. Here are two examples:

- Importing pictures of real-world, three-dimensional objects into the computer without having to photograph them on film, and then scan

- Grabbing images from video sources, such as videotape, camcorders, or still video cameras

The resolution of images which come from video is fixed at approximately 640 by 480 pixels, and color fidelity is generally poor, so the image captures may not be of print quality.

DIGITIZERS AND FRAME GRABBERS

Digitizers and frame grabbers are similar in function. A typical frame grabber has onboard RAM memory for storing at least one (if not more) digitized images. A digitizer simply allows you to grab a frame of video and bring it into computer RAM. Boards that allow you to grab several sequential frames and combine them into a single image yield better results.

Digitizers and frame grabbers that use NuBus cards are the preferred devices for video input, and are typically offered as 8-bit grayscale, 8-bit grayscale/color, 16-bit grayscale/color, and 24-bit grayscale/color. The software included with these devices usually offers the ability to save images in either PICT or TIFF format. Check with the board manufacturer for availability of a Photoshop plug-in. Newer AV computers have onboard video digitizers built in and can output back to video.

STILL VIDEO CAMERAS

Still video cameras are analog cameras that capture images in a format called NTSC Still Video. A good example is the Canon RC-570, which records images on 2-inch floppy disks, a standard for all manufacturers. The floppy disk holds either 25 or 50 images and can be downloaded directly from the camera through a video-digitizing board or disk renderer/digitizer and software for Macintosh or PC. Newer AV models of Macintosh have digitizing cards built in. The standard NTSC format means the images can be played back on TV. Still video cameras have the advantage of relatively low cost and convenience. The 640 × 480 pixel 8 bits per channel image quality is fine for video, multimedia, or lower-quality publication, but is probably not sufficient for medium- to high-quality needs.

TIP: Some Nubus boards can convert digital images to analog on the 2-inch floppy disk used by still video cameras. This is a convenient way to create presentations and play them on a television directly from the camera.

Frame-grabbed video images are generally of poor quality for print work, but the roughness actually seems to encourage more vigorous painterly manipulation. Artists often find that this low image resolution is not an issue if image manipulation—filter application, image overlay, and combining elements—is going to take place. Shooting with a camcorder can provide for hundreds of pose choices quickly at minimal expense. Bill Niffenegger demonstrates the use of low resolution video images in "Summer Fishing Fun" (Figure 4–15).

Niffenegger began this Norman Rockwell–inspired image by posing the "dad" and the "daughter" during separate shoots on a white background, which he frame-grabbed with a Sony TR101 High 8 camcorder, along with the various other elements in the composition (see Figure 4–16).

Niffenegger simplified the component images using posterization, despeckling, and diffusion-filtering before he began the painterly manipulation. All elements were composited together. To complete the effect, he painted in the fishing lines and color-corrected the entire image for final print output.

Niffenegger ©1993

Figure 4–15 "Summer Fishing Fun" was created from low-resolution video captures. (© Bill Niffenegger)

Figure 4–16   The various elements that Bill Niffenegger photographed with a video camera for "Summer Fishing Fun" (© Bill Niffenegger)

Digital Cameras

A growing technology for capturing images is digital photography. Unlike still video cameras which require a separate digitizing card, digital cameras digitize within the camera itself. A wide range of digital cameras is now available on the cost/quality continuum and new models are frequently announced.

TIP: A digital camera on a copy stand can double as a scanner.

Low- to mid-priced digital cameras are most useful for applications like newsletters or real estate listings where the advantages of speed and convenience outweigh image quality, which is lower than that of analog cameras.

A camera that has attracted much attention because of its relatively high image quality for a good price (approximately $700) is Apple's QuickTake 100. Like most digital cameras it uses a CCD array to sample an image. The CCD captures a 640 × 480 pixel, 8-bit per channel image. It is also very fast and lets a user shoot and store up to eight images with an interval of only a few seconds between shots. Quality is limited by a fixed-focus lens, and images must be decompressed and interpolated when they are transferred to a Macintosh or Windows-equipped PC with a serial cable.

Higher resolution (and priced) digital cameras are aimed at the graphic arts, photography, and journalism markets. The Kodak DCS 420 digital camera uses a large CCD array of 1524 × 1012 pixels to capture a 12 bits per color RGB image (36 bits total). This image when acquired into Photoshop produces a 4.4 megabyte file. The camera stores its images on a PCMCIA removable hard drive. Voice notations can be added to each image through a built-in microphone in the camera. Data and comments can also be stored with each image (Figure 4–17).

Other high-resolution digital cameras utilize monochrome CCD arrays and make three separate exposures through red, green, and blue filters. These slow cameras need to be attached directly to a computer, making them best suited for the studio camera market. These cameras work well for catalog photography and other high-volume controlled environments. Leaf Systems has released the Lumina, which uses standard Nikon 35mm lenses, for about $7,500. It captures a 2700 × 3400 pixel, 12-bits per channel image (Figure 4–18).

The Dicomed Digital Camera Back (approximately $21,500) also works best in a studio environment because of slow exposures. This camera back can fit onto any 4 × 5 view camera and can capture a maximum 6000 × 7520 pixels at 12 bits per channel. Photographer Stephen Johnson has been pushing the limits with the Dicomed camera by taking it out in the field to

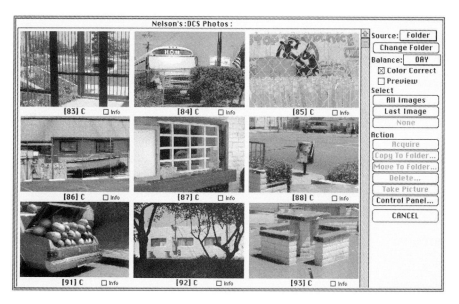

Figure 4–17 The Acquire interface for the Kodak DCS420 digital camera. Images can be opened directly from the camera or the entire file of images can be saved to a hard disk. Data and comments can be stored with each image.

Figure 4–18
This fantasy scene was
photographed with the
Leaf Lumina Camera
courtesy of
Nelson's Photo.
(© Mark Siprut)

photograph the landscape in much the same way that pioneer photographers ventured out at the turn of the century. In the photograph "Yosemite Falls," the slow scanning speed recorded the blur of the waterfall as the eastwind blew the fall diagonally during the entire time of the exposure (Figure 4–19).

Importing Images

So far we have been talking about importing images using scanners, CD-ROM sources, on-line services, video and digital cameras. However, you may need to open an image in Photoshop which has already been scanned or created in another program. You can also open and rasterize (convert into a bitmap) images from vector (smooth art) applications, from both specialized formats and the Clipboard.

PHOTOSHOP FILES

If you are opening Photoshop files, the best format to open and save in is the Photoshop 3.0 format (Photoshop's default file format). The Photoshop 3.0 format supports all of Photoshop's modes and can include layers, channels, and paths. It also compresses files on disk, saving space.

TIP: Although Photoshop 3.0 files are compatible across platforms, be aware of platform differences regarding file names. The current version of DOS and Windows 3.1 only support 8-character file names and Photoshop for Windows requires a .PSD extension. Follow this rule when saving Macintosh work that you intend to transfer to Windows. For example, the file name SAMPLE.PSD is in the correct format. The Macintosh file name My New Samples is not correct because it is too long and doesn't have the required extension.

Figure 4–19
"Yosemite Falls" showing
off during the long
exposure of the Dicomed
digital camera back
mounted on a 4 × 5 inch
view camera.
(© Stephen Johnson)

The Photoshop 2.0 format is available for backward compatibility with earlier versions of Photoshop, but doesn't support features added in Photoshop 2.5 and 3.0. Embedded in the Photoshop 3.0 file is also the 2.5 format, enabling Photoshop 2.5 and other programs (such as Adobe Premiere) to open Photoshop 3.0 files.

BITMAPPED FILES FROM OTHER APPLICATIONS

Photoshop opens and saves a wide variety of bitmapped file formats from applications on several computer platforms (Appendix A gives a complete description of each format). To open them, choose Open under the File menu and select the file. The TIFF format is usually a good choice for interchange because it supports all of Photoshop's modes except Multichannel and Duotone modes. The TIFF format can be imported and exported by almost every image editing application on the major computer platforms.

If you receive bitmapped files from other sources to include in a Photoshop image, be sure they are the same resolution. If not, the artwork could appear at a smaller or larger size than you expect.

OPENING FILES CREATED ON ANOTHER PLATFORM

Many raster or vector files created on a Macintosh or PC can be moved back and forth, to and from the other platform. Because of the wide variety of bitmapped file formats and variable standards, the best solution in a multi-platform publishing environment is to use Photoshop on both platforms to create your art and transfer the native file (.PSD). If both platforms don't use Photoshop, the TIFF format (.TIF in Windows) is the best choice. For example, the Windows screen captures for this book were created with WinCapture by Jasc Inc. This utility generates .TIF files which were transferred to the Macintosh (no translation required) and opened in Photoshop.

TIP: Software publishers would like us to believe that transferring graphics is a seamless procedure that always works properly. A prudent approach, however, is to test these procedures before you start a job. Record the problems and solutions, using these as guidelines for real jobs.

In addition to finding a common file format, you must also deal with the issue of reading physical media across platforms. Most Macintosh computers contain a 3.5 inch Super Drive which is capable of reading (mounting) DOS disks provided the proper software is loaded. Apple's Macintosh PC Exchange or DOS Mounter Plus accomplish this task. Once these extensions are installed, simply drag the file from your DOS disk to your Macintosh desktop and open the file with Photoshop. No translation is required. Transferring these files from the Macintosh to Windows is accomplished exactly the same way using a DOS formatted disk.

As noted above, DOS is limited to an 8-character file name and 3-character extension. Most Windows applications (including Photoshop) require the proper extension. For example, change the Macintosh file name of a TIFF image from *5 Fold Brochure* to 5FOLDBRO.TIF to properly open this document in Photoshop for Windows. (See Appendix A for a list of extension names.)

Using a Macintosh-formatted disk or SyQuest cartridge on a PC requires special software to transfer files. Mac-In-Dos and Conversion Plus are two Windows applications that accomplish this task. Remember, no translation is required in the transfer.

You can use removable media to transfer files between platforms. Unfortunately, many Macintosh-only service bureaus don't know how to properly use a DOS-formatted SyQuest cartridge on their Macintoshes. This often leads to frustration and lost data. The first step is to configure your PC's SCSI (Small Computer Systems Interface) card so your SyQuest drive is a fixed disk. Next use the DOS FORMAT command to prepare the cartridge for data. Proprietary formatting software for your SyQuest cartridge is not recommended as it often leads to lost data when the cartridge is used on a Macintosh. To properly mount (use) your cartridge the service bureau technicians must properly install either DOS Mounter, Plus/Multi Mounter, or Access PC *before* they attempt to mount your cartridge.

VECTOR FILES FROM ADOBE ILLUSTRATOR

You may need to incorporate some hard-edged vector graphics into Photoshop from illustration programs like Adobe Illustrator, Aldus FreeHand or CorelDRAW!. The EPS format has become a standard for vector graphics. The only EPS format that Photoshop imports is Adobe Illustrator EPS files. The one important problem is that when the objects come into Photoshop, they lose their vector properties (clean edges) and become part of the bitmap (raster).

Following are some reasons to rasterize vector illustrations in Photoshop:

- Ordinarily you cannot see overprinting information either on a computer monitor or on a digital color proof. For example, you cannot see the overprinting strokes created in vector art programs to build traps. When Photoshop rasterizes an Illustrator file, it shows two overprinting colors as a third color, as would print on a printing press. Therefore, you can use this Photoshop feature to preview trapping.

- Blends or gradients created in vector art programs are limited to 256 shades of a color (this is a limitation in PostScript). But the bands of color created are too perfect. When there are an insufficient number of steps, shade-stepping (banding) occurs when output to film. If you open an Illustrator file in Photoshop, it will open in CMYK mode. You can open the darkest channel and apply the Add Noise or a Blur filter to eliminate the banding. (You can also add noise to the other channels, but be careful not to overdo it. Also, do not add noise to a channel if there is no image.) Usually an Amount setting of 2 or 3 is sufficient. The added noise or blurring will break up the regularity of the steps, making them look smoother. Be aware, however, that there is a penalty: The resolution necessary for high-quality printing means the file size will now be much larger!

- Occasionally, a complex Illustrator file may be impossible to RIP (process) on an imagesetter. Converting it to a Photoshop bitmap at the appropriate resolution will often solve the printing problem.

There are three ways to bring Adobe Illustrator documents into Photoshop.

1. The Open command in the File menu allows you to open an Adobe Illustrator file as a new Photoshop document. When you open an Illustrator EPS file, it is rasterized into a bit-map—the pattern of pixels on a grid in Photoshop. You are asked to specify the file dimensions and resolution. Select the Anti-aliased option to improve the quality of the image being rasterized (Figure 4–20).

2. The Place command in the File menu places an Illustrator file as a floating selection on top of an existing Photoshop document. The Illustrator file comes in at the resolution of the image in which it is placed. Like any other floating selection, you can resize and move the selection. Once you have positioned it, clicking inside the selection box (the pointer becomes a gavel) confirms the placement. To cancel, move the pointer outside the box and click (the pointer becomes a No symbol). Then the Illustrator graphic can no longer be edited.

3. You can copy Illustrator 5.0 or 5.5 (Macintosh) images to the Clipboard and paste them into Photoshop. (You now have the choice of rasterizing these images or bringing them in as paths.) You may experience limitations with the Windows Clipboard. See "Importing with the Clipboard" below.

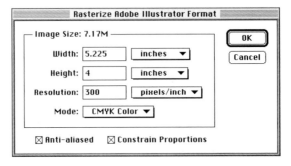

Figure 4–20
The Rasterize EPS File dialog that appears when opening an EPS file.

TIP: Be aware of some limitations of the rasterizing process: You cannot import patterns, stroked text, or any graphic that has been placed in the Adobe Illustrator document. Photoshop 3.0 can rasterize Illustrator gradients (earlier versions of Photoshop could not do this).

VECTOR FILES FROM MACROMEDIA FREEHAND AND CORELDRAW!

Adobe Photoshop will only reliably open or place Adobe Illustrator EPS files. If you use Macromedia FreeHand 4.0 CorelDRAW! 5.0 you must export your graphics to an Illustrator 3 format. In FreeHand 4.0, choose Export from the File menu, then choose Adobe Illustrator 3 as the file format. In CorelDRAW! 5.0 make the same choice, and CorelDRAW! will export an .AI (Adobe Illustrator-formatted) file. Then you can use the process described above to open or place FreeHand or CorelDRAW! files in Photoshop.

TIP: If there is any text in the FreeHand or CorelDRAW! document, avoid problems by exporting it to Adobe Illustrator format and then resaving the file. If you do not have Illustrator, the safest way to handle type is to convert your type to outlines (curves).

ACQUIRE ANTI-ALIASED PICT (MACINTOSH ONLY)

The PICT format on the Macintosh is sometimes used to store vector images created by basic drawing programs. The Anti-Aliased PICT Acquire module rasterizes a PICT graphic into a soft-edged anti-aliased file. Because the entire PICT image must be in memory for the rasterization to take place, you are limited by the memory of your computer as to how large an image you can handle.

To import a PICT image, choose Acquire under the File menu, then select Anti-Aliased PICT (Figure 4–21). You can choose the image dimensions, and whether to open it as Grayscale or RGB. This module is not available for Windows.

ACQUIRE PICT RESOURCE (MACINTOSH ONLY)

On the Macintosh, the PICT Resource Acquire module imports PICT resources from files. Often applications store PICT images in their resource fork. The Scrapbook is an excellent example of this. To open a PICT resource, choose Acquire under the File menu, then select PICT Resource. The PICT Resource dialog box lets you choose which resource to open

(Figure 4–22). The Preview button lets you scroll to the left and right through the PICT resources in the file. Clicking OK opens the displayed resource. This module is not available for Windows.

TIP: **The PICT Resource Acquire module used with the Scrapbook is a good way to edit sequential images for animation and multimedia. To store images in several Scrapbooks use SmartScrap from Portfolio Systems Inc., which allows you to create and save several Scrapbooks (Figure 4–23).**

ACQUIRE QUICK EDIT FILES (TIFF AND SCITEX ONLY)

The Quick Edit module allows you to open a portion of a large image, work on it, and then seamlessly insert it back into the main file. This is a good approach to working with large, high-resolution files that only need manipulations in certain sections of the file. The module works with uncompressed TIFF images and files stored in the Scitex CT file formats. Quick Edit does not work with files stored in the Photoshop 3.0 format.

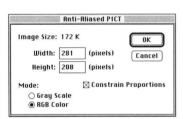

Figure 4–21
To open a vector PICT file in Photoshop, choose Acquire under the File menu, then select Anti-Aliased PICT. You can specify the dimensions and mode.

Figure 4–22
The PICT Resource Acquire module allows you to open PICT images stored as resources in other files, such as the Scrapbook. Click on the arrows to scroll through a series of images.

Figure 4–23
SmartScrap from Portfolio Systems Inc. allows you to create, name, and save several Scrapbooks. These file can be opened directly into Photoshop by using PICT Resource Acquire.

TIP: Use Quick Edit to test a Photoshop effect on a small part of an image before taking the time to apply it to the whole picture.

To use this module, choose Acquire under the File menu and select Quick Edit. Select the file to be opened, and the Quick Edit dialog box will appear (Figure 4–24). Drag with the cursor to select the portion of the image to be opened. The pixel dimensions of your selection and the file size are displayed. You may also check the Grid check box, in which you define a grid of *x* by *y* rectangles and select one of the grid rectangles to be opened for editing. Click OK to open the selected portion of the image as a new Photoshop document. After all work is completed, choose Quick Edit Save in the Export submenu under the File menu to place it back into the original file in perfect registration.

TIP: Total Integration, Inc. offers acquire modules that let you edit portions of documents in various file formats. After editing the section gets saved back into the original in perfect registration. FastEdit/TIFF supports RGB, CMYK, Grayscale and Bitmapped TIFF files. FastEdit/DCS allows you to edit a section of an image that has already been color-separated into the DCS (Desktop Color Separation) format. FastEdit/CT allows you to edit portions of files saved in the Scitex CT format.

Figure 4–24   Quick Edit Acquire allows you to work on a portion of a large document without opening the entire document. This will speed up your work. When editing is finished the section is saved back into the original document precisely in register.

IMPORTING WITH THE CLIPBOARD

In Photoshop you can use the Macintosh Clipboard for cutting, copying, and pasting selections between Photoshop images. You can also copy PostScript artwork to the Clipboard from Adobe Illustrator 5.0 or 5.5, Adobe Dimensions, and Adobe Type Align. A Postscript Clipboard image is rasterized as it is pasted into a Photoshop document. This is the same process discussed above for importing Adobe Illustrator graphics.

Two choices in Preferences affect this process: the Anti-Aliased PostScript option and the Export Clipboard option. These preferences are discussed in the section on setting preferences in Chapter 3, "Configuring Photoshop."

The basic function of the Windows Clipboard is identical to that of the Macintosh Clipboard. The Windows Clipboard does a great job in transferring text between applications. When it comes to graphics, however, it's a different story. The Windows Clipboard has no system level support for PostScript. In general, each application handles the Clipboard differently; many create a private Clipboard that is not available to other applications. If you create some PostScript art in CorelDRAW! and copy it to the Clipboard, it is converted to raster format (.BMP) and vector format (.WMF). This conversion sometimes changes your art. The Windows Clipboard is also very sensitive to available system resources and memory, which sometimes alter images in unpredictable ways. For these reasons we suggest that you avoid the Clipboard and export your PostScript art as an Adobe Illustrator file (.AI) or .TIF and then open or place this image in Photoshop.

WINDOWS TIP: If you use another raster program like Aldus PhotoStyler to create art and plan to modify this art in Photoshop, the Windows Clipboard may fail. The Windows Clipboard is not yet robust enough to handle a 10 MB file, and running two large applications at the same time really stresses the computer. Copying this file to the Clipboard may alter the image or even cause Windows to crash. We suggest you save your work as a .TIF, close the application, and then start Photoshop.

The Process of Digitizing Images

Input and output are intimately related in Photoshop. The very first step is to determine how you will use the image. Next choose methods of input and output. To achieve quality results, you should consider the following three points *before* you do your input:

1. You should calibrate your system so that you can achieve consistent and predictable results.

2. You should understand that the quality of your source image and how skillfully it is scanned will have a significant effect on your final result.

3. You should understand the concepts of resolution and file size so that you can create a file that will be appropriate for your intended output method.

The second and third points are discussed below. See Chapter 3, "Configuring Photoshop," for a description of the steps required to calibrate your system.

Start with a Good Original

GIGO (garbage in, garbage out) applies when choosing a source image for input. Whenever possible, select the best image you can find as the source for your scan or other input. With photographs, you will save a great deal of time and end up with a better result if your photographer shoots an extra roll of film to get a well-exposed and well-developed image, as opposed to your having to correct a bad image in Photoshop (even though Photoshop gives you tremendous capabilities to do just that).

The goal is to start with an original photograph with a full range of tones, good contrast and color balance. Bracketing, a technique used by professional photographers, can help achieve a good original. By shooting the image at a variety of exposure settings, the photographer has a better chance of capturing on film the ideal range of tones for scanning and reproduction.

If possible use original film for scanning rather than a print. The dynamic range of film is much greater than that of a prints. Photographic paper does not record the tonal information contained in a negative as well as a good scanner. By the time a print is made, a great deal of data is lost. For example, a typical black-and-white negative may be able to record 12 F stops of tonal information, but a print may only be able to record 8 F stops of information.

If you use transparencies, scan an original (rather than a duplicate) for the best dynamic range. Use a larger format transparency, such as a 4×5 inch, if your image will be enlarged. When 35mm slides are enlarged excessively, you can see the grain of the film.

TIP: When photographing an image in which the colors are critical, it's useful to include a grayscale control card in the shot. When the image is scanned and color corrected, you can match the gray card in the image with the real gray card. You can buy an 18% gray card from a photography supply company. See Chapter 8, "Color," to learn how to use a gray card to balance color.

Scanning Skill and Quality

Another important factor in achieving quality input, and therefore output, is the skill of the scanning operator. A bad scan made on a drum scanner may be worse than a good scan made on a less expensive scanner. If you are doing the scan yourself, learn how to use the software which comes with your scanner or other image digitizer.

If you purchase drum or desktop scans, make sure the operator is skilled in scanning for your desired output. For example, an image to be output through a film recorder should be scanned differently from one to be color-separated digitally.

Scanning Guidelines for Color and Tone

The task in scanning is to match the range of tones and colors in the original image to the capability of your scanner and to the ability of Photoshop to understand those scanned tones and colors. That information should then match the potential of your final output device.

CAUTION: Do not trust your monitor unless you have calibrated it to your output device or proofing method.

The ideal scan is one that needs no tone or color adjustments in Photoshop. Following are some tips for optimal scanning:

- Most scanning programs have an automatic function, which produces satisfactory rough scans (they tend to loose tones in the highlight and shadow areas). The automatic feature is not usually good enough for critical work.

- Most scanning programs have some controls for Brightness (exposure), Contrast, Gamma control, Curve adjustment, Color balance, and/or Sharpening, as well as Histogram readings.

- For critical work most images need fine tuning. To assess the range of tones, read the Histogram in Photoshop (some scanner software also have a built in histogram reading). The optimum is to have the highlight and shadows as close to the endpoints as possible without clipping the ends. If the Histogram reading does not reflect this goal, make corrections using the controls in the scanner software and then rescan (Figure 4–25). Generally, you can make adjustments using Curves, Gamma and/or Exposure. Most scans also need midtones lightened. Do this by adjusting the midpoint up or down in Curves or by changing the Gamma setting. Some scanning programs allow you to import curves created and saved in Photoshop. Avoid using the Contrast control.

- To get the color balance correct, it is best to have a neutral gray area in the picture. After scanning, read this area with the Info palette in Photoshop (your scanning program may have a similar tool). A neutral

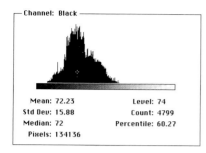 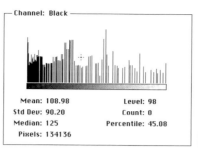 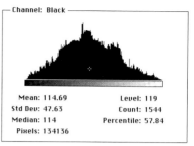

Figure 4–25 Histograms showing from left to right: less than a full range of tones, highlights and shadows clipped (burned-out highlights and poor shadow detail) and a good scan with a full range of tones.

area will read equal levels for all three RGB values. Another sure fire method of obtaining a neutral area in an image is to place an 18% gray card in the photograph at the time of the shoot (available at photography supply stores). Place it on an edge that you can crop out or shoot one picture with it and the next without it. Scans of similar photographs taken in the same lighting conditions should have similar tone and color balance. Adjust the curves and/or exposure for each color channel to correct the color. Rescan and then check the gray patch again. Some scanner software have a gray balance control. Choose it and then click on the gray patch. The gray balance control will automatically shift colors toward the neutral hue. See Chapter 8, "Color ," for more on correcting colors.

- To calibrate or set up your scanner to capture a full range of tones and balanced color, scan a grayscale (a series of steps ranging from black to white, available from Kodak as well as other manufacturers) and a standard image such as the Kodak Q-60 Color Input Target (includes a gray scale) or the Macbeth ColorChecker. Adjust the exposure/brightness, curves and color balance as necessary to yield the desired results for your output device. Judge the desired result by printing the image to your output device, or by making a proof print from separated film. Once you have achieved satisfactory results, save or note down the scanner settings to repeat them on future scans. If future images are correctly exposed and have good color balance these settings should get you close. See Chapter 3, "Configuring Photoshop."

TIP: Scanning a grayscale will show you the dynamic range capability of your scanner (Figure 4–26). See how many of the steps it can record, especially in the highlights and shadows.

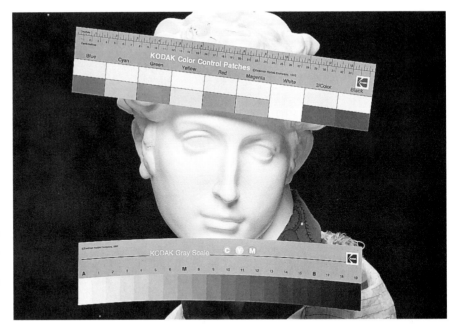

Figure 4–26
Scan a grayscale to
check the dynamic range
of your scanner and to
learn how to capture a
full range of tones.
Include a color chart to
balance the colors.
(© Craig Carlson)

Correct Image Resolution

Choose a resolution that will be appropriate for your image's intended use. If you create an image which has too low a resolution, it will appear pixelated, or coarse, when printed or displayed. Pixelated means that you can see the actual pixels that make up the image. On the other hand, if you create an image with too high a resolution, the file size will be larger than necessary, so Photoshop will require more of your computer's RAM. This slows down all operations, especially if the program has to use the scratch disk for virtual memory. The larger file will also be much larger to transport, take up valuable storage space, and print more slowly. Table 4–1 provides a handy reference for calculating appropriate image file sizes.

SCREEN

If you are creating an image that will only be displayed on a computer screen, such as for a presentation or video project, your choice is straightforward—choose the resolution that matches your monitor. For most Macintosh computers, you should choose 72 pixels per inch (ppi). Creating images that will be displayed on a PC/Windows computer screen is more complex. The first consideration is the video resolution that Windows and Photoshop both use. Two common video resolutions are 640 by 480 and 800 by 600. These two video resolutions normally display your image at 96 ppi. If you run Windows at a video resolution of 1024 by 768 your image normally displays

1 bit images — Line Art

Image	Image Dimensions				
Resolution	1 x 1"	2 x 2.5"	4 x 5"	5 x 7"	8 x 10"
100 ppi	2K	7K	25K	44K	98K
150 ppi	3K	14K	56K	97K	220K
200 ppi	6K	25K	98K	173K	391K
300 ppi	12K	56K	220K	386K	879K
400 ppi	20K	98K	391K	684K	1.53M
600 ppi	45K	220K	879K	1.51M	3.43M
1200 ppi	176K	879K	3.43M	6.01M	13.7M

8 bit images — Grayscale

Image	Image Dimensions				
Resolution	1 x 1"	2 x 2.5"	4 x 5"	5 x 7"	8 x 10"
75 ppi	6K	28K	110K	193K	440K
100 ppi	10K	49K	196K	342K	782K
150 ppi	22K	110K	440K	770K	1.72M
200 ppi	40K	196K	782K	1.34M	3.05M
300 ppi	88K	440K	1.72M	3.00M	6.87M
400 ppi	157K	782K	3.05M	5.34M	12.2M

Table 4–1 File Sizes of Scanned Images Use this chart to calculate the file sizes of scanned images. The intersection of the image dimensions and the image resolution will show you the file size for 1-, 8-, 24-, or 32-bit images. If you have an image size not listed, use the value for 1" x 1" and multiply the file size by the number of square inches in your image. For example, if you want to calculate the file size for a grayscale scan of a 4" x 4" image at 300 ppi, multiply 88 KB by 16 (the area in square inches).

24 bit images — RGB Color

Image	Image Dimensions				
Resolution	1 x 1"	2 x 2.5"	4 x 5"	5 x 7"	8 x 10"
75 ppi	17K	83K	330K	577K	1.29M
100 ppi	30K	147K	586K	1.00M	2.29M
150 ppi	66K	330K	1.29M	2.25M	5.15M
200 ppi	118K	586K	2.29M	4.01M	9.16M
300 ppi	264K	1.29M	5.15M	9.01M	20.6M
400 ppi	469K	2.29M	9.16M	16.0M	36.6M

32 bit images — CMYK Color

Image	Image Dimensions				
Resolution	1 x 1"	2 x 2.5"	4 x 5"	5 x 7"	8 x 10"
75 ppi	22K	111K	440K	770K	1.72M
100 ppi	40K	196K	782K	1.34M	3.05M
150 ppi	88K	440K	1.72M	3.00M	6.87M
200 ppi	157K	782K	3.05M	5.34M	12.2M
300 ppi	352K	1.72M	6.87M	12.0M	27.5M
400 ppi	625K	3.05M	12.2M	21.4M	48.8M

at 120 ppi. Because of these differences it's very important to determine the video resolution at which your images will actually be displayed. Your images won't be distorted if you create them at 640 by 480 (96 ppi) and display them at 1024 by 768 (120 ppi)—they will just look smaller on the screen.

BLACK AND WHITE LASER PRINTER

If your final output device is a black-and-white laser printer, your image must be halftoned for printing. (See Chapter 11, "Output," for a discussion of the digital halftone process.) The rule of thumb is to choose a scanning resolution between 1.5 and 2 times the lines per inch (lpi) of the halftone screen used for reproduction. The normal halftone screen for a 300 dots per inch (dpi) laser printer is between 53 and 75 lpi, so a scanning resolution between 80 and 150 ppi is appropriate. A 600 dpi laser printer may use a halftone screen between 85 and 100 lpi, so a resolution between 125 and 200 ppi would be best.

DIGITAL COLOR PRINTER

Less expensive digital color printers may use a halftone dot for imaging, so their output is relatively coarse. Use the same formula above to calculate resolution (lpi × 1.5 to 2 = scanning resolution). Higher quality digital color printers print with continuous tone (each pixel can be any of over 16 million colors), but they are still relatively low resolution. An image resolution between 150 and 200 ppi is usually adequate for imaging. On the very highest quality printers, you might go up to 300 ppi.

FILM RECORDER

If your output is a film recorder you need to match the resolution of the image with that of the film recorder. See "Resolution and Aspect Ratio for Film Recorders" later in this chapter.

HIGH-RESOLUTION IMAGESETTER

If your image will be sent to a high-resolution imagesetter for film output— whether in grayscale or a color separation—you again need to use 1.5 to 2 times the halftone screen formula. First find out from your printer what screen frequency is required for the press and paper that will be used for reproduction. For photographic magazine reproduction, you will need to refer to the specifications provided by the magazine. For example, if your image will be reproduced at 150 lpi, an image resolution of between 225 and 300 ppi should be fine.

SCALING YOUR IMAGE

The above formulas are for scanning your image for reproduction *at same size*. You may want to scale the picture larger or smaller to place it into a page layout program. Or you may wish reduce or enlarge the image at the time of printing. In these cases the scaling factor must be taken into account.

If you want to print a 2 × 3 inch image with a 150 lpi halftone screen, and you scanned it at 250 ppi, your scanner would sample the artwork at 250 samples per inch. If you placed that image in a page layout and then scaled it to 200% size, your 250 samples per inch would now spread over an area of 4 × 6 inches. Your effective resolution would decrease to 125 ppi, and the image would probably look pixelated.

To compensate for the effect of scaling up or down, multiply your scanning resolution by a scaling factor. In the preceding example, you should scan at 250 ppi times a scaling factor of 2, or 500 ppi, to compensate for the enlargement.

RESOLUTION FOR LINE ART

When discussing bit depth earlier in this chapter, a line art scan was described as a 1-bit scan. Selecting the correct scanning resolution for line art is different than for artwork which will be reproduced with halftone dots; no halftones are required because there are no graytones. For line art scans, a higher scanner resolution will produce fewer "jaggies," particularly along diagonal edges.

To reproduce line art on a 300 dpi laser printer, scanning at 300 ppi is the maximum required because the resolution of the printer (300 printer spots per inch) limits the quality of the image. However, to reproduce line art on an imagesetter, plan on scanning at least 800 ppi to avoid the jaggies. (Imagesetters use printer resolutions in the range of 1200 to 3600 dpi.) If your scanner doesn't scan at that high a resolution, you can photographically enlarge the artwork before scanning, then scale down the result in Photoshop to achieve a higher resolution.

TIP: **You may get better results reproducing line art if you trace it into a vector program (rather than leaving it in bitmapped form). You can manually trace or use the autotracing feature in Adobe Illustrator, Macromedia Freehand, or Corel Draw. Adobe Streamline will autotrace more complex images. Vector art, unlike bitmap art, can then be rescaled to use at any size without losing quality.**

RESOLUTION AND FILE SIZE

The size of the file you create is a product of three factors:

1. the dimensions of your image

2. the bit depth of your image

3. the resolution of your image

The first factor is pretty simple to understand. If you double the size of an image in both dimensions, the area of your image (width times height) will be four times as large. Therefore, the file size will quadruple.

Grayscale images contain 8 bits of information for every pixel. RGB images record 8 bits for each red, green, and blue channel, so each pixel requires 24 bits of information. Thus RGB images are three times as large as grayscale images with the same dimensions. If you convert from RGB to CMYK, you go from three channels of information to four (from 24 to 32 bits), and your file size increases by one-third.

Finally, it is important to understand the relationship between resolution and file size. If your resolution is twice as high as necessary, you will quadruple your file size! And since Photoshop's RAM requirements are related to file size, you will need four times as much RAM to manipulate the document.

TIP: To make things easier, you can use Photoshop to handle the complexities of figuring out how large a file will be. Choose New from the File menu. Enter the dimensions of the image that you want to use. Select the mode you will be working in, either Bitmapped, Grayscale, RGB, CMYK, or Lab. Then enter a value for resolution. Photoshop will calculate the file size.

RESOLUTION AND ASPECT RATIO FOR FILM RECORDERS

Resolution and aspect ratio are critical in the preparation of images for a film recorder. Like other issues of resolution, it is important to consider the output resolution on the film recorder at the time the image is created or digitized. Film recorders expose images on film at fixed output resolutions on a pixel grid of a fixed size (*x* pixels wide by *y* pixels high). If your image is smaller than or equal to the height and width of the pixel grid, you can output at the resolution of the pixel grid.

The resolution you choose depends on the quality requirements of your job and your computer's ability to handle the file size. Consider also that the price of a slide or transparency is more expensive for higher resolutions. Ideally you should create your image at the exact pixel size of the resolution you intend for output. The chart below shows the pixel dimensions of each resolution and the approximate file size for a 24-bit (RGB) image. The resolution choices (2K, 4K, and 8K) refer to the number of pixels on the long side of the image:

35mm Slides

Resolution	Pixel Dimensions	File Size
2K	2048 × 1364	8.0 MB
4K	4096 × 2728	32.0 MB
8K	8192 × 5456	127.9 MB

4 × 5 and 8 × 10 Transparencies

Resolution	Pixel Dimensions	File Size
2K	2048 × 1536	9.0 MB
4K	4096 × 3072	36.0 MB
8K	8192 × 6144	144.0 MB

Images can be enlarged for film recorder output either in Photoshop or, as the file is imaged, by the film recorder. Photoshop uses interpolation to resample the image (see Chapter 2, "Setting Up Your System"). As with output for prepress, outputting a low-resolution image at a high resolution on a film recorder will not give the image any more detail; it will only create a larger file size and cost more.

35mm slides have an aspect ratio of 3:2; 4 × 5 and 8 × 10 transparencies have an aspect ratio of 4:3. If your image does not match the aspect ratio and pixel dimensions of the recorder resolution, the film recorder service bureau can either crop to fill the frame or resize to fill the frame in one dimension. The other dimension will appear black. For a slide presentation, cropping the image to match the aspect ratio of the slide is usually the best choice.

Resampling an Image

Sometimes you will capture more information with your scanner or image digitizer than you need. Other times you may want to use an image in more than one way or at more than one size. In these cases, it is very easy to "sample down" an image in Photoshop. See "Resampling" in Chapter 7, "Image Processing."

If an image will be used at different resolutions and sizes, scan or create the image at the resolution needed for the largest size or for the highest resolution required. For example, you may be preparing your image for color separations (which require the highest resolution), but you may also want to create a color comprehensive which will be printed on a digital color printer at a service bureau. Because you are printing with a 150 lpi screen, you need 300 ppi image resolution for the color separations. It is not necessary, however, to send all the information in the high resolution file to a service bureau for the color comprehensive. Simply make a lower resolution version.

Summary

A myriad of source material for input is now available to digital artists and designers. Whether these images are digitized by digital cameras or recorded on film and scanned later Photoshop can accept many input options.

- Choose a method of scanning or digitizing that is appropriate for your subject, your eventual output, and the quality requirements of your project.

- When moving and importing files that have already been created, choose a file format compatible with the applications and platforms you are using. Double-check to see if the format is usable in your receiving application.

- For best results, start with original images that are well exposed and have good contrast and color balance. Scan original film instead of prints for the highest dynamic range.

- Learn how to use your scanner software or find a skilled operator to do your scanning.

- Scan images to maximize the dynamic range of the scanner and the tonal range in Photoshop.

- Scan your images at the proper resolution, based on your eventual output. Too high a resolution creates large files. Too low a resolution creates coarse, pixelated images.

As you can see, input is closely tied to output. For a more complete understanding of input, see Chapter 11, "Output." In the next chapter, "Tools," you will be introduced to the basic tools with which to edit, paint, and manipulate your digitized images within Photoshop.

5

Tools and Palettes

Photoshop's tools can literally work miracles. They can help you retouch images as well as create images from scratch. For example, Dick and Summer Todd used just about every tool in the Toolbox to retouch a severely damaged antique photograph of the founder of the city of San Diego (Figure 5–1). They selected areas with the various selection tools, feathered, used the Rubber Stamp tool, painted with the paint tools, lightened, darkened, softened, and enhanced with the editing tools, added gradients, etc. The undamaged hand was cloned and flipped to replace the missing hand.

At the end of this chapter you will find case studies of artists who create from scratch. However you use Photoshop's tools, you'll be amazed at their power.

Introducing the Tools and Palettes

Tools and palettes are analogous to a T square and X-acto knife, a hammer and drill, or beater and paring knife. They are the instruments you use to affect visual information. Like any tool in your studio, garage, or kitchen, it takes practice to master Photoshop's tools for maximum speed, control, and accuracy, so don't try to learn everything at once. Choose a few you will use most often in your work, and gradually add to your skill repertoire. Fortunately, many of Photoshop's tools are similar to tools in other graphics programs.

Adobe has improved the Toolbox in Photoshop 3. The Move and Sponge tools were added, and Photoshop 3's palettes have been revised to perform more specialized functions.

Figure 5–1   Most of the tools in the Toolbox were used to repair this damaged antique photograph of Alonzo Horton. (© Photo retouched by Dick and Summer Todd. Original photograph courtesy of the San Diego Historical Society.)

When you begin working with Photoshop, you should probably use the tools and palettes in their default states before changing their settings and positions. Remember that each tool has many working modes and options controlled by the palettes, so proceed patiently.

It is probably easiest to get a handle on Photoshop's tools through the palettes in relation to those tools. Because understanding palettes is crucial to using the tools effectively, we begin with a discussion of how palettes affect the tools.

Tools and Palettes in the Windows Version

The Windows tools and palettes in Photoshop are almost identical to those in the Macintosh version. The only difference is the procedure to close a palette. All the floating palettes and windows contain a Control menu, the box containing the dash in the upper-left corner of your palette. Double click on this box to close a palette or window.

Remember that throughout this book we use Macintosh keyboard instructions which are easily translated for those of you using the Windows version. Two global assumptions about keyboard instructions can be made for the Windows user: where you see the Command key mentioned substitute the Ctrl key; and where you see the Option key discussed, substitute the Alt key.

Working with Palettes

A palette is an interactive floating information window that you can move around the screen. In addition to the Toolbox, there are ten palettes that are essential to interfacing with Photoshop's tools. In default mode they are Brushes and Options (grouped in one window); Picker, Swatches, and Scratch (grouped in one window); Layers, Channels, and Paths (grouped in one window); the Info palette; and the Commands palette (Figure 5–2).

The palettes are grouped because they relate to each other intimately. In fact, in previous versions of Photoshop some of these features were combined into single palettes or dialogs. The Brushes and Options palettes control characteristics of particular tools such as size and shape (Brushes), and opacity and paint mode (Options). Picker, Swatches and Scratch all relate to choosing and mixing colors. Layers, Channels and Paths all concern selection, masking, shuffling images around and knowing where you are painting.

Palette Shortcuts and Helpful Hints

Because palettes are almost always involved with your tools, review the following shortcuts and helpful hints to increase your efficiency when working with any of the palettes:

- In general, you will increase your working speed if you keep your most-used palettes open in an unobtrusive place on the desktop. Of course, if you are working with a smaller monitor, the palettes may get

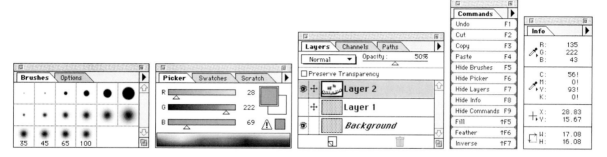

Figure 5–2   In default mode, the palettes are logically grouped. They are (from left to right) Brushes and Options; Picker, Swatches, and Scratch; Layers, Channels, and Paths; Info, and the Commands.

in the way. You can alternatively collapse and grow the palettes by clicking on the Zoom box on the right side of the palette window Title Bar or by double-clicking on the palette's Tab.

- To make all the palettes disappear, including the toolbox, press the Tab key. Press Tab again to make them all reappear. To hide individual palettes, select the palette's Hide command from the Window menu or click its Close box (Figure 5–3). Click on the Zoom box (right side of the Title bar) or double-click on the palette tab to collapse and expand the palette (Figure 5–4). The commands associated with a palette are accessed by pressing on the small black triangle near the upper-right corner of its window. This is referred to as a pop-up menu (Figure 5–3).

NOTE: When a palette is open, the Windows menu will display a command to "Hide" the palette; when a palette is closed, the menu will display a command to "Show" the palette.

- To make open palettes reappear in the same positions when you close and reopen Photoshop, make sure the Restore Palette & Dialog Positions button is checked in the General Preferences dialog box under the File menu (you must click on "More" to get this button).
- The default positions for the palettes are logically oriented along the bottom of your screen. Although you can move these around, the bottom of the screen is a good place to start because clicking on the Zoom box or double-clicking on the palette tab hides the window down below the screen, giving you more room to work.

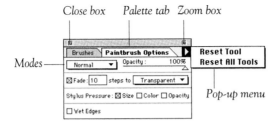

Figure 5–3
The components (parts) of a palette

Figure 5–4
Click on the Zoom box at the right side of the Title bar or double click on the palette tab to collapse and expand the palette.

Figure 5–5

Drag a palette by the tab
to separate it into its
own window. Drag a
palette over another
palette to group them
into a single window.

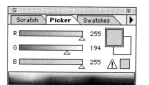 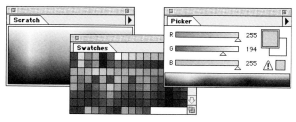

- If you have a keyboard with function keys, you can make the palettes (as well as many other features in Photoshop) appear without using the menus. Photoshop comes with some commands preassigned to function keys. To change or create new assignments to F keys, select New command from the pop-up menu in the Commands Palette.

- Some pre-assigned function keys for the palettes are as follows:

  Show Brushes, press F9.
  Show Picker, press F10.
  Show Layers, press F11.
  Show Info, press F12.

- Separate and move a palette by dragging it by its tab. Each palette can float alone or can be grouped with any other palette by dragging it over the other (Figure 5–5).

Brushes Palette

The Brushes palette controls the selection of brush shapes, sizes, parameters, and spacing. From the Brushes Palette and its pop-up menu (Figure 5–6), you can create and delete brushes, define brush options, and save and load sets of brushes.

To access the Brushes palette, select Show Brushes from the Palettes submenu under the Window menu.

To choose a Brush shape, click on the desired shape. Numbers inside a circle (diameter) indicate a brush too large to be shown in the palette.

ADDING, EDITING, AND REMOVING BRUSHES

Select New Brush from the Brushes palette pop-up menu to create a new brush. To modify an existing brush, click on it and then choose Brush Options from the pop–up menu or simply double-click on the brush icon. The New Brush or Brush Options dialog box will appear as in Figure 5–7 (they are identical). Any new brushes will appear in the lower part of the palette window.

The lower-left preview in the Brush Options dialog box shows the current brush angle and roundness. The lower-right preview displays the brush

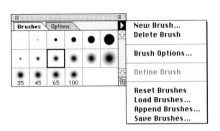

Figure 5–6
The Brushes palette

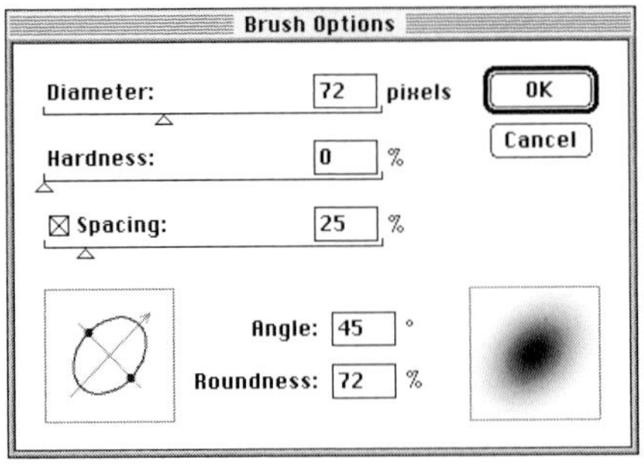

Figure 5–7
The Brush Options dialog box

hardness. As you change the settings the previews will simultaneously show the effects.

The **Diameter** slider changes the brush size from one to 999 pixels. In the case of an oval-shaped brush, the value indicates the longer dimension.

The **Hardness** slider softens the edges of a brush beyond the built anti-aliasing. The value reflects a percentage of the brush's diameter (0–100%). A small number yields the softest edge, and 100% will have a slight anti–aliased edge (Figure 5–8). The Hardness slider does not affect the Pencil tool which is never anti–aliased.

The **Spacing** slider controls the distance between brush marks. Specify the spacing with a percentage of the brush's diameter from 1 to 999. The higher the value entered, the more space to be added between brush marks. Click the check box next to Spacing to turn off its function. With Spacing off, the mouse will be sensitive to the speed at which it is moved, causing it to skip more pixels at faster speeds (Figure 5–9).

Figure 5–8
Hardness settings in Brush Options (left to right): 0%, 25%, 50%, 75%, and 100%

Figure 5–9
Spacing in Brush Options set to 25%, 100%, 200%, and 400%

Figure 5–10
Angle settings in Brush
Options from left to right, 0°,
45°, 90°, and 135°

Figure 5–11
Roundness settings in the Brush Options.
From left to right: 0%, 25%, 50%, 75%,
and 100%

The **Angle** setting is like varying the angle of a brush in your hand as you paint. It is measured as an angle from the horizontal. This setting must be on an oval shape to have an effect (it will not affect a circular brush). (Figure 5–10).

The **Roundness** setting varies the shape as an oval anywhere from a circle to a straight line. A 100% setting will be a perfect circle, and a small number will be a thin oval (Figure 5–11).

To delete a brush, click on it and then choose Delete Brush from the pop-out menu.

CUSTOM BRUSHES

Create custom brushes by selecting part of an image. A selection with soft edges (light gray) will simulate an anti-aliased brush. Although a custom brush can be made from any selection, they are usually better against a white background.

Use the Define Brush option from the Brushes palette pop-up menu after making a selection to create a custom brush (Figure 5–12).

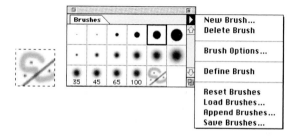

Figure 5–12
Make a selection and then choose Define Brush in the Brush Palette pop–up menu. The Custom brush will appear as a new brush shape in the Brushes palette.

Brush Options for custom brushes can be set in the Brushes palette pop-up menu or by double-clicking on the brush's icon (Figure 5–13). Spacing and Anti-aliasing are the only options. Large brushes cannot be anti-aliased.

TIP: **Photoshop comes with some sets of custom brushes. Look for them in the folder "Brushes and Patterns." Use** Load Brushes **from the pop–up menu to open the custom brushes (Figure 5–14).**

SAVING BRUSHES

Save Brushes and Load Brushes commands in the Brushes palette pop–up menu allow you to save a palette of brushes and then load it later for use with any other document. Although the Brushes palette can hold as many brushes as you need, it will be more efficient if you group and create your own saved personal sets of brushes.

Brushes stored in a file can be opened by choosing Load Brushes or added to the current palette with the Append Brushes command. Remember, you can always load the Default Brushes file by choosing Reset Brushes.

Options Palette

The Options palette, new with Photoshop 3, consists of several of the controls that were formerly part of the Brushes Palette. The Options palette also contains the controls previously found in the Options Dialog Box of each tool: Paint modes, Pressure, Opacity, and Stylus Controls on a digitizing pen. The controls in the Options palette vary to correspond with the current selected tool. For a specific discussion of how the Options palette works for each tool, refer to the "Individual Tool Overviews" section later in this chapter. Double-click on a tool to quickly open the Options palette.

To reset the options for a tool to its default setting, choose Reset Tool in the pop-up menu. To reset all tools to their default settings, choose Reset All Tools in the pop-up menu.

Control the use of a cordless pen on a pressure-sensitive digitizing tablet, such as the Calcomp, Kurta, and Wacom tablets, in the tool's Options palette. You have the option to set the variation in pressure to affect the size, color, and opacity of the tool. Set the stylus pressure options for the Pencil, Paintbrush, Airbrush, Rubber Stamp, Smudge, Blur/Sharpen, and Dodge/Burn/Sponge tools (Figure 5–15).

TIP: **The brush size in the Brushes palette also affects the dynamics of the stylus on a digitizing tablet. Try using larger brush sizes. If a small brush size is selected the range of the tools will be limited.**

Figure 5–13
The Brush Options dialog for a custom brush. Anti-aliasing is not available for larger brushes.

Figure 5–14
Photoshop ships with some sets of custom brushes. Use the Load Brushes command in the Brushes palette pop-up menu to open them.

Figure 5–15
The Pencil Options palette

OPACITY, PRESSURE, AND EXPOSURE CONTROLS

The **Opacity** slider control appears when the Paint Bucket, Gradient, Line, Eraser, Pencil, Paintbrush, and Rubber Stamp tools are selected. The percentage of opacity will determine the transparency of the paint laid down by a particular tool in relation to the underlying image (Figure 5–16). For example, when a solid black is the Foreground color and the Opacity is set at 30%, the result will be a 30% black blended over the parts of the image affected by the tool. Opacity can also be controlled with the number keys on the keyboard. By pressing a number from 1 through 0 before you use the tool, you will set the transparency from 10 to 100 percent. For example, before you paint with the Paintbrush tool, press the 4 key and your painting

Figure 5–16
A brush stroke with the Foreground color set to 100% black and the Opacity set to 30% over a 10%, 25%, and 50% black panel.

opacity will be set to 40 percent. Be aware, however, that this sets the opacity for that tool until it is changed again.

Pressure appears when the Airbrush, Smudge, Blur/Sharpen, and Sponge tools are selected. Pressure controls the "force" with which a tool is applied to the surface. For example, in the case of the Smudge tool, a higher pressure setting will spread paint farther (see Figure 5–83). With the painting tools, higher settings result in more paint applied to each stroke.

Exposure is used by the Dodge/Burn tool. A higher number equals a stronger effect. To lighten or darken an area with subtlety, set the exposure to a small number (try 10%). The exposure can be set to affect either the highlights, midtones, or shadows.

PAINTING AND EDITING MODES

The Options palette also controls how existing pixels in an image are affected by the foreground color when painting or editing with a tool. The modes also apply to the Fill command and Layer Options discussed in Chapter 6, "Image Selection and Masking." See Figure C–1 in the Color Section to see how the modes affect colors.

When using a tool, you can apply the foreground color in one of several modes, which are chosen from a pop-up menu in the Options palette. The mode choices change depending on the tool in use (Figure 5–17). The painting and editing modes do not affect selection or navigation tools.

- The modes for most of the painting and editing tools are Normal, Dissolve, Behind, Multiply, Screen, Overlay, Soft Light, Hard Light, Darken, Lighten, Difference, Hue, Saturation, Color, and Luminosity.

- In addition to the above modes, the Paintbucket and Line tools have the Clear mode.

- The Eraser tool does not have paint modes. Rather, it simulates the tools in the Toolbox: the Paintbrush, Airbrush, Pencil, and Block.

Figure 5–17
The paint modes change along with the Options palette, depending on the tool selected in the main toolbox.

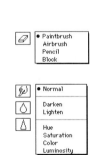

- The modes for the Smudge, Blur, and Sharpen tools change to Normal, Darken, Lighten, Difference, Hue, Saturation, Color, and Luminosity.
- The modes for the Dodge and Burn tools are Shadows, Midtones, and Highlights.
- The modes for the Sponge tool are Desaturate and Saturate.

Following is a brief description of each painting and editing mode.

Normal: The Normal mode, the default setting, applies the current Foreground color as a solid, opaque color using the painting tools.

Dissolve: The Dissolve mode works like the Airbrush tool in the original MacPaint program by randomly replacing the original pixel colors with the Foreground color. This dithered effect is most effectively used by setting the Opacity to a low percentage and selecting a large brush shape and painting with the Paintbrush or Airbrush tool.

Behind: Behind works only on Layers that have transparency (Preserve Transparency must not be clicked). The appearance is like painting on the back of glass that has the existing image on the front. You see the effect only in the transparent areas.

Clear: Fill or draw a transparency with the Clear mode. You must be on a layer for this mode to work.

Multiply: The Multiply mode creates a darker color by multiplying the Foreground color with the existing color. Multiplying with black results in black. Multiplying with white does not effect the existing color. Repeated strokes over an area builds progressively darker colors, similar to painting with marker pens.

Screen: Screen mode (opposite of Multiply) lightens the colors in an image by inverting the combination of the Foreground color and the existing color. Screen with white results in white, and with black leaves the existing color unchanged. Repeated strokes over an area progressively lightens it.

Overlay: Overlay combines the Foreground color with the existing color by Multiplying or Screening, depending on the existing color. This effect retains the lights and darks of the existing color, changing other colors depending on their hue and value.

Soft Light: Soft Light simulates illuminating the painted area with a diffused light. Painting or filling with a color lighter than a midtone gray lightens the existing color slightly, tinting it toward the paint or fill color, and painting or filling with a color darker than a midtone gray darkens the existing color slightly.

Hard Light: Hard light is more dramatic than Soft light. It simulates a brighter, more severe light source. Painting or filling with a color lighter than a midtone gray lightens the existing color slightly, tinting it toward the paint of fill color, and painting or filling with a color darker than a midtone gray darkens the existing color slightly. Highlights and shadows are accentuated.

Darken: Darken mode applies a tool only to pixels lighter than the current Foreground color, while pixels darker will not change.

Lighten: Lighten mode applies a tool only to areas that are darker than the current Foreground color. Lighter pixels will not change.

Difference: The Difference mode subtracts the existing color from the Foreground color or vice versa depending on which is brighter.

Hue: Use Hue mode to change pixels to the Foreground color. The Saturation and Luminosity values are left unchanged.

Saturation: Only the Saturation of pixels you paint will change in the Saturation mode. The Hue and Luminosity will not change.

Color: Use the Color mode for tinting or changing existing colors. In this mode, only the Hue component (or actual "color") is applied to the image, leaving the values untouched. When colorizing grayscale images, use the Color mode to apply "transparent" tints of the current Foreground color. The Luminosity of the image remains intact, while the Hue and Saturation values change.

Luminosity: The Luminosity mode is the opposite of the Color mode. When you paint in the Luminosity mode, only the Lightness of the existing pixels change, while the Hue and Saturation are unaffected.

TIP: If you encounter a problem with tools that do not seem to be drawing on the screen when used, check your mode settings (Darken, Lighten, Hue, etc.) to make sure that you are not using a setting that prohibits the tool from applying paint as expected.

Shadows: Shadows represent the darkest part of an image.

Midtones: Midtones are values located halfway between the shadows and highlights.

Highlights: Highlights represent the lightest part of an image.

Desaturate: Desaturate removes color from an image, neutralizing the color, making it grayer.

Saturate: Saturate takes neutral grays out of a color, making it more intense.

Layers Palette

The Layers palette shows all the layers in a document, controlling characteristics of how a layer combines with other layers: alignment, colors, tones, and opacity (Figure 5–18). A layer displays a composite of all visible channels. A normal color image is usually a composite of the red, green and blue channels.

The Layers palette lets you know which is the active target layer and which layer(s) you are viewing. Your tools can only paint or edit on one layer at a time, the target layer. If you are using layers, you should keep the Layers palette open at all times.

Following are some guidelines when using layers with the painting and editing tools. For a full discussion on using layers and the Layers palette, see Chapter 6, "Image Selection and Masking," and Chapter 10, "Compositing."

LAYERS CONTROL

- When opening a new document, you are automatically in the Background layer.

- Add a new layer by clicking on the New Layer icon at the foot of the Layers palette or Choose the New Layer command in the pop-up menu. Delete a layer by dragging it to the Trash at the bottom of the palette or by choosing Delete Layer in the pop-up menu.

- Click on a Layer name, such as "Layer 3," to make it the target layer. It will be highlighted by turning gray on the Macintosh and white in Windows.

- Click in the far left hand column of the Layers palette to show icons of an "eye." If the eye is showing, the layer is visible, but that doesn't mean it is also your target layer. It is possible to view one or more layers while working on a layer that is hidden from view.

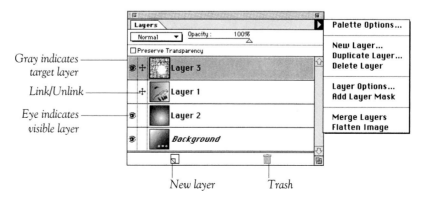

Gray indicates target layer

Link/Unlink

Eye indicates visible layer

New layer   Trash

Figure 5–18
The Layers palette

Figure 5–19
Use the Transparency
Options in the
Preferences submenu
under the Edit menu to
set the preferences for
how Photoshop displays
transparent areas
in Layers.

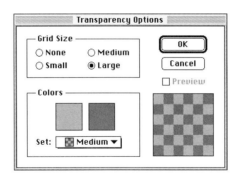

TIP: Keep the Layers palette open at all times to help you discern the target (active) layer. You can only work on one layer at a time, so you must pay attention to which layers are visible and which layer you are working on. It is easy to accidentally edit one layer while viewing another.

- When viewing one or more layers without the background layer, any transparent areas will show up as a checkerboard. To control the checkerboard pattern choose Transparency Options, a submenu of Preferences under the File menu (Figure 5–19).

- Click the Preserve Transparency button to paint or edit only areas that are not transparent, otherwise the tool will affect any part of the layer (Figure 5–20).

- You can only paint or edit on the target layer, but the Paintbucket, Magic Wand, Smudge, Rubber Stamp, and Blur/Sharpen tools have an option to sample from all visible layers.

Figure 5–20
If the Preserve
Transparency button is
clicked in the Layers
palette, painting and
editing will only affect
areas that are not
transparent. The image
on the left had Preserve
Transparency off and the
image on the right
had Preserve
Transparency on.

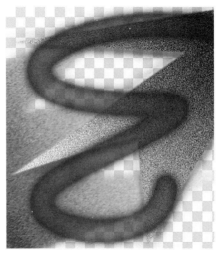

- The Layers palette shows the order in which the layers are stacked. You can change the order by dragging a layer to a new position. The uppermost layer in the palette is on top.

- Use the Move tool to move a layer. To link two or more layers in order move them as a unit, click in the second column from the left for each layer to activate the Link icon.

- Choose Layer Options in the pop-up menu in the Layers palette to control the Modes, Opacity and Blend parameters for your target layer. You can also group this layer with the previous layer. The Mode and Opacity controls are also available at the top of the Layers palette. See Figure C–1 in the Color section, the previous section entitled "Painting and Editing Modes," and Chapter 6, "Image Selection and Masking," for more information on Mode, Opacity and Blend control.

CAUTION: The Layers palette also has Modes and Opacity controls. The effects of these controls will compound the effect of the Modes and Opacity settings in the Options palette for specific tools. For example, you can paint with a tool at 50% Opacity, and have the layers set at 50% Opacity, and the result will be 25% Opacity when the layer is combined with other layers.

Channels Palette

The Channels palette (Figure 5–21) shows all the channels in a document. A channel is identical to a 256-level grayscale document, unlike layers, they contain no colors. A normal color image is usually a composite of the red, green and blue channels, each of which has 256 tones representing values in its designated color. Additional channels, up to a maximum of 24 channels, can be used as masks. As with layers, channels can be made visible or invisible, as well as editable or uneditable.

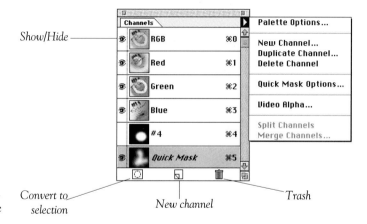

Figure 5–21
The Channels palette

Show/Hide

Convert to selection

New channel

Trash

Following are some basic guidelines when using channels with the painting and editing tools. For more information on using channels see Chapter 6, "Image Selection and Masking," and Chapter 10, "Compositing."

CHANNEL CONTROL

- An "eye" icon indicates that the channel is visible. On the Mac, a solid gray tone indicates that a channel is active and can be edited; in Windows, a white channel indicates that it is active and can be edited. It is possible to view one channel while working on another channel, ensuring perfect registration. Unlike layers, multiple channels can be edited simultaneously.

  TIP: **Pay attention to which channel is active. It is easy to accidentally edit the wrong channel. For quick access to a channel, use its keyboard shortcut shown on the right side of the palette.**

- Any of the painting and editing tools that apply to grayscale images can be used in channels (including Quick Mask and Layer Mask). Remember, no colors in individual channels. Painting colors in the composite channel automatically adds the correct value in each of the corresponding primary color channels. See Chapter 8, "Color," for more on color basics.

- To create a new channel, click on the New channel icon at the bottom of the palette or choose New Channel in the pop-up menu.

- To delete a channel, drag the channel to the Trash icon at the foot of the palette or choose Delete Channel in the pop-up menu.

- Selecting the Quick Mask mode in the toolbox will add a temporary channel to the Channels palette.

- Adding a Layer Mask to a layer in the Layers palette, actually adds the mask as a channel, applicable only to its corresponding layer.

- When in any layer or channel, channels can be loaded as selections by choosing the Load Selection submenu under the Select menu, by dragging the channel to the Convert icon at the foot of the palette, or by Option-clicking on the layer or simply pressing the Command-Option keys and the number of the channel.

- Selections can be saved as channels by choosing the Save Selection submenu under the Select menu or by clicking on the Convert icon at the foot of the palette.

Figure 5–22
The Paths palette

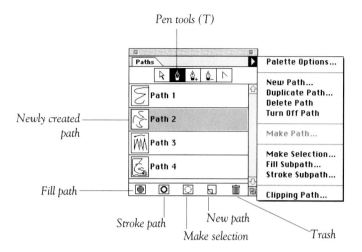

Pen tools (T)

Newly created
path

Fill path

Stroke path

Make selection

New path

Trash

Paths Palette

The Paths palette (Figure 5–22) allows you to use the Pen tool to draw precise, smooth-edged vector paths. The Pen tool is similar to the Pen tool in Adobe Illustrator and Aldus FreeHand. Paths made in either Photoshop or Illustrator can be swapped easily. Accurately drawn paths can be converted to selections for more precision, as opposed to using the Lasso tool to define a selection. Paths can be saved and then recalled for editing or exporting. Exported paths can be used as clipping paths to mask a Photoshop image that will be used over other images or colors in another program.

A complete discussion of the Paths palette is found in Chapter 6, "Image Selection and Masking."

TIP: To instantly select the Pen tool (which opens the Paths palette) and also toggle between the Pen tool and Path Select tool, type T on the keyboard.

TURNING PATHS INTO PAINTING AND EDITING TOOLS

For accurate control of any of the painting and editing tools, apply the tool with all its attributes to a path with the Stroke Path command in the pop-up menu in the Paths palette (Figure 5–23).

1. Click on a saved path in the list in the Paths palette or draw a new path with the Pen tool.
2. Select a tool, set its brush size and attributes in the Brushes and Options palettes. Choose a Foreground color.

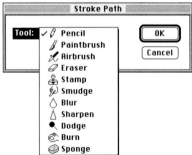

Figure 5–23
Examples of the Brush, Airbrush and Rubber Stamp tools applied to the Stroke Path command

Figure 5–24
The Stroke Path options dialog box showing the available tools

3. Choose Stroke Path (or Subpath) from the pop-up menu or hold the Option key and click the Stroke path icon at the base of the Paths palette. The Stroke Path dialog box will open (Figure 5–24)

4. If you selected a tool it will appear in the Tool pop-up menu, which also allows you to switch tools. Click OK and the tool with all its attributes will be applied to the path.

TIP: To bypass the Stroke Path dialog box, select a tool, its color and attributes, and click on the Stroke path icon at the base of the Paths palette (or drag the path to it). Successive clicks on the icon will build up the opacity and thickness of the stroke.

Swatches Palette

The Swatches palette, formerly part of the Colors palette, (Figure 5–25) allows the selection of foreground and background colors from a specific palette of colors. You can create customized palettes by adding, modifying or deleting colors. Palettes can be saved and then reloaded for use at a later time on any image.

Figure 5–25
The Swatches palette

CHOOSING A COLOR

To change the Foreground color, click on a color in the palette. To change the Background color, hold the Option key and click on a color in the palette.

ADDING, MODIFYING, OR REMOVING COLORS

- To add a color to the palette, mix the desired color using the Picker or the Scratch pad, then click on an empty box in the swatches palette to fill it with your mixed color.

- Hold the Shift key and click on an existing color to change it to the foreground color. Hold the Option and Shift keys and click on a color to add the color to the palette. All the colors will move over one space to give to new color a spot.

- You can create your own custom palettes, save and load them into future projects. Choose Save Swatches to save a custom palette. To load a custom palette into the Swatches Palette, select Load Swatches from the pop-up menu. Append Swatches adds a palette to the current palette. Photoshop comes with Custom palettes created to assist in specifying printing ink colors, such as the ANPA, Pantone, Toyo, Focaltone, and Trumatch color systems.

A complete discussion of color in Photoshop appears in Chapter 8, "Color."

Picker Palette

In the Picker palette (Figure 5–26), choose foreground and background colors by dragging the sliders below the color bars. The Picker palette allows the selection of colors from the RGB (Red, Green, and Blue), HSB (Hue, Saturation, and Brightness), CMYK (Cyan, Magenta, Yellow, and Black) and Lab (Lightness and Chroma) color models, as well as the Grayscale model. The pop-up menu allows you to switch color models.

- You can also pick colors from the color bar at the base of the palette or by clicking on the Foreground or Background color icons to open the Color Picker.

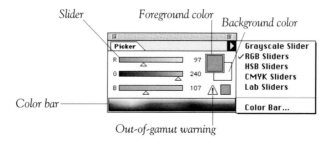

Figure 5–26
The Picker palette

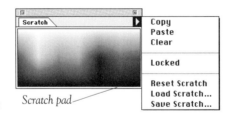

Figure 5–27
The Scratch palette

Scratch pad

- An exclamation point in a triangle indicates you have selected an out-of-gamut color—a color that cannot be printed using CMYK colors. Next to the triangle appears the closest CMYK equivalent. Click on this box to change the foreground color to this new CMYK color.

You should find the Picker palette easier to use than the Color Picker in the toolbox. For more on Color see Chapter 8, "Color."

Scratch Palette

You can mix your own custom colors in the Scratchpad by using any of the painting tools (Figure 5–27). You can also copy and paste in the palette as well as use it to define brushes or patterns.

- Use the Zoom and Hand tools to navigate around the palette with a close up view.
- Paint all the colors that you will use in a document in the Scratchpad. Copy small sections of color from an image and paste them into the Scatchpad. Use the Smudge tool to mix the colors.
- Once you have created a custom Scrachpad save it for later use by choosing Save Scratch in the pop-up menu. Choose Load Scratch to open a saved Scratchpad. Reset Scratch will load the default Scratchpad.
- To pick a foreground color from the Scratchpad, click on the color with the Eye Dropper tool. To pick a background color, hold the Option key down while using the Eyedropper tool.

For more on Color see Chapter 8, "Color."

Info Palette

The Info palette (Figure 5–28) provides image data, including the precise position of the pointer on the screen and the color values of pixels. Use the Info palette to measure angles of rotation, size, and distance, depending on the tool in use. These values are expressed in the x and y coordinates of the pointer's position using the current ruler units. The Scale command causes the height and width of a selection to appear, as well as the amount (percentage) of change. Use the information in the Info palette as an on-screen densitometer and tape measure.

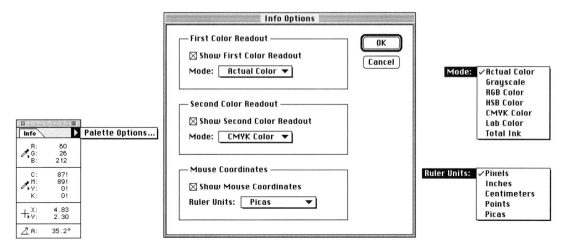

Figure 5–28
The Info palette

Figure 5–29
The Info Options dialog box

TIP: Leave the Info palette open at all times. Once you get used to it, it will help you control color output and the size and position of elements.

Color information is an important aspect of the Info palette and is displayed in two modes simultaneously. Usually the first color shows the current display mode data and the second the desired destination mode data. This gives you access to color values prior to actually converting a document. The color values for pixels can be shown in Grayscale, RGB, HSB, CMYK, total CMYK ink, and Lab modes. An exclamation point (Gamut Alarm) next to a CMYK color value indicates a nonprintable process color.

To change the color modes for the readouts and the measurement units, select Palette Options from the pop-up menu (Figure 5–29) or press on the Eyedropper and crosshair icons on the left side of the palette. Use the Info palette to show the before and after effects of color adjustments.

NOTE: If you are in RGB color mode and the values in the second color readout are set to CMYK Color mode, they are affected by the Printing Inks Setup and Separation Setup Preferences under the File menu.

Commands Palette

The Commands palette (Figure 5–30) allows you to add function keys to any menu item if you are using a keyboard that has function keys on it.

To add a command, select New Command from the pop-up menu and then choose the desired command from any menu or submenu (Figure 5–31). Designate an available F key. The new command will appear in the Commands palette.

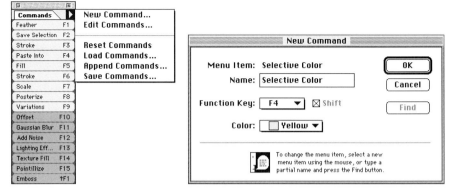

Figure 5–30
The Commands palette with
the Design Essentials
Command set loaded

Figure 5–31
The New Command dialog box

Save Commands in the pop-up menu will save a set of command for later use. Load Commands will open a saved set of commands. If you work on different types of projects that require completely different sets of menu shortcuts, this could be handy. Photoshop ships with several handy sets of commands palettes, such as the Design Essentials set shown in Figure 5–30.

The Toolbox

The Toolbox (Figure 5–32) contains icons for selection, painting and editing tools, and provides access to the Color Picker (see Chapter 8, "Color"), the screen display modes (covered in Chapter 3, "Configuring Photoshop"), and the Quick Mask mode. The Selection tools in the Toolbox, the Marquees. the Lasso and the Magic Wand, and the Quick Mask Mode will be discussed in depth in Chapter 6, "Image Selection and Masking."

TIP: **Each tool has a keyboard letter associated with it. Type the letter to instantly select the tool.**

Common Tool Factors

Photoshop provides standards that apply to the operation of most of the tools in the Toolbox.

- By pressing the Tab key you can make the Toolbox (and any other open floating palette) disappear from and reappear on the screen.
- To use a tool, simply click on its icon in the Toolbox and move the cursor into the active image area.

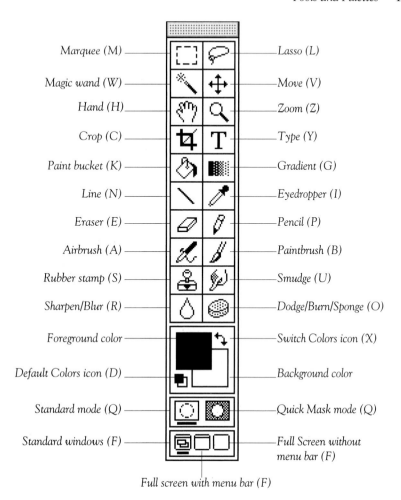

Marquee (M) — Lasso (L)

Magic wand (W) — Move (V)

Hand (H) — Zoom (Z)

Crop (C) — Type (Y)

Paint bucket (K) — Gradient (G)

Line (N) — Eyedropper (I)

Eraser (E) — Pencil (P)

Airbrush (A) — Paintbrush (B)

Rubber stamp (S) — Smudge (U)

Sharpen/Blur (R) — Dodge/Burn/Sponge (O)

Foreground color — Switch Colors icon (X)

Default Colors icon (D) — Background color

Standard mode (Q) — Quick Mask mode (Q)

Standard windows (F) — Full Screen without menu bar (F)

Full screen with menu bar (F)

Figure 5–32
To instantly select a tool
in the toolbox, type the
letter in parenthesis.

- Each tool has a unique icon. When using a tool on the screen, your cursor will usually be represented by the specific tool icon. To provide maximum accuracy when using most of the tools, you can replace the tool icon with a brush size that reflects the specific size and shape of the tool or a precise crosshair. The center point of the crosshair is the "hot spot."

- To choose the brush icon or shape select General Preferences under the File menu, and click on the desired tool attributes in the Tool Cursors box. If you prefer to use the actual tool icons, Figure 5–33 shows the hot spots of each tool.

TIP: Toggle between two tool shapes by pressing the Caps Lock key. Be aware that any type will appear in all caps!

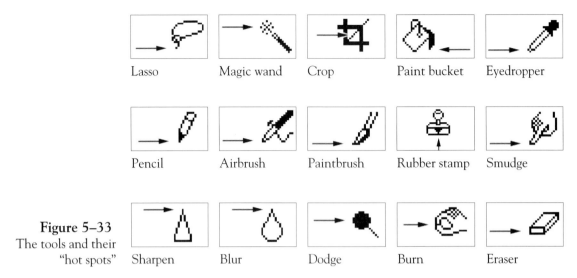

Figure 5–33
The tools and their
"hot spots"

Lasso Magic wand Crop Paint bucket Eyedropper

Pencil Airbrush Paintbrush Rubber stamp Smudge

Sharpen Blur Dodge Burn Eraser

- While using the drawing tools, you can temporarily change the current tool into an Eyedropper if you want to select a new Foreground color from a color found in the image by pressing the Option key. Clicking on a color will make it the active Foreground color.

   TIP: While using the Eyedropper tool, you can click on image windows other than the one you are currently working within in order to pick up colors not found in your working document. Using this capability, you can make a document with your preferred color palette, and select colors from this document at any time.

- If you want to use a tool to draw a straight line (or in the case of the softening or sharpening tools, to apply the effect in a straight line), choose the tool and click once where you want the effect of the tool to start. Then hold down the Shift key and click an end point. The result will be a straight line between the two points.

- Hold down the Shift key while painting to constrain movements to 90 degree increments; release the Shift key to continue in the freehand mode. Holding down the Shift key while painting with the Line tool will constrain its movement to 45 degree increments.

- If you press a number from 1 through 0 before using a tool, you will set the Opacity (transparency), Pressure, or Exposure (depending on the tool in use) from 10 to 100 percent. For example, before you paint with the Paintbrush, press the 4 key and your painting Opacity will be set to 40 percent.

- Double-clicking on most tools in the toolbox will opens the tool's Options palette, allowing you to modify controllable parameters that affect the way the tool works. For example, in the Paintbrush or Airbrush Options palette you can specify the Paint Fade-Out rate and Stylus Pressure options. The Fade-out rate determines the distance the tool can go before the "ink" flow gradually runs out.

- Many of the tools are really several tools in one. For example, the Dodge/Burn/Sponge tool has three separate but related functions. Hold the Option key and click on the tool in the toolbox or press the O key to toggle through the different functions.

- Tools will only affect areas inside an active selection.

> **TIP:** If a tool does not appear to function, check to see if you have an active selection somewhere in your image and that you are on the correct layer.

- If you are working on an image that has a floating selection, hold down the Command key to invoke the arrow. This will allow you to move the selection without switching tools manually.

- If you draw too fast or are working on a slow machine, the tools will remember the path of your stroke, even though the screen drawing lags behind.

- Artist Sanjay Kothari offers this tip: "Any tool applied in excessive amounts can be a creative effect." Have fun!

Individual Tool Overviews

The following overview discusses all the tools in the Toolbox. For more detailed information about using the selection tools, Marquee, Lasso, and the Magic Wand, please refer to Chapter 6, "Image Selection and Masking."

Marquee Tools

Use the Rectangular and Elliptical Marquee tools to make selections of all or parts of an image. Choose between the two shapes in the Marquee Options palette (Figure 5–34).

Under Style in the Options palette you can choose Constrained Aspect Ratio to specify the ratio of a rectangular or elliptical selection. For example, 1 to 1 will produce a perfect square or circle. Fixed Size allows you to specify the exact selection size in pixels. You can also indicate Feather amount in pixels and choose Anti-aliased edges. To deselect a selection, with the Marquee or Lasso tool active, click anywhere in the document outside of the selected area or choose None (Command–D) under the Select menu.

Figure 5–34
The Marquee
Options palette

Lasso Tool

Use the Lasso tool to make freehand selections in an image. You can make irregular polygon selections by holding down the Option key and plotting corner points by clicking the mouse. The Lasso Options palette (Figure 5–35) allows you to enter a Feather amount and choose Anti-aliased edges.

Magic Wand Tool

The Magic Wand tool allows you to select areas without tracing outlines. The tool analyzes the color and tone similarities between adjacent pixels and selects all similar pixels.

The Magic Wand Options palette (Figure 5–36) contains tolerance settings and the anti-aliased option. The Sample Merged button allows you to take a reading from all visible layers. Remember, any manipulation will still take place on the target layer.

To deselect a selection, with the Magic Wand tool active, click anywhere in the document inside of the selected area or choose None under the Select menu.

Move Tool

The Move tool is new to Photoshop 3. By pressing and dragging, it moves a selection. It nothing is selected, it will move the entire target layer or linked layers. If there are no layers, it moves the background.

TIP: If you move part of an image off the page, the image still exists out of the visible frame and you can move it back into the frame. However, if you use another tool on the image, anything that has been moved off the page is erased.

Hand Tool

Use the Hand tool to move a document page that is too large to fit in the active window. By pressing and dragging, you can move an image in the window so that you can see the rest of it. As you drag, you may need to continue to move the hand outside of the active window to see more. The Hand Tool Options palette (Figure 5–37) has two zoom controls, Zoom to fit the window and Zoom to a 1:1 pixel ratio.

TIP: By double-clicking on the Hand tool icon, you will return the magnified detail of an image to fit entirely within the document window.

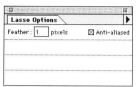

Figure 5–35
The Lasso Options
palette

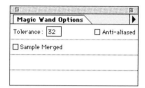

Figure 5–36
The Magic Wand
Options palette

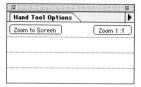

Figure 5–37
The Hand Tool Options
palette

NOTE: Don't confuse the Hand tool with the Move tool. The Move tool actually moves the pixel data in the document. The Hand tool scrolls the image within the active window—no pixels are actually moved on the document.

Zoom Tool

The Zoom tool and the zoom commands in the Windows menu are used to magnify and reduce your view of parts of an image when you need to work on small details or see the entire image. When using the Zoom tool you are not changing the actual size of a document, just how you are looking at it.

The magnification factor of an image is shown in the document's Title Bar. Photoshop allows magnification and reduction up to 16 times the original view of a document. For example, a 4:1 ratio shown in the title bar results in a magnification factor of 4. This means the image is being viewed at four times the original size, or 400 percent. A 1:4 ratio shown in the title bar displays the image reduced four times, or 25 percent. A 1:1 view of a document, or 100 percent, matches the resolution of the image to the resolution of your screen, not to the dimensions of the document. Since screen resolution is usually about 72 pixels per inch, documents having a high image resolution will show up larger when viewed on-screen than those with lower image resolutions.

To use the Zoom tool, click on its icon in the toolbox and move the cursor into the active image area. You will notice that inside the circle of the magnifying glass icon, a plus symbol appears. With each click of the mouse, the view of the image will magnify by a factor of 2. Now, hold down the Option key while clicking on the mouse and the symbol inside the circle of the cursor will change to a minus sign. Click on the mouse and the view of the image will reduce by a factor of 2.

The area of the image you magnify or reduce is the area on which you click. When you cannot magnify or reduce the view of an image any further, the circle of the cursor will appear blank.

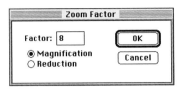

Figure 5–38
The Zoom Factor dialog box

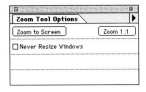

Figure 5–39
The Zoom Tool Options
palette

TIP: By double-clicking on the Zoom tool icon in the toolbox, you will return to a 1:1 view. To zoom in while using any other tool, press and hold the Command and Spacebar keys and click on the desired area. To zoom out, press and hold the Option, Command, and Spacebar keys and click on the image.

Drag a rectangle with the Zoom tool cursor in an image to select an area to magnify up to a factor of 16, depending on the size of the area you select.

You can also magnify and reduce your view of a document by choosing Zoom In, Zoom Out, or Zoom Factor (Figure 5–38) found under the Window menu. These commands will change your view by factors of 2. The Zoom Options palette (Figure 5–39) has two zoom controls, Zoom to fit the window and Zoom to a 1:1 pixel ratio.

Cropping Tool

As the name implies, this tool eliminates unwanted parts of an image. The Cropping tool is an expanded version of the Crop command found under the Edit menu. With the Crop command, you use the Rectangular Marquee tool to select the part of the image that you want to keep, then select Crop from the Edit menu. But by using the Cropping tool, you can determine the resolution of the final cropped image, and adjust the cropping area with the resizing handles before actually completing a crop.

TIP: To reduce a document's size, crop an image before placing it into a page layout program, rather than cropping it in the page layout program.

To use the Cropping tool, drag the Cropping tool over the area to be cropped (Figure 5–40); the very center of the tool is the "hot spot." Four handles will appear at the corners of the selection after releasing the mouse button. Drag the handles independently to redefine the selected area. Move the cursor into the selected area to transform it into scissors and then click.

TIP: When cropping an image, the selected area will be the new image size. If you want white space around an image, add to the document's dimensions in

Figure 5–40   On the left is the image before cropping showing the crop handles. On the right is the image after cropping. (© Mark Siprut)

the Canvas Size dialog box under the Image menu. See the discussion of Canvas Size in Chapter 6, "Image Selection and Masking."

In the Cropping Tool Options palette (Figure 5–41) you can enter values into the Width and Height fields (which can be specified in a variety of units selectable from the pop-up menus next to the fields), and crop images to a predetermined size. The resolution field allows you to specify the final resolution of the cropped image. You can crop and resample the image in one step.

TIP: To crop and rotate at the same time, drag a box with the Cropping tool, then hold the Option key and drag a handle to rotate the selection box. Click inside this box and your image will be both rotated and cropped.

Figure 5–41
The Cropping Tool
Options palette

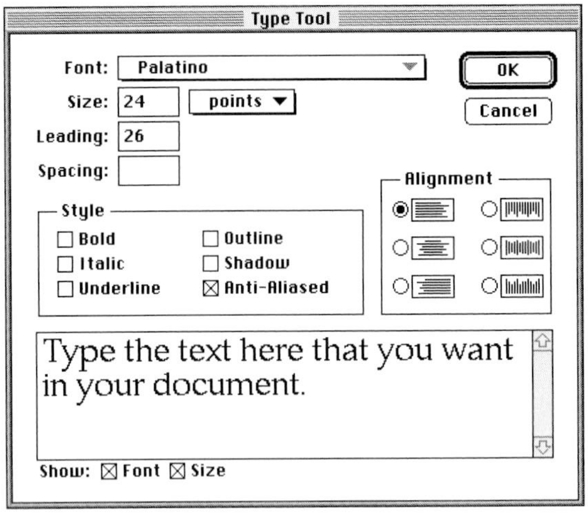

Figure 5–42
The Type Tool
dialog boc

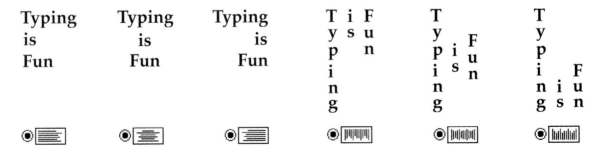

Type Tool

Unlike other raster programs, Photoshop allows you to create anti-aliased type in a variety of resolutions. Using the special effects filters, you can also produce innovative display typefaces in a myriad of colors and textures. Once you create type in Photoshop it becomes part of the bitmapped image (in vector programs type is retained in an editable format). Bitmapped type is treated just like any other graphic image in the program. Photoshop uses Adobe Type Manager (ATM) to draw a bitmapped font based on the Postscript vector font (See Chapter 2, "Set up and Document Management," for more on font management). Since Photoshop rasterizes type, do not expect the quality and type controls you find in object oriented programs.

When you click anywhere in the image with the Type tool, the Type Tool dialog box appears (Figure 5–42). Specify the Font, Size, Leading (line spacing), letter Spacing, Alignment (justification and rotation), and Style (Figure 5–43). You can create type in sizes between 4 and 1000 pixels. You specify type size in either pixels or points by pressing on the pop-up menu

Figure 5–43   Examples of alignment possibilities

next to the size number field. Click on Show Font and Size to view the text in the actual size in the dialog box.

CAUTION: You can stack type vertically with the Type tool, but unless it is a short word or phrase, you will find it hard to read.

TIP: In addition to normal Bold or Italic versions of a font, you can apply the Bold or Italic options to the Bold or Italic versions of a font in the Type Tool dialog box for an exaggerated effect.

Enter text by typing in the text field in the lower portion of the dialog box. Standard editing techniques apply. Although the Edit menu is not available while you are in the Type tool window, the keyboard equivalents for Cut, Copy, and Paste function on highlighted text.

CAUTION: Although the type in the text field automatically wraps, it does not wrap when placed on the image; you must type a carriage return to get a new line.

TO CREATE AND MANIPULATE TEXT:

1. Select the desired color for your text (the current foreground color), and click the Type tool on an image.
2. Type your text in the Type tool dialog box, and choose your font, size, alignment, and style. Click OK.
3. The type will appear on the image as a floating selection filled with the current foreground color. To change the color, click on the current Foreground color, pick another color, and then select the Fill command from the Edit menu. You can continually change the color of the type as long as you do not deselect it (if you click anywhere on the background image outside of the text, the text will be deselected and become part of the surrounding pixels).
4. Since the type is a floating selection and treated the same as any other graphic, any image processing, filter effect, calculations, layer combinations, and channel combinations can be applied. Use the following suggestions as a starting point. Experiment, but don't over do it.

KERNING

Once you create type, you can manually adjust the spacing between letters. Kerning is an addition to the Spacing option in the Type tool dialog box, which globally adjusts the spacing in a body of type.

1. Apply some type on the page and leave it as a floating selection.

2. Press the command key to turn the cursor into a lasso, then lasso a letter to deselect it. Move the type in relationship to the deselected letter. Use the arrow keys on the keyboard to move the letters. Repeat process for all letters you want to adjust.

3. OR hold down the Shift and Command keys to lasso the letters that will remain selected. Adjust as necessary.

TYPE GUIDELINES

- If you are running ATM normally with the rest of your system, it will automatically be used by Photoshop. To get the highest quality type, though, make sure to activate the anti-aliased checkbox in the Type Tool dialog box.

TIP: If you want to see the way type will look on a background without deselecting it, use the Hide Edges command in the Select menu (Command-H). Even though the "marching ants" selection effect is hidden, the type remains selected and can be moved into a new position.

- All characters typed in a text field must have the same style specifications. To create blocks of type with different styling, make multiple blocks of type and combine them manually.

- The text will appear as a floating selection to be moved around the screen. You can use any of Photoshop's tools or controls to modify the floating type or delete it by pressing the Delete key on your keyboard, which will not disturb the image behind it.

- Since type is a floating selection, you can apply filter effects and paste unique textures into or behind the type.

- Place the type on a new layer to control and change the way the text interacts with the underlying image. Using the Layer Options pop-up menu, vary the transparency of the text, allowing the background to show through. Or, by using the modes, you can apply the type as a tint or drop it out of the background.

- When creating large-sized type, it is preferable to specify the size, as opposed to scaling it. Enlarged type will result in jagged edges.

TIP: For unity and harmony, stay with one typeface in a design, creating variations in size, style, alignment, etc. Do not use more than two fonts on a design, one for most of the text and the other for emphasis or contrast. When

Figure 5–44
An example of a serif
font (left) and a sans-
serif font (right)

Palatino = Serif　　Avant Garde = Sans-serif

using two fonts in a design choose one as a serif font and the other a san serif font. **Do not use two different serif fonts or two san serif fonts in the same design (Figure 5–44).**

CREATIVE OPTIONS WITH TYPE

Reverse type: Choose a foreground color lighter than the background color on a page to create reverse or drop out type (Figure 5–45).

Translucent type: Give a transparent effect to type by using the Opacity or Mode controls.

1. Apply type over an image and then drag the Opacity slider in the Layers palette to a desired percentage. A low number will render with more transparency (Figure 5–46).
2. Another method for creating transparent type is to apply type over an image and then choose one of the Mode options in the Layers palette. Try Multiply, Screen, Overlay, Soft Light, etc . . . . Experiment.

Pattern: In addition to filling type with any color, fill it with a defined pattern.

1. To define a pattern, select an area from an image and choose Define Pattern under the Edit menu
2. Apply type over an image and leave it as a floating selection.

Figure 5–45
Reverse type

Figure 5–46
Translucent type

3. To fill with the pattern, choose Fill under the Edit menu to open the Fill dialog box and select Pattern in the Contents pop-up menu (Figure 5–47).

Paste Into: Using a clipboard image, you can paste it inside type.

1. Copy any image into the clipboard.
2. Apply type over an image and leave it as a floating selection.
3. Choose the Paste Into command under the Edit menu. The clipboard image will only appear inside the type (Figure 5–48).

Filter Effects: Filters offer numerous possibilities for special effects on type. Refer to Chapter 9, "Filters and Plug-ins," for more ideas. Here are three possibilities:

1. Apply any of Photoshop's filters to the floating type to affect only the inside portions.
2. Deselect (Command-D) the type and apply filters to distort the type's shape and integration with the background.
3. Select specific areas of the type and apply filters for localized distortion (Figure 5–49).

Dynamic Effects: As a floating selection, type can be distorted using the any of Photoshop's dynamic effects.

1. Apply type over an image and leave it as a floating selection.

Figure 5–47
Type filled with a
defined pattern

Figure 5–48
The Clipboard image
pasted into the type

Figure 5–49
The section of type crossing the water was selected, feathered, and then distorted with the Diffuse and Facet filters (© Dennis Haradyn and Kelley Advertising).

2. Choose the Scale, Skew, Perspective, or Distort command from the Effects submenu under the Image menu. Handles will appear on the four edges of the type. Drag on a handle to manipulate the text (Figure 5–50). When using the Scale command, hold the Shift key while dragging a corner handle to constrain the movement keeping the type's original proportion.

3. To rotate the type, choose one of the submenus in Rotate under the Image menu. Arbitrary allows you to enter an exact rotation angle, while Free allows you to drag a corner handle to the desired angle.

CAUTION: Anytime you stretch or distort an image in Photoshop the pixels are getting shuffled around by the interpolation methods discussed in Chapter 3, "Configuring Photoshop" (Figure 3-16). Too many repeated distortions can degrade the image quality.

Feather: Feathering softens the edges of type.

1. To feather the floating type, drag the Opacity slider in the Layers palette to 1% for the floating selection.

2. Apply the Feather command under the Select menu.

3. Choose a foreground color and then select Fill under the Edit menu (Figure 5–51).

Figure 5–50
Skew, Perspective, Distort, and Rotate were applied to the type.

Skew Perspective Distort Rotate

Figure 5–51
The Feather command
softened the type.

Feather   Feather   Feather

Shadow effects: A shadow behind type will make it appear to float above the page.

1. To create a shadow effect, set some type on the page and deselect.
2. Choose a different foreground color and click with the Type tool again. The original text will still be in the Type Tool dialog box. Click OK.
3. Move the new floating type over the original type with a slight offset. The arrow keys on the keyboard work well for slight nudges.
4. Shadows are more effective if the type below has a slight feather applied to it prior to placing the type on top (Figure 5–52).

TIP: For better control of layering type for shadow effects, apply the type to different layers. This will allow you to experiment without making a commitment.

Glow effect: To create a glow effect, use the Feather effect on placed type, change the foreground color, and then apply the type again. For more control, put each on a separate layer. Try this effect on a dark background (Figure 5–53).

Figure 5–52
A drop shadow will
make type appear to
float above the page.

Figure 5–53
A Glowing effect

Three-Dimensional type: Create three-dimensional contoured type with the Lasso, Feather command, and Paintbucket. This effect works best on soft rounded type (Figure 5–54).

1. Apply some type on the page and leave it as a floating selection.
2. Fill the selected type with a light gray or color and deselect.
3. In the Lasso Options palette, set the Feather to a low value and turn on Anti-aliasing.
4. Using the Lasso tool, select the edges of the type (use the Shift key with the Lasso to add to the selected areas). Be sure to include a portion of the white with the selection.
5. Choose a dark color as the foreground color. Use the Paintbucket tool to fill the selection by clicking on the gray or colored portion within the selection. The fill will only change the color, leaving the white areas unaffected.
6. For a highlight, choose white as the foreground color and apply light lines along the edges opposite the shadows with the Airbrush tool.

Embossed type: Type can appear to emboss or deboss a surface (Figure 5–55).

1. To create an embossed effect, place some type over a background image or texture and leave it selected.
2. Drag the Opacity slider in the Layers palette to 1%.

Figure 5–54   Create three-dimensional contoured type with the Lasso, Feather command and Paintbucket.

Figure 5–55
Embossed type

3. Choose Save Selection under the Select menu. Save it as a new Channel in the same document.

4. While the type is still a floating selection, choose Feather under the Select menu and use a 2 to 5 pixel radius.

5. Copy the feathered type to the clipboard and then Choose Load Selection under the Select menu. Choose the original saved channel, which will bring back the original unfeathered version.

6. Fill the selection with black or a dark color. Choose Paste Into from the Edit menu to paste the feathered version inside the unfeathered type. Use the arrow keys on the keyboard to offset it slightly.

For more information on using channels refer to Chapter 6, "Image Selection and Masking."

Type to Paths: Once type is created and becomes a floating selection, you can convert the selection to a path. Paths can be saved and used for path features: as a clipping path to mask other shapes, to export paths to Illustrator, or for careful manipulation of shapes with the anchor points of paths. Following are the steps to make a clipping path.

1. Apply some type on the page over an image and position it exactly over the area you want to mask, leaving it as a floating selection.

2. In the Paths palette choose the Make Path command in the pop-up menu of the paths palette. Turns the letter forms into a vector path.

3. Choose Save Path in the pop-up menu.

4. With the Arrow tool in the Paths palette you can move anchor points and change a curve by dragging direction points.

5. Choose Clipping Path from the pop-up menu and select the saved path from the path menu in the Clipping Path dialog box.

6. Choose Save As from the File menu. Save the document as an EPS file.

7. You can now place the masked image in an illustration or page layout program (Figure 5–56).

Figure 5–56
A clipping path was made from the outline of the letter form to mask the shape out of the photograph. (Photo courtesy of PhotoDisc, Volume 6)

Paint Bucket Tool

The Paint Bucket Tool uses the foreground color to fill the area over which it is applied (see Figure 5–54). Unlike its predecessors in other paint packages, Photoshop's Paint Bucket has Tolerance and Anti-aliased settings, which are available in the Paint Bucket Options palette (Figure 5–57). In most other paint programs the bucket will fill only the exact color over which it is used. The Tolerance setting allows additional colors and values to be filled. The higher the tolerance setting, the farther a dropped Paint Bucket will spread. A low tolerance setting will fill only tiny portions of modulated color.

If the Sample Merged button is deselected, the fill will be determined by the colors in the target layer. If the button is checked, the fill area will be determined by the selected colors in all the layers in the image, although only filling in the target layer.

The Anti-aliased setting will make the outside edges of the fill appear fuzzy. The Contents option fills the selected area with the foreground color or with a defined pattern.

The Modes and Opacity settings in the Options palette will also control characteristics of the fill color. See figure C-1 in the Color Section for examples of modes and opacity settings.

Gradient Tool

The Gradient tool blends color to assist you in creating believable images. The surface color of any object diminishes in intensity as it moves away from the light source. Even a subtle gradient will add dimension to a shape.

Gradients are attained by selecting a starting and an ending color. The starting color is the current Foreground color and the ending color is in the Background color. In the Foreground to Background style, red as the Foreground and blue as the Background will result in a range of purple shades blending from red into blue.

Use the Gradient tool to create large blend areas such as skies, an effect traditionally achieved with an airbrush. Use the Gradient tool in a press-and-drag fashion. The first press of the mouse button lays down the Foreground color. Dragging across a space with the button depressed will produce a line that follows the movement of the mouse. The length of the line determines the area of transition and the direction of the line determines the direction of the fill. Releasing the mouse button activates the fill.

There are two types of fills: Linear and Radial. The Linear fill will create transitions in straight lines that follow the direction in which the fill was applied. The Radial will make a fill of concentric tones as in a sunburst effect.

In both types of fill, the Midpoint Skew can be defined within the Gradient Options palette (Figure 5–58). This sets the point at which there is an even mix between the foreground and background colors; 50% is the default. A lower percentage will set the midpoint closer to the starting point.

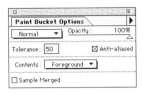

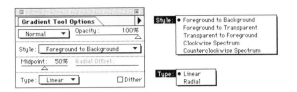

Figure 5–57
The Paint Bucket
Options palette

Figure 5–58
The Gradient Options palette

For example, 25% will set the midpoint one-quarter of the way from the start to the end of the fill. A higher percentage sets it away from the start. Use a 50% midpoint skew to create a perfectly even blend (Figure 5–59).

You also can select one of five Style options in the Gradient Options palette. The Style option determines how the fill makes the transition. The style options are: Foreground to Background, Foreground to Transparent, Transparent to Foreground, Clockwise Spectrum, and Counter Clockwise Spectrum.

If the Dither button in the Option palette is checked, the pixels in the blend will be dithered, or smoothed out. The dithering can be seen when you posterize the blend.

Modes and Opacity settings are also set in the Options palette (see Figure C–1 in the Color Section).

Figure 5–59
Blend with different
Midpoint Skews

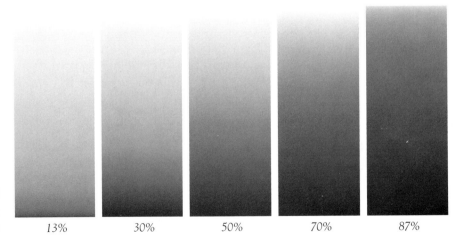

13%   30%   50%   70%   87%

LINEAR FILL EXAMPLE

"Visa Card" by Adam Cohen is an example of a linear fill.

1. Cohen began by sketching his ideas digitally. He traced over the sketch, copied it to a new window, and duplicated each shape to a new window.
2. He applied a dark green to white gradient on a slight diagonal.

TIP: Cohen advises filling selections only once—select Undo if it isn't right the first time.

3. He then sprayed white with a large airbrush to smooth out banding.
4. He added two or three levels of Noise to each of the CMYK channels to get rid of banding.
5. The globes are not radial fills, but flat solid colors airbrushed with large and then small brushes. Cohen drew a circle for the highlight and feathered it. He again added noise to get rid of banding (Figure 5–60).

Figure 5–60   Visa Card illustration showing a linear blend (© Adam Cohen)

RADIAL FILL EXAMPLE

Using radial fills within selections you can create a 3-D sphere with a soft shadow, a basic exercise for any art student.

1. Open a new grayscale document that is at least 600 pixels square. Set the Foreground color to white and the Background color to black.

2. Create a new layer in the pop-up menu in the Layers palette. Make the new layer the target layer by clicking on it (it will be highlighted).

3. In the Marquee Options palette, choose the Elliptical shape. Set the style to Constrained Aspect Ratio width 1, height 1. Create a circle selection by dragging the mouse.

4. Click on the Gradient tool. In the Gradient tool Options palette, choose the Radial Fill option with a 60% Midpoint Skew, and a 10% Radial Offset. Drag the Gradient tool across the selection, starting at the point that will be the highlight and ending at the shadow. Leave the sphere selected (Figure 5–61).

5. To create the reflection on the underside of the sphere (Figure 5–62), use the Gradient Tool Options palette to change the Style to Transparent to Foreground and the Radial Offset to 75%. Drag Diagonally across the selected circle from beyond the upper left to beyond the lower right. (Undo and try again if it's not quite right.)

6. Now that you have created the sphere, make the shadow cast on the surface beneath it. Make the background the target layer by clicking on it in the layers palette. You should now be able to see the sphere work on the background layer. The eye should be showing on both layers and the Background layer will be highlighted.

      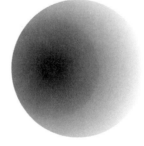

Figure 5–61
The selection filled a Radial blend.

Figure 5–62
The sphere with a subtle reflection on its underside

Figure 5–63
Create the shadow on a separate layer so that it can be distorted and moved with the Perspective and Scale commands.

Figure 5–64
The completed sphere
with its shadow

7. Using the Elliptical Marquee tool, draw an oval for the shadow. Choose Feather under the Select menu and set it to 10 pixels.

8. Set the foreground color to black and the background color to white. In the Gradient Tool Options palette change the Radial Offset to 10%. Drag the Gradient tool from an off-center point to the edge of the oval. Leave it selected (Figure 5–63).

9. Choose Perspective in the Effects submenu. Alter the shape of the shadow until it appears to lie on a flat surface. If the shadow is too small, use the Scale command in the Effects submenu to alter its width and height. Use the Move tool to position the shadow correctly under the sphere (Figure 5–64).

TIP: Create three-dimensional shapes in 3-D programs such as Alias Sketch, Ray Dream Designer, Strata Vision 3-D, MacroModel 3D, and Infini-D. Once created in the 3-D program with lighting, surface modeling, and textures, the images can be imported into Photoshop to be edited or combined with other images.

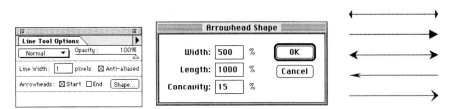

Figure 5–65
The Line Tool Options palette

Figure 5–66
The Arrowhead Shape dialog box

Figure 5–67
Examples of different arrowheads

Line Tool

Use the line tool to draw straight lines. The parameters of this tool are again found in the Line Tool Options palette: Opacity, Mode, Line width in pixels, Aliased, or Anti-aliased (Figure 5–65).

You can draw arrows with the Line tool. Click on the Start and/or End button to place arrowheads on the tips of a line. Then click on the Shape button, which opens the Arrowhead Shape dialog box (Figure 5–66), to control the shapes of the arrowheads. Modify them into various shapes and styles by adjusting their Width, Length, and Concavity (Figures 5–67).

TIP: You also can use the Line tool to measure distances in the document. To do this, define a Line Width of 0 in the Line Tool Options dialog box and choose Show Info from the Window menu. As you drag the pointer, the Info palette displays the *x* and *y* coordinates of the starting point, the change in *x* and *y*, the distance, and the angle.

Eyedropper Tool

Select colors from open documents for the foreground and background colors with the Eyedropper tool. As you click on parts of an image, the colors detected will be shown in the Foreground color box. Hold down the Option key and click to select a Background color. You may also select colors from other open Photoshop documents.

You can change the area the Eyedropper tool uses to sample a color through the Eyedropper Options palette (Figure 5–68). The pop-up menu has three options: the Point Sample option reads the exact value of any one pixel, the 3 by 3 Average option takes a 3-pixel by 3-pixel area and averages the values within it, and the 5 by 5 Average option averages the values in a 5–pixel by 5–pixel area. To see information about the pixels, use the Info palette in conjunction with the Eyedropper tool.

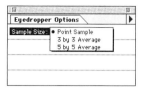

Figure 5–68
The Eyedropper Options palette

Figure 5–69
The Eraser Tool Options palette

TIP: The sampling size set in the Eyedropper Option palette controls the sampling area for the readouts shown in the Info palette. For accurate pixel information, set the sample size to Point Sample.

Eraser Tool

Drag the Eraser tool over any portion of the image to erase it. If the current background color is other than white, the Eraser will erase to that color.

TIP: Change the Background color of a layer by setting the Background color in the Toolbox and then click on the Erase Layer button in the Layer Options palette. This is much faster than filling a background with a different foreground color using the Paint Bucket tool or Fill command.

If you press the Option key, the Eraser becomes the Magic Eraser, turning the normal Eraser into a reverting tool. As you erase with the Magic Eraser, the image reverts to its last saved version on disk, regardless of the changes made to the image since the last time it was saved. The Magic Eraser will not work if the image has been resized or resampled. Neither will it work if the last saved version does not have a matching layer.

In the Eraser Options palette (Figure 5–69), you can change the brush type (Figure 5–70) to a Paintbrush (round anti-aliased), Airbrush (round anti-aliased that builds up with repeated stroking), Pencil (round jaggies), or Block (square hard-edged). You can control the Opacity, set the stroke to Fade in a designated number of steps. Control the Stylus Pressure of a pressure-sensitive digitizing pad. The Wet Edges button, available to the Paintbrush style eraser only, is transparent except at the edges of a stroke. There is a also button to erase the entire target layer.

Figure 5–70
Examples of Eraser
strokes with enlarged
detail. From left to right:
Paintbrush, Paintbrush
with Wet Edges,
Airbrush, Pencil ,
and Block

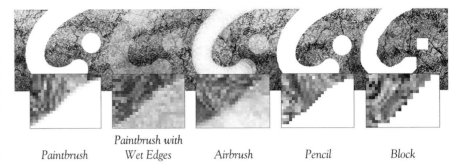

Paintbrush   *Paintbrush with*   Airbrush   Pencil   Block
                 Wet Edges

Pencil Tool

Photoshop's Pencil tool works like the pencil found in most graphics programs. As you drag across the screen, it paints with the foreground color. The Pencil tool does not have an anti-aliased option.

In the Pencil Options palette (Figure 5–71) you can make the pencil automatically erase specific colored pixels to the background color by selecting the Auto Erase option. First draw a line with the selected foreground color. If you start the next line on the previously drawn line, it will change to the current background color. If you draw any where other than on the previously drawn line, it will continue to fill with the foreground color.

Other parameters include paint Modes and Opacity settings. The Fade-out rate controls how far you can draw with the pencil before it fades out. Pressure-sensitive digitizing tablets with cordless pens also are supported by the Pencil tool. Set the Stylus Pressure to vary the Size, Color, and/or Opacity.

TIP: **When using a pressure-sensitive drawing tablet such as a Wacom tablet, you can vary the width of the Pencil tool by pressing down on the stylus depending on the default size. At the pencil's default brush size of a single pixel, pressure sensitivity does not function. You must change the size of the Pencil tool by choosing a large brush as the default. The Pencil will still draw a single pixel brush, but as you press down on the stylus, the brush size will increase up to the size of the largest default size selected.**

An exciting use of the Pencil tool is to create a pattern that begins with random pencil strokes processed through some of Photoshop's special effects filters (Figure 5–72). Other uses of the Pencil tool include pixel-by-pixel editing, or retouching precise areas of an image.

Remember, in the Brushes Palette you can choose the size and shape of the tool.

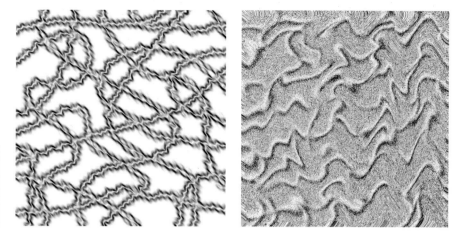

Figure 5–71
The Pencil Tool
Options palette

Figure 5–72
Examples of random Pencil strokes processed through some of Photoshop's filters

Airbrush Tool

The Airbrush is a seductive painting tool used to apply tones and colors gradually. The edges of a stroke are much softer than those of the Paintbrush, resulting in a simulation of the traditional airbrush effect. Depending on the Modes and Pressure settings, tones can be applied as soft, subtle sprays to add just a hint of color or as solid opaque stokes. The longer you hold the mouse button down, the more paint is applied, causing the stroke or mark to spread.

Some applications of this tool include adding make-up to skin tones, enhancing highlights and shadows, retouching, tinting areas with soft color, and simulating reflections on metal (Figure 5–73).

NOTE: Artists use the traditional (analog) airbrush to achieve smooth gradients for large areas such as skies. In Photoshop it is more effective to use the Gradient tool for large blends and the Airbrush tool for more detailed work.

Unlike its real-world counterpart, Photoshop's Airbrush can be accurately controlled. The Airbrush Options palette contains paint modes (see the discussion of paint modes earlier in this chapter and Figure C–1 in the Color Section), Pressure, and Fade Out Rate (Figure 5–74). Check the Fade box to control the distance of a stroke before it runs out of ink; the stroke can fade to transparent or to the background color. The Stylus Pressure selections will effect the color and pressure of a cordless pen on a pressure-sensitive tablet.

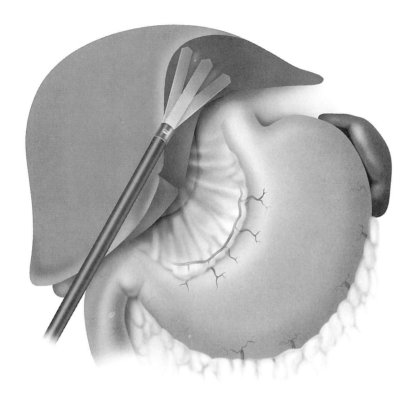

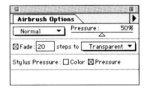

Figure 5–73
Terry Toyama used the Airbrush tool to model the shapes in this illustration of a stomach and liver. (© Terry Toyama and Krames Communication)

Figure 5–74
The Airbrush Tool
Options palette

Remember, in the Brushes Palette you can choose the size and shape of the tool, and make further parameter modifications by selecting Brush Options in the pop out menu.

Paintbrush Tool

The Paintbrush is very similar to the Pencil tool, except that the brush automatically has anti-aliased edges. The Paintbrush Options palette (Figure 5–75) controls the Opacity, paint Modes, Transparency, Stylus, and Wet Edges. Wet Edges simulates a build up of "paint" at the edges of the anti-aliased stroke.

By now you are probably wondering, What's the difference between the Pencil, Airbrush and Paintbrush tools? Here they are, side by side (Figure 5–76)

Remember, in the Brushes Palette you can choose the size and shape of the tool, and make further parameter modifications by selecting Brush Options in the pop-up menu.

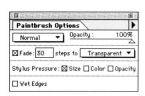

Figure 5–75
The Paintbrush
Options palette

Figure 5–76
From left to right, the Pencil, Airbrush, Paintbrush and Paintbrush with Wet
Edges with a detail of each

Rubber Stamp Tool

The Rubber Stamp tool duplicates pixels, a process sometimes referred to as cloning. There are seven different anti-aliased options in the Rubber Stamp Options palette: Clone (aligned), Clone (non-aligned), Pattern (aligned), Pattern (non-aligned), From Snapshot, From Saved, and Impressionist. Available for all the methods are paint Modes, Opacity control, Stylus Pressure for Size and Opacity (Figure 5–77).

If Sample Merged is clicked on (available only for cloning), the duplicated pixels will be from all visible layers, as if they were merged, and the result will appear on only the target layer. If Sample Merged is not clicked on, the duplicated pixels will be from the target layer only.

Remember, in the Brushes Palette you can choose the size and shape of the tool, and make further parameter modifications by selecting Brush Options in the pop-up menu.

CAUTION: If you change color modes, the Rubber Stamp tool will not work when sampling from one mode to another. The From Snapshot, From Saved, and Impressionist Rubber Stamps will not work if you crop or change the pixel resolution of the document.

CLONE (ALIGNED)

Use the clone function when you want to duplicate an image or retouch an area that has a texture. A typical situation might be to add a window to a wall (Figure 5–78) or remove a boat from the water. Some of the more

Figure 5–77
The Rubber Stamp
Options palette

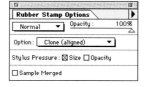

Figure 5–78   The window on the right was cloned from the window on the left using the Rubber Stamp tool set to Clone Aligned style. (© Mark Siprut)

problematic textures are water, cloudy skies, and skin. Be careful to clone from areas very close to the section to be retouched.

The Clone (aligned) option takes a sample of an image and applies it over another area, either from one document to another or within the same document. The tool uses a two-step process. First you place the Rubber Stamp tool over the area of pixels to duplicate, hold the Option key down, and click. Then move the cursor to the area to which you wish the clone to go. Press and drag and the image will appear, duplicating itself from the selected area. A crosshair shows the source of the pixels as you paint. The relationship of the initial sampling point is maintained, allowing you to stop and start, and even change brush shapes and modes.

TIP: Use the Rubber Stamp tool to retouch and repair spots and scratches in photographs. Option click as close to the spot as possible to match the tone. In the Rubber Stamp Options palette, set the mode to Darken if the spot is light and if the spot is dark, set the mode to Lighten. This method allows you to fill in the spots without affecting the surrounding areas.

You can clone from another file even though the other file is not an active window. The Rubber Stamp tool can pick up information from any part of the file, visible or not.

TIP: Although the Smudge tool may be used for retouching, it blurs the grain of the image. The Rubber Stamp tool, on the other hand, allows your image to retain its texture, so is ideal for retouching.

Figure 5–79
The final image on the right was created from the source on the left with the Rubber Stamp tool set to Clone Nonaligned. (Photo courtesy of PhotoDisc Volume 6)

CLONE (NONALIGNED)

The Clone (nonaligned) option is similar to the aligned option except it will always sample from the original point specified no matter where you paint with the tool. This sampling occurs even if the sampling point is not visible within the working window.

The Clone (nonaligned) option is very useful for applying the same sample to multiple locations in a composition (Figure 5–79).

PATTERN (ALIGNED AND NONALIGNED)

The Pattern (aligned) option allows you to define a pattern and repeat it as uniform tiles as you paint with the Rubber Stamp tool. To define a pattern select an area with the Marquee, choose Define Pattern under the Edit Menu, and deselect the selection.

As with the Clone options, the Patterns choice can be aligned and nonaligned choice. In Pattern Aligned, you can stop and start, and the grid will be maintained. In Pattern Nonaligned mode, every time you stop and restart will cause the pattern to begin from the center of the tiles (Figure 5–80).

Figure 5–80
Pattern Aligned on the left and Nonaligned on the right

FROM SNAPSHOT

The From Snapshot option is a method of capturing a selection, manipulating the image, then painting back in with the Rubber Stamp tool to revert as desired to the original captured state.

First make a selection and apply the Take Snapshot command under the Edit menu to temporarily store the data. Manipulate your image. At any point you can paint back in the original selection in exactly the same place with the Rubber Stamp into any layer of the same document. You cannot take a snapshot and use it in another document.

An effective technique using the Rubber Stamp tool in From Snapshot mode is to run a filter, take a snapshot, undo, and then set the Rubber Stamp tool to From Snapshot. This allows you to "paint in" a filter as though the filter efect was applied with a brush.

FROM SAVED

The From Saved option for the Rubber Stamp tool is similar to the Eraser tool's Erased to Saved mode (Magic Eraser). As you paint, From Saved restores an image to its last saved version. The main difference is that the Rubber Stamp can use the paint Modes with the From Saved option, while the Eraser has different brush types in the Erased to Saved mode.

IMPRESSIONIST

The Impressionist option for the Rubber Stamp is different from the other options, because it is similar to painting with a filter. It creates smudged organic patterns as the tool is rubbed over the image, simulating an Impressionist painting (Figure 5–81).

To give a photograph an effective painterly look, use a small brush size. A larger size results in a more chaotic appearance. A very large brush will obliterate the image. Use restraint with the Impressionist Rubber Stamp—try it in selected areas of an image and at various opacities.

Smudge Tool

Use the Smudge tool to push color, similar to rubbing a charcoal mark on paper with your finger. Setting the Pressure in the Smudge Tool Options palette determines how far the color will be pushed (Figure 5–82). A low setting gives a slight push or blurring action, and a high setting can smear a color across an entire document (Figure 5–83).

The Smudge Tool Option palette contains Stylus Pressure options, Opacity settings, and Finger Painting. Finger Painting smudges the foreground color in with the smudge (Figure 5–84). You also have the option of choosing Sample Merged which will include colors from all visible layers in the smudge but only apply the sampled colors to the target layer.

Figure 5–81
This photograph was painted over with the Rubber Stamp tool set to the Impressionist style. (© Mark Siprut)

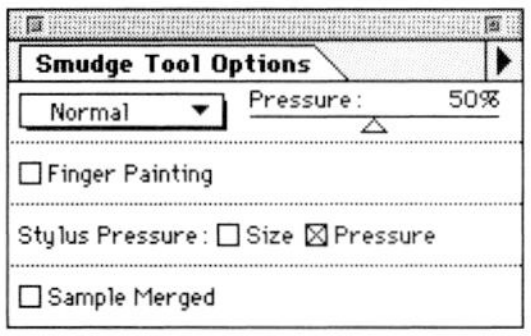

Figure 5–82
The Smudge Tool Options palette

Figure 5–83
A black line distorted with the Smudge tool at pressure settings ranging from 90% on the left to 10% on the right in 10% increments

Figure 5–84
An example of normal smudging on the left and smudging with the Finger Painting option selected on the right. The foreground color is set to 50% black.

Remember, in the Brushes Palette you can choose the size and shape of the tool, and make further parameter modifications by selecting Brush Options in the pop-up menu.

TIP: The Smudge tool can be used for small retouch details, but it wipes out the texture of the image. Try using the Rubber Stamp tool to retain grain in an image.

The Smudge tool cannot be used on a document in either the Bitmapped or Indexed color modes.

Blur/Sharpen Tool

The Blur/Sharpen tool facilitates softening or enhancement along the edges of shapes. Hold down the Option key and click on the Blur/Sharpen tool in the Toolbox to quickly switch between the two tools.

Use the Blur tool to soften harsh edges of an image or areas containing undesirable details. As you apply the Blur tool, the contrast between the pixels decreases, resulting in an overall smoothing effect. Set the Blur tool to a small brush size to soften the rough edges that are sometimes created when you paste one image on top of another.

Use the Sharpen tool to define edges of an image, simulating the effect of enhanced focus or clarity. As you apply the Sharpen tool the contrast between adjacent pixels increases, resulting in an overall sharpened effect.

NOTE: The Sharpen tool does not focus an image, but simulates sharpness by increasing the contrast along edges. You cannot actually focus of an out of focus photograph (Figure 5–85).

TIP: To sharpen large areas or an entire image, use the Unsharp Mask filter. See Chapter 9, "Filters and Plug-ins," for more on sharpening.

The options palette for Blur/Sharpen tools, called the Focus Tools Options palette (Figure 5–86), contains paint Modes, Pressure setting, a toggle to choose between Blur and Sharpen, Stylus controls (Size and Pressure), and Sample Merged. By clicking on the Sample Merged button

Figure 5–85
An example of the Blur tool on the left and Sharpen tool on the right

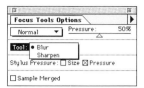

Figure 5–86
The Focus Tools
Options palette

Figure 5–87
The Toning Tools Options palette

you can sample the pixel tones or colors from all visible layers as if they were merged, putting the blurred or sharpened result into the target layer.

Don't overdo two things: the Pressure setting and repeated application over an area. Continually dragging the Sharpen tool over a specific area, you will strip away intermediate values, producing a harsh edge. Use the Blur/Sharpen tool at low Pressure settings to subtly build up to the desired effect.

The Blur/Sharpen tool cannot be used on a document in either the Bitmapped or Indexed color modes.

Remember, in the Brushes Palette you can choose the size and shape of the tool, and make further parameter modifications by selecting Brush Options in the pop-up menu.

Dodge/Burn/ Sponge Tool

The Dodge/Burn/Sponge tool goes beyond what was possible in a traditional photographic darkroom. By dragging the mouse over parts of an image, you have creative control over lightening and darkening specific areas. Traditionally, dodging and burning techniques let photographers correct tones in a photograph by increasing or decreasing the exposure of specific areas to achieve a complete range of highlight and shadow details. The Dodge tool lets you lighten areas of the image; the Burn tool lets you darken areas.

In addition, Adobe has added the Sponge tool in Photoshop 3, which increases or decreases saturation of color without affecting value (Dodge/Burn affects value without affecting color saturation). To switch among the three modes of the tool, hold the Option key and click on the Dodge/Burn/Sponge icon in the Toolbox.

The Toning Tools Options palette (Figure 5–87) allows you to control Dodging and Burning into the shadows, midtones, and highlights: Shadows will modify the dark pixels in an image, Midtones will modify colors in the middle range, and Highlights will modify only light pixels. You can set Exposure between 1 and 100% (a high number produces a stronger effect). Choose between Saturate and Desaturate for the Sponge tool. Control the intensity of the Sponge with the Pressure slider. Stylus Pressure has options for Size and Exposure (more pressure, more exposure).

TIP: **For best results with these tools set the Exposure or Pressure between 5 and 20 %. The effects are intended to be subtle.**

The Dodge/Burn/Sponge tool cannot be used on a document in either the Bitmapped or Indexed color modes.

Remember, in the Brushes Palette you can choose the size and shape of the tool, and make further parameter modifications by selecting Brush Options in the pop-up menu.

Color Controls

Just under the painting and editing tools in the Toolbox are the controls for choosing the foreground and background colors, for switching between them, and for returning to the default colors. To select a color, click on either the Foreground or Background color box (see Figure 5–32) and a Color Picker box will appear. Use the Foreground Color selection box for painting and filling. The Background Color selection box is the color that remains when you cut a selection out of an image, or erase from an image, or use the Pencil tool in the Auto Erase mode.

The colors in the Foreground and Background selection boxes are the two colors used to create a blend with the Gradient tool. Click on the Switch Colors icon to swap the foreground and background colors. Click on the Default Colors icon to return to the default black foreground and white background colors. For more information, refer to Chapter 8, "Color."

TIP: **It is easier to choose colors with the Picker, Swatches or Scratchpad palettes than with the Color Picker in the Toolbox.**

Creating from Scratch

When you create from scratch digitally you may feel like a painter facing a white canvas or a writer addressing a blank page. It can be scary. Many artists avoid the empty screen by scanning in a pencil sketch or a photograph for ideas. In any case creating from scratch refers to painting or drawing images with the tools, as opposed to imported and manipulating photographic images.

Following are several step by steps from artists that create from scratch using Photoshop's tools. Please see Chapter 13, "Case Studies," for more examples of how artists use Photoshop.

Using a Wacom Tablet

Francois Guerin sketched and painted freehand without using a template to create "Iced Tea" (Figure 5–88).

1. Guerin began by drawing with the Paintbrush tool using a Wacom Tablet to develop some ideas, sketching loosely.

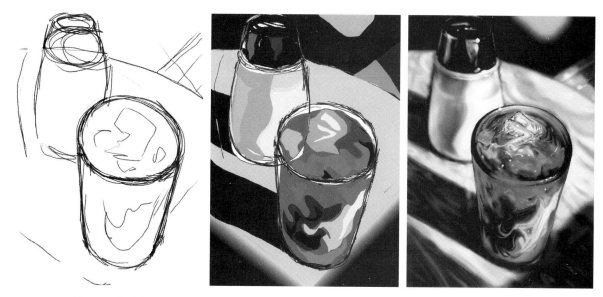

Figure 5–88   "Iced Tea" by Francois Guerin (© Francois Guerin)

2. Using the Lasso tool to draw basic shapes, he filled them with various colors, paying particular attention to the balance between brights and darks. Guerin repeated this step many times to develop a complex painterly image.

3. He used the Airbrush tool to achieve transparencies and model the shapes and the Blur tool to mix adjacent colors. For depth and softness he applied the Gaussian Blur filter to specific elements and areas.

Fantasy

Tom Cross was originally a zoologist. His images are filled with folklore and ecological references.

1. "Shell Caster" started from thumbnail sketches in a sketchbook and digital thumbnails drawn with a Wacom tablet.

2. Cross then scanned a conventional pencil sketch of the Shell Caster to use as a template to paint over in Photoshop (Figure 5–89).

3. Using the Airbrush tool at a 30% to 40% Opacity setting, he "glazed" color onto the sketch, painting gradually to build the values, sometimes employing the Darken and Lighten paint modes.

4. He then used other tools: the Paintbrush at 60% Opacity black to define and clean up edges, and the Smudge tool to blend tones in the face and skin. When he created a texture or color he liked, he painted with it in other areas by cloning with the Rubber Stamp tool. He also used the Dodge/Burn tools frequently, enhancing the highlights and shadows.

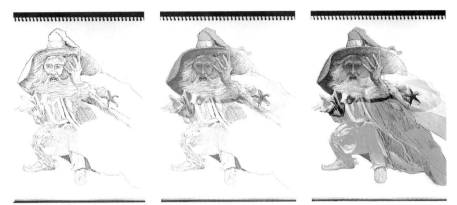

Figure 5–89
After scanning the
pencil sketch, Cross
gradually painted in the
colors and tones to
render the character,
Shell Caster.
(© Tom Cross)

Figure 5–90
The character
Shell Caster completed
prior to pasting him into
the background
(© Tom Cross)

Figure 5–91
The background
originated as composite
of seascape photographs
(© Tom Cross).

Figure 5–92   Shell Caster completed (© Tom Cross)

5. Cross pasted the Shell Caster (Figure 5–90) into the background, a composite of seascape photographs (Figure 5–91).

6. After creating and adding all the other elements, the final image was output as an IRIS print, at 150 ppi (Figure 5–92).

Technical Illustration

Terry Toyama, a medical illustrator, uses the following techniques for many of her anatomical and surgical illustrations.

1. Toyama began the Corneal Transplant illustration by making a pencil sketch on paper using medical and anatomical references (Figure 5–93).

2. The sketch was scanned in grayscale (which saves time) at 300 ppi.

3. She converted the file to CMYK Color mode.

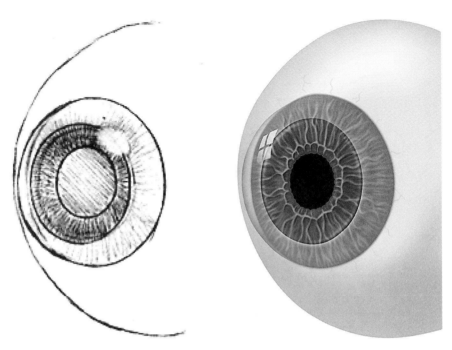

Figure 5–93
After scanning the
sketch, Terry Toyama
used the Paths, Airbrush,
and Eyedropper tools
with the TruMatch color
system to create this
illustration of a
corneal transplant
(© Terry Toyama
and Krames
Communication).

4. The Paths tool was used to trace over shapes in the sketch. Paths were saved in groups, such as bones, muscles, tendons, etc. Says Toyama, "I tend to use Paths more than Channels to save selections because they are not so memory intensive."

5. She deleted the pencil sketch from the document.

6. She chose a limited palette using the TruMatch color system: middle values, darks for shadow areas, and highlights (usually white).

7. She laid down the middle values by making selections from saved paths and filling them with the appropriate middle values.

8. The Airbrush tool was then used for modeling the highlights and shadows from her TruMatch palette.

9. Once the basic colors were applied, Toyama used the Eyedropper tool to choose colors and values between the middle, darkest, and highlight hues, by picking up the sprayed hues on the edges of the airbrush strokes. Later she picks other colors to avoid the monochromatic look.

10. After final art approval, the artist sent the file to the color house or printer for a Matchprint proof.

11. After seeing the proof, Toyama adjusted colors and tones as necessary. The final file was sent out again for another Matchprint proof (Figure 5–93).

Photorealism

Bert Monroy's illustration "The New York Deli" is a striking example of digital photo realistic painting from scratch (Figure 5–94).

1. He began by making a photographic study of the scene, shooting two or three overviews and many closeups for detail. He then taped the reference photos to the sides of his monitor.

2. When Monroy used to paint on canvas, he would sketch all the perspective lines and details over which he would paint. He still employs the same technique using Adobe Illustrator. For the Deli scene, the

Figure 5–94
Bert Monroy started "New York Deli" in Illustrator and finished it in Photoshop using the Line, Paintbrush, Airbrush, Pen, and Gradient tools. (© Bert Monroy).

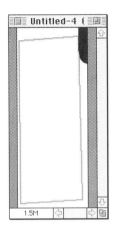

Figure 5–95
Monroy worked on small sections to conserve memory, selecting areas and applying blends with the Gradient tool.

Figure 5–96
Monroy started with the Pen tool, converted to a selection and used the Line, Paintbrush, and Airbrush to model and detail the shapes.

windows and the doorway were the only guidelines needed. Creating the type for the various signs was the majority of the work in Illustrator.

3. Once all the line work was created, the image was saved as an EPS file with Color Macintosh Preview.

4. Monroy opened the file in Photoshop to finish the artwork.

5. To conserve memory and bypass the slow processing speed of the Macintosh in handling large files, Monroy worked with sections of an image at a time, as it was unnecessary to have an entire 20 megabyte image open when working on a small section. He selected an area, copied it to the clipboard and pasted it into a new document (Figure 5–95).

6. He dropped in a blend for each area using the Gradient tool.

7. The bar on which the salami hangs was created with a variety of tools. First a wide dark colored stroke was laid down with the Line tool. With the Paintbrush, a soft light reflection was painted at the top of the bar. The bright highlight was created using the Airbrush tool with a Fade-out setting. The fade-out lets the strokes slowly diminish as they get away from the hot spot (Figure 5–96).

8. The salami hanging in the window and in the basket was created using the Pen tool. After drawing the shape, it was converted into a selection and filled using the Gradient tool. With the Airbrush tool he applied a highlight along the edge. For the finishing touch of realism, the Noise filter was applied with a low setting of about 16.

9. The salami was then cloned with a slight modification to each version (rotate, scale, etc.). The other items visible inside the window were created using similar techniques.

10. After completing detail sections, they were copied and pasted back into the main image precisely in register.

Naturalism

Sharon Steuer works as an artist both in digital imaging and traditional printmaking and painting. She created the painting "Ruffled in the Grass" (Figure 5–97) in three different programs.

1. Steuer began the portrait of the eagle in Aldus Freehand and Fractal Design Painter.

2. She imported the 8 × 10 inch rough image into Photoshop at 150 ppi and broadly painted in the landscape and details with the Paintbrush tool.

Figure 5–97
Sharon Steuer used the Paintbrush, Airbrush and Dodge/Burn tools with a Wacom Digitizing tablet to create "Ruffled in the Grass" (© Sharon Steuer).

3. Steuer then resembled the image to 300 ppi using Image Size under the Image menu, doubling the resolution to paint in the final details.

4. In the Options palette for all the painting and retouching tools, she set the parameters for her Wacom tablet stylus so that Stylus Pressure controlled Opacity: the heavier the pressure, the more opaque the effect; and the lighter the pressure, the more transparent the effect. She did not turn on the Size and Color options. She says the tablet "feels very much like a natural medium when used this way." She used the Airbrush tool for soft effects, the Paintbrush for crisper details in the foreground (such as the grass), and the Dodge/Burn tool for enhancing the feathers and grass (Figure 5–97).

Summary

- Once you develop your work habits and style, set your floating palettes in convenient places and leave them there. Remember that you can collapse and expand palettes by double-clicking on the palette tab. Assign well-used commands in the Commands palette to save time.

- To close a palette in the Windows version double-click the Control menu, the box containing the dash in the upper-left corner of the palette.

- Use a tool with the Options and Brushes palettes open at all times, as they control the function of the tool.

- Keep the Layers palette open at all times. For the most part, tools function on the target layer only. Control which layer you are working on and which layers are visible in the Layers palette.

- If you want to experiment, paint on a new layer. When satisfied, merge it with the other layers.

- Each tool produces many different effects. Choose the tools parameters in the Options and Brushes palettes. To build up an effect gradually, use the tool at less than full opacity.

- The Pencil Tool always has hard jagged edges, while the Airbrush and Paintbrush tools always have soft anti-aliased edges.

- Use the Eyedropper tool to pick up colors from your art, rather than remixing the colors each time.

- Learn the paint modes because they offer numerous possibilities for combining colors. Refer to the modes illustration C-1 in the Color Section.

- If you make a selection, a tool will only affect the selected area. See the next chapter, "Image Selection and Masking," for more on making selections.

6

Image Selection and Masking

A basic function of any graphics program is to select portions of an image to manipulate. If you have used other painting programs, you are probably accustomed to the standard Marquee and Lasso tools. In Photoshop the selection tools are more powerful and complicated than in other programs, but once mastered, these tools allow you to do what previously may have been difficult or impossible.

This chapter discusses the selection tools and how they can isolate areas as masks. These precise and sometimes complex selections can be filled, manipulated, filtered, layered, copied, and pasted into. You will learn how selections apply to layers, channels, and paths, and the basics of combining images. This chapter also discusses the difference between layers and channels, and introduces layer and channel management.

Dan Burkholder, a fine art photographer, demonstates selective masking in "Traffic Pursuing Molecules" (Figure 6–1). By selecting specific areas, applying more contrast and filter effects, and dropping in a new sky, he converted the Parisian expressway on the left into the dramatic night scene on the right.

Making a Selection

Making a selection means choosing an area in an image to edit, manipulate, or move. Make selections in the following ways:

- Use one of the three selection tools found in the toolbox: the Marquee, Lasso, or Magic Wand (Figure 6–2).

Figure 6–1   In "Traffic Pursuing Molecules," the image (left) was divided into three selection areas. The middle zone was solarized without affecting the new sky or street. The contrast was increased in the street selection to give it the wet street effect. The clouds and molecules were pasted into the sky.
(© Dan Burkholder)

- Use the Pen tool located in the Paths palette (Figure 6–2).
- The Paste commands under the edit menu will place the clipboard image as a floating selection on your document.
- The All command under the Select menu selects the entire target layer.
- The Color Range command under the Select menu will make selections based on colors or values.
- The Load selection command under the Select menu will turn a channel into an active selection.

How to Use Selections

You can then use selections for the following applications:

- To create complex photomontages with multiple elements from different sources
- To place objects against any background, creating seamless, smooth edges between foreground and background objects
- To construct on-the-fly masks for applying tint and color correction changes to specific portions of an image
- To save selection shapes as paths with a document—the paths will silhouette the shapes against backgrounds in other programs

Figure 6–2
Selection tools in the
Toolbox and
Paths palette

 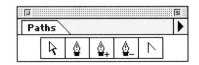

- To create vignettes with soft borders around selected areas
- To save selections as channels for future use in the current document or for combining with other documents or channels
- To specify selections to be copied, pasted, pasted into, pasted behind, pasted with special effects, pasted at various transparencies, and filled
- To apply dynamic effects such as scale, skew, perspective, and distort to selected areas
- To alter the selected portion of an image with the many filters available in Photoshop
- To draw geometric or organic shapes and fill or outline them with colors, gradients, patterns, or images (Figure 6–3 and 6–4)
- Fill selections at various Opacity and Mode settings for transparent and overlay effects (Figure 6–5).

Figure 6–3
Basic shapes with various
fills drawn with the
Marquee and Lasso tools

Figure 6–4
Selections with various
strokes applied

Figure 6–5
Transparency effects
using various Opacity
and Mode settings

Selection Creation Guidelines

Use the following guidelines when making selections:

- Double-clicking on a tool's icon opens the options palette, allowing you to control attributes specific to the tool.

- For selecting a shape with specific color or value or a shape against a solid-color background, use the Magic Wand tool or the Color Range command under the Select menu.

- For careful, delicate selections use the Pen tool to draw a path and then convert the path to a selection You can also use the Quick Mask mode with any of the paint tools to define careful selections.

  TIP: Once you have made a selection, save it as a channel or a path. You will always be able to get it back after deselecting.

- The Elliptical Marquee, Lasso, Magic Wand, and Pen tools have an anti-aliased option that will smooth the edges when making a selection.

- The Marquee, Lasso, and Pen tools can be feathered at the time you are making a selection, but all floating selections can be feathered by applying the Feather command under the Select menu.

- To move a selection, click on the Move tool or any of the selection tools (except the Magic Wand) in the toolbox and then drag from inside the selected shape (you will see an arrow).

- To move a selection by one-pixel increments, use the arrow keys on the keyboard. Selections can be moved with an arrow key while any tool is selected.

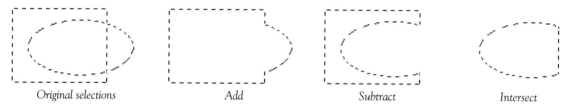

Original selections   *Add*   *Subtract*   *Intersect*

Figure 6–6 Add to an existing selection (left) by holding the Shift key (second from left); subtract from a selection by holding the Command key (second from right); and Intersect a selection by holding the Command and Shift Keys (right).

- A selection shape can be moved without actually moving the contents of the selection by pressing the Command and Option keys while dragging from the inside of the selected area.

  TIP: By using the selection tools and the Command and Option keys, you can create "cookie-cutter" masks consisting of the shape of a selected area. Move the selection area onto another part of the image and use color correction controls or filters to generate special ghosting and shadow effects.

- Add to a current selection with a new selection by holding the Shift Key in conjunction with a selection tool or command (Figure 6–6).
- Subtract from a current selection with a new selection by holding the Command Key in conjunction with a selection tool or command.
- Intersect a current selection with a new selection by holding the Command and Shift Keys in conjunction with a selection tool or command.

  TIP: You can begin selecting an area with one tool or command, and add to, subtract from, or intersect the selection area with any other selection tool or command.

- To deselect a floating selection, choose None under the Edit menu or click outside of the selection area with the Marquee or Lasso tools or inside the selection area with the Magic Wand tool.

The Selection Tools and Commands

The Lasso and Marquee are the standard tools for making selections in most raster graphics applications. In early paint programs, selecting a black-and-white image with a Lasso was a straightforward affair; the Lasso conformed to the shape of the black pixels, ignoring the surrounding white pixels in the process. When color painting programs appeared, the standard Lasso and

Marquee evolved so that they could select portions of an image by color components or by ignoring background colors.

Photoshop now offers robust controls for making selections based on specific parameters. You will find this selective control in the Magic Wand tool or the Color Range command. The familiar Lasso and Marquee tools take on many parameter controls not found in most other graphics programs.

In addition to making selections with the Marquee, Lasso, and Magic Wand tools, you can create a floating selection by pasting from the clipboard with the Paste command, by converting from a path in the Paths palette, by selecting the entire layer (Select All), or by loading a saved channel with the Load Selection command.

MARQUEE TOOLS

The two Marquee tools, the Rectangular and the Elliptical Marquees, allow you to select portions of an image for manipulation. Select an area by pressing and dragging diagonally from corner to corner or by holding the Option key and dragging from the center out. Hold the Shift key to draw a perfect square or circular selection.

These two anti-aliased selection tools have similar options. Double-click on the tool's icon to open the Marquee Options palette (Figure 6–7). Both tools have constrain parameters that allow you to select portions of an image with a predetermined selection size, as well as a fixed height-to-width ratio. The Constrained Aspect Ratio, found in the Style pop up menu, maintains the specified selection proportion. With a ratio of 1:1, the tool will select perfect squares and circles. The keyboard shortcut to maintain a 1:1 ratio is shift and drag from a selection corner.

The Fixed Size button forces the selection to the specified size. When you click the selection tool in the image, the predetermined Marquee appears on screen at the specified size and can be moved to the desired location on the screen. Clicking the mouse button outside the selection applies the selection.

TIP: If you are preparing images for boilerplate layouts, you may have already created sized place holders for graphic images that are optimized for the layout. By predetermining the size and aspect ratio of these two selection tools, you

Figure 6–7
The Marquee
Options palette

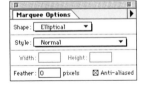

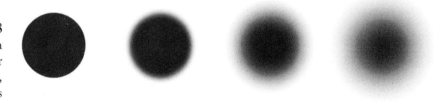

Figure 6–8
A selection filled with black with the Feather Radius settings at 1, 10, 30, and 50 pixels

don't need to waste time moving the image back and forth between Photoshop and your page-layout program.

The rectangular Marquee can be used to select individual one-pixel-wide vertical and horizontal bands of an image. This is useful for retouching images captured with video digitizers and frame grabbers, which sometimes contain signal distortions consisting of slightly shifted or offset scan lines. Once the scan line is selected, you can "nudge" it a pixel at a time in any direction by using the arrow keys on your keyboard.

The Feather Radius option defines how far to either side of the selection border the feathered edge will extend. You may also define a Feather Radius by choosing Feather under the Select menu after making a selection (Figure 6–8).

LASSO TOOL

Use the Lasso tool to draw a freehand, organic selection by pressing and dragging the mouse around a shape. The Lasso has an additional mode that allows you to toggle between the normal freehand mode and a "rubber-band," straight-line mode. To draw straight lines, hold down the Option key and plot points, clicking at the vertices of the polygons. When you release the Option key, Photoshop closes the current selection with a straight line between the first and last points. You may also release the Option key with the mouse button pressed down and continue making freehand selections.

NOTE: The Lasso tool does not automatically close in on an object against a solid background, as does the old MacPaint lasso. (For "autoselecting" a continuous color area use the Magic Wand tool.)

Double-clicking the Lasso tool opens the Lasso Options dialog (Figure 6–9). Feathering control and Anti-aliasing controls become available.

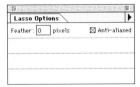

Figure 6–9
Lasso Options palette

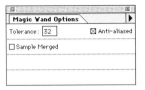

Figure 6–10
The Magic Wand
Options palette

Specify a Feather Radius to automatically avoid a harsh edge around a selection. Try a value of 1 for most basic selection tasks. To create a smooth transition between your selection area and the surrounding pixels, check the Anti-aliasing box.

MAGIC WAND TOOL

Use the Magic Wand to select contiguous areas of similar colors. Clicking on a color will automatically extend the selection to the borders of that color area. Select Anti-aliasing and adjust the spread factor sensitivity by double-clicking on the Magic Wand tool icon to bring up the Magic Wand Options palette (Figure 6–10).

The Tolerance control determines how far the selection area will spread. The values range between 0 and 255; lower values result in smaller selections (because fewer similar colors are selected) and higher values result in larger selections (Figure 6–11). When the sample merged box is chosen the Magic Wand tool will read the data from all of the visible layers but will

Figure 6–11
The Magic Wand tool set to a low tolerance on the left and to a high tolerance on the right

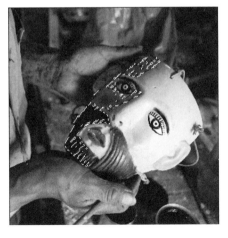

only make the selection in the target layer. If the box is not selected the Magic Wand tool will only sample from the target layer.

MOVE TOOL

Use the Move tool to drag a floating selection to a new position. If nothing is selected, the entire target layer can be moved. If another document is open, you can drag a selection or layer to the other document (drag and drop), bypassing the copy and paste command.

CAUTION: **If you drag a portion of an image out of the window area, you can drag it back. However, if you use another tool in the meantime, the outside portion will be cropped away never to be seen again.**

PEN TOOL

Use the Pen tool, accessed in the Paths palette, to draw smooth vector paths with the precision found in a drawing program. These paths can be saved as paths or converted to selections. The Pen tool in Photoshop functions similar to the Pen tool in most vector programs, such as Adobe Illustrator and Macromedia FreeHand. Plot points by clicking for corner points or dragging for curve points.

Drawing paths with the Pen tool allows you to work with precision over a bitmapped image without affecting the pixel information. The paths can be freely edited and moved around over the image. They can then be converted to selections, saved for future use, or filled, or stroked with any of the painting or editing tools.

Convert a path to a selection by choosing Make Selection in the Paths palette pop-up menu. See the "Paths" section later in this chapter for more information on creating and working with paths using the paths palette.

PASTE

The Paste command places a duplicate copy of the Clipboard contents in the center of the target layer (or document if there are no layers) as a floating selection.

SELECT ALL

The All command under the Select menu selects the entire currently active document, regardless of the current magnification. If the entire document is not visible, the selection marquee will extend beyond the visible boundaries of the window.

TIP: If you want to rotate or flip an entire document, do not use the All command to select the whole document for rotation—the All command will result in a cropped image when rotated.

COLOR RANGE

Color Range allows you to make a selection within a selection or an entire image based on a range of colors. Choose Color Range under the Select menu to open its dialog box (Figure 6–12).

The Select pop-up menu allows you to select colors based on sampled colors from the image, from a preset list of colors and tones, or out of gamut colors.

The Fuzziness slider will change the tolerance level of color recognition. A higher setting will allow for more color area to be selected.

The Preview will display either the current selection or the image. The preview in the document can use black matte to preview a selection against a black background (previews shades of white as shadows of black); white matte, which previews a selection against a white background (previews shades of black as shadows of white); and Quick Mask, which displays a selection with current quick mask settings.

The Eyedropper tools allow you to sample colors from the image to make the selection.

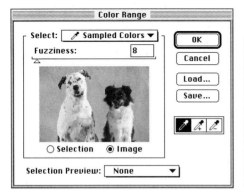

Figure 6–12
The Color Range dialog box

Figure 6–13
Color Range was used to select the blue background into which the background scene was pasted. (© Andrew Rodney)

Figure 6–14
The Clouds Difference filter was applied to the entire document in the top photograph. The selection in the center photograph was made with the Color Range command. In the bottom photograph, the Clouds Difference filter was applied to the selection, affecting only the selected areas. (© Craig Carlson)

The Color Range command was used to select the blue background behind the dogs, into which the background scene was pasted (Figure 6–13). Color Range was used to select the sky and its reflection in the photograph of the fisherman by Craig Carlson, prior to applying the Clouds Difference filter (Figure 6–14). For more information on using Color Range for color correction and replacement, see Chapter 8, "Color."

LOAD SELECTION

The Load Selection command converts a channel into an active selection. By saving selections as channels and then loading them when needed. Hours of work time can be eliminated because you do not have to reselect areas. See the "Channels" section later in this chapter for more details.

QUICK MASK

The Quick Mask mode allows you to make careful, precise selections by creating a temporary channel visible as a transparent overlay over the image. A Quick Mask automatically appears in the list of channels in the Channels palette. The Quick Mask mode allows you to refine and touch up selections with more precision and control than with the other selection tools in the toolbox.

After making a selection, click on the Quick Mask icon in the toolbox to create a Quick Mask. The selection instantly transforms into a transparent mask which you can edit with any of the painting tools. In the default mode, the dark colored areas (usually red) become the unselected areas and the clear areas become the selection. After editing the Quick Mask, click on the Standard Mode icon in the toolbox to return the mask to a selection. You can work back and forth without any problem.

NOTE: **In the default mode, painting with black in the clear area adds to the mask, decreasing the selection area. Painting with white or with the Eraser tool in the masked areas adds to the selection area.**

For more information on using the Quick Mask and channels see "Channels and Masking" later in this chapter.

Working with Selections

Once you have made a selection you can copy it, fill it, stroke it, move it, filter it, lighten it, darken it, adjust its tones and colors, colorize it, combine it with other images, paste into it, convert it to a path, save it a channel, use it on another layer or channel, add to it, subtract from it, delete it, use it to define a pattern, take a snapshot, crop it, vignette it with a soft feathered edge . . . .

Manipulating and Editing a Selection

Painting and editing tools, image processing commands such as Curves, Levels, Color Balance, and Filters only affect the inside of a selection (Figure 6–14). For example, in the photograph of the fisherman by Craig Carlson the Clouds Difference filter was applied to the selection, affecting the selected areas only (Figure 6–14).

WORKING WITH SELECTION GUIDELINES

Use the following basic guidelines when working with selections:

- If you move a selection, you will leave behind only the background color (usually white).

- Any area is automatically masked while selected; whatever you do will only affect the selected area. Paint tools, filters, and color correction controls only work within a selection. If nothing is selected, the manipulation will affect the entire layer (Figure 6–14).

   TIP: If you are in a magnified view and your current painting tool does not seem to be working, make sure that you do not have an area selected outside of your view. The tool works only within the selection area.

- Deselecting a floating selection will place it over the background, making it part of the background image. If you Undo the Deselect, you can delete the floating selection by pressing the Delete key (Backspace) on your keyboard, or by selecting Clear from the Edit menu. This will delete the floating selection and return the background to its original state.

- To move a selection click on any of the selection tools in the toolbox and then drag from inside the selected shape (you will see an arrow) or use the arrow keys on the keyboard to move a selection by one-pixel increments.

- To quickly duplicate a selection, press the Option key and drag the selection to a new position. You can also choose Float from the Select menu to duplicate a selection.

- Use the Move Tool or any of the selection tools to move a selection or an entire layer to a new position or to another document. Dragging a selection to another open Window leaves the original in place. This method, called "drag and drop," is new to Photoshop 3. Because you bypass the clipboard, drag and drop is faster than copy and paste.

- To see the effect of any manipulation or command without deselecting, use the Hide Edges command under the Select menu.

Edit Menu

The Edit menu has several commands that apply to active selections. These commands allow you to transfer, delete, fill, outline, define, and capture selections.

CUT AND COPY

The Cut and Copy commands allow you to capture a selection and temporarily store it in the clipboard.

Cut duplicates the selected area into the clipboard and removes the selection from the document, leaving the current background color (usually white) in its place.

Copy duplicates the selected area into the clipboard and leaves the original selection intact.

The clipboard image can then be pasted back into the same document, another layer, another channel, or another document. The resolution and color will remain intact unless you are transferring the selection to a program that does not support the color mode, color depth, or resolution of the selection.

The clipboard can only hold one image at a time. When you cut or copy a selection, the current clipboard contents are replaced. Photoshop has its own internal clipboard that works independently of the System Clipboard. When you leave Photoshop to go to another application, Photoshop exports its clipboard to the System clipboard (this can take a while if the clipboard image is large).

TIP: If you are working back and forth between applications and do not want to transfer the clipboard image, turn off "Export Clipboard" in the General Preferences submenu under the File Menu. The clipboard contents will then be deleted when you exit Photoshop.

CAUTION: The Windows clipboard is not robust enough to transfer Photoshop images to other programs. Crop the selection and save the file in an appropriate format.

PASTE COMMANDS

The Paste commands duplicate the contents of the clipboard into the current open document. (The clipboard contents remain intact until something else is cut or copied.) The clipboard can store raster images, vector images, or type. Images can be easily copied or cut from other applications to paste into Photoshop as long as the images are from raster programs. Vector images or type are not so simple. Here are some guidelines for pasting into Photoshop:

- Pasting is resolution dependent. Pixel for pixel replacement takes place. If two documents are different in size or resolution and you copy from one and paste in another, the size of the pasted image will change. Therefore, if possible copy and paste between documents of the same resolution.

- After pasting an image, it becomes a floating selection which you can then move precisely into position. In addition to the Mode and

Figure 6–15   The image on the left was copied and pasted to the center image. The floating selection was rotated and filtered. The Layers palette (right) shows the floating selection.

Opacity controls, you can apply any of the image processing and manipulation controls to the selection. Use the dynamic controls to stretch, distort, rotate, show perspective, and skew the image. Apply any filter or color control to the pasted image. Modifications will affect only the pasted selection and not the surrounding area (Figure 6–15).

- A pasted image also appears as a Floating Selection in the Layers palette (Figure 6–15). Blending between the pixels of the floating selection and the background are manipulated through the Layer palette using the Opacity slider and Mode pop-up menu.

- Once you deselect an image it becomes part of the bitmap. If you are not sure where the image should be placed, paste it on a new layer.

- After pasting an image, save the selection as a channel under the Select menu. You can then always get the selection shape back by selecting Load Selection.

- You cannot paste type from the clipboard directly on a Photoshop document. You must first open the Type tool dialog box, paste the type, and format it.

- When pasting a PostScript clipboard image copied from Adobe Illustrator, Adobe Dimensions, and Adobe Type Align, a dialog box appears asking if you want to paste the image as pixels (rasterize) or as a path (vector). For more information on using Photoshop with vector programs, see Chapter 11, "Output."

- Pasting vector clipboard images from applications other than those by Adobe is unreliable. It is better to save the image in a file format that Photoshop supports and then open it.

Figure 6–16 The Paste Into command placed the model and ground into the selected dark background to create "Hiding." (© Mark Siprut)

Paste: The Paste command places the clipboard image in the center of the current document as a floating selection over the current target layer. A floating selection is a temporary layer, so it will also appear as a Floating Selection in the Layers palette where you can apply the Modes and Opacity options prior to deselecting it. Deselect the floating selection to merge it with the layer beneath it.

Paste Into: The Paste Into command uses a selection as a mask by pasting the clipboard image inside an active selection (Figure 6–16). After applying the Paste Into command the pasted image becomes an active selection inside the previou selection. By dragging inside the floating selection, you can move it into the desired position. Any manipulation or painting tool can be applied to it before deselecting. When you modify the pasted image, you can undo the effect without deselecting the original selection.

Paste Behind: In earlier versions of Photoshop, Paste Behind command allows you to paste the clipboard image outside of a selected area. To paste behind a selection in Photoshop 3, hold the Option key while choosing the Paste Into command. The pasted image will be masked by the selected area in front of it. In Figure 6–17, the nineteenth-century engravings were pasted one at a time behind the selected leaves using the Paste Behind command.

Figure 6–17   To produce "Ant Stomp" (right), the Paste Behind command was used to place the figures behind the selected leaves. (© Ellen Landweber)

Paste Layer: The Paste Layer command allows you to paste the clipboard image directly into a new layer. In addition to the Mode and Opacity controls, you now have the Layer Options and other Layer palette controls available. See the Layers section later in this chapter for more information on how to use layers.

Pasting into Channels: You can paste a clipboard image into any channel on any layer. Since a channel contains only grayscale information, a color image will be converted to grayscale when pasted on a single channel. Pasting a grayscale image on a color document will place the image in the selection on all of the component color channels simultaneously. When pasting a selection on two or more channels simultaneously, the image within the selection will appear on the uppermost channel, and the selection shape will mask an area showing only the selection shape in the other channels (Figure 6–18). To paste the clipboard image on more than one channel (other than the color

Figure 6–18
Pasting on two channels simultaneously places the grayscale version on the uppermost channel and a silhouetted mask on the lower channel.

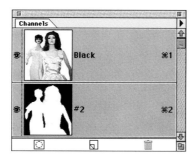

component channels such as RGB), you must paste the image on each channel one at a time.

TIP: To simultaneously paste a selection and save it as a channel, create a new channel in the Channels palette and make both the target channel and the new channel visible. The image will appear on the uppermost channel while the selection shape will become a mask on the new channel (Figure 6–18).

CLEAR

The Clear command replaces the selected area with the current background color. The selected area does not get captured to the clipboard. Do not confuse the Clear command with the Cut command (Cut duplicates the selection into the Clipboard).

FILL AND STROKE

The Fill and Stroke commands allow you to fill selections and their borders with colors, tones, and patterns. After making a selection, choose the Fill or Stroke command under the Edit menu to open a dialog box that specifies the fill options.

Click Preserve Transparency to apply the fill or stroke to the opaque areas of a layer only. Transparent areas shown as a checkerboard pattern will not be affected.

In the Blending section, set the Opacity (transparency) and fill Mode. Fill and Stroke use the same Opacity and Mode options available for the painting tools and for Layer Options.

To see how each mode affects an underlying color when filled see Figure C–1 in the Color Section. Each vertical band was cropped from various photographs or created with Photoshop's tools, commands, and filters. In each pair of horizontal bands the upper band was filled with solid green (100% cyan and 100% yellow) and the lower band was filled with the same green at a 50% Opacity setting. In each case the Mode setting at the right of each pair of horizontal bands was applied in the Fill dialog box when filling the selection with the color. Examine how each mode affects the fill color when combined with the colors and values of the underlying verticle bands.

For more information on blending modes, see Chapter 5, "Tools and Palettes," and "Layer Options" later in this chapter.

Fill: In the Fill dialog box (Figure 6–19), set the Contents to fill with either the Foreground Color, Background Color, a defined Pattern, a saved version of a file, a Snapshot, Black, 50% Gray, or White (Figure 6–21).

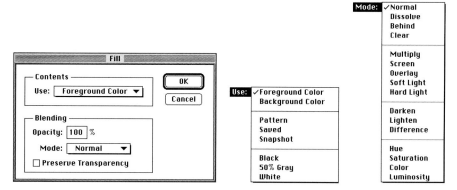

Figure 6–19
The Fill dialog box

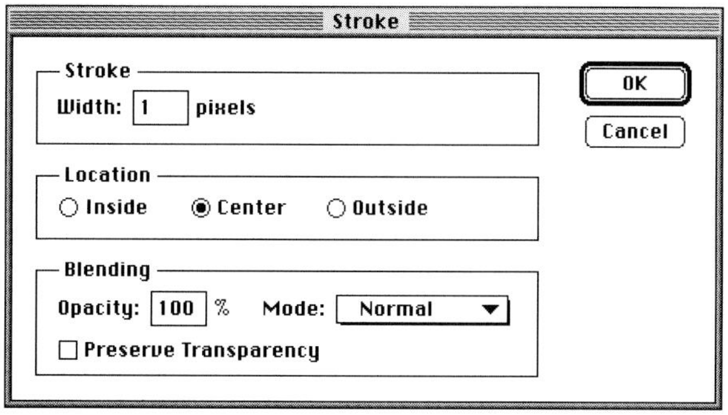

Figure 6–20
The Stroke dialog box

TIP: Fill a selection with a blend by dragging through the selection with the Gradient tool (Figure 6–3).

TIP: You can quickly fill any selected area with the current Foreground color at 100% opacity by pressing the Option and Delete (Backspace) keys. If you are on the background layer, press the Delete (Backspace) key to fill a selection with the background color. Deleting a selection while on a layer will make the selection area transparent. These shortcuts do not use any of the settings in the Fill dialog box.

Stroke: Set the stroke Width, Location, and Blending in the Stroke dialog box (Figure 6–20). The Foreground color will be applied to the edge of a selection (Figure 6–21).

CROP

Use the Crop command to retain the selected area as a document and eliminate the unselected areas. The Crop command functions with the Rectangular Marquee with no feathering only.

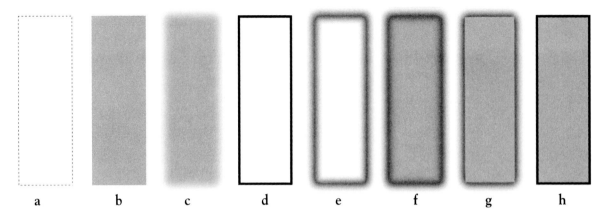

Figure 6–21   An area (a) selected with the Rectangular marquee; (b) Filled with 30% black; (c) Filled with 30% black using an 8 pixel Feather Radius; (d) No fill with a 5 pixel black Stroke; (e) No fill with a 5 pixel black Stroke and an 8 pixel Feather Radius; (f) Filled with 30% black, a 5 pixel black Stroke, and an 8 pixel Feather Radius on both; (g) Filled with 30% black, a 5 pixel black Stroke, and an 8 pixel Feather Radius on the Stroke only; (h) Filled with 30% black, with a 5 pixel black Stroke

TIP: To crop at to an exact resolution or to crop and rotate simultaneously, use the Cropping tool in the toolbox.

DEFINE PATTERN

Use the Define Pattern command to turn a selected area into a tiling component of a pattern (Figure 6–22). To define a pattern, select an area with the Rectangular Marquee (no Feather) and choose Define Pattern. This defined pattern can be used in any open Photoshop document. Use a defined pattern for the following:

- To fill a selection with a defined pattern with the Fill command
- To fill a color area with a defined pattern with the Paintbucket tool
- To paint with a defined pattern with the Rubber Stamp tool
- To create a custom halftone screen by converting a grayscale document to Bitmap mode

TIP: Photoshop ships with a folder of Postscript Patterns to define patterns. When you choose a document from this folder, the Rasterize Adobe Illustrator Format dialog box appears in which you should set the size, resolution, mode, and anti-aliasing.

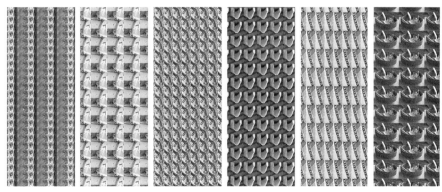

Figure 6–22   The defined pattern examples were all created from the image on the left. (© Mark Siprut)

TAKE SNAPSHOT

The Take Snapshot command captures the current selection or all visible layers (if no selection is made) to a temporary buffer. This temporary buffer, similar to but independent of the Clipboard, can temporarily store one image with each Photoshop document. The snapshot remains with the document, so if you have multiple open documents, each can have its own Snapshot. Use a Snapshot for the following:

- To fill a selection with a snapshot with the Fill command
- To paint with a snapshot using the Rubber Stamp tool (See Chapter 5, "Tools and Palettes.")

TIP: Use the Take Snapshot command prior to editing or manipulating an image and then paint back or fill desired areas with the snapshot image (Figure 6–23).

Figure 6–23
The original image (left) was captured with the Take Snapshot command and then filtered and manipulated (center). Areas were then painted and filled with the Snapshot image (right). (© Mark Siprut)

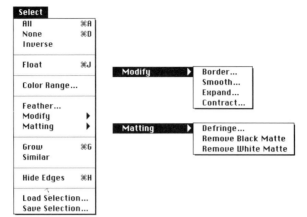

Figure 6-24
The Select menu

Select Menu

All of the commands in the Select menu (Figure 6–24) apply either to making selections or to working with selections. These commands allow you to modify, extend, duplicate, feather, inverse, hide, load, and save selections. Because the All and Color Range commands make selections, they were discussed in the "The Selection Tools and Commands" section earlier in this chapter.

NONE

Deselect any selected area by selecting None. Once applied, you can be sure that nothing is selected in the current document. The None command does not work, however, with selected paths.

TIP: You can also deselect by clicking anywhere outside of the selection area (inside of the document), unless you are using the Magic Wand tool, in which case click inside the selected area to deselect.

INVERSE

Inverse selects the exact opposite of the current selection. If you are working on a selected portion of an image and want to manipulate the rest of the picture, use the Inverse command. Switch back to the exact original selection by choosing Inverse again.

FLOAT AND DEFLOAT

After making a selection the Float command duplicates it, allowing you to move or manipulate the selection without affecting the original selected area. This floating selection also appears in the Layers palette as a temporary layer. A floating selection not in its original position has the Defloat command as an option. Selecting the Defloat command deletes the image defined by thelection shape, leaving the background color or transparency in the selection area after moving or deleting the selection.

TIP: To quickly duplicate a selection, hold the Option key down while dragging the selection to a new position. The original image will remain.

FEATHER

Feathering allows you to precisely determine how a selection's edges will blend with a background or underlying layer. With the Feather command, create variable soft edges for a selected area, resulting in "vignette" effects or seamless blending of images. When you choose Feather, a dialog box appears in which to specify the degree of feathering (Figure 6–25). Accepted values are 1 to 250 pixels. Higher numbers yield softer edges (Figure 6–26).

Use the Feather command to produce anything from smooth borders to glowing halo effects. In conjunction with other selection commands you can create special effects such as glows around shapes by combining the Feather and Border commands (Figure 6–30).

TIP: Apply the feather effect to the Marquee and Lasso tools when making a selection in their Options palette.

Figure 6–25
The Feather Selection
dialog box

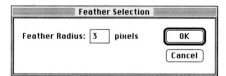

Figure 6–26
Feather examples with
the Feather Radius set to
5, 25, and 50 pixels

MODIFY

The Modify submenu provides commands for affecting the pixels that define the edges of a selection (Figure 6–24).

Border: The Border command creates a new selection along the edge of a selection. Choose the Border command and specify the desired width in pixels in the Border dialog box (Figure 6–27). Specify the border width between 1 and 64 pixels. This new selection is identical to any other selection; you can apply filters, feather, copy, and change color (Figure 6–28).

Smooth: The Smooth command looks for small artifacts along of the edges of a selection and either increases or decreases the selection area to smooth the edges. Choose the Smooth command to open the Smooth Selection dialog box and enter the Sample Radius from 1 to 16 in pixels. Photoshop looks for pixels within the specified radius that are either selected or unselected. If the majority of the pixels within the specified radius are selected, unselected pixels are included with the selection. If the majority of the pixels within the specified radius are unselected, selected pixels are included with the selection.

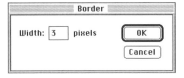

Figure 6–27
The Border dialog box

Figure 6–28
The Border command
was used to select the
area which was
manipulated with filters
and curves .
(© Mark Siprut)

Expand: Use the Expand command to enlarge a selection area by 1 to 16 pixels in all directions.

Contract: Use the Contract command to shrink a selection area by 1 to 16 pixels in from the selection edge.

MATTING

The Matting submenu provides commands for modifying the pixels at the anti-aliased edges of a selection showing traces of a previous background. Matting blends the selection seamlessly into a new background by changing the color or value of the edge pixels to match the new background. Matting becomes active only on a floating selection.

Defringe: The Defringe command analyzes the edge pixels and replaces any unrelated colors with the neighboring colors. Although you can specify from 1 to 64 pixels in the Defringe dialog box, one to two pixels will usually do the trick (Figure 6–29).

Remove Black Matte: Remove Black Matte removes the black halo fringe along the edges of a selection originating from a black background.

Remove White Matte: Remove White Matte removes the white halo fringe along the edges of a selection originating from a white background.

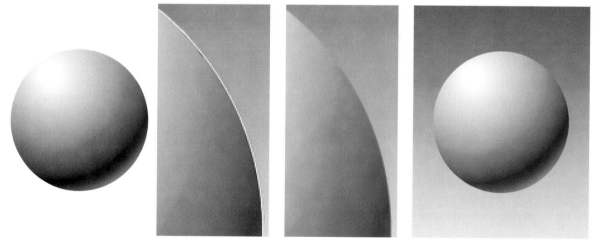

Figure 6–29   The sphere on the left, created on a white background, shows a light edge when pasted on a darker background. The Defringe command was applied at a two pixel setting to eliminate the fringe and produce a smooth edge.

GROW

Choose the Grow command when a selected area must be slightly larger. By choosing Grow, the selected area expands to adjacent pixels based on color and value. The amount of additional expansion as well as the degree of anti-aliasing is based on the tolerance setting in the Magic Wand Options palette (regardless of the selection tool in use).

SIMILAR

Choosing the Similar command causes Photoshop to search through the document and select all colors that are similar to the originally selected color or colors. Use this command if you want to change or manipulate a particular color in the entire document. As with the Grow command, set the sensitivity of the Similar command in the Magic Wand Options palette.

HIDE EDGES

Hide the "marching ants" animation of the selection border with the Hide Edges command. The area remains selected. Applications of the Hide Edges command include applying masked painting tools to a selection without seeing the selection edges, viewing text immediately after creating it without deselecting it, and previewing an area processed with any filter without the marching ants distraction. The Hide Edges command toggles to Show Edges when Hide Edges is active.

SAVE AND LOAD SELECTION

The Save Selection command converts the current selection into a new channel. A channel can be used as a selection at any time by selecting Load channel. View and edit the channel by choosing show Channels under the Windows menu and clicking on the desired channel in the Channels palette. See the "Channels" section later in this chapter for more details.

Glow Effect: Use the Save and Load Selection commands to create a glow effect around selections. This exercise will combine the Border and Feather commands (Figure 6–30).

1. Start by filling the background color to a dark gray or black.
2. Make a selection using the Elliptical Marquee and choose the Save Selection command to save it as a channel.
3. With the shape still selected, choose the Border command under the Select menu and enter a value of approximately 20. Choose the Feather command and enter a value of approximately 10.

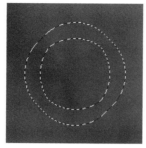

Figure 6–30 The Border and Feather commands were applied to the circle after saving it as a channel (left). The original circle was loaded and then filled with black (right) to achieve this glowing effect.

TIP: When using this technique, the size of the border determines the range of the glow. A good starting point for the Feather value is usually slightly less than half that of the Border value.

4. Choose a white as the Foreground color, and Fill the selection to achieve the glow.
5. Choose Load Selection under the Select menu to retrieve the original selected circle. Fill it with black.

You can use this technique with any selected shape. The shapes can be against solid or complex backgrounds. The glow technique also works well with type (Figure 6–31).

Figure 6–31
The Glow effect can be used on any selections by saving and loading them as channels.

Paths

Paths in Photoshop offer a mini vector (object oriented) program that works directly over Photoshop's primary function as a raster program. Paths and the Pen tool accessed in the Paths palette function as most other vector programs like Illustrator and FreeHand. The drawing, path editing, layering, and masking capabilities of vector paths registered directly over raster imagery give you precise control over how the paths interact with the pixels. Use paths for the following applications:

- Draw precise shapes that you would otherwise trace with the Lasso tool. Drawing with the Pen tool offers more control than does the irregular Lasso. After tracing a shape, convert the path into a selection.

- Convert selections into paths for fine-tuned, precise shape editing and then convert back to selections.

- Use the Paths palette to save paths defining hard-edged masks instead of saving them as channels. Paths use much less disk space than do channels.

- Paths can be scaled and rotated without any resolution or quality loss.

- Paths can be saved as clipping paths with the document, masking the Photoshop image when placed in another program.

- Paths can be exported to Adobe Illustrator as well as copied and pasted to or from Illustrator. Illustrator paths can be imported into Photoshop.

- Apply any of the painting or editing tools to a path for more precision than drawing with the mouse.

DEFINING A PATH WITH THE PEN TOOL

To define a path with the Pen tool select the Pen icon in the Paths palette (Figure 6–32). To preview a path before setting the next point, double-click the Pen tool to open the Pen Tool Options palette and click the Rubber Band box (Figure 6–33).

A path is defined by a series of points, called *anchor points*, which control the characteristics of the path, referred to as a *Bézier curve*. Bézier curves can describe any shape, retain all vector qualities, and are the core mathematical description of shapes in the PostScript language. The anchor points allow you to move the position of line segments, and, in the case of curve points, the *direction points* allow you to control the curvature of the path. Direction points are at the ends of a *direction line*, which is tangent to the path at the anchor point.

The following steps briefly describe how to draw a path:

1. Click the beginning point of the desired line.

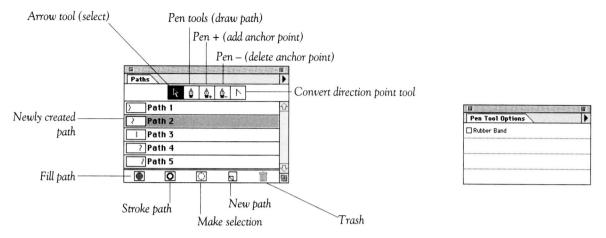

Figure 6–32
The Paths palette

Figure 6–33
The Pen Tool
Options palette

2. Continue clicking to create straight lines with corner points at each click. To plot anchor points with curved lines, press and drag at the points where the curve should change direction. Hold the shift key to constrain the plotting of points to 90° or 45° angles in relation to previous points (Figure 6–34).

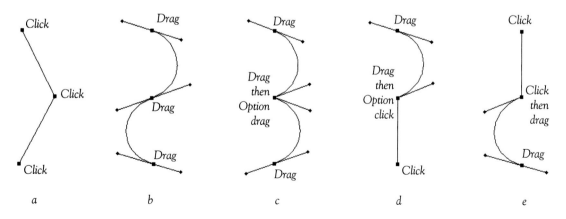

Figure 6–34　The above paths show anchor points for straight line segments (corner points) and anchor points with corresponding direction lines for curved segments (curve points). The mouse signals give the anchor point characteristics to describe the path (drawn from top to bottom).

3. To create a closed path, click on the beginning anchor point as the last link. A small circle appears to let you know that the path has been closed.

TIP: **If you select a New path from the Paths palette pop-up menu or click on the New path icon before you begin drawing, your path will automatically be saved.**

Use the following guidelines when drawing paths (Figure 6–34):

- Click with the Pen tool to draw corner points (a).
- Press and drag with the Pen tool to draw curve points (b).
- To change the direction of a curve at an anchor point, return to the last curve point, hold the Option key, and drag in the direction of the desired curved path (c).
- To draw a straight path from a curve point, return to the last anchor point, hold the Option key, and click on the point. Proceed with plotting the next point (d).
- To draw a curved path from a corner point, return to the last anchor point and drag, then plot the next point. A direction line appears (e).
- Plot as few points as possible for smooth paths .
- If you plan on filling a path or converting it to a selection, draw a closed path by clicking or dragging on the first anchor point on the path to close the loop.

EDITING PATHS

Each curve anchor point has a pair of lines with direction points at the ends. Corner points have no direction lines. Moving the anchor points will move the line segment associated with it. Moving the direction lines will adjust the curves.

By using the Arrow, Add point (the pen with a plus), Delete point (the pen with a minus), and Convert direction point tools, you can edit paths around odd and complex shapes with accuracy. Since anchor points define paths, moving or changing the characteristics of the points on a path will change the position and shape of the path.

Use the following techniques to edit paths:

- To move an anchor point or direction line, use the Arrow tool and drag the point to the new position. To temporarily change to the Arrow tool while using the Pen tool, hold the Command key. Move a point in one pixel increments with the arrow keys on the keyboard.

- To select multiple anchor points, select the Arrow tool, hold down the Shift key and click on the points, or press and drag a rectangular shape surrounding the points.

- To select all the anchor points on a path, select the Arrow tool, hold the Option key and click anywhere on the path. You can then drag the path to a new position.

- To change a point from a corner to a curve or vice versa, select the Convert direction point tool (on the far right side of the Paths palette) and click on the point you want to change.

- Hold down the Control and Command keys to switch to the Convert direction point tool.

- Change the direction of a curve by dragging on the direction point handles with the Convert direction point tool.

- To add a point to a path, use the Pen + tool and click on the segment of a line to which you want to add a point.

- To delete a point on a path, use the Pen – tool and click on the point you want to delete.

- Duplicate a path by holding down the Option key and dragging on a path.

SCALING, ROTATING, AND FLIPPING PATHS

Photoshop does not have a direct method of scaling, rotating, and flipping paths, but you can perform these functions on an entire document that includes paths. To scale, rotate, or flip a path choose Duplicate under the Image menu to create a new duplicate document. If you are working with a high resolution file with multiple layers, make only one layer visible in the Layers palette prior to duplicating. In the Duplicate dialog box, click on the Merge Layers button.

To scale the new document choose Image size under the Image menu. Make sure that File Size is deselected and then change the size or resolution. For accurate scaling, change to percent in the measurement units pop-up menu. Click OK and the entire document along with the path will change in size.

To rotate the new document choose one of the Rotate submenus under the Image menu except for Free Rotate. The entire document including the path will rotate.

To Flip the new document choose one of the Flip submenus under the Image menu. The entire document will flip.

To return the altered path to the original document, click on the path in the Paths palette, copy it, and then past it back into the original document.

NOTE: The above technique does not work with the other dynamic effects under the Image menu: Free Rotate, Scale, Skew, Perspective, or Distort.

DEFINING SELECTIONS AS PATHS

Convert a selection made with any of the selection tools to a path by choosing Make Path from the Paths palette pop-up menu. The Make Path dialog box will open (Figure 6–35)

A number from .5 to 10 pixels in the Tolerance box determines how accurately the path will follow the lines of the selection by plotting more or fewer anchor points. A higher value produces a smoother path, plotting fewer points, which results in less detail (Figure 6–36, center). A lower value produces a rougher path with more detail by using more points (Figure 6–36, right).

TIP: Too many anchor points in a path can cause problems when outputting to a PostScript printer from a vector program.

SAVING PATHS

A saved path will be saved along with the main document. The Paths palette and its pop-up menu offer controls for saving, duplicating, and deleting paths. After drawing a path, choose Save Path in the pop-up menu

Figure 6–35
The Make Path options dialog box showing the Tolerance control

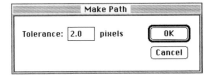

Figure 6–36
The shirt in the image on the left was selected and converted to a path at a five pixel Tolerance in the center and at a one pixel Tolerance on the right.

Figure 6–37
After drawing a path,
choose Save Path from
the pop-up menu in the
Paths palette.

or drag the temporary Work Path to the New path icon to add a path to the list of saved paths (Figure 6–37). To create a new saved path prior to drawing it, select New Path from the pop-up menu or click on the New path icon.

Duplicate a path by selecting it in the list and then choosing Duplicate Path in the pop-up menu or by dragging the path to the New path icon.

Delete a path by selecting it in the list and choosing Delete Path in the pop-out menu or by dragging it to the Trash icon.

Turn off a path by selecting it in the list and choosing Turn Off Path in the pop-up menu or by clicking inside the palette box rather than on another path name. A path will remain selected and displayed until you select a different path or turn it off.

TIP: To retain exact path and anchor point positions, save the path before you define it as a selection. Converting a selection back to a path creates a new and often different set of anchor points.

To use and save paths from other Photoshop documents or from Adobe Illustrator, copy them to the clipboard and then paste them into the current document.

APPLYING A FILL OR STROKE TO A PATH

Fill a path with a color or a defined pattern by using the Fill Path command. The Stroke Path command applies a stroke to a path. These commands are similar to the Fill and Stroke commands in the Edit menu, which apply to selections, but with some useful differences.

Fill Path: Click on a path in the list and select the Fill Path pop-up menu to open the Fill Path dialog box (Figure 6–38).

In the Contents pop-up menu, select either the Foreground Color, Background Color, Pattern, a saved version of a file, Snapshot, Black, 50% Gray, or White.

In Blending, select the Opacity and fill Mode. The Fill Path command uses the same Mode options available for the painting and editing tools, fills and layer blending. For a description of each mode, see "Layer Options" in the Layers section later in this chapter. If you want to fill a path using the current settings in the Fill Path dialog box, click on the Fill icon at the bottom of the paths palette and the path will automatically fill, bypassing the Fill Path dialog box.

Rendering allows you to choose anti-aliased to eliminate the jaggies and enter a Feather Radius to further soften the edges.

NOTE: If the path has not been saved or if only some of the points on the path are selected, the pop-up menu will read Fill Subpath and Stroke Subpath.

Stroke Path: Click on a path in the list and select Stroke Path from the pop-up menu to open the Stroke Path dialog box (Figure 6–39). The tools available in the pop-up menu function identically to the toolbox tools with settings controlled in the Brushes and Options palettes. The selected tool will be applied to the path using the attributes associated with that tool (Figure 5–23).

To bypass the Stroke Path dialog box, select a tool, its color and attributes and click on the Stroke path icon at the base of the Paths palette (or drag the path to it). Successive clicks on the icon will build up the opacity and thickness of the stroke.

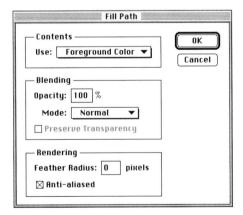

Figure 6–38
The Fill Path options dialog box

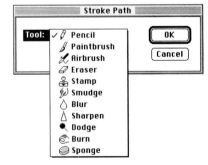

Figure 6–39
The Stroke Path options dialog box showing the available tools

CONVERTING PATHS TO SELECTIONS

Any path can be converted to a selection. A selected path can also be combined with or subtracted from a selected area.

To convert a path to a selection, click on it in the list and choose Make Selection from the pop-up menu. The Make Selection dialog box will open (Figure 6–40). Enter a Feather Radius and choose Anti-aliased to eliminate the jaggies.

TIP: To instantly convert a path to a selection, click on the path in the list and then press the Enter key on the numeric keypad or drag it to the Make Selection icon.

If you want to combine a converted path with a selection, select an area prior to choosing the Make Selection command. The dialog box will give you four options in the Operation area to define how the path and the current selection will combine to create a new selection. These options function the same as the Command and Shift keys when combining selections with the selection tools (Figure 6–6).

New Selection disregards the current selection and makes a new selection.

Add to Selection adds the path shape to the current selection.

Subtract from Selection subtracts the path shape from the current selection.

Intersect with Selection makes a selection only in areas where the current selection and the path overlap.

Figure 6–40   The Make Selection dialog box allows various ways to combine a path with an existing selection. In this case, the figure on the left is subtracted from the selection (See "Night Scene," by Adam Cohen, Figure 6–65).

CLIPPING PATHS

A clipping path saved with a document creates a mask that silhouettes the area inside the path against a transparent background (area outside of the path) when the Photoshop document is placed in an Illustration or page layout program such as Adobe Illustrator, Macromedia FreeHand, AdobePageMaker, or QuarkXPress. The silhouetted image can then be placed in front of other elements such as type, images, patterns, or a solid color (Figure 6–41).

Convert a saved path to a clipping path by selecting Clipping Path from the pop-up menu. The Clipping Path dialog box opens, allowing you to select the desired Path and Flatness setting (Figure 6–42).

Choose the Path to use as the mask from the Path pop-up menu. Its name then appears in outline type in the Paths palette list (Figure 6–32). It will also appear in the Paths pop-up menu when you save the file in the EPS format.

NOTE: **You can specify to include a clipping path with a file in either the Paths palette pop-up menu or in the Paths pop-up menu in the EPS Format dialog box that appears when saving a file in the EPS file format.**

The Flatness setting for clipping paths refers to the smoothness of the curves (created by short straight line segments) in the final output. A lower Flatness value creates shorter line segments, resulting in a smoother curve.

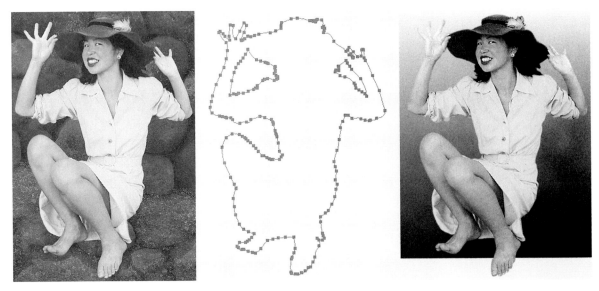

Figure 6–41   The model on the left was traced with the pen tool and then the path (center) was saved as a Clipping Path. The image was placed into Illustrator (right) against a blended background. (© Mark Siprut)

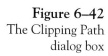

Figure 6–42
The Clipping Path
dialog box

You can enter a number from 0.2 to 100, but for high-resolution printing a maximum Flatness setting of 8 should be adequate. Use a setting below 3 for low resolution output. Leave the Flatness field blank to use a printer's default setting

TIP: To see the effects of a clipping path, the document must be saved as an EPS file and placed into another program such as Adobe Illustrator, Macromedia FreeHand, Adobe PageMaker, or QuarkXPress.

When saving the document with a clipping path for use in another program, use the EPS file format. More information on saving EPS files can be found in Chapter 11, "Output."

CAUTION: Clipping paths can cause printing problems typically associated with vector graphics. A limit check error may indicate a path too complex to print. To avoid this problem create paths with as few anchor points as possible and a higher Flatness setting. Printing to an older imagesetter might require the Even Odd plug-in included with Photoshop. Refer to the Read Me file with the plug-in for more information.

Layers

Layers new with Photoshop 3, maintain image data in a state of suspended space, similar to stacking images on sheets of film or acetate on top of each other. Layers contain actual portions of the document that exist independent of the background and of one another but appear as one homogenous layer on the screen or printed page. Placing image elements on separate layers without committing to merging pixels allows you to increase your productivity and creativity over previous versions of Photoshop.

Layers in an image could have many functions:

- You can composite images from different sources over each other without committing to their exact positions. Each element on a different layer can always be moved independently.
- When combining (pasting) two or more images onto each other, you can experiment with opacity, modes, blending, dynamic effects, posi-

tion, scale, brightness, contrast, and filter effects using layers without affecting the underlying layer.

- Duplicate or copy the actual data in the background to a new layer, apply various effects, and recombine at various Opacity or Mode settings.

- Place type on separate layers for drop shadows or special effects.

Working with Layers

Because the layers are independent (not a part of the background), they allow you to rethink and update your work as often as you like. You can move, color correct, retouch, create, recomposite, and reorder the layers as many times as necessary. Photoshop allows 99 layers plus the background, but you will probably run out of memory space before you run out of layers.

To work with and control the layers in a document you must have the Layers palette open (Figure 6–43). Open the Layers palette from the Palettes submenu under the Window menu. It's a good idea to keep it open at all times.

Although you can view more than one layer at a time, only one layer can be active at a time. The active layer, highlighted in the Layers palette with white on the Macintosh and gray in Windows is referred to as the *target layer*.

Use the following guidelines when viewing, editing, and moving layers:

- Click on a layer in the list to make it the target layer. You can only edit one layer, the target layer, at a time.

- Keep the Layers palette visible so that you always are aware of the target layer.

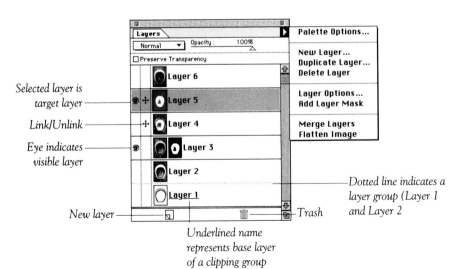

Figure 6–43
The Layers palette

Selected layer is target layer

Link/Unlink

Eye indicates visible layer

New layer

Underlined name represents base layer of a clipping group

Dotted line indicates a layer group (Layer 1 and Layer 2)

Trash

- If you add a new layer, it always appears in the list directly above the target layer, becoming the new target layer.

- To view a layer, click the Eye icon in the left hand column of the Layers palette. If you want to view one layer alone, hold the Option key and click on the desired layer's Eye icon. To make multiple layers visible or invisible in one mouse stroke, press on one of the Eye icons and drag down the column.

- The position of each layer in the Layers palette list determines the order in which the layers are stacked. The layer at the top is the uppermost layer of the document. Layers can be moved up and down in the list by dragging them to a new position. Be sure that you see a line appear between the layers before you release the mouse.

- If you want to move layers as a group, click in the second column of the Layers palette on any layers that you want to link with the target layer. A small version of the Move tool icon will appear in the column, linking the layers. You can then move the target layer along with any linked layers with the Move tool. Linked layers are useful with drop shadows and clipping groups.

- When viewing a layer without the background layer, transparent areas will display with a checkerboard pattern.

- Adding layers adds to the size and memory requirements of a file, but only by areas in layers that contain data. A layer with more transparent areas uses less memory then does a layer with more pixel data.

- Layers always have the same color mode and resolution as the background of the image.

Creating and Deleting Layers

In the Layers palette you can create new layers, duplicate layers, convert selections to layers and delete layers. In the Edit menu you can paste the clipboard into a new layer.

NEW LAYER

To create a new layer, choose New Layer from the pop-up menu or click on the New Layer icon at the bottom of the Layers palette. The New Layer dialog box opens and allows you to name the layer, set the blending mode, and group the layer with the previous layer. Group With Previous Layer is not available if the previous layer is the Background Layer.

Many effects and filters will not work on empty layers. The Fill With Neutral Color option allows you to fill the layer so you can apply effects to the layer. If no effects are applied to the layer the fill will not affect the overall image. The neutral color varies depending on the mode. Some modes, such as Normal, Hue, Saturation, Color, and Luminosity do not have a neutral color so this option is not available. For more information on modes see the "Layer Options" section and Figure C–1 in the Color Section. For more information on modes and neutral colors when combining images and applying special effects see Chapter 10, "Compositing."

Layers can also be dragged from one open document to another open document by clicking on the name of the layer in the list and dragging it over another document. When the layer is over the new document, the border of the document is highlighted, signaling that you can drop the layer. In the new document, the new layer comes in above the previous target layer and retains the name it had in the source document.

DUPLICATE A LAYER

To duplicate a layer, click on it in the list and choose Duplicate Layer from the pop-up menu or drag it to the New Layer icon.

FLOATING SELECTIONS AS LAYERS

To convert a floating selection to a layer, choose Make Layer from the pop-up menu, click on the New Layer icon or double-click on the floating selection's name in the list.

PASTE LAYER

Use the Paste Layer command under the Edit menu to paste the clipboard image directly into a new layer. The Make Layer dialog box will appear with options to name the layer, set the Opacity and Mode and Group With Previous Layer.

DELETING LAYERS

Click on the layer in the list and choose Delete Layer from the pop-up menu or drag the layer to the Trash icon at the bottom of the Layer palette.

Layer Transparency and Masks

Areas in a layer can be entirely transparent. A visible layer without the background showing will display a checkerboard pattern representing the transparent areas. To change the color or frequency of the checkerboard pattern choose Transparency Options, a submenu of Preferences under the File menu (see Figure 5–19).

In addition to the transparent quality, you can use the transparent areas in a layer as a mask and you also can create a custom mask to define the transparent areas of each layer.

TRANSPARENCY MASK

Each layer has a transparency "mask" associated with the transparent areas. To activate the mask while working on a layer, click the Preserve Transparency option. Any painting, editing, manipulating, filtering, or pasting will affect the image areas of the layer, leaving only the transparent areas untouched (see Figure 5–20).

Use the transparent areas as a mask to create an active selection in the target layer by choosing Load Selection from the Select menu, opening the Load Selection dialog box. Choose the Layer's Transparency from the Channel pop-up menu. Click OK and the image areas in the layer will become an active selection (Figure 6–44). A shortcut to load the image areas as a selection is to press the Command, Option, and T keys simultaneously.

LAYER MASK

A Layer Mask is an 8 bit grayscale channel attached to a layer that defines or customizes the transparent areas of the layer. To create a Layer Mask, click on the layer in the list and choose Add Layer Mask from the pop-up menu. A thumbnail icon will appear next to the layer icon with a highlighted black border (Figure 6–45).

With the Layer Mask icon highlighted, any editing will affect the layer mask. Click on the Layer icon (left) to edit the imagery on the layer. Double-click on the Layer Mask icon to open the Layer Mask Options dialog box (Figure 6–46).

The Layer Mask Options dialog box allows you to set how the mask will affect the transparent areas of a layer. Choose Hidden Areas if you want the color to indicate transparent areas. If you choose Visible Areas the color will

Figure 6–44
The transparent areas of a layer create a mask. Load the image areas of a Layer as a selection by choosing the Load Selection command.

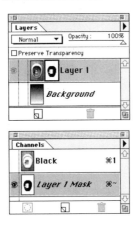
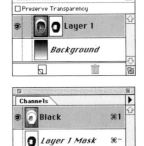

Figure 6–45
The Layers palette shows a layer and its Layer Mask, and the Channels palette shows the channel for the Layer Mask. On the left is the Layer Mask channel. In the center is the Layer showing the transparent area created by the Layer Mask. On the right, the background shows through the transparent area.

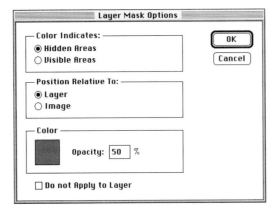

Figure 6–46
The Layer Mask Options dialog box

Figure 6–47
When discarding a Layer
Mask, click the Apply
button to apply it
permanently to the layer.

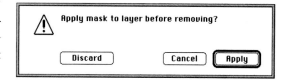

indicate non-transparent image areas. In the Position Relative To section, choose Layer to link the position of the mask to the layer when the layer is moved. Choose Image to allow the layer to be moved independently of the mask. The Color box allows you to set the color and transparency of the mask. If you click on Do not Apply to Layer, the mask will not affect the layer until the Layer mask is removed. A red X will appear over the Layer Mask icon. Holding the Command key and clicking on the Layer Mask icon will also temporarily turn off the mask.

Once your transparency is correct, you can apply the layer mask to make the transparency permanent by choosing Remove Layer Mask from the pop-up menu or by dragging the Layer Mask icon to the Trash icon. You will be given the option to Apply the Layer Mask or discard it (Figure 6–47).

To view the Layer mask as you edit it, click in the left column of the Layer Mask channel in the Channels palette to display an Eye icon. In the default mode, painting with black will add to the mask indicating transparent areas. Painting with white or with the Eraser tool subtracts from the mask, adding to the image areas. See the "Channels and Masking" section of this chapter for more information on working with channels.

CLIPPING GROUPS

By grouping layers, the transparent areas of the lowest layer will mask the image in all of the layers above it as a group. To define a clipping group, double-click on the layer that you want to be masked or select Layer Options from the pop-up menu and choose the Group With Previous Layer checkbox. The transparent areas of the underlying layer will mask the upper layer. As a shortcut, make sure the layer you want masked is directly above the masking layer, hold the Option key and click on the dividing line between the two layers. In a Clipping Group, the bottom layer name (the masking layer) is underlined and the dividing line between it and the masked layer appears as a thin dotted line (Figure 6–48). Add as many layers as desired (up to 99) to the clipping group. The background cannot be the basis of a clipping group because the background is, by definition, unmasked.

Figure 6–48
The original composite
of two layers on the left
was converted to a
clipping group on the
right, allowing the
background to show
through the transparent
area. The Layers palette
on the right shows the
clipping group.
(© Mark Siprut)

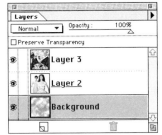

Layer Options

Layer Options in the Layers pop-up menu opens a dialog box to control the interaction between the pixels of a layer and the pixels of any visible layers below it. When composited, the pixels of the two images combine using the numerous options and settings (Figure 6–49).

The transparency of layers can be modified by using the slider at the top of the Layers palette or in the Layer Options dialog box. The blending modes of the layer which function the same as the fill and paint modes can

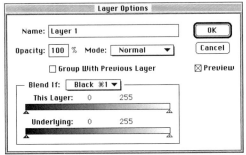

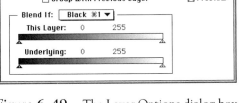

Figure 6–49   The Layer Options dialog box

also be changed by the pop-up menu at the top of the Layers palette or in the Layers palette. The Blend If: sliders control which tones of the selected layer blend with tones of the Underlying Layer. Grouping layers to create clipping groups was discussed in the previous section, "Clipping Groups."

NOTE: Filling a layer with a neutral color for the applicable modes is only an option when creating a new layer.

WORKING WITH LAYER OPTIONS

To apply Layer Options to a layer, click on the layer in the list and select Layer Options from the pop-up menu or double-click on the layer icon. Select the Preview button to see any modifications prior to committing the change to the image.

Layer Options affects the color or channel specified in the Blend If pop-up menu and the value range specified between the triangles in the upper (This Layer) slider in relation to the value range specified in the Underlying slider. Only active channels appear in the Blend If pop-up menu. The Gray option controls all colors in an image.

The sliders determine the values of the selected layer and the underlying image that will be affected. The full range of tones varies from 0 (black) to 255 (white). The space between the triangles determines which pixels will be changed. Pixels with values outside of the specified range will not be affected.

NOTE: When you paste a selection into a layer pay attention to the mode and opacity of the layer. The mode and opacity of the target layer will affect how the pasted selection will combine with other layers.

Opacity sets the transparency of the layer. A higher number makes the upper layer more opaque while a lower number makes it more transparent.

TIP: To quickly change the Opacity setting of a layer without using the Layer Options or Opacity slider in the Layers palette, type a number on the numeric key-pad of an extended keyboard: 1 equals 10%, 5 equals 50%, and 0 equals 100%.

Mode determines how pixels of the current layer will combine or blend with pixels of the underlying layer. These modes function the same as the modes available in the Fill dialog box and in the Options palette for painting tools. See Figure C–1 in the Color Section.

LAYER OPTIONS EXAMPLES

Use the following exercises to view the effects of the Opacity, Mode options and blending sliders. The examples focus on grayscale combina-

Figure 6–50   Create a blend on the background layer and posterize the bottom half (second from left). On a new layer draw a circle and fill it with a radial blend (third from left). Use this combination (right) for the following exercises.

tions, but once you understand the issues you can go through the exercises, substituting various colors for the upper and lower layers.

1. Create a new square grayscale document and fill it with a linear blend from black to white using the Gradient tool.

2. Select the bottom half with the Rectangular Marquee and choose the Posterize command, a submenu of Map under the Image menu. Set the posterization to 11 steps (Figure 6–50, left).

3. Make a new layer and draw a circle with the Elliptical Marquee. Using the Gradient tool create a radial blend from white in the center to black at the edge (Figure 6–50, center).

4. Choose Layer Options from the pop-up menu. Make sure the Preview box is selected. Use this configuration to test and explore the various options in the following examples. After each exercise, return the settings to the original default positions.

Opacity: Try various Opacity settings between 1 and 100% (Figure 6–51). Lower percentage numbers make Layer 1 more transparent and higher numbers make it more opaque.

Figure 6–51
A 60% Opacity setting applied to Layer 1 (left), a 30% Opacity setting applied to the Layer 1 (center,) and a 10% Opacity setting applied to the Layer 1 (right)

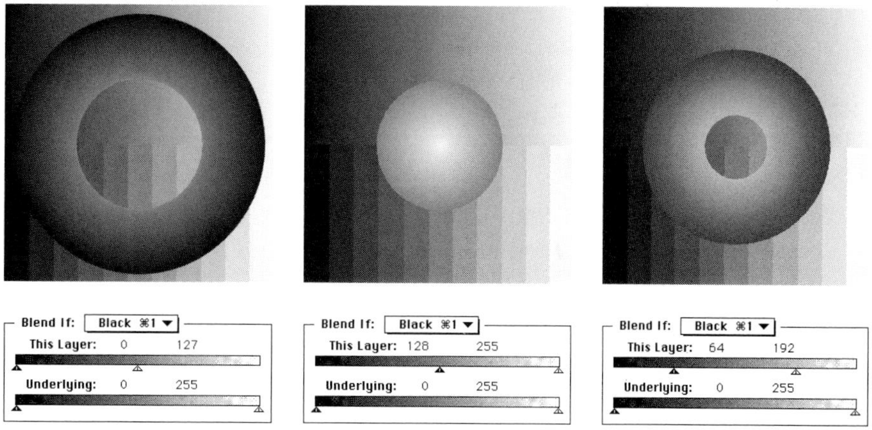

Figure 6–52
Setting the slider for Layer 1. Only values between the triangles will show when combined with the background.

This Layer: Experiment with the This Layer slider (Layer 1) by moving it to various positions.

1. Move the right triangle to middle gray (127). Only values between black (0) and middle gray (127) of Layer 1 will be visible over the Underlying layer (Figure 6–52, left).

2. Move the right triangle back to its original position (255) and move the left triangle to middle gray (128). Only values between middle gray (128) and white (255) of Layer 1 will be visible over the Underlying layer (Figure 6–52, center).

3. Move the left triangle to dark gray (64) and the right triangle to light gray (192). Only values between dark gray (64) and light gray (192) of Layer 1 will be visible over the Underlying layer (Figure 6–52, right).

4. Repeat the above steps, but this time hold the Option key and drag the inner triangle in to the specified positions. You will see a similar effect, with the exception of a blend of tones between the split triangles (Figure 6–53).

Underlying: Experiment with the Underlying slider by moving it to various positions.

1. Move the right triangle to middle gray (127). The values between black (0) and middle gray (127) of the Underlying image will be changed to the pixels values of Layer 1 (Figure 6–54, left).

2. Return the right triangle to its original position and move the left triangle to middle gray (128). The values between middle gray (128) and white (255) of the Underlying image will be changed to the pixel values of Layer 1 (Figure 6–54, center).

Figure 6–53
Setting the slider for
Layer 1. Only values
between the triangles
will show when
combined with the
background. Values
between the split
triangles will blend.

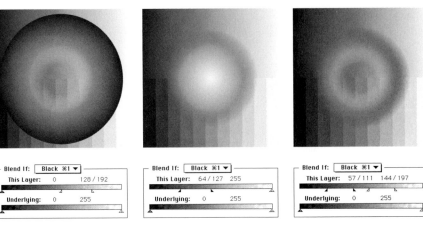

Figure 6–54
Setting the slider for the
Underlying Layer. Only
values between the
triangles will be changed
when combined with
Layer 1.

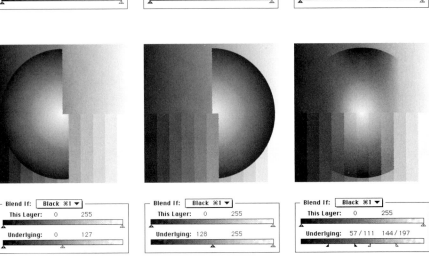

3. Move the left triangle to dark gray (64) and the right triangle to light gray (192). The values between dark gray (64) and light gray (192) of the Underlying image will be changed to the pixel values of Layer 1 (Figure 6–54, right).

4. Do the above exercise again holding the Option key and dragging the inner triangle in to the specified positions. You will see a similar effect with the exception of a blend of tones between the split triangles (Figure 6–55).

Mode: Choose the various Mode options to learn how the pixels of Layer 1 change or combine with the Underlying layer (Figure 6–56). Shown are Modes that work in black and white: Dissolve (at 50% Opacity), Multiply, Screen, Overlay, Soft Light, Hard Light, Darken, Lighten and Difference. The choices in the Mode pop-up menu function the same as those available

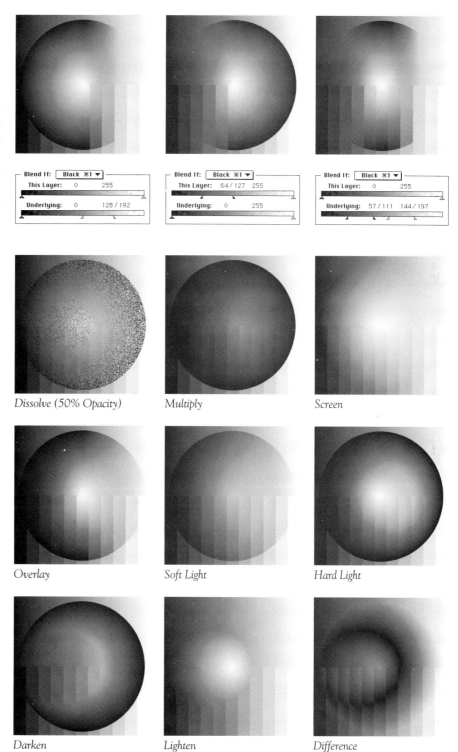

Figure 6–55
Examples of setting the slider for the Underlying Layer. Only values between the triangles will be changed when combined with Layer 1. Values between the split triangles will blend.

Dissolve (50% Opacity)   *Multiply*   *Screen*

Overlay   *Soft Light*   *Hard Light*

Figure 6–56
Examples of blending modes

Darken   *Lighten*   *Difference*

for the painting tools and the Fill command. See Chapter 5, "Tools and Palettes," for an explanation of each of the modes and the example Figure C–1 in the Color Section.

Merging Layers

To keep file sizes down as much as possible, merge layers that are final in their relationship to one another. To merge layers, click the Eye icons on the Layers palette to make only the desired layers visible. Choose Merge Layers from the pop-up menu. Layers not visible will remain intact.

Flatten Layers allows you to merge all visible layers and throw the other layers away at the same time. All file formats except the Photoshop 3 format require flattened documents. Therefore, documents with layers must be flattened before saving in another format. Otherwise, save in the Photoshop 3 format.

Channels and Masking

When a selection is made it creates a mask. Any manipulation takes place only within the selection's boundaries. Use selections to isolate certain areas of an image to paint, apply color changes, filters, or any other image processing command. To use a selection at a later time, save it as a channel. When activated, a channel becomes a normal selection.

Channels

Although any selection in an image is a temporary mask, a selection converted to a channel can be saved with an image file for later use. Use channels to isolate and mask parts of an image (Figure 6–57), to overlap shapes, to collage various images, and to apply image processing effects to specific areas. A channel, sometimes referred to as an alpha channel, can be viewed or edited by activating it in the Channels palette (Figure 6–58). Open the Channels palette by choosing the Palettes submenu under the Window menu.

NOTE: Don't get channels and layers confused. In general use channels for masking components of an image. Use layers for the actual components of the image.

Figure 6–57
The channel on the right was used as a mask to isolate the baby from the background.
(© Joseph Tracey)

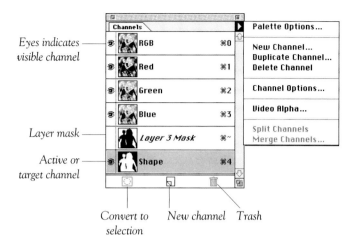

Eyes indicates
visible channel

Layer mask

Active or
target channel

Figure 6–58
The Channels palette

Convert to   New channel   Trash
selection

As introduced in Chapter 1, all Photoshop documents (except for Grayscale and Bitmapped) consist of multiple channels, each of which is an 8-bit image. In the RGB Color mode, you can create and edit full 24-bit color pictures because the image is actually made up of three 8-bit channels, red, green, and blue. When viewed as a composite image, these RGB layers display the full spectrum of visible colors. Photoshop can work with documents containing up to 24 channels. In a 24-bit RGB image, three channels are occupied (for the RGB layers), leaving 21 channels that can be used for masking and special effects. A document in CMYK Color mode uses four channels, one each for cyan, magenta, yellow, and black, leaving 20 channels available for other uses.

NOTE: Channels use memory. Each new channel is equal in size to an existing channel. In a grayscale document, adding a channel doubles the size of the file. In an RGB image, each channel occupies one-third of the document's size. Each channel maintains the resolution of the main image.

Channels can be combined in various ways by using the Apply Image and Calculations commands under the Image menu. Refer to Chapter 10, "Compositing," for information on combining images, channels, and layers.

CREATING AND USING CHANNELS

Create a new blank channel by choosing New Channel from the pop-up menu in the Channels palette or by clicking on the New Channel icon at the foot of the palette. The Channel Options dialog box will appear (Figure 6–59). You can also create a new channel by making a selection with any of the selection tools and choosing Save Selection under the

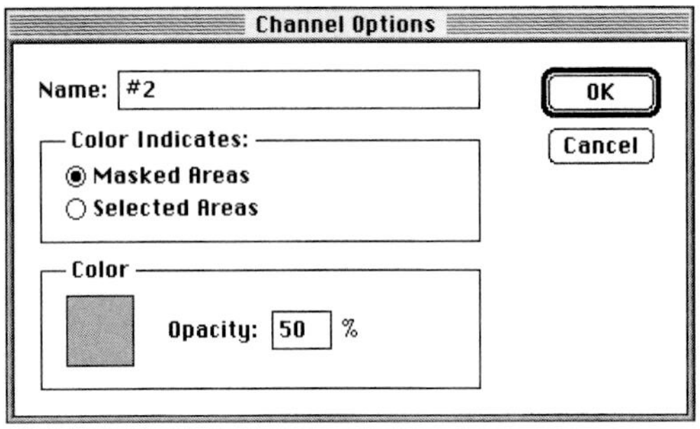

Figure 6–59
The Channel Options
dialog box

Select menu, or by clicking on the Convert to Selection icon. Use any tool, filter, or command that works in the Grayscale mode in a channel.

To view, edit, or manipulate a channel, click on it in the Channels palette or use its keyboard command (next to the channel number). When a channel is visible on the screen, an Eye icon is visible in the far left column. To make any channel invisible, click on the Eye icon for its channel. To edit a channel, click on its name and it will turn gray on a Macintosh and white in Windows. Any number of channels can be viewed or modified simultaneously. You can even view one channel while modifying another.

TIP: Be careful to view and edit the desired channels. It is easy to accidentally manipulate a channel other than the one viewed.

The pop-up menu in the Channels palette allows you to delete channels, set channel options, split and merge channels, and even copy a channel to a 32-bit video card.

DELETE CHANNEL

To delete a channel, click on it in the Channels palette list and choose Delete Channel from the pop-up menu or drag it to the Trash icon at the bottom of the palette.

CHANNEL OPTIONS

The Channel Options dialog box appears when you create a new channel, by clicking on a channel in the list and choosing Channel Options or by double-clicking on the channel name in the list (Figure 6–58). The dialog box allows you to name channels, select what color indicates either a masked area or a selected area, and to set the opacity of the channel's color.

QUICK MASK MODE

The Quick Mask mode generates a temporary channel that allows you to instantly see both your working image and the mask (temporary channel) at the same time. Quick Mask is the fastest method of generating a channel from a selection. The Quick Mask can be edited and then instantly returned to a selection, or it can be saved as a normal channel with the image.

To create a Quick Mask, make a selection with any selection tool or command and click on the Quick Mask icon in the toolbox. The selection instantly transforms to a transparent mask over the image and appears in the Channels palette list as a "Quick mask." The name in italics will remind you that it is a temporary channel (with all the properties of a normal channel).

To convert the Quick Mask to a normal channel, click on it in the list and select Duplicate Channel from the pop-up menu or drag it to the New channel icon. It will appear as a new duplicate channel with the Quick Mask still active.

Double-click on the Quick Mask icon in the toolbox or the Quick Mask channel in the Channels palette, or choose Quick Mask Options in the Channels pop-up menu to open the Quick Mask Options dialog box, which is identical to the Channel options dialog box (Figure 6–58). The specified color shows either the selected areas or the masked areas. The default overlay color, red (similar to a rubylith), masks the image, and the clear areas represent the selection (editable) area.

VIDEO ALPHA COMMAND

The Video Alpha command in the pop-up menu allows you to copy a channel into the extra 8 bits provided by a 32-bit video card that supports the use of an alpha channel. Use an alpha channel to control the transparency of an image when combining it with a video source.

NOTE: **Video Alpha command only applies to video cards that are made to handle an alpha channel.**

SPLIT CHANNELS

The Split Channels command in the pop-up menu separates all the channels in a document into individual grayscale documents, each of which can then be edited and saved under its own name.

Figure 6–60
Specify mode and number of channels in the Merge Channels dialog box.

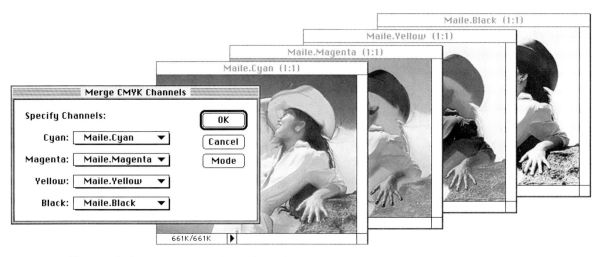

Figure 6–61   The Merge dialog box allows you to specify which channel each document will become.

MERGE CHANNELS

Choose Merge Channels in the pop-up menu to convert up to four separate grayscale documents into channels of a single file. A dialog box appears in which to specify the Mode from a pop-up menu and the number of channels (Figure 6–60). If you enter a number other than the number of channels that compose a color mode, the Multichannel mode will become the only option. Click OK and the next Merge Channels dialog box allows you to choose an open document for each channel (Figure 6–61).

NOTE: **All documents that you want to merge into a single file must be open, exactly the same size and resolution, and in Grayscale mode with no extra channels.**

Masking Examples

"NIGHT SCENE" BY ADAM COHEN

Adam Cohen, a digital illustrator, used several masking techniques to produce "Night Scene." He drew paths around the elements and saved the paths to use them as selections. After converting paths to selections to mask areas, Cohen used various painting tools to define the forms (Figure 6–62). After

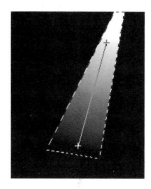

Figure 6–62
After converting the path to a selection, Cohen used the Airbrush tool to define the figure.

Figure 6–63
After selecting an area for the light beam, it was saved as a channel.

Figure 6–64
A Linear blend was applied to the channel with the Gradient tool.

selecting the areas for the light beams, he saved them as channels (Figure 6–63). Linear blends were applied to each channel with the Gradient tool (Figure 6–64). The channels were loaded as selections, feathered, and then lightened with the Brightness/Contrast command (Figure 6-65).

NOTE: Cohen warns that filling a channel with a blend leaves white edges which usually need touching up.

"LEONARDO PIX" BY KAI KRAUSE

Kai Krause, a Photoshop master, demonstrates some of the complexities of image selection and masking in "Leonardo Pix" (Figure C–25 in the Color Section).

Krause started with a small scan of Leonardo da Vinci's famous study of anatomy (Figure 6–66). He created a duplicate copy to a second channel on which he applied the Levels command to whiten outside shades and darken inside shades to black. With some retouching this black mask channel made it easier to isolate, manipulate, and compose the final figure on to any background.

In experimenting with images, Krause recommends that you "let yourself be guided by the process—let it come back to surprise you all by itself!

Figure 6–65
Several masking
techniques were used to
create "Night Scene."
(© Adam Cohen)

Rather than trying to achieve a pre-contemplated effect, be open to merely steering the path of the process and with complex combinations of the elements it will reach completely unexpected results. To that end, first create a number of ingredients to work with: a plain mask, maybe several shrunken or expanded sharp masks, blurred copies which can be blended, outlines, shadows, highlights, depthy curvature, and maybe some preferred textures or scans. Then plug and play with the elements, or rather plug and pray you have enough time and disk space to see it all and keep all the good stuff. . . ."

Figure 6–66   Krause started with a drawing by Leonardo da Vinci. The mask isolated the figure from the background. Then Levels, Curves, and filters were applied to distort the image.

Summary

- A selection masks an area so that manipulations affect only the inside of the selection.
- Save selections as channels or paths to be retrieved in the future.
- Create vignettes or seamlessly blend images with the Feather command.
- The blend Modes function the same in each paint tool's Options palette, Fill command, and Layer Options.
- For precise, careful selections use the Pen tool or the Quick Mask mode.
- To select areas by color or tone use the Magic Wand tool or Color Range command.
- Moving a selection deletes the background unless you duplicate or float the selection. Deselecting a selection merges it with the target layer.
- Keep the Layers palette open at all times. You can only work on one layer at a time, the target layer. Be careful not to accidentally work on one layer while viewing another.
- When working with channels, keep the Channels palette open at all times. You can edit and view any combination of channels at one time. Be careful not to accidentally alter one channel while viewing another.
- Save solid shapes as paths because they use less memory.
- To silhouette a Photoshop image when placed in another program use a clipping path.

- The transparent areas of a layer are automatically a mask: Turn on the mask in the Layers palette with the Preserve Transparency button, load the mask with the Layer Mask command in the pop-up menu, load the transparency as a selection with the Load Selection command, or mask with the transparent areas by creating a clipping group.

- Only the Photoshop 3 format will retain layers. To save in other formats you must flatten the document.

For more information on combining images with layers, channels, calculations, and other programs, see Chapter 10, "Compositing." The next chapter focuses on how to process and manipulate your selections.

7

Image Processing

Image processing can mean many things. Scientists use image processing to analyze images to "see" things that are not immediately apparent. Prepress professionals use image processing to make color and tone corrections on images. Photographers and artists use image processing functions and techniques to creatively manipulate images.

This chapter discusses several controls to change, or process, images in Photoshop found under the Image menu. These controls include the Map commands, Adjust commands, Flip, Rotate, Effects, Image Size, Canvas Size, and Histogram.

Some of the image processing commands are demonstrated in Figure 7–1. After cropping the original photograph (left) with the Canvas Size command, and the easel paintings were selected, enlarged, and distorted with the Scale and Distort commands. The tones in the foreground were brightened with the Curves command; the background tones were subdued with the Levels command. To add depth the background was softened with the Gaussian Blur filter while the foreground was sharpened with the Unsharp Mask filter. When completed the high-resolution file was resized to the proper resolution to be printed in this book, using the Image Size command.

Commands that combine or move documents, layers, and channels (Duplicate, Apply Image, and Calculations) are discussed in Chapter 10, "Compositing." Other image processing controls include the Sharpen/Blur and Dodge/Burn/Sponge tools (discussed in Chapter 5, "Tools and Palettes") and Filters (discussed in Chapter 9, "Filters and Plug-ins").

The "Adjusting Tones" section of this chapter focuses on value adjustments without regard to color. The commands that apply to color controls are discussed in Chapter 8, "Color."

Figure 7–1   The original image on the left was processed through a variety of commands to create the final version on the right: the Scale and Distort commands on the easel with the paintings, Curves and Levels to adjust contrast and brightness, and the Gaussian Blur and Unsharp Mask filters to soften the background and sharpen the foreground. (© Mark Siprut)

Image Processing Guidelines

Photoshop's image processing controls have a number of common features:

- If a selection is active, all of the image processing controls, except the Image Size and Canvas Size commands, affect only the selected area. If nothing is selected, a command may affect either the entire target layer or the entire image. For example, the Rotate command rotates an entire document if nothing is selected, while the Levels command affects only the target layer.

  TIP: Because image processing affects only the target layer, you must merge layers or flatten the document if you want to affect more than one layer. Once you merge or flatten the layers and apply effects, you cannot return to the original layers. If you want to apply an effect to multiple layers but keep the layers separate, apply the identical command to each of the layers individually.

- Many of the image-processing control dialog boxes have Preview buttons. Click on the Preview button to see the changes exclusively in the currently active document or selection area. By using the Preview button, you can experiment with different effects without leaving the dialog box. Some filters have a small preview within their dialog boxes.

TIP: Make a quick comparison of a manipulation to the original by applying the color adjustment, value change, or filter effect to a small selected area. Select Undo to get back to the original.

- The current document's Scroll Bars, Hand, and Zoom tools are active in an image-processing dialog box. You can scroll around a document and zoom into an area to see the effects of an image-processing change without closing the dialog box.

- When you move the cursor over an active document, the Show Info palette displays readouts of color values and cursor position.

- Cancel settings made in a dialog box without closing it by holding the Option key and clicking on the Cancel button (which changes to a Reset button). Some filters do not have a Reset option.

- If you run Photoshop on a black-and-white Macintosh, most of the map and adjustment controls are not interactive; you must use the Preview command to see the changes made. Although you cannot see color, you can work with it on a black-and-white system by interpreting numerical color values.

- If you turn on Video LUT Animation in the General Preferences dialog box, all open Photoshop documents will show changes in real time (except for filters), if the Preview button in the command you're using is deselected. If Video LUT animation is off, no changes will be visible unless the Preview button is selected.

TIP: If you use a 24-bit or 32-bit video card and have problems with previews, try resetting the Monitors control in the Control Panels. Click another display mode and then reselect the desired mode. Video LUT in the General Preferences also should be deselected.

TIP: Before pressing the Preview button after changing a slider or other control, you can do a quick before-and-after comparison of the change by pressing on the Title Bar of the control dialog box (with Video LUT Animation on). The screen will temporarily revert to the normal, unaffected display mode.

- To apply identical color corrections or value adjustments to a number of images, use the Save and Load features in many of the image-processing dialog boxes. Save settings by clicking the Save button and then name them. To apply the settings to the same command in another document, click the Load button in the dialog box to locate and apply the settings.

TIP: To automate repetitive work to an even greater extent, check out software that allows you to record a series of keystrokes to perform a function. For example, PhotoMatic from DayStar records a series of events as a script which can then be performed on other images automatically. QuicKeys from CE Software, Inc., provides a number of options to speed through repetitive work. If you have many images that require the same types of color corrections and tone adjustments, try DeBabelizer from Equilibrium Technologies. This helpful program facilitates batch processing of multiple documents.

CAUTION: Do not trust your monitor for color and tone adjustment unless you have calibrated your system. See Chapter 3, "Configuring Photoshop," for instructions on calibration.

Overview of Image Processing

Let's say you get a scan and it's less than perfect. For some reason you cannot rescan the image, so you have no choice but to use Photoshop's image processing tools for tone and color corrections. Or maybe the scan is perfect, but the original is flawed or damaged. Or maybe you just want to manipulate the image somehow. Following is a brief overview of the various tools and techniques you might apply to improve an image's quality.

CAUTION: The best quality image will usually be realized by making corrections at the scanning stage. Once a scan is complete, Photoshop has a fixed amount of data with which to work.

- **Identify the Image Type**—Analyze the tones and colors in an image with the Histogram and the Info palette. The Histogram graphically represents the tones in an image. The Info palettes displays readouts of colors and tones for the position of the cursor over the image.
- **Adjust the Tones**—Photoshop has several tools for altering the tones or density of a file. The quickest and simplest methods are the Equalize, Brightness/Contrast, or the Auto Levels commands. You can achieve more control over tonal adjustments, however, with the Levels or Curves commands, which offer precise control of highlights, midtones, and shadows.
- **Correct the Color**—Photoshop has numerous tools and commands for altering the color balance of images. They range from simple tools for minor corrections (Color Balance) to those that control specific colors in an image (Selective Color).
- **Remove Defects**—Use the Despeckle filter to remove the screening effect found in pre-printed material or the unwanted grain in a photograph. (Be aware that previously printed artwork is most likely

copyrighted material!) Photoshop 3's Dust and Scratches filter removes imperfections, dust, scratches and damage automatically. Use the Rubber Stamp tool to clone over defective parts of the image, replacing unwanted pixels with neighboring pixels. Occasionally you may want to blur parts of an image to remove defects, suggest movement or distance/perspective, or to emphasize the non-blurred areas.

- **Manipulate the Image**—This is your chance to be creative. Select parts of an image to scale, skew, rotate, or duplicate. Copy and paste other images to create composites. Apply special effect filters to all or parts of the image.

- **Set the Resolution and Size**—The actual resolution of a file is determined at the scan stage. The best image quality and quickest results will be achieved if the correct size and resolution of a file is set when scanning an image. Sometimes, however, Photoshop must be used to resize or resample a scanned image. Each different output device and printing method may require a different resolution. Use the Image Size command to resize or change resolution.

- **Sharpening**—Most scanned images require some degree of sharpening. The most common way to sharpen a file is to use the Unsharp Mask filter. The degree of sharpening is determined by the final output method. Although you may think you can't over-sharpen a file, such a file may reproduce worse than an original file with no sharpening.

CAUTION: Using the monitor to judge the degree of sharpening can be deceiving because undoing an applied sharpen effect makes an image seem relatively too soft.

Adjusting Tones

A primary aspect of image processing is adjusting the tones and colors in an image. Before adjusting colors, you should first learn how to adjust tones, because an RGB color image is really just three grayscale documents on top of each other, one each for red, green, and blue. Once you have a handle on tone adjustments, move on to Chapter 8, "Color."

To adjust tones in an image, first analyze the actual pixel data, then use the proper command to make the adjustment.

CAUTION: Every time you use a command to adjust the values in an image, you are changing the actual pixel data. Repeated applications will deteriorate an image.

Examining the Image Data

Before you start adjusting the tones and colors of an image that appear wrong on your monitor, analyze the actual pixel data. The Histogram gives you an overall visual graph of the distribution of values of your image. The Info palette gives you specific readouts for any area of your image.

The meaning of the values in the various dialog boxes can be confusing. No matter what mode you are working in, the monitor projects values of Red, Green, and Blue. If you working in grayscale, you can use either percentage values from 100% (black) to 0% (white) or levels values from 0 (black) to 255 (white). Sometimes only one of these options is available and you will have to cross reference. For example, the Levels dialog box uses level values, but you may want to make an adjustment based on a percentage value. Use Table 7–1 to cross reference grayscale values.

NOTE: The values in the Table 7–1 are true if you have Use Dot Gain for Grayscale Images turned off in the Printing Inks Setup preferences dialog box under the File menu. If this option is turned on, levels and RGB values will reflect a compensation for the specified dot gain. Turning on this option means that you want your monitor to display tones as they would print, which means that you have calibrated your monitor. Do not use a dot gain value less than 22%.

THE HISTOGRAM

The Histogram window (Figure 7–2) plots out the distribution of pixels based on their brightness for all visible layers in the current selection or active document (if nothing is selected). Use the Histogram to analyze the tones and colors in an image. Analysis should be made both before and after adjusting tones as a gauge to check for optimum brightness, contrast, and tonal range.

In a color image, the Histogram shows data from all color channels combined if Gray is selected from the Channel pop-up menu. Choose any other color channel from the pop-up menu to view the Histogram for an individual color channel. To view the Histogram for a channel other than a color channel, click on the channel in the Channels palette to make it active

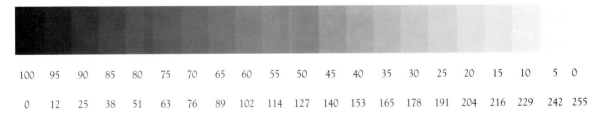

100	95	90	85	80	75	70	65	60	55	50	45	40	35	30	25	20	15	10	5	0
0	12	25	38	51	63	76	89	102	114	127	140	153	165	178	191	204	216	229	242	255

Table 7–1   The upper row of numbers shows percentage values and the lower row shows the equivalent levels or RGB values.

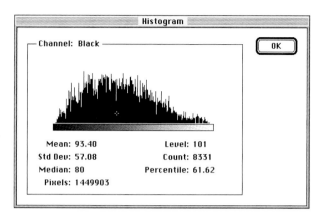

Figure 7–2
The Histogram window
shown with the cursor
selecting a pixel which
activates the Level,
Count, and
Percentile displays.

(the eye icon should be visible) and then open the Histogram window. If you make a selection and then open the Histogram, data from only the selected area will be displayed.

The horizontal axis displays values from black (0) at the left to white (255) at the right. The vertical axis displays the total number of pixels for each value. A dark image typically displays a Histogram with a heavy emphasis on the left side of the graph. Lighter images display uneven balances toward the right side of the graph.

As you move the mouse over the Histogram, the numerical readouts at the lower right inform you of the brightness value (Level), number of pixels (Count), and percentage of pixels less than the Level displayed (Percentile) of the current pointer location.

The information in the lower left refers to brightness values of the entire selected area or document. The Mean takes into account the entire range of values and shows the middle value. The Standard Deviation (Std Dev) displays how much the values in the image vary. The Median gives a middle value. The Pixels value shows the total number of pixels in the selection or document.

TIP: The Histogram shows pixel data for the discernible parts of visible layers only. Areas hidden from view will not affect the Histogram. To evaluate an individual layer, make it the only visible layer.

INFO PALETTE

By moving the cursor around the image, you can get specific pixel values in the Info palette (see Chapter 5, "Tools and Palettes"). The palette can display values in two modes simultaneously by specifying them in the pop-up menu. The two modes are especially useful if you are working in RGB Color mode and will be converting the image to CMYK Color mode. By reading specific areas, you can determine if localized tone or color correction is necessary.

CAUTION: Info palette values for color modes other than the current mode (Actual Color) reflect settings made in the Printing Inks Setup and Separation Setup Preferences commands under the File menu.

The readouts for the sampling area of the cursor position in the Info palette are dependent on the settings in the Eyedropper tool Options palette. You can set the Eyedropper tool to sample a single pixel or a larger area. If you want to sample single pixels, set the Sample Size to Point Sample. To avoid a single unusual pixel value throwing you off, set the Sample Size to 3 by 3 Average. The value displayed in the Info palette will then reflect the average value of a 3 by 3 pixel square.

Evaluating the Image

Examine an image to determine what corrections are necessary. Is it too dark or too light? Is there too little contrast or too much? Is there a color cast that should be removed? Are there areas of the image that must be selectively corrected?

Perhaps the most important image correction is to match the range of tones to the capability of the reproduction process. The problem is that we see more tones than can be captured on film; other tones are lost when the image is digitized by a scanner, and even more tones are lost when the image is printed on paper.

An image that is too flat, too high in contrast, too bright or too dark may need tonal correction.

In a color image you are likely to detect discrepancies between the actual and expected colors in specific areas, particularly in neutral tones, skin tones, and colors of particular concern for the person judging the image.

READING THE HISTOGRAM

Use the Histogram to determine if the scanner captured enough information, to see if an image has been previously overcorrected, or to identify the *image type*.

If there are gaps in the Histogram, it may be because the scanner didn't capture 256 levels of information for each channel. Or you may be examining an image that has already been corrected. The bigger the gaps, the fewer the tones. In a Histogram of a scanned image, the pixels should be represented smoothly along the entire graph. Most unaltered photographs have the majority of pixels in the midtones, producing a bell curve histogram (Figure 7–2).

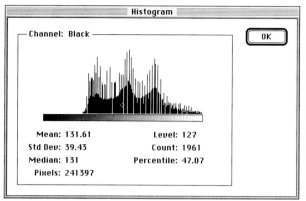 

Figure 7–3   The Histogram shows that the image on the right (too light) has no dark values.

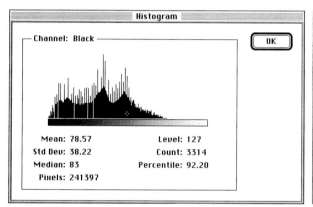 

Figure 7–4   The Histogram shows that the image on the right (too dark) has no light values.

An irregular Histogram indicates that an image might not reproduce well. Some problem Histograms include the following:

- If the left side of the Histogram is completely flat (no indication of any pixels), no data exists in that portion of the image, indicating that the image is missing dark values (Figure 7–3).

- If the right side of the Histogram is flat (no indication of any pixels), the image is missing light values (Figure 7–4).

- If the Histogram has solid lines all the way to the left side (clipped), the image might be missing shadow detail.

- If the Histogram has solid lines all the way to the right side (clipped), the image might be missing highlight detail.

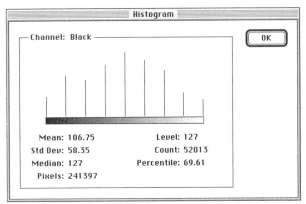

Figure 7–5   The Histogram shows that the image on the right has been posterized

- A histogram with gaps represents an image that has probably been manipulated or poorly scanned: some tones are missing and some tones are present in great quantities (Figure 4–26).
- A Histogram that looks like blades of grass represents a posterized image (Figure 7–5).

IDENTIFY THE IMAGE TYPE

Image type is a method of describing how values are distributed in an image and to help determine how they might be adjusted.

An *average key* image has an even balance of light and dark tones. The Histogram displays most of the pixels in the middle tones with less at the dark and the light ends. If all the pixels are evenly distributed between dark and light, the mean would be 128. For average key images, often only the highlight and shadow points need to be set without adjustments to the midtone.

A *low key* image has mostly dark tones. The Histogram will display most of the pixels on the left side of the graph. Low key images might need adjusting to lighten the midtones and increase detail in the shadow areas (Figure 7–6).

A *high key* image has mostly light values. Since the majority of the pixels in the image are light, they will appear toward the right side of the Histogram. High key images might need adjusting to darken the midtones and bring out the detail in the highlight areas (Figure 7–7).

NOTE: Sometimes high or low key images are desirable, such as a photograph of a polar bear in the snow or a black cat in a coal mine. Since judging the tones in an image is subjective, the content of the image should always be considered when making tonal adjustments.

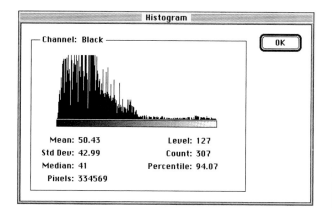 

Figure 7–6 In a low key image most pixels are located toward the left end of the Histogram.

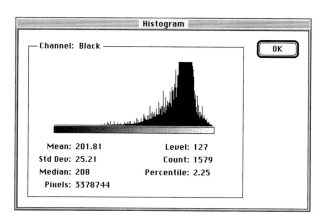 

Figure 7–7 In a high key image more pixels are in the light end of the Histogram. (© PhotoDisc Digital Stock Photography)

A *low contrast* image appears gray with no highlights or shadows. Most of the pixels in the Histogram will appear clustered in the center area with few or no pixels at either end (Figure 7–8).

A *high contrast* image has very dark and light areas with few middle tones. Most of the pixels in the Histogram will be at either end with few in the center (Figure 7–9)

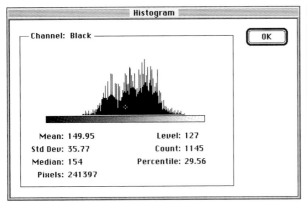

Figure 7–8   In a low contrast photograph the pixels will appear clustered in the center area of the Histogram.

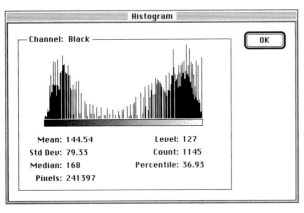

Figure 7–9   In a high contrast photograph the pixels will appear at the ends of the graph with few or no pixels in the center area of Histogram.

The Map Commands

The commands found in the Map submenu (Figure 7–10) allow simple modifications to the colors or brightness levels in an image. In the Map submenu you will find the Invert, Equalize, Threshold, and Posterize commands.

INVERT

This command inverts the values of the pixels in an image or selection area. You can make a positive image negative, or convert a negative into a positive image. With a color image, the Invert command will change all the colors to their opposites or complements on the color wheel (Figure 7–11).

Figure 7–10
The Map commands

Figure 7–11
The image on the left, "Lightning Dancer," was inverted to create the negative on the right. (© Cher Threinen–Pendarvis)

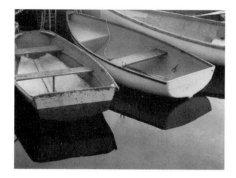

Figure 7–12
The Equalize command was applied to the original Boats on the left, to automatically adjust the tones and produce the version on the right. (© Michael Roney)

Figure 7–13
The Equalize dialog box

EQUALIZE

The Equalize command balances the brightness and contrast values of an image to Photoshop's analysis of the optimum settings. For example, if a scanned image appears darker than the original, use the Equalize command to automatically redistribute the balance of brightness and contrast values, resulting in a lighter, more balanced image. The Equalize command sets the darkest value to black, the brightness value to white, and redistributes the in-between values to an even range of tones (Figure 7–12).

Besides applying the Equalize command to the entire image, additional tone controls become available by selecting a portion of an image. In the Equalize dialog box (Figure 7–13), values in an entire image can be equalized based on values in a selected area. Conversely, the selected area itself can be equalized without affecting the rest of the document (Figure 7–14).

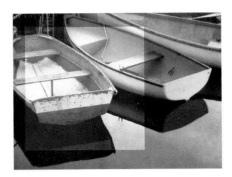 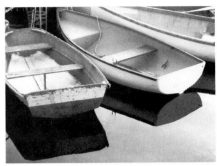

Figure 7–14
The Equalize command applied to the selected area only on the left and then to the entire image on the right based on the selected area

TIP: Although Equalize facilitates the correction of a scanned image, the results may be brighter or darker than expected, and therefore unusable. For more accuracy, use the Levels or Curves commands discussed later in this chapter.

THRESHOLD

Threshold allows you to create high-contrast black-and-white versions of a grayscale or color image. Selecting Threshold temporarily converts the screen into a 1-bit, black-and-white display mode and opens the Threshold dialog box (Figure 7–15).

This dialog box displays a Histogram and a Threshold Level text field showing the value of the slider position below the Histogram. The position of the slider represents the brightness level at which tones will become either white or black. A lower Threshold Level produces more white areas and a higher Threshold Level produces more black areas. The midpoint is 127 in a range of 0 to 255 (Figure 7–16).

POSTERIZE

The Posterize command (Figure 7–17) allows you to specify the number of colors or gray levels (brightness values) used to represent the value range of an image or selection area. Typically, the Posterize command is used to reduce the

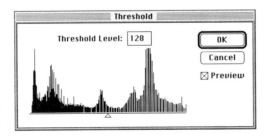

Figure 7–15
The Threshold dialog box

Figure 7–16
In this photograph the Threshold slider was set to a light Threshold Level on the left, medium in the center, and dark on the right. (© Varden Studios)

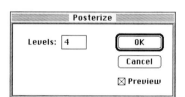

Figure 7–17
Enter the number of gray levels in the Posterize dialog box.

Figure 7–18
The image shows a posterization with four levels of gray. (© Mark Siprut)

number of levels of gray in a grayscale image, but can also create special color effects. The tones in the image will appear in distinct steps (Figure 7–18).

The Adjust Commands

The commands found in the Adjust submenu (Figure 7–19) include commands that are used for value adjustments, color correction, and color changes. These include Levels, Curves, Brightness/Contrast, Color Balance, Hue/Saturation, Replace Color, Selective Color, Auto Levels, Desaturate, and Variations.

Figure 7–19
The Adjust Commands

This section presents only the commands used for adjusting tones: Levels, Curves, Brightness/Contrast, and Auto Levels. The commands that control color are discussed in Chapter 8, "Color."

LEVELS

Use the Levels command (Figure 7–20) to precisely adjust the highlight, midtone, and shadow values in the target layer of an image. For most images these controls give you good tone correction capability.

The Levels dialog box displays a Histogram for the target layer in the current document or selection area. The Channel pop-up menu allows you to control individual channels or all color channels combined. The left side of the Histogram represents the darker areas of the image, and the right side represents the lighter areas. A value of 0 is black, 255 is white, and numbers in between correspond to varying degrees of brightness. Below the Histogram is the Output Levels slider which controls the tonal range of the image after applying the Levels command. It also has a range from black (0) to white (255). Click the Preview option to view the effects in real time within the selection or current document only.

Levels Sliders: Along the bottom line of the Histogram are three triangular sliders. The black slider represents the darkest value (shadows), the

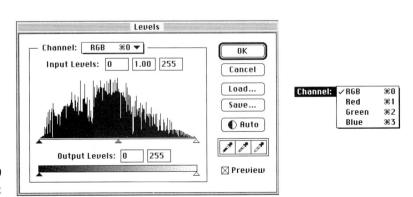

Figure 7–20
The Levels dialog box

Figure 7–21
This Levels dialog represents a dark image lacking good highlights. To lighten the image, drag the white triangle to match up with the lightest value represented in the Histogram.

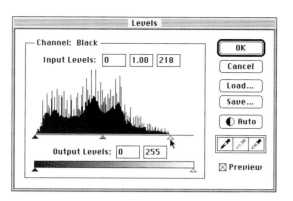

Figure 7–22
The dark car on the left was lightened to produce the car on the right with the Levels command.

gray triangle represents the midtones (gamma), and the white triangle represents the brightest values (highlights). At the top of the Levels dialog box you will find three input level values for the three triangular slider controls.

The positions of the sliders in relation to the Histogram represent the Input Levels. In an optimum situation move the triangles so that the darkest actual value in the image (pure black) is directly over the black triangle, and the lightest value in the image (pure white) corresponds to the position of the white triangle.

In a Histogram of an image that is too dark the brightest mapped value in the image might be to the left of the white triangular slider on the right side (Figure 7–21). To lighten the image, drag the white triangle slider to the left until it lines up with the lightest values represented in the Histogram. You may also need to adjust the gray midtone triangle to compensate for the newly brightened image (Figure 7–22).

The Output Levels slider at the bottom of the Levels dialog box adjusts the output tones of the image. The area between the triangles in the slider represents the range of tones in the image after performing this function. To achieve the highest contrast, set the triangles at the extreme ends. Move the triangles in to lower the contrast or decrease the value range.

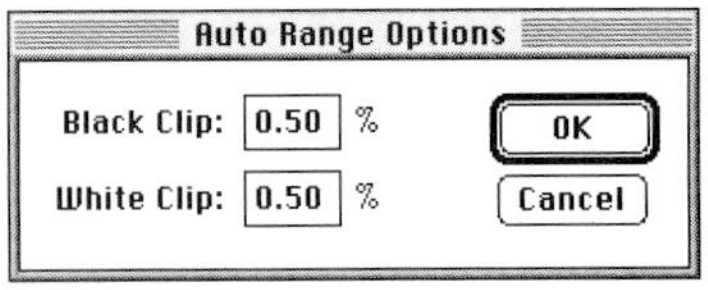

Figure 7–23
The Auto Range
Options dialog box

Black and White Points: To reproduce well, an image should have a full range of tones from black to white. Click on the Auto button to set the black and white points automatically. The darkest pixels in the image will be adjusted to black and the lightest pixels will be adjusted to white. This function is preset to clip the values by .5%. To change this default value, hold the Option key, click on the Auto button, and the Auto Range Options dialog box will appear (Figure 7–23). Type in a percentage between 0 and 9.99.

TIP: To find the highlight and shadows in an image, evaluate tones in specific areas by moving the cursor around in the image and reading the values in the Info palette.

To set the black and white points individually, which is more accurate than using the Auto button, click on the black Eyedropper in the dialog box and then click on the darkest part of the image. That point will become black. Similarly, set the white point with the white Eyedropper tool by clicking on the lightest part of the image to make it white. To preview where the shadow and highlights appear in your image, deselect the Preview button and hold the Option key while dragging either the black or white triangles (Figure 7–24).

Offset printers usually do not want an image with a tonal range from pure white to black. They prefer halftone dots in the highlights and shadows. Provide this by setting the black and white points to be other than pure white or black. Consult your printer in advance to find out what values should be set for the highlights and shadows. For example, printing on a coated paper stock might require a 5% highlight dot and a 95% shadow dot and printing on an uncoated paper might require a 10% highlight dot and a 90% shadow dot.

Change the value of the black or white points of the Eyedroppers by double-clicking on them to open the Color Picker. You can then set the values to be other than pure black or white. For example, to set the shadow value to 95%, double click on the black Eyedropper tool and enter 12 in each of the R, G, and B text fields. To set the white value, double click on the white Eyedropper tool and enter 242 in each of the R, G, and B text fields. Refer to Table 7–1 for percentage-to-levels conversion values.

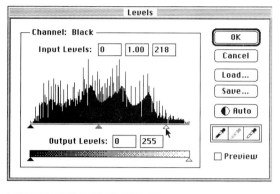

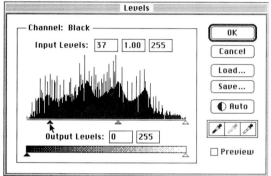

Figure 7–24 Preview clipped highlights and shadows by deselecting the Preview button and holding the Option key while dragging either the black or white triangle sliders below the Histogram.

NOTE: When working in Grayscale or RGB Color modes, use the above recommendations for setting the values in the Color Picker (do not use CMYK values). When working in CMYK Color mode, use CMYK color values.

TIP: Sometimes you might not want to choose as a highlight value the very brightest part of an image. There are some parts of an image that are called *specular highlights*. These are areas where, when the image is reproduced, you don't want to have a halftone dot. They are areas so bright that for them to be properly viewed, they should be printed as paper white—with no ink at all. If you choose a specular highlight as your lightest value, the resulting image will tend to look too dark in the highlight to midtone areas.

To manually set the output value of the black and white points, use the Output slider at the bottom of the Levels dialog box (Figure 7–25). Drag the black triangle to the desired level, such as 12 for a 5% halftone dot. Drag the white triangle to 242 for a 95% halftone dot (see Table 7–1).

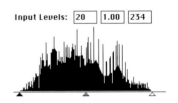

Figure 7–25
Manually set the output values of the darkest and lightest tones by moving the black and white triangles in the Output slider at the bottom of the Levels dialog box.

Figure 7–26
If the tones in the image or selection do not reach black or white, manually darken the shadow and brighten the highlight by dragging the black and white triangle sliders to meet the last tones at the ends of the Histogram.

The image will reproduce too dark or light if the vertical lines in the Histogram fall short at either end. Manually darken the shadows and brighten the highlights by moving the black and white triangle sliders under the Histogram graph to the last vertical lines at the ends of the graph. Set the triangle just to the outside of the last value to avoid clipping (Figure 7–26). If you want to clip some of the shadow and highlight tones, position the triangles inside of the Histogram endpoints.

Adjusting the Midtones: Midtones are the values halfway between the highlights and the shadows. In the Levels dialog box, the midtones are controlled by the middle (gray) Input slider triangle. The middle input value, referred to as the *gamma* value, is also displayed in the middle Input Levels text field above the Histogram. If your image is too dark, move the middle triangle to the left or enter a value greater than one in the gamma text field (middle) above the Histogram. If your image is too light, move the middle slider to the right; the gamma value will change to a number less than one.

If you are preparing an image for offset printing, you also need to compensate for *dot gain* by lightening the midtone values (move the center triangle to the left) to compensate for the darkening of the tones that will occur on the printing press. Dot gain is greater in the midtones and also varies depending on the paper and press conditions. Consult with your printer for specific dot gain compensation instructions. For more information on dot gain, refer to Chapter 11, "Output."

Neutral Gray Point: Remove a color cast from an image by setting a neutral gray point. Click on the middle Eyedropper tool in the dialog box and then click on the desired middle gray point in the image. The colors at that point will be adjusted to middle gray and, therefore, all colors in the image will be adjusted accordingly toward the neutral color. To change the color setting of the Middle Eyedropper, open the Color Picker by double-clicking on the tool. See Chapter 8, "Color," for more information on correcting colors.

TIP: The most accurate method of placing a neutral gray in your image is to physically put a neutral gray card in the photograph at the time of the shoot.

CURVES

The Curves command provides an intuitive, visual graph to precisely adjust the input to output relationship of the values in the target layer of an image. The Curves dialog box (Figure 7–27) displays a pop-up menu for the separate color channels in the document. You can adjust the map for the overall image or for each individual color channel. A straight diagonal line from the lower-left to the upper-right corners represents an unchanged distribution of brightness values.

In addition to controlling the highlight, midtone, and shadow values in an image, you can control the values at any point on the graph. The horizontal axis represents input values (original tone) and the vertical axis represents output values (revised tones). The values, read from left to right and bottom to top, are represented as levels from black (0) to white (255) or percentages from white (0%) to black (100%). Toggle between the levels and percentage readouts by clicking on the graduated bar below the graph (Figure 7–28).

When you move the cursor into the map area, it turns into a crosshair by default. Change the curve with this crosshair by dragging any point on the line to a new position. This new curve changes the brightness values represented in the image. You can plot up to 15 points on the line. To see where

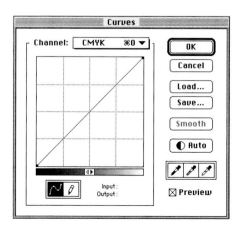

Figure 7–27
The Curves dialog showing an unchanged distribution of brightness values.

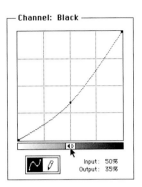
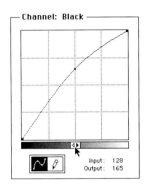

Figure 7–28
Toggle between the levels and percentage readouts by clicking on the graduated bar below the graph in the Curves dialog box.

a value on the image falls on the graph, click on the image and a small circle will appear on the line with the corresponding Input and Output values displayed below the graph.

Select the Pencil tool at the bottom of the mapping area (Arbitrary Map option) to draw lines with the Pencil in the graph area. Try drawing the following line: Click the Pencil in the upper-left corner of the map area. Hold down the Shift key (constrains the lines drawn with the pencil to 45° and 90° angles), and click the Pencil in the lower-right corner of the map area. This will draw a straight line exactly the inverse of the normal map, resulting in an inverted, or negative, image (Figures 7–29 and 7–30).

By using the Pencil to draw irregular maps (Figure 7–31), you can achieve a variety of tonal effects similar to the solarization effect in darkroom photography (Figure 7–32). Click on the Smooth button to smooth out the abrupt, jagged, straight lines, creating smoother transitions between tones.

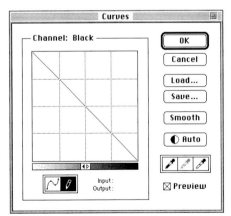

Figure 7–29
The Curves dialog box showing a reversed 45° line

Figure 7–30
Reversing the 45° line creates a negative image.

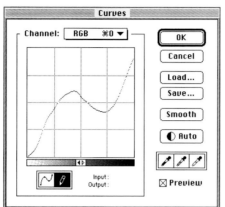

Figure 7–31
The Curves dialog showing an irregularly drawn map

Figure 7–32
Examples of effects you can achieve using the pencil tool to alter the Curves map

Black and White Points: As discussed in the "Levels" section earlier in this chapter, an image should have a full range of tones from black to white to reproduce well. Set the black and white points automatically with the Auto button. To set the black and white points individually, which is more accurate than using the Auto button, click on the black Eyedropper in the dialog box and then click on the darkest part of the image. That point will become black. Similarly, set the white point with the white Eyedropper tool by clicking on the lightest part of the image to make it white.

Refer to the Levels section for details on setting the parameters for the Auto button and the Eyedropper tools. They function identically in the Curves dialog box as in the Levels dialog box.

To manually set the white and black points in an image drag the ends of the diagonal line to the desired values (Figure 7–33). For example an offset printer might advise you to set the highlight to 5% and the shadow to 95% for a coated paper; or set the highlight to 10% and the shadow to 90% for an uncoated paper. Consult you printer for specific parameters.

Adjusting the Midtones: Midtones are the values halfway between the highlights and the shadows. In the Curves dialog box, control the midtones by dragging the diagonal line from the center of the graph. For example, if

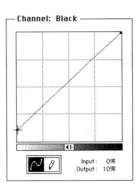 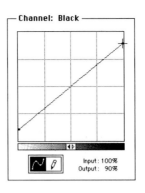 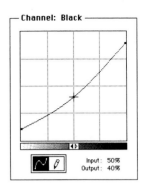

Figure 7–33
The Curves dialog box set to output 10% in the highlight and 90% in the shadow. The midtones are lightened slightly to compensate for dot gain.

the Curves readouts are set to the percentage mode (white on the left and black on the right), dragging the center point down will lighten the midtones, and dragging it up will darken the midtones (Figure 7–33). If you are preparing work for offset printing, manually compensate for dot gain by lightening the midtones. Consult with your printer for specific dot gain compensation instructions. For more information on dot gain, refer to Chapter 11, "Output."

Neutral Gray Point: Remove a color cast from an image by setting a neutral gray point. Click on the middle Eyedropper tool in the dialog box and then click on the desired middle gray point in the image. The colors at that point will be adjusted to middle gray and, therefore, all colors in the image will be adjusted accordingly toward the neutral color. To change the color setting of the Middle Eyedropper, open the Color Picker by double-clicking on the tool. See Chapter 8, "Color," for more information on correcting colors.

BRIGHTNESS/CONTRAST

The simplest tool for altering tones or the density of a file is the Brightness/Contrast command. This dialog box controls the overall brightness and contrast values of either an entire image or a selected area (Figure 7–34). Current numerical values are displayed above the respective sliders.

Although this command works well for simple adjustments, the Brightness/Contrast command's linear correction can result in data loss if over-used. The file's data is moved entirely in one direction or the other to make the file lighter or darker or to alter the contrast. In other words, if

Figure 7–34
The Brightness/Contrast command dialog box

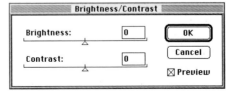

you use Brightness/Contrast to lighten an image by 25%, all the pixels in the file are equally affected by 25%. You can achieve more control over tonal adjustments with the Levels or Curves commands.

AUTO LEVELS

The Auto Levels command operates identically to the auto button found in the Levels and Curves dialog boxes. Although Auto Levels is a quick and convenient way to correct the tonal range in an image, Levels and Curves offer precise manual control.

Resolution and Size

The essential relationship between the size and resolution of an image is not immediately obvious. The physical size of an image is measured by the number of pixels, inches, or centimeters that make up the dimensions of an image. The resolution of an image refers to the pixel density of an image. For example, a 3 x 4-inch image can vary in the number of pixels that fill that area, even though the size is fixed. A 3 x 4 inch image with a resolution of 72 pixels per inch (ppi) has fewer pixels, takes up less disk space, and contains less detail than the same size image at 300 ppi.

The actual resolution of a file is determined at the scan stage or when a new document is created. Often, however, a scanned image must be resized in Photoshop. Reducing the size of an original scan will not appear to lose image quality because unneeded pixels are removed. On the other hand, try to avoid resizing a file to larger than an original scan because Photoshop must create new pixels (resample) by examining adjacent pixels and creating new pixels in between by interpolation (see Chapter 3, "Configuring Photoshop").

TIP: A small dose of the Unsharp Mask filter can overcome some of the softness that can result in resampling a file. Also make sure you have Bicubic resample selected in the preferences for the highest quality.

Canvas Size

In most cases the Canvas Size reflects the exact size of the image. Use the Canvas Size command to add extra working space outside the image area or to crop an image to a specific size without changing its resolution (Figure 7–35).

The Canvas Size dialog box displays the current canvas size in the measurement units specified in the Units Preferences dialog box under the File menu. Enter the desired size in the New Size area fields in the unit of measurement chosen from the pop-up menus.

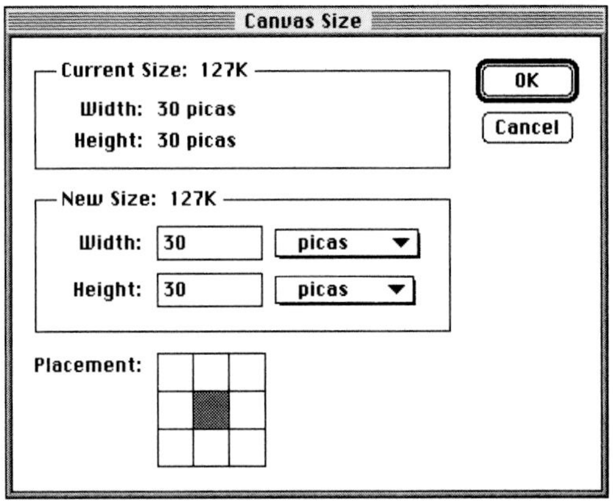

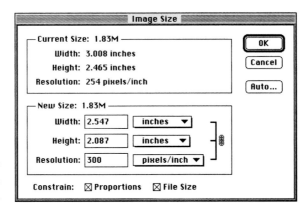

Figure 7–35
The Canvas Size
dialog box

The nine squares below the New Size selection area show where the image will be placed on the new canvas. Change this location by clicking on one of the boxes.

Image Size

Use the Image Size command to resize an image while controlling its resolution or to change an image's resolution while maintaining its size. Remember that you can only see your image at the resolution of your computer monitor. Changes to the resolution or size of an image may not be readily visible on your monitor, but will show up when printed.

The Image Size dialog box (Figure 7–36) contains the current information on the width, height, and resolution of the image, as well as choices for a new width, height, and resolution.

Choose the measurement units from the pop-up menus next to the New Size values. The Width pop-up menu includes a Columns measurement choice based on the values entered in the Width and Gutter fields found in the Units Preferences dialog box.

Figure 7–36
The Image Size
dialog box

The Constrain options, located under the New Size options area, allow for scaling an image proportionally, without losing resolution or file size. Click in the Proportions box to keep the width and height aspect ratio constant when making size or resolution changes. The File Size option allows changes to the dimensions or the resolution without resampling the image (see "Resampling" below). Photoshop will automatically update the parameters based upon entries without removing or adding information to the original image.

RESAMPLING

Resampling means increasing or decreasing the resolution of an image through interpolation. When the resolution is increased, Photoshop inserts new pixels with intermediate values between existing pixels. When you resample an image with the File Size checkbox deselected, the document's printed size (dimensions) stays the same, but the amount of information (number of pixels) in the image changes. Therefore, the file size changes.

When the resolution of an image is decreased, there is a loss of data, thereby creating a smaller file size. In other words, pixels are removed from the document.

You can see the results of a resampled image by holding down the Option key and clicking on the Size Indicator in the lower-left corner of a document window immediately before and after resampling. Any changes in physical dimensions and file size will be reflected in this window. Resampling will also be evident when viewing an image at a 1:1 zoom factor, as displayed in the Title Bar, because at a 1:1 ratio every pixel of the monitor displays a pixel of the document.

To resample by specified percentages or numbers of pixels choose the percent or pixels options in the Units pop-up menu next to the text fields for width and height. Choosing the percent or pixels options will always resample an image.

TIP: When resampling, keep an original version of the image and resample it as necessary for output. Resampling an image down in resolution, and then resampling it back up again, results in image degradation.

When you resample, rotate, or apply special effects filters such as Perspective or Skew to an image, Photoshop creates new pixels to fill in areas. Photoshop decides where to place these new pixels based on one of three methods of interpolation specified in the General Preferences dialog box under the File Menu. (Refer to the General Preferences section of Chapter 2, "Setup and Document Management," for a detailed discussion of interpolation methods.)

RESOLUTION FOR PRINTED OUTPUT

The optimum resolution of an image to be printed on a printing press is usually determined by three factors:

- The resolution of the image
- The resolution of the output device
- The halftone screen frequency of the final output

For offset printing the optimum resolution of an image should be twice the desired line frequency of the halftone screen (although in some cases, you *may* be able to get by with 1.2 times the frequency). For example, to print an image at 150 lines per inch (lpi), you should be working with a 300 ppi image. Keep in mind that the 300 ppi is relevant to the final size. If the photo you scan is 2 x 3 inches and you want to print it at 4 x 6 inches, you must scan the original at a 600 ppi. When you double the size of the 600 ppi scan, the resolution will be cut in half to 300 ppi.

AUTO RESOLUTION

By clicking the Auto button in the Image Size dialog box, Photoshop will automatically determine the resolution for an image. Click the Auto button to open the Auto Resolution dialog box (Figure 7–37). You may enter the final output halftone screen resolution in the Screen value box and select a measurement from the pop-up menu. Remember that the value entered will only be used to calculate a resolution value for the image. If you want to set a halftone screen frequency for final output, use the Halftone Screens dialog box in the Page Setup dialog box.

The Quality options include the following:

- Draft, for a resolution that is one times the screen frequency up to 72 ppi, resulting in the lowest resolution
- Good, for a resolution setting that is one and one-half times the screen frequency, which may be used for noncritical situations
- Best, which results in a resolution two times the screen frequency and is the optimum setting for standard offset printing applications

Figure 7–37
The Auto Resolution dialog box offers an easy method for calculating the resolution of an image that will be halftoned when printed.

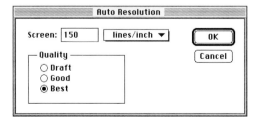

After you enter the desired Auto quality and click the OK button, you will return to the main Image Size dialog box, with the new resolution entered in the resolution field.

CAUTION: Once a file has been resampled down in resolution, pixel information is lost and can never be retrieved in its original form.

Image Transformations

Under the Image menu you will find the commands to flip, rotate, scale, stretch, skew, change the perspective, and distort portions of images. Following are some basic rules to remember:

- The Flip, Rotate, and Effects commands, otherwise referred to as the Dynamic effects commands, can be applied to any selection.

- The Interpolation method specified in the General Preferences dialog box under the File menu affects the rendering quality of the dynamic effects. Nearest Neighbor is the fastest method but gives the poorest results; Bilinear is a reasonably fast method with reasonable quality; and Bicubic is the slowest method with the best quality. (Refer to Figure 2–11 to compare the visual differences in these methods.)

- To flip or rotate an entire image, apply the command without making a selection (Figures 7–38 and 7–39). Photoshop will automatically adjust the document area to accommodate the image. If you select the entire image (with the Select All command) and apply an arbitrary or a 90° rotation, the resulting image will be cropped.

- CW stands for "clockwise" and CCW means "counterclockwise."

- When applying any of the manual dynamic effects (Free Rotate, Scale, Distort, Perspective, and Skew), handles appear on four corners of a selection's bounding box. As you drag the corner handles into the desired position, the image redraws itself when you release the mouse button. If you hold down the Option key while dragging handles, the image will not redraw until all of the handles have been placed and the Option key is released. This improves efficiency when distorting a high-resolution image to a predetermined shape.

- When using any of the Effects commands, you can continually change a selection by dragging the handles to new positions. Click inside the selection to render the effect. After rendering, the Undo command negates all of the consecutive changes of the specific command, returning the image to its initial state. Pressing the Command and Period keys before clicking in the selection to finalize the effect achieves the same result.

Figure 7–38
The original image on
the left was flipped
horizontally (center) and
vertically (right).

Flip

The Flip commands flops an image horizontally or vertically. Be careful not to include text in a flopped image (Figure 7–38).

Rotate

ARBITRARY ROTATE

Arbitrary Rotate allows you to specify rotation of image in degrees (Figure 7–39). The acceptable value range for the Arbitrary Rotate command is –359.99° to 359.99°. Note that you can also specify fractions of a degree.

To rotate an entire document, do not make a selection. Choose Arbitrary Rotate and specify an angle. Photoshop will automatically

Figure 7–39
The image on the left
was rotated 30° and -15°
on the right.

enlarge the Canvas Size to accommodate the rotated image. If you make a selection before rotating, you might crop the image.

FREE ROTATE

Free Rotate allows you to rotate a selection freehand. After choosing the Free Rotate command, determine the angle of rotation by dragging one of the four handles. Click inside the selection to render the command.

Effects

SCALE

Use the Scale command to stretch or compress a selection (Figure 7–40). Hold the Shift key when scaling to constrain the effect to the aspect ratio of the original selection. Be aware that enlarging a selection spreads the pixels apart. Through interpolation, new pixel data is invented so that the resolution of the enlarged selection matches that of the host file. Reducing a selection removes pixel data matching the resolution of the selection to the host file.

CAUTION: Most photographers do not like their images stretched out of proportion. Use the Shift key when scaling to constrain the effect, maintaining the original aspect ratio.

SKEW

The Skew command allows you to slant an image in a vertical or horizontal direction (Figure 7–41). The first time you use this command, the horizontal and vertical pairs of handles will be coupled. Moving one handle also moves the coupled handle. The handles are then decoupled and allow you to choose an individual handle, causing the Skew command to behave like a constrained Distort. Recouple the handle pairs by pressing the Shift key while dragging a handle.

Figure 7–40
Scaling examples: A selection from the original was enlarged (left), while the image was stretched out of proportion horizontally (center) and vertically (right).

Figure 7–41
The image on the left
was skewed horizontally
and on the
right vertically.

PERSPECTIVE

The Perspective commands allow you to move two corners of a selection in opposite directions simultaneously to give the selection a three-dimensional appearance (Figure 7–42). After making a selection, choose the Perspective command and drag a corner handle either out or in. The adjacent corner handle will move in the opposite direction.

Figure 7–42
Perspective
command examples

Figure 7–43
Distort
command examples

DISTORT

The Distort command allows you to drag any of the corner handles on a selection independently of each other (Figure 7–43).

Summary

- Develop a strategy for processing your images. Calibrate your system and make tests to insure predictable results. Determine the image type and the desired result before applying affects to the actual image.

- Most image processing commands work on selection areas as well as the entire target layer.

- Most image processing commands work on only one layer at a time, the target layer. To affect the entire composite image or multiple layers, merge the desired layers or flatten the document. In contrast to layers, multiple channels can be affected simultaneously.

- Evaluate the tones in an image with the Histogram and Info palette.

- Use the Levels and Curves commands to adjust tones for accuracy. The Brightness/Contrast command or Auto Levels will not be as precise.

- When resizing an image, you can reduce the file without loss of detail but if you enlarge an image, pixelation may result due to the reduction in resolution.
- Scan at two times the halftone screen frequency for optimal results.
- Every image processing command changes the pixel data. Repeated applications can deteriorate an image.

Now that you know how to adjust tones, you will be more effective in adjusting color, the subject of the next chapter.

CHAPTER 8

Color

One of the most exciting aspects of Photoshop is creating, manipulating, and editing images in color. Color often communicates information more effectively than black-and-white, adding visual excitement and emotion to images. But color can also be confusing and intimidating.

This chapter helps you understand the basics of color: different color systems, the color wheel, and how to select, sample, and mix colors in Photoshop for any project. It discusses Photoshop's eight different color display modes, which allow you to edit images by manipulating different aspects of color and tone characteristics. Converting from one mode to another and process color separations are also covered in this chapter, as are strategies to perform color corrections on images, to remove color biases, and to detect and correct out-of-gamut colors.

First, let's define color. . . .

Color Systems

Color is light. More accurately, color is light within the visible spectrum as we perceive it. The electromagnetic spectrum contains waves of different frequencies. Some frequencies, such as X-rays and cosmic rays, are shorter than visible light. Infrared and radio waves are longer than visible light.

We say "an apple is red" as if this were an attribute of the apple. Actually an apple's color is a complex interaction of its surface characteristics, the particular kind of light that is shining on the apple, and the person who is observing the light reflected off that apple.

Most perceived colors are reflected. But light can also be transmitted, as when it passes through a pane of glass or a photographic transparency. Furthermore, color can be emitted from objects like computer monitors and televisions.

How Color Is Described

One of the most important contributions to color science was made by Sir Isaac Newton. He performed a series of color matching experiments in which he found that most, but not all, colors can be produced by mixing combinations of red, green, and blue lights. When the three lights were all turned on, the result was seen as white. With all the lights off, black was perceived.

Much later, scientists studying the human eye found three types of *cones*, the light-sensitive receptors with which we see colors. The sensitivity of the three cones types overlap, but generally correspond to the red, green, and blue portions of the spectrum. Referred to as the *tristimulus* nature of color, color can be described by three values or as having three dimensions. The most common three component color descriptions are *additive color* and *subtractive color* (Figures 8–1 and 8–2).

ADDITIVE COLOR (RGB COLOR)

Computer monitors and televisions function much like the lights in Newton's experiments. Electron guns vary in intensity as they sweep the surface of the picture tube exciting red, green, and blue phosphors. The

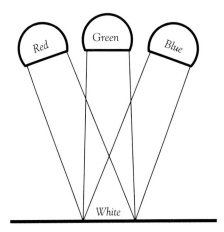
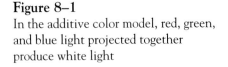

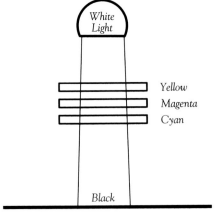

Figure 8–1
In the additive color model, red, green, and blue light projected together produce white light

Figure 8–2
In the subtractive color model, projecting white light through cyan, magenta, and yellow filters produces black.

phosphors emit colored light which our eyes "mix" visually so we perceive different colors.

Red, green, and blue are the *additive primaries*. If you select an area in Photoshop and color it bright red, the red phosphors are turned on to maximum intensity. If you turn on both red and green phosphors to full intensity, your eye perceives the result as yellow. If red, green, and blue phosphors are turned on to the maximum, the result is white. The three additive primaries added together in different mixtures can produce more than 16 million colors on a monitor. Also referred to as RGB (for red-green-blue) color, additive color is also used by devices like scanners, digital cameras, and film recorders.

SUBTRACTIVE COLOR (CMYK COLOR)

Colors reproduced on paper cannot use the RGB system. Digital color printers, printing presses, and photographic media use cyan, magenta, and yellow colorants (and sometimes black, as explained below) to produce colors. These three colors are the *subtractive primaries*.

Inks, dyes, toners, or other colorants act as filters (absorbers). They absorb (subtract) certain wavelengths of light and allow other wavelengths to pass through to the paper. For example, red ink absorbs or subtracts the cyan wavelengths and reflects the red light—we perceive the result as "red." Subtractive color can be referred to as CMY (cyan, magenta, and yellow) color. Figure 8–2 demonstrates the effect of projecting white light through cyan, magenta and yellow filters.

According to color theory, mixing full saturations of cyan, magenta, and yellow should result in black. Each color should subtract out its complementary color from white (cyan subtracts red, magenta subtracts green, and yellow subtracts blue), leaving no color to reflect back to your eye. In practice, however, full saturations of the subtractive primaries produce a muddy brown color because of impurities of the inks or other colorants. Most digital color printers and printing presses use a fourth color, black, to create true blacks and properly saturated shadow areas. The fourth color, black (K), is sometimes referred to as the *key color*.

THE COLOR WHEEL

The primary colors of the additive and subtractive models interrelate as shown in a circle called the *color wheel*, where colors are arranged in order of hue (Figure 8–3). The wavelength frequencies increase starting from the lowest frequency color, red at 0°, and moving counterclockwise. Each color (hue) can be identified by an angle. The order of the colors is the same as the order of the colors in a rainbow or light going through a prism.

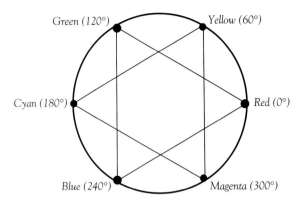

Figure 8–3
The color wheel shows the interrelationship of the primary colors. Each hue is identified by an angle on the color wheel.

Colors directly opposite each other on the color wheel are called *complementary colors*. Complementary colors placed next to each other tend to vibrate; and when mixed with each other they produce a neutral tone. Colors next to each other are called *analogous colors* and tend to be more harmonious when placed next to each other.

HUE-SATURATION-BRIGHTNESS (HSB COLOR)

Although the RGB system makes sense for a machine like a monitor or scanner, RGB isn't necessarily easy to work with intuitively. (Try picking colors by moving red, green, and blue sliders. . . .) Other three-dimensional color systems have been developed to describe color. Photoshop uses a system called HSB (Hue-Saturation-Brightness), a more intuitive variant of the RGB system.

In these systems one dimension represents the lightness/darkness (*luminance*) of a color and two other dimensions represent the *chrominance*, or the color component of the color. In Photoshop, the luminance component is called Brightness and has values from 0% (black) to 100% (white).

Chrominance consists of two components, Hue and Saturation. Hue is the color name, such as "orange" or "green," that scientists call the wavelength of the color. The hue aspect of HSB Color is described by an angle on the color wheel (Figure 8–3). The second chrominance component, Saturation, represents the strength or purity of a color. Saturation has values between 0% (no color) and 100% (fully saturated).

COLOR GAMUT

Color gamut refers to the range of colors that a particular monitor, digital color printer, or other device can reproduce. None of these devices can reproduce all the colors our eyes can see in nature. Pure cyan, for example, cannot be represented in the RGB color space of monitors. Similarly, there are many bright blues and reds which cannot be represented using the CMYK color space of most printers. Photoshop has several tools to determine when your an RGB color is *out of gamut*, meaning it cannot be printed on the currently chosen CMY(K) printer. You can use Photoshop's color correction tools to alter these colors.

DEVICE-INDEPENDENT COLOR

Color scientists need to describe colors in a precise, measurable way that reflects how the human eye perceives color. In 1931 the Commission Internationale de L'Éclairage (CIE) developed a system describing colors based on color matching experiments performed under specific conditions of lighting and viewing angle. A later modification of this standard, CIE L*a*b, was established in 1976.

Photoshop uses this system, which it calls Lab Color, as its internal color description. As described in the "Process Color Separations" section of this chapter, Photoshop uses Lab color as an intermediate step when converting between color modes.

Lab Color has several advantages. First, unlike RGB or CMY(K) colors that vary with the displaying or printing device, Lab Color is device independent. Second, Lab Color contains all the colors we see. Lab color description is also more precise because tonal differences are detectable with color measuring devices like colorimeters or spectrophotometers. Finally, CIE L*a*b and related device-independent color systems are used by color management systems.

Lab Color, like the HSB Color, has one dimension representing color lightness/darkness (*luminance*) and two other dimensions, a and b, representing the *chrominance*, or the color component of the color. The a dimension represents colors along the magenta/green axis of the color wheel. The b dimension represents colors along the yellow/blue axis of the color wheel. With these three coordinates, *L*, *a*, and *b*, any color can be described.

NAMED COLOR SYSTEMS (CUSTOM COLORS)

Another color description method, popular among graphic arts professionals, uses systems of color swatches called *named color* systems (each color has a distinct name or number associated with it). Photoshop calls these *custom colors*.

These widely used systems can be divided into two broad classes based on the two basic methods used to print colors on a printing press: *process colors* and *spot colors*. In process color printing, all colors are broken into CMYK color components. Process color is used when a full color image will be printed on a digital color printer or the printing press. Designers specify spot color printing when printing one, two, or three ink colors, or when printing colors that cannot be accurately printed with CMYK inks. You can print spot colors in Photoshop by printing or saving from the Duotone mode, or by printing individual channels.

Custom Colors

Specify Custom printing colors in the Custom Colors dialog box (Figure 8–4) accessed by clicking the Custom button in the Photoshop Color Picker. The closest custom color to the current color selected in the Picker will be displayed. Select a custom color by typing the number of the color you want (you must type relatively quickly), or by dragging the triangle sliders along the vertical scroll bar which controls the set of colors along the left. Click on the desired color swatch to select the color and then click OK. At any time, click on the Picker button to return to the Photoshop Color Picker.

Custom color systems specify either process color mixes (CMYK) to create desired colors or specific custom ink colors. Each color system has corresponding reference books that show swatches of the printed colors. The printed color swatchbooks have numbers for each swatch that can be specified in the Custom Colors dialog box.

CAUTION: Although a custom color ultimately describes a process color mix or a custom ink color, it is displayed on a monitor with RGB colors. Do not depend on the monitor — odds are you will not be able to match the colors exactly. Calibrating your monitor will help get predictable colors, but for accuracy always use a printed swatchbook as a reference.

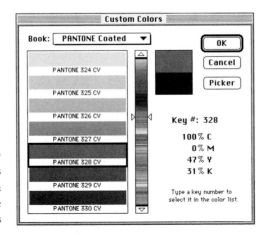

Figure 8–4
The Custom Colors dialog box with a scrollable list of Pantone Coated color swatches

PROCESS COLOR MATCHING SYSTEMS

Trumatch, Pantone Process, Pantone ProSim, Focoltone, DIC, and ANPA color systems are created by mixing tints of each of the CMYK process color inks.

Obviously, CMYK colors can be specified as percentages of each component in the Color Picker or Picker palette without using one of the above color systems, but refer to the color swatchbook designed to facilitate the choosing of colors within a logical system.

Trumatch: The Trumatch CMYK-based swatchbook shows over 2,000 achievable computer-generated colors. The Trumatch Color Finder is organized into 50 hues which are numbered sequentially around the color wheel. Each hue section displays up to 40 tints and shades based on saturation and brightness. The swatchbook also has a section to specify four color grays, normally difficult to produce. The Trumatch system was also designed specifically for digital output. The finer screen tint increments allow for subtler variations in colors than do the 5% to 10% steps available with conventional screens.

Pantone Process: The CMYK-based Pantone Process color swatchbook displays over 3,000 colors in the industry-standard 5% increments (with a few at 3%).

Pantone ProSim: The Pantone ProSim color system gives you the best possible CMYK color match to the Pantone Matching System (PMS) solid colors. Only approximately 50% of the PMS colors can be matched accurately with CMYK colors. To specify a color, first find the desired color in the PMS swatchbook and then pick the same color in the ProSim Custom Color dialog box. The appropriate CMYK mix will be selected.

Focoltone: The Focoltone color system, originally created for the traditional printing industry, facilitated a designer's color selection by providing combinations made with common components. The stripper at the print shop could easily eliminate or add screen tint components to make any color changes. Focoltone's CMYK-based swatchbook displays 763 colors that can be selected in the Custom Colors dialog box. Focoltone also provides custom color formulas to match the process colors with solid-ink spot colors.

DIC Color Guide: The DIC Color Guide, produced by the Dainappon Ink and Chemical company from Japan, provides a system of selecting process colors popular in the Japanese graphics industry.

ANPA Color: The ANPA Color system in Photoshop is based on the ANPA Color Ink Book Volume 7, which has been replaced by the Newspaper Association of America (NAA) Color Ink Book Volume 8. The

Volume 8 reference book contains 41 colors created from nine base colors: the process colors plus some special spot colors. Use the Volume 8 reference book to specify CMYK colors for daily newspapers that print color on newsprint paper, rather than the ANPA color palette in Photoshop.

Each page in the book shows a single-ink spot color and, when applicable, the process color mix that most closely matches it. Printing on newsprint requires special consideration in color selection and output due to the highly absorbent quality of the paper. The absorbent paper causes more than normal dot gain (ink spread). See Chapter 11, "Output," for more information on dot gain.

SPOT COLOR SYSTEMS

A spot color refers to a custom ink color printed on a printing press or other reproduction process such as silkscreen printing, letterpress, etc. The two systems discussed below, the Pantone Matching System and the Toyo 88 Color Finder system, are designed for offset printing.

There are two ways to print or save a file for spot color output in Photoshop: from the Duotone mode or by printing or saving extra channels.

TIP: If you want to specify a metallic, custom pastel, or varnish ink, simply identify it with any spot color and then tell the printer how you want the plate printed. If you want to apply a varnish to a process-color separation, create a new channel with the masked area and then print it separately. If you are printing from QuarkXPress, you can export the extra channels with the PlateMaker export plug-in (described in the "Spot Color Separations" section in Chapter 11, "Output").

When working with spot colors in the Duotone mode, be consistent in your color-naming conventions if you will be exporting the image to another program for spot color output. Color names must match letter for letter and space for space.

CAUTION: When working in modes other than the Duotone mode, Photoshop converts spot colors into RGB or CMYK colors. These converted colors may not match the original spot colors. Beware of selecting colors in this unreliable fashion.

Pantone Matching System: The Pantone Matching System (PMS) provides over 1,000 spot-color inks. This international color language accurately specifies, communicates, and matches color. The Pantone company does not produce inks; it produces the color swatchbooks with specifications for the ink colors. Ink companies make and sell the ink products to printers.

Ink colors vary depending on the paper on which they are printed. The PMS swatchbooks display colors on both coated and uncoated paper. Colors may be selected in Photoshop for either paper type. Be careful not to switch between color selections in Pantone Coated and Pantone Uncoated because Photoshop changes the color name as it attempts to match the look of the ink on the monitor.

TIP: **To ensure that the Pantone names match their spelling in other programs, select Short PANTONE Names in the General Preferences dialog box under the File menu.**

TIP: **To reproduce PMS colors using CMYK colors, use the ProSim Color System.**

Toyo 88 Color Finder: The Toyo 88 Color Finder system from Japan consists of 1,050 spot-ink colors blended with Toyo bases and intermediates. This is the only system available in Photoshop that uses its own inks. The organization of the Color Finder into two categories, high and low chroma, has its roots in psychological research done in color perception.

The Toyo colors also seem to be brighter and more vibrant than those found in other systems. To ensure the best match, specify a Toyo Ink from a certified blender and a printer who uses Toyo inks.

Choosing Colors

Photoshop provides a variety of methods to choose colors. Colors can be selected from either the standard Apple or Windows Color Picker or the Photoshop Color Picker. Select the desired Color Picker in the General Preferences submenu under the File menu. In addition to the Color Picker, Photoshop provides the Picker, Swatches, and Scratch palettes and the Eyedropper tool to pick colors.

Apple Color Picker

Apple modified the Color Picker with System 7.5, making it extensible. In the new Apple Color Picker (an extension that can also be used by earlier system versions) you can choose color picking systems by clicking on the More Choices button and then on an icon in the scrollable field along the left side of the dialog box. Two systems are provided with the picker, the Apple HSL (Figure 8–5) and Apple RGB (Figure 8–6) systems.

The Apple Color Picker offers the advantage of visualizing colors based on their relationship on the color wheel. However, converting to CMYK Color mode when using the Apple Color Picker is problematic, because it doesn't show CMYK values and will not warn you of out-of-gamut color selections.

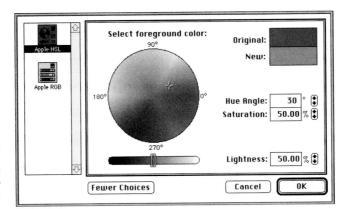

Figure 8–5
The Apple HSL mode
for the Apple Color
Picker in System 7.5

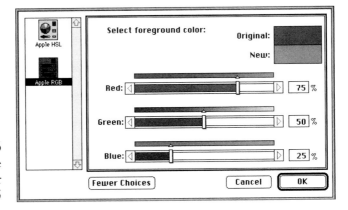

Figure 8–6
The Apple RGB mode
for the Apple Color
Picker in System 7.5

The **Apple HSL** (Hue-Saturation-Lightness) system provides a color wheel display (Figure 8–5). You can select colors by clicking on the wheel or typing in numbers. Hue is specified by an angle, and Saturation and Lightness by percentages.

Drag the mouse around the perimeter of the color wheel to change Hue. Move in toward the center to change Saturation. Drag the Slider under the color wheel to adjust the Brightness. The color box in the upper right splits in half, showing you the original selected color with the revised color above it.

The **Apple RGB** system allows you to mix colors with three sliders, red, green, and blue, in percentage values (Figure 8–6). The color box in the upper right splits in half, showing you the original selected color with the revised color above it.

Some companies are developing color tools which can be added to the new Apple Color Picker. For example, the software for Light Source's Colortron, a low-cost spectrophotometer (a device which measures the light waves of the visible spectrum), makes use of the new Apple Color Picker.

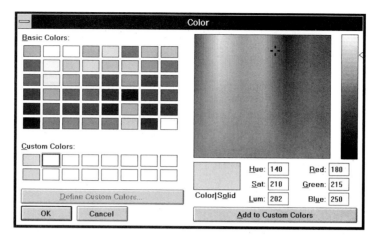

Figure 8–7
The standard Windows
Color Picker

Windows Color Picker

In the Windows Color Picker you can specify colors using the HSB or RGB color models (Figure 8–7). The current version of Windows does not contain any system-wide support for color management, nor does it have a gamut alarm or method of choosing CMYK colors.

CAUTION: Colors may not look the same on your screen when used in your target applications. Even exactly the same colors (RGB or HSB) created and displayed in Photoshop may not look the same when displayed in the Macintosh and Windows versions. Be sure to test your images before proceeding with a project.

Photoshop Color Picker

The Photoshop Color Picker, available on both Macintosh and Windows, provides a more stable and versatile method of color selection (Figure 8–8). A simultaneous display of a color's numeric mix in the various color modes allows you to select colors based on the HSB, RGB, Lab, or CMYK color

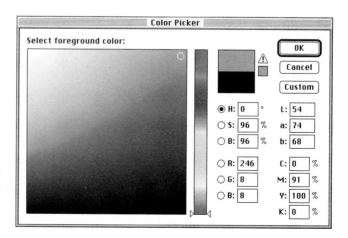

Figure 8–8
The Photoshop Color
Picker with an out-of-
gamut color selected

models. A warning alarm appears when you select a color that cannot be reproduced with CMYK colors.

To make the Photoshop Color Picker available, open the General Preferences dialog box under the File menu and choose Photoshop in the Picker pop-up menu. Click OK.

To set the Foreground color to black and the background color to white, click on the Reset Default Colors button in the Toolbox. Click on the Foreground color icon to open the Color Picker.

The Photoshop Color Picker consists of the following: the Color Field in the left side of the window, which in this case displays values of red; the Color slider, a vertical strip to the right of the Color Field; radio buttons with corresponding text fields for each of the color systems; two color swatches showing the original color and revised color; and a Custom button that allows you to pick colors based on named color systems.

Click in the upper-right corner of the Color Field to change the foreground color to red. The two color swatches in the upper-central part of the Color Picker dialog box display the new color above the original color. An exclamation mark in a triangle (a gamut alarm) appears when you select a color that cannot be reproduced with CMYK colors.

Colors may be selected visually from the Color Field and Color slider, which display components of either the HSB or RGB color models. Clicking on the various radio buttons changes the view of the color components.

- Click the Hue radio button (H) to set the Color slider to display hues, while the Color Field displays saturation and brightness values. The horizontal axis in this case reflects changes in saturation, while the vertical axis reflects changes in brightness. After selecting a desired hue, click anywhere in the color field to change its saturation and brightness.

- Click the Saturation radio button (S) to display a range in saturation in the Color slider. The color field displays changes in hue on the horizontal axis and changes in brightness on the vertical axis.

- Click the Brightness radio button (B) to display a range in brightness in the Color slider. The color field displays changes in hue on the horizontal axis and changes in saturation on the vertical axis.

- Click the Red radio button (R) to display a range of red values in the Color slider. The color field displays changes in blue values on the horizontal axis and changes in green values on the vertical axis.

- Click the Green radio button (G) to display a range of green values in the Color slider. The color field displays changes in blue values on the horizontal axis and changes in red values on the vertical axis.

- Click the Blue radio button (B) to display a range of green values in the Color slider. The color field displays changes in blue values on the horizontal axis and changes in red values on the vertical axis.

Choose colors at any time numerically by typing the appropriate number in the value fields. As you type in new numbers, Photoshop automatically recalculates the new color and updates the entire window.

- In the HSB mode, specify Hue by a color's angle (degrees) on the color wheel, and specify saturation and brightness with percentage values.
- In the RGB mode, specify a range of colors from 0 to 255 in each of the fields.
- In the Lab mode, specify Lightness (L) as a percentage, and the *a* and *b* components by values ranging from –128 to 127.
- In the CMYK mode, specify a percentage in each of the color component fields.

The settings made in the Printing Inks Set Up and the Separation Set Up preferences dialog boxes under the File menu affect how CMYK color values relate to the other color models. See Color Separations later in this chapter for more information about how those preferences affect mode conversions.

The Floating Color Palettes

Photoshop 3 provides three floating color palettes, the Picker, Swatches, and Scratch palettes, that facilitate the choosing and mixing of colors. Display the palettes by selecting Palettes under the Windows menu and desired palette from the submenu.

TIP: Once you have an image open with colors in it, you can pick colors from the image with the Eyedropper tool.

THE PICKER PALETTE

You can select either the foreground color or background color quickly and logically in the Picker palette from color sliders or from a spectrum of colors in a color bar (Figure 8–9). Change the color mode of the slider controls to Grayscale, RGB Color, HSB Color, CMYK Color, and Lab Color using the pop-up menu on the right side of the palette. Click on the Foreground or Background color box to choose which will be affected by your selection.

TIP: Improve performance on a slow computer by deselecting the Dynamic Sliders in Picker button in the General Preferences dialog box under the File menu.

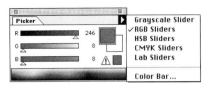

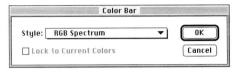

Figure 8–9
The Picker palette showing its pop-out menus

Figure 8–10
The Color Bar dialog box

Move the sliders to vary each of the color components. The range of values for RGB Color, HSB Color, CMYK Color, or Lab Color is basically the same as for the Photoshop Color Picker described above. An additional option, the Grayscale Slider, is available from the pop-up menu and provides a single slider which can be set between 0% (white) to 100% (black).

If you select or mix a color out of the CMYK gamut, an exclamation point in an alert triangle will appear on the right side of the palette. Next to it will be the closest color Photoshop can simulate. Click on it and the selected color will change to this new color. See the "Detecting Out-of-Gamut Colors" section later in this chapter.

TIP: To create a set of consistent pastel colors using the HSB mode, set the Saturation and Brightness to fixed light values and move the Hue slider to get the desired colors. To make lighter and darker tints and shades of a fixed color, use the Saturation and Brightness sliders while leaving the Hue constant.

The color bar along the bottom of the palette provides a gradient of colors from which to choose. When you choose Color Bar from the pop-up menu, the Color Bar dialog box appears (Figure 8–10). You can choose from four Styles: CMYK Spectrum provides a spectrum of CMYK (printable) colors horizontally which vary in saturation vertically. RGB Spectrum provides a spectrum of RGB colors horizontally which vary in saturation vertically. Grayscale Ramp provides a gradation from white to black. Foreground to Background provides a gradation from the current foreground color to the current background color.

TIP: Shift-clicking in the Color Bar toggles you through the gradient styles without going to the pop-up menu.

When you move the cursor over the color bar, it becomes the Eyedropper tool allowing you to choose colors. If you choose the Foreground to Background option, there is a checkbox to Lock to Current Colors. Checking the box locks the color bar to the chosen color range, even if the foreground or background colors change.

THE SWATCHES PALETTE

You can select colors from a set of color swatches (cells) using the Swatches palette (Figure 8–11). Use the default set of swatches or add, change, insert, or delete colors. You can also save, load, and append swatches of colors.

The cursor becomes the Eyedropper tool by passing it over the cells, allowing you to click on a color to select it as the current foreground or background color. It becomes a Paint Bucket tool over blank cells, allowing you to add new colors.

You can add, replace, insert, or delete colors in the swatches with the following keystrokes:

- To add a new color to a blank cell, move the cursor over it and the cursor will change to the Paint Bucket tool. Click on the cell to add the color.

- To change a cell's color mix to a new color, hold the Shift key to turn the cursor into the Paint Bucket tool and click on a cell.

- To insert a new color between existing cells, hold the Shift and the Options keys down and click on a cell. The new color will be added and the existing cells will move over.

- To delete a Color swatch, hold down the Command key to turn the cursor into the Scissors tool and click on the cell.

You can create your own custom palettes or load any of the existing custom color palettes, such as the ANPA, Pantone, Toyo, Focoltone, and Trumatch palettes. These palettes are found in the Color Palettes folder. You can also load color tables that you have created in the Indexed color mode (see the "Indexed Color" section later in this chapter).

Choose Load Swatches from the pop-up menu to load a new palette. Choose Save Swatches to save a palette to disk. You can combine palettes by using the Append Swatches command. The Reset Swatches restores the default palette.

TIP: Although the Color palette can be made as large as desired, you may find it more practical to make smaller palettes for individual projects.

Figure 8–11
The Swatches palette showing its pop-up menu

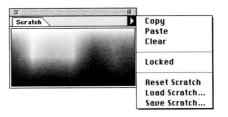

Figure 8–12
The Scratch palette
showing its pop-up menu

THE SCRATCH PALETTE

Use the Scratch palette as a custom-color mixing well (Figure 8–12). The Scratch palette contains an RGB spectrum by default.

Just as an artist uses a palette, you can use any of the painting tools to mix colors on the Scratch palette (try the Smudge tool or the Gradient tool). The Rubber Stamp tool allows you to copy portions of an image into the Scratchpad. The Move tool can be used to drag a selection from a document window. Zoom in or out for precise color selections with the Zoom tool. Change your view when you've zoomed in on a palette with the Hand tool.

TIP: **If you are mixing colors in the Scratch palette and adding them to the Swatches palette, save time by separating the two palettes by dragging one away from the palette's tab.**

TIP: **The Scratch palette is also a convenient place to define a custom brush shape or pattern.**

Scratch palettes can be saved to disk or loaded from the pop-up menu. You can use any of the selection tools except the Pen tool to make selections to be copied and pasted to another Scratch palette. You can reset the Scratch palette to the default by choosing Reset Scratch.

Lock a palette by choosing Lock from the pop-up menu. When locked, you can only pick up colors from the palette with the Eyedropper tool. If the palette is not locked, you can choose Clear from the pop-out menu to create a new palette. (The palette will be filled with the background color.)

Color Modes

Each color mode represents a color model that Photoshop uses to depict an image (Figure 8–13). The Bitmap, Grayscale, Duotone, Multichannel, and Indexed Color modes use one channel to describe a basic image. The RGB, Lab, and CMYK Color modes use multiple channels in combination to describe an image. In all cases except the Bitmap mode, additional channels

Figure 8–13
When converting from RGB mode, you can directly convert to Grayscale, Indexed Color, CMYK Color, Lab Color, or Multichannel mode. The other choices are grayed out.

can be used for masking and image compositing. Each color mode has particular applications that justify its use, and converting from one mode to another facilitates the use of each mode's attributes.

Mode Conversions

Converting from one mode to another should not be taken lightly. In most cases the pixel data is irreversibly changed. Be aware of the following issues and guidelines prior to making any mode conversions.

GENERAL CONSIDERATIONS

Changing modes allows you to create a variety of special effects, strip out or add color information, manipulate certain qualities of an image such as lightness (luminosity) or channel characteristics, or end up in the right number of channels (or the right number of colors) for your specific output.

To change modes, go to the Mode menu and choose the mode to which you want to convert. In some cases, you cannot convert directly; the destination mode may be grayed out so you must first convert to an intermediate mode and then to the destination mode. Following are the choices you will find when changing modes.

Bitmap: From Bitmap you can only convert to Grayscale.

Grayscale: From Grayscale you can convert to Bitmap, Duotone, Indexed Color, RGB Color, CMYK Color, Lab Color, or Multichannel.

Duotone: From Duotone you can convert to Bitmap, Grayscale, Indexed Color, RGB Color, CMYK Color, Lab Color, or Multichannel.

Indexed Color: From Indexed Color you can convert to Grayscale, RGB Color, CMYK Color, or Lab Color.

RGB Color: From RGB Color you can convert to Grayscale, Indexed Color, CMYK Color, Lab Color, or Multichannel.

CMYK Color: From CMYK Color you can convert to Grayscale, RGB Color, Lab Color, or Multichannel.

Lab Color: From Lab Color you can convert to Grayscale, RGB Color, CMYK Color, or Multichannel.

Multichannel: From Multichannel you can convert to Bitmap, Grayscale, RGB Color, CMYK Color, or Lab Color.

When converting to Indexed Color, Duotone, and Bitmap modes, you must choose how the conversion will be accomplished. For instance, when converting to Indexed Color choose the resolution, the palette, and the dithering method to be used. The choices are described with each mode later in this section.

GUIDELINES FOR SUCCESSFUL MODE CONVERSIONS

Keep in mind a few basic rules as you make mode conversions:

- Most important: always save a copy of your file in the source mode before you do a mode conversion. In many mode conversions, you are asked to discard color information or channels. For example, when you convert from a color image to Grayscale, you'll be asked to throw away your colors. To edit the colors again, you must return to the original file.

- Don't convert back and forth between modes. Sometimes you can convert between modes without any change in the data, but in most cases the data file gets changed. Generally, try to convert in one direction only, from the source mode to the destination mode. For example, if you convert from RGB Color mode to CMYK Color mode and back to RGB, your end result will not match your original. And the more times you convert, the farther from the original you will stray. On the other hand, you can convert freely between RGB Color and Lab Color without losing information.

- If your image contains layers, "Flatten visible layers and discard hidden layers?" will usually appear when converting between modes. If you click OK, the file will be flattened to one layer. Again, if you plan on editing the layers, save a copy of the file with layers before converting.

- If you can't convert directly to another mode, get there in two steps. For example, to create a duotone or work in the Bitmap mode, you must change to Grayscale mode first.

Bitmap

The Bitmap mode displays an image with a grid of 1-bit black or white pixels. No graytones exist in this basic display mode which is useful for high-contrast graphic images and custom halftone screens for special effects or refined control.

All color and grayscale information is removed from an image when converted to Bitmap mode. To convert a color image to Bitmap mode, you must first convert it to a Grayscale mode. When a grayscale image with 256 levels of gray is converted to Bitmap mode, levels 0 to 127 are converted to black and levels 128 to 255 are converted to white.

In addition to simple, low-resolution graphic images, the Bitmap mode allows you to create high-resolution halftoned black-and-white images. You have full control of the characteristics of the halftone dots used to render an image. The halftone dots can be any shape, dithered or customized from any pattern. After applying screen effects, a bitmap image can be converted to a color mode for special effects. Bitmap mode can be used to create halftones for non-PostScript printers.

You should do most of your image editing in Grayscale mode as there are few editing choices available in Bitmap mode. When converting an image to Bitmap mode, you can choose the output resolution used for the conversion process (Figure 8–14). The different settings result in various halftone dot sizes, angles, and shapes.

The default settings in the Input and Output fields correspond to the resolution of the image being converted. You can specify the units for output as either pixels per inch or pixels per centimeter by pressing on the pop-up menu button on the right-hand side of the units field. To change the input units, select the Image Size option under the Image menu and then change the unit format in the New Size area.

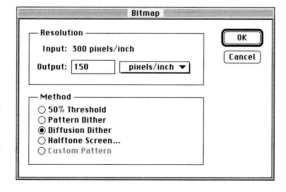

Figure 8–14
In the Bitmap dialog box set the output resolution, halftone, and dithering method.

NOTE: After conversion to Bitmap mode, an image might appear to have changed in size. In reality, the image is the same size. Press and hold the size indicator in the lower-left side of the image window to observe that the image matches the size of the original grayscale image.

Because all tones are converted to black and white, Bitmap mode creates the smallest file size of any mode.

Not all file formats can save images from the Bitmap mode. Bitmapped images can be saved at any resolution in the TIFF or EPS formats. When saving in the TIFF format, white areas will automatically be transparent in a page layout program. In the EPS format, the Save dialog box contains a Transparent Whites button which makes white areas either transparent or opaque white in a page layout program. The MacPaint format limits bitmaps to 72 ppi at 8" by 10". The PICT format can save at any resolution and size but should only be used for on screen presentations and not for print output.

DITHERING AND HALFTONING

When converting a grayscale image (Figure 8–15) to Bitmap mode, you can apply one of five types of dithering or halftone screens to the image:

50% Threshold: Converts the image into a high-contrast, non-textured bitmap. When analyzing the grayscale image, pixels with a value of 128 or higher are converted to white, and those with values of 127 or lower are converted to black (Figure 8–16.) This is called a *line shot* in conventional photography.

Pattern Dither: Converts grayscale values into "clumps," or geometric groups of black-and-white dots (Figure 8–17).

Diffusion Dither: One of the most visually pleasing conversion modes, reminiscent of the grainy feel of early digitized images. At higher resolutions the scattered pixels are hardly noticed, producing the appearance of a continuous tones (Figure C–7 in the Color Section and Figure 8–18).

Halftone Screen: Allows you to process an image through a variety of halftone screens. By screening an image through the Bitmap mode, you have full control over the halftone effect—anything from fine screens to course experimental effects. Using this technique you can print custom halftones on any non-PostScript printer, a feat impossible until the arrival of Photoshop.

When choosing this conversion method, you are presented with a dialog box containing the halftone options (Figure 8–19). You may enter specific halftone screen frequencies, measured in lines per inch, as well as the

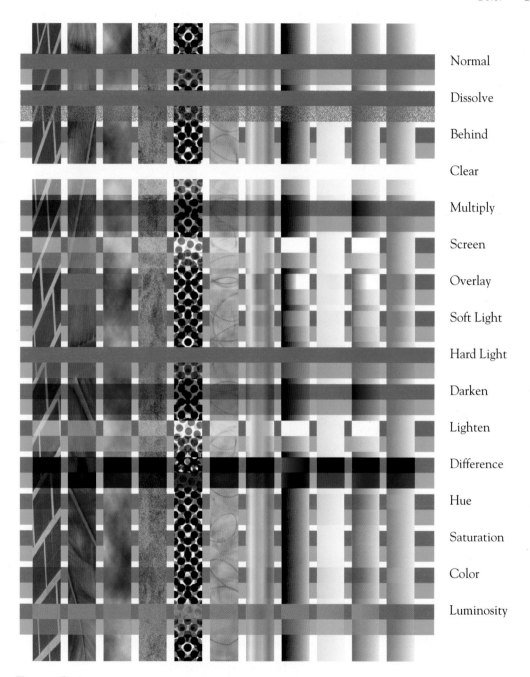

Normal

Dissolve

Behind

Clear

Multiply

Screen

Overlay

Soft Light

Hard Light

Darken

Lighten

Difference

Hue

Saturation

Color

Luminosity

Figure C–1
The Fill modes in Photoshop (see Chapter 6, "Image Selection and Masking").
In this chart, sample image selections, shown as vertical bands, are altered by
Photoshop's Fill modes, shown as superimposed horizontal bands. The top band
in each mode is filled with solid Green; the bottom is filled at 50% Opacity.

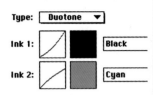

Figure C–2
The above Duotone
curves were applied to
the grayscale photograph
"Boats" by Merrill Nix.

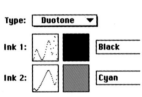

Figure C–3
The curves for this
Duotone were modified
more dramatically.

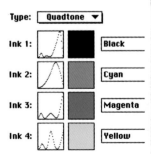

Figure C–4
The above curves resulted
in this Quadtone.

Figure C–5 (left)
In Lab Color mode, curves were altered for the **a** and **b** channels only, affecting only the colors and not the values.

Figure C–6 (right)
The values were altered with Curves in the Lightness channel only, leaving the colors unaffected.

Figure C–7
The "Dithered Pixels" technique explained in Chapter 11, "Output," was used to create this image. The sky (courtesy of CD Folios) was pasted into the background by defining the figure as a mask (see Figure 1–11).

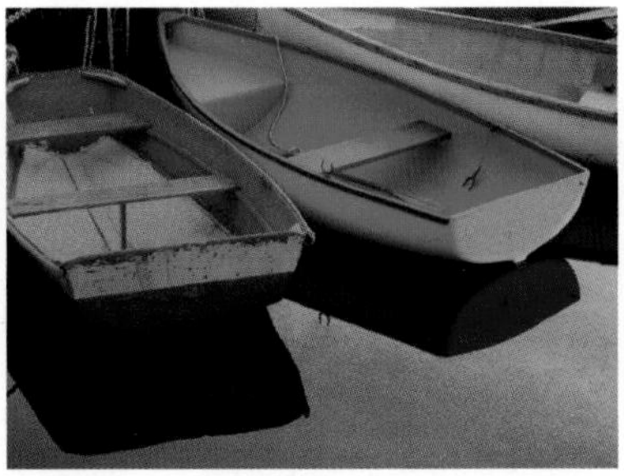

Figure C–8
The original grayscale "Boats" by Michael Roney was converted to Lab mode and then colorized by filling areas with the **a** and **b** channels active and the Lightness channel inactive.

Figure C–9
Only the colors in the above colorized photograph were inverted with the **a** and **b** channels active and the Lightness channel inactive.

Figure C–10
Only the values in the colorized photograph were inverted with the Lightness channel active and the **a** and **b** channels inactive.

Various filters were used to create these effects on Andrew Rodney's photograph, "Dog in Bowl."

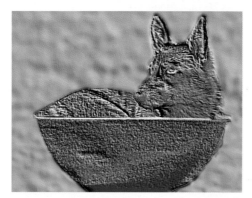

Figure C–11
Emboss and Trace Edges

Figure C–12
Pinch

Figure C–13
Aldus Gallery Effects Volume 1, Dry Brush

Figure C–14
Aldus Gallery Effects Volume 1, Mosaic

Figure C–15
Aldus Gallery Effects Volume 1, Splatter

Figure C–16
Aldus Gallery Effects Volume 2,
Glowing Edges

Figure C–17
KPT (Kai's Power Tools) Texture

Figure C–18
Find Edges and Invert KPT

Figure C–19
Andromeda 3-D Box and Sphere on Grid

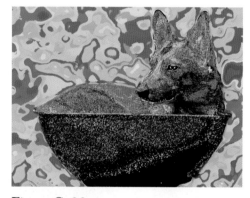

Figure C–20
Second Glance Chrommassage

Figure C–21
Xaos Tools Paint Alchemy Oil Canvas

Figure C–22
Xaos Tools Paint Alchemy Bubbles

© Bill Niffenegger

Figure C–23
Use the Variations command discussed in Chapter 8 to make a color cast and saturation test. The settings shown here are: 1, More Saturated; 2, Just Right; 3, Less Saturated; 4, More Blue to the Midtones; 5, More Green to the Midtones; 6, More Red to the Midtones.

Figure C–24
This sequence, created with a rotoscoping technique (see Chapter 12, "Multimedia"), uses the Filmstrip format saved from Adobe Premiere.

Figure C–25
To create "Leonardo Pix," Kai Krause used various channel operations (chops), as well as masking, Levels, Curves, and filters. See Chapter 6, "Image Selection and Masking."

© Kai Krause

© Chris Swetlin

Figure C–26
Each tool in this multimedia interface performs a metaphorical function (see Chapter 12, "Multimedia").

© Bellacera, Siprut, Stump

Spring Forth
Tom Cross

© John Lund

Locomotive
John Lund

© Lanny Webb

© Hiroshi Miyazaki

A 1993-Early November Dream
Hiroshi Miyazaki

Sunshine
Lanny Webb

© Diane Fenster

I Couldn't Stay in Miami
Diane Fenster

© Stephen Johnson

Fading Away
Stephen Johnson

© Sanjay Kothari

Wheels
Sanjay Kothari

Drive-In
Adam Cohen

Buffalo Transmitting Power to Man
Joseph Bellacera

Highrow Glyphics
Wendy Grossman

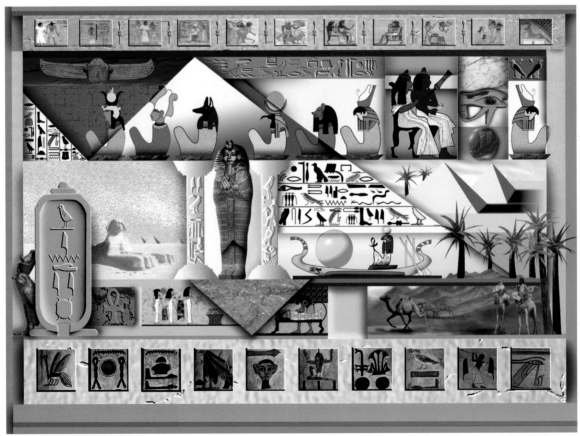

© Jean-Francois Podevin/Larry Scher/The Image Bank

The Sky is Page. . .
Jean-Francois Podevin
and Larry Scher

Motorola Frame Relay
Ed Foster

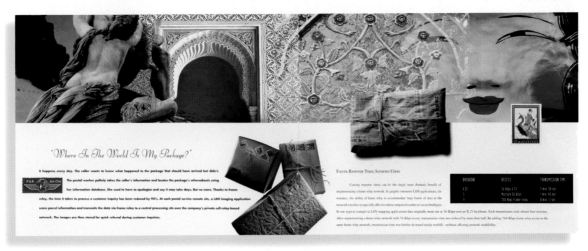

© Ed Foster

Akihabara
Bert Monroy

Peter Pan
Alan Brown

© Alan Brown/Photonics Graphics/Courtesy Erik Kaegler, Cincinnati Ballet

© Charly Franklin

Man on Ladder
Charly Franklin

© Andrew Rodney

Microsoft Office Ad
Andrew Rodney

Twisting Spine
Terry Toyama

Ephemera
Dorothy Simpson Krause

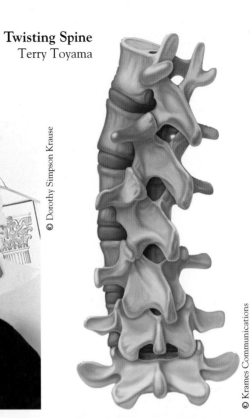

© Dorothy Simpson Krause

© Krames Communications

**Banks &
Terrorism**
Rick Nease

© RickNease/The Blade

© Ellen Van Going/Krames Communications

**Evolution of a Computer Virus
(a Harmless Variety)**
Ellen Van Going

Hardware Upgrade
Nick Fain

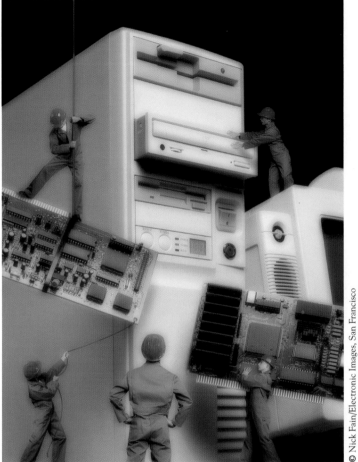

© Nick Fain/Electronic Images, San Francisco

© Jeff Schewe

Couch Potato Family
Jeff Schewe

© Philip Rostron

**Chestnuts
Roasting**
Philip
Rostron

© Greg Vander Houwen

Cloud Burst
Greg Vander Houwen

© Nino Cocchiarella

© Hagit Cohen

Kushi's Dream
Hagit Cohen

Black and White 1
Nino Cocchiarella

Figure 8–15
The original grayscale image

Figure 8–16
50% Threshold

screen angle of the halftone. Use different screen frequencies depending on the final output applications. For example, when preparing an image for output to a 300 dpi printer, a frequency value of 53 lines per inch and an angle value of 45 degrees will produce the best results. There are also six types of dot shapes (see Figure 11–26). Halftone screen settings can be saved and then loaded later for use with other images.

Figure 8–17
Pattern Dither

Figure 8–18
Diffusion Dither

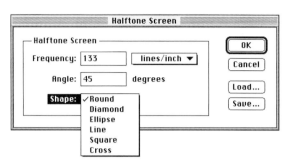

Figure 8–19
The Halftone Screen dialog box allows you to set the screen frequency, angle, and shape

Figure 8–20
A Custom Halftone screen was applied to this photograph.
(© Mark Siprut)

Custom Pattern: This option becomes available when you have defined a pattern prior to making the mode conversion. To define a pattern, select the desired area and choose Define Pattern under the Edit menu. Patterns used to define a halftone screen can create a myriad of effects (Figure 8–20).

Grayscale

The Grayscale mode uses up to 256 shades of gray for each pixel in an image. This mode contains one channel of information, called Black, in the Channels palette. Grayscale images can be obtained by digitizing a black-and-white image, opening a Photo CD file created from a black-and-white negative, converting a color image to Grayscale mode, or converting a Bitmap mode image into Grayscale mode.

Since there is only one channel of information, the file is one-third the size of an RGB image. All commands and tools are available except those

Figure 8–21
The Grayscale dialog
box when converting
from Bitmap mode

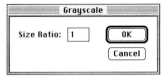

that apply specifically to color. For example, the Hue/Saturation and Color Balance controls are disabled when you are working in Grayscale mode.

TIP: **It is important to understand the Grayscale mode because an individual channel in any other mode functions as a grayscale document.**

When color images are converted to Grayscale mode, all color information is removed from the image. You will be prompted as you convert a color image whether you want to "Discard color information?" Be sure to save an original version if you need to use the color file again.

Instead of converting an RGB image to Grayscale mode directly, a better quality image might be achieved by using one of the following techniques.

- Convert the color image to Lab Color mode and use the Lightness channel, which has the tonal information in the picture. Duplicate the channel into a new document.

- Use the Channels palette to view each of the channels, red, green and blue, and choose the one which has the information you want to use.

- Duplicate two or more channels into layers of a new document and experiment with combining them using various blending modes and opacity settings.

When you convert a bitmap image into Grayscale mode, you can specify the size ratio to be used in the conversion process (Figure 8–21). The Grayscale dialog box controls the resolution of the resulting image. The default setting of 1 yields an image the same size as the original bitmap image. If you enter a value of 2, the resulting image will be scaled down 50%.

Duotone Mode

Duotones, tritones, and quadtones are used in offset printing to increase the tonal range and to add color to grayscale images. The monitor can display up to 256 shades of gray, but the printing press can only reproduce about 50 tones of gray (or an ink color). By printing the same image two times in register, the range of tones increases, rendering a richer, more saturated image.

Duotones can be created in Photoshop by starting with a grayscale image and then converting to Duotone mode. If you are starting out with an RGB or CMYK image, first convert to Grayscale mode, then convert to Duotone mode.

Duotones can take advantage of custom color inks such as those specified by Pantone and Toyo. Photoshop does not break each color out as a channel; rather it treats the duotone as a single 8–bit channel. The colors and tonal curves for the various plates are simulated as a composite on the screen. The separation to individual plates happens only at the time of printing. See the duotone examples in the Color Section (Figures C–2, C–3, and C–4).

CREATING A DUOTONE

To produce a monotone (one color), duotone (two colors), tritone (three colors), or quadtone (four colors), start with an image in Grayscale mode and then choose Duotone from the Mode menu to access the Duotone Options dialog box (Figure 8–22). In the Type pop-up menu, choose Monotone, Duotone, Tritone, or Quadtone. The Type choice will activate the ink color fields and Curve icon boxes.

Pick colors from the Custom Colors pop-up menu (see Figure 8–4). To choose an ink color from the Custom Colors dialog box, click on the solid color square for the desired ink. Click on the Picker button to mix your own color. Whether you use a custom color or define your own, the spelling of the color names must match the spelling of the same colors used in any other programs that will be used in combination with Photoshop to separate the file. Not all programs spell the custom colors identically. Check the naming conventions in the various programs you use or type in your own simple color names such as Color 1 and Color 2. Custom Colors are discussed earlier in this chapter.

TIP: When using Pantone colors, you can choose Use Short Pantone Names in the General Preferences dialog box to ensure that the spelling will match most other programs. Be sure to check the spelling; misspelled names could be a costly mistake.

Figure 8–22
In the Duotone Options dialog you can specify colors and tonal curves for monotones, duotones, tritones, and quadtones.

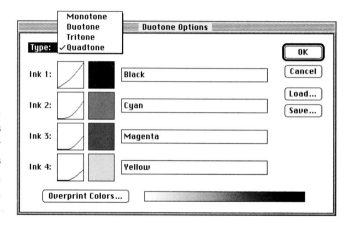

NOTE: Some of the custom colors in the menu, such as the Trumatch selections, are mixed with process colors (CMYK). Others, such as Toyo, are mixed with custom inks. In either case, be aware that the color on the monitor often does not match the printed ink color. Always refer to a printed swatch book when specifying ink colors.

TIP: If you are choosing a process color as an ink and wish to separate it on a process color plate, be sure to name it "Cyan," "Magenta," "Yellow," or "Black."

Next, adjust the relationship between input gray values and the output values for each of the inks by clicking on the Curve icon next to the ink color, opening the Duotone Curve dialog box (Figure 8–23). Make adjustments by clicking points on the graph or by entering numbers in the output percentage boxes. The x-axis (horizontal) refers to input values and the y-axis (vertical) refers to output values.

By default, the curve is a straight line indicating that, for each grayscale value, a halftone dot of the same value will be created for that ink. To lighten the midtone of a color, enter a value of 40 beside "50%," which indicates that wherever there is a 50% tone in the image (the input value) a 40% halftone dot will be created (the output value) for the indicated ink color. Usually, set darker colors to print heavier in the shadows (toward the right) and lighter colors to print heavier in the highlights (toward the left).

TIP: You can specify up to 13 points on the curve, but two or three are usually sufficient because Photoshop interpolates the in-between values into a smooth curve.

After setting the curve for a color, click OK to return to the Duotone Options dialog box. After setting the curves for each color, click OK once again to see a screen preview of your image.

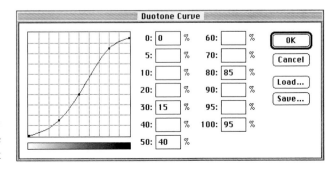

Figure 8–23
The Duotone Curve dialog box

NOTE: Set the way two overprinting colors will appear on the screen by clicking on the Overprint Colors button in the Duotone Options dialog box. Clicking on a swatch for an ink combination opens the Color Picker where color adjustments can be made. This color adjustment is best made if you have a printed sample to match your display against. These settings have no effect on output.

EXAMINING AND ADJUSTING A DUOTONE IMAGE

After examining your duotone image on screen, you may wish to make adjustments to the color curves. It's a good idea to use the Info Palette to analyze your image by viewing readouts from various points in the image.

To use the Info palette in Duotone mode, select the Options pop-up menu to open the Info Options dialog box. Choose Show First Color Readout and select Actual Color from the Mode pop-up menu. After you click OK, measure the amount of each color with the Eyedropper tool, indicated on the Info palette by the numbers 1, 2, 3, or 4, depending on how many colors you have specified.

It is possible to view individual plates as channels by converting to Multichannel mode. Be sure to save your document before doing this because you will need to revert back to the Duotone version. When converted to Multichannel mode, Channel 1 displays Ink 1, Channel 2 displays Ink 2, and so on. Do not attempt to adjust the image in multichannel mode—you must revert the image back to make the adjustments in the Duotone Options dialog box. Nor can you correctly print your image from Multichannel mode. This method can only be used for viewing individual channels. When finished, choose Revert from the Edit menu to return to your Duotone image.

TIP: An alternative if you do want to edit individual channels is to convert from Multichannel to CMYK and then output or save separations. You will not be able to preview the colors correctly but you can edit print the channels.

Once you have adjusted the color curves to your satisfaction, use the Save button on the Duotone Options dialog box to save curves for use on other images. Use the Load button to load duotone curves.

TIP: Photoshop ships with a number of curves for duotones, tritones and quadtones. Macintosh users can find them in the Duotone Presets folder inside the Goodies folder. Windows users can find them in the duotones subdirectory. These curves are created using shades of gray, process colors, and Pantone colors. Load them by clicking the Load button in the Duotone Options dialog box. Even if you choose not to use these curves, they are a great starting point.

PROOFING AND PRINTING A DUOTONE IMAGE

When you are satisfied with the effect on your monitor, print a color composite or output color separations. Either can be printed directly from Photoshop. However, be aware of these important warnings:

- Most digital color printers are CMYK printers. Some don't recognize duotone curve information. If not, these printers will only print the underlying grayscale image, ignoring the duotone curves. To print the color image, make a copy of your duotone image (retaining the original) and convert it to CMYK Color mode. Use this image to print color composites.

- Duotones are printed with halftone screens on top of halftone screens, just like process color printing. The screen angles must be set correctly to avoid moiré patterns. Normally, black or the darkest color should be set to 45°. Set the second darkest color to 75°, the third darkest color (for a tritone) to 15°, and the lightest color (for a quadtone) to 0°.

Often images must be imported into other programs to be combined with graphics and text. You must save a file from the Duotone mode in the EPS file format to save the duotone curve information and allow the file to be color separated (TIFF files will neither save duotone curves nor separate spot colors). When saving an EPS file, a dialog box will appear with various options. Set the Preview option for your computer platform. If you want to see the colors, choose 8–bit. Set the Encoding to Binary for most situations unless your setup can't handle it. Click Include Halftone Screens only if you have specified a halftone frequency and angle in the Page Setup dialog box. If you do not set the halftone angles and frequency in Photoshop, you will need to set them in the host application. (By default, spot colors separate at 45°, which will cause a moiré pattern if used for more than one color.)

Check with your service bureau or printer to find out how to handle the halftone screens. Refer to the section on "How to Save Your EPS File" in Chapter 11, "Output," for more information on printing composites and separations.

Indexed Color

Use the Indexed Color mode when you want to limit the number of colors used to display an image. An indexed color image consists of one 8–bit channel with a specific color lookup table, or fixed palette which can include up to 256 colors. Because Indexed Color mode has only one channel it creates a smaller file, one-third the size of an RGB file. Typical applications of Indexed Color mode include on-screen presentations and multimedia.

Many tools and commands do not function in Indexed Color mode. Tools that are not available include the Smudge, Blur/Sharpen, and Dodge/Burn/ Sponge tools. Commands that do not work include Filters, Apply Image, and Calculations. The Map and Adjust commands function only on the entire image and become disabled after making a selection. Indexed Color mode has only one layer, the background. When converting an image with layers to Indexed Color mode you will be prompted to flatten the image. Be sure to save an original version if you need to use the layers or perform any image editing not available in the Indexed Color mode.

TIP: **Because you have limited editing ability in Indexed Color mode, you can temporarily convert to RGB for most image editing and then switch back to Indexed Color mode.**

You can only convert to Indexed Color mode from Grayscale, RGB Color, or Duotone modes. If you are starting in other modes, convert to RGB Color or Grayscale modes first.

When you convert an RGB image into Indexed Color mode, you can determine how the colors in the original image will be represented and the type of color palette that will be generated (Figure 8–24). Specify the number of bits dedicated to each pixel, which determines the number of colors in the color palette. Four-bit color can use up to 16 colors per pixel, while 5-bit color yields 32 colors (2 to the fifth power). Odd numbers, such as 3, 5, and 7, are useful for saving images in some of the more esoteric modes, such as Amiga IFF and CompuServe GIF formats. The indexed color depths most used are 2, 4, and 8 bits. You can also specify the exact number of colors in the palette by choosing Other and specifying the number.

Figure 8–24
The Indexed Color dialog box that appears when converting to Indexed Color mode allows you to choose the pixel depth, palette, and diffusion dither.

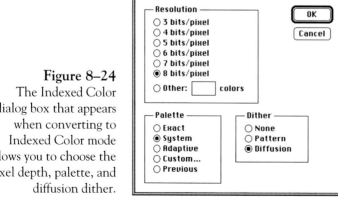

The palette and dithering options allow you to specify the type of palette that will result from the format conversion and the type of dither employed. Dithering simulates intermediate values of the colors, resulting in the illusion of more colors than are actually in the palette. Diffusion Dither tends to yield the smoothest image by scattering and intermixing the pixels (see Figure 8–18). The Pattern Dither produces a regular pattern similar to a canvas texture in an oil painting (see Figure 8–17). The None option results in a posterized appearance.

INDEXED COLOR PALETTES

There are five types of color palettes that can be used when converting to Indexed Color mode.

The **Exact palette** is an option when there are 256 or fewer colors in the image being converted. In this case Photoshop exactly matches the colors in the palette to the colors in the image.

The **System palette** consists of a predetermined set of colors that are supported by any application following the standard Apple programming guidelines. Object-oriented PostScript software such as Freehand and Adobe Illustrator use the standard System palette to display their entire color range on 8–bit displays. If you are not sure about which palette to choose, this is your safest bet.

Adaptive palettes are optimized to best represent the colors found in an image. When converting a 24-bit image to 8–bit indexed color, Photoshop analyzes the colors and creates a 256-color palette that best represents the colors found in the original file. An image with an 8–bit Adaptive Palette usually looks very much like the 24-bit image onscreen.

The **Custom palette** option allows you to create your own color table. The Color Table dialog box will appear after clicking the OK button with this option selected (see the next section "Editing the Color Table"). The Load and Save buttons allow you to access and save Color Tables for use in multiple documents.

The **Previous palette** is handy when converting more than one document with the same palette. Once a palette is applied to an image, subsequent conversions to Indexed mode have the Previous palette as an option.

TIP: To prepare images for screen presentations or multimedia, it is often helpful if multiple images use the same palette. Unfortunately, some programs have problems dealing with custom palettes and expect images to be mapped to the Apple system palette. Programs such as Macromedia Director can import and work with different palettes. See Chapter 12, "Multimedia."

EDITING THE COLOR TABLE

To view the currently active palette in Indexed Color mode, select Color Table under the Mode menu (Figure 8–25). This is the same dialog box that appears when you convert a color image to Indexed Color and choose the Custom palette.

Change individual colors in the table by clicking on the desired color, which opens the Color Picker. If you change a color in the Color Table, all occurrences of that color in the image file will be updated to reflect this new color.

You can also create gradients between two colors by selecting a range of colors in the table. This technique can be used in Macromedia Director to create smooth transitions when cycling colors. This feature can also colorize a grayscale image. Use the following steps to create a gradient between two colors in the Color Table:

1. Choose Color Table from the Mode menu. Press and drag from the first to the last color swatch for the desired blend (Figure 8–26). Any number of colors can be included for the blend.

2. The Color Picker will open and prompt you to "Select first color." Select the first color for the blend and click OK.

3. The Color Picker will open a second time, and prompt you to "Select last color." Select the second color for the blend and click OK. The

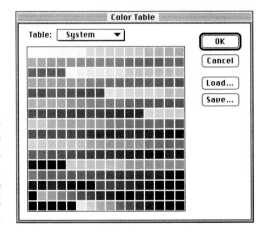

Figure 8–25
The Color Table allows you to edit the colors and make custom palettes for a document. Color tables can be saved and then loaded for future documents.

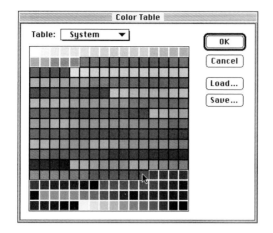 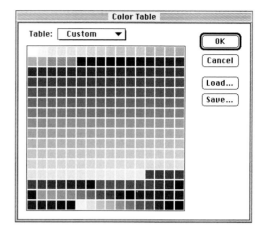

Figure 8–26   In the Color Table press and drag between two colors (left) to select a set for a blend (right).

program will automatically create the blend using the number of color cells selected.

4. Click OK again and the color table will be applied to the image. You can save and load custom color tables using the Load and Save buttons in the right-hand side of this dialog box.

TIP: Custom color tables can be opened in the Swatches palette mentioned earlier in the chapter. Thus, you can save a custom color table and load it in the Swatches palette, and then use that set of colors to paint with in any document.

BUILT-IN COLOR PALETTES

The black body, grayscale, spectrum, and system color palettes are built into Photoshop. Selecting one of them replaces the current palette with the chosen palette.

Black Body has its origins in physics. This table displays a transition of colors based on the nature of how heat is radiated from a body (like light radiating from a star). As a body heats up, such as an iron bar over a hot fire, it turns from black to red to orange to yellow to white. Desktop publishers can probably ignore this color table, but scientists might find it useful for image analysis problems.

Grayscale replaces the color range with a smooth 256-shade transition of grays from black to white.

Spectrum is a color table based on the colors that make up white light. If you observe light passing through a prism, you'll see a smooth transition between violet, blue, green, yellow, orange, and red.

System is the standard palette available in most applications. If your not sure, this is the safest palette to use.

RGB Color

RGB Color mode, the normal Photoshop working mode, describes an image by combining three channels, each representing one of the additive primary colors, red, green, and blue. When you open an image that has been digitized into Photoshop by a scanner or digital camera, you will usually be in the RGB display mode because these devices are designed to work with the additive colors. RGB Color mode gives you access to the full capabilities of all of Photoshop's tools and commands.

A 24-bit RGB image is composed of three separate 8-bit images (channels), one each of red, green, and blue, superimposed one on top of another to provide the full color image. RGB Color mode shows the three 8–bit channels as a composite, but you can also view and edit each channel separately (Figure 8–27). To view a channel, click to the left of a channel in the channels palette. The eye icon indicates that a channel is visible. To make a channel active for editing, click on the channel name. The channel in the palette will highlight (gray on a Macintosh and white in Windows) indicating that it is editable. Most tools and commands can be applied to individual channels.

TIP: Each channel can be viewed and manipulated in its appropriate color or in gray values. This choice is available in the General Preferences dialog under the File menu.

Figure 8–27
The Channels palette (left) showing an RGB Color image with one channel active (right)

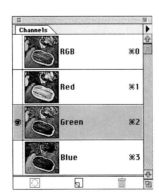

When the monitor is running on a 24-bit video display card, RGB Color mode is displayed on-screen with the full 24-bit color range. On an 8-bit system, a pattern dithering scheme is used to display the image with the best possible 8–bit (256 colors) quality. All tools work at a full 24 bits, regardless of the pixel/bit depth of the video card driving the monitor.

Many prefer to do their image editing and color correction in RGB Color mode. The file size of RGB files is smaller than in CMYK (see the tip in the next section). If the file is going to have multiple uses—for example, multimedia as well as print—RGB is a more general and flexible format. Finally, Photoshop 3 provides several tools to show you in RGB Color mode what the results will be when you convert to CMYK Color mode.

CMYK Color

The CMYK Color mode describes an image by combining four 8–bit channels, each representing one of the subtractive primary colors, cyan, magenta, and yellow, plus black. Most digital printers and printing processes use the CMYK colors (process colors) to reproduce full color images.

The CMYK image shows the four 8–bit channels as a composite, but you can also view and edit each channel separately (see Figure 1-12). To view a channel, click to the left of a channel in the channels palette. The eye icon indicates that a channel is visible. To make a channel active for editing, click on the channel name. The channel in the palette will highlight (gray on a Macintosh and white in Windows) indicating that it is editable. Most tools and commands can be applied to individual channels.

TIP: Each channel can be viewed and manipulated in its appropriate color or in gray values. This choice is available in the General Preferences dialog under the File menu.

Most images begin in the RGB Color mode but need to output from the CMYK Color mode in order to print to a CMYK digital printer or for color separations to make CMYK offset printing plates. The conversion to CMYK Color mode is controlled by the parameters set in the Monitor Setup, Printing Inks Setup, Separation Setup, and (if you are using it) Separation Table dialog boxes found in Preferences under the File menu. These settings should be set before you start working and should not be changed in the middle of a project.

NOTE: When you convert to CMYK Color mode, you end up with four channels instead of the original three. The document therefore becomes one third larger, processing more slowly than before.

When you have converted your image to CMYK mode, you do not see CMYK color. You are looking at a monitor displaying light with red, green, and blue phosphors—in other words, the display uses the RGB model. Photoshop has to use the same Preferences settings to convert the CMYK image to RGB values so you can see it.

CAUTION: Most CMYK files are targeted to particular settings for dot gain, black generation, and other printing issues set in the Preferences. If you subsequently change the preferences settings while in CMYK Color mode, you must go back to the original RGB file and reconvert it to CMYK in order for the new setting to affect the file.

Editing in CMYK mode also offers some advantages:

- If you are experienced, you can match printed halftone dot values. Use the Info palette to precisely measure the color values at critical places in an image—for example, if is important to reproduce flesh tones accurately. If you take a color reading with the Eyedropper tool and see that a Caucasian's skin tones measure C: 20%, M: 60%, Y: 62, K: 0, you would recognize that it looks sunburned—too red. From experience, or by referring to a process color tint chart, you might color correct the skin to C: 20%, M 40%, Y: 42, K: 0 to make it look more natural.

- If you have purchased a high-quality drum scan from a color service bureau or if you've rasterized a color image coming from an illustration program like Adobe Illustrator, you will mostly likely receive the file in CMYK Color mode. The service bureau will ask you what the target press and paper stock is before scanning, making appropriate settings in their scanner software to target that printing setup. If you have communicated well with your service bureau, you should not have to color correct the image. If you need edit or manipulate the scanned image, leave it in CMYK Color mode.

- You can produce smoother gradients for printed work if they are created in CMYK Color mode rather than in RGB Color mode.

Lab Color

The Lab Color mode is based on visual color perception using a standard created by the Commission Internationale de L'Éclairage (CIE). In CIE L*a*b, a revision of this standard adopted in 1976, color values are defined mathematically to exist independent of any device. Photoshop drops the asterisks and calls this standard Lab Color, using it as the internal standard for storing color values.

Conversions between RGB Color and CMYK Color are problematic because the gamut of colors available in RGB does not match the gamut available in CMYK, and because RGB and CMYK values are linked to particular devices. Lab Color provides a device-independent standard to create consistent color documents on different color devices. Transparent to the user, Photoshop uses Lab Color as an intermediate stage during mode conversions. Lab Color is also used by color management systems as a standard for defining colors.

The Lab Color mode describes an image by combining three 8–bit channels. A channel for *luminance* or Lightness controls the tonal range in the image. Two other channels control *chrominance* or color, an *a* channel, which controls the range from green to magenta, and a *b* channel, which controls the range from blue to yellow (Figure 8–28).

Because the luminance values (lightness) in an image are separated from the colors, you can adjust the lightness (or tones) without affecting the actual color components of the image using the following method:

1. Open a color image and convert it to Lab Color mode.

2. Open the Channels palette under the Windows menu. Click on the Lightness channel to activate it (make sure that the "eye" icon is visible and the channel highlighted).

3. Open the Curves dialog box under the Adjust submenu under the Image menu and make changes to the curve, altering the image. Click OK. Click on the Lab channel in the Channels palette to view the composite. The gray values in the image will appear distorted, but the colors will remain intact (Figure C–6 in the Color Section).

The color of the image can be manipulated without altering its Lightness channel by using the above method and altering the *a* and *b* channels only. The final image will have altered colors, but the value range will remain intact (Figure C–5 in the Color Section.).

Listed below are suggestions for using the Lab mode.

- Colorize black and white images by converting to Lab mode by isolating the *a* and *b* channels, and adding colors without affecting the gray values (Figure C–8 in the Color Section).

Figure 8–28

Here, the image from Figure 8–28 appears in Lab Color mode. Luminance is controlled by the Lightness channel; colors between green and magenta, by the *a* channel; and colors between blue and yellow, by the *b* channel.

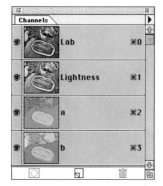

- Invert the *a* or *b* component of an image to substitute negatives (complements) of the colors, leaving the main detail of an image positive (Figure C–9 in the Color Section).

- Invert the Lightness channel only to create a negative of the image, leaving the original colors intact (Figure C-10 in the Color Section).

- Posterize the image with the Lightness channel isolated, and then apply the median filter. When you activate the color channels, the image will look hand-painted.

- Experiment with other filters and commands on the Lightness channel: Solarize, Find Edges, Invert, Brightness/Contrast, Gaussian Blur, and the various tools in the toolbox.

- Apply tools, commands and filters that keep the channels in register, such as Pointillize, Median, Threshold, Airbrush tool, Paintbrush tool, etc., to individual or combinations of channels.

After adjusting any of the channels, the image can be converted back to the original RGB Color mode. Because Lab Color is the standard reference for other Color models, it is safe to switch back and forth between Lab Color and RGB Color mode, or between Lab Color and CMYK Color mode.

CAUTION: Do not switch back and forth directly between RGB and CMYK Color modes. This will adversely affect the colors.

If you have a PostScript Level 2 digital color printer, you can print directly from the Lab Color mode. Lab Color is converted to CMYK in the printer using color rendering dictionaries built into the printer. At the time of this writing, you cannot print color separations to PostScript Level 2 imagesetters.

Multichannel

The Multichannel mode, the most generic display mode, contains up to 24 grayscale channels, each containing 256 levels of information (8–bit). The Multichannel mode frees all channels so that they can be moved, edited, or deleted without the limitations built into the color modes. The Multichannel mode has only one layer, the background layer, so whenever you convert to Multichannel mode any layers will be merged.

Some suggested uses and benefits of the Multichannel mode include the following:

- Use the Multichannel mode as an intermediate step when converting from one mode to another if you want to keep all of the channels intact. You can convert freely between the Multichannel mode and any other mode without loss of data.

- View individual duotone, tritone, or quadtone color plates as grayscale channels.
- Convert a duotone, tritone, or quadtone to CMYK Color mode by first converting to Multichannel mode from the Duotone mode.

TIP: To save a duotone image as a CMYK file or in the Scitex CT format, convert from Duotone to Multichannel and add blank channels so that you have a total of four channels. Convert the image to CMYK Color mode. You can then save it in the Scitex CT format, as well as EPS or TIFF. You must reassign the proper colors to the plates at the time of printing.

- To work with groups of grayscale images similar in size, create a single multichannel Photoshop document with a different image in each of the channels. Using this technique you can keep up to 24 related images together in one file.
- Create multichannel compositing and special effects.
- Temporarily convert RGB, Lab, or CMYK Color images to Multichannel mode to shuffle channels around in the Channels palette. Obviously this will change the final colors in the image.

NOTE: In earlier versions of Photoshop, if you deleted any of the component channels of an RGB or CMYK image, the image was converted automatically into the Multichannel display mode. In Photoshop 3, you must convert to Multichannel mode prior to deleting or shuffling any channels.

When converting to Multichannel mode any color names will be replaced by numbers. For example, an RGB image will have three channels labeled #1, #2, and #3.

It's not easy to print or save out of Multichannel mode. To print a multichannel document, you must print individual channels. Only the Photoshop native format, and TIFF and RAW file formats can save from Multichannel mode. Other applications cannot open or import Multichannel documents.

TIP: To save Multichannel mode documents for exporting to QuarkXPress use the PlateMaker export plug-in from In Software. The plug-in exports in the DCS 2.0 format to save multiple plates to be used as spot colors, varnish layers, or other. See the "Saving Spot Colors with the PlateMaker Export Plug-in" section in Chapter 11, "Output," for more information.

Process Color Separation

The process of converting an image from RGB Color to CMYK Color mode (or in some cases from Lab Color to CMYK Color) is called *color separation*. This complex conversion is important in preparing files for printing on a printing press or digital color printer.

Photoshop stores its files, regardless of their mode, in Lab Color because it is a device-independent color space with a larger gamut than any other color space (as discussed in earlier in this chapter). Lab Color ensures that files convert from one mode to another with a minimum loss of color information.

How Photoshop Converts from RGB to CMYK

Converting from RGB to CMYK takes two steps. First, Photoshop converts RGB information to Lab using the settings stored in the Monitor Setup Preferences. Second, the program converts the Lab information to CMYK using settings in Preferences for Printing Inks Setup and Separation Setup.

NOTE: If you are using a Separation Table, the information in the table will be used instead of the settings in the Printing Inks Setup and Separation Setup preferences. Separation Tables are discussed later in this section.

Once the image is in CMYK Color mode, you can't really see the image in CMYK because the monitor displays with red, green, and blue phosphors. To display your CMYK image, Photoshop must go backward using the preferences settings, and convert the CMYK values back to RGB values for the monitor.

While in the RGB color mode, settings for Printing Inks Setup and Separation Setup have no effect on the RGB data. The settings take effect only when you actually perform the RGB to CMYK conversion.

TIP: If you have converted an image to CMYK and you wish to make a change in your settings for Monitor Setup, Printing Inks Setup, or Separation Setup, you must reconvert from RGB to CMYK for the change to take effect. For example, if you change the dot gain value from 22% to 35% to print on newsprint instead of coated stock, you must return to the original RGB image and reconvert to CMYK for the new dot gain value to take effect.

Working in RGB Mode

In general, the best approach when working on images coming from desktop scanners or digital cameras is to edit primarily in RGB Color mode. With few exceptions, converting to CMYK should be one of your last steps before saving for printing.

There are several advantages to editing or color correcting in RGB. First, the file size is smaller and more flexible. Second, RGB is also the format needed for multimedia. Third, you can decide how to set up for printing as the last step.

When working in RGB, however, always be conscious of the difference between the available gamut of colors the monitor can display and those that can be printed on a CMYK digital printer or printing press using process colors. Each device or press setup has its own range of displayable or printable colors. Although most colors coming from scanners or digital cameras are usually within the gamut for printing, it's very tempting to create bright monitor colors which cannot be printed.

DETECTING OUT-OF-GAMUT COLORS

Fortunately, Photoshop provides several tools for detecting RGB colors that are unprintable or out of gamut. In the Photoshop Color Picker or in the Picker palette, if you select an unprintable color an alert triangle with an exclamation mark (!) appears indicating an out-of-gamut color next to the color choice (see Figure 8–8). Click on the small color square below the exclamation mark to choose the closest CMYK equivalent as the current color. If your image still has an out-of-gamut color, Photoshop will create a color as close as possible to your selection when the image is converted to CMYK by "clipping" the color to fit within the printable gamut of the chosen printer.

NOTE: The actual gamut of colors available will vary depending on the printer or press setup you have chosen in Printing Inks Setup and Separation Setup Preferences. If you choose a different printer, colors which were printable before may no longer be, and vice versa.

Keep the Info palette open at all times. As previously mentioned, the Info palette can show color values for two modes simultaneously. Set the first color to show the your current mode of RGB Color and the second to show CMYK Color values. This gives you access to the CMYK Color values prior to actually converting a document. If an out-of-gamut color is detected, an exclamation point appears beside the CMYK value (Figure 8–29).

The following steps point out some out-of-gamut colors. Luckily, Photoshop supplies you with six quickly accessible, unprintable colors to work with!

Figure 8–29
The Info palette shows that the first six swatches of the Swatches palette are out-of-gamut.

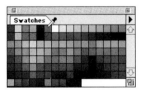

1. Open any RGB Color image.

2. Open the Swatches palette by choosing Palettes under the Window menu. If the Info palette is not open, choose the Show Info palette from the same submenu.

3. In the Info Palette Options pop-up menu, set the First Color Readout to RGB Color and the Second Color Readout to CMYK Color.

4. Choose the Eyedropper tool, and move it over any of the first six swatches of the Swatches palette. (If you no longer have Photoshop's default swatches, choose Reset Swatches from the Swatches palette pop-up menu.) In the Info palette, you will see that exclamation points appear next to the CMYK values for these colors, indicating that they are out-of-gamut (Figure 8–29).

There are two other methods of detecting nonprintable colors before doing a conversion to CMYK mode: Gamut Warning and CMYK Preview.

GAMUT WARNING

Gamut Warning displays all the areas of an image that are out-of-gamut for the currently selected printer.

1. Open any RGB Color image.

2. Choose Gamut Alarm from the Mode menu. All the unprintable colors will appear as a neutral color.

3. Make these areas stand out more definitely by changing the display color. Choose the Gamut Warning Preferences under the File menu. Click the color swatch to open the Color Picker (see Figure 3–18).

4. Choose a bright, contrasting warning color. You can also set an Opacity value between 0 and 100. An opacity value of less than 100 will reveal some of the underlying image. Click OK.

Use any of the color correction tools or commands to correct for nonprintable colors. (See the "Color Correction" section later in this chapter).

TIP: In the ColorRange dialog box (available under the Select menu), choose Out Of Gamut from the Select pop-up menu. All of the out-of-gamut colors will become a selection. Then use Sponge tool or an appropriate Adjust command to correct the colors.

CMYK PREVIEW

The CMYK Preview feature allows you to see how an image will look before actually converting from RGB Color to CMYK Color. The CMYK

Preview does not convert the colors, but previews them in their CMYK equivalent. If a color is clipped because it is out-of-gamut, you will see the color as less saturated and/or darker.

This feature is most effectively used when both the RGB Color and CMYK Preview images are viewed side-by-side.

1. Open or create a brightly colored RGB image.

2. Choose New Window from the Window menu to create a new window.

3. Move the new window so you can see both windows of the same image next to each other.

4. Click on the new window to make it active and choose CMYK Preview from the Mode menu. When compared to the original, notice that the out-of-gamut colors appear desaturated and muted in the CMYK Preview window.

Creating and Using a Separation Table

If you are accustomed to printing color images to different digital printers or to different paper stocks, you can save time and be more consistent if you save your settings for Printing Inks Setup and Separation Setup preferences into a Separation Table for each printer or press setup. Using a Separation Table replaces the choices you make in the Printing Inks Setup and Separation Setup preferences.

Separation tables function in the following cases: using a color management system like EfiColor, if you prefer to use the color separation algorithms of another color separation program, or if you want to build a custom table for your digital color printer or printing specifications.

To create a separation table using Photoshop's preference settings, follow these steps:

1. Choose the Printing Inks Setup Preferences from the File menu and make your choices in the Printing Inks dialog box. (These choices are described in the "Calibration" section in Chapter 3, "Configuring Photoshop.")

2. Choose the Separation Setup Preferences from the File menu and make choices from the Separation Setup dialog box. (These choices are described in the "Separation Setup" section in Chapter 11, "Output.")

3. Choose the Separation Tables Preferences from the File menu. The Separation Tables dialog box appears (Figure 8–30). Click the Save button. You can then name your separation table.

To use a separation table, choose the Separation Tables Preferences from the File menu. In the Separation Tables dialog box, click the Load button. Select the Separation Table you want to load and click OK.

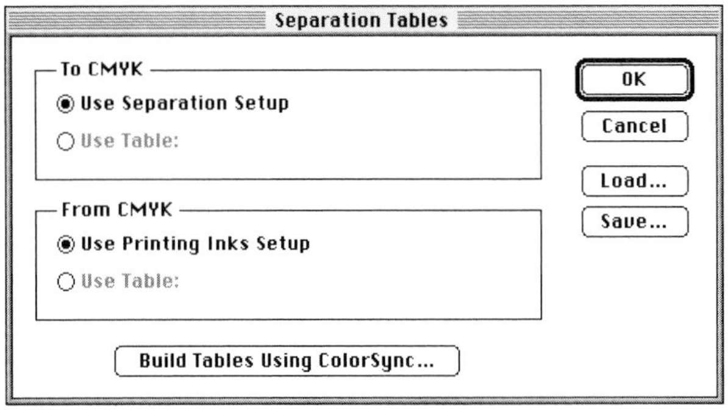

Figure 8–30
The Separation Tables
dialog box

Photoshop will build its internal table based on the information in your table. Separation Setup will now be grayed out in the Preferences submenu. You can choose Printing Inks Setup, but an alert dialog box will tell you that information in Printing Inks Setup won't be used in conversion to and from CMYK. Converting from RGB to CMYK (or back) will be based on the loaded Separation Table.

In order to use Printing Inks Setup or Separation Setup again, instead of a Separation Table, choose the Separation Tables Preferences from the File menu. In the To CMYK section, click the Use Separation Setup button. In the From CMYK section, click the Use Printing Inks Setup button.

SEPARATION TABLES FROM OTHER APPLICATIONS

If you use a color management system (CMS), you can to use the profile information provided by your CMS to generate a separation table to be used in Photoshop. For example, if you use EfiColor Works, which uses the EfiColor CMS, the EfiColor Profile Editor can generate a separation table for your specific printers or press setups. Load the separation table as described above. See the EfiColor Works documentation for more information on how to use the Profile Editor. (Color management systems are described in Chapter 3, "Configuring Photoshop.")

Tables created by the color separation algorithms used by other software such as Color Access or ColorStudio can be loaded into Photoshop. An Adobe Technical Note, "Using Separation Tables from Other Applications," describes the somewhat technical procedure by which color tables from these applications can be converted into Photoshop separation tables. The tech note is on the Adobe Photoshop Deluxe Edition CD-ROM, or is available from Adobe Technical Support.

CUSTOMIZED SEPARATION TABLES

The most ideal conversion from RGB to CMYK is made by developing a custom separation table for your particular printer or press setup. The choices in Printing Inks Setup are generalized for "ideal devices" in a laboratory and may not reflect how your printer actually prints colors. Or you may not see your printer listed in Printing Inks Setup. Here are two methods to create a custom separation table:

- If you use EfiColor Works, the EfiColor Profile Editor can customize a device profile. Start with a profile which approximates your device and then tailor the profile further. In the Profile Editor you can edit transfer curves for each color, dot gain settings, and GCR (gray component replacement) levels. (Transfer curves, dot gain, and GCR are discussed in Chapter 11, "Output.") After completing your custom profile, generate a Separation Table as described above.

- If you are fortunate enough to have access to a colorimeter or spectrophotometer (precise color measurement devices), you can measure CMYK color swatches from a printed proof and use those values to customize Printing Inks Setup and a Separation Table. This method may soon be a more widely viable option with the advent of inexpensive hand-held spectrophotometers, such as the Colortron from Light Source.

Use the following steps to create a custom ink setting in the Printing Inks Setup Preferences.

1. Print a proof of the *Olé No Moiré* image described in the Calibration section in Chapter 3, "Configuring Photoshop."
2. Choose the Printing Inks Setup Preferences from the File menu. In the Printing Inks Setup dialog box, select Custom from the Ink Colors pop-up menu. The Ink Colors dialog box appears (Figure 8–31).

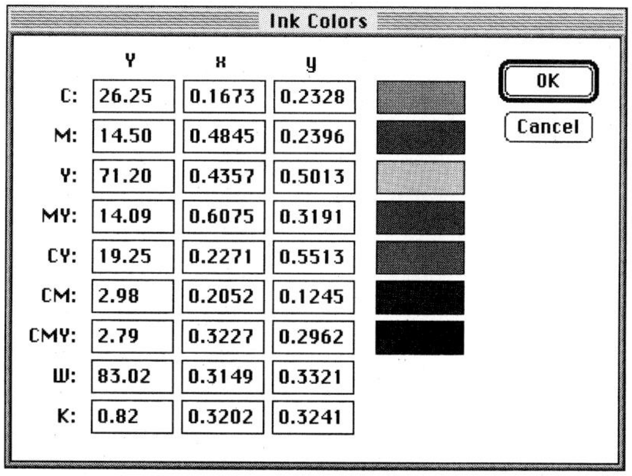

	Y	x	y		
C:	26.25	0.1673	0.2328		OK
M:	14.50	0.4845	0.2396		Cancel
Y:	71.20	0.4357	0.5013		
MY:	14.09	0.6075	0.3191		
CY:	19.25	0.2271	0.5513		
CM:	2.98	0.2052	0.1245		
CMY:	2.79	0.3227	0.2962		
W:	83.02	0.3149	0.3321		
K:	0.82	0.3202	0.3241		

Figure 8–31
The Ink Colors
dialog box

The Ink Color dialog box displays various combinations of CMYK and their corresponding CIE chromaticity values. These are similar to Lab Color values, but are mathematically transformed. Colors are defined by three coordinates: *x*, *y*, and *Y*. *Y* is the luminance coordinate and *x* and *y* are the chrominance coordinates.

3. Measure the CIE values of the CMYK patches on the printed proof with a colorimeter or spectrophotometer, and enter these values into the Ink Color dialog box. Click OK.

4. Save a Separation Table using this Printing Inks Setup information.

Trapping

The Trap command becomes an option only in the CMYK Color mode. Trapping creates a slight overlap in adjoining colors to compensate for misalignment that might occur on the printing press. This misalignment will be apparent where two unrelated solid colors butt against one another. In most cases you do not need to set a trap. If you have solid colors in your image, consult your printer for the specific trap value to enter. For more information on trapping, refer to Chapter 11, "Output."

The Adjust Commands

Use commands under the Adjust menu (Figure 8–32) for tonal adjustments, color correction, special effects, and color enhancement. Image processing commands that apply to tone control only (Levels, Curves, Brightness/Contrast, and Auto Levels) were discussed in Chapter 7, "Image Processing."

TIP: The most accurate controls to adjust values are the Levels and Curves commands. Use either to adjust both grayscale and color images.

Figure 8–32
The Adjust Commands

Adjust Guidelines

- Adjust commands apply only to the target layer. You cannot apply a command to more than one layer simultaneously. To apply the same command to multiple layers, apply the command to each layer one at a time, or merge the layers prior to applying the command. Remember that merging layers is irreversible.

- As a safeguard always make a duplicate copy of your document (or duplicate the Layer) before making changes. Open both windows side by side to compare corrections.

- Be careful not to overdo tone or color correction. Repeated corrections can reduce the number of tones in an image, resulting in banding or shade stepping. Histograms of over-corrected images will show gaps for missing values.

- Many of the Adjust commands have Save and Load buttons. Once you have established settings you can save and then load them into future documents for identical corrections.

- To make localized color changes, use any of the selection tools or commands prior to applying the color change; only the selected portion of the image will be affected.

- The current document's Scroll Bars, Hand, and Zoom tools (including keyboard shortcuts) are active while working in any of the Adjust commands.

- Keep the Info palette open for before and after readouts for any pixel values while an Adjust command dialog box is still open.

- Cancel any settings made in a dialog box without closing it by holding the Option key and clicking on the Cancel button (which changes to a Reset button).

Levels

The Levels command adjusts the highlight, midtone, and shadow values in an image. In a color image, these controls can apply to all channels at once or to individual channels (Figure 8–33). Refer to Chapter 7, "Image Processing," for basic instructions on how to use the Levels command.

ADJUSTING COLOR

Because all colors in an image are made by compositing values from the red, green, and blue channels or, in the case of CMYK images, from the cyan, magenta, yellow, and black channels, colors can be adjusted by changing the values with the Levels command. For example, in an RGB image, if you move the midpoint slider to the left for the Red channel, it will brighten the red values in the midtones making the image more red

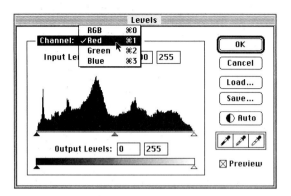

Figure 8–33
The Levels command
can edit values for
individual channels.

while simultaneously reducing the cyan (the complement of red). If you move the slider to the right the opposite will happen: the middle values of red will darken, making the image less red and more cyan.

RGB: If you lighten a channel (it adds the color), the colors will adjust toward the channel's color and away from its complement. If you darken a channel, the colors will adjust toward the complement and away from the channel's color.

Lab: In the Channel pop-up menu, choose the *a* channel. If you move the middle input slider to the left, the image will become more magenta and less green. If you move the middle input slider to the right, image will become more green and less magenta. In the Channel pop-up menu, choose the *b* channel. If you move the middle input slider to the left the image will become more yellow and less blue. If you move the middle input slider to the right, the image will become more blue and less yellow. Adjusting the Lightness channel affects only brightness and not color balance.

CMYK: If you darken a channel the colors adjust toward the channel's color and away from the complement. If you lighten a channel, the colors adjust toward the complement and away from the channel's color. Adjusting the Black channel affects only brightness and not color balance.

TIP: To evaluate colors pass the cursor over areas in the image and read the adjusted values in the Info palette. It displays both before and after values.

NEUTRAL GRAY POINT

Remove a color cast from an image by clicking on the desired middle gray point in the image with the middle Eyedropper tool in the dialog box. Or set the neutral value manually for each individual channel. All colors in the image will then be adjusted toward the neutral color. (Unless your photograph has an exact neutral gray card in it, defining the neutral value can be subjective.)

To change the color setting of the Middle Eyedropper (Neutral Gray Point), open the Color Picker by double-clicking on the tool. For an RGB Color image set the neutral gray to equal values of red, green, and blue. Generally middle gray is set at 127 or 128, but you can set it to any desired value or color.

For CMYK Color images, accurate color balance can be attained if you adjust each channel individually by matching the color values to a printed screen chart, a printer's specifications, or a reference table such as Table 8–1. For example, middle gray based on Table 8–1 (shown later in this chapter) is cyan: 46, magenta: 33, yellow: 33, and black: 9.

BLACK AND WHITE POINTS

To reproduce well, an image should have a full range of tones. To set the black and white points, ensuring a full coverage of tones, use the Auto button, the Black and White Eyedropper tools, or set black and white points manually. Follow the instructions in the "Levels" section in Chapter 7, "Image Processing," for basic instructions on setting black and white points and using the black and white Eyedropper tools.

For grayscale and RGB Color images you can use the black and white Eyedropper tools to set the black and white points, but for greater accuracy and especially for CMYK Color images, set the black and white points manually by adjusting each channel individually.

To set the Black Target Color for the Black Eyedropper tool, double click on the Black Eyedropper. The Color Picker will open. Enter the desired values in the RGB text fields. To set the White Target Color for the White Eyedropper tool, double-click on the White Eyedropper. The Color Picker will open. Enter the desired values in the RGB text fields.

Set the Black and White Point values manually by selecting channels one at a time from the Channels pop-up menu. For each channel, move the black and white input triangle sliders to the desired value. To find the shadow and highlight values in the image, pass the cursor over the likely areas and read the values in the Info palette. Set the output values by dragging the black and white output sliders to the correct values. (If you're working in CMYK, you must translate percentage values to levels. See Table 7–1 in Chapter 7, "Image Processing.")

TIP: **If you have difficulty finding the shadow and highlight areas in an image, use the threshold method. With the Preview button deselected, hold the Option key and drag the black or white input sliders. The black or white clipped values will appear in high contrast in the image (see Figure 7– 24).**

Curves

The Curves dialog box provides the most control of all of the image editing commands because it allows you to adjust any value in any channel independently. In the composite channel you can adjust the tones for the all channels at once. Or you can adjust channels individually by selecting each separately from the channels pop-up menu. Editing an individual color channel is identical to editing a grayscale document. Refer to Chapter 7, "Image Processing," for instructions on how to use the Curves command.

The basic steps using Curves are similar to those described for Levels: (1) Use the Eyedropper to measure the pixel values in the lightest and darkest parts of the image. (2) Set the target printing values for shadow and highlight. (3) Set the highlight and shadow points. (4) Make midtone adjustments if necessary. (Setting the target values for the Black, White and Gray Eyedropper tools is identical in Curves to the setting target values in Levels.)

To manually set the shadow, highlight and midtone for each individual channel follow the procedure for grayscale images described in Chapter 7, "Image Processing." Set each channel to the specific output values desired for any point on the Curve. To see where a value on the image falls on the graph, click on the image and a small circle will appear on the line with the corresponding Input and Output values displayed below the graph.

ADJUSTING COLOR

Adjusting colors with Curves follows the same principles described in the previous section on Levels. The main difference being that instead of only darkening and lightening the midtones, you can darken and lighten any value in the image by moving the curve up or down with up to 16 different points. An advantage of the Curves command is that you can adjust certain parts of the curve while locking other parts into position.

NOTE: In Lab mode, moving the curve up and down makes the colors more magenta or green for the *a* channel and more yellow or blue for the *b* channel.

Color Balance

Remove unwanted color casts from an image with the Color Balance command. For example, in a photograph of a child wearing a bright yellow jumper surrounded by big red balloons, light bouncing off the balloons may adversely affect the color of the jumper. This reaction of light and color is known as *color contamination*. With Color Balance, color contamination can be corrected by pulling out the unwanted colors.

The Color Balance command adjusts the balance of the colors that make up an entire image, layer, or selection. Color Balance works best on images in which precise color correction is not required. You can remove

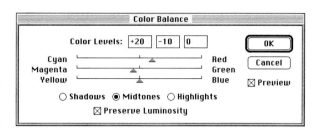

Figure 8–34
The Color Balance
dialog box

undesired color in an image, brighten dull colors, or use the controls to affect changes in the shadows, midtones, or highlights. Choose Color Balance to open the dialog box (Figure 8–34) and move it to see the image. Make sure the Preview option is selected.

The Color Balance command works with RGB, CMYK, Lab, and Indexed Color images. When used with a Lab Color image, the sliders represent the *a* (Green/Magenta) and *b* (Blue/Yellow) channels. Each slider represents colors directly across from each other on the color wheel. The Color Balance can be changed by moving the slider controls or by entering numbers between +/–100 in the boxes above the sliders. Moving a slider toward a color increases the amount of that color while decreasing the amount of the complementary color (opposites on the color wheel). The Preserve Luminosity check box prevents changes from affecting the tonal balance in the image. (Color changes will not darken or lighten the image.)

Hue/Saturation

The Hue/Saturation command allows you to make color adjustments based on the HSB color model. Hue/Saturation works most accurately in RGB Color mode. With the Hue/Saturation command (Figure 8–35) make global or selective color changes to hue (color tint), saturation (purity of color), or lightness (value). You can also tint a selection with a solid color by using the Colorize command found in the lower-right side of the dialog box. This is similar to filling an area with the Color Only option, except that with Hue/Saturation you can dynamically change the color using a slider control.

Make adjustments to all of the colors in an image or to specific primary color components. Adjust all colors by clicking on the Master radio button.

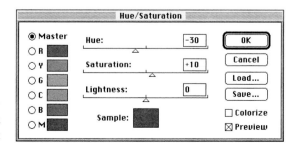

Figure 8–35
The Hue/Saturation
dialog box

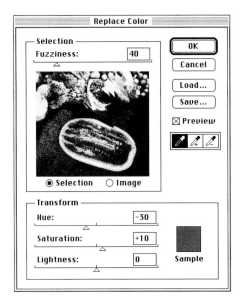

Figure 8–36
The Replace Color
dialog box

Select individual primary colors along the left side of the dialog box. The Sample box displays the current foreground color which can be changed by sampling a color from the image with the Eyedropper tool.

The **Hue** slider shifts the colors around the color wheel. As you move the Hue slider, all the colors change with respect to one another. This rotation, measured in + or – degrees, is displayed in the text field next to the slider.

The **Saturation** slider controls the purity (intensity) of the colors. Move the slider to the right for brighter, richer colors and to the left for duller, muted colors. The text field uses numbers between +/–100.

The **Lightness** slider controls the brightness (values) of the colors. Move the slider to the right for lighter colors and to the left for darker colors. The text field uses numbers between +/–100.

Replace Color

The Replace Color command allows you to build a temporary mask based on particular colors and then adjust those colors using the HSB color model. In the Replace Color dialog box, you can display either the image or the selection by clicking one of the two radio buttons under the preview. The Selection button should be checked to see the mask in the preview. Make sure to click the Preview check box to view changes in the image (Figure 8–36).

Using the three Eyedropper tools, select areas to mask. The + (plus) and – (minus) Eyedropper tools add or delete colors from the mask. The Eyedropper tool with the Shift key adds to the selection and with the

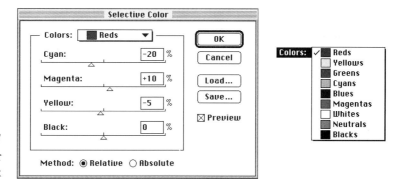

Figure 8–37
The Selective Color
dialog box

Command key deletes areas from the selection. The Fuzziness slider controls the tolerance of the mask much like the Magic Wand tool.

Once a temporary mask is created, the Hue, Saturation, and Lightness sliders can change those color parameters within the masked area. These controls operate just like the Hue/Saturation command. Use the Load and Save buttons to save the color adjustments for other images.

Selective Color

Selective Color, a new feature in Photoshop 3, borrowed from high-end color systems, allows you to selectively modify specific colors without affecting other colors. In the Selective Color dialog box, pick the color to modify from the Colors pop-up menu (Figure 8–37). In addition to the additive and subtractive primaries available in high-end color correction, Selective Color allows you to adjust black, white, and neutral colors. Once selected, only that color can be modified with the Cyan, Magenta, Yellow, and Black sliders. The Selective Color command is optimized for CMYK Color correction. It generally has more effect on saturated colors than on neutral colors. Selective Color will only work on the composite color channel.

There are two ways this command can be applied. If you select the Absolute option, color percentage corrections will be applied to the selected color by the amount shown. If you select the Relative option, corrections will be applied proportionately to the color value. For example, with the Absolute method, a 10% decrease of magenta to a color with 50% magenta would produce 40% magenta. With the Relative method, the same adjustment would produce 45% magenta (it would be reduced by 10% of 50%). Because black and white have no color components, the Relative method does not produce any changes. The Selective Color Parameters can be saved and loaded for use on other images.

Desaturate

The Desaturate command removes all color from an image or a selection. This has the same effect as converting to Grayscale mode without actually changing modes or as moving the Saturation slider to –100 (no saturation) in the Hue/Saturation dialog box. Use the Desaturate command to convert selected areas to grayscale while retaining colors in the other areas.

Variations

The Variations command, allows you to visually adjust the color balance, contrast, and saturation of an image or selection by clicking on small color corrected preview thumbnails. The Variations dialog box (Figure 8–38) not only shows changes as they are applied to an image, but also a number of the optional sample corrections, which are continuously updated as you make changes.

Although not as accurate as other commands, Variations does provide an obvious way to see your options. Each thumbnail displays subtle differences in the color, saturation, or contrast settings. For example, to make a color correction that adds red to your image, click on the thumbnail image that says More Red. A redder image (the Current Pick) will appear next to the Original image. The color options correspond to the position of the colors in the Apple Color Picker.

The radio buttons to the right of the top two thumbnail images give you the choice of adjusting the Shadows, Midtones, Highlights, and Saturation of your image. The slider below these radio buttons controls how small or large these incremental changes will be displayed and applied.

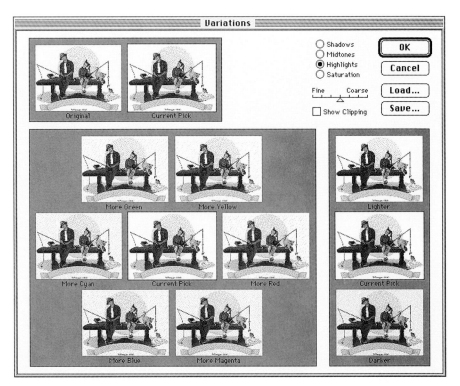

Figure 8–38
The Variations dialog box displays different color and value options.

The controls in the Variations command window change for Grayscale or Duotone mode images. In these cases, the only options available for adjustment are the highlights, midtones, and shadows. You cannot use the Variations command with Lab Color, Index Color, or Bitmapped modes.

The Show Clipping checkbox controls whether or not to preview areas in an image that will be clipped (changed to black or white when an adjustment is applied). Because highlights and shadows can get too light or too dark, the Show Clipping checkbox will show which areas are being clipped. Photoshop will display neon colors in these areas when you are pushing values too far.

TIP: After experimenting, simply click on the Original image to return the Current Pick back to the original.

You can save and load Variations settings for use at a later time. For the Variations command to be visible under the Image menu, the Variations plug-in must be located in Photoshop's Plug-ins folder.

TIP: The Variations command can be used for color separation insurance. Bill Niffenegger offers the following advice: "When using a new printer or color house, strike an agreement to run an 8 ½"x 11" film separation and Matchprint test. Make a composite image using the most sensitive areas of all the image files that will be used in the final job. Use the Variations command to bracket different saturation levels and color casts of the composite file (similar to a photographer bracketing a photo shoot) and place it into the page layout software that will be used for printing the job. Note the settings used for each step in the test. When the Match print test is returned and the most accurate strip is picked, apply the same settings to images throughout the job." See Figure C–26 in the color section.

Strategies for Correcting and Changing Colors

You will often want to change colors or tones of images in Photoshop, correcting for deficiencies in preparation for reproduction. You can also enhance an image and create special effects, mood, or atmosphere. Perhaps an image should not just reflect reality, but look better than reality! These subjective color corrections are more art than science.

Here are some steps to help you develop a strategy for color-correcting an image:

Calibrate your monitor to output: Otherwise, you cannot trust the image you see on the screen. Calibration is described in Chapter 3, "Configuring Photoshop."

Start with a good original: Digitize the image to capture as much tonal and color information as possible. Tone and color corrections will not recover sufficient detail in a poorly scanned image. Guidelines for achieving proper input are given in Chapter 4, "Input."

Learn how to read the Histogram, Info palette and Color Picker values. Practice with the Adjust commands (particularly Levels and Curves) and the Dodge/Burn/Sponge tool. Understand color theory and how Photoshop works with color.

Evaluate the image: Examine the quality of the image and decide what specifically must be corrected. Decide whether to work in RGB or CMYK. Use the Histogram and Info palette to help evaluate the color values in an image.

Identify the image type: High key, low key, average key, high contrast, and low contrast images all have different correction requirements. Image types are discussed in Chapter 7, "Image Processing."

Adjust the tones in the image: Set the highlight (the lightest parts of the image), the shadow (the darkest parts of the image), and the midtone values.

Correct for color imbalance. Decide which corrections should be made to the entire image, to selected areas of the image, or to particular colors. Necessary color changes may be *global*, meaning they affect all colors in an image. Or color corrections may be *local*, applied to specific selections. Color changes can also be *selective*, applied to all occurrences of a particular color in an image.

Convert from RGB to CMYK: If the final target is the printing press, at some point an image must by be converted to CMYK. Convert only once with the correct settings. You may then need some final color corrections in CMYK Color mode.

Color Correction Guidelines

Following are some ideas and tips for making global, selective, and local color and tone corrections:

- If evaluating the image as a whole seems daunting, look at the Histogram or Info palette to evaluate tone and color values.

- In a color image, increasing or decreasing the tonal values in a channel changes the color balance of the entire image. Similarly, changing the color balance of an image changes the tonal values in each of the channels.

- Either adding a color (red, for example) or subtracting its complement (cyan) adjusts colors toward the color (the image becomes redder).

- Either subtracting a color (red, for example) or adding its complement (cyan) adjusts colors toward the complement (the image becomes more cyan).

- Adding equal amounts of two analogous colors on either side of a color is the same as adding the color itself (for example, adding green and blue is the same as adding cyan). Subtracting equal amounts of two analogous colors on either side of a color is the same as subtracting the color itself (subtracting green and blue is the same as subtracting cyan).

- If the hue of a color is slightly off, try tweaking it toward one of its analogous colors.

- To make local corections, use any of the selection tools to select an area to modify and then apply a color adjustment tool or command.

- Select and change areas of a specific color throughout an image (selective correction) with the Color Range command under the Select menu or by clicking on a color with the Magic Wand tool and then choosing Similar under the Select menu.

- Apply color correction to specific colors throughout an image by using the Selective Color command.

- Replace specific colors throughout an image with the Replace Color command.

- The Sponge tool will either add saturation to a color or desaturate a color. Desaturate a color that is out-of-gamut.

- Dodge and Burn is an excellent localized tone-control tool.

- Fill areas with color with the Paint Bucket tool or Fill command under the File menu. Use the various modes and opacity settings to control how the fill color combines with the underlying color.

- Many of the tools and commands can apply color and tone changes to specific highlights, midtones, or shadows.

Correcting for Color Imbalances

Once you have corrected the tones of an image, you should correct or enhance the colors. Correcting for color casts or enhancing special colors or areas depends on how you want the image to be perceived. Who is the audience for the image? Will viewers appreciate subtlety or do they needed to be shocked by color? In most cases you will try to match your image to a digitized print, transparency, or real-life scene. Focus your attention first on the colors that count the most: neutrals, memory, and special colors.

NEUTRALS AND GRAY BALANCE

A *neutral* color, produced by a *gray balance*, has no color bias or cast. Gray balance means creating a balance of red, green, and blue values for RGB images, or a balance of cyan, magenta, yellow, and often black values for CMYK images, to create a neutral color. Whites, grays, and black are all neutral colors.

Representative Neutral Values

Grayscale	RGB	C	M	Y	K	Dot Area
95%	13	67	55	54	85	Shadow
90%	26	67	54	53	72	
80%	51	64	51	50	49	
75%	64	61	49	47	39	3/4-tone
70%	77	58	46	45	31	
60%	102	53	40	39	18	
50%	128	46	33	33	9	Midtone
40%	153	38	27	27	4	
30%	179	30	20	20	1	
25%	191	25	16	16	1	1/4-tone
20%	204	20	13	13	0	
10%	230	10	6	6	0	
5%	242	5	3	3	0	Highlight

Table 8–1
Values for CMYK and RGB that produce a neutral color for various gray levels

TIP: To ensure a neutral area in a photograph it helps to take the picture with a gray card or grayscale step wedge in the frame.

Table 8–1 lists the CMYK and corresponding RGB values needed to achieve gray balance. These values can be observed either in the Photoshop Color Picker or by setting the Info palette to display both RGB and CMYK values. Use any of the Adjust commands to globally, selectively, or locally correct the colors to end up with the desired neutral values. The most accurate commands are Levels and Curves when applied to individual color channels.

Neutrality is easier to understand in the RGB color model. A neutral value has equal amounts of red, green, and blue. But, in the case of CMYK Color images, observe that in highlights, cyan should be 2 to 3% greater than the other primaries. In the midtones and shadows cyan must be 12 to 14% greater than magenta and yellow values. The cyan ink must print heavier than the magenta and yellow to achieve a true neutral color because of impurities in printing inks.

NOTE: The Grayscale equivalent of the RGB values given in Table 8–1 are true if Use Dot Gain for Grayscale Images is turned off in the Printing Inks Setup preferences. The RGB column represents equal values for red, green, and blue. The CMYK values result from converting the RGB values to CMYK with

Printing Inks Setup preferences set to 25% Dot Gain and Separation Setup preferences set to the default settings (Separation Type: GCR, Black Generation: Medium, Black Ink Limit: 100%, Total Ink Limit: 300%). Use this table as a general guide but consult with your printer and service bureau for specific recommendations for your situation.

MEMORY AND SPECIAL COLORS

Memory colors are colors that we tend to remember because they are attributes of common objects, such as blue sky and green grass. Other common memory colors are the colors of food and flesh tones. Because of their psychological importance, memory colors should look as realistic as possible.

Also put in this category other special colors that will make a difference to the person who will judge the image. If you're reproducing a company's logotype or a product which is color critical, such as clothing or a car, the colors of these objects must receive special attention.

To match specific colors, refer to a color chart or swatchbook printed on your target printer or printing press. For example, for offset printing refer to a screen tint book of process colors to get the CMYK mix of a particular color, then match the CMYK values in Photoshop. For a digital printer, refer to a chart printed on that specific printer for an exact match. Use the Info palette to see if the values of the desired color match the values of the printed reference.

TIP: **Many digital printers and service bureaus supply color charts. You can also get software that will print charts on any printer from color matching system companies such as Pantone, Trumatch, and Focoltone. If you can't get a color reference chart for your situation, make your own.**

Summary

- The color wheel, defined by hue (the color), saturation (purity of the color), and brightness (degree of lightness or darkness), shows the relationships between additive and subtractive colors, and complementary and analogous colors. This information is necessary to correcting, enhancing, or altering colors.

- The additive colors, red, green, and blue, are best for on-screen work and presentations. The subtractive colors (or process colors), cyan, magenta, and yellow with the addition of black for shadow detail, are best for printed reproduction.

- Custom colors, also referred to as spot colors, are special inks printed on a printing press.

- Monitor colors have a wider color gamut than printed colors. Photoshop gives you many tools to detect and correct out-of-gamut colors.

- It's vital to understand Photoshop's color modes and how to change between them.

- Analyze the color values in an image with the Histogram and Info palette. Use the Info palette systematically to monitor color values for both the color mode in which you are working and, if applicable, the CMYK color equivalents.

- Apply color changes globally to affect the entire image or layer, selectively to affect only certain colors in an image, or locally to affect only selected areas.

- Develop a strategy for color and tone correction. Overcorrecting can destroy image data. There are many color correction and tools to perform any desired result, but the most accurate are the Levels and Curves commands.

Now that you have learned to correct tones and colors, you are ready for some of Photoshop's most creative tools: filters and plug-ins.

9

Chapter 9: Filters and Plug-ins

Photoshop's filters and plug-ins can produce results which are subtle or dramatic. Many yield unexpected visual effects, while others assure consistent and time-saving production results. Although filters are fun to play with, don't be tempted to use one just because it produces a "cool" effect if that effect doesn't relate to the content of your image.

To appreciate the power of the filters and plug-ins, practice using them individually and in combinations on many types of images. Try experimenting with filter effects on one or more translucent layers superimposed on your base image. Exaggerate effects through repeated applications or by using high settings (Figure 9–1).

Most filter plug-ins are accessible from the Filter menu. Some plug-ins, mostly device interfaces and file converters, can be accessed under Acquire or Export submenus under the File menu, or appear as new menus or when saving documents. Photoshop's open architecture allows third-party companies to add to the program's function.

There are two types of filters and plug-ins: *native* and *plug-in* modules. Native filters, programmed directly into Photoshop, cannot be removed. Modular filters (plug-in modules) are separate little programs that can be added to Photoshop's imaging arsenal at any time by placing a plug-in module in Photoshop's Plug-ins folder (Macintosh) or PLUGINS directory (Windows) (see Figure 1–10). Some filters and plug-ins require a math coprocesor, which may or may not be present in your model.

Figure 9–1
Guy Powers masked out the background in the studio shot on the left and applied the Unsharp Mask filter at a high setting (Amount: 400%, Radius: 4 pixels, Threshold: 0 levels) to boost highlights and exaggerate contrast. He then applied the Motion Blur filter to create "Flying Car" on the right.
(© Guy Powers)

This chapter looks at Photoshop's native and plug-in filters supplied by Adobe, as well as some of the more popular and useful plug-ins available from third-party manufacturers. Unless indicated, the filters and plug-ins are available for both Macintosh and Windows platforms.

NOTE: If a filter module does not appear in the Filter menu, make sure that the filter file is in the Plug-ins folder or PLUGINS directory. If it still does not appear, the filter file may be corrupted (unlikely, but possible). Try installing a fresh copy of the filter file. Or, on a Macintosh, you can restart Photoshop while holding down the Command key, which flushes the cache of plug-ins that Photoshop stores. This forces Photoshop to rescan all the files in the Plug-ins folder. A third solution is to throw away the Adobe Photoshop Prefs file in the Preferences folder of the System Folder.

Guidelines for Using Filters

Keep in mind the following when working with Photoshop filters:

APPLYING FILTERS

- Filters do not work in Bitmap and Indexed Color modes. To apply a filter to an image in Bitmap mode, you must first convert the image to Grayscale. To apply filters to an Indexed Color image, you must first convert it to RGB Color mode, apply the desired filters, and then convert the file back to Indexed Color mode. Some filters, such as Gallery Effects and Lens Flare, won't work in CMYK Color mode.

- Filters can be applied to any selected portion of an image, including masked areas, layers and channels. If nothing is selected, the filter will be applied to the entire target layer.

  TIP: **Try applying filters to individual component channels of color images for glowing special effects.**

- When applying a filter to a selection, feather the selection for a smoother transition into the background.

- Use low settings for subtler effects. Higher settings can completely obliterate an image or produce dramatically exaggerated effects..

- To instantly stop the processing of a filter, press the Command and Period keys. The image will revert to its prefiltered state.

- Filters only work on one layer at a time but can work on multiple channels simultaneously.

- To quickly test a filter effect, select a small area and apply the filter. Use the Undo command under the Edit menu to get a quick before-and-after appraisal of an applied filter effect.

- After applying a filter, it appears at the top of the filter menu so you can quickly reapply it. By applying a filter multiple times, you can exaggerate, simplify, and abstract an image.

- Some filters perform immediately while others have user-specified parameters. For example, Blur and Blur More begin processing immediately after selected from the menu, but Gaussian Blur has a control dialog box that asks you to specify the degree of blurring.

- After applying a filter, choose Take Snapshot from the Edit menu and then choose Undo from the Edit menu. You can now fill the image or selections with the filtered version of the original image by choosing Snapshot in the Use pop-up menu in the Fill dialog box under the Edit menu.

- To dilute or soften the effect of a filter on an image, duplicate the image to a new layer, apply a filter to the duplicate layer and change the Opacity or Mode settings. The duplicate layer will combine with the original.

PAINTING WITH FILTERS

- Create several layers of the same image with different filters applied. Use the Eraser tool at various opacity settings to remove areas of one layer, allowing other layers to show through.

- Paint with a filter using the Rubber Stamp tool. Open a file and duplicate the background to a new layer. Apply a filter to the new layer. Select the Rubber Stamp tool (make sure it is set to Clone Aligned), hold the Option key and click on an exact spot that you can find again (use the Info palette to get the exact x and y coordinates). This registers the image from which to clone. Next, click on the layer you wish to paint on in the Layers palette, place the Rubber Stamp tool on the original spot (using the Info palette to find it) and click. Now you can paint the filtered image onto the original image in exact alignment.

- Apply a filter to a duplicate copy of an image and select an area with the Marquee tool. Choose Define Brush from the Brushes palette pop-up menu. The filtered selection will appear as a new brush in the Brushes palette. You can now paint with the new brush on your original image (or any other document).

- Apply a filter to an image, choose Take Snapshot from the Edit menu and then choose Undo from the Edit menu. Select the Rubber Stamp tool. In the Rubber Stamp Options palette, choose From Snapshot in the Options pop-up menu. You can now paint with the filtered version of the original image.

- Before applying a filter, save your document. Apply the filter and then choose the Rubber Stamp tool. In the Rubber Stamp Options palette, choose From Saved in the Options pop-up menu. You can now paint back the original image.

Adobe Filters

The native and plug-in filters included with Photoshop are categorized in the submenus under the Filter menu. The basic filter categories are Blur, Distort, Noise, Pixelate, Render, Sharpen, Stylize, Video, and Other.

Many of the filters, both old and new, sport a redesigned interface in Photoshop 3. These filters have a dialog box composed of a preview of the underlying image which can be moved with a hand tool that appears when the cursor is placed inside the preview window. A "+" and "−" button allow you to zoom in or out. The zoom ratio is shown in between these two zoom controls. The effect of the previewed filter can be toggled on and off by clicking and holding the hand tool in the preview window. However, you should inspect the preview in the 1:1 zoom ratio at some point in the process, since this will be most accurate indication of the filter's effect.

Figure 9–2
The Blur filters

Blur

The Blur filters can soften an image or eliminate unwanted textures (Figure 9–2).

BLUR

Use the Blur filter for subtle smoothing and softening of images (Figure 9–3). Blurring lightens the pixels found next to the hard edges of well-defined lines and shaded areas. The Blur filter effect is subtle, when compared to Blur More and Gaussian Blur. The Blur filter can smooth out regions of noise (grain) from a less than optimum scan. By using this filter in conjunction with the Defringe command under the Select menu, you can effectively blend the edges of a pasted image with the background.

BLUR MORE

Blur More is equivalent to multiple passes of the normal Blur command (Figure 9–3). Use the Blur More filter for a stronger and faster blurring effect.

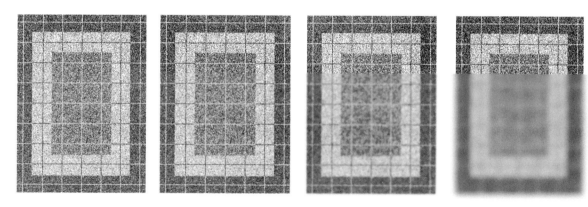

Figure 9–3   The lower sections of these four examples show various degrees of blurring. Shown from left to right: Blur, Blur More, Gaussian Blur with a 2 pixel Radius setting, and Gaussian Blur with an 8 pixel Radius setting.

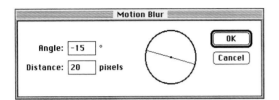

Figure 9–4
The Motion Blur dialog box

Figure 9–5
The Motion Blur filter was used to simulate the movement of this old car.

GAUSSIAN BLUR

Gaussian Blur smoothes in variable amounts. Unlike the other blurring filters, you can specify the degree of blurring. Accepted Radius values range between 0.1 to 250. Using this filter, you can create very subtle or overwhelmingly blurred variations of an image (Figure 9–3).

MOTION BLUR

Motion Blur creates the illusion of movement by distorting the image. The human eye does not perceive a moving object in focus. Motion Blur simulates movement at various speeds, in a specific direction (Figure 9–4).

The two variables, Angle (measured in degrees between –90° and 90°) and Distance (measured in pixels between 1 and 999), control the direction and amount of blurring (Figure 9–5).

RADIAL BLUR

The Radial Blur filter creates the effect of zooming or moving a camera rapidly. There are two blur options, Spin or Zoom. Spin blurs along circular lines while Zoom blurs back and forth. The Amount field can accept values from 1 to 100, and controls the direction of rotation if the Spin option is selected or the amount of the blur if Zoom is selected. A higher value causes more blur. The Quality field has three options: Draft, Good, and Best. Draft is the fastest method but produces additional grain. Good and Best produce less grain and a smoother blur, but take longer to apply. By dragging on the small dot in the Blur center box, the origin of the blur can be moved (Figures 9–6 and 9–7).

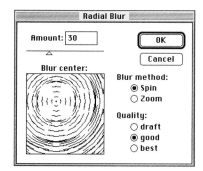

Figure 9–6
The Radial Blur
dialog box

Figure 9–7   The lower sections of these four examples show various applications of the Radial Blur filter. From left to right: Spin with Amount set to 3, Spin with Amount set to 15, Zoom with Amount set to 8, and Zoom with Amount set to 25.

Distort

Geometry forms the basis of the Distort filters, each of which has a dialog box to control the parameters (Figure 9–8). The Photoshop package includes some fantastic Distortion Plug-in modules that should be placed in the Plug-ins folder: Displace, Pinch, Polar Coordinates, Ripple, Shear, Spherize, Twirl, Wave, and ZigZag. You can verify which plug-in effects modules are currently loaded by opening the About Plug-in command under the Apple menu. Under Windows, verify through About Plug-ins under the Help menu. Credits for each plug-in will appear in the window.

DISPLACE

Displace refers to another image to control the distortion. Color values read from a displacement map (the reference image) displace the values in the affected image. Values range from 0 (negative displacement) to 255 (positive displacement) with no affect at 128. After setting the parameters

Figure 9–8
The Distort filters

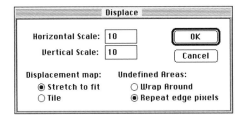

Figure 9–9
The Displace dialog box

 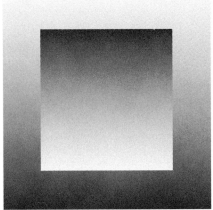 

Figure 9–10   The Displace filter was applied to the Blends image (center), using the silhouetted figure on the left to create the final image on the right.

in the Displace dialog box (Figure 9–9), you will be prompted to choose a file to use as a reference image. Any Photoshop file (it must be in Photoshop format) except for images in Bitmap mode can be used as a displacement map (Figure 9–10).

PINCH

Pinch distorts an image toward or away from the center of a selection area. Accepted values range from –100% to +100%. Negative values pinch the selection toward the center and positive values push it outward (Figure 9–11, 9–12, and C–12 in the Color Section).

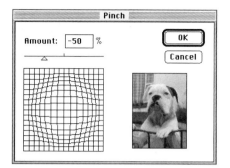

Figure 9–11
The Pinch dialog box

Figure 9–12
The Pinch filter was applied to the two dogs in this photograph. A positive value was used on the left and a negative value on the right.

POLAR COORDINATES

Polar Coordinates converts an image from a horizontal and vertical coordinate orientation to a polar orientation. It can also look at an image as if it were in a polar orientation and convert it to rectangular coordinates. Using this filter, you can create an *anamorphosis*, a popular art form from the eighteenth century that requires a cylindrical mirror to view the image (Figures 9–13 and 9–14).

RIPPLE

Ripple breaks up an image with a fluid, liquid effect. The accepted values range between –999 and 999. You can also choose the Size of the ripple effect, Small, Medium, or Large (Figure 9–15). Use this filter to create textures and patterns (Figure 9–16).

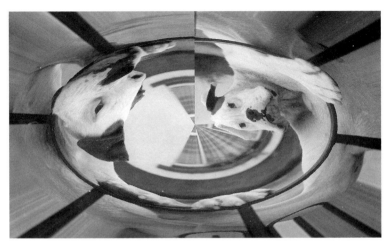

Figure 9–13
The Polar Coordinates dialog box

Figure 9–14
The Polar Coordinates filter was applied to the photograph of the two dogs. To view this anamorphosis, place a mirrored cylinder in the center of the picture.

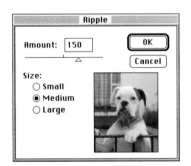

Figure 9–15
The Ripple dialog box

Figure 9–16
The Ripple filter was applied to the photograph of the two dogs at a Small size (left) and a Large size (right).

SHEAR

The Shear filter allows you to wrap or distort an image along a curve created in the Shear dialog box. The line (band) running along the grid can be moved along any point along the bottom of the grid, or points can be added to the line to create a curve that sets the direction of the distortion

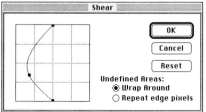

Figure 9–17
The Shear dialog box

Figure 9–18
The Shear filter was applied to the two dogs in this photograph at different settings.

(Figure 9–17). Wrap Around fills empty space with imagery from opposite sides while the Repeat Edge Pixels extends the pixels along the edge of the image (Figure 9–18).

SPHERIZE

Spherize maps a selected area onto an imaginary spherical surface, similar to a photograph taken with a fisheye wide-angle lens. Values between –100% and 100% can be specified in the Spherize dialog box (Figure 9–19). Negative percentages render a concave effect and positive a convex effect (Figure 9–20).

TWIRL

Twirl spins an image toward the center of the selection area. The rotation is greater nearer the center. You can specify values between –999 and 999. Positive values yield a right-hand twist, and negative numbers result in a left-hand twist (Figures 9–21 and 9–22).

WAVE

Wave works like a programmable Ripples filter through which you can create rich organic textures. The turbulence effect is a mathematical concept based on chaos theory. Turbulence abounds in the natural world—wisps of smoke, patterns formed by pressurized water, mixing oil and water.

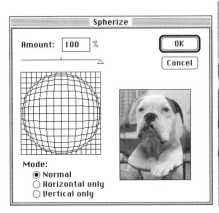

Figure 9–19
The Spherize dialog box

Figure 9–20
The Spherize filter was applied to the dogs in this photograph.

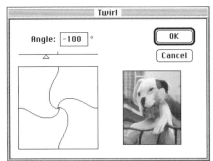

Figure 9–21
The Twirl dialog box

Figure 9–22
The Twirl filter was applied to the dogs in this photograph. A negative percentage rendered the concave effect on the left and the positive percentage rendered the convex effect on the right.

The Wave dialog box has a number of controls (Figure 9–23). The Number of Generators specifies how many strange attractors will be used for a wave pass. You can specify up to 999 generators. Higher numbers of generators produce more complex patterns.

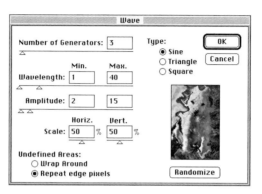

Figure 9–23
The Wave dialog box

Figure 9–24
The Wave filter was applied to the background in this photograph.

NOTE: The Wave filter is similar to the Ripple filter when applied once, but multiple passes yield smooth, liquid effects. Each pass modulates the previous pass. Think of a pond of water into which you drop many pebbles into the water at the same time. Even though each splashing pebble produces a simple radial wave pattern, the combined effect of many radial waves crashing into each other produces more complex patterns.

The Wavelength and Amplitude fields allow you to enter minimum and maximum values ranging from 1 to 999. Photoshop uses the values within the specified range on each of the generators. A greater range between the minimum and maximum values yields a more random and chaotic effect. The Random Start Phase checkbox causes each pass of the filter to be based on a different set of locations for the generators. The Scale values allow you to determine the separate horizontal and vertical emphasis of the filter effect. Specify the type of waveform used by the effect: Sine, Triangle, or Square. Each yields an entirely different effect. You can also choose to Wrap Around the pixels in a selected area or Repeat Edge Pixels. This determines what happens on the edges of the selected areas. Wrap Around preserves the visual continuity of an image (Figure 9–24).

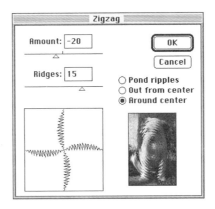

Figure 9–25
The ZigZag dialog box

Figure 9–26
The ZigZag filter was applied to
this photograph.

ZIGZAG

ZigZag is like dropping a rock into the center of a glass disk filled with water which is on top of an image. The waves ripple away from the point where the rock hits the water (Figure 9–25).

You can specify the Amount of the effect (–100 to 100) and the Ridge of the waves (1–20). The larger the amount, the more evident the waves; the larger the ridge, the more wavy the edges of the waves. You also have three different types of ZigZag: pond ripples, out from center, and around center (Figure 9–26).

Noise

Noise refers to the random texture that appears in an image. This texture, referred to as grain in photography, can be smooth, subtle, or extreme. The noise filters can add, emphasize, subdue, or eliminate the grain in an image (Figure 9–27).

Figure 9–27
The Noise filters

Figure 9–28
The Noise filter was applied to these blends in varying amounts. Shown from left to right: 8 Gaussian, 25 Uniform, 80 Gaussian, and 200 Uniform.

ADD NOISE

The Add Noise filter introduces random pixels to an image. It can be used after blurring, softening, or combining images from different sources to simulate the grain usually found in photographs. When processed through some of the other filters, such as Blur, Gaussian Blur, and Find Edges, noise becomes a useful source for organic patterns otherwise difficult to create from scratch. Applying small amounts of noise (amount set between 10 and 40) to grayscale images enhances the overall texture, producing a stippled effect. A checkbox labeled Monochromatic produces a noise effect with no coloration to the pixels.

Specify the amount of noise applied by entering numbers ranging from 1 to 999. Uniform noise tends to be more ordered than the more chaotic Gaussian method. Gaussian noise also slightly lightens the image (Figure 9–28).

DESPECKLE

The Despeckle command subtly blurs an image without affecting distinct areas of contrast. Use this filter to remove unwanted noise (grain) from an image without affecting major areas of detail. Grainy or old photographs are prime candidates for the Despeckle filter. It can also help stabilize images captured with a frame grabber from video sources or to remove a moiré pattern.

DUST & SCRATCHES FILTER

The Dust & Scratches filter, new to Photoshop 3, removes dust and scratches from the image so you don't have to do this time-consuming task by hand. A large preview with zoom controls allows you to move about the image and see the effects of the filter on the preview (Figure 9–29). Two slider controls adjust the degree to which this filter affects the image:

Figure 9–29
The Dust and Scratches
dialog box

Figure 9–30
The Dust and Scratches filter was applied to the vintage image from PhotoDisc on the left by Bill Niffenegger for the cover of this book.

Radius determines the size of the dust or scratch that will be recognized and Threshold sets the difference between the element and the surrounding area. Setting the Threshold level too low causes an apparent softening of the image. Try applying the filter only to severely damaged areas rather than to the entire image. With practice, this filter can magically clean up a dirty image in short order (Figure 9–30)!

MEDIAN

The Median filter can help reduce the amount of noise in an image. Specify a Radius (1–16) for it to blend and discard pixels (Figure 9–31). Pixels that vary too much from adjacent pixels are discarded. Higher values cause more averaging, which makes the image look more blurred (Figure 9–32).

Figure 9–31
The Median dialog box

Figure 9–32
The Median filter was applied to the dog photograph at various radius settings. Shown from left to right: 1 pixel, 4 pixels, 8 pixels, and 16 pixels.

Pixelate

These filters produce various special effects by manipulating the values of image pixels with common properties (Figure 9–33).

COLOR HALFTONE

The Color Halftone filter creates the effect of enlarged halftone screens. The filter converts each CYMK channel of the image into a series of halftone dots. The dialog box has a field for entering the maximum radius of the halftone dots from 4 to 127 (Figure 9–34). The angle for the screens can be configured for each channel. This filter applied to an RGB image uses the values in the first three channels of the dialog box. If applied to a grayscale image, it uses the information in the first entry only.

CRYSTALLIZE

The Crystallize filter groups pixels into a polygon shape. The actual size or cell is set using the Slider or by entering a number (3 to 300) into the Cell Size box. Smaller numbers render more subtle effects (Figures 9–35 and 9–36).

FACET

The Facet filter analyzes an image, determines major areas of solid or similar colors, and emphasizes them using flat, geometric color, shapes (Figure 9–37).

FRAGMENT

Fragment makes four copies of an image and places them slightly offset from each other. It is similar to a photographic star filter (Figure 9–38).

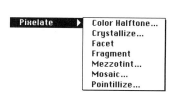

Figure 9–33
The Pixelate filters

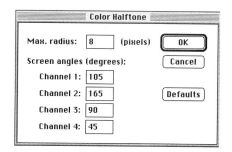

Figure 9–34
The Color Halftone dialog box

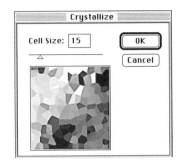

Figure 9–35
The Crystallize
dialog box

Figure 9–36
The Crystalize filter was
applied to the dog
photograph at various
Cell Sizes. Shown from
left to right:
8, 16, and 32

Figure 9–37
The Facet filter was applied several
times to this photograph.

Figure 9–38
The Fragment filter was applied to
this photograph.

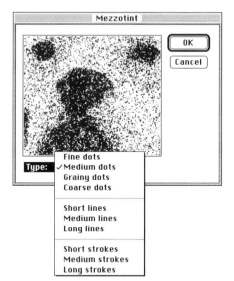

Figure 9–39
The Mezzotint dialog
box showing the screen
patterns available in the
Type pop-up menu

MEZZOTINT FILTER

The Mezzotint filter produces three groups of different Mezzotint effects (different dots or screen effects in a continuous tone image). The Mezzotint filter opens with a large preview of the image and a pop-up menu that allows you to pick a screen type: dots, lines, or strokes (Figure 9–39). Among each of these three groups, you can further specify the strength of the effect by choosing fine, medium, grainy, or course dots, and long, medium, or short lines and strokes (Figure 9–40).

MOSAIC

The Mosaic filter turns an image into pixelated squares. In the dialog box, you can set the Cell Size in pixels from 2 to 64 (Figure 9–41).

Create variations on the square cell by resizing the image by 50% horizontally or vertically, applying the Mosaic filter, and then resizing the image back to the original size. Or rotate the image, apply the Mosaic filter, and then rotate the image back to the original orientation (Figure 9–42).

POINTILLIZE

The Pointillize filter creates random dots throughout the image. The size of the cell can be from 3 to 300 pixels. Note that the background canvas color is used between the dots (Figures 9–43 and 9–44).

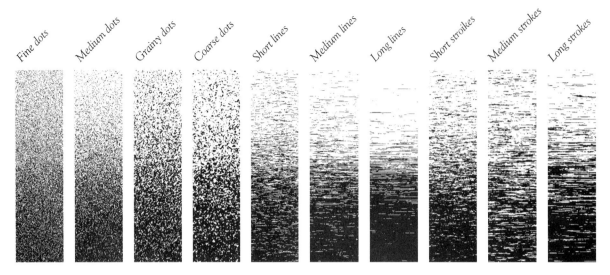

Figure 9–40 The Mezzotint filter applied at the settings shown

Figure 9–41
The Mosaic dialog box

Figure 9–42
The Mosaic filter applied to the dog photograph (left to right): Cell Size 10 pixels, Cell Size 10 pixels after a 45° rotation and then rotated back to the original angle, Cell Size at 20 pixels after a horizontal stretch and then returned to original proportions.

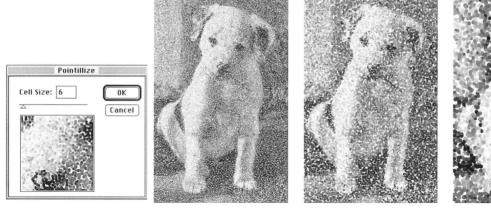

Figure 9–43
The Pointillize
dialog box

Figure 9–44
The Pointillize filter was applied to the dog photograph. Shown from left to right:
Cell Size at 3 pixels, 6 pixels, and 12 pixels

Render

The Render menu, new in Photoshop 3, contains filters that create or mimic natural effects (Figure 9–45).

CLOUDS FILTER

The Clouds filter produces soft cloud-like patterns by varying the values of the foreground and background color palette (Figure 9–46). Strengthen the effect by holding down the Shift Key when choosing the Clouds filter. Various cloud effects can be generated by repeatedly applying this filter, since the effect is random for each application.

Figure 9–45
The Render filters

Figure 9–46
Repeated applications of
the Clouds filter

Figure 9–47
The Difference Clouds
filter applied to an image

DIFFERENCE CLOUDS

The Difference Clouds Filter also creates random cloud effects but blends the effect with existing pixels in the source image using the Difference apply mode (Figure 9–47). The first time the filter is used, the image is inverted but repeated applications create a marble like texture. This filter does not work in Lab Color mode.

LENS FLARE

The Lens Flare filter creates an effect similar to the circular refractions that appear when bright light shines into a camera lens. There are several parameters in the dialog box (Figure 9–48). Enter a value (10% to 300%) for Brightness or use the slider. Drag the crosshair in the thumbnail to set the center of the Flare. The Lens type changes the size of the flare and the number of refractions. Flare only works on color images (Figure 9–49).

LIGHTING EFFECTS

The Lighting Effects filter allows you to place up to 16 different light sources in an RGB image. This filter can be configured with different light intensities, light colors, light angle, light shapes, ambient colors, and so on (Figures 9–50 and 9–51).

In the Style section, begin by picking one of several preset styles from the pop-up menu. The light sources display their color and illuminated areas on the preview image. Drag the light sources to any position on the image. Add a new light by pressing on the light bulb below the preview and dragging it into position over the preview image. Delete a light source by dragging it to the trash icon below the preview. New or revised light styles can be saved by clicking the Save button; styles can be deleted by clicking the Delete button.

Figure 9–48
The Lens Flare dialog box

Figure 9–49
The Lens Flare filter was applied to this photograph with Brightness set to 100% and the Lens Type at 50–300mm zoom.

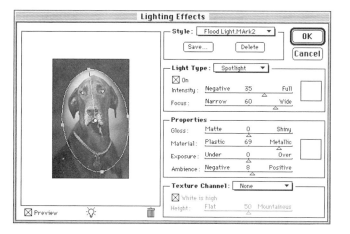

Figure 9–50
The Lighting Effects dialog box

In the Light Type section, choose one of three types of light from the pop-up menu for each light source. Directional light produces the effect of a single light source and angle like that of the sun. The Omni light shines in all direction much as a bare light bulb radiates light in all directions. The Spotlight is a combination of Directional and Omni—the light has a definite angle with some spill to the sides in the shape of an ellipse.

The light types have provisions for changing the shape, direction, and size of the illuminated areas by dragging the points on the ellipse or the point at the end of the direction line. Change the color of a light source by clicking on the color swatch at the right side in the Light Type section. Sliders control the intensity of each light and, in the case of a Spotlight, the focus.

The Properties section has the following controls:

- The Gloss slider sets the reflectance of the surface upon which the light is shining from glossy to matte.
- The Material property slider sets the object's and light's reflectance. The slider goes from Plastic, which reflects the color of the light, to Metallic, which reflects the color of the objects.
- The Exposure slider controls the amount of lightness and darkness of the light.
- The Ambience slider controls how the light source mixes with ambient light. A higher positive setting will illuminate the image with more ambient light. A lower setting will illuminate the image more with the light sources. Negative settings illuminate the image with the compliment of the ambient light color. Set the color of the ambient light by clicking on the color swatch at the right side in the Properties section.

The Texture Channel section offers controls for creating a textured light effect. In the pop-up menu select a channel in the image to mask the projected light, producing textured bumps in the image. Any channel containing texture or imagery can be used. The Mountainous slider will vary the texture from Flat to Mountainous, resulting in a more profound texture effect. The White is High check box sets the white in the texture channel as the high points; otherwise, the black in the channel is the texture high point. To use other grayscale documents as a Texture Channel, first use the Texture Fill filter to load the document as a channel. It will then appear in the Texture Channel pop-up menu (Figure 9–52).

TEXTURE FILL

Texture Fill provides a quick method of loading a grayscale image into a channel of an open document. This channel can be used as the primary image, as a selection mask, in channel operations or as a bump map to be applied with the Lighting Effects filter. Texture Fill will only recognize Photoshop 2.5 or 3.0 grayscale documents (Figure 9–53).

Figure 9–51
Example of the Lighting Effects filter

Figure 9–52
The lighting effect Filter with a
Texture Fill used as a bump map

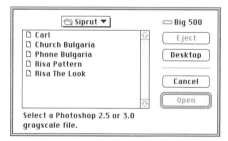

Figure 9–53
Open the Texture Fill dialog box to
load a grayscale Photoshop document
as a channel.

Figure 9–54
The Sharpen filters

Sharpen ▸	Sharpen
	Sharpen Edges
	Sharpen More
	Unsharp Mask...

Sharpen

By increasing the contrast of neighboring pixels, especially at edges, the sharpen filters produce the illusion of increased sharpness (Figure 9–54).

NOTE: Although the Sharpen filters can improve the apparent sharpness of an image, they are not a substitute for a high-quality scan of a focused photograph.

SHARPEN

The Sharpen filter sharpens blurry images by increasing the contrast of adjacent pixels (Figure 9–55).

SHARPEN EDGES

Sharpen Edges applies a sharpening filter only to the areas of major brightness change, the same edges that the Find Edges filter picks up (Figure 9–55). It sharpens an image without affecting smooth soft areas.

SHARPEN MORE

Sharpen More is equivalent to applying the normal Sharpen filter several times (Figure 9–55).

UNSHARP MASK

Unsharp Mask, the most accurate way of controlling the sharpening effect, has its origins in traditional noncomputer photographic techniques. The process consisted of taking a film negative, creating a blurred positive version

Figure 9–55
The Sharpen filters at various settings. Left to right: Sharpen, Sharpen Edges, Sharpen More, and Sharpen More applied three times.

of the image, sandwiching the two together, and shooting the results onto a higher-contrast photographic paper.

Photoshop's Unsharp Mask filter essentially does the above process digitally. The image is copied, made negative, blurred, and averaged with the original image (behind the scene). The resulting image is brightness-balanced and appears sharpened only in areas of substantial brightness differentiation (you control the threshold value).

The Amount field controls the intensity of the tonal change. Higher percentages result in more pronounced sharpening (within the areas affected based on the radius setting). The acceptable range of values for Amount is 1% to 500%. A setting of 100% to 200% is a good starting point. Setting Amount too high can introduce unwanted noise.

The Radius field controls the distance from each side of an edge that will be affected by the tonal change (0.1 to 250 pixels). Higher Radius values render stronger sharpening effects. Lower radius numbers produce less noticeable sharpening. A high setting can result in an oversharpened image. A 1 to 2 pixels radius is a good starting point.

The value specified in Threshold (0 to 255) controls the brightness level difference that must exist between shapes before the filter will take effect. Lower numbers yield a sharper image, while higher numbers will have less sharpening (Figures 9–56 and 9–57).

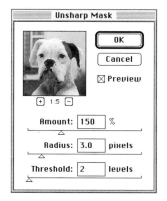

Figure 9–56
The Unsharp Mask dialog box

Figure 9–57
The Unsharp Mask filter. Amount, Radius, and Filter settings shown left to right: 50%, 2 pixels, 5 levels; 50%, 4 pixels, 0 levels; 100%, 4 pixels, 0 levels; 500%, 2 pixels, 40 levels.

Figure 9–58
The Stylize filters

Stylize

Use the Stylize filters to distort and abstract images or selections. Some create the appearance of drawings, paintings, or photographic filter effects (Figure 9–58).

DIFFUSE

Diffuse randomly jitters the pixels. Repeated application of this filter gradually breaks up the image until it looks as if it were drawn with crayon or charcoal.

There are three options in the Diffuse dialog box. Normal breaks up all of the pixels in the image. Darken Only breaks up darker parts of the image more than lighter areas. Lighten Only breaks up lighters parts of the image more than darker areas (Figure 9–59).

EMBOSS

The Emboss filter makes images appear engraved or raised by darkening the traced edges of an image and subduing the colors and tones. The Emboss dialog box has three parameters (Figure 9–60). Use a positive angle or move the line clockwise to raise the surface. Use a negative angle or move the line counter clockwise to lower the image. Enter the desired angle in the Angle field or move the line in the circle to a new angle.

Figure 9–59
The Diffuse filter was applied to the dog photograph at various settings. Shown from left to right: Normal, Lighten Only, and Darken Only.

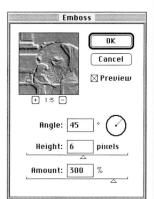

Figure 9–60
The Emboss dialog box

Figure 9–61
The Emboss filter was applied to the photograph of the two dogs. On the left, the settings were Angle 45°, Height 2 pixels, Amount 500%; and on the right, Angle 155°, Height 10 pixels, Amount 150%.

The Height field sets the depth of the emboss and can accept a value from 1 to 10 pixels. The Percentage field can accept values from 1 to 500%; the lower figure produces the least amount of color or tonal changes around the emboss edges, and the higher figure produces a more pronounced color effect (Figure 9–61 and Figure C–11 in the Color Section).

EXTRUDE

The Extrude filter creates 3-D shapes in Blocks or Pyramids. The dialog box has several options for setting the parameters (Figure 9–62). The Size box, in pixels from 2 to 255, sets the length of the selected shape's base. A higher number will produce fewer but larger objects. The Depth box, in pixels from

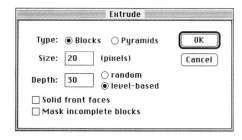

Figure 9–62
The Extrude dialog box

Figure 9–63
The Extrude filter was applied at various settings. Left to right: Size 30 pixels, Size 15 pixels, and Size 15 pixels with Solid front. The Type was set to Blocks and the Depth at 30 (level based) on all three.

0 to 255, controls how far the shapes appear to protrude from the surface. The Random button will create the depth effect indiscriminately. The Level-Based check box matches the depth of the shapes to the overall brightness of the image (darker shapes will appear deeper). The Mask Incomplete Blocks masks blocks at the edges of a selection so they do not appear cut off (Figure 9–63).

FIND EDGES

Find Edges finds the significant brightness transitions (edges) in an image and darkens them, while lightening the flat areas (Figure 9–64).

Figure 9–64
The Find Edges filter was applied to this photograph.

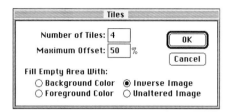

Figure 9–65
After applying the
Solarize filter, the photo
was lightened with the
Levels command.

Figure 9–66
The Tiles dialog box

SOLARIZE

The Solarize filter has its roots in the photographic darkroom as a technique for altering the tones on a photograph to achieve special effects. In the darkroom, the print or film is exposed with a flash of light in the development process. This exposure quickly darkens only the lighter portions of the image causing a reversal of the tones. The shadow areas retain normal values.

Since the Solarize filter darkens the lighter values in an image, it usually appears too dark after applying the filter. To adjust the values after applying the filters, use the Levels, Curves, or Brightness/Contrast commands under the Image menu (Figure 9–65).

TILES

The Tiles filter fragments an image into square shapes. The first parameter in the dialog box (Figure 9–66) specifies the number of tiles to be generated. Maximum Offset sets the distance the tiles should be offset from each other. The last option, Fill Empty Area With, controls how the areas between the tiles are filled (Figure 9–67).

TRACE CONTOUR

Trace Contour finds major brightness changes (edges) and draws thin lines around them, changing the remainder of the image to white. You can specify the threshold level and which side of the edge to highlight (Figure 9–68).

Figure 9–67
The Tiles filter was applied to the dog photograph using these Number of Tiles, Maximum Offset, and Fill Empty Area with settings (left to right): 10/10%/Foreground Color, 8/20%/Background Color, and 4/50%/Inverse Image .

WIND

The Wind filter gives the illusion of wind blowing by creating small horizontal lines across an image (Figure 9–69). In the dialog box, choose the strength of the filter, Wind, Blast, or Stagger, as well as its direction.

Figure 9–68
The Trace Contour filter

Figure 9–69
The Wind filter was applied to the dogs photograph.

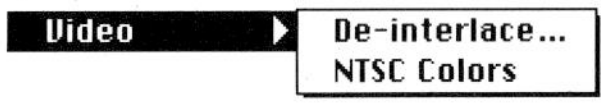

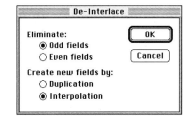

Figure 9–70
The Video filters

Figure 9–71
The De-Interlace dialog box

Video

Images captured from a video source might not appear correctly on a computer, and computer images might not appear correctly when output to video. The following filters can help correct images transferred from one environment to another (Figure 9–70). For more information on working with video, refer to Chapter 12, "Multimedia."

DE-INTERLACE

De-Interlace smoothes an image, removing either the even or odd interlaced lines by copying and pasting one set of lines onto the other. Specify whether the lines should be replaced by Duplication or Interpolation (Figure 9–71).

NTSC COLORS

NTSC Colors remaps the colors in an image to match the gamut of colors that can be reproduced by a television. The NTSC palette (a palette of colors set by the National Television System Committee) must be used in order to specify predicable reproducible colors for playback on a television screen. This limited color gamut keeps oversaturated colors from bleeding into neighboring areas. Refer to Chapter 12, "Multimedia," for more on preparing art for video output.

Other

These filters allow you to make custom filters, abstract images, affect masks, and offset images (Figure 9–72).

Figure 9–72
The Other filters

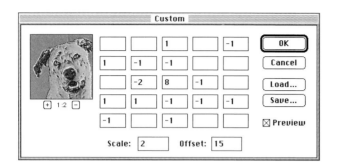

Figure 9–73
The Custom filter dialog box

Figure 9–74
The Custom filter was applied to this image using the settings in Figure 9–73.

CUSTOM

The Custom filter opens a programmable matrix to create special effects, custom blurring, and sharpening filters (Figure 9–73). The text fields multiply an individual pixel's brightness values by the number entered (–999 to 999) (Figure 9–74). By using the Save and Load buttons, custom filters can be saved for use at another time.

HIGH PASS

High Pass is a filter that originated in engineering. It allows the high-frequency portion of a signal to get through, blocking out lower frequencies. The High Pass filter finds areas of major brightness changes (edges) and highlights them, while it softens and neutralizes areas of low contrast. In the accepted range of 0.1 to 250, lower numbers emphasize the edges more and remove more color. Higher numbers retain more colors and affect the edges less (Figures 9–75 and 9–76).

MAXIMUM

Maximum spreads lighter areas by converting adjacent darker pixels to lighter ones. Specify the number of pixels to be converted from 1 to 10 (Figures 9–77 and 9–78).

MINIMUM

Minimum is the opposite of the Maximum filter. Darker areas are spread by converting lighter adjacent pixels to darker ones (Figures 9–79 and 9–80).

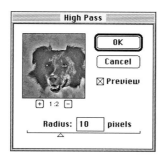

Figure 9–75
The High Pass filter
dialog box

Figure 9–76
The High Pass filter was applied to this
image using the settings in Figure 9–75.

Figure 9–77
The Maximum filter
dialog box

Figure 9–78
The Maximum filter was applied to this
image using the settings in Figure 9–77.

Figure 9–79
The Minimum filter
dialog box

Figure 9–80
The Minimum filter was applied to this
image using the settings in Figure 9–79.

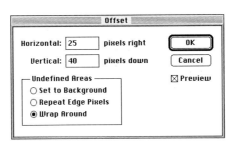

Figure 9–81
The Offset filter dialog box

Figure 9–82
The Offset filter was applied to a
selection in this image using the
settings in Figure 9–79.

OFFSET

Offset shifts the image or selection by the number of pixels set in the dialog
box. Move image or selection precisely in horizontal or vertical directions
with this filter (Figures 9–81 and 9–82).

Filter Factory

For those who love special effects, like to create their own Photoshop filters, and have a knack for the mathematical underpinnings of digital image
editing, Adobe has created Filter Factory, a plug-in that comes with the
Deluxe CD-ROM version of Photoshop 3 for the Macintosh. Accessed
from the Synthetic submenu under the Filter menu, Filter Factory lets you
create formulas for manipulating pixels in the red, green, blue, and alpha
channels of an RGB image, save the settings for later reuse, and create your
own plug-in filters, complete with slider bars and preview windows.

Filter Factory is not for Photoshop beginners or the faint of heart. Similar
in concept to the Custom filter (mentioned earlier) and featuring a dialog
box built around sliders and formula fields, Filter Factory has the raw power
of HSC Software's KPT Convolver custom effects generator (mentioned
later in the chapter), but without Convolver's intuitive ease of use.

Nevertheless, Filter Factory has already developed an enthusiastic following of creative and digitally sophisticated users, as evidenced by the
hundreds of formulas and filter-creation tips posted in America Online's
Photoshop forum. Filter Factory is a powerful tool for serious digital imagers
and production-oriented users who want to create custom tools without
conventional programming.

Third-Party Filters and Plug-ins

Adobe has created a technology that has become a standard for the graphics industry: the open architecture plug-in format. It allows for addition of filters and mini programs to Photoshop. This format is used by Photoshop, as well as other programs such as Adobe Premiere, SuperPaint, PageMaker, EFI Cachet, Color Studio, Specular Collage, Fractal Design Painter, QuarkXPress, StrataVision 3-D, and many other Macintosh and Windows applications. Although Adobe offers some plug-in filters, most must be purchased from third-party vendors. Following is a discussion of the most popular and useful plug-in modules for image processing, production and special effects.

Gallery Effects

The Gallery Effects filters from Adobe Systems, available in three separate volumes, offer a myriad of special effects plug-in filters. All filters share an easy-to-use interface that has sliders to change settings and an interactive preview to see the effects before actually applying the filter. The filter parameters can be saved and named for later use.

GALLERY EFFECTS: CLASSIC ART VOLUME 1

Gallery Effects: Classic Art Volume 1, a set of 18 filters, imitates various art styles (Figure 9–83). The Gallery Effects Graphic Pen, Dry Brush, Chalk & Charcoal, and Charcoal all reduce a color image to simple shades and tones to create a stroked effect. The Water Color filter transforms a color photograph into a pseudo watercolor painting, and the Poster Edge filter creates a somewhat similar effect. The Smudge Stick filter is a more intense alternative to

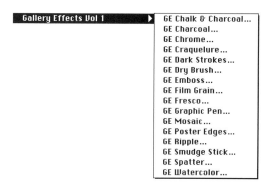

Figure 9–83
The Gallery Effects Volume 1 filters

Figure 9–84
The Graphic Pen filter

Figure 9–85
The Mosaic filter

Figure 9–86
The Ripple filter

the native motion filter (Figures 9–84, 9–85, and 9–86, and also Figures C–13, C–14, and C–15 in the Color Section).

CLASSIC ART, VOLUME 2

Gallery Effects: Classic Art, Volume 2, contains an additional 18 filters (Figure 9–87). The Volume 2 filters have excellent on-line help and useful tips accessible from within each filter's dialog box (Figure 9–88). Several of the filters create striking effects with continuous tone images, such as the Diffuse Glow and Grain filters. Although Volume 1 had a Film Grain filter, the Grain filter in Volume 2 creates colorful noise more suitable for color images. PhotoCopy, Stamp, Note, and Bas Relief reduce continuous-tone

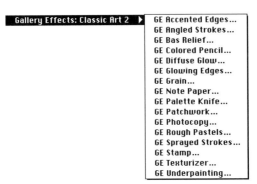

Figure 9–87
The Gallery Effects Volume 2 filters

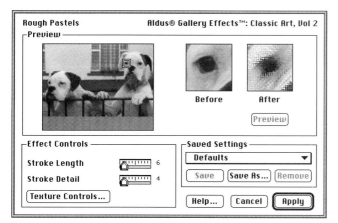

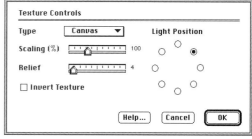

Figure 9–88
The Gallery Effects Volume 2 dialog box for the Rough Pastels filter

Figure 9–89
The Texture Controls dialog box accessed by clicking on the Texture Controls button in the previous dialog box

color images to simple graphic images, textures, and shapes much like Graphic Pen, Dry Brush, and Charcoal filters in Volume 1.

Don't overlook textures provided by the Rough Pastels, Texturizer, and Underpainting filters. By clicking on the Texture Controls button in their dialog boxes, you can access an additional dialog box with a pop-up menu of several textures such as Brick, Canvas, or a PICT file that can be loaded as a texture (Figures 9–89, 9–90, 9–91, and 9–92, as well as Figure C–16 in the Color Section).

Figure 9–90
The Bas Relief filter

Figure 9–91
The Glowing Edges filter

Figure 9–92
The Palette Knife filter

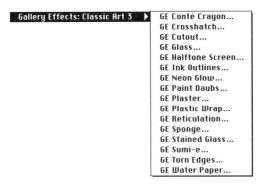

Figure 9–93
The Gallery Effects Volume 3 filters

CLASSIC ART, VOLUME 3

Gallery Effects: Classic Art, Volume 3, offers an additional 18 filters (Figure 9–93). Volume 3 includes Conte Crayon (crayon on a textured rough surface), Crosshatch (crosshatching drawn through an image), Cutout (cut-outs of colored papers), Glass (image viewed through glass), Halftone (halftone dots), Ink Outline (a fine narrow line around details), Neon Glow (a soft glow near the edges of dark and light areas), Paint Daubs (various paint brush styles), Plaster (three-dimensional plaster casting, darker areas appear raised while lighter areas appear lowered), Plastic Wrap (wrapped in a shiny plastic material or coating), Reticulation (mimics a photographic condition in which the emulsion of the film contracts and distorts during processing, producing a cracking effect), Sponge (a textured sponge), Stained Glass (backlit stained glass with simulated lead separating the panes), Sumi-e (mimics the Japanese painting style characterized by rich blacks and soft edges), Torn Edges (edges of shapes resemble torn paper), and Water Paper (the image painted on a damp textured paper, producing blurred and soft colors) (Figures 9–94, 9–95, 9–96).

ANDROMEDA SERIES 1 FILTERS

Andromeda

Andromeda Series 1 Filters mimic photographic optics and camera filters (Figure 9–97). The number of effects possible with Andromeda filters far exceeds those available with camera filters. A dialog box offers numerous controls to modify the filters, displaying effects in a preview window (Figure 9–98).

The plug-in filters included in the package are Velocity (one- or two-way smears simulating motion), Halo (diffuses and spreads highlights into darker portions of an image), Star, Rainbow (translucent rainbow), Diffract, sMulti (breaks up areas into multiple straight lines or patterns),

Figure 9–94
The Conte Crayon filter

Figure 9–95
The Plaster filter

Figure 9–96
The Stained Glass filter

Figure 9–97
The Andromeda Series 1 submenu showing the 10 available filters

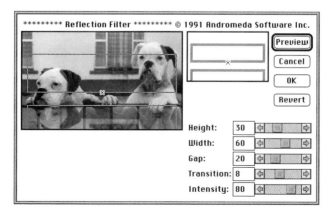

Figure 9–98
The Andromeda Reflection filter dialog box

Figure 9–99
The Reflection filter was applied to this photograph of the dogs.

cMulti (breaks up areas into multiple circular elements), Reflection (reflects part of the image in a pool of water, Figure 9–99), Prism (breaks up the image slightly while intensifying the spectral colors), and Design (creates dimensional patterns).

ANDROMEDA SERIES 2

The Andromeda Series 2 Filter creates true 3-D surface mapping within Photoshop. The plug-in produces 3-D effects with variable viewpoints and shading controls, mapping an image onto shapes such as a sphere, cylinder, plane, or box.

Upon choosing the filter, a single dialog box offers numerous controls to modify the filter's function, displaying the effects in a preview window (Figure 9–100). The viewpoint control allows you to "fly" around the surface, select a camera viewpoint, and take snapshots of the 3-D scene. The surface, or image on the surface, may be resized, shifted, rotated, or scaled. A movable light source allows you to control the object's lighting and shading. In addition to affecting the ambient light, the light source has a specular (hot spot) that can be moved onto the surface for special glossy or matte shading effects, controlling the depth and shading of the object. Choice of surfaces, shading effects, viewpoint, and distance provide flexibility to create quick 3-D scenes and single animation frames (Figure 9–101 and Figure C–19 in the Color Section).

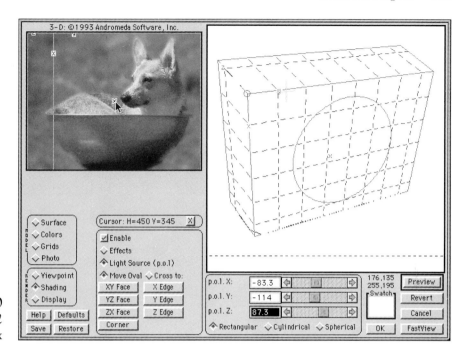

Figure 9–100
The Andromeda Series 2
Filter dialog box

ANDROMEDA SERIES 3

Andromeda Series 3 contains a single but complex filter called Mezzo, which allows you to produce and mix numerous high-quality mezzotint (halftone screen) effects from grayscale images. Initially, the filter opens in the Novice mode with a series of preset Mezzotint screen choices preview windows (Figure 9–102). Control the parameters for blends, lines, and text effects as well as the halftone screen frequency (LPI). A helper box recommends

Figure 9–101
The Andromeda Series 2
Filter applied to a box on
the left and to a sphere
on the right

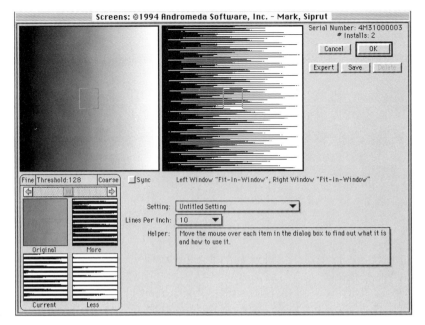

Figure 9–102
The Andromeda Series 3
Mezzo filter dialog box

which LPI setting should be used with each preset and which preset should be used for a desired effect.

Click on the Expert Mode button for more options to create screen effects (Figure 9–103). The Enhance Photo Window allows you to apply Unsharp Masking to the image using Amount and Radius sliders. The Output Image Window controls the contrast of the final image using pattern and threshold sliders. Settings can be saved and loaded for later use.

AutoMask

AutoMask from Human Software (Macintosh only) automatically creates soft edge masks for quick photoelectronic masking and removal of backgrounds on photos. It also creates montages of two images with transparency effects. AutoMask works in RGB or CYMK and supports Tiff, ScitexCT, and Photoshop 2.0 files (Figure 9–104).

AutoMask has three modes for creating masks and composites: Touch Tone Masking (Mask) and B&W Mask creation (B&W) for creating masks, and Image Composition (Image) for compositing two pictures without creating a mask. The Ghost field controls the transparency overlay effect (from 0 to 100%) for merging images. Imported images can be scaled by entering figures in a series of four fields. These four fields relate pixel count as well as enlargement/reduction ratios.

Figure 9–103
The Andromeda Series 3 Mezzo filter applied at several settings (Photo courtesy of CMCD)

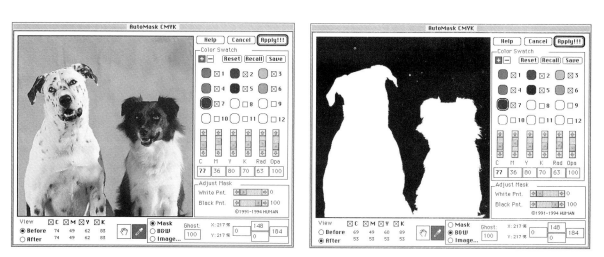

Figure 9–104   The Automask dialog box

Black Box

Black Box from Alien Skin Software, a set of six plug-in filters, produces effects achieved previously only with multiple layer or channel operations (Figures 9–105 and 9–106). For example, drop shadows, normally created using several layer or channel operations, can be created in a single step with Black Box's Drop Shadow filter (Figure 9–107).

Figure 9–105
Example of the Black
Box filters from Alien
Skin Software

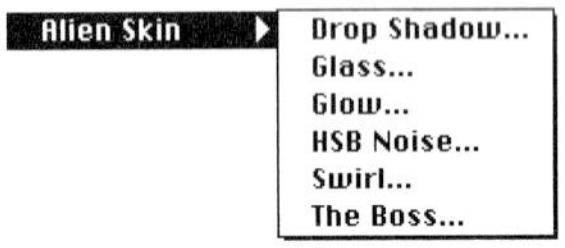

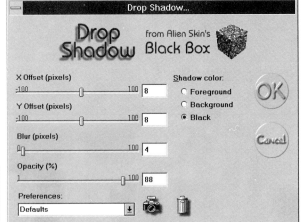

Figure 9–106
The Black Box submenu

Figure 9–107
The Black Box Drop Shadow dialog box for Windows

The Glow filter creates a radiating glow around a selection. You can specify the drop off of the glow as well as the opacity. In addition, there is control for anti-aliasing the glow which removes some abrupt jumps in brightness which are most noticeable in thin bright glows.

TIP: The Glow filter gives type more punch if it is difficult to read because of a busy background. If the type is light, put a 25% opacity black glow around it. If the type is dark, put a 25% opacity white glow around it. The resulting increase in contrast should make the type more readable.

Emboss applies a 3-D effect to a selection with controls for lighting, depth, bevel shape, and smoothness of edges. The Glass filter, similar to the

Emboss filter, creates a transparent 3-D effect above the unaltered underlying selection. HSB Noise adds noise with adjustments based on Hue, Saturation and Brightness. The Swirl filter creates and then smears random whirlpools in a selection.

TIP: Most of the Black Box filters deselect the floating selection after the application of the filter. To avoid losing the selection, save it as a channel prior to applying the filter.

CD-Q

CD-Q from Human Software is an acquire module for importing Photo CD images. It can also acquire files over a network. One of CD-Q's strengths is the ability to acquire the YCC color space of Photo CD image packed as CYMK files. You have a great deal of control over how the YCC data is converted to CYMK for the press, such as Gray Component Replacement (known as GCR), Black level adjustment and White and Black point selection. CD-Q acquires files from YCC to RGB and Grayscale. Although it's possible to acquire YCC to RGB and then use Photoshop to convert the file to CYMK, doing the conversions directly in the acquire stage saves time and generally results in superior quality.

CD-Q allows you to select images on the Photo CD in either an overview format or as individual images. The overview option displays all the pictures on the CD on a grid of thumbnails from which to select the images (Figure 9–108). Upon choosing an image pack, a conversion panel opens, allowing you to control the conversion into Photoshop. In addition to cropping, rotation, resolution and sharpening controls, you can specify

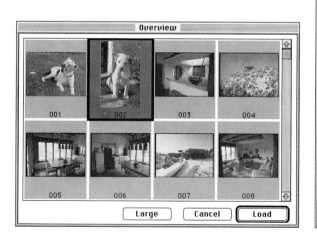

Figure 9–108   The CD-Q dialog boxes for opening a Photo CD into CMYK Color mode

the conversion color space. Curves and previews for each color channel allow you make color corrections or adjustments.

Another plug-in, CD-Q RGB, is similar to CD-Q but provides color space conversions from RGB to CYMK using many of the same controls and features found in CD-Q. Rather then beginning with a Photo CD YCC image, CD-Q RGB requires you begin with an RGB Tiff file.

Chris Cox

Chris Cox, a freelance programmer, created a set of free plug-in filters (Chris will, however, take donations). His professionally executed set of 18 filters for the Macintosh only are spread throughout Photoshop's various filter menus (Figure 9–109).

BLUR

Average averages all the colors in a selected area and fills the selection with that color. It was created to turn photos into images resembling stained glass.

UnAlias blurs edges using an edge detector with a threshold value. Use it to remove jaggies from images.

OTHER

Checkers creates a checkered pattern over an image using the foreground and background colors.

BitShift rotates the bytes that make up the image by a specified value from 1 to 8.

Grid creates a grid over the image. The spacing and width of the horizontal and vertical lines can be specified, and the colors of the grid are controlled by the foreground or background color.

Figure 9–109
Examples of some of Chris Cox's filters. Left to right: Checkers, Grid, and Psycho

NOISE

Add More Noise is similar to Photoshop's Noise filter but offers more control.

Total Noise replaces the image or selection with a totally random uniform noise.

Fractal Noise generates grayscale noise that appears very cloud-like, and looks a similar to the new Photoshop Cloud filter when colored.

Plaid is a noise filter that makes symmetrical patterns of each color channel.

STYLIZE

Psycho produces a random sine-wave-based color map which can best described as psychedelic (hence the name). This filter is perfect for producing images reminiscent of the 1960s.

CUSTOM

Edge3x3 works much like Photoshop's Find Edges filter but is built for speed.

Erode reduces dark areas in an image based on a threshold value. If the area of the image exceeds the threshold value, the filter sets those pixels to white.

Dialate operates in an opposite fashion from Erode, enlarging the dark areas of the image.

Skeleton is a cousin to Erode and Dilate. Again, a threshold is specified and the dark areas of the image are reduced to an approximate centerline or skeleton. Erode, Dilate, and Skeleton are recognition algorithms for such uses as OCR, but of course also produce some weird effects.

VIDEO

ColorKey, ChromaKey, and FastKey, found in the Video menu, create masks which can also be used for channel calculations.

ColorKey turns the filtered image into a mask based on the foreground color. By selecting a foreground color with the eyedropper, calling up the filter, and entering a tolerance of between 0 to 999, you can create a mask based on the color selected.

ChromaKey also creates a mask based on the current foreground color with a controlled technique based on hue, saturation, and value tolerances.

FastKey, producing a mask based on a color value, is faster than the other filters because it has no provisions for any tolerances.

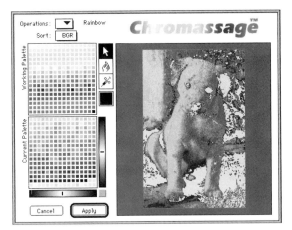

Figure 9–110
The Chromassage
dialog box

Chromassage

The Chromassage plug-in by Second Glance Software (Macintosh only) remaps colors in an image. It presents a preview with a small tool set and a large single image (Figure 9–110).

The Current color palette contains 256 of the most common colors in the image. The Working palette contains 256 color squares to define changes to the original. When first opened, both palettes have the same 256 color squares arranged in a sorted order that can be changed through the Sort pop-up menu. For example, the colors can be arranged by RGB, GRB, BGR, etc. The resorted palettes affect how you control the remapping of colors.

Next to the Current palette are two Jog Wheels, one horizontal and one vertical. The vertical Jog Wheel shifts the hue of the current palette much like a color wheel. The horizontal jog wheel cycles the color squares; each square is replaced by the one before it. In addition, a pop-up menu contains many preset palettes such as rainbow, pastel, and so on. With selection tools, move some or all of the colors of an existing color palette to your palette, and view the color changes on the preview (Figure C–20 in the Color Section).

ColorMatch

DayStar Digital's ColorMatch plug-ins (Macintosh only) offer you an integrated color management system to control calibration, input of scanned images, color optimization, output preview, and color space conversion. DayStar licensed the KCMS (Kodak Color Management System) technology from Eastman Kodak and created the ColorMatch filters to produce accurate color results from scanner to monitor and to output device. The filters work with device profiles called Precision Transforms (PTs). For example, you pick a specific PT for the type of input device and a specific PT for an output device to ensure that the output matches the input. The ColorMatch system also allows you to calibrate the monitor and create a specific monitor PT so that when the system is running, what is seen on screen is what will print on output: true WYSIWYG color.

Figure 9–111
Set the scan source and the monitor in use.
The ColorMatch for Display filter will optimize
the display of your image.

Figure 9–112
The ColorMatch Preview filter will display a soft proof
next to the original, showing how the image will print.

NOTE: Do not use Photoshop's RGB to CMYK Color mode conversion when
using ColorMatch.

Once the monitor has been calibrated with the ColorSet calibration
application, an image opened into Photoshop is then adjusted with the
DayStar ColorMatch for Display filter (Figure 9–111), if an input PT has
been used. The filter will adjust the color content of the file to produce
color optimized for the currently selected monitor.

NOTE: Use the ColorMatch for Display filter only if an input PT is used.
The file must be scanned for the large color gamut of KCMS, which the filter
optimizes to the gamut of the monitor. A file scanned for KCMS will appear
inaccurate without the use of this filter. A scan which was not scanned with
KCMS will display the RGB data correctly.

If you want to see how the file will appear printed, the ColorMatch
Preview filter allows you to select the PT for the intended output device
(Figure 9–112). For example, if the file will be printed on an offset printing
press, select the SWOP coated PT. ColorMatch will create a "soft proof" on
screen next to the original file showing how the image will print. Out-of-
gamut colors or color differences between a monitor and a specific output
device become more obvious with this filter.

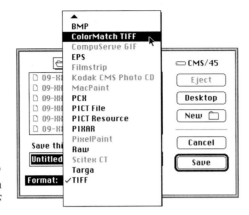

Figure 9–113
Saving a file as a
ColorMatch TIFF

The final step is to save or print the file. To save the file, select ColorMatch TIFF from the file format list in the Save As dialog box (Figure 9–113). At this stage, the corrections (actually the transforms) built into the CMS take effect, optimizing the conversion from a large color gamut (interchange RGB) to the gamut of a specific calibrated output device or to another color space. Because the image is saved with color tags as a special TIFF file, the original file does not get altered.

ColorMatch Print, available as an Export submenu under the file menu, prints the optimized file directly to the output device, avoiding the process of creating a tagged TIFF file.

The ColorMatch system can be greatly accelerated by a DayStar Charger DSP board (See "Acceleration" in Chapter 2, "Setting up Your System"). For superior results, Kodak's PICC (Precision Input Color Calibration) software will work with ColorMatch by allowing you to produce a custom input PT for any scanner. (See "Color Management Systems" in Chapter 3, "Configuring Photoshop.")

CyberMesh

CyberMesh from Knoll Software, an Acquire module (for Macintosh only), transforms grayscale files into 3-D images. CyberMesh operates by interpreting the gray levels in an image as heights: Black is the lowest level, and white is the highest level (Figure 9–114). The 3-D models created are rectangular, cylindrical, or spherical, accomplished by generating a polygon for each pixel in the image. The resolution pop-up menu, which varies from 10% up to "Full" resolution (with ten steps in between), allows the image to be previewed with greater speed by rendering fewer polygons.

A tool bar changes the view of the image preview and the display mode setting. Familiar tools such as a magnifying glass and scrolling hand tool operate just like Photoshop's tools. A View Rotator tool allows you to rotate the view of the model around the X, Y, and Z axes.

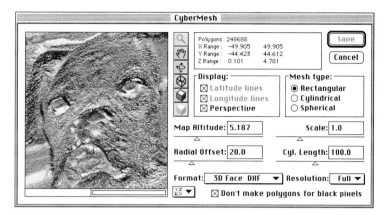

Figure 9–114
The CyberMesh
dialog box

There are three display modes for viewing the model. Wireframe produces the fastest preview and is useful for quick manipulations. Solid with lines is the slowest preview mode but shows the image shaded with the polygons outlined in black. Solid is the most readable display and is previewed with a single shaded light source. Map Altitude, Scale, Radial Offset, and Cycl. Length sliders produce an almost endless number of alterations. Once the model is to your liking, select the specific file format required and the image will be exported and saved. CyberMesh can save the file in the DXF format.

DayStar Charger

Many of the DSP Accelerators, made specifically to speed up Photoshop functions, have their own filter versions, which appear under the Filter menu. The DayStar Charger DSP has a plug-in called the PowerPreview (Macintosh only), a submenu of DayStar Charger under the filter menu (Figure 9–115).

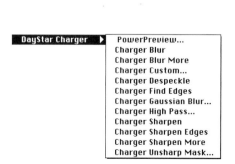

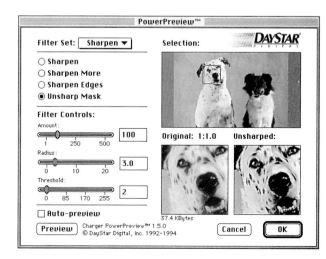

Figure 9–115   The DayStar Charger filters and the PowerPreview dialog box

When selected, a large dialog box appears with three previews in which you can move a smaller, sizable marquee around a preview and see the filter effects on two smaller previews, a before and after view.

Charger filters can be accessed from the DayStar Charger submenu or from filter sets in the PowerPreview dialog box provided by a pop-up menu. Filters sets are Blur, which includes Gaussian Blur; Sharpen, which includes Unsharpen Mask; and Other, which includes Despeckle, Find Edges, and High Pass.

In the Custom filter you can input numeric values into the various fields and see the effect on the preview in real time. DayStar Charger filters provide accelerated filtering of Grayscale, RGB, Lab, and CYMK files. Various DSP boards can be used with PowerPreview in addition to DayStar's line of Charger cards. The software also supports multiple DSPs.

Epilogue PS

Epilogue PS Acquire module from Total Integrations (Macintosh only) allows Photoshop to access and rasterize any PostScript or EPS file using a software-based PostScript Level 2 Interpreter from Adobe. (Rasterizing is necessary to convert a vector graphic to a bitmapped image for use in Photoshop.) Files can be rasterized into RGB or CMYK Color modes. Epilogue PS works with a separate application called Epilogue Server, which supports variable resolutions and is only limited by available hard disk space. The Epilogue PS package also includes a utility called FASTview that allows the user to view on screen any PostScript or EPS file prior to actual RIP and can even report the processing times for the actual interpretation.

Intellihance

Intellihance from DPA software (Macintosh only), a set of three packages, automatically corrects images. These filters automatically adjust images for contrast, color cast, brightness, sharpness, and speckle removal. The filters include Intellihance Pro GS (for Grayscale), Intellihance Pro RGB, and Intellihance Pro CYMK (three additional packages, called "LE" editions, which have fewer options are not discussed here). Each plug-in can be used for the appropriate color space of the file you wanted to correct (Figure 9–116).

Intellihance is "an intelligent filter" because it only corrects the limitations found in a given image. For example, if the image doesn't need sharpening but it does need contrast corrections, Intellihance will only correct for contrast, making the files more uniform when output.

The three filters have similar dialog boxes with pop-up menus to set how the files will be processed by Intellihance. The Pro RGB settings include Descreen to remove a halftone screen from an image, Contrast to set the contrast and flatten the shadows or highlights for special reproduction needs like newspaper printing, Brightness to set the output brightness or

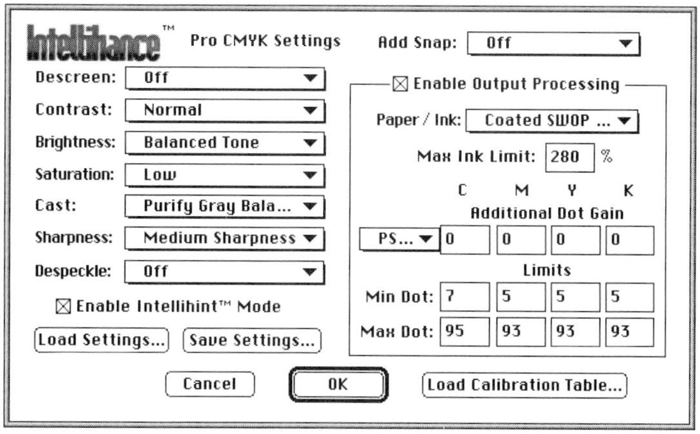

Intellihance™ **Pro CMYK Settings**

Add Snap: [Off ▼]

Descreen: [Off ▼]

Contrast: [Normal ▼]

Brightness: [Balanced Tone ▼]

Saturation: [Low ▼]

Cast: [Purify Gray Bala... ▼]

Sharpness: [Medium Sharpness ▼]

Despeckle: [Off ▼]

☒ Enable Intellihint™ Mode

[Load Settings...] [Save Settings...]

☒ Enable Output Processing

Paper / Ink: [Coated SWOP ... ▼]

Max Ink Limit: [280] %

　　　　C　　M　　Y　　K

Additional Dot Gain

[PS... ▼][0][0][0][0]

Limits

Min Dot: [7][5][5][5]

Max Dot: [95][93][93][93]

[Cancel] [OK] [Load Calibration Table...]

Figure 9–116
The Intellihance Pro
CYMK dialog box

exposure, Saturation, Cast to remove unwanted color casts, Sharpness, Despeckle to reduce noise, and Add Snap to add a final touch of contrast. On the CYMK and gray scale filters, a menu called Press Calibration controls the compensation for dot gain. This works in conjunction with the Press Gain menu and Dot Gain & Limits field. The type of selection made with the Press Calibration menu will automatically place a figure into the press Gain Field. For example, selecting Coated offset 133 lpi automatically places a figure of 10% Dot Gain in the Press Gain Field.

A check box called "Enable Intellihint Mode" previews the tone curve Intellihance has chosen for the image before processing the entire image. Controls are provided for manual correction for greater control over tone curve corrections. A Marquee tool can select a specific area that the filter uses to judge its corrections. In addition three Eyedropper tools allow you to set the black point, midtone, and white point respectively. The Eyedropper tools operate as densitometers, producing readings in either percentages (0% for White, 100% for black), or as the actual pixel levels from 0 to 255.

Intellihance also offers scanner calibration (the program comes with a calibration strip for scanning), batch processing using either QuicKeys or Tempo II, various separation tables that can be loaded into Photoshop to do RGB to CYMK conversions, and monitor calibration tables for many popular proofing systems.

Kai's Power Tools

Kai's Power Tools (KPT), a set of special effects and production filters, appears in KPT's own submenu as well as scattered about in various native filter submenus (Figures C–17 and C–18 in the Color Section). Convolver, new to the KPT family, is also discussed below.

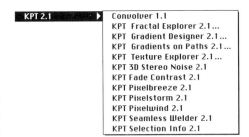

Figure 9–117
The KPT (Kai's Power
Tools) submenu showing
the 12 available filters

KPT

The KPT submenu contains the core filters (Figure 9–117). Many of these filters have real-time previews showing how an effect will be applied to the image. The filters function efficiently in CYMK color mode as well as in RGB. Most come with preset parameters that you can add to, save, and name as custom effects. Numerous calculation modes (or Apply modes) are available, such as Subtract, Multiply, Screen, and Lighten only. The program adds real time previews for all apply mode effects.

The **KPT Gradient Designer**, a filter used to create blends or gradients, goes far beyond Photoshop's Gradient tool. The Blend tool can create a gradient with two colors, but the KPT Gradient Designer can assign any number of colors throughout the blend, as well as control the transparency, direction, origin, number of repetitions, and more. KPT refers to this filter as "analogous to Lego building blocks" because it builds upon other filters to accomplish its tasks.

The **KPT Texture Explorer** uses an innovative interface which allows you to shuffle various texture permutations (Figure 9–118).

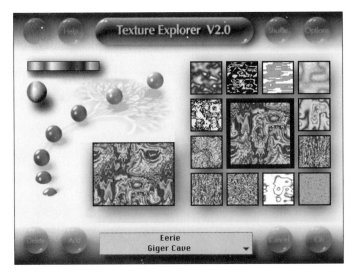

Figure 9–118
The KPT Texture
Explorer dialog box

Figure 9–119
KPT filters effects shown
from left to right:
Pixelbreeze, Pixelwind,
and Glass Lens Soft with
Hue Protected
Noise Maximum

Fractal Explorer provides a series of controls for the production of fractals, which are mathematically created patterns of infinite detail. This filter is another in the "Lego block" style already described. Fractal Explorer contains many of the various controls found in the Texture Explorer and Gradient filters, such as preset options, real-time previewing, opacity control, and preview and shuffle options.

Pixelstorm, **Pixelwind**, and **Pixelbreeze** filters diffuse and displace pixels (Figure 9–119).

NOISE

In the Noise submenu you will find seven different noise filters, including the **KPT Special Red, Green, and Blue**, which add intense noise with a dominate color. The three Hue-protected filters, Maximum, Medium, and Minimum, generate noise based upon the hue of the selected image, causing random noise. The **3-D Stereo Noise** filter creates a special displaced 3-D noise effect with grayscale images. The **KPT Grime Layer** also produces a dark transparent noise over the image—a subtle texture with effect intensity operated by the numeric key pad.

KPT Hue Protected Noise filter is a set of three filters that operate much like Photoshop's noise filter except Hue Protected Noise preserves the hues in the image—ideal when noise is needed but the color or hue should be retained.

KPT Special Noises, a set of three filters which produce unusual noise textures, is useful to create the look of sandstone or as an intermediate stage for building up a texture.

BLUR

Gaussian Glow, Gaussian Electrify, and Gaussian Weave are found under the Blur menu. Each applies different blurring or softening to lighter or darker areas. Gaussian Glow produces the effect of a faded photo by producing a smooth blur in darker areas of the image. Gaussian Electrify produces a glowing effect by blurring lighter areas of an image. Gaussian Weave produces directional blurs: horizontal, vertical, and a blending of the two.

Also in the Blur filter submenu are four KPT Smudge filters: Darken Left, Darken Right, Lighten Left, and Lighten Right. Each creates subtle motion blur effects with control over direction and density.

DISTORT

Vortex Tiling, new in version 2.1, produces a two-step image distortion. The image is first mirrored and then an imaginary circle around the center of a selection flips the image inside out. The amount of vortex tiling is controlled with the keyboard numeric key pad—lower numbers create a small circle.

KPT Glass Lens (Bright, Normal, and Soft) creates 3-D spheres using a special ray tracer (Figure 9–119). The intensity of the spectral highlight in the sphere depends on the filter used and the direction set using the keyboard, with ten different options possible.

KPT Page Curl simulates the effect of a page peeled back. A highlight and shadow produce a 3-D effect.

SHARPEN

KPT Sharpen Intensity produces stronger contrast and brighter colors. Use it to add snap to an otherwise dull-looking image.

STYLIZE

KPT Diffuse More, similar to the Diffuse filter in Photoshop, works with a larger number of pixels which yields a stronger effect.

KPT Find Edges Charcoal produces a similar effect to Find Edges but with a faint grayish looks much like charcoal on white paper.

KPT Find Edges Soft is similar to the other find edges filters but less harsh and intense.

KPT Find Edges and Invert is similar to Photoshop's Find Edges, but combines the Invert function at the same time. The Caps Lock key toggles the Invert on or off.

KPT Scatter Horizontal diffuses the image on the horizontal axis but includes a lighten mode.

KPT Convolver

Convolver, an amazing plug-in from the developers of Kai's Power Tools, provides access to limitless kernel-based effects at the same time, like sharpen, blur, emboss, find edges, saturation, color contrast, etc. The manipulations can be used separately or in combinations.

The interface, similar to Kai's Texture Explorer filter, operates in three modes: Explore, Design, and Tweak (Figures 9–120 and 9–121). Buttons, rolling balls, sliders, and pop-up menus set the parameters, allowing you to preview an unlimited number of custom filter effects.

Explore mode automatically cycles through effects and displays them in 15 different mini previews. Toggle the various controls and instantly see changes or *mutations* applied to the previews. Simply click and watch Convolver work its magic until you see a desired effect.

Design mode gives you specific controls to manually set the filter parameters while providing 15 variations in the mini preview windows. You can set the parameters for such effects as blur, sharpen, edge effects, relief effects, hue angle, saturation, brightness, and contrast.

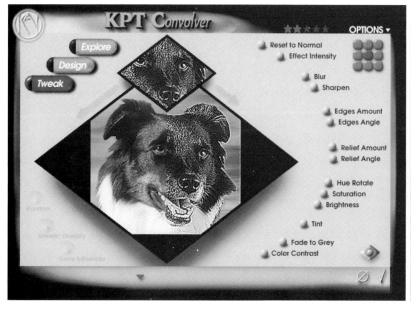

Figure 9–120
The KPT Convolver dialog box

Figure 9–121
The Convolver filter was applied
to the dog photograph
(© Andrew Rodney).

Tweak mode works with a single, large preview and set of rolling balls to fine-tune effects in real time. Every possible filter effect can be controlled, whether subtly or radically.

NOTE: There are some "surprises" in the software. Over time, hidden features are revealed offering further controls, tools, and even some just plain fun . . . .

KEPS Precision

DayStar Digital has several sets of additional filters for use with the Charger PFS accelerator board. These filters (Macintosh only) were originally developed by KEPS, a Kodak company, for their high end imaging workstations. Several function like the filters found in Photoshop (such as Precision Blur, Blur More, Gaussian blur, Sharpen, Sharpen More, and Unsharp Mask), but are greatly accelerated and more precise.

In addition, the Precision Adaptive Sharpen filter allows you to create a custom curve that affects what areas of an image undergo sharpening. For example, you could produce a curve that would sharpen midtones more than highlights while applying no sharpening to the shadows. The Precision Rotate & Resize filters allow you to do both of these operations in one step.

Paint Alchemy

Paint Alchemy from XAOS Tools (for the Macintosh only) is a single Photoshop plug-in composed of five different filters for customized effects: Brush, Color, Size, Angle, and Transparency. Paint Alchemy is described as a painting system in the form of a plug-in. It applies brush strokes to selected areas of the image using *control cards* to generate an unlimited set of parameters. The sheer number of different parameters available in Paint Alchemy for manipulating an image is staggering! Not only does it allow custom, user-defined styles to be saved, but it comes loaded with 75 styles.

Paint Alchemy has a preview similar to Gallery Effects with a larger window showing the entire image and two smaller windows showing the unaltered and manipulated images. Move from card to card in any order. Configure the parameters and preview the changes until you find the ultimate effect (Figure 9–122).

The **Brush** card is the first to appear and generates the greatest effects on the image (Figure 9–123). Although there are six standard brushes, any PICT file of any size can be loaded as a brush. Brush controls include Density, Positioning, Randomizing, and Layering.

The **Color** card is used for creating the base color of each brush stroke. You can apply a solid color or a color from the image and adjust its hue, brightness, and saturation.

Figure 9–122
The Oil Detail style was applied to the dogs in the foreground, while the Watermarker style was applied to the background.

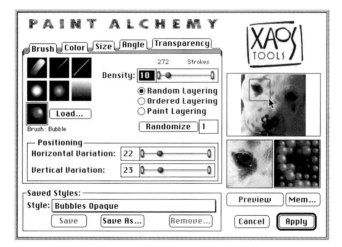

Figure 9–123
The Paint Alchemy Brush card

The **Size** card sets the size of the brush strokes through a pop-up menu. For example, by setting the size to Radial Distance, the brush strokes change in size in a circular fashion from the center gradually outward to the edges.

The **Angle** card is used to specify the orientation or rotation of the brush strokes, from no variation to random strokes. A pop-up menu similar to that of the size card allows for variance like the radial distance, and provides controls to vary vertical or horizontal position.

The **Transparency** card sets brush stroke transparency with controls similar to those already mentioned.

Paint Alchemy works only in RGB Color mode. To manipulate an image in another mode, convert it to RGB, apply the filter effects, and then convert it back to its original mode. (Figures C–21 and C–22 in the Color Section.)

Pattern Workshop

The Pattern Workshop plug-in from MicroFrontier (Macintosh only) creates patterns and texture effects in Photoshop. Found under the Pattern Workshop filter submenu are the Pattern Edit and the Pattern Fill filters (Figure 9–124).

Pattern Edit creates new patterns or edits the many patterns that come loaded with the filter. The Pattern Set pop-up menu contains 10 sets each with 16 different patterns. In addition, new sets can be created and loaded into this menu. An existing pattern can be edited. A portion of the image or the entire image can become a pattern using the "Grab from Image" button.

Pattern Fill applies the patterns to an existing file. Like Pattern Edit, a pop-up menu selects the pattern required (Figures 9–125 and 9–126).

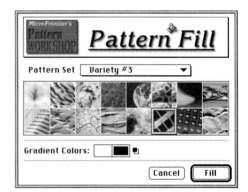

Figure 9–124
The Pattern Filter submenu

Figure 9–125
The Pattern Fill dialog box

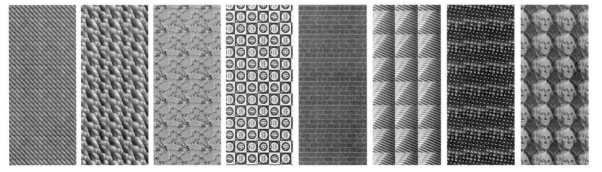

Figure 9–126   Examples of some of the many Pattern Fill filters

Figure 9–127
Examples of Paul Badger's shareware filters. Shown from left to right: VectorGraph, Radar, and Lumpy Noise.

Paul Badger

Paul Badger offers a set of three Mac-only shareware filters (Figure 9–127).

VectorGraph, found in the Stylize menu, maps the direction of an image's shading. This filter creates a 3-D look much like an emboss filter. Paul recommends using VectorGraph on a single channel of an image.

Radar, found in the Other menu, is designed for animators to create the effect of a radial sweep. A dialog box allows you to configure the effect; Start and end gamma, skew and angle fields allow you to specify the Radar effect.

Lumpy Noise found in the Noise menu, controls the size of the grain created when applying noise to an image. Lump value, color depth and color convergence controls modify the effect. Using check boxes, a darker or lighter mode can be applied. This filter can produce a different looking random noise effect.

PhotoFusion

The PhotoFusion plug-in from Ultimatte (Macintosh only) creates masks for compositing photographs with the method known as *blue screen* compositing. Blue screen masks have been used in the motion picture special-effects industry for decades. Like its counterparts in the film industry, PhotoFusion works with a special blue-painted background—you must photograph a subject against a special blue screen. Rosco manufactures Ultimatte Blue paint to create this background.

A photograph shot against the special blue background is opened into Photoshop with PhotoFusion in the Acquire submenu (Figure 9–128). The plug-in creates an accurate grayscale mask based on the blue areas in the image, which can include transparent objects, soft edges and extremely fine detail in the foreground subject (Figure 9–129).

The precise mask can be saved as a channel or as a separate file for minor corrections. For example, Photoshop's paint tools could be used to quickly edit the mask of an image photographed using wire to hold up a prop.

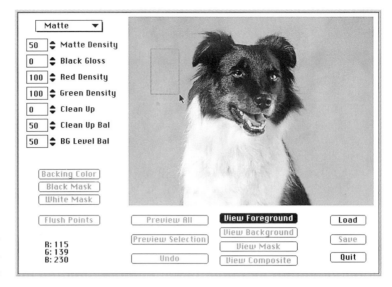

Figure 9–128
The PhotoFusion
dialog box

Figure 9–129
Left to right: the original
studio photograph of the
dog shot against a
background painted with
Ultimatte Blue; the
mask generated by
Photofusion; and the
final image of the
masked dog pasted into
the background created
with KPT Bryce .
(© Andrew Rodney)

PhotoLab

PhotoLab from Silicon Wizards (Macintosh only), a set of eight filter-based photographic methods, can manipulate and modify RGB or CYMK files (Figure 9–130). The dialog box for all the filters share a common interface with Before and After preview screens allowing you to see effects prior to actually applying the filter (Figure 9–131). The filters come preloaded with example parameters, and user-defined parameters can also be saved and loaded. Most of the filters have an AI (Artificial Intelligence) mode, which functions like an auto exposure mode on a camera.

Gradtone replaces or modifies the colors in an image by replacing selected luminance values with color hues.

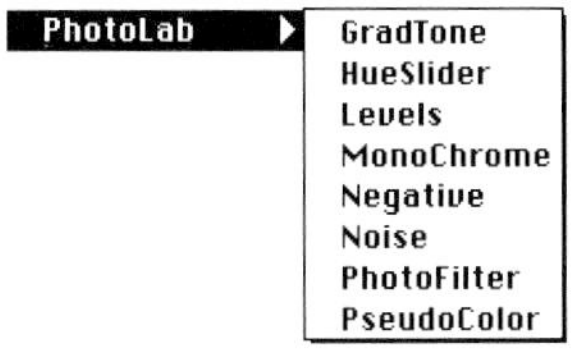

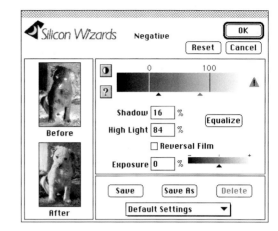

Figure 9–130
The PhotoLab submenu

Figure 9–131
The PhotoLab Negative filter is useful for inverting scanned negatives.

HueSlider moves all the colors in an image toward a selected color. Select the color by moving the Red, Green, and Blue sliders. A fourth slider controls the amount of color mixing and saturation. Use this filter to remove a tint or to match another portion of an image.

Levels produces two different but related effects. The first increases or decreases separation or contrast between colors and the second sharpens the image. The filter examines similar colors (controlled with sliders) and combines them into a single color. Negative shadow values and positive highlight values increases sharpness. Using these sliders along with the overall exposure control manipulates the gamut or contrast of the image. Increased contrast will appear to sharpen an image.

MonoChrome produces a monochromatic (one color) image, using a Hue slider to specify a color and controls for Saturation and Exposure.

Negative converts a scanned negative to a positive image with control over highlights, shadows, and midtones to counter the tonal compression found in negative film. Unlike Photoshop's Invert command, this produces superior results with color negatives, which have an orange mask in the base of the film stock (Figure 9–131).

Noise filter creates random groups of colored pixels throughout the image. A Hue slider and controls for Saturation and Brightness allow unlimited options for specifying the colors of the noise.

PhotoFilter modifies a group of colors, changing their overall color cast. In addition to adding or subtracting specific colors, you can also manipulate the exposure of the image. The PhotoFilter comes preset with several color filter effects based on the color correction filters used in photography

PseudoColor filter distorts the colors in a file. This filter can be used for pop art effects or to mimic the look of infrared film.

PhotoMatic

PhotoMatic, a scripting utility from DayStar Digital (Macintosh only), allows you to automate Photoshop operations. For example, a PhotoMatic script might open eight files, rotate them, convert them from RGB to CYMK Color mode, apply some filter effects, and save the files in a different file format. PhotoMatic can run its script automatically without user intervention while Photoshop is running in the background. The program can also run on a network.

By choosing Start under the Record menu (shown at left), PhotoMatic creates a script by watching you perform a series of tasks. Choose the Stop command and a standard save dialog box opens to save the script. The script can be edited with the AppleScript Editor that comes with PhotoMatic (it requires AppleScript to operate) or any word processing program.

PhotoMatic comes with its own application which allows you to batch process with various scripts and multiple files. Select a number of files that need processing and place them into the PhotoMatic folder using Apple's Drag and Drop method and select a script to run.

Pixar Classic Textures

Pixar Classic Textures Volumes One and Two, collections of photographic textures provided on CD-ROM readable by both Macintosh and Windows platforms, feature a plug-in that automatically tiles the textures into an area of any size or resolution with no visible seams (Figure 9–132). The textures, photographed from original material, incorporate a patented Pixar technology that provides seamless tiling when used with the Pixar Textures filter (Figure 9–133).

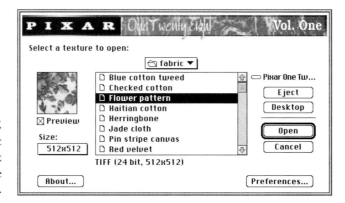

Figure 9–132
The Pixar Classic Textures filter dialog box will open any TIFF file and seamlessly tile it.

Figure 9–133   Examples of Pixar Classic Textures available on CD-ROM

ScanPrep Pro

ScanPrep Pro from ImageXpress, an Acquire module, automatically optimizes files for specific output requirements using what ImageXpress calls a "Smart Agent Processor." ScanPrep Pro completely and automatically sets all the necessary parameters for any scanned or PhotoCD image with up to 23 processing techniques so that files are ready for output. Once you specify the intended input (the scanner used) and the intended output, ScanPrep Pro creates a duplicate file and takes over Photoshop in an *auto pilot* mode (Figure 9–134).

ScanPrep Pro comes loaded with a database of lithographic information that it uses to correct a file for output using color separation tables developed by Rochester Institute of Technology. ScanPrep Pro can correct existing scanned images or work with many desktop scanners, making corrections at the scan stage by over-ridding the scanner's default software.

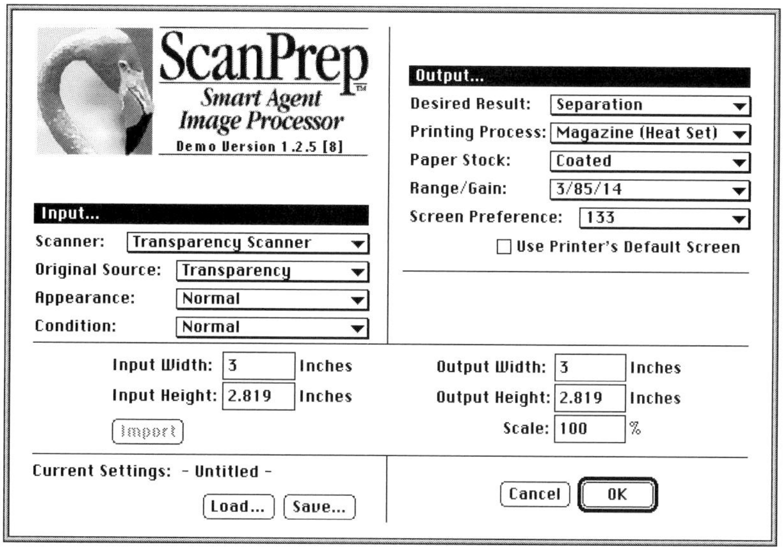

Figure 9–134
The ScanPrep dialog box

ScanPrep Pro will analyze the resolution of a file and warn you if the new output scaling is too large.

The Desired Output field contains options for Line Art, Halftone, Separation (for 4 color work), Custom Separation (user defined), and RGB Color. The Halftone output can be further defined as specular, Dropout, or Full Range. Each option handles the generation of a dot in pure whites and blacks. Drop out is useful when subjects have been photographed on a white background and that background needs to be stripped-out.

The Separation option sets the output for CYMK, SWOP printing. Custom Separation allows you to create separation parameters and save them for future use. The Custom Separation Setup dialog presents controls for GCR, UCR, Black Generation, Total Ink Limit, and other custom separation options.

The Printing Process and Paper Stock menus, linked to the Desired Result menu, tell ScanPrep Pro the type of output devices to be used, with options for Newspaper, Magazine, Brochure, Printers (like dye sublimation), and Film Recorders, and the specific paper stock that will be used for printing, such as Coated, Non coated and Newsprint. The dot gain compensation is either set automatically or you can manually set the parameters for highlights, midtones and shadows. A halftone screen frequency from 53 dpi up to 200 dpi can be selected in 11 different steps. ScanPrep Pro even has provisions for Stochastic Screening.

ScanTastic

ScanTastic from Second Glance Software (Macintosh only), an Acquire plug-in module, allows you to scan directly from Photoshop. Plug-ins are available for most most flatbed scanner models. It provides control of resolution, bit depth, scaling, brightness and contrast, and transfer curves for each of the RGB channels. Scanned images automatically become an open Photoshop document (Figure 4–11).

Select

Select, a powerful and simple-to-use color correction filter from Human Software (Macintosh only), allows you to apply selective color corrections as well as *gradation* (global) corrections to CYMK images.

The Gradation dialog box presents four color channels represented as curves in a small window (Figure 9–135). You can create or remove any number of points along the curve of each color plate to modify the shape and thus affect the colors in the image. Five fields define points in the curve. Or you can enter numeric figures for curve generation. You shape some or all of the curves, and clicking on the Preview button presents a before and after thumbnail of the image corrections. In addition, a Sup Cast button can examine the entire image and automatically set the curves to remove an unwanted color cast in the file.

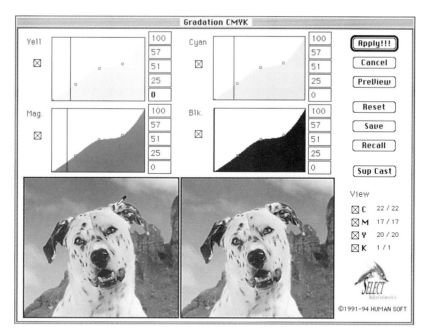

Figure 9–135
The Select Gradation
dialog box for color
correcting
CMYK images

The Selective correction mode mimics features found on high-end systems. This is known as *local color correction*; it allows you to apply a color correction within a color range without affecting other colors in the image, such as the yellow in the reds of an image. An Eyedropper tool allows you to read color values and pick colors to modify.

SpectrePlug-ins

Pre-Press Technologies offers two plug-ins (Macintosh only) for image processing, SpectrePlug-in Color Correction and SpectrePlug-In Unsharp Masking (Figure 9–136).

SPECTREPLUG-IN COLOR CORRECTION

SpectrePlug-In Color Correction changes specific colors in a CYMK file. The filter creates a color correction table with up to six primary and six user-definable colors to modify CYMK values. The densitometer allows you to select color areas to correct or replace.

SPECTREPLUG-IN UNSHARP MASKING

SpectrePlug-In Unsharp Masking has capabilities not found in other Unsharp Masking filters (Figure 9–137). This filter allows you to smooth, sharpen, or do both at the same time. This filter can affect some or all of the color channels or *plates* (as they are called in the dialog box). The filter

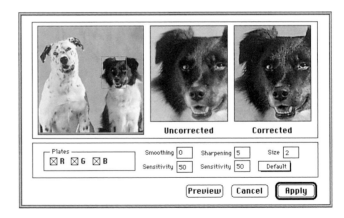

Pre-Press Technologies ▶ **Color Correction...**
Unsharp Masking...

Figure 9–136
The Select Gradation dialog box for
color correcting CMYK images

Figure 9–137
The SpectrePlug-In Unsharp Masking dialog box.

comes loaded with preset sharpening and smoothing parameters. You can
also create and save your own parameters for latter use. This filter will only
operate with CYMK or RGB images.

Terrazzo

Terrazzo, a plug-in from Xaos Tools (Macintosh only), creates regular patterns from a selected area in an open document. These patterns can be used
to create backgrounds, design fabrics and other kaleidoscopic looking images.

Control Terrazzo with a single easy-to-use dialog box. A large preview
shows the source image next to a large destination image, where all effects
can be seen in real time. You can pick 17 Symmetries (basic tiling patterns), each with an infinite number of possible patterns, opacities and
color effects (Figure 9–138).

A Feather slider controls the transitions between tiles. An Opacity slider
controls the opacity of a pattern applied to the source image. Common
Photoshop apply modes such as Lighten, Darken, Hue, Saturation, Color,
Multiply, and so on are available from a pop-up menu. Tiles can also be
saved as PICT files.

WaterMark

The WaterMark filter, a shareware product from John Dykstra Photography
(Macintosh only), places a © (copyright) symbol into a selection or over an
entire image. This filter allows you to submit images for examination to
potential users but prohibits them from reproducing the images. The two
controls provided are Opacity, which controls how light or dark the symbol
appears on the image, and Repeat, which controls the number of symbols
appearing on the image. Although not impossible, it would be very difficult
to retouch out this symbol (Figure 9–139 and 9–140).

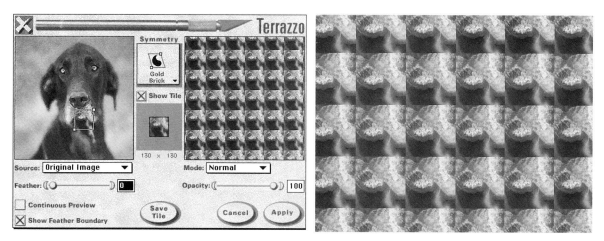

Figure 9–138   The Terrazzo dialog box showing the selected area that generated the tiled pattern on the right

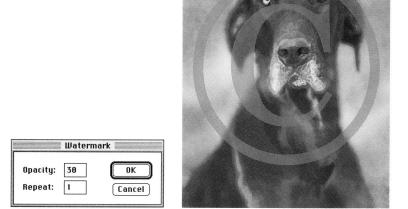

Figure 9–139
The Watermark dialog box

Figure 9–140
The Watermark filter can protect an image from unauthorized use.

Summary

This chapter provided overviews of Photoshop's native filters, as well as descriptions and techniques for using the many filters and plug-ins available from third-party manufacturers.

- There are two types of filters: *native* and *plug-in* modules. The native filters are programmed directly into Photoshop and cannot be removed. Plug-in modules are separate little programs that can be added to Photoshop by placing a plug-in module in Photoshop's Plug-ins folder (Mac) or PLUGINS directory (PC).

- Most filters appear under the Filters menu, although a number of plug-ins appear under other menus, such as the Acquire or Export submenus.

- Production filters and file converters generally appear under Photoshop's Acquire or Export menus.

- Most filters feature dialog box previews that allow you to preview the filter's effects before actually applying it to the entire image.

- Filters do not work in Bitmap and Indexed Color modes.

- Filters can be applied to a selection or the entire image.

- Experiment with filter settings. Low settings yield subtle results and high settings produce exaggerated effects (they can also destroy an image).

- Filters only work on one layer at a time but can work simultaneously on multiple channels.

- To test a filter effect, select a small area, apply the filter, then Undo.

In the next chapter learn how to combine your filtered effects with other images using paste controls, layers, channels, channel calculations, and other programs.

Compositing

Almost all digital artists work with multiple image elements and isolated special effects, requiring some masking and compositing to produce a final, polished product. Photoshop 3 makes compositing much easier with the Layers palette, which allows up to 99 layers in a document. Each layer can be moved and edited independently, stacked, merged, or grouped, have its own painting mode or mask, and be used as a mask for other layers. At the same time, Photoshop's calculation commands also provide controls for combining channels and layers.

This chapter presents tips and techniques for combining images using layers and channels. It begins with techniques that are layer-based, and then progresses to compositing techniques with the calculate commands: Duplicate, Apply Image and Calculations. The chapter concludes by describing how Photoshop interacts with some other applications.

This chapter assumes that you are familiar with the basic function of layers and channels as discussed in Chapter 6, "Image Selection and Masking."

Planning a Composition

Before getting to the technical issues, let's talk about combining images from an aesthetic, graphic point of view. We have all seen digital art that looks like a cluttered grade school collage: without a sense of composition, without regard to perspective, without a clear statement. Photoshop gives you incredible power to produce the most fantastic images, but simplicity is often the most powerful visual effect. Be a ruthless editor when you combine images. Planning also helps keeps the size of your files down.

Figure 10–1   In "Step Out of the Picture" David Herrold collaged elements photographed
separately from above in his carefully planned composition. (© David Herrold)

Begin developing an image by establishing a clear purpose. If the image
is to be realistic, pay attention to lighting sources and perspective.
Consider dominant and subordinate elements, cropping, the arrangement
of space; all design principles apply in the digital arena.

One artist who plans his compositions very carefully is David Herrold, as
is evident in "Step Out of the Picture" (Figure 10–1). The artist preserves a
plausible sense of perspective in a composition by using photos shot from a
similar camera elevation. In this case, Herrold photographed models, an
interior, props, and a landscape from above, collaging them together to produce a surreal psychological drama.

Says Herrold, "Even when the inaccuracies of lighting and perspective
are kept below the threshold of viewer awareness, the composite image
acquires a different feel than straight photography has. I regard this different
feel as a characteristic that should not be suppressed . . . but retained as a
declaration that the image is fiction and not a straight photograph that lies."

Working with Layers and Channels

Use layers and channels for combining images, masking, or creating special effects by placing elements on different layers and channels. Layers allow interactive compositing of layer elements that required multiple irreversible steps in previous versions of Photoshop. Channels provide a quick method of storing selections and image elements independent of the composite image or layers. You can even use layers and channels to store components of images as an "image library" to be incorporated in other compositions. Control most layer operations in the Layers palette and channels operations in the Channels palette.

Layers and Channels Guidelines

Layers display the channels that combine to make a color image (composite channel) such as the red, green and blue channels of an RGB Color image. In the case of a grayscale image, a layer displays the data that is in the Black channel (Channel 1). All extra channels function independently of layers. A channel can be attached directly to a layer by creating a layer mask.

In addition to being controlled by their palettes, layers and channels can be moved and combined with the calculation commands: Duplicate, Apply Image and Calculate. The calculate commands are discussed later in this chapter.

Although many creative possibilities exist, in general you should use layers for compositing image elements and use channels for storing selections for masking.

LAYER GUIDELINES

Using the Layers Palette you can create, copy, merge, order, and delete layers, and even create masks. Use the following guidelines when combining images or creating special effects with the Layers palette:

- To change the order of multiple layers, select the layer in the Layers palette, and drag it to a new position in the palette relative to the others.
- You can only edit one layer, the target layer, at a time. Make it active by clicking on its name in the palette or on the image element from the desired layer in the document window with the Move tool while pressing the Command key.
- To copy a layer between documents, select it in the Layers palette and use the Copy/Paste commands. When the layer is pasted into the target document, it will come in as a Floating Selection. To come in as a new layer in that document, use Paste Layer from the Edit menu. You can also copy a layer from one document window to another by dragging

the layer with the Move tool from the Layers palette to the open window of the destination document.

- To duplicate a layer drag it from the Layers palette to the document window, drag it to the New Layer icon at the bottom of the palette, or choose Duplicate Layer from the pop-up menu.

- When combining layers you can use the modes, opacity, and blend controls in the Layer Options dialog box or Layers palette to help blend images. Combination effects can be restricted or amplified on specific values or colors on any layer independent of other elements, values, or colors.

- When creating a new layer, the New Layer dialog box allows you to specify the Opacity, Mode, and grouping for the layer. Some Modes also provide an option to fill the layer with a neutral color. A layer filled with a neutral color for its assigned Mode will have no visible effect on underlying layers unless the values are changed, such as painting or applying a filter. Some tools, commands, and filters do not function on empty layers; by filling the layer with a neutral color, no visible change occurs until the layer is altered.

- The transparent areas of a layer can be used as a mask. If the Preserve Transparency box is checked, any painting or editing will effect only the portions of the layer containing pixels or color values. If you leave the Preserve Transparency box unchecked, any painting or editing will effect the entire layer. Use the transparent areas of a layer to mask other layers by creating a clipping group. The transparent area in the lowermost layer will mask all elements from the grouped layers. Group a layer with a previous layer in the Layer Options dialog box.

- Create a customized mask for a layer by assigning it a Layer Mask. A Layer Mask creates a channel which applies a mask to its assigned layer only.

CHANNEL GUIDELINES

Using the Channels Palette you can create, duplicate, order, and delete channels. Channels are ideal for storing selections and 8-bit image elements independent of layers. Under the Select menu, use the Save Selection command to convert a selection to a channel and the Load Selection command to convert a channel to a selection.

- To change the order of multiple channels, select the channel in the Channels palette, and drag it to a new position in the palette relative to the others.

- Painting tools, editing tools, and many of the image processing and filter commands can affect multiple channels simultaneously. Some filters and commands affect only one channel at a time. Make a channel active (target channel) by clicking on its name in the palette. To make multiple channels active, press the Shift key and click on the desired channels.

- To copy a channel to another document: Click on its name in the palette, Select All, copy it, and then paste in the desired channel of the destination document; drag the channel from the Channels palette over the open window of the destination document (it will automatically come in as a new channel); or click on a channel name, choose Duplicate from the pop-up menu, and select the destination document from the Document pop-up menu in the Duplicate Channel dialog box.

- To duplicate a channel, drag it from the Channels palette to the document window, drag it to the New Channel icon at the bottom of the palette, or choose Duplicate Channel from the pop-up menu.

- Combine channels as masks by loading them one at a time with the Load Selection command under the Select menu and using the Operation options in the Load Selection dialog box. Combine channels into new channels by using the Copy/Paste or Calculate commands.

- When creating a new channel, the Channel Options dialog box allows you to choose a mask color for the channel and specify whether the color indicates the selection or the mask areas.

- To convert the transparent areas of a target layer into a channel, select Load Selection under the Edit menu, choose the layer transparency from the Channel pop-up menu, click OK and then Choose Save Selection also under the Select menu. Specify New in the Channel pop-up menu. Or, make the layer active in the Layers palette, press Command-Option-T to load the transparency as a selection, and then save the selection.

- When a layer with a Layer Mask assigned to it is selected as the target layer, the Layer Mask appears as a channel in the Channels palette. The Layer Mask functions like any other channel except that it automatically masks its layer. Convert a Layer Mask channel to a normal channel by dragging it to the Duplicate Channel icon.

Layer and Channel Techniques

Previous to Photoshop 3, some of the program's most popular techniques, such as fading one image into another and creating drop shadows, required building complex channels that were manipulated and calculated onto one another. Once an image was altered, there was no way to revert because the new data had replaced the original data. Thanks to layering,

Figure 10–2
Create some type on a new layer.

most compositing is now interactive and intuitive. And, provided you have the memory, every step can be modified or reversed.

CREATE A DROP SHADOW WITH LAYERS

Type is used in this example, but the same technique applies to any other shapes, such as buttons for multimedia.

1. Place some text in your image using the Type tool. The type will be highlighted as a Floating Selection on the Layers palette.
2. Convert the Floating Selection to a new layer by dragging it to the New Layer icon at the bottom of the palette (Figure 10–2).
3. Duplicate the layer by dragging it from the Layers palette to the document window or to the New Layer icon at the bottom of the palette. This will create a copy of the layer directly on top of the original type layer (Figure 10–3).

Figure 10–3
Duplicate the type layer to create the shadow layer.

Figure 10–4
Offset and blur the shadow layer.

 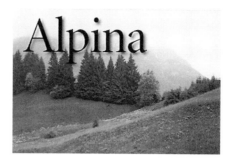

Figure 10–5
Link the type layer with the shadow layer by clicking in the column next to the eye icon and then change their position by dragging with the Move tool.

4. Using the Move tool, drag the shadow layer slightly to offset it from the type layer. Now you have a simple drop shadow which can be modified if desired.

5. For a soft shadow, choose the Gaussian Blur filter from the Filters menu, align the preview window to show a portion of the shadow, and choose a Blur Radius that produces the desired effect. Once the shadow is blurred, you can easily change its color and opacity without damaging the type or the underlying image (Figure 10–4).

6. Link the Type layer with the Shadow layer by clicking in the column next to the eye icon. You can now drag the type and its shadow together with the Move tool (Figure 10–5).

CREATE A DROP SHADOW WITH CHANNELS

Type is used in this example but this technique will work on any selection shape.

1. Place some text in your image using the Type tool. The type will be appear as a Floating Selection.

2. Make the selection transparent by dragging the Opacity slider in the Layers palette to 1%.

3. Choose the Save Selection command under the Select menu, choose New from the Channel pop-up menu and click OK.

4. Apply the Feather command under the Select menu. Try a Feather Radius of 3 to 5 pixels.

5. Fill the feathered selection with a dark color.

6. Choose Load Selection under the Select menu and select the channel to which the type was saved.

7. Press and hold the Option and Command keys while moving the selection slightly to offset it.

8. Fill the selection with a color.

CREATE A LAYER GROUP

Once you have a layer in an image, it can be used as a mask for layers above it. The following example shows how to apply a texture to a sphere created in a layer using a Clipping Group.

1. Create a new layer in a background image and name it Sphere. Leave it as the target layer.

2. To draw a sphere, make a circular selection with the Elliptical Marquee and fill it with the Gradient tool set to a Radial blend from white to black (Figure 10–6).

3. Open a file of a texture to map onto the sphere and with the Move tool, drag it into the sphere image. It will appear as a new layer, named Granite in this example (Figure 10–6).

4. Open the Layer Options dialog box for the granite layer, select the Group with Previous Layer check box and set the mode of the layer to Overlay (Figure 10–7).

The transparent areas of the Sphere layer will mask the texture so that the texture appears within the shape of the sphere only.

Figure 10–6
Draw a sphere on a new layer above the background image (left). Place a texture (center © LetraSet clip art CD) on a new layer above the sphere layer as shown in the Layers palette (right).

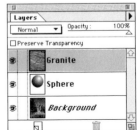

Figure 10-7
Click the Group with
Previous Layer button in
the Layer Options dialog
box. The transparent
areas of the sphere layer
will mask the texture,
causing the texture to
appear on the
sphere only
(© Matt Brown).

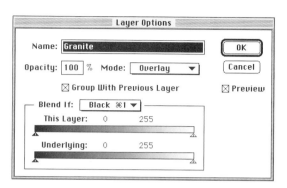

CREATE MOVABLE EMBOSSING WITH LAYERS

Using layers, quickly create an embossing that is also movable. Layers allow
you to interactively change the effects as often desired without making the
data a permanent part of the image.

1. Create a new layer in an image and name it Emboss. Leave it as the
   target layer.
2. Using any of the selection tools or the Type tool, create a selection
   shape and fill it with black or white.
3. Apply the Emboss filter to the layer.
4. Set the blending mode of the embossed layer to Overlay or Soft Light
   (Figure 10-8).

The embossed layer can be dragged around the image with the Move
tool, embossing its shape into the underlying image.

CREATING A FLOATING LENS FLARE WITH A NEUTRAL LAYER

The Lens Flare filter can put a finishing photographic touch to an image.
With layers, you can experiment with the Lens Flare, turning it on or off,
adjusting its strength, and moving it as necessary.

Figure 10-8
For a moveable embossed
shape, apply Emboss to a
solid black or white
shape on a layer set to
Overlay or Soft Light
mode. (© Mark Siprut)

Figure 10–9
New Layer dialog box
with "Fill with Screen-
neutral color (black)"
checked on

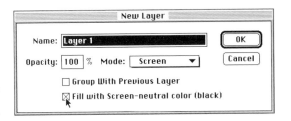

1. Open an image and then create a new layer by clicking on the New Layer icon on the bottom of the Layers palette, or by selecting the New Layer command from the pop-up menu.

2. In the New Layer dialog box, set the mode of the new layer to Screen and check "Fill with Screen-neutral color (black)" and click OK (Figure 10–9).

3. Apply Lens Flare to the new layer.

The effect in the new layer can now be moved, edited and viewed independently of the image. Other filters such as Add Noise and Texture Fill can be applied in the same manner (Figure 10–10).

DODGE AND BURN WITH NEUTRAL LAYER

The Dodge/Burn tools irreversibly change the pixel data in an image, but an obscure technique using layers to store dodging and burning effects will avoid altering the actual pixel data of an image. You can use the layers iteratively, adding additional layers and duplicates of layers to increase the effects of the dodging and burning, or to keep the edits to specific states until you decide on a final version. Instead of using the Dodge/Burn tools, this technique calls for painting with lighter and darker values on a layer set to the Soft Light mode and filled with its Neutral color — 50% black. Blending with the Soft Light mode will lighten areas painted with lighter values and darken areas painted with darker values (Figure 10–11).

Figure 10–10
The Lens Flare filter
applied to a new layer set
to Screen blending mode
and filled with neutral
black (left) creates a
moveable filter effect over
the background image
(right). (© Matt Brown)

Figure 10–11
The original (left), the
layer with lightened and
darkened areas (center),
and the final
version (right).

1. Open an image to lighten and darken in specific areas (dodge and burn).

2. Create a new layer by clicking on the New Layer icon on the bottom of the Layers palette, or by selecting the New Layer command from the pop-up menu.

3. In the New Layer dialog box, set the mode of the new layer to Soft Light and check "Fill with Screen-neutral color (50% gray)" and click OK (Figure 10–12). Since the layer is filled with its neutral color, it will have no affect on the underlying image until you darken or lighten areas. Keep this layer as the target layer.

4. To lighten (dodge) or darken (burn) an area, use the Airbrush or Paintbrush tool set to the appropriate size at a low Opacity setting such as 5% to 15%. You will have more control if you build the values in subtle amounts as opposed to using higher Opacity values. Painting with lighter values will dodge the underlying areas and painting with darker values will burn the underlying areas.

Because the effects of the blending modes on layers are cumulative, you can add more layers and try different versions. The image display will be affected but each layer will be stored independently without affecting the actual data of the image in the background layer.

Figure 10–12
New Layer dialog box
with "Fill with Screen-
neutral color
(50% gray)" checked

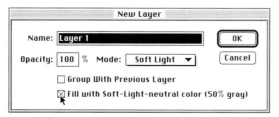

USING LAYERS TO CROSSFADE IMAGES

1. Open two images to crossfade into one another. If the two files are not the same size, resize or crop one to fit the other.

2. Using the Move tool, drag one of the images over the other. This will create a new layer in the destination document.

3. In the Layers palette, click on the upper layer to make it the target layer and then select Add Layer Mask from the pop-up menu. Nothing will visibly change in the image, but if you have thumbnails turned on in the Layers Palette Options dialog box you will see a new thumbnail next to the original thumbnail representing the mask. Note that the border around the new thumbnail is highlighted, indicating that the layer mask is active (Figure 10–13).

4. Select the Gradient tool and set it to a Linear blend. Set the foreground and background colors to black and white. Draw a gradient across the image. Because the Layer Mask is active, the blend will be drawn in the channel assigned to the Layer Mask. The mask (blend), having varying degrees of transparency will vary the blending of the two images producing a crossfade effect (Figure 10–14). If the images don't blend exactly the way you envisioned, you can redraw the blend.

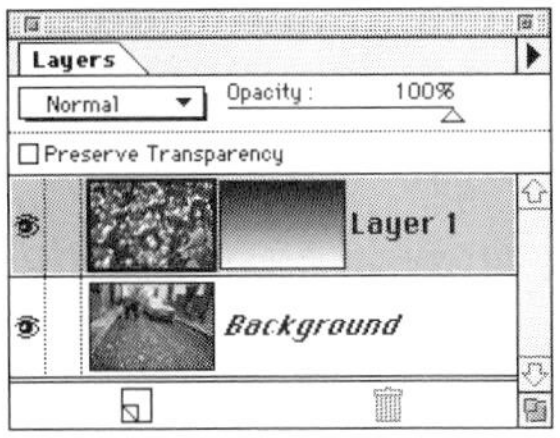

Figure 10–13
Layers palette with a layer mask active

Figure 10–14
Finished crossfade between the two images (© Mark Siprut)

Figure 10–15
Channel Gradient
technique used to blur
and filter portions of the
these images using the
channel on the left
as a mask

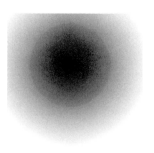  

5. Once the image is blended together, you can apply the layer mask to the image by selecting Remove Layer Mask from the pop-up menu on the Layers palette and choosing Apply.

APPLY A FILTER THROUGH A CHANNEL WITH A GRADIENT MASK

Selectively apply a filter to an image by applying a gradient to a channel and then loading it as a selection.

1. Open an image and create a new channel in the Channels palette.
2. Click on the new channel to make it active and apply a radial blend with the Gradient tool.
3. Click on the composite channel to make it active and then choose Load Selection under the Select menu. Load the channel with blend.
4. Apply any filter or image processing command (Figure 10–15).

Calculate Commands

The calculation commands provide a mathematical method of moving, duplicating and combining layers and channels. Most calculation effects, with the aid of the Opacity and Blend modes, can be achieved by copy and pasting, stacking and combining layers, and saving and combining selections and channels, all of which use memory and processing time. Calculations, although more abstract, allow you to composite and move images at warp speed (bypassing the clipboard). And now with Photoshop 3 you can even preview most effects prior to actually applying the command.

The calculation commands compare corresponding pixels of channels and layers (the *source*) and, depending on the function, place the results into a destination document (the *target*). The comparison of pixel values can be from channels and layers in the same document or from any other open document, as long as the dimensions in pixels match exactly.

CAUTION: The calculation commands function only if all the source and target document's dimensions in pixels are identical. If you try to combine two files that are off by even a single pixel you will not see the files in the pop-up menus.

The three calculation functions in Photoshop are the Duplicate, Apply Image, and Calculations commands.

- **Duplicate** makes a copy of the current document, layer or channel and places it in a destination document.
- **Apply Image** combines layers and channels from a source document with the current active document, placing the results in the current active layer and channel (target).
- **Calculations** combines pixel values of two source channels from any open document of identical dimensions and places the results in a target channel.

In addition to combining pixel values by comparing their brightness values, the Apply Image and Calculations commands also have an option to include a document's channel as a mask.

The Apply Image command results in either a composite channel, such as an RGB Color image, or a single channel. The Calculations command always results in a single channel.

You can use the Apply Image and Calculations commands on both color and black and white images, but they are not accessible to images in the Indexed Color mode (in this case convert to RGB Color mode) or the Bitmap mode (convert to Grayscale mode). The Duplicate command under the Image menu is available in all modes.

The Apply Image and Calculations commands have controls for Opacity and Blend Modes. Both function as in the Layers palette and Layer Options dialog box.

Duplicate

Make an exact duplicate of a document, layer or channel with one of the Duplicate commands. To duplicate an entire document, choose Duplicate under the Image menu. To duplicate a layer, choose Duplicate from the pop-up menu in the Layers palette. To duplicate a channel, choose Duplicate from the pop-up menu in the Channels palette.

TIP: Keep your current working document from getting too large by creating a separate multichannel and/or multilayer document in which to store image elements. To retrieve channels or layers use the Apply Image or Calculations

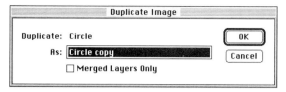

Figure 10–16
The Duplicate Image
dialog box

commands. The Load selection command under the Select menu can convert a channel from any open document into a selection as long as the pixel dimensions of the source document match the current active document exactly.

DUPLICATE THE DOCUMENT

Choose Duplicate under the Image menu to duplicate the entire active document. The Duplicate Image dialog box (Figure 10–16) opens, allowing you to name the resulting document and choose to merge all visible layers. If you leave the Merged Layers Only button unchecked, all layers in the document will be included in the resulting file. If you check Merged Layers Only, all visible layers will be merged into one layer in the resulting file. In either case, all of the channels will stay intact.

DUPLICATE LAYER

Choose Duplicate from the pop-up menu in the Layers palette to duplicate the current target layer. The Duplicate Layer dialog box opens (Figure 10–17) allowing you to name the resulting layer and specify a destination. The destination can be the same document or any other open document or new document of exactly the same pixel dimensions.

DUPLICATE CHANNEL

Choose Duplicate from the pop-up menu in the Channels palette to duplicate the selected channel. The Duplicate Channel dialog box opens (Figure 10–18) allowing you to name the resulting channel, invert it, and specify a

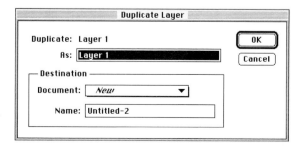

Figure 10–17
The Duplicate Layer
dialog box

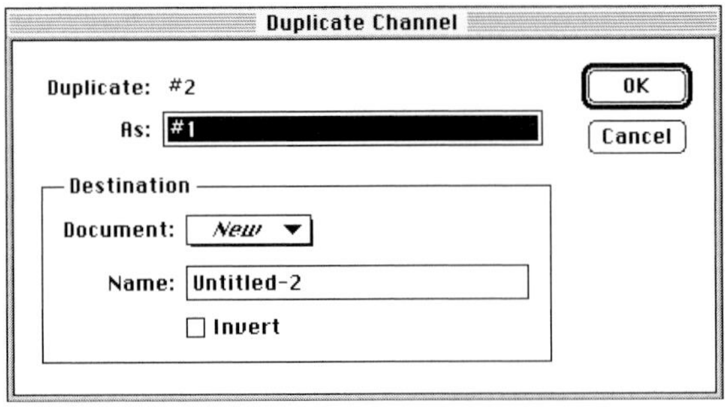

Figure 10–18
The Duplicate Channel
dialog box

destination. The destination can be the same document or any other open document or a new document of exactly the same pixel dimensions.

Apply Image

The Apply Image command combines pixel values from a source to the target layer in the current active document. The Apply Image command always uses the current active document as the result (target). The source layer and channel can be from the same document or any other open document (as long as the pixel dimensions match the target exactly).

The Apply Image command can be applied to the composite channel (for example the RGB composite channel) or any other single channel. If more than one channel is active, the Apply Image command becomes unavailable.

USING THE APPLY IMAGE COMMAND

1. Open both a source document and target document. A single document may be used if it has multiple layers or channels. Make the target document, including its target layer and channel active.

2. Choose Apply Image under the Image menu to open the Apply Image dialog box (Figure 10–19). Notice that the Target shows the current target layer and channel that will be affected by the command.

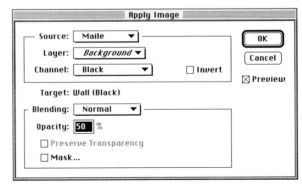

Figure 10–19
The Apply Image
dialog box

Source

Target

Figure 10–20
The source image (top left) was applied to the target image (top right) with the Apply Image command set to Normal at 50% Opacity. The lower right image resulted by inverting the source.
(© Mark Siprut)

Normal, 50% Opacity

Normal, 50% Opacity, Source inverted

3. In the Source pop-up menu, choose an open document; in the Layer pop-up menu, choose a source layer; and the Channel pop-up menu, choose a source channel. To instantly convert the source into a negative, click the Invert button (Figure 10–20).

4. Choose a Blending mode from the pop-up menu and specify an Opacity. The source layer and channel pixel values will blend with the target pixel values based on the selected Blending mode (see the following section on Calculation Blending Modes) and Opacity percentage (Figure 10–20).

5. The effect can be masked by clicking the Preserve Transparency and/or Mask buttons. Click the Preserve Transparency button to apply the operation only to the opaque areas in the target layer. Click the Mask option to expand the dialog box (Figure 10–21), allowing you to choose a document, layer and channel from pop-up menus to mask the effect of the command. For example, in Figure 10–22, the source image in Figure 10–20 was applied to the same target with the Apply Image command through the mask (a saved channel in the target document) shown in Figure 10–23 (right). The resulting image on the left was set with the Blending to Multiply at 100% Opacity and the resulting image on the right was set to Subtract at 100% Opacity, Scale 1.5 and Offset 127.

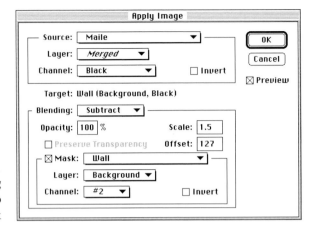

Figure 10–21
The Apply Image dialog
box expanded to
include a mask

Figure 10–22
The source image in
Figure 10–20 was applied
to the same target with
the Apply Image
command through the
mask shown in Figure
10–23 (right).

Multiply, 100% Opacity　　　　*Subtract, 100% Opacity, Scale 1.5, Offset 127*

COMBINING MASKS WITH APPLY IMAGE

The Apply Image command provides a quick method of combining masks
saved as channels from the same document or any other open document of
the same size to the current active document. The following example
demonstrates a basic mask combination. Discover more by experimenting.
For more masking combination ideas, see the upcoming section on
Combining Masks with Calculations (Figures 10–24 and 10–32)

1. Open two documents of identical dimensions. Make a selection in
   each document and save each as a new channel (Figure 10–23).

2. Choose one of the two documents as the target, make it active and
   then make the channel with the mask active. The result of the calculation will appear in the selected active channel.

3. Choose the Apply Image command under the Image menu and select
   the desired source document from the Source pop-up menu. Choose
   the channel with mask in the Channel pop-up menu.

Figure 10–23
The image on the left, Channel #2, was used as the source and Channel #2 from another image (right) was used as the Target in the mask combination examples in the following figure.

Source   *Target*

Normal 50% Opacity   *Multiply, 100% Opacity*

Figure 10–24
These examples demonstrate masking combination possibilities with the Apply Image command using the source and target images in Figure 10–23.

Multiply, 50% Opacity, Source inverted   *Difference, 100% Opacity*

4. Experiment with Blending modes, Opacity settings and Invert options. Click the Preview button to interactively preview your experiments. The resulting channel can then be loaded as a selection in the main image to apply any effects (Figure 10–24).

Calculations Command

The Calculations command combines pixel values from two source channels and places the results in a target channel. The source channels can be in the same document or in any other open document of the same dimensions. The target channel can be in the same document as either of the

Figure 10–25
The source images for the following examples: Source 1 on the left and Source 2 on the right

Source 1   *Source 2*

source channels, in any other open document of the same dimensions, or in a new document. The result of the Calculations command is always a single channel, although the composite channel (listed as Gray) can be used in either Source 1 or Source 2.

USING THE CALCULATIONS COMMAND

1. Open two source documents or channels (Figure 10–25) and the target document. A single document may be used as a source if it has multiple channels. The same document or any other document may be used for the target channel. If you do not have a target document in mind, the Calculations command can create a new document as part of the operation.

2. Choose Calculations under the Image menu to open the Calculations dialog box (Figure 10–26)

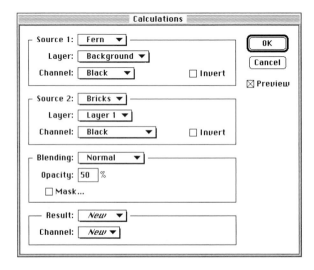

Figure 10–26
The Calculations dialog box

Figure 10–27
The Calculations
command set to Normal
at 50% Opacity on the
left and Multiply at
100% Opacity with
Source 1 inverted
on the right

Normal, 50% Opacity   *Multiply, 100% Opacity, Source 1 inverted*

3. In the Source 1 pop-up menu, choose an open document; in the Layer pop-up menu, choose a source layer; and the Channel pop-up menu, choose a source channel. To instantly convert the source into a negative, click the Invert button (Figure 10–27, right, and Figure 10–30).

4. Repeat the above steps to specify the channel for Source 2.

5. Choose a Blending mode from the pop-up menu and specify an Opacity. The two source channel pixels values will blend with each other based on the Blending modes (see the following section on Calculation Blending Modes) and Opacity percentage (Figure 10–27).

6. Clicking the Mask option expands the dialog box (Figure 10–28), allowing you to choose a document, layer, and channel from pop-up menus to mask the effect of the command (Figure 10–29).

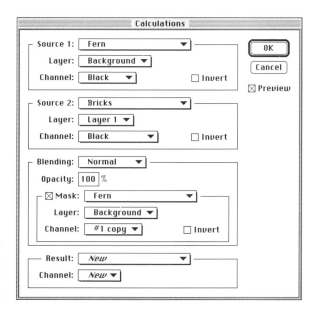

Figure 10–28
The Calculations dialog
box expanded to
include a mask

Figure 10–29
The channel on the left was used as a mask in the calculation that produced the resulting image on the right. The Blending mode was set to Normal at 100% Opacity.

Mask

Normal, 100% Opacity

Figure 10–30
The channel shown in Figure 10–29 was used as a mask in these calculations. Source 1 was also inverted to produce the left image, and Source 2 was inverted to produce the right image.

Source 1 inverted

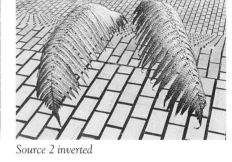

Source 2 inverted

7. Choose a target document from the Result pop-up menu and a target channel from the Channel pop-up menu. Note that you have the option to create both a new document and a channel from the operation. You can also create an active selection in the target document by choosing Selection from the Channel pop-up menu.

8. Experiment with various options with the Preview button clicked to learn how images and masks can be combined (Figure 10–30).

COMBINING MASKS WITH CALCULATIONS

The Calculations command provides a quick method of combining masks saved as channels from the same document or any other open document of the same size. The following examples demonstrate some common basic mask combinations (Figure 10–32).

NOTE: The following examples demonstrating various mask combinations can also be achieved with the Apply Image command.

1. Create two new source documents of identical dimensions with black backgrounds.

Figure 10–31
Source 1 on the left and
Source 2 on the right
were used for the
calculations shown in
the following figure.

Source 1   *Source 2*

2. In the first document, draw a rectangle with the Marquee tool. Fill it with white. This will be Source 1 in the calculations (Figure 10–31).

3. In the second document draw a circle with the Marquee tool and fill it with white. This will be Source 2 in the calculations. Make sure that the area of the circle will overlap the area of the rectangle in Source 1 (Figure 10–31).

4. Open the Calculations command under the Image menu and choose the rectangle image as Source 1 and the circle image as Source 2 from the pop-up menus.

5. Experiment with Blending modes, Opacity settings and Invert options. Click the Preview button to interactively preview your experiments. Choose New from the Result pop-up menu to create a new document with each trial (Figure 10–32).

Calculation Blending Modes

The calculation Blending modes available in both the Apply Image and Calculations commands function identically to the Paint, Fill and Layer Options modes. Options not found elsewhere in Photoshop are the Add and Subtract modes. Since the calculations affect only grayscale blending, modes designed for color blending are not found in the Calculation Blending modes. The options below are available in both the Apply Image and Calculations commands (Figures 10–33 and 10–34).

NORMAL

Normal applies the source pixel values to the target. At 100% Opacity, the result will be identical to the source. The effect of the Normal mode is more apparent when the Opacity is varied. Try 50% Opacity for an equal mix of two channels.

MULTIPLY

The Multiply mode simulates superimposing two film transparencies over each other and then projecting light through them. The overlapping tones

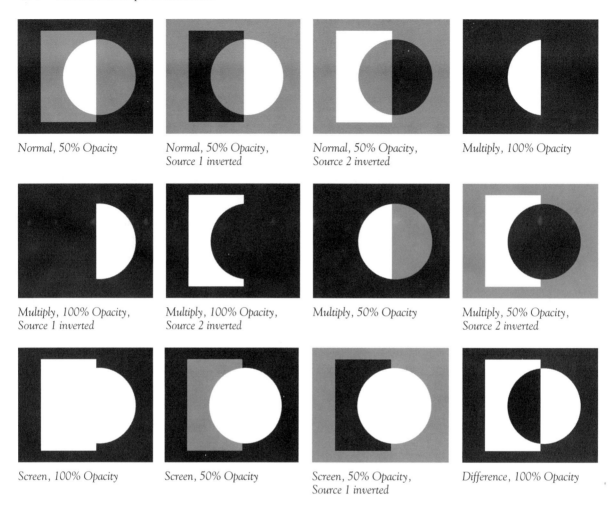

Normal, 50% Opacity

Normal, 50% Opacity,
Source 1 inverted

Normal, 50% Opacity,
Source 2 inverted

Multiply, 100% Opacity

Multiply, 100% Opacity,
Source 1 inverted

Multiply, 100% Opacity,
Source 2 inverted

Multiply, 50% Opacity

Multiply, 50% Opacity,
Source 2 inverted

Screen, 100% Opacity

Screen, 50% Opacity

Screen, 50% Opacity,
Source 1 inverted

Difference, 100% Opacity

Figure 10–32   These examples demonstrate masking combination possibilities with the
Calculations command using the source images in Figure 10–31.

create even darker areas, common light areas are light, overlapping dark
and light areas are medium dark, and overlapping dark areas are the darkest. The result of Multiply is always darker than either of the source images.
Mathematically, corresponding pixel values of the two channels are multiplied and then divided by 255.

SCREEN

The Screen mode is the opposite of the Multiply mode. Overlapping values
are lightened rather than darkened. The result of Screen is always lighter
than either of the source images. Screen is like projecting two transparencies

Figure 10–33
The source images used for the calculations shown in Figure 10–34 (© PhotoSphere)

Source 1

Source 2

Normal, 50% Opacity

Multiply

Screen

Overlay

Soft Light

Hard Light

Darker

Lighter

Add, Scale1.5, Offset 127

Subtract, Scale 1.5, Offset 127

Subtract, Scale 1, Offset 255

Difference

Figure 10–34   The Blending modes

onto a wall or like a photographic print made from a negative that is double exposed. Mathematically, the inverse of corresponding pixel values of the two channels are multiplied.

OVERLAY

The Overlay mode is a combination of the Multiply and Screen modes. Light areas get lighter and dark areas get darker, and highlights and shadows are retained.

SOFT LIGHT

Soft Light functions like the Overlay mode, but with a little less contrast. Light areas get slightly lighter and darker areas get slightly darker.

HARD LIGHT

Hard Light functions like the Overlay and Soft Light mode but is stronger. Light areas become much lighter and darker areas become much darker.

DARKER

The Darker mode compares the corresponding pixel values in the two channels and places the darker of the two in the target channel.

LIGHTER

The Lighten mode compares the corresponding pixel values in the two channels and places the lighter of the two in the target channel.

ADD

The Add mode adds corresponding pixel values in two channels resulting in lighter values where shapes overlap. The Add mode has two addition options, Scale and Offset, to precisely control the calculation based on the existing tonal range and the desired effect. The sum of the corresponding pixel values in the two channels is divided by the Scale value and then added to the Offset value. Scale has a range from 1.000 to 2.000. Higher numbers darken the image. Offset has values from -255 to 255. Negative numbers darken the image and positive numbers lighten the image.

SUBTRACT

The Subtract mode subtracts corresponding pixel values in two channels resulting in darker values where shapes overlap. Similar to the Add mode, the Subtract mode has two addition options, Scale and Offset, to precisely connote the calculation based on the existing tonal range and the desired effect. The difference of the corresponding pixel values in the two channels is divided by the Scale value and then added to the Offset value. Scale has a range from 1.000 to 2.000. Higher numbers darken the image. Offset has values from -255 to 255. Negative numbers darken the image and positive numbers lighten the image.

DIFFERENCE

The Difference mode subtracts the values in one channel from the values in the other channel and displays the resulting absolute value (absolute value is always a positive number). For example, if two corresponding pixels are both black the result is black (0 – 0 = 0). If two corresponding pixels are both white, the result is also black (255 - 255 = 0). If two corresponding pixels are dark gray and white, the result would be light gray (64 – 255 = 191).

You can use the Difference mode to discern tonal differences between two similar images (any differences will be lighter than black).

Kai's Chops

Kai Krause, Photoshop wizard and developer of Kai's Power Tools, offers a series of techniques for using the Calculations command, which he refers to as "Chops."

ALL'S WELL THAT BLENDS WELL WITH NORMAL

The Normal Blending mode in the Apply Image or Calculations commands will add together the brightness values of each pixel in two images (similar to Add) and allow you to shift the relative dominance of either one, by entering a percentage. At 50% they are usually equally strong. Use the Calculations command with the Normal Blending mode at 50% Opacity for all of the following calculations. In each case, set the Result document and Channel to New.

1. Open a new small Grayscale document and type a large "G" filled with black. Duplicate and invert the original image to produce the exact opposite in the second document (Figure 10–35).

2. Choose the Calculations command and use the Normal Blending mode at 50% Opacity to blend the original G (Source 1) with the duplicated and inverted version (Source 2). Combining each corresponding pixel pair results in the average of the two, which in this case is an even shade of gray (Figure 10–35). Vary the percentage

Figure 10–35
Duplicating and inverting the original G (left) produces the G in the center. Blending the two with Normal at 50% Opacity yields gray (right).

for the negative or positive versions to achieve varying degrees of contrast between the G and the background.

3. The original G (Source 1) blended with solid gray (Source 2) yields a toned version of the original (Figure 10–36).

4. The inverted G blended with gray produces a toned version of the inverted G (Figure 10–37).

5. Duplicate the original G to retain the document image size and then fill it with a black to white gradient. Blend the original G (Source 1) with the gradient (Source 2) to produce a version toned by the gradient (Figure 10–38).

6. Using the Offset filter or Move tool, offset one of the original source images by a few pixels both horizontally and vertically. Combine the two source images again as in step 1. If the two source images are

Figure 10–36
Blending the original G (left) with the gray in the center yields a toned version of the original (right).

Figure 10–37
Blending the inverted G (left) with the gray in the center yields a toned version of the inverted G (right).

Figure 10–38
Blending the original G (left) with the gradient in the center yields a version toned by the gradient (right).

exact opposites, they cancel each other, producing 50% gray, but if they are not exactly registered by slightly offsetting one from another, the result will appear embossed (Figure 10–39).

7. Apply the Gaussian Blur filter (set to 4) to the original inverted G and offset the resulting blurred shape by –4 pixels horizontally and –3 pixels vertically (left and up). Use the original G as Source 1 and the inverted blurred version as Source 2. The result has a light corona effect and a shadowed curve on the right (Figure 10–40).

8. Experiment by varying the offset and blur amounts. Any of the resulting files can also be used for further blends (Figure 10–41).

Figure 10–39
Blending the original G (left) with the inverted offset version in the center produces a relief effect (right).

Figure 10–40
Blending the original G (left) with the inverted, blurred, offset version in the center produces a soft relief effect (right).

Figure 10–41
Continue to blend the various resulting images for more possibilities.

Using Photoshop with Other Programs

You will probably need to use other programs along with Photoshop to achieve types of imagery, effects, or processes not available or inefficient in Photoshop. You can use Photoshop as an intermediate step to transfer an image from one program to another. Important issues when working in other programs include saving in the correct file format, retaining the intended color depth and palette, and maintaining the correct size and resolution. When using other applications with Photoshop, make sure they can open and save in a compatible file format. For information on file formats refer to Appendix A, "File Formats." For a description of how Photoshop interacts with animation and multimedia programs, see Chapter 12, "Multimedia."

Output Programs

You can combine Photoshop images with other images and text in a design or layout for output, or make prints larger than the paper size of your printer. Page layout programs such as PageMaker or QuarkXPress allow you to combine images and text and output at high resolutions. Programs such as PosterWorks and most page layout programs allow you to tile output on multiple pages to make larger prints. You will usually need to save a Photoshop file in a TIFF or EPS file format for the output program to recognize it. For more information on using Photoshop with programs for output, refer to Chapter 11, "Output."

Vector Illustration Programs

Photoshop, a raster program, does not have the resolution independent flexibility and object oriented precision provided by vector graphics programs such as Adobe Illustrator, Macromedia FreeHand and CorelDRAW! You might find it necessary to work back and forth between these programs and Photoshop. Photoshop can interact easily with Illustrator, but other vector program must be saved in the Illustrator EPS format in order to be opened in Photoshop. Save Photoshop files in the correct format for the intended program. For example, files saved in the TIFF format can be place in FreeHand but not in Illustrator. Files saved in the PICT or MacPaint format are appropriate for use as templates in Illustrator. Paths can be copied and pasted back and forth between Illustrator and Photoshop.

Many artists use vector programs prior to finishing their illustrations in Photoshop. For example, in "New York Deli" (Figure 5–94) Bert Monroy drew most of the guidelines for the windows and doorways and created the type for the signs in Adobe Illustrator (Figure 10–42). Sharon Steuer began the portrait of the eagle in "Ruffled in the Grass" (Figure 5–98) in Macromedia Freehand, softened the strokes in Fractal Design Painter, and finished it up in Photoshop (Figure 10–43).

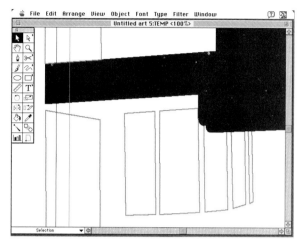 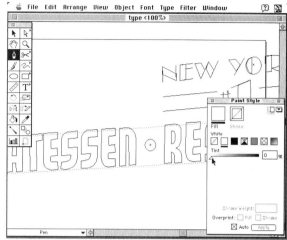

Figure 10–42   Monroy drew the guidelines for the doors, windows and type for the signs in Adobe Illustrator for the illustration "New York Deli" (Figure 5-94).

Three Dimensional Programs

You can draw three dimensional forms in Photoshop, but the effects are limited and the work laborious. Three dimensional programs such as Ray Dream Designer, Strata Vision, StrataStudio Pro, MacroModel, Infini-D, Caligari TrueSpace, Electric Image, Adobe Dimensions, Pixar Tapestry, and Ray Dream addDepth can create and render believable 3-D forms with lighting, shadows, textures and environments from a variety of viewpoints.

After creating shapes in a 3-D program the images can usually be saved in a compatible file format to facilitate opening them in Photoshop. Wendy Grossman created the three dimensional elements in "Foxwood" for *Connecticut Magazine* in Adobe Dimensions and Ray Dream Designer and

Figure 10–43
Sharon Steuer began the portrait of the eagle in "Ruffled in the Grass" (Figure 5-98) in Macromedia FreeHand (left), softening the image in Fractal Design Painter before finishing the illustration in Photoshop.

Figure 10–44   The three dimensional elements in "Foxwood" were created in Adobe Dimensions, and Ray Dream Designer (left) and then placed into the Photoshop to finish the illustration (right). (© Wendy Grossman)

then combined them with other elements in Photoshop to complete the illustration (10–44).

Photoshop images can be projected onto shapes as texture maps in most 3-D programs, as well as projected onto the backgrounds as environment maps (Figure 10–45). Greg Notzelman creates room environments in Macromedia MacroModel and renders then in Electric Image using patterns and surface textures created in Photoshop. After rendering the image, final tonal adjustment are made in Photoshop (Figure 10–46).

Raster Programs

Although Photoshop is a raster program, other raster programs provide tools and functions not available in Photoshop. For example, you can use Jagg II to smooth out the Jaggies in an image, the layering features in Specular Collage for quick compositing, special paper effects in Fractal Design Painter, or the blazing speed of HSC Live Picture to manipulate large files.

Figure 10–45
A Photo CD image of the building was saved as a PICT file, imported into StrataStudio Pro as a texture map, and projected on the sphere. The same image was also projected on the background as an environment map. (© Mark Siprut)

Figure 10–46
This room environment was created in Macromedia MacroModel and rendered in Electric Image. The brick and floor patterns were created in Photoshop and tiled as texture maps. Final tonal adjustments were made in Photoshop. (© Micro Mentor and Greg Notzelman)

Specular Collage, a great program for layering and compositing, exports files in the Photoshop 3 format with all the layer data intact. You can therefore do initial quick compositing in Collage at low resolution and then export to Photoshop for final touch-ups (Figure 10–47).

For loose painterly effects use Fractal Design Painter. Cher Threinen-Pendarvis demonstrates the program's painterly look in "Laughter," which is part of a series of portraits focusing on human emotion (Figure 10–48).

Threinen-Pendarvis scanned a damaged photographic portrait into Photoshop, adjusted the contrast with the Levels command. Opening the image in Painter, she chose clone, filling the background with black and

Figure 10–47
The layers in Collage (left) all transfer to Photoshop (right) when saved from Collage in the Photoshop 3 format.

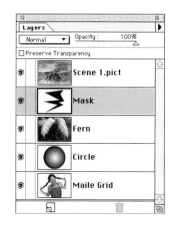

Figure 10–48
To create "Laughter," Fractal Design Painter was used to paint over and clone a scanned photograph prior to final tonal adjustments in Photoshop. (© Cher Threinen-Pendarvis)

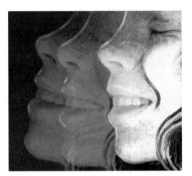

turning on the tracing paper option. (This option is similar to using a light table, allowing you to see your original.) Using the charcoal brush and a rough paper texture she painted with white over the photograph. She toggled between the cover and cloning methods in the Brush palette to alternately paint and clone with her strokes. The image was masked, copied, floated and rotated slightly to suggest movement at 50% and 30% opacity. The image was then opened again in Photoshop for final tonal adjustments.

NOTE: Painter opens RGB and grayscale images only. It cannot open CMYK, rasterized EPS, or JPEG files. Painter exports RGB rif, RGB tiff, PICT, Photoshop 2.0 and 2.5, MBP, PCX and Targa files. It exports EPS/DCS, five part files for color separations (CMYK).

Anna Stump used Fractal Design Painter with a Wacom tablet to draw from a live model. After doing the sketch, she transferred it to Photoshop and then applied the Gallery Effects Watercolor Filter (Figure 10–49).

Live Picture from HSC software facilitates working with large 24-bit color images. The program uses a mathematical representation of the pixels, which allows editing and effects in real time. Because of its speed,

Figure 10–49
A live model sketched on a Wacom tablet using Fractal Design Painter and Photoshop (© Anna Stump)

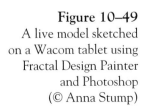

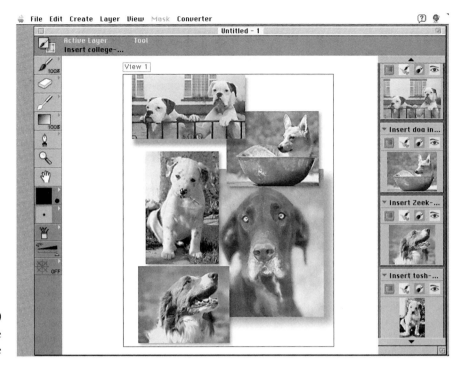

Figure 10–50
The Live
Picture interface

artists that need to work with large files (such as 100Mb to 300 Mb) will benefit by doing initial compositing in Live Picture and finishing work in Photoshop (Figure 10–50).

Unlike Photoshop, Live Picture does not work with actual pixel based files. Neither does it use proxies or low resolution files like Collage. Instead, large bitmapped files are converted to a proprietary format called IVUE; Live Picture applies all manipulations to a FITS file, a mathematical representation of the work.

Live Picture is able to work with virtually any sized file with no speed limitations; a 10 Mb file and a 100 Mb file can be manipulated at virtually identical speeds. However, because Live Picture never actually works with individual pixels, you must use Photoshop for work that requires editing at the pixel level. You can do distortions, sharpening, blurring and some special effects in Live Picture using brushes, as well as color correction and color separations.

Pattern and Image Generation Programs

Pattern and image generation programs automatically create imagery that can then be used in Photoshop compositions, as backgrounds, details, surfaces, etc. KPT Bryce mathematically renders three dimensional landscapes, producing fantastic terrain and environments (Figure 10–51). Specular TextureScape (Figure 10–52) and Adobe TextureMaker (Figure 10–53) create textures, such as marble, wood, fabric bricks and water, by tiling modular components.

Figure 10–51
Images generated in KPT
Bryce can then
be used in
Photoshop compositions.

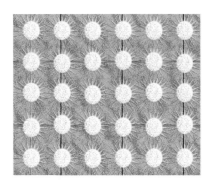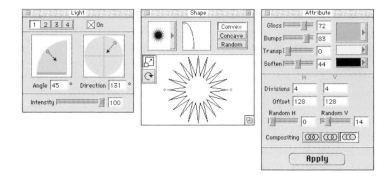

Figure 10–52   The Specular TextureScape interface

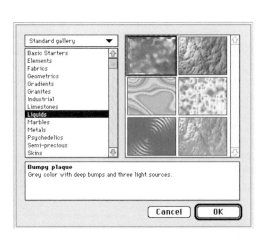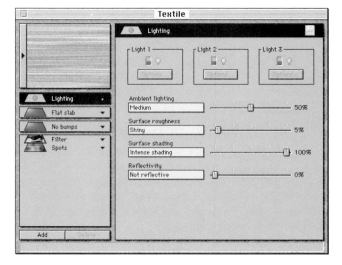

Figure 10–53   The Adobe TextureMaker interface

Summary

- Plan out your idea before creating many layers, channels and extra files. Try sketching some possibilities on paper or working in low resolution and then recreate your rough at high resolution. Combining images and effects can be exciting, but without some organization it's easy to create a multimegabyte mess.

- Layers allow you to save your work as independent elements that can be changed and edited as often desired.

- Many complex techniques that would have required advanced channel calculations in previous versions of Photoshop can now be accomplished with layers. Layers allow you to see what you are doing as you do it.

- The Preserve Transparency option on the Layers palette will allow you to paint or edit without effecting the transparent portion of the layer. Any manipulation, painting or filter will only affect the opaque areas in the target layer.

- Each layer can have its transparency loaded as a selection. This can then be used to mask other layers or as a component in calculation commands.

- When using Calculations or Apply Image, be sure that all source and target images are exactly the same size in pixels.

- Use Calculate when you are working with channels. Use Apply Image when you want to affect the composite channel in color images.

- When using other applications with Photoshop, make sure they can open and save in a compatible file format.

Now that you have created a masterpiece, let's try to print it. For help see the next chapter.

C H A P T E R **11**

Output

You have created a masterpiece in Photoshop. The final step is to get the image out of the computer and onto paper or other media. Of course, you do not have to wait until your project is completed to output it. Several output methods can be employed as a project progresses, such as creating comprehensives or proofs.

You have the following output options:

- Prepare your image for a transparency film recorder.
- Prepare your image for presentation graphics or multimedia (see Chapter 12, "Multimedia").
- Save your image and edit it further in another bitmapped image editing program.
- Print black-and-white halftone prints on a PostScript laser printer or on a high-resolution imagesetter.
- Print on a non-PostScript printer with a dithering pattern.
- Print color prints directly to an RGB, CMY, or CMYK PostScript digital printer.
- Print color prints on a non-PostScript continuous-tone printer.
- Separate color images into four process color separations for offset printing.
- Import your Photoshop image into a page layout or illustration program, combine it with text and vector graphics, and output either a color digital print or color-separated film as a composite finished document.

This chapter discusses how to set up your system for whatever output you choose. You will be introduced to different kinds of printers and output devices, and the imaging methods they use. The chapter will discuss how to output from within Photoshop and how to save Photoshop documents to use or print from other applications. It also covers the complexities of process and spot-color separations, how to create them in Photoshop, and how to print or save them from Photoshop.

Calibration

A key issue that arises in the preparation of images for output is calibration. The original artwork, the scanned artwork viewed on a computer screen, and a proof print will probably end up looking somewhat different in color or tone at each stage.

The complex issues of calibration in the production process become most important when using Photoshop to separate a color image into process colors (converting to CMYK Color mode). But calibration also affects the output of grayscale images, printing to film recorders, and printing to digital printers as well (Figure 11–1).

If you haven't calibrated your system yet, go back to the Calibration section in Chapter 3, "Configuring Photoshop," and follow the described procedures. Otherwise, you can never trust that what you see on your computer screen will have a consistent relationship to what will be printed. Reviewed in brief are the steps to follow:

1. Choose Monitor Setup in the Preferences submenu under the File menu and enter values for the gamma and white point of your monitor.

Figure 11–1
To ensure that output from you printer resembles what you see on the monitor, you should calibrate your system. Shown here is the SuperMatch Proof Positive printer with the PressView 21T monitor.
(© Radius)

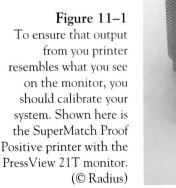

2. Choose Printing Inks Setup in the Preferences submenu under the File menu and select a target printer or press setup.

3. Choose an image that has a wide range of colors or tones like the *Olé No Moiré* image that comes with Photoshop. Print the image to your digital printer or have your service bureau make color separations, printing them to a laminated proof.

4. Compare your monitor display to the laminated proof and adjust the monitor to look like the proof.

Printers and Other Output Devices

Although working in Photoshop is fun, having a print in your hands completes the cycle (except for those pesky multimedia artists who don't believe in prints). Presented below are a number of options available for producing hard copy.

Dot Matrix

Who can forget about the good, old ImageWriter? The dot-matrix printer, which uses small pins striking against a ribbon, is still a viable way to output images created in Photoshop. In fact, it may be just the thing to add that special, retro-computer flair to your prints. While most dot-matrix printers produce black-and-white output, single-color and even four-color ribbons are available. Adobe even provides an ImageWriter color export module for the Macintosh version of Photoshop to print to an Apple ImageWriter using a color ribbon. If you're into economy, try using a dot-matrix printer with Photoshop.

Inkjet

The inkjet printer is a couple of steps above the dot-matrix printer used with the color ribbon mentioned above. The quality of inkjet output can rival that of thermal wax printers described below. Inkjet printers use tiny jets to spray color inks onto paper to produce full-color output. The price of a color inkjet printer is near that of a good color dot-matrix printer, making decent color printing a viable option

Laser

With resolutions from 300 to 600 dots per inch (dpi) and even higher, laser printers provide good output for grayscale images. The latest laser printers from Apple and Hewlett-Packard, for example, can print images using a greater number of shades of gray, achieving remarkable quality. If you produce a newsletter or other publication that uses black-and-white photos, consider outputting your halftones to your laser printer. Photoshop has numerous controls for adjusting the quality of halftones, and you may be surprised at what you can get away with.

Printer manufacturers like QMS, Xerox, and Hewlett Packard are beginning to introduce color laser printers as well.

Thermal Wax Color

Thermal wax color printers are an inexpensive way to get a good quality color image output on paper. Using special color-impregnated ribbons to produce slick prints, thermal wax printers are available from many manufacturers at prices that rival regular laser printers. With color becoming more and more popular, the prices for thermal wax printers have fallen sharply.

Thermal wax printers generally require that a special paper be used. This paper is sometimes flimsy and shiny, but recently some companies are touting their printers' ability to use good, laser bond paper. Thermal wax printers produce excellent color transparencies.

Phase-Change Color

Phase-change color printers are a relative newcomer to the color printer field. Using colored wax sticks instead of ink or ribbons, phase-change printers produce excellent quality prints on a variety of plain paper or transparencies up to 11 by 17 inches in size. One drawback to phase-change printers is that they generally don't do a great job on transparencies.

Dye-Sublimation Color

Dye-sublimation printers produce some of the best color output. The quality of the prints produced by these printers rivals those produced in a traditional darkroom. Using expensive ribbons and special paper, dye-sublimation printers are generally employed by those who require the best possible output, at the highest cost per page. Dye-sublimation printer prices have been steadily falling, but if you can't afford one yourself, you can get a dye sublimation color print at a service bureau.

Other High-End Printers

Color copiers that have PostScript interfaces provide a quick way to proof images. Usually too expensive for the average user, color copiers are widely available in service bureaus. Although not highly color accurate unless used in conjunction with a color management system, they can provide an economical way to print multiple copies of a color image.

Very precise high-end inkjet printers are used to make color proofs of advertisements and newspaper pages before they are printed. These printers cost anywhere from $30,000 on up. Digital artists often choose the Iris inkjet printer, in particular, to make color prints of their work. It produces color-accurate output on a variety of different papers, including fine art and handmade papers.

Imagesetters

Imagesetters are specialized machines optimized for high-resolution output of images and text. In an imagesetter a focused laser light imposes a very fine grid of printer dots in black and white onto photographic film or paper.

After being developed in a photographic film processor, the film or paper is used to make printing plates. These plates in turn are mounted on a printing press and used for reproduction onto different kinds of paper. Resolutions of 1200 to 2400 dpi are common for imagesetter output, with even higher frequencies possible.

To produce process color or spot-color separations of Photoshop images, you must output imagesetter separations onto film. If you use Photoshop to output to an imagesetter, become familiar with the requirements of the output device. A service bureau can give you good advice. In particular, be sure the imagesetter is calibrated so it produces the halftone dot values that are being requested by Photoshop (see the "Halftones" section later in this chapter).

Film Recorders

You can prepare artwork in Photoshop for imaging with a film recorder on 35mm or larger film, which can be used for making photographic prints, slide presentations, backlit displays, or scanning back into the computer. There are several advantages to creating a film transparency. Since it is continuous tone, a transparency can be scanned to different sizes and screen frequency requirements. A predictable light source is all that is required for viewing a transparency. Furthermore, the format is well understood and easily handled by graphic arts professionals.

A film recorder consists of a cathode ray tube (CRT) attached to a camera back. The recorder produces a continuous-tone image on slide film or on a negative of a particular size. Better quality film recorders address a larger and higher pixel count with a smaller spot size (the size of the pixel on the CRT). High-end film recorders do not use a CRT. For example, the LVT uses a light valve technology and the Fire 1000 uses a similar light source.

Slide film recorders always image in RGB, so prepare your image in RGB Color mode. If you are beginning with a drum scan, have it stored on disk in RGB (not converted to CMYK as the scanner's color computer would normally do for color separations). Ideally, your image resolution should match the output resolution of the film recorder. Refer to "Resolution and Aspect Ratio for Film Recorders" in Chapter 4, "Input," for more information on preparing files for output to film recorders.

TIP: The software which drives film recorders can vary. Some film recorders have a Photoshop plug-in, so the Photoshop bit-map information can be sent directly to the film recorder. Other software would convert a Photoshop file to PostScript before sending it to the film recorder. Because of these differences consult with your film recorder service bureau to prepare your file to their specifications.

Methods of Output

Among this wide variety of printers and output devices, there are several methods of converting the tones and colors on your monitor into a printed image. Reproduction methods include continuous-tone, halftone dots, and dithered patterns.

Continuous Tone

Any photograph, illustration, or graphic that consists of a wide range of tones or gradation of tones is called *continuous tone*. Our eyes see the world as continuous tone. The photographic process produces images on transparencies and prints which are also continuous tone. More expensive digital printers—most color copiers and dye-sublimation printers and the Iris inkjet printer, in particular—can vary the intensity of spots used to create an image to produce continuous-tone output.

Halftones

Many output devices use a method of reproducing continuous-tone images called *halftoning*. In the nineteenth century, printers discovered that a photograph had to be represented by a pattern of dots to be printed on a printing press. Presses cannot print continuous tones; ink is either there or it isn't.

In this century, photographic techniques were developed for producing the dots, called *halftone dots*. The size of the dots determines the tonal values. For instance, a cluster of large dots that leaves little white space between dots reproduces a dark area. An area composed of tiny dots where the white area is stronger produces a light gray area. Varying the size of halftone dots results in a print with multiple tones (Figure 11–2). Halftone dots are arranged in a fixed grid with a certain number of rows of dots in an inch.

Figure 11–2
A halftone
screen close-up
(© Chris Swetlin)

Laser printers and imagesetters also produce halftones digitally rather than photographically. PostScript printers create the halftone patterns at the time of printing. These printers image with tiny dots—sometimes called spots or printer pixels—produced by a laser. (Thus, their resolution is measured as dots per inch, or dpi.) To produce halftones, printer dots are grouped together into *halftone cells*. By imaging different numbers of printer dots in a halftone cell, postScript printers replicate photographic halftones. For example, to represent a 50% tone, a properly calibrated PostScript imagesetter would create a halftone cell in which half of the printer dots were "turned on," creating a 50% halftone dot on film. The technology of digital screening has developed rapidly in the past few years, and professionally produced digital screening can now exceed the quality of halftones produced photographically.

Whether produced photographically or digitally, halftone screens are measured in lines per inch (lpi), the number of rows of halftone dots in an inch. Halftone screens vary in frequency in order to meet the requirements of various forms of printing. Newspapers, for instance, require a coarse dot screen, usually between 65 and 85 lpi, because newsprint paper is very absorbent and cannot reproduce well with screens that are too fine. Halftone screens used on uncoated stock are between 100 and 133 lpi. The coated or glossy stock used in magazines can hold a small tight dot, usually 133 or 150 lpi, thus attaining much finer detail in reproduction. Certain presses can achieve even higher halftone screens on coated stock (175 to 200 lpi or even higher) for the highest quality of reproduction.

Halftone screens are set at a particular screen angle, relative to the edge of the image or page (Figure 11–3). Black is usually printed at a 45° angle. Rotating the screen makes the halftone dots less obvious to the eye, and increases the illusion of continuous tone. Process color separations print colors from four halftone screens: cyan, magenta, yellow, and black. The

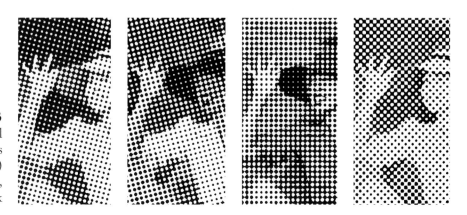

Figure 11–3
The conventional halftone screen angles for (left to right) cyan, magenta, yellow, and black

angles of the screens are critical. If not set correctly, an interference pattern between the screens, called a *moiré*, is produced.

Traditionally the screen angles for process colors are set 30° apart, except for yellow which differs by 15°. Various imagesetters use somewhat different screening methods, frequencies and angles. Because of these differences, let the color service bureau or printer handle these settings at output time or get specific instructions on the required settings.

Halftones also have a dot shape. PostScript halftone dots are usually clustered in the center of the halftone cell. In special halftone dot shapes, the printer dots may be arranged in other patterns (see Figure 11–26). See the "Halftone Screens" section later in this chapter for a discussion on how to specify halftones in Photoshop.

Dithering and Stochastic (FM) Screening

Besides halftoning, there are several other methods to reproduce continuous-tone images. These methods, called dithering, create tonal values using a pattern of printer (or monitor) dots. Create dithered patterns in Photoshop by converting from Grayscale to Bitmap mode and clicking on either the *Pattern Dither* or *Diffusion Dither* options. Pattern Dither has an ordered appearance and Diffusion Dither has a random or disordered pattern (Figure 11–4). The "Bitmap" section in Chapter 8, "Color," describes how to create these halftone patterns in Photoshop. Non-PostScript printers and computer displays often represent tones or colors with dithering patterns.

Another form of dithering called *FM (frequency modulated)* or *stochastic screening*, has been introduced for PostScript imagesetters. In normal digital halftones the size of the halftone dots varies (the number of printer dots in the halftone cell which are "turned on"), but the grid of the halftone dots remains consistent. With FM screening different tones are represented by differing numbers of small microdots; more microdots clustered together

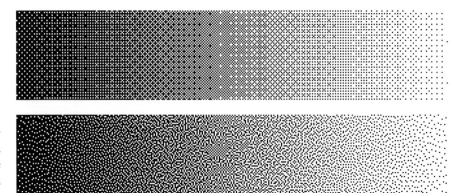

Figure 11–4
The top band shows a pattern dither and the bottom band a diffusion dither.

create a darker tone, fewer create a lighter tone. Because there is no grid as with halftone dots, the dots appear to be distributed randomly.

A benefit of FM screening is the absence of moiré patterns. Since there is no grid of halftone dots, there is no possibility of an interference pattern from misaligned halftone screens. Moirés can also arise in reproduction from the interference between halftone dots and grids which appear in the image as well (like the pattern of a fabric, for example); FM screening eliminates these moiré problems as well. Some printers who are early users of this technology also appreciate the option to run higher ink densities than are possible with halftone dots, which produces more saturated colors.

There are new production issues raised by FM screening, however. The tiny dots produce more dot gain (see the "Dot Gain" section later in this chapter), and many proofing systems cannot reproduce the fine dots. If you plan to use FM screening, work closely with the printer to make sure you prepare your file correctly.

Printing from Photoshop

Photoshop provides a complete set of controls for printing to different output devices, including producing spot and process color separations. Although most printing choices are made in the Page Setup and Print dialog boxes, you can also print to some devices via the Export submenus.

Page Setup Dialog Box

When printing an image from within Photoshop, you will make most of your settings by choosing Page Setup from the File menu. In the Page Setup dialog for both platforms, choose whether to print positives or negatives, labels, or marks which a commercial printer would use in the reproduction process, create a border or bleed, and set the halftone screen and transfer function.

By default, when you print an image all visible layers and channels will be printed. To print individual layers or channels, see the "Spot Color Separation" section later in this chapter. To print a selection of an image, see the "Print Dialog Box" section.

PAGE SETUP/MACINTOSH

Figure 11–5 shows the dialog box on the Macintosh with a PostScript printer selected. The top portion of the dialog is the standard LaserWriter Page Setup. You select paper size, scaling, Orientation, and Printer Effects. The dialog box will look somewhat different with a non-PostScript printer selected.

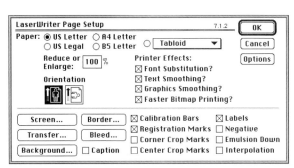

Figure 11–5
The Macintosh Page Setup dialog box

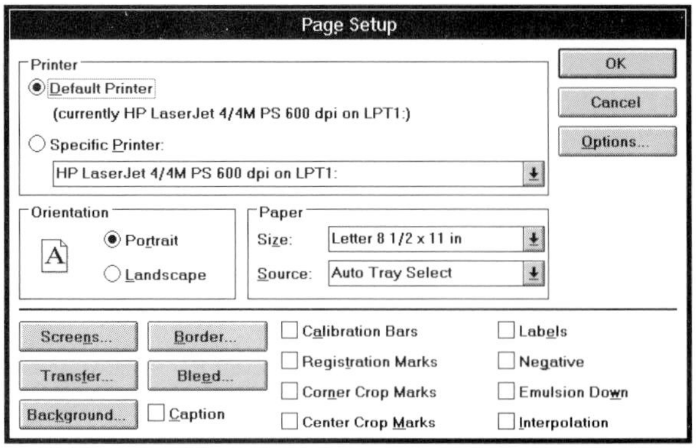

Figure 11–6
The Windows Page Setup dialog box

PAGE SETUP/WINDOWS

The Page Setup dialog box in Windows contains a Printer section which permits you to change your target printer (Figure 11–6). You can set additional options for your target printer via the Options button. Clicking the Options button takes you to the Options dialog box if you are using the Windows PostScript driver or to the Setup dialog box if you are using the Adobe PostScript driver (Figures 11–7 and 11–8). The Adobe PostScript driver offers several significant advantages over the Windows PostScript driver:

1. Printing is faster to PostScript Level 2 devices.
2. Fonts don't have to be listed in your WIN.INI file.

Figure 11–7
The Adobe PostScript driver Setup dialog box

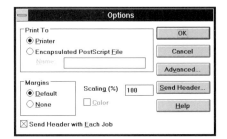

Figure 11–8
The Windows PostScript driver Options dialog box

3. Binary and JPEG encoding is supported for faster printing (encoding is discussed below).

4. You can create .PRN (print to disk) files for Level 2 printers.

WINDOWS TIP: If you own a Hewlett Packard LaserJet 4, 4M, 4ML, 4P, or 4MP call HP (303-353-7650) and they will send you the Adobe PostScript Driver for Windows free. It's the same driver Adobe sells (minus written documentation and support for imagesetters). You can also download this driver from CompuServe. Type go hpspecial at the ! prompt.

HALFTONE SCREENS

As described above, halftone screens that print grayscale or color images to PostScript printers have a screen frequency, an angle, and a dot shape. If you are producing an image for a printing press, these choices should be determined by the requirements of your commercial printer.

To print a grayscale image, enter the screen settings in the Halftone Screen dialog box, accessed by clicking the Screen button in the Page Setup dialog. You will be presented with the Halftone Screen dialog box (Figure 11–9). Make choices for the frequency, angle, and dot shape for a single halftone screen. Photoshop can call out dots which are round, elliptical, or diamond-shaped, or dots in a line, square, or cross pattern. If you can program in the PostScript page description language, you can enter your own code for a halftone screen in the Custom option. There are also buttons to Save and Load halftone screens to use your parameters with different images.

Two checkboxes suit special situations. To use the default screens built into the PostScript printer, check Use Printer's Default Screens. If printing to an imagesetter that has a PostScript Level 2 or Emerald processor, check the Use Accurate Screens option.

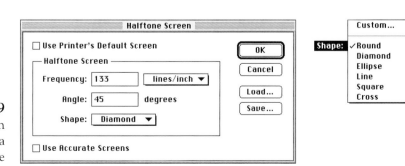

Figure 11–9
The Halftone Screen dialog box for a grayscale image

TIP: If you send your image to a color service bureau or printer for output, have them choose the halftone dot settings based on their experience and assessment of your reproduction needs. They may have imagesetters which use different screening technologies.

You may want to print a composite image to a color printer for an image in Indexed Color, RGB Color, Lab Color, or CMYK Color. The screen frequency choice will affect your output only if your printer uses halftone screens to render an image. The screen frequency choice will be ignored by your printer if it renders images with continuous tones or dithered patters.

To print a color separation for commercial printing from any of the color modes, choose Screen on the Page Setup dialog to open a slightly different dialog box (Figure 11–10). This sets halftone screens for four plates—cyan, magenta, yellow, and black. Again the choices should be dictated by your commercial printer's needs. You may either (1) choose the color of the screen from the Ink pop-up menu and enter the frequency and angle values manually, or (2) click the Auto button and enter the resolution of the printer and the screen frequency at which you wish to print. Photoshop will calculate the values automatically.

The same choices for Use Printer's Default Screen and Use Accurate Screens are also available when printing color separations, as well as options for saving and loading screens settings. There is also a checkbox to choose the same dot shape for each ink.

TRANSFER FUNCTION

Clicking the Transfer button in the Page Setup dialog box takes you to the Transfer Functions dialog box. This function is used occasionally to calibrate imagesetters in order to produce accurate gray values. Most service bureaus and printers, however, usually use third-party imagesetter calibration software

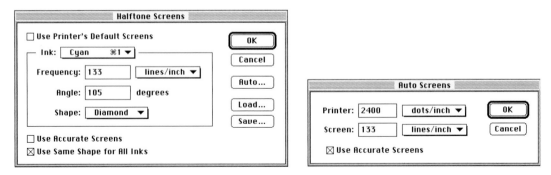

Figure 11–10   The Halftone Screens and Auto Screens dialog boxes for a color image

to accomplish this function. In some limited cases, the Transfer Function dialog box can also be used to compensate for dot gain which occurs in the reproduction process. (Dot gain and the use of the Transfer Function dialog box is discussed in the "Process Color Separations" section of this chapter.)

PRINTERS' MARKS

When printing film separations, Photoshop allows you to include a number of printers' marks around your image by choosing check box options in Page Setup. These marks are useful to the commercial printer for cropping the image, for making sure that the negatives and printing plates are properly in register, and for ensuring that color is printing accurately on press.

- Crop marks indicate where an image should be trimmed. Photoshop allows you to print two kinds of crop marks—corner and centered.
- A calibration bar is an 11-step grayscale bar that represents the transition in density from 0 to 100% in increments of 10%. When printing color separations, a progressive color bar is also printed. These bars can be measured with a densitometer during the color calibration process.
- The Registration Mark option includes targets to line up the four individual plates insuring correct registration on the printing press.

TIP: Preview printers' marks, labels, negative, emulsion, borders, and bleeds by pressing and holding the mouse button on the file size indicator displayed in the bottom left corner of the Photoshop document window. You will get a preview of the relative size of the image on the currently selected page size. All visible settings in Page Setup will also be displayed (see Figure 3–10).

LABELS

Choosing the Labels option in the Page Setup dialog box prints the file name beside the image as well as the channel name when printing separations.

CAPTION

If you have entered information for Caption in the File Info dialog box it will print next to the image. This feature is discussed in "Entering File Information" in Chapter 3, "Configuring Photoshop."

BACKGROUND COLOR

If you click the Background button in Page Setup, you will be presented with the Color Picker dialog box. You can select a background color for your image which will be applied at the time of printing. (The image itself remains unchanged.) Selecting a background color can be useful in preparing images for a film recorder.

BORDER

If you would like a black border printed around an image, click the Border button. You can specify the border width in the units of your choice up to a maximum of 10 points.

BLEED

Crop marks are normally printed to line up with the edges of the image area. If you choose Bleed you may choose a width value with which the crop marks will cut into the image. This bleed area allows the image to extend slightly beyond the trim edge up to a maximum bleed of $1/8$ inch.

NEGATIVE AND EMULSION

Usually, images printed directly to film for offset printing are output as negatives. For special prepress situations, foreign printers, or silkscreen printers, your commercial printer might request positives. When printing directly to paper, a positive is best.

   The emulsion side of the film or paper is sensitive to light and will record the image. When the emulsion is up, any type on the image is readable. Text reads as a mirror image when the emulsion side is down. Emulsion down is often the preferred format when printing to film, but check with your printer to see which emulsion option they prefer (Figure 11–11).

Figure 11–11
From left to right: examples of output printed as a positive emulsion up, negative emulsion up, positive emulsion down and negative emulsion down.

 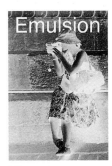  

Positive, emulsion up   *Negative, emulsion up*   *Positive, emulsion down*   *Negative, emulsion down*

INTERPOLATION

When printing to some (but not all) PostScript Level 2 printers, checking Interpolation can smooth a low-resolution image by resampling up at the time of printing. On most other printers Interpolation will have no effect.

Print Dialog Box

Some additional printing options are available from the Print dialog box in Photoshop. Choose Print from the File menu. Figure 11–12 shows the Print dialog when a PostScript printer is selected on the Macintosh.

The Windows Print Dialog box (Figure 11–13) is similar to the Macintosh version, but there are a few differences. It does not contain an Options button or the Print Selected Area option. The Print Quality drop-down list permits you to change the resolution of your print job if your printer supports this feature. The Windows version does not have a Paper Source section in this dialog box; rather this option is located in the Page Setup dialog box. To create a PostScript file click the Print To File check box. If you are using the Windows PostScript driver with either a PostScript Level 1 or 2 printer, remember that this driver does not support Binary or JPEG encoding. Use ASCII encoding for all your print jobs or PRN files.

In either platform, if an image is in Grayscale mode Photoshop prints it to the selected printer. In Indexed Color or RGB modes, you must click a button that determines whether you print in Gray (grayscale), RGB, or CMYK. In Lab mode, click a button to choose between printing in Gray, Lab, or CMYK.

TIP: If you choose to print in CMYK from an image in RGB, Indexed, or Lab Color mode, be sure you have chosen the proper printer in the Printing Inks Setup Preferences submenu. Photoshop converts to CMYK at the time of printing based on preferences settings. See Chapter 8, "Color," for more information on mode conversion.

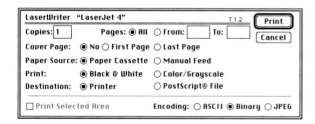

Figure 11–12
The Print dialog box on the Macintosh

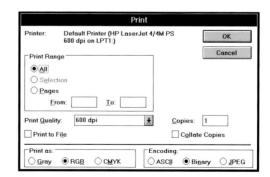

Figure 11–13
The Print dialog box in the Windows version of Photoshop

In CMYK or Duotone Color mode there is a check box for printing color separations. Check Print Separations to print a color-separated image to your imagesetter or printer. Uncheck this option to print a composite print to either a black-and-white or color printer.

ENCODING

Encoding refers to the manner in which image data is sent to the printer. There are three choices for Encoding: *ASCII, Binary,* and *JPEG.* Binary produces a file that is half the size of ASCII and prints faster. In most cases Binary is the best choice on the Macintosh. Old versions of some applications, like PageMaker and FreeHand and some spooling software, cannot use Binary, so ASCII must be used. If you are in Windows, the Adobe PostScript driver supports Binary, but the Windows PostScript driver only supports ASCII encoding.

JPEG compression can be used when sending directly from Photoshop to PostScript Level 2 printers. (JPEG is explained in Compression section of Chapter 3, "Configuring Photoshop".) A JPEG-encoded image is compressed by Photoshop and then is uncompressed as the image prints. Photoshop always uses the high-quality setting for JPEG compression of your print jobs. Don't use this option for PostScript Level 1 printers. In Windows, you can use JPEG encoding with the Adobe driver, but not with the Windows driver.

PRINTING A SELECTED AREA

You may print a selected part of an image in the Macintosh version of Photoshop by selecting the area with the Rectangular marquee tool and then clicking Print Selected Area in the Print dialog box. This option works only on unfeathered rectangular selections.

Printing with Export Plug-ins

Another method of printing images from Photoshop is with specialized Export plug-ins. Certain digital color printers and film recorders print directly from Photoshop through Export plug-ins. Adobe includes in the Macintosh version of Photoshop an Export plug-in for printing to a ImageWriter II with a color ribbon. Most of these plug-ins are only available for the Macintosh version of Photoshop. Check the documentation for your printer or output device to verify if an output plug-in is provided. Figure 11–14 shows an Export plug-in for a 3M Rainbow dye-sublimation printer.

The advantage of using Export plug-ins is speed. Photoshop images are already composed of pixels. With a plug-in the raster information can be sent directly to the printer without the extra step of converting to a PostScript file which the PostScript processor must rasterize again. To speed up printing through an Export plug-in, you should usually send the

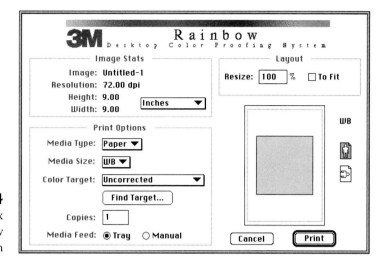

Figure 11–14
The export dialog box
for the 3M Rainbow
Export Plug-in

data at the printer's resolution. For example, for the 3M Rainbow, which prints with a 300 dpi resolution, create or resample your image in Photoshop to 300 ppi.

If your printer uses an Export plug-in, place it in the Acquire/Export folder within the Plug-Ins folder. Then choose your plug-in by choosing Export from the File menu.

OTHER EXPORT PLUG-INS

Photoshop has a few built-in Export filters for writing to specialized file formats. These include modules to export Amiga HAM (Hold and Modify), to export pen paths to Adobe Illustrator, and to save Quick Edit files in Scitex and uncompressed TIFF formats. Exporting pen paths is discussed below in "Preparing Images for Use in Other Applications." Quick Edit files are discussed in Chapter 4, "Input." Use the Export plug-in to save an image opened through the Quick Edit Acquire module. The quick-edited image section is seamlessly replaced in the original image.

Process Color Separations

Process color separation and printing—printing images by creating four printing plates in cyan, magenta, yellow, and black—has traditionally been done by professionals with many years of color experience. This was necessary because of the complexity of the process. Theoretically, it should be possible to convert from the RGB to the CMY color model easily for printing on a digital color printer or printing press, but there are several issues that complicate the process.

First, the inks and pigments used in the printing process are impure. If you printed full saturation (100%) each of cyan, magenta, and yellow, you should theoretically get black. Real inks, however, will print a dirty brown. A black plate (K for key color) must be generated to produce a true black, extend tonal range, and improve shadow detail.

A second problem is that several inks cannot print in full saturation on top of each other without creating press problems. Most printers request that print jobs have no more than 240 to 320% ink coverage to prevent these problems. This percentage is called the *total ink limit*.

There are two ways to deal with these problems. Certain amounts of cyan, magenta, and yellow are removed from neutral gray areas wherever black will print to reduce the ink coverage. This approach is called *under-color removal* (UCR). The second approach, called *gray component replacement* (GCR), sees a neutral component wherever a pixel contains cyan, magenta, and yellow. Some or all of this component is printed with black, reducing the CMY components.

A third complication is that different printers and press setups printing on different presses and papers will produce different colors. This phenomenon is caused by the interlinked issues of *color gamut* and *dot gain*.

Color gamut is the range of color that can be displayed on a particular monitor, printed on a particular digital printer, or printed on a printing press. When images are converted from RGB to CMYK, the gamut of colors is considerably decreased. Each printing choice has its own gamut of colors. Chapter 8, "Color," describes how to color-correct an RGB image in Photoshop for the smaller gamut of CMYK.

Dot gain refers to what happens to halftone dots through the production process. Halftone dots usually swell as they hit the paper, darkening the tones of a grayscale image or the color of a color image. Compensating for dot gain is described below.

STRATEGIES FOR DOING COLOR SEPARATIONS

Learning how to deal with these reproduction problems can be daunting to anyone who is new to working with color images! All of the choices made in Photoshop's controls for Monitor Setup, Printing Inks Setup, and Separation Setup affect the final quality of your color separation. You must decide whether to take on the responsibility for making these decisions or find another way to create color separations. Fortunately, there are at least three strategies for handling color separations in Photoshop.

Strategy 1: Learning to Do Color Separations in Photoshop

1. Calibrate the image you see on the screen to printed output. Go through the calibration process described in Chapter 3, "Configuring Photoshop." If not, you'll be continually frustrated in your attempts to achieve predictable output.

2. Gather some essential information from your commercial printer to make the proper settings in Photoshop:

   - Find out what *screen frequency* the press can handle in printing your image. Use this information at the scanning stage to scan at the proper image resolution (Chapter 4, "Input").

   - Ask the printer how much *dot gain* to expect from the *film stage* to press sheet in the midtones. Printers are used to talking about dot gain from *proof stage* to press sheet, but this is not the correct value to use for Photoshop. If you cannot determine this, try the default values for your paper stock in Printing Inks Setup preferences.

   - Your printer can also tell you what the recommended *Black Ink Limit* and *Total Ink Limit* are for the press that will output your image. Enter this information in the Separation Setup dialog box. A small print shop may not be able give you this information. If you cannot determine this, use the default value.

   - Ask your printer whether they prefer you to use GCR or UCR to generate the black plate, and then make this choice in the Separation Setup dialog box.

3. Make the proper choices of monitor and printer or press setup in the Preferences for Monitor Setup and Printing Inks Setup. See the "Calibration" section in Chapter 3. Make the proper settings in the Preferences for Separation Setup, described below.

4. Convert your image from RGB to CMYK. This process is described in the Mode Conversion section of Chapter 8, "Color."

5. If you didn't do color correction in RGB Color mode, you can do it in CMYK. This is described in the color correction sections of Chapter 8, "Color."

6. Usually you must sharpen your image. Sharpening and Unsharp Masking are described in Chapter 9, "Filters and Plug-ins."

7. If necessary, create traps in your image. This process is described below.

8. Print color separations to film on an imagesetter as described earlier in this chapter. Be sure to include the necessary printers' marks. If you are placing your images into another application, see "Preparing Images for Use in Other Applications" below.

9. Have a laminated proof made from your separation films to check color and halftoning issues such as color balance, moirés, registration, and trapping.

DOT GAIN

Dot gain is the growth of halftone dots through the printing process. There are many potential sources of gain—an uncalibrated imagesetter can produce a halftone dot different from one called out in the image, for example. The greatest source of dot growth, however, happens when the dot lands on paper. The pressure of the press forces ink into the absorbent paper which causes the inked halftone dots to spread outwards. The degree of dot growth will depend on the kind of press, the nature of the ink, and the paper used on the press. This is why you must ask the printer for the dot gain value.

How much does the dot grow? Halftone dots grow most in the midtone because this dot has the longest perimeter. Small highlight dots grow much less. Large shadow dots overlap each other and show little gain. The greatest dot gain is with a 50% dot; dot gain disappears with a 0% or 100% dot.

A dot gain percentage refers to the *additive increase* in midtone (50%) dot. A measurement of a 20% dot gain means that a 50% midtone dot will print on paper as a 70% dot. (It doesn't mean that a 30% dot will increase to 50%.)

Industry surveys of printers and the SWOP standards used for printing in North America show a typical dot gain from film to press of 18–25% in the midtone, when printed on coated stock. Dots grow more when printed on uncoated stock, and on coarse newsprint dot growth is even greater. Figure 11–15 shows enlargements of the same image printed of three different paper stocks.

COMPENSATING FOR DOT GAIN IN ADOBE PHOTOSHOP

Photoshop offers you three ways to compensate for dot gain:

1. Photoshop uses a built-in dot gain compensation (which you can alter) when an image is converted from RGB to CMYK mode.

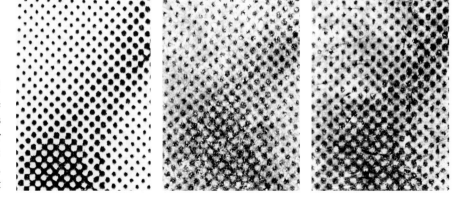

Figure 11–15
Enlargements of the same halftone dots printed on three paper stocks: (left to right): coated, uncoated, and newsprint

2. You can manually compensate for dot gain by changing the tonal range in the image using the Curves or Levels commands in the Adjust submenu under the Image menu.

3. You can set the Transfer Function to compensate for dot gain.

A good first step is to consult with your service bureau and/or printer about dot gain compensation. If they have no preference, the methods used below will work well in most situations.

Whichever method you use, remember that the dot gain value that Photoshop needs is the one which occurs *between film and press sheet*.

DOT GAIN COMPENSATION FOR RGB IMAGES

Whenever you convert from RGB Color mode to CMYK Color mode, Photoshop uses a built-in compensation for dot gain. The conversion is optimized for dot gain values of 20% or more. The exact value is set in the Printing Inks Setup preferences under the File menu (Figure 11–16).

Always choose the appropriate target in Printing Inks Setup prior to converting your image to CMYK Color mode or printing directly to a digital color printer. If you do not have dot gain values from your printer, try the following settings.

- For printing on coated stock, choose SWOP (Coated). Photoshop's default dot gain of 20% appears. You may increase the setting up to 23%.

- For printing on uncoated stock, choose SWOP (Uncoated). Photoshop's default dot gain or 25% appears. You may increase the setting up to 30%.

- For printing on newsprint, choose SWOP (Newsprint). Photoshop's default dot gain of 30% appears. You may increase the setting up to 35%.

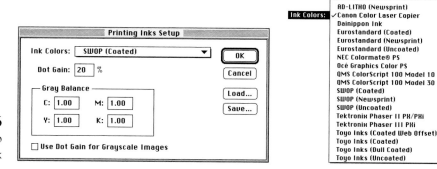

Figure 11–16
The Printing Inks Setup
dialog box

- When printing a proof to a digital color printer, select the model of printer that most closely matches your color printer, and the dot gain for that printer will appear.

For the best results, run test proofs to check image quality. Laminated proofs, generally the most accurate, have dot gain built in; find out how much from the color service bureau or printer. If the proof reasonably simulates the dot gain of the press printing on coated paper, the printer should come close to matching the color and tone of the proof on the press.

As a result of proofing or consultation with the printer, if you find you need to change the dot gain value, set the new dot gain value in Printing Inks Setup and reconvert the original RGB image to CMYK mode again.

NOTE: Once you are in CMYK Color mode, the settings in Printing Inks Set-up have no effect on the data, but they do affect the image's display on the monitor.

COMPENSATING FOR GRAYSCALE OR DUOTONE IMAGES

Photoshop does not automatically compensate for grayscale or duotone images. For these images, calibrate your monitor to a laminated proof as described in the "Calibration" section of Chapter 3, "Configuring Photoshop." By matching your display to a laminated proof which has dot gain built in, the monitor will simulate the image printed on coated paper stock. The monitor can be adjusted to simulate various dot gain condiitions in the Printing Inks Setup preferences dialog box. Enter the dot gain value and turn on Use Dot Gain for Grayscale Images. Percentage values will remain the same, but RGB values used to display the gray values will change. Manually compensate for dot gain using the Curves or Levels commands described in the next section.

MANUALLY COMPENSATING FOR DOT GAIN

There are situations when you may need to manually compensate an image for dot gain. This could happen, for example, if you have calibrated your monitor to a laminated proof, but must print an image on a paper that has more dot gain, such as uncoated or newsprint stock. This technique could also be used if you have not calibrated your monitor to a proof. Choose Curves in the Adjust submenu under the Image menu and use the following technique:

1. Open the Curves dialog box. It is easiest to adjust the tonal curve for dot gain compensation by entering values as a dot percentage by clicking the bar beneath the curve to toggle (transpose) the graph

from levels to percentages. In this orientation, original input values are displayed with light values (highlights) on the left and dark values (shadows) on the right, output values are displayed with light values on the bottom and dark values on the top.

2. Drag the curve down with the crosshair at the 50% level to the desired percentage. Consult your printer to find out what percentage dot will increase to a 50% dot when printed to a specified paper stock (Figure 11–17).

You can also compensate for dot gain manually using the Levels command in the Adjust submenu under the Image menu:

1. Open the Levels dialog box. The Histogram at the top displays the distribution of values in the image. The top slider adjusts the input values and the bottom slider controls the output values.

2. Drag the center triangle in the top slider slightly to the left (to the desired midpoint output level) to lighten the midtones in the image (Figure 11–18).

SETTING THE TRANSFER FUNCTION

You can also compensate for dot gain by setting a transfer function in the Transfer Functions dialog box accessed in the Page Setup dialog box under the File menu (Figure 11–19). Click the Transfer button. Although the transfer function may work for dot gain compensation in specialized situations, there are potential problems: (1) To save the transfer function in an

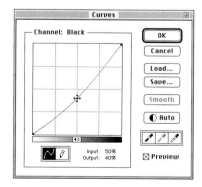

Figure 11–17
Drag the midpoint in the Curves dialog box down to the desired output percentage to manually compensate for dot gain.

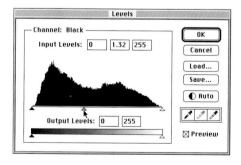

Figure 11–18
Compensate for dot gain in the Levels dialog box by dragging the center triangle in the top slider slightly to the left, which will lighten the midtones in the image.

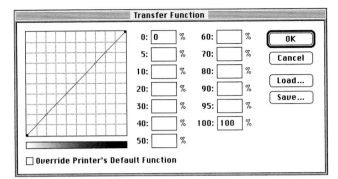

Figure 11–19
The Transfer Functions
dialog box

image to print it in another application, you must save the image in EPS format. You must check the Include Transfer Function box in the EPS Format dialog box. (2) Occasionally saving a transfer function out of Photoshop can interfere with imagesetter calibration software. In most cases, it's better to use the settings in the Printing Inks Setup preferences or to manually adjust the tones using Curves or Levels.

TIP: Don't use the Transfer Function to adjust dot gain if you are compensating for dot gain by using the Printing Ink Setup preferences or making manual adjustments in Curves or Levels.

OTHER FACTORS IN WORKING WITH DOT GAIN

There are some other factors to consider when working with dot gain:

- Dots change in the highlight and shadow areas of a halftone. Dots smaller than a certain size will disappear on the press. Dots larger than a certain size can't be distinguished and will be filled with ink. This is usually handled when you choose a true highlight and shadow area to maintain detail in the image. See the Tone Control and Adjustment section in Chapter 8, "Color," for instructions on setting highlight and shadow dots.

- Halftone dots grow in size even more at higher screen frequencies. When dots are smaller, the spaces between dots are smaller and fill up with ink quickly. For a job with a very fine line screen, be sure to consult with your printer about the expected dot gain.

- A new technology called stochastic, or FM screening, doesn't use conventional halftone dots. FM screening has greater dot gain than does conventional halftoning.

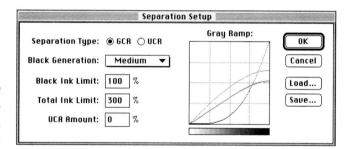

Figure 11–20
The Separation Setup
dialog box with
GCR selected

SEPARATION SETUP

Photoshop's Separation Setup dialog box (Figure 11–20) contains controls for undercolor removal (UCR) or gray component replacement (GCR). In this dialog box you may set Separation Type—either UCR or GCR.

NOTE: Settings in both Separation Setup and Printing Inks Setup affect only the conversion of RGB color information to CMYK color mode, including printing to a CMYK printer from RGB color mode.

For UCR separations, you only have the choices *Total Ink Limit* and *Black Ink Limit*. Total Ink Limit refers to the total percentages of cyan, magenta, yellow and black ink on any one spot. As previously described, this should normally be between 240% and 320%. Photoshop's default is 300%. Black Ink Limit is the largest amount of black allowed on any one spot. The default is 100%.

For GCR separations, select the degree of Black Generation—Light, Medium (the default), Heavy, None, Maximum, or Custom. The Medium option should work well for most images. If you choose None, no black plate will be printed. The Custom option allows you to adjust the black generation curve manually. For GCR separations, you may also select *undercolor addition* (UCA), which adds cyan, magenta, and yellow in dark areas of the picture after removing some black, creating a richer black than black ink alone can provide.

TIP: You can observe the results of the settings in the graph on the right side of the Separation Setup dialog box—experiment with different settings (Figure 11-20).

There are also buttons for saving and loading the Separation Setup options, useful if you need to apply custom separation curves to several images.

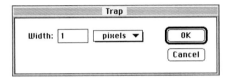

Figure 11–21
The Trap dialog box

SEPARATION TABLES

Information in Photoshop's Printer Ink Setup and Separation Setup determines how RGB or Lab Color modes get converted into CMYK Color mode. These preference can be saved and loaded using Separation Tables preference. See the "Mode Conversions" section in Chapter 8, "Color."

TRAPPING

Printing technology, although quite good, cannot ensure perfect registration. A slight printing shift may cause solid butting colors to leave a gap between them. A slight overlap of the butting colors, typically called *trapping*, will help avoid the gaps from appearing.

Trapping in Photoshop is controlled with the Trap command. After converting an image to CMYK Color mode, the Trap command, found under the Image menu, becomes active. When selected, the Trap dialog box appears (Figure 11–21).

TIP: The Trap command works only in the CMYK Color mode—it's only relevant when color separating an image, and has no effect on on-screen editing. Trapping also cannot be seen on most digital color printers when you're making a composite print.

To use the Trap command, simply enter the value to compensate for misregistration. You can specify the amount of trapping in pixels, points, or millimeters; the default is one pixel. Your commercial printer will supply the necessary value based on the amount of misregistration expected from the printing press. Applying the Trap command is normally the last step before printing color separations.

NOTE: Trapping is not necessary unless there are sharp transitions of flat color in your image. Consult your commercial printer to see if trapping should be applied. Create the smallest trap necessary to avoid artifacts in the image. The trapping value is dependent on image resolution: One pixel will create a much greater trap at 72 ppi than in a 300 ppi image.

Strategy 2: Use a Color Management System to Create Color Separations

A new class of software is now available: color management systems (CMS). For average color quality requirements, a CMS will not require you to get involved with color complexities—such as GCR, UCR, and color gamut issues—in order to obtain relatively consistent color display and print. Refer to Chapter 3, "Configuring Photoshop," for a discussion of color management systems.

While the components of CMSs vary, they usually have much in common:

1. Color Management Systems make use of a device-independent color space, called CIE color (Lab color in Photoshop is one variant of CIE color).

2. CMS's have profiles (or they allow you to generate profiles) that record the exact color-gamut and color-rendering characteristics of devices like scanners, monitors, and printers.

3. CMS's have an "engine" that is capable of transforming color from one color space to another.

COLOR MANAGEMENT SYSTEMS WITHIN PHOTOSHOP

CMS systems work with Photoshop in a variety of methods. Some bypass Photoshop's preferences by adjusting the colors or converting to CMYK mode when opening a document. Some bypass Photoshop's preferences by adjusting color values or converting to CMYK when printing or saving. Others work within Photoshop by replacing the preferences with custom tables.

- Kodak Color Management System (KCMS) uses Device Color Profiles (DCP) that mathematically describe the color gamut of scanners, monitors, and output devices. KCMS is automatically available in Photoshop, primarily to open Photo CD images (see Chapter 4, "Input") but an additional product called Precision Input Color Characterization (PICC) allows you to create an input Precision Transfer for any scanner. The basic KCMS does its work when a document is opened in Photoshop (see Figure 4–15).

- DayStar's ColorMatch runs on the Macintosh using the Kodak Color Management System (KCMS) as a basis engine, providing an integrated color management system to control monitor calibration, input of scanned images, color correction, output preview, and color space conversion, providing optimum files for specific output devices. ColorMatch installs as a plug-in module, appearing in the Filter menu for color correction and output preview, in the Save As dialog box to save files in the ColorMatch TIFF format, and in the Export submenu to print using ColorMatch Print.

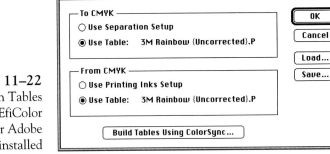

Figure 11–22
The Separation Tables
dialog box with EfiColor
for Adobe
Photoshop installed

- EfiColor Works from Electronics for Imaging (EFI) uses Separation Tables that replace the selections usually made in Monitor Setup, Printer Ink Setup, and Separation Setup (Figure 11–22). First specify your monitor in the Monitor Setup dialog box. Then choose the digital color printer or press setup that matches your output, and the separation table will convert the image to CMYK, taking into account the color gamut and dot gain for the chosen printer or press.

Strategy 3: Get a CMYK Scan from a Drum Scanner

Another strategy for creating color separations is to buy color scans from an experienced color service bureau that uses a drum scanner. Drum scanners were described in Chapter 4, "Input." This is the best choice for critical prepress work. Your service bureau will provide you with a high-quality CMYK image that you can manipulate in Photoshop. Since the image is already in CMYK Color mode, you do not have to deal with the complications of the mode conversion.

TIP: Remember that this scan is already preseparated, so keep it in CMYK Color mode as you work. You will lose quality if you convert it to RGB and back again.

Proofing

Whichever method you choose to produce your process color separations, you should have a proof made of your image. It is much less expensive to catch mistakes early on in the proofing process than finding them in a piece on the press! There are four principal ways of proofing color separated images: (1) digital proofs, (2) overlay proofs, (3) laminated proofs, and (4) press proofs.

DIGITAL PROOFS

Digital proofs are made on composite color printers. As described in "Printers and Other Output Devices" above, there are a wide variety of printers on which you can print your image.

Unless you use a color management system or have made special compensation for a digital printer's color gamut in Photoshop, digital color printers may or may not give you a good idea of the image's color. Also, digital printers that print as continuous tone will look different from an image printed with halftone dots on a printing press. Digital printers usually have no way of showing the effect of dot gain and most cannot show the overprinting used in trapping.

OVERLAY PROOFS

Overlay proofs, commonly referred to as *Color Keys*, are made from film separations printed on an imagesetter. Each channel of color appears on an acetate sheet. Four sheets of acetate on top of each other in register on a white base create a full color image. Examples of overlay systems are 3M Color Keys and Hoechst Naps.

The advantage of overlay proofs is that you can view each color plate separately. The disadvantage is inaccurate color because you must look through several acetate layers.

LAMINATED PROOFS

Laminated proofs, the industry standard for proofing an image prior to committing it to the printing press, are made from the same color-separated film used to expose the printing plates. The images on the four pieces of film are sequentially transferred onto white base material with cyan, magenta, yellow, and black colorants. A final laminate layer fuses the layers. Laminated proofing systems include 3M MatchPrint, Hoechst PressMatch, Dupont Chromalin, and Fuji Color Art.

Sometimes referred to as "contract proofs," laminated proofs provide an agreement between the printer and customer as to how an image (or page) will print. Most printers prefer this system because of accurate color and dot gain simulation. Laminated proofs also preview possible halftone-related press problems like moirés and banding. Traps created in an image to compensate for press misregistration can be viewed. Sometimes a different base material can simulate the actual paper on which a job will be printed.

PRESS PROOFS

Press proofs are made by actually printing an image on a press, sometimes using a special kind of printing press called a proofing press. Press proofs are sometimes required for approving color-critical jobs. These proofs are very expensive and, in most situations, have been replaced by laminated proofs.

Spot Color Separations

Spot Color

Spot color separations print with two, three, or more custom colors. Sometimes spot color separations create a fifth, sixth, or more plates for extra colors or varnish layers which also can be used with process color separations.

There are several ways to print spot color separations from Photoshop:

1. You can create duotones, tritones, or quadtones and print them from Photoshop or save them for printing in another application.

2. You can create channels or layers and print them individually out of Photoshop.

3. You can create a CMYK file with additional channels, an Indexed color file, or a Multichannel file and, using an Export plug-in, save spot color plates for use in a page layout program such as QuarkXPress.

DUOTONES

Duotones, tritones, and quadtones use two, three, and four colors to reproduce a grayscale image in a way that increases the tonal range or to add colors. Refer to the "Duotones, Tritones, and Quadtones" section in Chapter 8, "Color."

Since duotones usually print with halftone screens, screen angles and frequencies must be set to avoid moiré patterns. Imagesetter screening technology varies among vendors and devices, requiring specific screen frequency and angle settings. Consult your printer and service bureau to determine the optimal settings.

To set screen angle and frequency, click the Screens button in the Page Setup dialog box under the File menu (Figure 11–23). The Ink pop-up menu allows you to set the parameters for each color. Normally, set the angle for black or the darkest color at 45°, the second darkest color 30° apart (often at 75°). In a tritone, set the third darkest color 30° from the second color (often

Figure 11–23
The Halftone Screens
dialog box for a
quadtone image

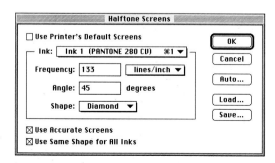

15°) and in a quadtone, the lightest color 15° from the third color (usually 0°). Click the Auto button to have Photoshop determine the optimal frequency and angle settings based on the printer resolution. Your service bureau will tell you whether or not to click the Use Accurate Screens button (see the "Page Setup" section earlier in this chapter).

To print a composite image from the Print dialog box, do not check the Print Separations option. To print separate plates, check Print Separations. To save duotones for printing in another application, save in the EPS file format (see "Preparing Images for Use in Other Applications" below).

Duotones can be proofed on digital printers, but since most digital printers print in CMYK, they may not produce accurate color for duotones created using Pantone colors.

TIP: Many digital color printers cannot print duotones if you are in duotone mode or if you have saved your image as an EPS file with duotone curves included. Make a copy of your file (saving the duotone information in the original) and convert the copy to CMYK Color mode. Use the CMYK version to print to the digital printer.

The best way to proof duotones is to make spot color separations and proof with a Dupont Chromalin proofing system. This system uses color toners which include Pantone colors, producing the most color-accurate proof. A simpler and less expensive option is to make overlay proofs (Color Keys).

LAYERS AND CHANNELS

Photoshop's default is to print all visible channels and layers. You can print spot colors by creating each color in a separate channel. In the Channels palette, select only one channel to be visible, and then print that channel after making the appropriate choices in Page Setup and Print dialogs. Repeat the process until all the channels have been printed.

Another method is to make each spot color a separate layer. Normally Photoshop prints all visible layers, but if a layer is hidden it will not be printed. Make each layer visible, one at a time, and print them individually.

With both of these methods, remember to set the screen angle and frequency to avoid a moiré pattern.

SAVING MULTIPLE SPOT COLORS

Saving duotones, tritones, or quadtones in the EPS format allows up to four colors for an image. Additional separations for spot colors, varnishes, or plates for die cuts can be printed from channels manually, but if you need to save a document with multiple channels representing spot colors for separations in a page layout program, such as QuarkXPress, you must use an export plug-in like PlateMaker (Mac only) from In Software. Another method of saving multiple spot color separations is to save individual, separated files from an image with a limited color palette. This can be done manually or with an export module such as PhotoSpot (Mac only) from Second Glance Software.

If you will be printing separations from QuarkXPress, use PlateMaker to export from Photoshop in the DCS 2.0 format (a newer version of Desktop Color Separation (DCS) format described later in "Preparing Images for Use in Other Applications"). The DCS 2.0 format supports saving extra plates which can be used for spot colors, varnishes, die cuts, or other specialized effects.

PlateMaker will export any CMYK, Indexed Color, or Multichannel document for printing plates in QuarkXPress (or that support the DCS 2.0 format). In a CMYK file, you can also save up to 20 additional grayscale channels. In a Multichannel file, you can create up to 24 grayscale channels. Indexed Color files can contain up to 256 colors in the Index channel and up to 23 additional grayscale channels. Documents can be saved with clipping paths. Figure 11–24 shows the PlateMaker dialog box used for exporting a CMYK file with two additional channels for Varnish and Pantone color plates.

PhotoSpot from Second Glance Software, an export plug-in module, separates colors from an image with a limited color palette into distinct separate documents in the TIFF or native Photoshop formats (Figure 11–25). TIFF

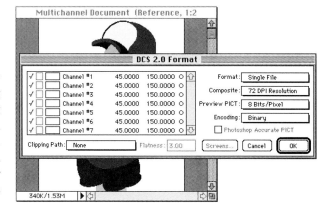

Figure 11–24
The PlateMaker dialog box when exporting CMYK document as an EPS DCS 2.0 format, which will separate with extra channels for additional spot colors

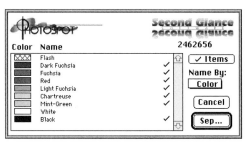

Figure 11–25
The PhotoSpot dialog box when exporting a document with a limited color palette which creates separate documents for each color

files must then be individually imported into a page layout program, tagged with a color, and stacked in register. The page layout program will then print the colored layers as separations, provided you have specified colors to over-print in the page layout program. To create a document with a limited color palette, convert to Index Color mode and use the Posterize command or color reduction filters such as PaintThinner, Acetone, or Turpentine, also from Second Glance Software.

Halftone Screen Alternatives

Whether photographic or digital, a halftone screen produces a series of dots that vary in size but remain constant in frequency. Halftone screens do not have to be round—other shapes available in Photoshop include a diamond, ellipse, line, square, and cross, as well as user-defined custom shapes (Figure 11–26). You can specify a halftone dot shape (as well as frequency and angel) prior to printing or saving from Photoshop by clicking the Screens button in the Page Setup dialog box. To include these setting when saving a document, save in the EPS format and click on the Include Halftone Screen button. You can also apply a halftone screen with any shape, angle, or frequency when converting from Grayscale to Bitmap mode (see Chapter 8, "Color.").

CUSTOM PATTERNS

You can create a custom halftone screen when converting a grayscale image to the Bitmap mode with the Define Pattern command under the Edit menu. Any pattern or texture can be defined as a Custom Pattern and then be used as a custom halftone screen

1. Start with a texture or pattern (Figure 11–27). Select the pattern with the Marquee tool, and choose Define Pattern under the Edit menu.
2. Open an image in Grayscale mode to be processed through the defined pattern. A color image must be converted to Grayscale mode.
3. Choose the Bitmap mode from the Mode menu. Click the Custom Pattern option in the dialog box.

DITHERED PIXELS

Another halftone screen alternative when converting to Bitmap mode is to screen the image with dithered pixels. In this case, you define a resolution, but not a dot shape. The size of the dithered pixels remains constant while their position, or frequency varies.

When converting to the Bitmap mode, a Grayscale document can generate a pattern dither (Figure 8–17) or diffusion dither (Figure 8–18). Refer to the "Color Modes" section in Chapter 8, "Color," for more information on

Figure 11–26
These gradients have
various halftone
screens applied.

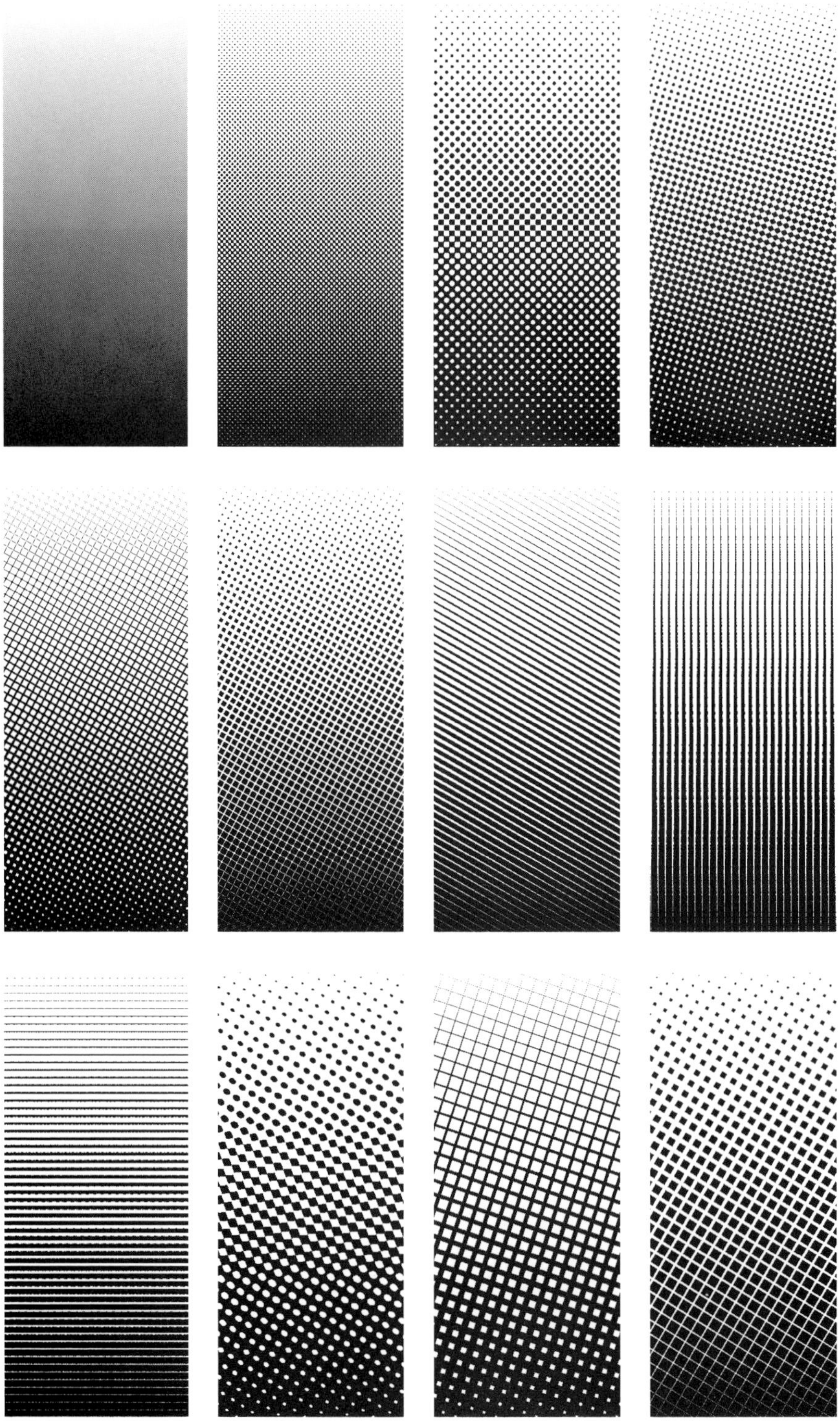

Left to right:
Round, 45°, 133 lpi
Round, 45°, 53 lpi
Round, 45°, 25 lpi
Diamond, 15°, 25 lpi

Left to right:
Cross, 30°, 25 lpi
Square, 30°, 25 lpi
Line, 30°, 25 lpi
Line, 90°, 25 lpi

Left to right:
Line, 0°, 25 lpi
Ellipse, 30°, 15 lpi
Cross, 15°, 15 lpi
Square, 30°, 15 lpi

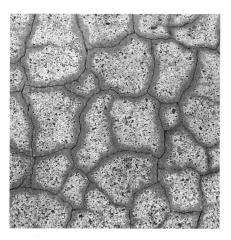
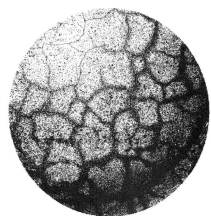

Figure 11–27
The original scanned texture on the left was used to define a custom halftone screen when the image of the sphere on the right was converted to Bitmap mode.

converting to Bitmap mode. Since the conversion to Bitmap mode must be from the Grayscale mode, color images must be separated into individual grayscale documents, one for each color. The following example illustrates the process using a color image (See Figure C–7 in the Color Section).

1. Starting from a CMYK Color image, open the Channels palette and choose Split channels from the pop-up menu (Figure 11–28). This creates four separate grayscale documents, each representing a channel (see Figure 1–12).

2. Convert each of the documents to Bitmap mode, choosing Diffusion Dither and the desired resolution in each dialog box (Figure 11–29). Use a resolution equal to or less than the resolution of your output device.

3. Each of these bitmap documents must now be converted back to Grayscale mode at a Size Ratio of 1. After converting all four files back to the Grayscale mode, choose Merge channels from the pop-up menu in the Channels palette (Figure 11–30). Choose CMYK Color mode from the pop-up menu in the Merge Channels dialog box

Figure 11–28
Choose Split Channels from the pop-up menu in the Channels palette to create four separate grayscale files from a CMYK document.

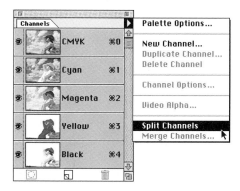

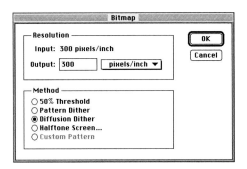

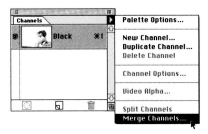

Figure 11–29
Click Diffusion Dither and the desired resolution in the Bitmap dialog box.

Figure 11–30
Choose Merge Channels in the Channels palette pop-up menu to combine the four separate files into one.

(Figure 11–31). The Merge CMYK Channels dialog box will open (Figure 11–32). Make sure that the proper document appears in the pop-up menu next to each corresponding channel.

4. You can now print color separations of the resulting document; each separation will have the dithered effect.

MEZZOTINTS

A mezzotint is another type of halftone screen with irregularly shaped dots. When you create a mezzotint screen a defined Custom Pattern breaks up the tones in an image into random shapes. Included with Photoshop are some pattern documents that can be used as custom patterns. Two of them, Mezzotint dot and Mezzotint shape, can be used to define a pattern that

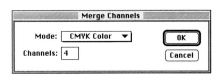

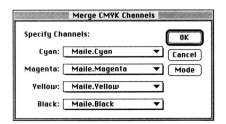

Figure 11–31
Specify the color mode in the Merge Channels dialog box.

Figure 11–32
In the Merge CMYK Channels dialog box, link each document with its corresponding channel.

Figure 11–33
A custom mezzotint
halftone screen was
applied when converting
this image
to Bitmap mode.
(© Mark Siprut)

will simulate a mezzotint. Use the following method to create your own pattern and resulting mezzotint on an image (Figure 11–33).

1. Open a new grayscale document to be used as a pattern. Make it the same size as your image. Choose Add Noise in the Noise submenu under the Filter menu. In the dialog box, set the desired amount and the distribution to Gaussian. Apply the Blur filter to soften the pattern.

2. Choose Select All under the Select menu and then choose Define Pattern under the Edit menu.

3. Open the Grayscale image to be screened and convert to Bitmap mode. In the dialog box click on the Custom Pattern option and enter a resolution. (Adobe recommends a higher resolution than the input value.)

To apply a mezzotint to a color image, follow the above steps under Diffusion Dither, substituting the Custom Pattern option for Diffusion Dither in the Bitmap mode dialog box.

Preparing Images for Use in Other Applications

Images created in Photoshop are often transferred into other applications prior to final output. To move a Photoshop image to another program, you must either save it in the proper format, use an export plug-in module, copy it from Photoshop and paste it in the destination program, or create a live link with Publish and Subscribe on the Macintosh. Following are some typical scenarios:

- You might save an image to be opened in another raster (bitmap) program such as Specular Collage or Fractal Design Painter. When you move a Photoshop image into a raster-based program, the image remains an editable bitmap at its original resolution.

- You may wish to place a Photoshop image into a vector-based (object-oriented) illustration program like Adobe Illustrator, MacroMedia FreeHand, or CorelDRAW! When you place a Photoshop file in a vector program, you will no longer be able to edit it.

- You might import your image into a page layout program like QuarkXPress or PageMaker to print a document such as a newsletter or advertisement. An imported image will usually no longer be editable (if you choose the TIFF format for a black-and-white or grayscale image, you might be able to colorize it or do elementary tone adjustment in the page layout application). If you Publish the image (using Create Publisher under the Edit menu on the Macintosh), and then Subscribe to it in the page layout document, you will have created a live link that is automatically updated whenever the original is altered and saved.

- Finally, you might be preparing your image for presentation or multimedia applications. Some applications such as Macromedia Director allow image editing, whereas others, such as Adobe Persuasion, do not.

Cross-Platform Issues

Transporting files between the Windows and Macintosh platforms is significantly easier today then it was a few years ago. Remember to thoroughly test these procedures *before* you start a job using sample files representative of your project. Testing involves placement of your art on the destination platform and proofing the image. It also involves using the latest version of your destination application or import/export filters. Developers usually update these filters to solve problems that may arise. (Fortunately you use Photoshop, a program most developers are anxious to properly support.) Find a file format that works and produces repeatable results; this becomes your standard—do not deviate from it!

The best solution is to transport Photoshop's native file format (.PSD) between the Macintosh and Windows platforms. If neither platform uses Photoshop, then the RGB or CMYK .TIF format is your best solution, followed by the .EPS format. These formats work properly in many Windows applications as long as you avoid JPEG encoding your .EPS files since no Windows applications currently support this. For a discussion of file formats, see Appendix A, "File Formats."

SCITEX TIP: LineWorker from In Software, a plug-in module, allows Photoshop (Macintosh only) to import and export Scitex Linework files.

Preparing for a Raster-Based Program

To save a Photoshop file to open in a raster-based program, you must consider issues of file format, mode, and resolution.

If your image is grayscale or RGB, the ideal file format to use in another program may be the TIFF format (.TIF in Windows). TIFF is recognized on both the Macintosh and PC platforms by virtually every bitmapped application. Other commonly recognized formats for grayscale and RGB are the PICT format on the Macintosh, and the Photoshop 2.0 format.

If your image is CMYK, many raster applications will not open it. Check to make sure that your destination program will accept a CMYK image.

If you place an image into an existing raster file, make sure that the resolutions are the same. Otherwise, the image could open up larger or smaller than expected.

Preparing for a Vector-Based Illustration Program

When preparing Photoshop images for vector (object-oriented) programs you should be aware of file format, color mode, resolution, and rotation.

If you are printing color composites or color separations, always convert your images to CMYK before saving them. Photoshop usually does a better job of converting colors than do the default settings of most digital printers for color composites. Save in CMYK for images to be color separated by illustration applications or utilities like Adobe Separator. Following are the file formats that common illustration programs accept:

- Adobe Illustrator on the Macintosh only opens EPS files, but can read MacPaint and PICT files as templates.
- Adobe Illustrator for Windows can open Photoshop files in the EPS (preferred), BMP, PCX, and TIFF formats.
- Macromedia FreeHand on the Macintosh supports MacPaint, TIFF, PICT, and EPS images. Black-and-white or grayscale MacPaint, TIFF and PICT images can be monochromatically colored in FreeHand. Tones can be adjusted on grayscale TIFF files.
- Macromedia FreeHand for Windows supports .TIF, .EPS, and .BMP formats. It has the same abilities to colorize and adjust tones as the Macintosh version.
- CorelDRAW! accepts .TIF or .EPS files.

Take enlarging or reducing images into account when the images are scanned. If you enlarge an image, you may end with a "pixelated" image because the scaling has reduced the image resolution. Follow the guidelines in Chapter 4, "Input," regarding image resolution.

You can usually rotate bitmapped images after placing them in an illustration program, but the rotation can greatly increase printing time. If possible, rotate ahead of time in Photoshop.

Exporting Paths to Vector Programs

Adobe provides two ways to move vector Pen tool paths created in Photoshop into Illustrator. You can export paths with the Paths to Illustrator Export plug-in. Or, if you are working on the Macintosh, you can copy your path to the Clipboard and then paste into Illustrator.

The Export plug-in is available for both Macintosh and Windows through the following steps:

1. Create a Pen tool path and save it in the Paths palette (Figure 11–34) as described in Chapter 6, "Image Selection and Masking."

2. Choose the Paths to Illustrator Export submenu under the File menu. Choose the desired path from the Write pop-up menu, and name and save the file into the folder of your choice. By default, Photoshop appends ".ai" to the name of your file. Click Save, and the path will be saved in Illustrator 3 format (Figure 11–35).

3. In Adobe Illustrator, choose Open under the File menu (don't choose Place) and select the saved Photoshop path. You can now apply any of Illustrator's vector effects: stroking, filling, adding type to the path, and so on. Notice that the path includes crop marks that designate the boundaries of your original document (Figure 11–36). Do not move the path or the crop marks if you want to use the path in the original Photoshop document in its exact position. Since Macromedia

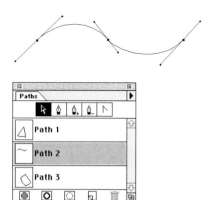

Figure 11–34
Save a path in the Paths palette and also save the Photoshop document.

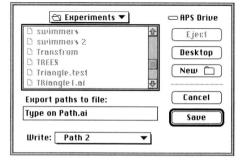

Figure 11–35
In the Paths to Illustrator dialog box, choose the path to export in the Write pop-up menu.

FreeHand and CorelDRAW! can read Illustrator 3 format, they can also open Photoshop paths.

You can now either use the art in Illustrator (for example, you can use the path to create a mask) or you can save your additional vector-based effects back to the exact position in the original Photoshop file.

To return the Illustrator art and path to Photoshop:

1. In the Illustrator document, choose Save As to save the revised path with any art, type or enhancements.

2. Open the original Photoshop image with the path. Choose the Place command under the File menu and select the saved Illustrator file. The enhanced path will be rasterized into its correct position in the original file ready for more Photoshop effects (Figure 11–37).

NOTE: Macromedia FreeHand will not export the file with the proper bounding box (crop marks) to place it in into Photoshop in position.

Exporting with the Clipboard

On the Macintosh you can use the Clipboard to copy paths from Photoshop to Illustrator:

1. In Photoshop select the path you want to transfer to Illustrator.

2. Choose Copy from the Edit menu to copy to the path to the Macintosh Clipboard.

3. Open Illustrator and choose Paste from the Edit menu to paste the path into your file.

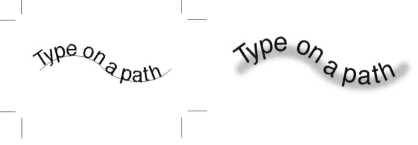

Figure 11–36
In Illustrator, type is added to the path originally created in Photoshop

Figure 11–37
The Illustrator file, placed into the original Photoshop file in its exact position on the original path, stroked with the Airbrush tool with a gray tint.

This method will not work with Macromedia FreeHand. Nor will it work on a PC because the Windows Clipboard is not robust enough to reliably copy Photoshop graphics to other applications.

Preparing for Page Layout Programs

Most of the previously mentioned issues in preparing Photoshop images for illustration programs also apply to placing images into page layout programs: file format, color mode, resolution, and rotation. Page layout programs usually accept more file formats, but TIFF and EPS are again preferred. They also work across computer platforms.

As with illustration programs, the effect of scaling an image in a page layout program should be taken into consideration when digitizing the image. Rotation should take place in Photoshop rather than in the page layout program for faster printing.

Whether to Save in TIFF or EPS Format

Save in TIFF formats for a non-PostScript printer, as it will not understand PostScript commands in the EPS format. If you're printing to a PostScript printer, consider the following:

- Either CMYK TIFF or EPS files can be printed to color PostScript printers. Convert color images to CMYK Color mode and save as a single-file EPS for best results (see the next section).

- CMYK files in either the TIFF or EPS formats can be color separated by most page layout programs. The DCS format of EPS (see the next section) will print faster to imagesetters.

- To print both a high-resolution CMYK digital print and color separations, the CMYK TIFF format is the best choice.

- To colorize black-and-white or grayscale images with a single color, or do minor tone adjustments in QuarkXPress or PageMaker, save in the TIFF format. However, you will have more control if you execute these functions in Photoshop.

- If you use a color management system to adjust image colors for printing to a target device profile, you should usually save in the TIFF format. For example, DayStar Color Match has a specially tagged version called ColorMatch TIFF. Refer to your CMS manually for specific instructions.

- If you have saved a clipping path using the Paths palette to silhouette an image, save the file in EPS format in order to print it correctly in another application.

- Save a duotone, tritone, or quadtone in the EPS format for it to correctly separate into the desired colors.

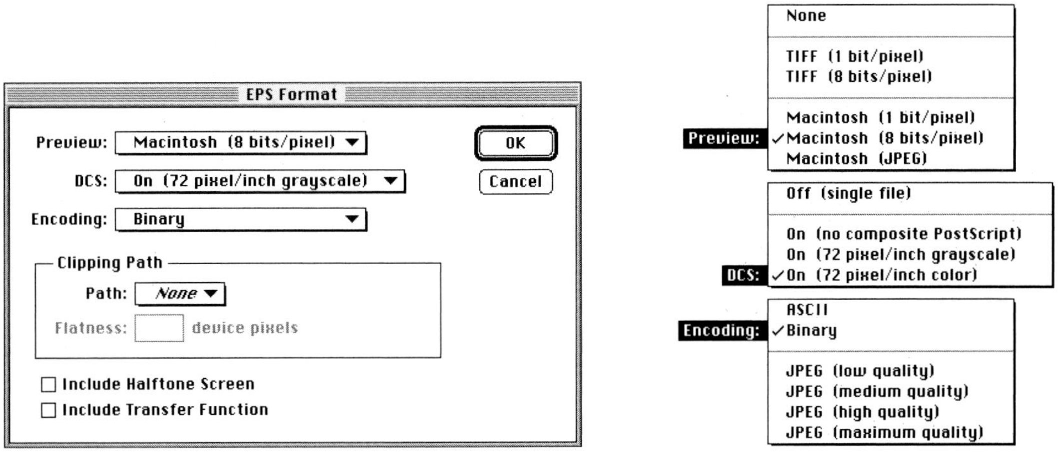

Figure 11–38 The EPS Format dialog box for the Macintosh

How to Save Your EPS File

Saving a file in the EPS format presents you with a dialog box (Figure 11–38). The Preview pop-up menu gives you choices for 1-bit (black-and-white), 8-bit (color) or JPEG preview for Macintosh, and 1-bit or 8-bit TIFF for IBM PC-compatible computers (Figure 11–39). If you plan to place the EPS file in another application, Preview will provide a low-resolution representation of the image to display in your illustration or page layout program. The JPEG form of compression can be used as a preview to create a smaller file than an 8-bit preview, but the file will place into another application somewhat slower because it must decompress. Not all applications support a JPEG preview (no Windows applications do), so you should test this procedure.

When saving a CMYK image in the EPS format, the DCS pop-up menu becomes an option. DCS, an abbreviation for Desktop Color Separation, is a special version of the EPS format originated by Quark Inc. which has become a standard for saving color images.

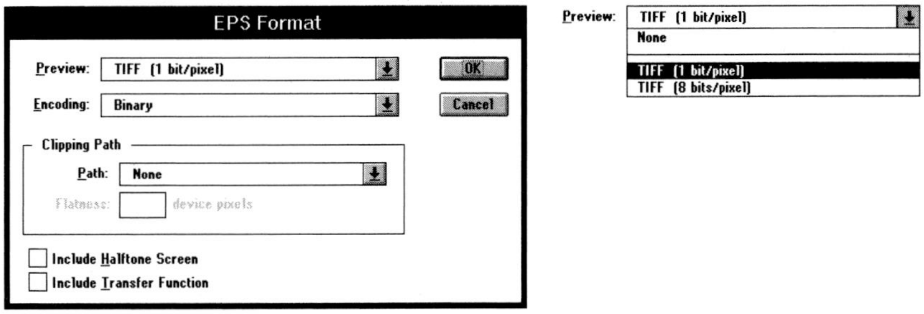

Figure 11–39
The Windows EPS Format dialog box does not contain the three Macintosh preview options in the Preview drop-down list box.

If you save a file for process color separations, choose the option labeled "On (72 pixel/inch color)." This creates five separate documents. Import the low-resolution color "master" file into your illustration or page layout program. The other four files (cyan, magenta, yellow, and black) contain the high-resolution information to be sent to the imagesetter when the color separation is printed. By pre-separating the high-resolution image, printing it from an illustration or page layout program becomes more efficient.

When using the DCS option, you also have the option of selecting "On (no composite PostScript)," which saves no preview image for placement (saves memory), or "On (72 pixel/inch grayscale)," which saves a grayscale preview for placement.

If you want a high-quality digital color print of your image placed into another application, select "Off (Single file)." This choice produces a single high-resolution file, instead of five files.

The Encoding pop-up menu chooses how the image data is saved to go to the printer. See the previous discussion in the "Print dialog box" section about the choices for Encoding. In most cases, Binary is the best choice, but if your setup can't handle it, choose ASCII. Another option is JPEG with four different levels of compression—low, medium, high, and maximum. Currently, you can use this option for printing a composite proof to a Postscript Level 2 color printer. You should, however, avoid the JPEG option for printing separations because no application can currently read and separate JPEG-encoded EPS files.

If your image includes Pen tool paths, the Clipping Path option allows you to choose which path will be saved with the file as a clipping path. You can also specify a flatness value. A clipping path will silhouette an image when it is placed in another application. Chapter 6, "Image Selection and Masking," describes how to create and save clipping paths.

TIP: **To prevent "limitcheck" PostScript errors on high-resolution imagesetters, save clipping paths with a higher flatness value. Flatness refers to how accurately the curves will be rendered. A value of 6 to 8 will print smoothly at high resolution on an imagesetter even though it would look rough on a lower-resolution printer.**

If you select Include Halftone Screens, the choices you make in the Screens dialog box (an option in the Page Setup dialog box) will be saved with the EPS file. Otherwise the image will print with the screen frequencies and angles set in the application printing the color separations.

Click Include Transfer Functions if any adjustments were made in the Transfer Functions dialog box. Check with the service bureau or printer that will output your documents to see if you should save this information with your file. Halftone Screens or Transfer Functions are usually *not* clicked when saving an EPS file.

Preparing Images for Screen Presentation

When preparing images for presentation graphics, multimedia, video, or animation, your final output will usually be on a computer monitor or television. When saving a Photoshop image, you should set the proper file format, resolution, color mode, and color depth.

- Most presentation, multimedia, and animation programs on the Macintosh prefer the PICT format for importing images. Most Windows applications prefer the .TIF format, but some also prefer .BMP or .PCX files.

- The resolution of the image should match the resolution of the display. For example most Macintosh computers display at 72 dpi. PCs can display at resolutions ranging from 72 to 120 dpi.

- Since monitors display with red, green, and blue primary colors, save images in the RGB or Indexed Color modes.

- Match the color depth of the saved image to the capability of the presentation program and display hardware. (RGB Color mode is 24 bit and Indexed Color mode is 8 bit.)

For more information on presentation graphics, multimedia, video, or animation refer to Chapter 12, "Multimedia." For information on file formats, see Appendix A, "File Formats."

Summary

- A wide variety of printers and other output devices can be used to print images created in Photoshop. They range from dot matrix printers on the low end to imagesetters and film recorders on the high end. Choose an output method appropriate to your project and within your budget.

- Be sure to calibrate your system for consistency and predictability.

- Learn how to use Photoshop's controls for the printing process, such as the Page Setup, Print, Printing Inks, and Separation Setup dialog boxes.

- Before outputting film separations for commercial printing, consult with the printer and service bureau about halftone screen frequency, halftone screen angles, dot shapes, ink limits, dot gain, printing emulsion up or down (as a positive or negative), file formats, resolution, etc.

- Choose a strategy for separations that matches your quality requirements and skills. If you are making the separations yourself, learn the technical issues that will produce acceptable results.

- When saving your image for use in another application, choose a file format compatible with your applications and platforms.

If RGB to CMYK conversions make your head spin, try working in multimedia, the subject of the next chapter.

Multimedia

Multimedia, the buzzword for the newest forms of mass communication in a fast evolving electronic era, depends heavily on visuals. The creation and production of visuals for multimedia demands an understanding of digital imaging. Most images used for video, film, television, interactive CD-ROMs and computer presentations must be processed in a program such as Photoshop.

In general, multimedia presentations involve the normal design considerations of print, plus issues of motion, sound, and timing usually associated with video. For purposes of this book, multimedia includes interactive computer presentations, television, CD-ROM, interactive on-line, slide show presentations, animation, video, and film.

How Photoshop Fits into Multimedia

The unifying factor between all forms of multimedia is that images (often with sound and text) are presented in sequence, from a simple slide show with a few images to a video animation that displays 30 images per second. Each change, even the slightest, requires a new graphic to bridge from one idea to the next, and Photoshop is one of the tools to create that bridge.

Macromedia Director, Authorware, VideoFusion, Adobe Premiere, Adobe Persuasion, DIVA VideoShop, Vividus Cinemation and other multimedia and animation authoring programs require quality images. Although primarily designed for print production, Photoshop's tools and special effects are essential for multimedia production. In addition to functioning as a basic multimedia image preparation program (sizing, cropping, retouching, color correcting, etc.), Photoshop can also create backgrounds, screen interfaces and buttons. More elaborate effects include animated filter effects, dynamic effects with the Stretch, Perspective and Distort commands, channel masks, layer effects, and rotoscoping.

This chapter gives you an overview of basics issues in multimedia, including sequential imaging and timing, delivery, and using Photoshop in conjunction with some multimedia programs. The chapter also discusses the preparation of images for video, film, animation, interactive CD-ROM and computer slide show presentations. First, however, it's important to understand how to organize an interactive multimedia presentation through storyboards, navigation and interface graphics, layering, and transitions.

Interactive Multimedia

Preparing for print media is simple in theory because you create a physical document that someone will read, hopefully, from start to finish. Video, film and animation also function in a linear fashion and are planned with the storyboard. A storyboard, drawn like a cartoon strip, describes a film or video production with a series of key images along with accompanying text, sound effects, and transitions.

Interactive multimedia, on the other hand, is nonlinear; the user should be able to move in many different directions. Interactive multimedia adds new design considerations to the digital process: navigation and branching. Most interactive multimedia presentations and storyboards are constructed like a family tree that branches, rather than like a linear cartoon strip. You begin with a single concept, like great-great-great grandma. She had ten children, and each of them had families, with the average number of divorces and second families. . .it can get complicated if you don't have that initial family tree diagram. And an interactive piece doesn't have to start with great-great grandma; it can start anywhere and go anywhere.

In any case, a script, storyboard and/or branching diagram will help you plan a successful multimedia production.

Navigation and the Screen Interface

The screen interface—the main screen, or series of screens, of your production—provides access to deeper levels of information. The participant will return to the interface again and again, so it must be consistent, compelling, and obvious. An interface that is transparent (used without noticing it) allows the user to focus on the content, whether it be computer-based training, a marketing presentation, sales brochure, or entertainment.

For example, the screen interface of the interactive CD-ROM *Color Made Easy* by Apple Computer contains compelling visuals and informative text to demonstrate the basics of color. (Figure 12–1). Each object in the still life scene has a problem: over pixelation, off registration, poor color

Figure 12–1
In the *Color Made Easy* multimedia interface for Apple Computer, clicking on each object leads the user to another level of information. (© Hagit Cohen, Grace Chen and Art Lab)

range, etc. The user clicks on an object or a button for a demonstration of the problem, and explores methods to correct the problem. The icon with six squares to the left of the still life takes the user back to the main menu.

Navigating through a production, the user must have a secure sense of his or her location at all times. Try to keep your show as simple as possible, building more layers and branching only if logic demands that you provide deeper levels of discovery. If possible, keep navigation controls to all the levels visible. Always have an escape for the user to get back to the top level without going through intermediate levels. The navigation paths may be apparent to you because you built the presentation, but a user who can't find his or her way around immediately will find the quickest way to quit (Figures 12–2 and 12–5).

Figure 12–2
Keep navigation controls visible at all levels and always have an escape for the user to get back to the top level or to quit (© Gary McDaniel)

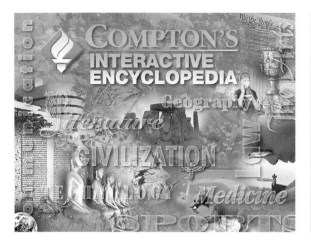 

Figure 12–3   The title page on the left uses text as a background to produce a mood and suggest the richness and depth contained in *Compton's Interactive Encyclopedia*. The text in the boxes on the right can be scrolled to read more, to be searched, listed in outline form, linked with images, and printed. (© Compton's New Media, produced by Raquel Aceves)

Text and Narration

Education, training, marketing, and research presentations usually require text as a main component. But let's face it: text can be difficult to read from glowing phosphors on a screen or a television projection. In most multimedia presentations, especially those designed for entertainment, text should be kept to a minimum. Give the user visual and audio instructions if you have the storage room by reinforcing text with narration.

Text can be integrated into backgrounds, appear as distinct narrative text fields (Figure 12–3), or function as simple graphic elements (Figure 12–6).

TIP: Narration and text together have more impact than does either alone, but they should either be identical word for word, or very different. If slightly different, the listener/reader will be disoriented and understand neither the visual nor the aural message. One strategy is to give detailed audio with basic text, or provide detailed text with basic audio.

Backgrounds

Backgrounds should be unified throughout a presentation. If your interface background graphic is low contrast (very light, very dark or mostly midtones) it will be easier to incorporate into your overall design. A simple method of designing a background is to take an image from the production and adjust its values in Photoshop with any of the image processing commands such as Brightness/Contrast, Levels or Curves. In Figure 12–4 the background was created by enlarging, adding noise and lightening one of the frames in the animation.

Figure 12–4
The background was created by enlarging, filtering and lightening one of the animation frames (© Mark Siprut).

Buttons

Navigation buttons like *Forward*, *Backward*, *Quit*, and *Help*, should appear in the same place on every screen (Figure 12–5). Similarly, type and levels of graphic information should always pop up in the same place, allowing the user to focus more on content than navigation.

Buttons should be obvious to use and easy for the mouse (or fingers) to click on. Buttons are satisfying if they depress visually, change color, or are accompanied with a sound (click, scream, word, explosion, meow...) when clicked. Words can also be buttons. Provide a visual clue that a word is hot (a button) by making it a different color or bold. For example, when the word "impact" is clicked in the MediaWeave show, broken glass appears with the word "POW" along with a sound affect (Figure 12–6).

An interface design for a touch screen kiosk should have large simple buttons. Figure 12–7 shows an interface from a kiosk where visitors to county buildings can access available county social services. The produc-

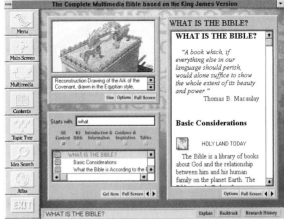

Figure 12–5   Navigate through this multimedia presentation, *The Complete Multimedia Bible based on the King James Version*, by clicking the buttons that appear along the left side throughout the production. (© Compton's New Media, produced by Raquel Aceves)

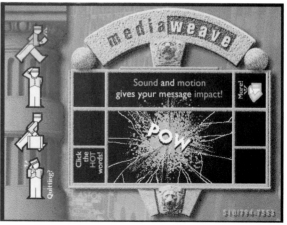

Figure 12–6   Buttons should be simple to use. Words and graphics can also be buttons—clicking on the word "impact" causes an explosion with broken glass and the graphic word "POW." (© Chris Swetlin, Mediaweave)

Figure 12–7   The large buttons for this touch screen kiosk are always in the same place, and facilitate navigation by children, elders, or anyone who might have problems activating the buttons. (© Chris Swetlin, Mediaweave)

tion is trilingual (English, Vietnamese, Spanish) to serve the agency's clientele. The large buttons are in the same place throughout the entire production to facilitate navigation. All graphic elements are as large as possible to accommodate children using the touch screen and to avoid problems with mistaken selections.

TIP: Buttons can also be invisible, appearing only when the user drags the cursor over them. This encourages exploration and can add mystery.

Buttons can be designed in many creative ways. Use Photoshop to draw, retouch and mask interesting shapes. In Figure C-26 (in the Color Section) Chris Swetlin created the tools in the red toolbox by placing actual tools on a flatbed scanner, and then masking, retouching, and compositing them in Photoshop. Each tool is a button that performs a metaphorical function when clicked.

Sequential Imaging

Sequential images produce animations, one of the most exciting features of a multimedia presentation. Sequential imaging is effective when most of the elements are consistent (such as the background, the sound, the colors, etc.) but the area you want to be noticed changes.

TIP: Keep your animations simple. Your client or other circumstances (such as delivery, memory, or money) could force you to change your design. Also, the simpler the animation, the less data must be jammed through your computer.

FILE SIZES VERSUS SPEED

Normal animation for video runs at 30 fps (frames per second), but animation run at 15 fps or less can look very credible. Animations that start small and grow to fill the entire screen will bring your computer to its knees; as more and more screen must be redrawn your CPU has to sprint to keep up, and will ultimately lose the race. To facilitate running animation sequences at faster rates, use an image area smaller than the full screen. The smaller the image area, the faster and smoother the animation will run. In the bubble gum transition of an animated button (Figure 12–8), there are only four frames and a "pop, " but the viewer connects all the images and perceives that the bubble grows much larger than the actual display size.

Figure 12–8   There are only a few frames and a "pop" in this interactive button, but the viewer connects all the images, perceiving that the image grows much larger than actual size.(© Eric Benson).

Figure 12–9   A simple sequence of looped drawings keep the screen alive during an introduction discussing coffee in a travelogue presentation. (© Anna Stump)

The challenge of imbedding animations and movies into a multimedia presentation is to make them a part of the whole piece, not just appendages that move outside the context of the rest of the design. Try revealing the animation by wiping part of the background away, like a sliding door. Or design the background of the animation to be the same color as the interface background.

CONSTANT MOVEMENT

Interactive multimedia requires that the viewer be constantly stimulated, whether visually, aurally, or tactilely. Because we have been so heavily influenced by the television culture, we need a constant flow of images to stay interested.

In general, something should move on the screen in your multimedia presentation at all times. Even a small element will capture the users attention or act as a vehicle to take him or her to the next idea. Looping a simple 2-D animation can do the trick, such as looping several drawings of the same object (Figure 12–9).

TRANSITIONS AS MOTION

Transitions get the user from one idea to the next in a smooth, logical manner. Transitions should advance your story unobtrusively (you want the user to focus on the idea, not the flash).

The most basic transitions are simple cuts and dissolves. To get an idea of how universal and effective these transitions are, watch television for a minute and count the cuts. It's tempting to use the fancy effects possible with Photoshop and multimedia programs, but roll downs, explosions, and peel backs get old fast. Waiting for an image to change, even a few seconds, can be frustrating. The user wants instant feedback or gets bored.

Effective transitions gradually reveal another image or part of an image. For example, the rain drops falling on the panoramic series of Crater Lake gradually reveal the background (Figure 12–10).

Figure 12–10   Rain drops reveal the background in this interactive interface of Crater Lake (© Eric Benson).

Delivery   Knowing the delivery platform is as important as identifying your target audience. Output possibilities can include television, computer screen, slide shows, film, video projection systems, CD-ROM, disk, video tape, slide shows, etc.

You should design for output on the lowest common denominator if you don't know the final platform for display or if it will change. For example, if you do all your development on a Power Macintosh or Pentium computer and don't take into consideration that someone may be viewing your production on a Mac Classic, you will have a very disappointed and confused audience because the display will be in black and white and cropped.

Many multimedia applications do not require a great deal of memory, such as a touch screen kiosk or interactive games that contain lower resolution graphics, and few digital video movies and sound files. If you are delivering your product on CD-ROM, you don't have to be as thrifty with your data as you do when sending an electronic brochure out on a 1.4 Mb floppy disk.

Preparation for Television

Color television screens and computer color monitors function differently (otherwise we would not pay up to ten times more for the latter). Knowing a little about the technical differences between the two will better prepare you to create images that will transfer from your computer to and play well on a television screen.

Both monitors and television screens use red, green, and blue (RGB) electron guns to paint the dots (pixels) on the screen creating a color image. Both paint one line of pixels at a time, from left to right, starting at the top and going to the bottom of your screen. The similarity ends there.

The National Television System Committee (NTSC) sets the standard and defines how color is encoded for television playback in the United

States, Mexico, Canada and Japan. Discussed below are some pitfalls that can occur when transferring from computer (RGB) to television (NTSC) or vice versa, and how to avoid them.

TIP: Consider purchasing an output device (a small television) for your computer that will allow viewing of images in real time on an NTSC monitor. You will be able to see problems as they are occur and make corrections on the spot.

Fixing Flickering Images

When running an animation, the computer monitor displays each frame in passes of one-pixel lines from top to bottom. A regular television set uses two passes to paint each frame. The odd-numbered lines are painted first, and then even numbered ones are painted as the odd ones fade out. This process is called interlacing.

If one-pixel-width lines or very small serif type are present, there will be a flicker on the screen because the one-pixel-wide parts of the image are being painted on every other pass. Because this occurs very quickly, it appears as flickering or shimmering. If those lines were two pixels wide, at least half of the line would show up each time, greatly reducing the flickering effect. So when you develop images for television or NTSC format (i.e., computer to videotape), avoid one-pixel horizontal lines and fine serif typefaces.

When working with an image captured from NTSC with something less than a frame-accurate video deck, use the Photoshop De-Interlace filter from the Video submenu under the Filter menu to remove either the odd or the even lines. This filter will then replace the lines removed by duplicating the existing lines or by interpolating between lines. Try it both ways to see which works best for your file.

Avoiding Bleeding Colors

NTSC uses a reduced range of colors (gamut) to produce the best possible images within the medium's inferior capabilities. Computers can use millions of colors and some are too bright when played on an NTSC system. The color gamut of RGB Color does not match the gamut of NTSC Color. The colors will either change to a different hue or the color from one bright pixel may bleed over and impact on neighboring pixels, causing the image to look fuzzy. Greens, blues, and yellows are also easily oversaturated. The NTSC Colors filter, in the Video submenu under the Photoshop Filters menu, restricts colors to those acceptable for the television standard.

Normally, the relative lack of resolution of standard NTSC video is a drawback in terms of quality. However, the softening effects of NTSC may actually improve the overall image quality of animation files created with the standard Macintosh system color palette.

To optimize hard disk space when creating lengthy animations use 8-bit palettes, especially when outputting to low-end video peripherals. There is a major drawback to working in 8-bit when designing for video: dithering. Dithered 8-bit images often look fine when viewed in RGB, but can become really obnoxious on video. Dithering creates many single pixels, much like the fine serifs and single-pixel lines mentioned earlier, and will cause the same offensive flickering or shimmering, even in relatively low-end video formats such as VHS or Hi-8.

Creating Readable Type

Computer screens have a higher resolution than television screens. Small text may look fine on a computer screen, but when transferred to television (NTSC) text might become unreadable. Use at least 18-point type for text; 24- to 96-point type is even more desirable. For smaller type use sans serif fonts instead of serif. Use drop shadows or 3-D lettering to set titles apart from the background.

Using the NTSC Safe Area

When images transfer from computer to NTSC, 10 to 20% of the image will crop. To ensure that an image is properly displayed, it should be designed appropriately. When using the Macintosh standard 640 x 480 pixels (13-inch) monitor, anything outside 576 x 432 pixels will not show up on an NTSC monitor. Stationary text should be limited to a 504 x 384 pixel area. Consider using a channel mask as a visual reminder of these borders.

Video Capture and Recording

Some video capture cards manage a full 32–bits of information (like NuVista, RasterOps and Radius). This means that along with 24 bit RGB information they can store an additional 8–bits that can function as a channel (i.e., 32 bit board). The extra 8– bits can be used from Photoshop by selecting Video Alpha from the pop-out menu in the Channels palette.

Serious animators who already have a Macintosh II or higher with a video capture board, a video to NTSC output device, and a video tape recorder (VTR) can add DQ–Animaq video animation controller (NuBus board) and QuickPass software with Photoshop plug-ins from DiaQuest. By working through these special plug-ins, frames can be captured directly from videotape. They can then be edited, and recorded back to a different place on the same videotape without leaving Photoshop. The QuickPass software can bypass the normal pre-roll procedures in the animation rendering process, significantly reducing rendering times.

Animated Sequences Created with Photoshop

This section offers some suggested tools and techniques for creating animated sequences in Photoshop. Any effect applied repeatedly and saved each time as a new file can provide a series of images for a multimedia or video presentation. In general, the more increments used, the smoother the overall effect. Be sure to save the files in a file format, color depth and resolution compatible with your authoring program.

Using Filters

Although Photoshop's special effects filters do wonders with still images, they truly come to life in creating animation. Most useful are filters that have adjustable parameters, so you can gradually modify an image over time by processing it through a filter, increasing (or decreasing) the parameter increments (or decrements) with each pass while saving each iteration.

The general flow of the process is as follows:

1. Open an image into the RGB Color or Grayscale mode and then select, crop, and size it as required.

2. Save the image to a disk in the Photoshop format.

3. Determine how long the animated effect will last and how many frames you will need. For example, for a two second long sequence at 15 frames per second, you must create 30 individual frames. Thus you have 30 incremental changes to make over 30 separate files. Determine the increments you will use for the filter, choose the filter from the Filter menu, and enter the desired parameter values in the filter dialog box.

4. Once the filter effect has been applied to the image, if necessary convert to Indexed Color mode under the Mode menu, and choose the appropriate options (Resolution, Palette, and Dither) from the dialog box.

5. Select the Save a Copy command under the File menu. Choose the appropriate file format from the Format pop-up menu and name the file, adding a sequence extension number to keep the files in numerical order.

> **TIP:** Good file-naming habits save time and frustration in the long haul. For example, if more than 100 and less than 999 images are to be used, begin the numbering with 001 instead of 1 (e.g., Animate.001).

6. After saving the file, choose the Revert command under the File menu to reopen the original file.

7. Apply the next filter pass, and repeat the conversion and saving process above. Repeat these steps for the number of frames needed.

8. Finally, sequence these frames in an animation program such as Macromedia Director or Adobe Premiere.

Most filters in Photoshop can be used for animation effects. (Refer to Chapter 9, "Filters," for more information on using filters.) Filters can also create an infinite range of backgrounds for your presentations (look ahead to Figure 12–15). Experiment and use your imagination, starting with the following suggestions:

GAUSSIAN BLUR DISSOLVES

By taking advantage of the programmable Gaussian Blur filter, you can create an animated "blur-on" effect that is distinctly different from the various dissolve transitions found in animation programs. Enter different amounts into the Radius factor in the Gaussian Blur filter dialog box as follows: Start by determining the number of steps for the dissolve (5 to 10 frames work well); use a Gaussian Blur setting of between 20 and 30, and in increments of 4 to 5, gradually decreasing the blur factor until the image is normal. You can also reverse this sequence starting with a normal image and going to a full blur (Figure 12–11).

MOTION BLUR

The Motion Blur filter produces the illusion of something moving past you at high speed by blurring the moving object or the background. This filter can compensate for large pixel jumps in frame-by-frame animation to give the appearance of smoother motion. The Motion Blur filter allows you to determine the angle and distance of the blur effect. The longer the distance, the more "trail" is left behind the moving object. You can also blur the background while the moving object remains sharp. The angle relates to the motion of the object, so if the object is moving at a 30° angle with respect to the horizontal plane, then the blur should also be at 30° (Figure 12–25).

RADIAL BLUR

Similar to the Motion Blur, the Radial Blur gives the illusion of rotation around a definable center point or zooming-in on the defined point (Figure 12–12).

Figure 12–11
The Gaussian Blur technique (at 4, 10 and 30 pixels) was applied to the original image on the left
(© Sally Everding)

Figure 12–12
The Radial Blur technique was applied to the original image on the left with the amount set at 10, 50 and 100 (© Sally Everding).

Figure 12–13
The Twirl filter was applied at 60°, 100°, and 500° to the original image on the left (© Sally Everding).

TWIRL

Use incremental steps of 10 to 50 in the Twirl dialog, up to a maximum of 999, for a dramatic twirl effect (Figure 12–13). An alternative is to use the twirl filter in reverse sequence, creating an animation that starts with a fully twirled image and ends with the original untwirled image. Words can twirl onto the screen out of a misty background by gradually building up the brightness or transparency of the twirling image as it unfurls.

PLUG-IN FILTERS

Plug-in filters, such as Andromeda, Kai's Power Tools, Aldus Gallery Effects, Second Glance Chromassage, and Xaos Tool's Paint Alchemy, add tremendous flexibility and power to Photoshop. Placed in the Photoshop plug-ins folder on the Macintosh or the PLUGINS directory on a PC, they become available under the Filters menu. Many Plug-in filters also work in other programs such as Fractal Design Painter and Adobe Premier. For example, the plug-in filter Paint Alchemy has sliders that can yield a different result when manually changed over time (Figure 12–14).

Figure 12–14
An animation sequence created with Xaos Tool's Paint Alchemy.

Dynamic Effects

By incrementally applying any of the dynamic effects under the Image menu, Rotate, Scale, Skew, Perspective and Distort, the viewing angle of forms can appear to change. Shapes can actually appear to move as three dimensional forms as they go through a series of distortions. Some examples include turning a page of an illustrated book, spinning a plate with an image mapped onto its surface, text in perspective rolling in from the background, and images mapped onto the sides of flying shapes (Figure 12–15).

Layers and Channels

The multiple layers possible in a single Photoshop document naturally facilitate creating animations in Photoshop. Layers function like sheets of clear acetate overlaid on each other in perfect registration, as in conventional cell animation. Traditional animation effects can be created in Photoshop, including independent movement of foreground elements in relation to the background, tracing scanned or video captured images (rotoscoping), transitions, and multiple blending effects.

Photoshop's masking capabilities with channels can augment complex layered image effects. Channels can be combined by copy and pasting, drag and dropping, or with the Calculations command. Loading a selection from a channel offers additional masking options.

MOVING ELEMENTS INDEPENDENTLY

Animate an image independent of the background by placing it on a new layer over the background layer. Multiple layers can be used for multiple

Figure 12–15   An animation sequence created with the Rotate, Scale, Perspective and Distort commands

Figure 12–16   By placing each image on a different layer, it can be moved independently for each frame. (Rabbit and turtle courtesy of CMCD, Inc.)

images at different distances from the viewer (Figure 12–16). The following steps suggest the use of layers to give a sense of depth to movement:

1. Open an image to use as a background. Create a new blank layer.

2. Open or draw an image that you want to move across the background. If its not already silhouetted, carefully trace or mask the shape, select and then paste it on the blank layer in the background document.

3. Add more images, each on its own layer for a greater sense of depth.

4. Use the Move tool to change the position of the foreground shapes. After each changed position, choose Duplicate under the Image menu and click the Merged Layers Only button. This will flatten the visible layers in the duplicated documents. Save each version (in an appropriate file format) with a new number after it.

TRACING

Scanned drawings, photographs or video clips can be traced on a new layer over the original scan. To draw animated variations of an image, create a new layer over an image on the Background layer. Change the blending mode to Multiply or use Normal at 50% Opacity. You can now draw on the layer while tracing the background layer. After completing the tracing make another new layer and repeat the process. Continue making new layers and tracing for each frame. Duplicate each layer as a new document and save each as a separate numbered file in an appropriate file format.

A traditional animation technique, *Rotoscoping*, uses original filmed sequences as a basis for drawing animations. Use the above technique over each frame of a scanned film sequence or digitized video (Figure 12–23). For more on Rotoscoping, see the section later in this chapter on Video and Animation.

Figure 12–17   Use the Opacity control and Blending modes in the Layers palette to incrementally blend one image into another. (Trees and leaf courtesy of Digital Stock)

TRANSITIONS

Two images on independent layers over each other can be gradually blended from one to another using the Opacity control and Blending modes in the Layers palette or Layers Options dialog box. Start with a mild change and gradually increase the settings, saving a copy each time, until a complete change is accomplished (Figure 12–17).

FILTER DISTORTIONS

To achieve filter distortions duplicate the image on the background layer to a new layer several times. On each layer, apply a slightly different filter effect. When you have the desired effect, duplicate each layer to a new document and save each with a new number after the name. Try combining some of the layers with Opacity or Blending modes and then use the Duplicate command under the Image menu to duplicate only the merged layers.

MASKING AN ANIMATION WITH A LAYER MASK

Mask a moving image inside of another shape by attaching a Layer Mask to a layer (Figure 12–18). Visualize yourself sitting in a train, viewing the scenery that appears to flow past the window. This effect might be used for a logo, in which the text of the logo is like the train window.

1. Open a document to use as a background, such as a landscape, wall, pattern or texture.
2. Create a new layer in the Layers palette and enter some large black type or create a solid black graphic.
3. Create another new layer in the Layers palette and in the New Layer dialog box, clicking the Group With Previous Layer button. Grouping this layer with the layer beneath will convert the transparent areas in

Figure 12–18
A Layer Mask was used to mask the background from the shape of the letters so that the movement appears only inside the letters.

the lower layer into a mask. Any imagery on the upper layer will appear only in the unmasked areas.

4. Open or create an image to animate inside the masked graphic and copy it to the Clipboard. Use an image at least twice the size of the graphic. Paste the Clipboard image onto the upper layer. It will appear as a masked shape.

5. Select the Offset filter in the Other submenu under the Filter menu. Click the Wrap Around option and enter 2 to 5 pixels in the Horizontal text field. Click OK. The image will move horizontally only within the masked area.

6. Choose the Duplicate command under the Image menu with the Merged Layers Only option clicked. Save the duplicated document in an appropriate file format with an extension number such as .01.

7. Repeat steps 6 and 7 for each frame. Each time you select the Offset filter, the image on the upper layer will move to the right inside of the masked area. The Wrap Around feature causes a duplicate of the moving image to come in as the original moves out of the scene. One full cycle will create enough frames to loop the sequence in a multimedia or animation program.

A FILTER EFFECT COMBINED WITH A CHANNEL MASK

Here is another example using two effects at the same time: distorting one image with the Twirl filter while dissolving it into a second image. Getting the second image to fade in can be somewhat challenging. One method is to use the Threshold command with a channel mask presenting increments of the second image over the first image. Adjustments of the Threshold

Figure 12–19 Each frame in this animation sequence was created by rotating the image in Layer 1, copying it to a new channel to make a mask with the Threshold command, and then reloading the mask to clear the areas showing the image in the Background Layer. (© Bruce Powell)

command in each increment will cause a little more of the second image to appear in the first with each step (Figure 12–19).

1. Open two different images that are the same size. Copy one to a new layer of the other. You should have a document with an image in the Background Layer and a second image in Layer 1. Save this document as "Original."

2. Choose Duplicate under the Image menu. Flatten the image (Layers palette pop-up menu) and save it in an appropriate file format for your destination animation or multimedia program, giving it an extension number such as .01.

3. Return to the original document and duplicate it. In the duplicate document, make Layer 1 the target, apply the Twirl filter at 50° and copy it to the Clipboard. In the Channels palette, make a new channel and paste the Clipboard image.

4. With the new channel active, select the Threshold command in the Map submenu under the Image menu. Move the slider to the right so that only a small area in the image turns white. Click OK.

5. Make the composite channel (color) or the Black channel (grayscale) active and choose Load Selection under the Select menu. (Layer 1 should still be the target layer.) Load the channel with the threshold mask. Choose Clear under the Edit menu (or use the Delete key). The image on the Background layer will show through the transparent (cleared) areas.

6. Flatten the image (Layers palette pop-up menu) and save it in an appropriate file format and give it an extension number such as .02.

7. Repeat the process starting at step 3 through step 6 for every frame, giving each the next sequential number with the document name when saving. Add 50° each time to the Twirl filter, giving each frame a greater rotation angle. When applying the Threshold command to the channel, move the slider slightly more to the left each time, leaving more white area. Each subsequent frame should have a greater rotation and show more of the background image until the last frame, which should show only the background image.

Using Photoshop with other Programs for Multimedia

You can use a variety of methods to exchange images between Photoshop and other programs when creating multimedia presentations or animations. Before starting on a project learn which formats are required to transfer images between the various programs and platforms to be used. Since most images prepared for presentation graphics, multimedia, video, or animation will usually be displayed on a computer monitor or television you should set the proper resolution, color mode and color depth.

Most presentation, multimedia, and animation programs on the Macintosh prefer the PICT format for importing images. Most Windows applications prefer the .BMP, .PCX, or .TIF file formats.

On the Macintosh, multiple images can be copied to a scrapbook file to be imported all at once by some programs. Use a scrapbook management program such as Smartscrap from Solutions Inc. to create and file separate scrapbook files. A Scrapbook file can be accessed In Photoshop by choosing the PICT Resource command in the Acquire submenu under the File menu. Each image can be opened as an independent file (Figure 12–26).

Files can also be transferred between Macintosh and Windows platforms in various file formats. Like Photoshop, many programs such as Macromedia Director, Adobe Premier, MacroModel and Kodak Arrange-It function almost identically on both platforms. When transferring projects between platforms, be aware that fonts, color palettes or color depth may not work the same on the other platform. Developing a project on the delivery platform will insure more predictable results.

Multimedia

Macromedia Director, a two-dimensional interactive multimedia and animation authoring program available both for Macintosh and Windows, provides up to 48 layers, or channels, of independent movable objects (sprites) on the screen at once, as well as simultaneous sound effects from two sound tracks (Figure 12–20). Director also has an extensive English-like programming language, Lingo, which allows creation of elaborate interactive presentations that can also control external electronic devices.

Director can import a variety of image and animation file formats, as well as sounds, palettes, and other Director movies to be orchestrated into interactive animated presentations. On the Macintosh, Director can import PICT, MacPaint, Sound, Scrapbook, PICS, and QuickTime movie files (Figure 12–21). In Windows, Director can import bitmaps (.BMP), metafiles (.WMF), MacPaint (.PNT), Macintosh PICT (.PCT), TIFF (.TIF), Encapsulated Postscript (.EPS), PC Paintbrush (.PCX), Photo CD (.PCD), GIF (.GIF), Sound (.AIF and .WAV), Digital Video movies (.AVI and .MOV), and Animator movies (.FLC and .FLI) files.

Color palettes are an important issue to consider when creating graphics for Director. Because most CD-ROM's must be playable on 8–bit color systems, animations/movies are usually created in Director in the 8–bit (256

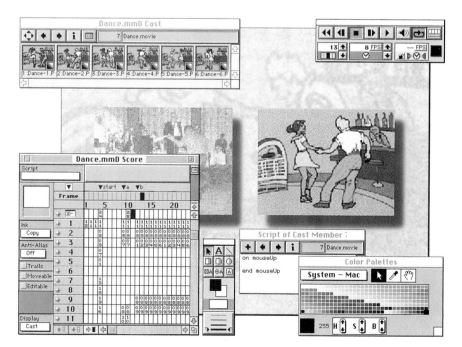

Figure 12–20
The Macromedia
Director interface
showing the Stage, Cast,
Panel, Color Palette,
Tools, Script, and
Score windows.

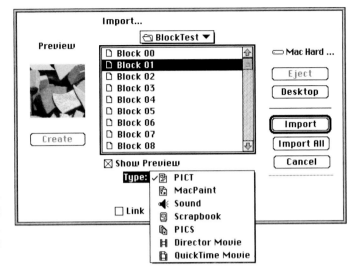

Figure 12–21
The Macromedia Director Import command accesses a variety of formats including sounds.

color) mode. You can import 24–bit images directly into Director and resample them to 8–bit within the program, but Photoshop resamples more efficiently than Director. Director can also play in the 24–bit mode if you have a fast computer system with a 24–bit monitor.

Good multimedia shows tend to have the fewer palettes. Director can handle more colors than the standard system color palette contains, but with drawbacks: palette changes slow down the overall flow of the presentation, use up valuable castmember positions, consume more memory, and usually cause visual discomfort during the palette transitions. To manage the color palette situation effectively, without having to use the system palette, set the color palettes in Photoshop first or make a custom palette in a program like DeBabelizer from Equilibrium.

TIP: When converting an RGB Photoshop file to Indexed Color mode, the number of bits of color information per pixel can be specified from 3–bits (8–colors) to 8–bits (256–colors). Although 8–bits are normally used for images ending up in Director, converting images to 6 or 7 bits reserves color palette positions for consistent or recurring colors in the Director animation (such as control buttons for interactive presentations that are always the same color).

Video and Animation

Adobe Premiere combines video, audio, animation, still images and graphics into movies on both the Macintosh and Windows platforms (Figure 12–22). Use Photoshop along with Premiere to touch up still images, create special effects, produce animated sequences, and create transitions.

Video clips from Premiere can be imported into Photoshop in the Filmstrip format for retouching, filter effects, color correction or use as a

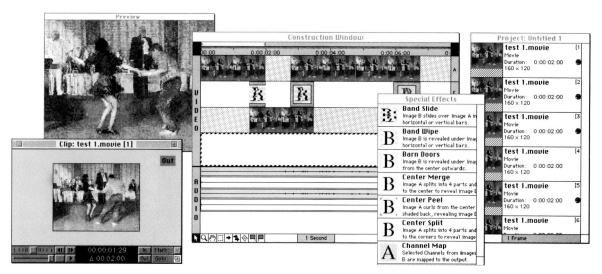

Figure 12–22   Adobe Premiere with the Preview, Clip, Construction, Special Effects and Project windows open.

template to draw cartoon type animation, a conventional technique called *Rotoscoping* (the traditional animation technique of tracing from individual frames of a film). After editing the filmstrip in Photoshop it can be exported back to Premiere in the Filmstrip format. No audio associated with that movie will be transferred, but as long as the number of frames in the filmstrip has not been changed, the filmstrip links back up with the original sound in Premiere.

The following Rotoscoping technique uses a video clip from Premier, saved in the Filmstrip format. The RasterOps 24XLTV card was used to digitized the original video into the QuickTime format (Figure 12–23 and C–24 in the Color Section).

1. Begin in Premiere by creating or opening a QuickTime movie to be edited. Use the Clip window to locate the section of the movie you want to edit. Mark the 'In' and 'Out' points to specify the sequence to be exported. With the Clip window still open, use the Export command to create a Filmstrip export file.

2. Open the file in Photoshop. It will display as a series of frames with a scrolling window (Figure 12–23a). Filmstrips automatically open in the RGB Color mode as the Background Layer with an additional fourth channel masking each frame (Figure 12–23b).

CAUTION: You can edit and manipulate a Filmstrip file in Photoshop with most tools and commands, but do not scale, crop, or

Figure 12–23
An example of the
Rotoscoping technique.
Left to right: (a) the
original Filmstrip from
Adobe Premiere open in
Photoshop in the
Background Layer; (b)
filmstrips automatically
open with a fourth
channel masking each
frame; (c) the
Background Layer is
lightened and traced
over in a new layer;
(d) after drawing the
main characters,
repeating elements are
drawn and pasted into
each frame.

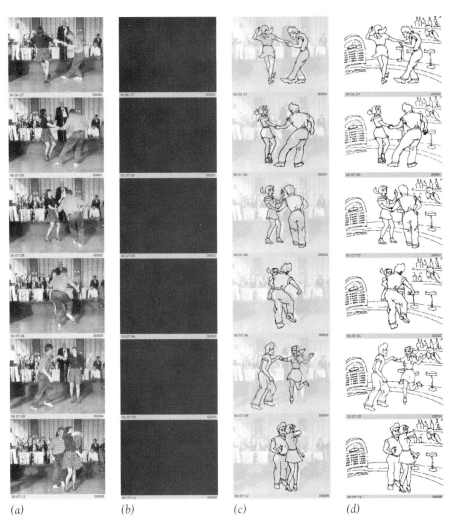

(a)   (b)   (c)   (d)

change the resolution of the document. **Any size or resolution changes will make the file unsaveable in the Filmstrip format.**

3. Create a new layer in the Layers palette. Leave the new layer as the target layer and keep both layer visible. Trace over each frame to create new characters. Any repeating elements can be copied and pasted to each frame. As you draw try changing the Opacity or Blending modes in order to see your work. You can also lighten the background with the Brightness/Contrast command.

4. After drawing all elements, add colors. Return to the Blending mode to Normal and Opacity to 100% (unless you want to blend your drawing with the original).

5. Choose Flatten Image in the Layers palette and save the file in the Filmstrip format.

6. Import the file into Premiere. The sounds, if any, can now be linked back up with the movie as long as the length has not changed.

TIP: To determine the number of frames to edit, Multiply the length of the effect times the frames per second (playback rate). For example, if an animated character should appear for 3 seconds on a filmstrip that will play at 15 fps, 45 frames will require editing. Frame by frame editing is tedious, so prepare yourself to invest some time.

DIVA VideoShop, a HyperCard based program for the Macintosh, can add rotoscoping to QuickTime movies using a similar method. Instead of a Filmstrip filter plug-in, a 'QTime' plug-in filter provided by Diva is placed in Photoshop's Plug-ins folder. Select a portion of a QuickTime movie in VideoShop and copy it to the Clipboard. The movie opens within Photoshop by first opening 'QTime' from the Acquire menu and choosing Clipboard. After editing the segment in Photoshop, choose 'QTime' from the Export menu. This saves the strip as a standard QuickTime movie. It can be brought back into VideoShop for further editing along with other movies, images, effects and sounds.

Morphing

Morph, a Macintosh and Windows program from Gryphon Software, starts with two different images and creates a series of in-between frames that can be animated as a movie. These in-between images appear as a gradual metamorphosis or transformation between the two original images. To produce the best looking Morph, the beginning and ending images should be exactly the same size, with the same or similar backgrounds. Use Photoshop to prepare (retouch, edit, scale and crop) the two images before morphing them (Figure 12–24).

Figure 12–24   Create in-between frames between two images with Morph.

Figure 12–25
The airplane, created in
Topaz on an IBM PC,
was saved in the TGA
format and then pasted
in the farm photograph.
The Motion filter was
applied in increasing
amounts to each frame
in the background only
(© Chris Swetlin and
Mark Siprut)

3-D Animation

Use Photoshop to edit or manipulate images created in 3-D programs. Most of the current programs such as Specular Infini–D, MacroModel, Ray Dream Designer, Specular LogoMotion, StrataVision, and Strata Studio Pro can save animation sequences in a variety of file formats compatible with both Photoshop and most multimedia authoring programs. You can also use Photoshop to create backgrounds to paste into a 3-D program prior to generating an animation sequence (Figure 12–25).

Most 3-D program file formats for still images will open directly into Photoshop, but at first glance multiple images stored on the Mac in the Scrapbook or PICS format seem inaccessible. Use the Acquire submenu under the File menu and choose PICT Resource. Select a Scrapbook or PICS file and Open. All frames will be available for editing one at a time in Photoshop (Figure 12–26). After clicking the Preview button in the dialog, click the arrow buttons to view each of the pictures in the file. Stop at the picture to be edited and click OK. Each image will open as an independent file.

Batch Processing

PhotoMatic from DayStar can automate most functions in Photoshop on the Macintosh. Any repetitive task can be automated by recording a script from a menu within Photoshop. PhotoMatic can also batch process a series of files by placing them into the PhotoMatic folder. The entire folder of images can then be processed in the background and placed automatically into another folder of finished work.

Figure 12–26
On the Macintosh, the
PICT Resource Acquire
command will open a
series of image stored in
a Scrapbook or in the
PICS format.

DeBabelizer from Equilibrium provides automated graphics batch processing, manipulation, and translation on the Macintosh. It indexes
(converts 24–bit images to 8–bit images) and creates a superpalette that
works for all the 8–bit images in a chosen file. All image work is first
done in 24–bit color in Photoshop and then transferred to DeBabelizer
for batch processing to reduce each image to its own 8–bit adaptive
palette (indexing). DeBabelizer creates a single superpalette, optimized to
work for all images in a project. Other DeBabelizer features include:
scripting; automated batch processing such as cropping, scaling, and saving in a variety of formats; cross platform translation; and automated use
of Photoshop plug-ins.

Adobe ScreenReady can automatically rasterize files from most programs
and file formats (even EPS file) to prepare them for use in multimedia, animation, or video authoring programs.

Screen Capture

CameraMan from Motion Works can record anything appearing on the
screen, including menus and dialog boxes, and save a recording as a movie
or capture a still shot. On the Macintosh, CameraMan can save a recording
in the QuickTime or PICS format or in a series of still frames as PICT files.
On the Windows platform, CameraMan can save a recording in the Video
for Windows (.AVI) format and capture still shots in the Bitmap (.BMP)
format. Start recording with a definable function key and stop recording
with another function key. CameraMan has simple editing tools as well as
sound recording features.

Capture from Mainstay on the Macintosh allows you to record any
image, including menus and dialog boxes, and save the image in a variety
of file formats as well as to the Clipboard or Scrapbook.

Windows has a built in screen capture feature (press the Print Screen key), which records the screen to the Clipboard which can then be pasted into Photoshop. Several shareware screen capture utilities such as WinCapture from Professional Capture Systems are also available.

Summary

- To produce a successful multimedia production, plan a project with a script, storyboard, or branching diagram.
- Create simple buttons and backgrounds that are easy to see and use. Pay attention to size, contrast and colors when creating elements intended to facilitate navigation.
- In an interactive presentation, keep buttons in the same place and always provide an escape button to return to the top level without going through intermediate levels. Don't forget a Quit button.
- Save files from Photoshop in the proper file format, resolution, color depth, and size required by the destination multimedia or animation authoring program.
- Design and create presentations for the specific final display program and platform. If you don't know the final platform for display or if it will change, design for the lowest common denominator, such as the smallest display, slowest machine or least number of display colors.
- When preparing images for television output make sure that the colors are within the gamut of NTSC reproducible colors.
- Any effect in Photoshop applied repeatedly and saved each time as a new file can provide an interesting series of images for a multimedia or video presentation.
- Trace scanned images or sequential video frames by placing the original on the Background Layer and drawing on a new layer.
- Use a batch processing program to process several images or repetitive tasks automatically.

Good luck on your multimedia productions. For some Photoshop tips and techniques from other artists that you may be able to incorporate into your work, check out the final chapter of this book, "Case Studies."

CHAPTER 13

Case Studies

This chapter presents images from a cross section of Photoshop users: well established and emerging artists, illustrators, graphic designers, educators, medical illustrators, journalists, and photographers.

All of these artists offered hints, explanations, and ideas. We would like to thank these busy people for their contributions.

A Note on the Artistic Process

In the early years of digital imaging, programmers and artists began experimenting with the new technology and tools. The digital process was often more analytic than artistic, and digital images were criticized for their lack of serious artistic merit and mature design sense.

But as technology and mediums such as Photoshop have matured and become available to a wider range of people from diverse backgrounds, digital artwork has come closer to pure art. Artists are now aware that they are contributing to a new aesthetic and ideology. There is more doubt and, therefore, more searching and self exploration in the media rather than of the media.

Photographer Stephen Johnson expresses the responsibility he feels when he creates digital images:

> I wonder how this work will stand the test of time. Sometimes I do feel as though I'm flailing about, casting nets as far as I can throw just to see what happens. The danger is that the work will become the products of the tools, rather than the imagination. To some degree that is inevitable, the media always limits. It is sad, but at this point in the development of digital imagery, the tools and techniques almost completely dominate the

discussion, and the images. That is clearly a measure of how early on we are in this process, and how far this new media has to go to mature. It is now mostly possibility.

Black and White Gallery

"RACCOON LAKE" BY DAVID HERROLD

David Herrold (Figure 13–1) received his MFA from Wichita State University in Kansas and his BS from Emporia State University in Kansas. He is currently an Associate Professor of Art at De Pauw University, Greencastle, Indiana.

Herrold's system includes a Mac IIfx with 8 Mb RAM, HP ScanJet Plus scanner and HP LaserJet 4MP printer.

Step by Step

1. Herrold began with 8 × 10 inch black-and-white prints shot with a 35 mm Nikon N6006. After deciding on a general idea and collecting the necessary photographs, he scanned them. He then used the computer to experiment with different compositions at 50% of the final scale (low resolution).

2. The first rough composite of the background for "Raccoon Lake" was made with four prints photographed in panorama (Figure 13–2).

3. The edges between the prints were fused together and cleaned up with the Rubber Stamp tool (Figure 13–3).

Figure 13–1   "Raccoon Lake" by David Herrold

Figure 13–2
Rough composite of four
separate photographs

Figure 13–3
The edges were blended
with the Rubber
Stamp tool.

Figure 13–4
Herrold experimented
with composition
and perspective.

4. Herrold added several potential objects to experiment with the composition. Elements were resized, rotated, and moved about on top of the background both to get a feel for how they looked and to resolve the perspective (Figure 13–4). He pasted the clipboard images with the Floating Selection slider in the Paste Control dialog box (Photoshop 2) set to 254 or less to remove the white area surrounding the object being pasted.

NOTE: Paste Controls in Photoshop 2.0 was changed to Composite Controls in Version 2.5. In Photoshop 3.0 this feature is in the Layer Options palette.

5. The Trees were all based on a single image (Figure 13–5). It was photographed against the sky to be sure that the detailed parts were already

Figure 13–5   The newspaper, woman and tree were masked and copied out of other documents. The tree was bent and stretched with the Skew command.

against a white background— otherwise it would have been difficult to separate it as a distinct shape. The lower part of the background was removed by tracing around the tree with the Lasso tool. Herrold then altered the one tree by selecting branches, moving them to away from the tree slightly and extending existing edges with the Rubber Stamp tool.

6. The Tree appears bent by the pressure of wind because the artist selected successively smaller parts of the upper foliage and used the Skew command to stretch and distort it. The Blur tool was used to soften the edges of the pasted elements.

7. In the final version the woman was placed behind the picnic table. The table was copied from an earlier version and pasted on top again. Herrold added the overcast sky, suggesting a diffuse light source, so the strong shadows under the picnic table were eliminated.

Thoughts of the Artist

I have collected an archive of prints filed by category: people, trees, cars, complete backgrounds, etc. Completing an image often involves returning to a site with a printout in progress in order to retake a shot from a different angle to solve a perspective or lighting problem. Most of the time and effort is spent making the original photographs and playing with ideas.

I am interested in landscape imagery that reflects large scale human activities: industrial, agricultural, and so on. My approach is somewhat like a short story fiction writer in the sense that I invent spaces and activities that are not true taken as a whole but draw on facts that work together in a way that is plausible. I try to retain a sense of photographic factual truth but at the same time create a surreal atmosphere with mildly contradictory perspective or lighting between elements. Although the images refer to human interaction with the landscape, they are not documentary so I try to avoid political/ecological overtones.

"ESTO NO ES BERLIN" BY CRAIG FREEMAN

Craig Freeman received his BA from the University of California at San Diego and his MFA at the University of Colorado, Boulder. He is currently a Professor of Art at the University of Florida in Gainesville.

"Esto No Es Berlin" (Figure 13–6) is a proposal for a public art project at the San Ysidro, California/Tijuana, Baja California border. The final images would measure 8' × 24' and would be attached on the fence that separates the USA and Mexico. Says Freeman, "The project is designed to raise debate about the environmental and social issues that surround free trade."

Step by Step

1. The components were shot on Kodak Plus X film with a Mamiya RB67 camera. The negatives were printed in a darkroom and scanned with a Microtek 600ZS flatbed scanner into Adobe Photoshop on a Macintosh IIci.

2. Freeman began the composite by optimizing the tonal range of the background image with Curves and cropping it into the 1 × 3 aspect ratio. He then matched the tonal range of the remaining components (Figure 13–7 and 13–8).

3. He selected the Calaveras and the toxic drum with the Lasso tool set with a 1 pixel feather and saved the selections as channels.

4. He copied and pasted each image into new and separate documents, saving them as PICT files to be viewed sequentially with KPT QuickShow to assure smooth transitions.

5. The mural images will be printed on a Hewlett-Packard DesignJet 650C Plotter.

Thoughts of the Artist

I find the computer much more versatile than the conventional darkroom. However, there is also a danger that digital imaging brings to the field of photography: It seems all too often these days that content and image meaning are being eclipsed by a fetish obsession with gadgets and glitzy affects. Photography is about ideas and the computer is just another tool to express those ideas.

Figure 13–6
"Esto No Es Berlin" by
Craig Freeman

Figure 13–7   The background image for "Esto No Es Berlin"

Figure 13–8   The original sequential images of the Calaveras

"PLAYGROUND, TEXAS" BY DAN BURKHOLDER

Dan Burkholder attended Franklin and Marshall College in Lancaster, Pennsylvania, and received his BA and Master's Degrees from Brooks Institute of Photography in Santa Barbara, California. He teaches photography at the University of Texas at San Antonio.

Burkholder photographs with a 35mm camera because of its spontaneity and wide lens availability. He works exclusively in black and white, making enlarged negatives for contact printing to his platinum/palladium prints. To prepare the prints, prior to exposure Dan hand-coats a premium quality 100% cotton rag paper, adding small amounts of gold, lead, and mercury to fine-tune the image contrast and color. His most recent work combines digital imaging with the platinum printing process (Figure 3–9).

The Platinum/Palladium print is one of photography's oldest printing processes. Unlike the conventional black and white print, in which the tones of gray and black are comprised of metallic silver, in the platinum/palladium print the final image tones are the actual metals, platinum and palladium. This not only lends the print its unique qualities of softness and warmth, but also makes the most permanent image.

Burkholder's system includes a Nikon F4S, 20mm Nikon lens, Santos Mira 35 film scanner, Power Mac 7100 with a Radius Rocket accelerator, NEC 4FG and Radius 21-inch Grayscale monitors, SyQuest drive, 600 Mb magneto-optical drive, and an Art-Z digitizing tablet.

Step by Step

1. Burkholder exposed the original T-Max 100 black-and-white negative on a foggy morning just a few hundred yards from his home (Figure 13–10). Since it was exposed with a 20mm wide angle lens, there was an exaggerated perspective to the scene: the background items seem distant and divorced from the carousel in the foreground. Says Burkholder, "This was the desired effect, in part because it helps feed people's perception of Texas as an expansive and desolate landscape."

Figure 13–9   "Playground, Texas" by Dan Burkholder

Figure 13–10
Burkholder's original
photograph

2. He scanned the original negative into Photoshop on the Mira 35, a 10 bit, 2700 ppi scanner. The image was rich in grays but lacked bite in the highlights and shadows.

3. He selected the Jungle Jim and trees with the Lasso tool using a fairly large Feather radius. He then floated the selection, flipped it horizontally, and copied it to the clipboard.

4. Next, he made a path around the concrete pipe on the left, working at 1:1 or higher magnification for precision. He converted the path to a selection with a one pixel feather radius and used Paste Behind to place the Jungle Jim and trees (clipboard image) behind the pipe.

TIP: To paste behind a selection in Photoshop 3.0, hold the Option key down and choose Paste Into under the Edit menu.

5. The next job was to add some drama to the top third of the image. First, using the Pen tool he made paths around each Jungle Jim set, the original and the "cloned" one. Making a Quick Mask, he used the Gradient tool to create a progressive mask that could be applied to the top part of the image. With this mask, any effect would be applied in a smooth fashion rather than with a hard edge.

6. Before applying the Quick Mask to the image, Burkholder modified the mask around the outbuilding by creating a long horizontal selection,

feathered it, and then filled in that part of the mask with black. The modified mask would not apply any effect to the lower part of the building and would help create the halo effect behind it. He converted the mask to a selection, then loaded the Jungle Jim paths. Make Selection was chosen in the Paths pop-up menu; the artist set a low feather value and clicked Subtract from selection. This subtracted the Jungle Jim shapes from the active selection.

7. With the modified selection in place, he used the Curves dialog to invert the tones, playing with the curve to get just the right effect. The progressive nature of the selection made the tonal values change from negative to positive smoothly, something that would be very tricky to perform in the conventional wet darkroom.

8. A radical curve was applied in the Curves dialog to elevate the shadows and flatten the highlights. The image was then sampled up to 12x18 inches and converted to Bitmap mode at 1200 ppi.

9. The resulting file was output on an Agfa SelectSet 5000 running at 2400 dpi. The negative was contact printed on hand coated platinum/palladium paper as the final step.

Thoughts of the Artist

My primary concern is with the discovery of beauty—recording it, and controlling its elements of form and tonality using both traditional and digital photographic techniques.

I am fascinated by photography's ability to "fossilize light" as in no other medium, and find the qualities of the platinum/palladium print particularly suited to my vision of reality, whether literal or romanticized.

"TRANSITION" BY EMIL IHRIG

Emil Ihrig is a photo illustrator, book designer, author, and the co-owner of VersaTech Associates, a book packaging and graphic design house in Prescott, Arizona.

Ihrig's digital studio is comprised of a Macintosh Quadra 950 with 72 Mb of RAM, 1.2 Gb hard drive, Radius Intellicolor 20-inch monitor, UMAX PowerLook scanner, CalComp Drawing Board II, CD ROM drive, 230 Mb magneto-optical drive, SyQuest drive, and Fargo color printer.

"Transition" (Figure 13–11) reflects a metaphysical interpretation of a person crossing over to another realm of existence after physical death. The elderly woman is successively metamorphosing from the physical state to the universal elements. The face at the left of the image can be interpreted in many different ways—the mystery of what lies beyond, meeting a loved one, a deity, etc.—depending on the viewer's own outlook.

Figure 13–11   "Transition" by Emil Ihrig

Step by Step

1. Ihrig started with a Photo CD photograph of the clouds and sky, which he had originally shot from an airplane window (Figure 13–13). He applied the Unsharp Mask filter and then the Facet filter to give the sky a painterly look.

2. He opened a second image of an elderly woman crossing the street. He used the Lasso tool to isolate her from the background and saved the masked image as a separate file with the figure saved as an alpha channel (Figure 13–14).

3. The artist copied the female figure to the clipboard and pasted her into the background image bleeding off the right side. With the female figure selected, he used the Border command to create a border selection area 30 pixels wide and then feathered this by 15 pixels. He used the Paint Bucket tool to fill this feathered border selection with a warm gold color simulating an aura.

Figure 13–12
Face of store window
mannequin

Figure 13–13
Cloud formations photographed out of an airplane window

Figure 13–14
An elderly woman
isolated from her
original background

4. To intensify the aura, he pasted a second copy of the female figure directly over the first and again created a 30-pixel border area with a 15-pixel feather, filling it with the same gold color. Pasting a third copy of the female figure on top of the first two preserved the woman's outline without sacrificing the feathering effect of the aura.

5. Ihrig then returned to the image of the elderly woman, scaled the figure downward while maintaining the aspect ratio, gave it a one-pixel feather, and copied this smaller-size figure to the clipboard.

6. He pasted the smaller female figure onto the background image slightly below and to the left of the first figure. With the figure still selected, he applied the Luminosity mode at a 58% opacity.

7. Once again he scaled down and feathered the female figure, this time to an even smaller size. He copied this figure to the clipboard and pasted it onto the background image, placing it below and to the left of the other two.

8. To this smallest female figure (floating selection), he applied the Screen mode at 80% opacity, creating the impression that she is blending into the clouds.

9. In the third and last source image—a photo of a male mannequin's face in a department store window—he selected and isolated the

lower part of the face, omitting the eyes to lend this mask-like image an impersonal look (Figure 13–12).

10. He copied and pasted this mask to the cloud image, feathering it slightly and applying the Luminosity mode at 50% opacity.

Thoughts of the Artist

I prefer to create compositions that are spare, not busy. My digital artwork tends to have a single focus of attention. I feel it's important for the artist to have a concept in mind before approaching the computer. Without first developing a concept, one can easily get lost among tools, filters, and techniques used for their own sakes.

"THE UPSTAIRS ROOM SERIES, #116" BY MARGARET EVANS

Margaret Evans received her MFA from Rochester Institute of Technology and her BA from Goddard College in Vermont. She is currently an Adjunct Professor of Photography at Rochester Institute of Technology.

Evans' system includes Macintosh computers, Kodak and Nikon film scanners, and a Canon CLC 500 color laser printer.

"The Upstairs Room" (Figure 13-15) is part of a series of images created by Evans while she was a resident at the Art/Omni, International Artists' Center in Upstate New York. Evans considers this series of photographs of three young women dressed in white and placed in a room as "still-image choreography." The windows are filled with recognizable photographs of women that span the early history of photography. These historical views represent photography's "window" on the world of women, a tradition that has existed since the inception of the medium.

Step by Step

1. Evans used a Kodak film scanner to scan the original black and white negative of the three women in the room (Figure 13–16). In Photoshop she sized the original to 6 × 10 inches, adjusted for brightness and contrast, and made a print of one of these images to measure the windows to fit the historical transparency images.

2. She then scanned transparencies of the historical images. These were cropped, sized, adjusted for brightness and contrast, despeckled, and unsharp-masked.

3. To insert these images into the windows she created paths that masked the blank spaces, leaving the interior and the figures intact. The paths were converted to selections with a one-pixel feather

Figure 13–15 "The Upstairs Room Series, #11B" by Margaret Evans includes historical images in the windows (from left to right): "A Study in Sunlight" by Heinrich Kühn (1905), "Letitia Felix" by Clarence White, and "Portrait (Miss N.)" by Gertrude Käsebier.

radius. Each image was then pasted into its window. While still a floating selection the artist moved it into position and adjusted the perspective (Effects under the Image menu).

4. The ceiling was copied from a still video capture, originally an out-of-focus image of a colorful collage. The floating globes were obtained from a similar image. In some instances the "Composite Controls" were used to make the ceiling "color" translucent, allowing the original image to show through. In keeping with the ethereal nature of the image, edges along the ceiling and around the windows were blurred, and additional "sunlight" color was airbrushed throughout the room.

"The Upstairs Room" includes the historical images "A Study in Sunlight," by Heinrich Kühn (1905), "Letitia Felix" by Clarence White (1903), and "Portrait (Miss N.)" by Gertrude Käsebier (1903). All photos were originally published in early issues of *Camera* magazine.

Figure 13–16
Evans shot many different poses of the three women in the room.

Thoughts of the Artist

I caution myself that the easy versatility, flexibility, and speed of the machine may perhaps generate a relaxed attitude towards creating new images. Lighting effects, texture, blending, dynamic tension, and composition are issues that must be considered aesthetically. The computer cannot make those decisions. The computer cannot remedy a fundamentally uninteresting or technically poor image. Tools that feather, blur, pointilize, posterize, size, colorize, and create dramatic backgrounds and drop shadows are surely useful to the creative photographer. Yet none of these effects outmode the craft of photography. A negative with no shadow detail is as flawed on the monitor as in the enlarger. The new electronic medium remarkably enhances our work, energizing new and unforeseen directions, not by abandoning the past, but by building on it.

"DEPRIVED" BY MARK SIPRUT

Mark Siprut received his BA from Humboldt State University in California and his MFA from the University of California at Santa Barbara. He currently teaches in the School of Art, Design, and Art History at San Diego State University.

Siprut's system includes a Quadra 800 with 56 Mb RAM, 1.7 Gb hard disk, running an 80 MHz Daystar PowerPro 601 Power PC Processor, Fujitsu Dynamo 128 Magneto Optical Drive, SyQuest drives, Radius SuperMatch PressView 21-inch monitor with a Thunder II GX 1360 video card, Wacom ArtZ Digitizing Tablet, Mac II accelerated with Daystar 40 MHz Turbo 040 accelerator, Microtek ScanMaker 45T film scanner, ScanMaker 35T film scanner, and a Hewlett-Packard ScanJet IIc flatbed scanner.

Figure 13–17   "Deprived" by Mark Siprut

"Deprived" (Figure 13–17) is part of a series of photographic collages by the author mixing portraits of old and young people, often using toys as a metaphor to bridge the gap between the generations.

Step by step

1. The girl in the hut and the dolls were photographed in Mexico with 35mm Tri-X film and scanned on a Kodak Rapid Film scanner (Figure 13–18).
2. The girl in the hut was put on the background layer. Siprut put each group of dolls on separate layers (Figure 13–19). The dolls on Layer 1 were positioned with the Move tool over the stack of wood at 50 percent opacity. A layer mask was used to isolate the dolls on Layer 2 and then the Find Edges filter was applied.
3. Two masks were created on channels (Figure 13–19). The first isolated the fireplace to increase the contrast and apply dodging and burning. The second channel contained a blend which, when loaded onto the

document, allowed the Ripple filter to subtly texturize the wood, the girl's legs, and the ground.

4. The smoke from the pot was enhanced with the Dodge tool. Unsharp Masking was selectively applied to finish the image.

Figure 13–18
The original photographs of the child in a hut and the dolls

Figure 13–19
The Layers palette (left) shows the girl on the background layer and each doll group on separate layers. The Channels palette (right) shows the masks used to isolate parts of the composition.

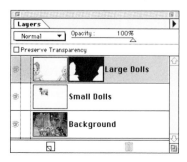
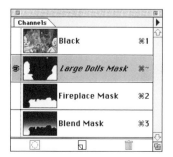

Color Gallery

The following images can be found in color in the Color Gallery insert.

"SPRING FORTH" BY TOM CROSS

Tom Cross has a degree in zoology. He is an active artist and formerly taught at the Ringling School of Art and Design in Florida.

Cross' system includes a Quadra 700, Daystar 040 accelerator upgrade, 68 Mb Ram, SyQuest, 128 magneto-optical drive, Microtek scanner, video digitizing board, and Sony Camcorder.

"Spring Forth" was created for a series of prints representing the four seasons reproduced as offset lithography in a limited edition for Mill Pond Press.

Step by Step

1. Cross began by making a pencil thumbnail in his sketchbook. He then created more low resolution thumbnails on the computer with reference photos, video captures, and colorized sketches.

2. Each character was then created separately, from a drawing using a Wacom tablet, a video capture, or scanned photo (Figure 13–20). Says Cross, "I use photos as sophisticated underpaintings." He doesn't want his images to look like montages, even though the initial images

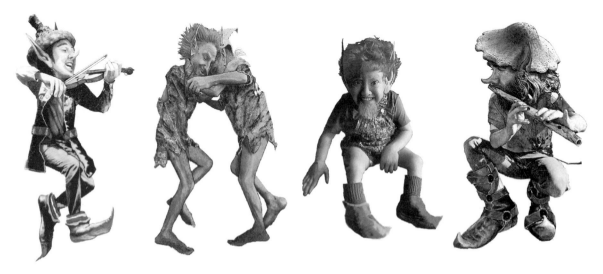

Figure 13–20   Cross created each character using video captures, scanned photos and a Wacom digitizing tablet.

come from diverse sources. In general, his source images are deliberately low resolution.

3. The artist then created a background using a combination of reference photos, video captures and drawings (Figure 13–21). This background was later scrapped and replaced by a simpler solution (see the Color Gallery).

4. Cross combined all the parts by pasting into selections, experimenting in channels and masks, and cloning with the Rubber Stamp tool.

Figure 13–21
A busy background was replaced by the simpler sky shown in the final piece.

5. He added stars and bubbles in Channels from a template, and applied various filters from Andromeda, Paint Alchemy, and Kai's Power Tools on selections from the saved channels.

6. Finally, Cross magnified the image and cleaned up edges.

7. The printer output 10 to 15 IRIS tests to get the color correct (artist proofs). The artist then chose the proof he like the best and worked on it by hand with watercolor, acrylic, or colored pencils. The original was then coated with a sealer. From this one-of-a-kind hand-painted IRIS print the final lithograph was printed by Harvest Productions in Anaheim.

Thoughts of the Artist
I've gone from acrylic paint, to combining photographs with painting, to digital. Now I can finally realize my visions.

"LOCOMOTIVE" BY JOHN LUND

John Lund has a degree in English literature. He currently owns an advertising photography studio in San Francisco specializing in digital work.

"Locomotive" was commissioned by SuperMac Technologies for use in collateral material and brochures. The piece was art directed by Amber McLain.

Step by Step

1. Lund traced the locomotive with the Pen tool and converted it to a selection (Figure 13–22). He used Curves and Hue/Saturation to alter the colors. The train was flipped so that it would head in the right direction. The letters on the train were then flipped back to read correctly.

2. He copied a sunrise shot, flipped it horizontally, increasing the saturation, and then pasted it behind the train selection (Figure 13–23).

3. The cloud slab was constructed by making selections from a cloud image and darkening and lightening sections to give a 3-D effect. Lund then pasted the slab on top of the locomotive as a floating selection at 50% Opacity. He then cut out the slab around the front of the train, and returned the slab to full Opacity. He used the Pen tool to create a path around the slab, deselecting it (Pen Tool palette pop-up menu) with a feathered edge.

4. He created selected shapes from the cloud image, colorizing them with Hue/Saturation. The light beam is a selection lightened with Brightness/Contrast.

Figure 13–22
The original train photograph was
flipped and masked as a selection.

Figure 13–23
The sky was pasted behind the train.

5. The steam was hand painted with the Airbrush tool set to white at
various opacities.

Thoughts of the Artist
When I started out as a photographer, I was against using filters. But the
more I use a computer the less conservative my vision gets, and the more
I appreciate work that is unusual.

"A 1993-EARLY NOVEMBER DREAM" BY HIROSHI MIYAZAKI

Hiroshi Miyazaki received his BA from Aoyama Gakuin University, Tokyo,
Japan, and a second BA and his MA from San Diego State University. He
is currently a fine arts professor at San Diego Mesa College.

Miyazaki's system includes a Macintosh IIsi, 9 Mb of RAM, 240 Mb hard
disk, and ArtZ Wacom digitizing tablet. Besides Photoshop, he used Fractal
Design Painter and Aldus PageMaker to create this piece.

"A 1993-Early November Dream" is part of Miyazaki's "Dream" series, in
which he has been chronicling social and political issues that have affected
him personally. The image, with accompanying text, illustrates how, with
diligence and discipline, Japan has emerged out of the complete destruction
of WW II as one of the super-power nations of the world.

The accompanying text reads as follows:

One night, in one of my recent, recurring dreams, I found myself among
old classmates, in a small classroom of an elementary school in my native
country, Japan. While pounding on the podium, the teacher gave her

daily admonition in a loud voice, and said, "Shonen yo, taishi wo idake—Boys, be ambitious." I am a firm believer that the Japanese spirit of accomplishment is due in part to this Japanese admonition of the past, with, perhaps, an American twist. At a time when the United States had newly been recognized as a world power and industrial giant, and greatly admired by the Japanese, I might add, Americans were working in a manner similar to that of the Japanese at that time. So greatly admired was the American system that the Japanese government invited an American educator, a Dr. Clark, to come to Japan to assist in the modernization of the educational system. The above phrase was introduced to all Japanese students. Perhaps, Americans would do well to heed the words of their compatriot, Dr. Clark; words which in this more enlightened time, would more appropriately be, "Boys and girls, be ambitious."

Step by Step

1. Miyazaki scanned Figure 13–24 and manipulated the images.
2. He then added several quick strokes in different colors using the Wacom digitizing tablet and pressure-sensitive pen.
3. He pasted the completed image on a background of paper texture created in Fractal Design Painter.
4. The final composited image was imported into PageMaker to add the text.

Figure 13–24
Original photograph of
the child

Thoughts of the Artist

Because I'm primarily a studio-artist, I use the computer as another medium or tool, such as pencil and paint, for expressing my ideas. I also like to incorporate a computer in teaching my painting course. Computer technology allows the students to explore different versions of their paintings on the monitor before making a commitment on canvas.

"SUNSHINE" BY LANNY WEBB

Lanny Webb received his BA from Atlanta School of Art and his MFA from Georgia State University. He is currently Coordinator of Electronic Design and Associate Professor of Graphic Design at the University of Georgia in Athens.

Webb's system includes a Mac IIcx with 32 Mb RAM and 300 Mb external hard drive, Daystar 68040 CPU accelerator with a static RAM cash card and NuBus imaging accelerator, Nikon Cool Scan, La Cie Silverscanner II, and Canon CJ10.

"Sunshine" is a self portrait of Webb in front of one of his digital photographs. This promotional piece for an exhibition is an exaggeration of the influence he feels light has on a subject.

Step by Step

1. Webb scanned a lake-scape (Figure 13–25), and created a frame and shadows around it with the painting tools and feathered fills.

2. He then scanned a self portrait (Figure 13–26), "cleaned it up, did a little cosmetic surgery," and pasted it in front of the lake-scape.

Figure 13–25
Webb's original lake-scape

Figure 13–26
Webb's original self-portrait

3. Using a series of paths converted to feathered selections, he varied the brightness and saturation to form the sun rays.

4. Finally he used the Rubber Stamp tool set to the "from Saved" option on low opacity on selections of the figure to suggest that the sun's rays are being blocked by his head and shoulders. Final output was to Iris inkjet printer.

Thoughts of the Artist

All my drawings, whether traditional or digital, try to depict a specific mood or character of a subject or place. For this feeling or character to be apparent in my work, I must focus on its "essence" by deleting or adding information or, in many instances, combining elements from several sources.

Digital technology allows you to draw or paint with areas of digitized photographs as your pigment. I feel the ability to work with this "photo pigment" is the heart and power of digital image making.

I have always had a fascination, if not an obsession, with light and how it affects the spirit of a subject. Our perception of a subject is determined by its lighting, and yet we frequently are unaware of this ever-present but subtle force. The essence of any subject can change poetically, dramatically, or mystically depending on the quality of light.

"I COULDN'T STAY IN MIAMI" BY DIANE FENSTER

Diane Fenster received her BS in biology. She currently works as a graphic artist for the School of Science at San Francisco State University and is a freelance illustrator and fine artist.

Fenster's system includes a Macintosh 840 AV with 64 Mb RAM, a 1.2 Gb drive, CD ROM drive, Syquest, and 128 MO drive.

"I Couldn't Stay in Miami" is from the "Ritual of Abandonment" series, a work in progress which Fenster views as a two-dimensional performance piece. Embedded within each image is a present day fairy-tale of love and abandonment, each written by a different person especially for this project. Although some are true and some are fiction, all speak of the human situation of falling in love and thereby putting oneself at risk.

Concurrent with the creation of the printed images is the production of a "virtual artist's notebook." This CD-ROM will include an electronic copy of the images, background information on the formation of the series, and QuickTime movies of the authors reading their stories.

Step by Step

1. Fenster photographed the nudes and the train tracks with a Canon Xapshot still video camera. The images behind the story texts were

captured from video images. The handwritten text (provided by the individuals who wrote the stories) and other objects were scanned.

2 The typed text of each story was set up in PageMaker, laser printed, and scanned back into Photoshop.

3. The nude was merged into the train by pasting it and then gradually deleting it with a feathered Magic Wand tool to fit the forms. Details were extended with the Rubber Stamp tool by cloning.

4. To produce the graytone and neon effect the artist pasted the Zapshot image over a solarized grayscale version of the same image. While the Xapshot image was still a floating selection, she set it to the Color mode and moved it to slightly offset the grayscale version.

5. The streaks of color were produced by selecting clumps of pixels, feathering, pasting, and stretching them to get flashes of color.

6. The text was colorized by selecting and copying an interesting clump of colored pixels, pasting it into the type, and stretching it with the Bicubic Interpolation setting in Preferences to get a full color range within the type. The type was then manipulated with the Solarization filter and the Hue/Saturation command.

7. The final images were output on a film recorder from Photoshop files to 4×5 inch transparencies from which a limited edition of 30×30 inch Fujichrome prints were printed.

The text in "I Couldn't Stay in Miami" is a story by an author who wishes to remain anonymous:

> When I was 22 I took a 6 day train trip from Miami, Florida to Reno, Nevada to start a new life.
>
> When I was 20 I thought I had found the answer to my unhappiness and loneliness, I fell in love with Dottie. It seemed that I had found the only person who would love me and I couldn't imagine us ever separating. After 2 years and reasons I'm still not sure of, she told me that she had to go away to school in Tennessee and didn't want to see me anymore.
>
> I couldn't stay in Miami, where I had lived all my life. I called my aunt and uncle who I had only met once and asked if I could stay with them in Reno while I looked for a place to live.
>
> I decided that I would take the train in order to distance myself from Miami and my former life. I spent the 3 weeks before leaving saying good-bye to friends and visiting places for the last time. I got on the train in North Miami for the 3 day trip to Chicago. Through the south the train was dirty and the people not very friendly. We were stopped for a whole night due to a freight train derailment. We sat on the track next to the derailed train looking at broken cars.

By the time we got to Chicago I had just enough time to run and catch the train bound for Reno, the Zephyr. Immediately everything looked more positive, the train was clean and the cars had western decoration inside. The people on the train were very friendly and I found myself sitting in the observation car and meeting new people as we made our way from the midwest into the real west.

I could feel the past being distanced behind me. I ate trout in the dining car and sang with 2 girls between train cars as we entered Colorado. It really felt like a new life was beginning. After Colorado we went north to Wyoming, across Utah, through the middle of the Great Salt Lake and into Nevada. I arrived in Reno early on Sunday morning and started the second part of my life.

I wrote to Dottie, but she never wrote back. After 5 years I had given up, but not forgotten Dottie, when she called. I was flying back to Miami to visit my parents before I married Jeanne and Dottie said she wanted to see me. She was having a difficult time and said she wanted to marry me and would live anywhere I wanted. I met her in Miami and told her I was getting married.

Five years later she committed suicide.

Thoughts of the Artist

When I experiment with layers and calculation commands, I try every one. Sometimes the unexpected is the most successful.

Push the medium. Just running a filter on something isn't doing digital art. Exposing one's heart and soul is.

"FADING AWAY" BY STEPHEN JOHNSON

Stephen Johnson has a BA and MA in Art from San Francisco State University and currently works as a fine arts photographer, photography teacher, and designer in Northern California.

Johnson created "Fading Away" as a fine art piece to express the loss he felt when his father left. "Staying up late one night in yet one more attempt to come to terms with my past," he combined his only family portrait with a photograph taken through a window at Striped Butte in Death Valley which reminded him of that loneliness. The working title was "Dad Left in 1962."

Step by Step

1. Johnson started with scans of the desert scene he photographed through the window. He then scanned the family portrait, photographed by his grandmother, Mary Johnson (Figure 13–27).

Figure 13–27
The original image of Striped Butte Johnson photographed through a window and the family portrait, photographed by his grandmother, Mary Johnson.

2. He masked the background in the window.

3. The first attempts at combining the two images didn't work. He tried to make the family into big cutouts that would progressively collapse onto the desert. "As it turned out," says Johnson, "something much simpler was stronger." He simply faded his father out of successive images with the Rubber Stamp tool's From Saved option, increasing the Opacity setting of the revert as the images drifted back, thus the title, "Fading Away."

Thoughts of the Artist
For the first time in my career I am having to really work to express ideas—straining to give visual vent to deep emotions set loose by these new possibilities. For me, photography had largely been a witnessing—intense and interpretive, but nonetheless I always knew I was on the sidelines, the creator was the planet itself. This is different. My images are trying to be much more the product of my brain and my heart. There is a new visual vocabulary to work out, and a new sense of how I want my audience drawn in. There is a darkness to peer into and a sadness to illuminate. There are demons to engage and villains to expose. There is a whole wide universe of wonder to ponder.

"WHEELS" BY SANJAY KOTHARI

Sanjay Kothari received a degree in engineering in India, then attended the New England School of Photography in Boston and Rutgers University in New Jersey. He is currently a freelance photographer and digital artist in New York and is represented by R. Greenberg Associates.

Kothari states: 'Wheels' evokes the comic/absurd nature of modernity in India, the odd juxtaposition of technology and tradition. The image also imitates the sets of traveling photographic studios in Indian carnivals wherein the village folk have themselves photographed inside of cars with glamorous cityscapes in the background."

Step by Step

1. Kothari began by creating low-resolution thumbnails, which provided freedom for ideas to flow quickly. Once the direction was established he switched to high-resolution files.

2. The image was constructed in three layers: the ornament arch as the background, then the street scene, then the car.

3. He created the outer arches by flipping a doorway twice (Figure 13–28).

4. The inner arches and street scene were constructed from a second photograph (Figure 13–29).

5. Kothari enhanced the color using the Curves and Hue/Saturation commands. To model the columns and give them depth he used the Dodge and Burn tools and spherized on the vertical axis only.

6. The wheels and ground were copied and pasted in from another image (Figure 13–30).

7. The entire image was warmed up by pushing up the separate yellow and magenta curves in the Curve dialog.

8. He then applied Unsharp Mask at about 50% two or three times at a 0.5 radius and a Threshold setting of zero, building up the effect gradually.

Thoughts of the Artist
Photography has finally become what it was meant to be.

Figure 13–28
One doorway was flipped to create the outer arches.

Figure 13–29
The inner arches were repeated and the background extended in the final.

Figure 13–30
The wheels and ground were pasted in from this photo.

"BUFFALO TRANSMITTING POWER TO MAN" BY JOSEPH BELLACERA

Joseph Bellacera received his BA from the Humboldt State University in Arcata, California and his MFA from University of California at Santa Barbara. He currently works as a painter and graphic designer in Sacramento.

"Buffalo Transmitting Power to Man" is part of a series of images that Bellacera calls Ancient Rhythms. Based on pictographs and petroglyphs by North American Indians, the series represents the artist's attempt to bring this unique primitive art form into a contemporary perspective.

Says Bellacera, "I am attracted to rock drawings because they represents a time when people had an unbroken sense of unity between themselves and nature, and between nature and the spiritual."

Step by Step
Many of the pieces in the series are monoprints. The images are digitized, manipulated, and output as color laser prints, then painted over by hand.

1. Bellacera began by doing a black and white sketch of an ancient Indian rock painting located on the Churchill River Saskatchewan (Figure 13–31). He scanned it and colorized it in Photoshop.

2. He used various tools and filters to produce a series of colored versions of the petroglyph.

3. He then inverted the image to get its opposite color effect, which left a black border. He painted the edges with white using the Airbrush tool to reduce the impact of the black.

Thoughts of the Artist
Any tool or medium, whether painting, photography, printmaking, or digital image making, which can help express the feelings and interpretations an artist has in relation to his or her life experiences is fair to use. I am not a purist when it comes to technique or mediums; I set my parameters or limitations in other ways. It is the process which is of primary importance to me. In fact, I often paint over my digitized images. That way I get the best of both worlds.

Figure 13–31
The artist drew a sketch of the Indian petroglyph.

"DRIVE-IN" BY ADAM COHEN

Adam Cohen received his BFA at Tyler School of Art, Temple University, Philadelphia. He currently works as a fine artist and illustrator in New York.

"The Drive In" is a personal piece that incorporates an earlier artwork on the movie screen.

Step by Step

1. Cohen began by sizing a new document, divided it in half, making selections for each, and saving each half as a channel.

2. He created a ground texture by mottling with the Airbrush tool, adding noise, and removing some saturation. He scaled this texture to be larger in front and smaller in the back, and pasted it into the bottom selection.

3. He created three different models of cars in three color combinations in separate documents. First he created masks with the Pen tool for each section of a car by saving paths, and turned them into selections as needed (Figure 13–32).

4. He filled each selection with a solid color, air brushed the edges, and cut out the car windows.

5. He pasted the figures inside the cars.

6. The tires and headlights were filled circles made with the Elliptical Marquee.

7. He added hand drawn details with a Wacom digitizing tablet.

8. The sky was a graduated blend created with the Gradient tool.

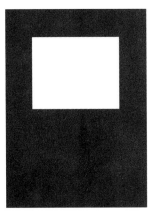

Figure 13–32   The masks for three different car styles, the cars, the mask for the movie screen, and the detail from a previous illustration that was pasted into the screen

9. Cohen drew the columns for the movie screen, used the Gradient tool for form, and cut off the bottom of the columns to add shadows.

10. He drew a square for the screen with the Marquee tool and saved it as a channel. He then copied a detail section from an existing illustration, cleaned up the details (because he greatly enlarged the detail), and made it into a slightly bluish monotone for a Hitchcock effect. He pasted it into the selected screen and scaled it to fit.

11. He pasted the cars into the piece, scaled for perspective in rows. The cars were saved as a Channel to mask the ground. This allowed him to add shadows under the cars.

12. He placed the speaker poles next to each car as transparent selections, zoomed in and cut along the edges to fit them in. He used the painting tools to draw the electric wires.

13. The stars were created with a feathered brush. The moon was two circles made with the Elliptical Marquee, one subtracted from the other.

"HIGHROW GLYPHICS" BY WENDY GROSSMAN

Grossman attended Boston Institute of Art and the School of Visual Arts. She is currently an instructor at the School of Visual Arts in New York.

Grossman's system includes a Quadra 700 with 20 Mb of RAM, Wacom Tablet, SyQuest drive, NTR laser printer, and an Apple 14" monitor. Besides Photoshop, she used Adobe Illustrator, Adobe Dimensions, and Ray Dream Designer to create this piece.

"Highrow Glyphics" was inspired by a 9-year-old girl, Amy Singh, who approached Grossman with a school project on Egypt. The girl was so enthusiastic that Grossman tacked the report on her studio wall, and immediately began working on the piece.

Step by Step

1. Grossman began by scanning in a traditional pencil sketch. She saved it as a PICT file and opened it in Adobe Illustrator as a template (Figure 13–33).

3. She constructed all the separate parts in Illustrator (Figure 13–34).

2. She also drew all the basic graphic components in Illustrator, adding flat color to make the underpainting (Figure 13–35). It was saved as an Illustrator 5 file.

3. In Ray Dream Designer, the artist created the three-dimensional elements: the scarab beetle and the palm trees.

Figure 13–33
Grossman scanned a
traditional pencil sketch
to use as a template in
Adobe Illustrator.

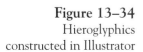

Figure 13–34
Hieroglyphics
constructed in Illustrator

4. Grossman the opened the Illustrator file in Photoshop and pasted all
   the photo imaging and 3D files. She used the Airbrush tool and the
   Dodge/Burn tool, building up light layers of low opacity color.

   TIP: To get seamless, translucent edges, Grossman begins shading with a
   100 pixel brush at 3% Opacity. Then she paints with a 80 pixel brush at
   7% Opacity, then with a 50 pixel brush at 11% Opacity, etc.

5. Once the elements were in place, she applied the filter Aldus Gallery
   Effects: Classic Art Volume 2 to the columns (Figure 13–36).

6. To get the embossed effect on the hieroglyphics strip, the artist
   applied the Emboss filter to the selection, copied it to the clipboard,

Figure 13–35
In Illustrator all flat tones were blocked based on the sketch.

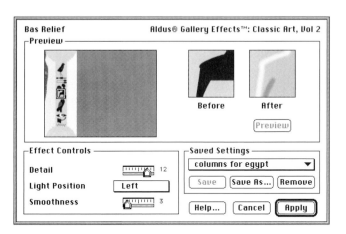

Figure 13–36   Aldus Gallery Effects applied to the columns

and then pasted the clipboard image back with Color Only at 100% opacity (Figure 13–37).

Grossman combines her fine art, which has a "cubist flair," with photo illustrations. "Before I discovered digital imaging, my work was schizo-phrenic: it was fine art or it was illustration. Photoshop lets me do more

Figure 13–37   The Emboss filter applied to the hieroglyphics strip

crossover." She employs unusual paper in fine art prints of her work, including papyrus, fig tree bark, and raw silk.

"THE SKY IS PAGE . . ." BY JEAN-FRANCOIS PODEVIN AND LARRY SCHER

Jean Francois Podevin received his degree from Ensag Ecole Nationale Superieure d' Arts Graphiques in Paris. He is now a designer and illustrator in the Los Angeles area.

Larry Scher received his BA from the University of California, Los Angeles and his MBA at Valley State. He teaches video production at Rio Hondo College and owns Timestream Video, a video production company.

Podevin and Scher collaborate, the former emphasizing the concept and aesthetic, and the latter the technical and applications. Their system includes a 50Mhz 486 computer with 32 Mb Ram and a 32 bit True Vision AT Vista board with 14 Mb of Video Ram. Besides Photoshop, the artists also used Vista Rio and TimeArts Lumina.

"The Sky is Page . . ." was commissioned as a New Year's greeting card for Cindy Csurak of the Image Bank. The goal was to use as many different photographs as possible. Podevin designed the image based on a poem of Anna Fontescal:

> The sky is page,
> the ink light,
> the fields unlimited . . .
> and the bridges span rivers of eternity.

Rather than opt for stereotypical holiday symbols, Podevin chose to illustrate the calendar cycle. The peacock's feathers represent a series of time lapse pictures of the days of the year and the four directions: sunrise east, sunset west, noon, north light, zenith, etc. The peacock functions as a metaphor for radiance, color, beauty and illusion, qualities which are applicable to image making.

Step by Step

1. Podevin created a pen sketch on paper with notes indicating possible photographs (Figure 13–38).
2. Based on the sketch, he selected the photographs from the Image Bank library, and had them scanned to a Photo CD (Figure 13–39).
3. Podevin made small prints of all the images, cut out sections of the sunsets, fields, and trees, and made a traditional collage (Figure 13–40).
4. The collage was then recreated in Photoshop. Each image was masked and cut out. Some painterly effects were applied with brushes in Fractal Design Painter.

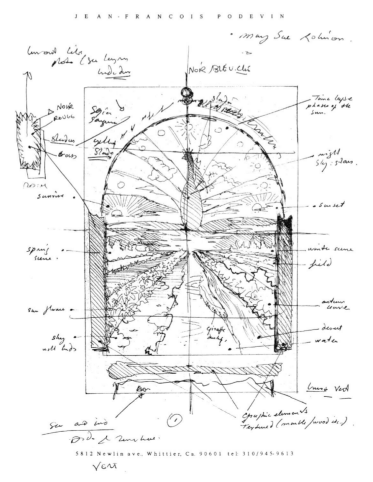

Figure 13–38
Podevin created a sketch with notes indicating possible photographs.

Figure 13–39   The photographs from Image Bank (left to right): Sunset by Grant Faint, Peacock by Ulf E. Wallin, Waterlilies by Luis Padilla, and Sunflowers by Giuliano Colliva

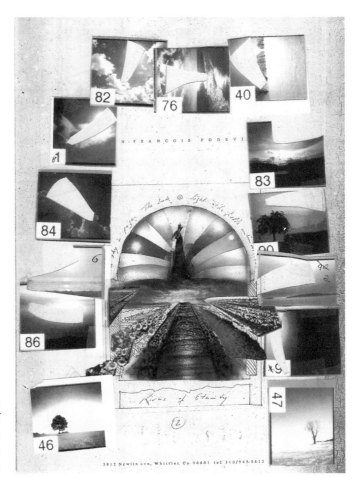

Figure 13–40
Podevin's collage of cutouts from the prints of the Image Bank photographs

5. The files were then assembled in Vista Rio, using the sketch as a layout (much like assembling a stained glass window).

6. The image was touched up as a single 24 Mb file in Lumina. It was returned to Rio and the type and graphic elements on the sides and bottom added. It was output on a film recorder as a 4 × 5 inch transparency from 20 floppy disks.

Thoughts of the Artist

Podevin believes that all media, traditional and digital, should be incorporated into image making:

> When we look at something we naturally focus on it and ignore everything else around. But while we're focusing, the whole world exists around us, the fleeting textures and states of feeling we're hardly even aware of. The camera deals with what we're looking at, and sketching deals with the overall surrounding. And computers are the tool of integration. They are a kind of super-media that works in a very spontaneous, Zen mood.

"MOTOROLA FRAME RELAY" BY ED FOSTER

Ed Foster has a BA from Massachusetts College of Art. He now owns a graphic design business in Boston.

"Motorola Frame Relay" was created as a horizontal spread (22 × 8.5 inch) in a Motorola Codex product brochure. The challenge was to convey the theme of "around the world" in a unique way through textures, incorporating stock photography.

Says Foster, "Photoshop and stock photography allowed us to do a higher end image than the budget would have allowed with traditional photography."

Step by Step

1. Foster began the piece in a new horizontal document by laying down the tiles and the statue first.

2. Then he pasted other patterned images using Lighten and Darken modes to print into the statue but not into the live area next to it.

3. The woman's face was stretched horizontally prior to copying it, copied, and then pasted in using lighten only to give it a transparent effect over the pattern. Where the face didn't appear on the solid white area, he pasted again using the Paste Into command.

4. The temple had a slice of pattern missing and was cloned using the Rubber Stamp tool to replace it. The flowers were cloned and placed over transparent areas to give a layered effect.

5. A package was photographed in the studio, silhouetted, and then pasted on top of a created shadow.

6. Once the collage was completed, Foster made an assessment of needed improvements. He then recreated the entire collage after enhancing the colors on the original independent files.

Foster believes that creativity is still the key. His company will remain small and flexible, flowing with technological changes, to best serve his clients.

He advises employee hopefuls that obtaining practical work experience may be more important to their careers than finishing a college degree.

"AKIHABARA" BY BERT MONROY

Bert Monroy has been an advertising art director and creative director in New York. He currently works as a digital matte artist and multimedia producer in San Francisco.

Monroy's main system includes a PowerPC 8100 with 96 Mb RAM, Internal 250 Mb Drive, PLI 1.3 Gig drive, Quantum 1 Gb. drive, Bernoulli 150, SyQuest, PLI Infinity Optical, and Apple CD-ROM drive.

"Akihabara" was created for *Step-By-Step Japan* Magazine.

Step by Step

1. Monroy began "Akihabara" by shooting several photographs on location. He used them as reference on which to base the work.

2. He drew all the perspective lines in Adobe Illustrator, saving the document as an EPS file.

3. He opened the file in Photoshop. To conserve memory, the artist worked on small sections of the image by copying them into separate documents.

4. First he dropped a blend into each small shape in the sketch using the Gradient tool. Then, using the Pen, Paintbrush, and the Airbrush, tools, he added highlights, shadows, and details. He then added noise to some areas.

5. After finishing the small area, it was copied and pasted back into the main image precisely in register. Thus Monroy slowly constructed this piece, which took more than 150 hours to complete (Figure 13–41).

Thoughts of the Artist
My selling feature as an illustrator is my ability to achieve a photo realistic effect whether the subject is an existing place or a fictitious scene.

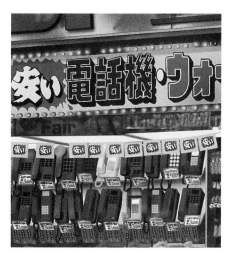 

Figure 13–41
Two magnified details
of "Akihabara"

For my own personal art, I prefer to recreate scenes which do exist. I feel our society has become so fast-paced that we do not take time to look at where we are. I force people to stop and look. The scenes I paint usually ask me to be painted. My eyes are always roving my surroundings and sometimes a particular building or scene will just capture my attention and unfold itself as a painting.

"CINCINNATI BALLET'S PETER PAN" BY ALAN BROWN

Alan Brown received his BS from Syracuse University in New York. He now owns Photonics Graphics, Inc., a computer illustration and advertising photography company in Cincinnati.

Brown's system includes a Quadra 840 and a Power Mac 7100, with 74 Mb RAM in each, 24 bit color cards by Radius, assorted peripherals, and a Howtek flatbed scanner.

"Cincinnati Ballet's Peter Pan" was designed for the cover of the ballet company's season brochure and advertising campaign.

Step by Step

1. The dancer was photographed as a 2.25 inch color negative (Figure 13–42). Brown made an 11 × 14 inch color print, which was then sent to a color separation house to be scanned on a Hell drum scanner.

2. The sky and clouds was a 35mm in-house stock shot which Brown had put on Photo CD (Figure 13–43).

3. The dancer was outlined in Photoshop and masked. Brown did some dental work to improve his smile.

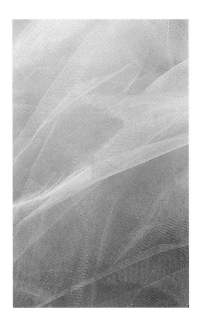

Figure 13–42
The original dancer

Figure 13–43
The sky and clouds background

Figure 13–44
The original background fabric

4. The dancer and sky were assembled in Specular Collage, taking advantage of its layering feature.

5. Returning to Photoshop, the artist then applied the Aldus Gallery Effect Plastic Wrap to the image. It was placed in front of a floating fabric and shadows were added (Figure 13–44).

Brown works extensively with 3-D programs, combining photographs with 3-D images. "Digital imaging has changed my whole way of working. In the last six years I have gone from mostly photographic to mostly illustrative images."

"MAN ON LADDER" BY CHARLY FRANKLIN

Charly Franklin began working as a photographer in England and Ireland when he was 17 years old. He now owns a photography studio in San Francisco.

Franklin's system includes a Quadra 950 with 140 Mb RAM, two 1 Gb drives, one dedicated as a scratch disk for Photoshop, Pinnacle 650 Mb magneto-optical drive, SyQuest drive, and a Bernoulli.

"Man on Ladder" was created for Computer Sciences Corporation in Los Angeles as a visual metaphor for the idea of insurance.

Figure 13–45
The pristine beach without footprints

Figure 13–46
The model on the ladder
with supports

Step by Step

1. Franklin began by constructing a ladder with bolted poles which would stand up at an angle by itself. He then went on location to shoot the scene at the beach.

2. Before introducing the ladder, the pristine scene was photographed without footprints (Figure 13–45).

3. Franklin added the ladder to the scene, careful not to get footprints in the sand where the shadow would fall. The model climbed the ladder to pose for photographs (Figure 13–46).

4. The images were scanned on a Nikon 3510 scanner.

5. The model on the ladder was copied and pasted into the pristine background and then color corrected.

6. The ladder supports were removed with the Rubber Stamp tool by cloning the surrounding areas. Franklin used masks during retouching as friskets (Figure 13–47).

7. Later Franklin was able to create another version with a different sky.

Figure 13–47
The masks used for
retouching the ladder,
model and shadow

Franklin's photographic style and subject have not changed drastically with the advent of digital imaging: "I used to do stuff like this without Photoshop but it was really difficult. I've always been trying to get this kind of control." He warns about the danger of sitting too many hours in front of the computer at the expense of going out and taking pictures.

"MICROSOFT OFFICE AD" BY ANDREW RODNEY

Andrew Rodney graduated from Art Center College of Design in Pasadena, California. He currently works as an advertising photographer in New Mexico.

Rodney's system includes a Quadra 900, 40 Mb RAM, Raven 1 Gb array drive, DayStar Charger PFS DSP board, Wacom digitizing tablet, 13– and 17-inch Apple monitors.

This photo illustration was created for a direct mail advertisement for Microsoft Office to illustrate the capabilities of the Microsoft Office product in a graphic and humorous fashion.

Step by Step

1. The model was photographed in the studio in color with Fujichrome 120 film (Figure 13–48). Rodney also made an identical shot without the model because the client needed two versions: one with the man, and one with only the graphics.

2. The image was scanned on a Crosfield drum scanner to the RGB Color mode and opened in Photoshop.

3. Rodney created each floating element digitally. Some were screen dumps from actual Microsoft products, sized and cleaned up. Others were created with Photoshop's Type tool.

Figure 13–48
The model
photographed in
the studio

4. All elements were saved as paths so that the second image (without the man) could be created exactly the same way by copying and pasting all elements from one file into the other. To do this Rodney converted the paths to selections and then copied the selections.

"EPHEMERA" BY DOROTHY SIMPSON KRAUSE

Dorothy Simpson Krause received her Ph.D. from Pennsylvania State University, her MA from University of Alabama, and her BA from Montevallo University in Alabama. She currently is a Professor of Computer Graphics and Design at Massachusetts College of Art.

Step by Step

1. The scanned components include a photograph of a Medici palace from Florence, bits of imagery Krause collected in Italy, real glasses, leaf, dried flower, and a strip of black handmade paper for contrast.

2. The separate scans were composited on a Macintosh IIfx using Photoshop and Color Studio.

3. The final three megabyte file was printed on an Iris printer at 28 × 32 inches on handmade bark paper by Nash Editions. Gold leaf was added to the fleur-de-lys.

Thoughts of the Artist

My work is based upon the premise that our similarities are greater than our differences and that, at this time in history, electronic media enables us to transcend our separateness and to understand, as at no time in the past, our interdependence.

Although I was trained as a painter, I have always been a collage-maker, both in my art work and in my life. I work with what I have and what I find. I use historical and current images as the source material for my work, enlarging on the fragmented political, ethical, and social meanings they suggest by combining, layering, manipulating, and merging them into provocative statements or questions. Fragments of written language, signs, symbols, charts, and diagrams are embedded in our consciousness and in my images.

I want my work to have the quality of allegory; not to be factual, but to be truthful in character . . . .to question the issue of power and how it is implemented.

"TWISTING SPINE" BY TERRY TOYAMA

Terry Toyama received her BA from the University of California San Diego and her MA from Johns Hopkins University in Baltimore, Maryland. She currently works in the San Francisco bay area as a medical illustrator.

The "Twisting Spine" was used in a patient education booklet for people with back problems.

Step by Step

1. Toyama began by creating a pencil sketch from a skeletal model (Figure 13–49).

2. She scanned the sketch at 72 dpi grayscale to be used as a template for the final art.

3. She resampled the sketch to 300 ppi using the Image Size command and then converted it to CMYK Color mode.

4. For middle values, shadows, and highlights, she chose colors from the Trumatch Color system book (which are also palettes in Photoshop).

5. Toyama then created paths to serve as "friskets" for the illustration. The paths were converted to selections and then filled with solid colors from her limited Trumatch color palette.

6. Using the Eyedropper tool to choose colors from the artwork, she painted with the Airbrush tool to model the shapes and define the highlights and shadows.

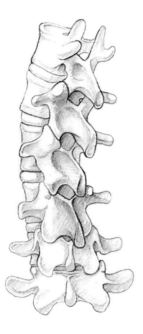

Figure 13–49
Toyama's original
pencil sketch

"BANKS & TERRORISM" (© 1993 THE BLADE) BY RICK NEASE

A self taught artist, Rick Nease is currently the editorial art editor at *The Blade*, a newspaper serving the entire Northwest Ohio's community.

Nease's system includes a Quadra 950 with 40 Mb RAM and 250 Mb Hard Drive. Besides Photoshop, he used Adobe Illustrator and Adobe Dimensions to create the piece.

"Banks & Terrorism" was created as an illustration for *The Blade*'s "Behind the News" Sunday section. The story analyzed the increasing terrorist attacks on many large banks and the resulting effects on the international banking community.

Step by Step

1. Nease started with an 3-D model created in Adobe Dimensions (Figure 13–50). The Columns and dollar sign were designed in Illustrator and brought into Dimensions and extruded. All other shapes were created in Dimensions, including the dynamite. Nease forced the general perspective, rendered the model, and opened it in Photoshop.

2. Nease created a mask for the background, selected it, and added a gradient color (fire orange to yellow).

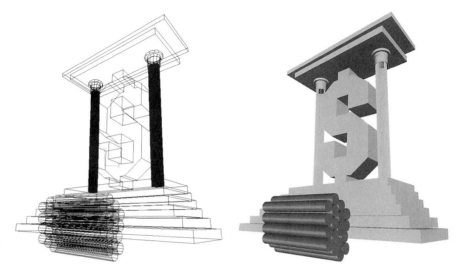

Figure 13–50
Nease created and
rendered the bank in
Adobe Dimensions and
then opened it in
Photoshop to finish
the piece.

3. Photos of actual terrorists caught on surveillance cameras from the Associated Press were cut out and placed in the background, stretching and distorting the shapes to follow the lines of the "bank" model. The tail end of the "terrorists" was then pushed around with the Smudge tool to achieve a painterly finish.

4. Nease selected the mask again and applied a displacement map Tile with an offset of 10, 10. This added the streaky texture and feathered the bank model into the background. He then inverted the selection and reversed the mask, applying the same displacement map with different settings (Tile-20-20, and offset of 20, 20) to help retain the detail of the "bank."

5. Finally, the artist added highlights with the Airbrush tool. To create the dynamite fuses, he made selections with small paths and added gradient blends.

Thoughts of the Artist

My Photoshop editorial illustrations vary in topics from AIDS to Zebras. Photoshop gives me the ability to create striking images under daily deadlines.

Some people in the arts community do not recognize computer illustration as a real art form. Even in *The Blade* the arts writer has referred to computer art as an oxymoron. Those who trash computer art are probably the same people who scoffed at airbrushes when they were first invented. But no matter the technology, the artist's eye is and will remain the most important tool known to artists. Without that, there aren't enough Mb in the world that will create good art.

"EVOLUTION OF A COMPUTER VIRUS (A HARMLESS VARIETY)" BY ELLEN VAN GOING

Van Going received her MA from the Johns Hopkins University, School of Medicine in Baltimore, Maryland. She currently works as a medical illustrator in the San Francisco area.

Van Going's system includes a Quadra 950 and a Microtek 600 flatbed scanner. In addition to Photoshop, she used Kai's Power Tools in the creation of this piece.

"Herpes" was created for the cover of a booklet describing the derivation, dynamics, and prevention of this viral disease. It was originally produced as reflective art for Krames Communications. The artwork was requested for re-use by Time-Life Books, so was recreated and modified digitally with permission from Krames Communications.

The image shows the herpes virus leaving a dead host cell, where it has replicated itself many times by taking over the host cell's genetic material. As the newly formed viruses move on to invade and destroy other healthy host cells, they are accosted and destroyed by the body's host defense mechanism, the immune system.

Step by Step

1. The final output size of the document was determined to be 5 × 7 inches at the 300 ppi. Van Going made a tissue sketch indicating positions of viruses to be added to the original image. She used a photograph of her original artwork, taken several years ago.

2. The artist scanned the photograph of her artwork into Photoshop.

3. Van Going worked from the specific to the general to rebuild and modify the image. She used the Pen tool to outline the inner crystalline structure of the herpes viruses, converted the path to a selection, and saved it as a separate channel. She then selected the outer capsules, nuclei, and cytoplasmic structures of all the cellular elements and also saved them as separate channels.

4. To the crystalline structure the artist applied first a feather of 12 pixels and then the Extrude Filter with Pyramid, Size 100, Depth 110 settings.

5. The outer circular capsule (with spikes) was enhanced with the Airbrush, Paintbrush, and Blur tools.

6. Van Going copied the finished herpes virus element several times at various sized to suggest the ubiquity of the viral invasion.

7. She next manipulated and enhanced the host defense cell and the macrophage using a combination of the KPT Texture Explorer Filter for nuclear texture and the KPT Glass Lenses Filter.

8. She enhanced highlight and shadow areas throughout the image using the Airbrush tool at various opacities and brush sizes.

9. Finally the entire image was brightened and color enhanced using the Curves Command. Afterward, Van Going applied a soft glow around the major herpes viruses to suggest their infective properties.

Van Going says, "Upon finishing this piece, I realized that, indeed, I had created yet another 'computer virus,' but with a happy ending—it is harmless in digital form!"

"HARDWARE UPGRADE" BY NICK FAIN

Nick Fain has a fine art background and worked as an illustrator and designer for 15 years before switching to electronic photo illustration. He was one of the first beta test sites for Photoshop.

"Hardware Upgrade" was created for *Multimedia World* magazine to illustrate the physical improvements to the PC computer.

Step by Step

1. Fain shot a 4 × 5 inch transparency of the computer and component parts (Figure 13–51). He shot 35mm photographs of a single model in the studio, asking him to take poses based on the computer background photograph (Figure 13–52).

2. The photos were scanned into Photoshop, cleaned up, retouched, and silhouetted.

3. The artist placed the workers into the composition and made minor adjustments in arm and leg positions. Masks for each figure were saved as a selection, feathered, and inverted, and then cast shadows were created.

4. When all the elements were composited, Fain floated the entire composition and applied a Gaussian Blur of 10 to 20 pixels at 50% Opacity on Lighten only. This produced a bright glow with a soft focus. Because Gaussian Blur tends to flatten out contrast, he went back into the image and added contrast where needed.

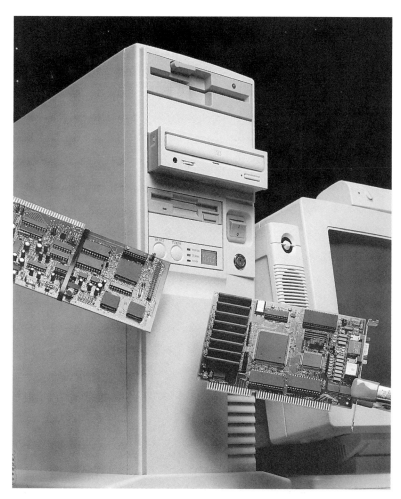

Figure 13–51
The computer was photographed with the hanging upgrade boards.

Figure 13–52 One model was photographed in various poses in the studio.

Thoughts of the Artist

Photoshop 3.0 is a high-end professional tool. Anything at the pro level requires more computer power, processing power, and RAM. Get the fastest Power Mac you can afford and jam as much RAM as possible into it.

In general I recommend that designers come to electronic imaging with a firm background in conventional printing, production, and illustration.

In the near future we will see quantum leaps in hardware and technology, affordable digital cameras for various applications, 64 bit color, and digital prints on par with darkroom prints. We'll go beyond CMYK gamut printing. Digital imaging is on the cusp of a new plateau.

"COUCH POTATO FAMILY" BY JEFF SCHEWE

Jeff Schewe received his BS at Rochester Institute of Technology. He is now an advertising photographer in Chicago.

Schewe's system includes a Quadra 950, 256 Mb RAM, arrayed 1.6 Barracuda 1 drives, dual monitor setup—14 and 21 inches—and a Wacom digitizing tablet.

"Couch Potato Family" was created as an ad for potato fungicide for Bader/Rutter Advertising in Milwaukee. The image had to be shot in multiple photos and collaged together because of the different sizes of the objects.

Step by Step

1. Schewe began by shooting the elements that would go into the composition (Figure 13–53). He sent the film out for scans at a service bureau.

2. He cleaned up the scans in Photoshop and saved low-resolution versions for sizing and roughing in the composition.

3. He created paths to outline the various shapes, used these paths to create feathered selections and pasted the elements into the background shot of the television.

4. Schewe then composited low resolution images for the client.

5. After approval, he assembled the final images at film recorder resolution and sent out for film output to an 8 × 10 inch transparency.

Thoughts of the Artist

My approach is to work as photographically realistic as possible to create surreal imagery impossible to do with traditional photography. Digital imaging offers more total control over the final image. There really aren't any good excuses left as to why something can't be done . . . which puts a lot of pressure on creators.

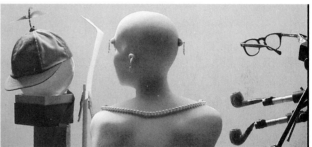

Figure 13–53   The television, the potatoes, and costume elements

"CHESTNUTS ROASTING" BY PHILIP ROSTRON

Trained in London, Philip Rostron now owns a photography and digital imaging studio in Toronto.

Rostrum's system includes a Quadra 950, 200 Mb RAM, a 2 Gb twin array hard drive, 5.25 inch 650 Mb optical drive, SyQuest, screen accelerators, and a 21-inch monitor. In addition to Photoshop he uses Live Picture.

"Chestnuts Roasting" was created as a promotional Christmas card.

Step by Step

1. Rostron began by photographing a fireplace in an old mansion. The fire and legs were shot in the studio (Figure 13–54).

2. The fireplace had to be expanded by cloning stonework with the Rubber Stamp tool. The fire was built out of dozens of flames for a "cartoon look."

3. He pasted all the elements together, added motion with the Motion Blur filter and touched it up, adding shadows to the legs.

Figure 13–54   The fireplace, boots, and fire photographs Rostron used to create "Chestnuts Roasting."

"CLOUD BURST" BY GREG VAN DER HOUWEN

Greg Van der Houwen owns Interact, a computer graphics firm outside of Seattle. He went to the School of Hard Knocks and "has yet to receive a degree."

Vander Houwen's system includes a Mac IIci, Power Mac 7100, Wacom digitizing tablet, and Minolta 35mm SLR camera. In addition to Photoshop, he used Adobe Illustrator and Fractal Design Painter to create the piece.

Vander Houwen grew up in the semi desert of central Washington state, where the foreground of "Cloud Burst" was photographed: "When it rained in the spring the landscape seemed to bloom. I remember the sweet smell, the sudden color change, the contrast between bone dry and wet. As a child I remember thinking of rain as water from heaven, probably due to how rarely it rained there." The image was created from these memories.

Step by Step

1. This image was composed from four elements: the clouds, the waterfall, the desert, and the stars (Figure 13–55). Vander Houwen started with a background composite of the desert and the sky.

2. Vander Houwen extracted selection masks from the composite and applied various filters to them. He then painted in fog to appear as though it had settled into the small valleys.

3. In a second document he retouched the waterfall to separate it from its background. It was then opened in Fractal Design Painter, where he applied a paper texture.

4. After compositing the waterfall into the desert and sky scene through a semitransparent mask, he painted it into the background.

Figure 13–55
The original
photographs of the
waterfall, sky, and desert

5. The stars were created in Adobe Illustrator where they were distorted and scaled for placement into Photoshop. The Illustrator document was pasted into an alpha channel and used as a mask to make hue and tonal adjustments to the main image.

6. The file was output to a 4 × 5 inch transparency on the LVT film recorder. The image is about 60 Mb as an uncompressed TIFF file.

"BLACK AND WHITE 1" BY NINO COCCHIARELLA

Nino Cocchiarella attended the North Carolina School of Arts. He currently works as a designer in Indiana and uses both an IBM PC-compatible and a Macintosh computer.

Cocchiarella's system includes American Megatrends EISA 486, 66 MHz with 64 Mb of RAM, American Megatrends EISA fast SCSI II caching controller with 4 Mb cache, Matrox MGA 64-bit video card, Fujitsu 1 Gb hard drive, Fujitsu 128 Mb optical drive, Wacom digitizing tablet, Screen DT-S1015AI drum scanner, and Umax 840 scanner. In addition to Photoshop his software includes Adobe Illustrator, Fractal Design Painter, and QuarkXPress.

"Black and White 1" was produced in Adobe Photoshop 3.0 for Windows.

Step by Step

1. Cocchiarella began with an image from a series of photographs based on hand-painted stones (Figure 13–56). Using a 4 × 5 camera,

Figure 13–56
The background layer is
a Polaroid photograph of
a hand painted stone.

he shot Polaroid-type 55 Positive/Negative film, which provides a "Polaroid edge."

2. He scanned the negative on his drum scanner for a high-quality image as the background layer.

3. He created a second layer, Layer 1, to add color to the black-and-white image (Figure 13–57). Setting the Layer Option to Soft Light, the artist stretched the Gradient Tool from red to blue across the image diagonally, colorizing the image without effecting the white area.

4. Next he used the Pen tool to outline the hand-painted design on the stone, making a selection with a four-pixel feather. He then applied another gradient in the opposite direction. Then the "up" text was added to Layer 1.

5. Layer 2 contains the majority of the text and shadowed text (Figure 13–58). The Layer Option was set to Normal.

6. The words were created and enhanced with the new Lighting Effects filter, and a texture map (bump map) applied to produce a 3-D effect.

7. In layer 2 the word "lights," along with its soft shadow, were originally placed closer to the other text. The selection had been dropped, but

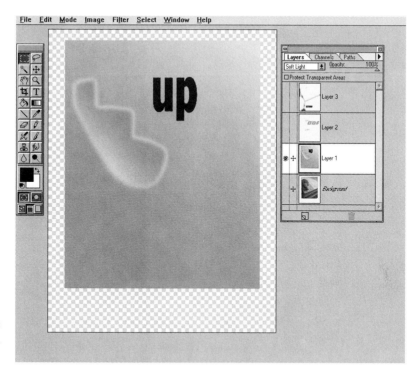

Figure 13–57
On Layer 1, the
gradients and the word
"up" were added .

Figure 13–58
Layer 2 contains the text
and shadows.

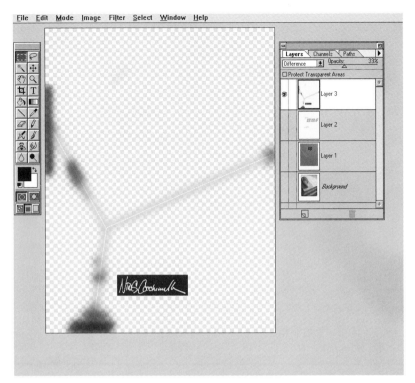

Figure 13–59
Layer 3 contains the
laser beams
and touchups.

later Cocchiarella decided to move it. He selected the small part of that layer containing that text and shadow with the Marquee and moved it, without effecting anything else. States the artist, "Never again will those horrifying words 'dropping the selection' be spoken again!"

8. Laser-beam-looking lines were created using the Pen tool to make paths stroked with the Airbrush tool set at different sizes and colors (Figure 13–59). This layer was set to the Difference mode at 33% Opacity in the Layer Options (like painting with a negative brush). Other touchups were done on this negative layer as well.

"KUSHI'S DREAM" BY HAGIT COHEN

Hagit Cohen received her MA from Rochester Institute of Technology in New York. She currently works as a designer in San Francisco and for Pineapple, a multimedia producer in Israel.

Her system includes a Macintosh Centris 650 with 24 Mb RAM.

"Kushi's Dream" is part of a series of work that Cohen refers to as "collaborative portraiture." She photographs personal acquaintances holding objects closely related to them against a neutral background, and then interviews them about their childhood memories, their dreams, and where

Figure 13–60
The original
photographs of the sky
and daisy field

they see themselves in their lives. She then constructs a background based on her impressions of this information.

Step by Step

1. Cohen constructed "Kushi's Dream" pasting the component images of sky, daisy fields photographed in Israel, and Kushi using Composite Controls (Photoshop 2.5), layering with the Brightness only and Darkness only settings (Figure 13–60).

2. She scanned a photograph of plastic horses and tinted them with the Brush tool set to Color Only at various opacities. After distorting them slightly she pasted these horses into the sky above the fields.

In general, Cohen is not interested in the computer except as a tool that allows tremendous freedom. She is more concerned about "quality art" and what it expresses; how the art is created is almost meaningless to her.

She advises, "Have a style of your own and something to say first. Don't worry about how many programs you have to learn or how much RAM you have."

"PHOTOSHOP HANDBOOK COVER" BY BILL NIFFENEGGER

Bill Niffenegger considers himself a perpetual student. He is the CEO of the award-winning Niffenegger Studios, a design, illustration and training firm in Cloudcroft, New Mexico. He is the author of *Photoshop Filter Finesse* and *Kai's Power Tools Finesse, The Official Book/ CD.*

Niffenegger's system includes a Quadra 800 with 74 Mb RAM, Radius SuperMac PressView Monitor with a Thunder II GX 1360 card, a Wacom ArtZ tablet, Barracuda drives, a MicroNet 1.3 Gb Optical drive, a Microtek 45T Transparency scanner, and a two-page SuperMac Proof Positive Printer.

"Photoshop Handbook Cover" was commissioned by the cover designer, Amy King, and Random House. Niffenegger used many of Photoshop 3's

Figure 13–61
The original base photograph from the Italian Fine Arts, Prints and Photographs CD Rom from PhotoDisc. (© PhotoDisc)

Figure 13–62
The Dust & Scratches filter was applied to the entire layer to clean up the image.

new tools. The goals in conceptualizing the image were to portray sophisticated fun and unique effects.

Step by Step

1. The base image (from PhotoDisc's Volume 13, Italian Fine Arts, Prints and Photographs), a vintage photograph of a man viewing a photo album, was chosen for its nostalgic look and the distressed condition of the old, worn image (Figure 13–61).

2. Niffenegger opened the image from the CD at its largest size and then used the Image Size command to further enlarge the image to the size of the book cover (plus a little extra for printer bleed). He left the image in the RGB mode and duplicated the background layer to make a new layer.

3. The new layer was selected and the Dust & Scratches filter applied to the entire layer at a setting of Radius 15 pixels and a Threshold of 20—a high setting, but the old daguerreotype had pronounced deterioration and scratches (Figure 13–62).

4. The entire new layer was colorized using the Airbrush tool with the mode set on Color. This layer was then duplicated for the next phase.

5. The new layer was partially removed using the Lasso tool while drawing a line which looked torn. The remaining portion of the man's arm

Figure 13–63
After colorizing the selection, the
Pointillist filter provided the texture.

Figure 13–64
The fairy figures were produced from a
font letter to which a mable-like texture
was applied.

was color enhanced using Curves to bump up the color to make it
more confetti-like.

6. The background was colored blue and the Pointillist filter applied.
   The torn edge was darkened with the Burn tool to give it a shadow
   (Figure 13–63).

7. The colorized layer was selected and the torn edge formed by the top-
   most pointillism layer. The edge was lightened using the Dodge tool
   to highlight the edge.

8. The colorized layer was cut away in the top third with the Lasso tool
   to reveal the original image. The edges of both layers were dodged
   and burned to give the illusion of torn dimensional layers.

9. The picture areas of the photo album were selected and made into
   new layer. Images from Niffenegger's arsenal of archival digital paintings were resized, skewed and rotated to fit within the active areas of
   the layer (pictures in the book).

10. The fairy-like figure was created from a Fontbank Font letter in the shape
    of a dancing figure. It was altered in black-and-white to the final shape
    and painted with highlights and shadows to appear more three-dimen-
    sional. Kai's Power Tools Texture Explorer in the procedural apply mode
    gave the figure the custom marble-like texture. The figure was then dupli-
    cated in increasingly more transparent percentages (Figure 13–64).

11. The dancing figure was pasted into the composition. An airbrushed touch of yellow with the Dissolve mode setting finished the piece.

12. The file was converted to CMYK Color mode using the SWOP Coated EFI Profile for Photoshop and saved as a TIFF file for importing into QuarkXPress.

Thoughts of the Artist

Amazing tools await the rabidly interested artist. Photoshop 3 is an astounding set of tools for imaging and of course a powerful repository for special-effects filters. While this book may be ending with an appropriate ride off into the sunset, I see a bright horizon over the bend for imaging.

Appendix A:
File Formats

File formats allow opening, importing, placing, saving, exporting, copying, and pasting graphic documents between programs.

Unless otherwise stated, you can assume that the following file formats are available with both the Macintosh and Windows versions. Depending on the file format, when you save, a dialog box like the one in Figure A–1 appears with various options. Although they look different, these dialog boxes provide the same options on both the Mac and Windows platforms.

When saving in a particular format on the Mac, you can include an abbreviation of the file format name as an extension to the name of your file, such as "house.PICT", to serve as a reminder.

When working on a PC under Windows, an extension is automatically added to a file name when saving.

Figure A–1
Although they look different, the save dialogs on both the Mac and Windows versions provide the same saving parameters.

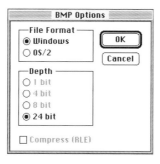
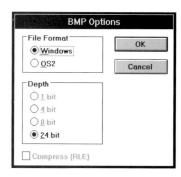

If you are saving a file on the Mac to be used on the a PC, it is critical that you save the file with a maximum of eight characters plus a three character extension divided by a period (example.TIF). On a PC the proper extension is essential for recognition of the file format. The extension for each file format is included below.

.PSD	Photoshop
.AI	Adobe Illustrator
.IFF	Amiga IFF
.HAM	Amiga HAM
.BMP	BMP
.RLE	BMP
.GIF	CompuServe GIF
.EPS	Encapsulated PostScript
.FLM	Filmstrip
.JPG	JPEG
.PCD	Kodak Photo CD
.MPT	MacPaint
.MAC	MacPaint
.PCX	PCX (originally PC Paintbrush)
.PCT	PICT File
.PICS	PICT Resource File
.PXR	Pixar
.PXI	PixelPaint
.RAW	RAW
.SCT	Scitex CT
.TGA	Targa
.VDA	Targa
.ICB	Targa
.VST	Targa
.TIF	TIFF

Photoshop 3

The native Photoshop 3 format is preferable when saving images in any color mode that you do not plan to export to another application. Only the Photoshop 3 format supports layers created in your document. It will also store any layers, channels, and paths in your image. (Layers, channels and paths are described in Chapter 6, "Image Selection and Masking".) The image will always retain the full color information it started with, whether imported into Photoshop as a 256-color indexed image, grayscale, 24-bit or even 48 bit file. This is the only format that supports all of the display modes. When you are working in Photoshop, Photoshop 3 files can be opened and saved much quicker than in any other file format. It is also the preferred format for moving Photoshop files between Macintosh and Windows platforms.

Some programs recognize the Photoshop format. For example, Specular Collage version 2.0.1 and later can save in Photoshop 3 format, and retain the layers created in Collage when then the document is opened in Photoshop. Adobe Premier also recognizes Photoshop 2.5 format.

Included with Photoshop 3 format, by default, is a flattened version of the image readable by programs that can recognize the Photoshop 2.5 format. This feature increases the file size of the document. Turn off this feature to save space if you are working only in Photoshop 3 by choosing General Preferences under the File menu and then click the More button. A Photoshop 3 file can be saved in Photoshop 2.5 format if it doesn't have layers.

CAUTION: **Photoshop 3 can have up to 24 Channels. Since Photoshop 2.5 can only open files with a maximum of 16 Channels, a file with more than 16 channels will not open. Opening and saving a file in Photoshop 2.5 format flattens the image, discarding all Layers.**

If you need to save the file in another format, always retain the original in the Photoshop 3 format. Choose the Save a Copy command to save a version in another format without losing the original document attributes and to keep the original open on the monitor. When saving a file in another format, be sure to give it different name if you want to keep the original.

Photoshop 2.0

Save a file in this format with the Macintosh version only if you need to open it in Photoshop 2.0 or 2.5 for the Macintosh . This format will retain all of the features available in Photoshop 2.0, discarding everything else. Note that you cannot save in this format while in the Lab mode, because the Lab mode does not exist in version 2.0. If you Save an image with layers into this format, you will merge all your layers and flatten your image because layers were not supported before Photoshop 3.

Furthermore, all duotones saved as EPS files will lose their color between Photoshop 2.0 and 2.5 formats because the duotone information is in the resource fork in 2.0 and in the data fork in 2.5.

Adobe Illustrator

Adobe Illustrator, an application available on both Macintosh and Windows, stores files using Adobe's Postscript code. Adobe provides a way to open and import vector art from Illustrator (or from Aldus FreeHand and CorelDRAW!, when saved in Illustrator 3 format) into Photoshop. Illustrator can also save in the EPS format which Photoshop can open.

Illustrator files can be opened with the Open command from the File menu, which will create a new Photoshop document, rasterized into a bit-map at the specified resolution. You can also choose the Place command in the File menu, which places an Illustrator file as a floating selection on top of an existing Photoshop document. On the Macintosh, it's also possible to copy Illustrator 5.0 or 5.5 images to the Clipboard and paste them into Photoshop.

Photoshop files cannot be saved in Illustrator format because it is a vector format. However, you can export pen tool paths created in Photoshop with the Paths to Illustrator Export plug-in. If you are working on the Macintosh, you can also copy your path to the Clipboard and paste it into an Illustrator file. You can also copy Illustrator paths into Photoshop via the clipboard. See Exporting Paths to Vector Programs in Chapter 11, "Output."

Amiga IFF

The Amiga Interchange File Format (IFF) is the standard raster file format for the Commodore Amiga. Use this format to transfer images between the Macintosh/Windows and the Amiga. Some paint programs on IBM computers also support this format. RGB, Indexed Color, Grayscale and Bitmapped modes can be saved in this format.

There is a special compressed form of IFF called HAM which is an export module; see Amiga HAM below.

Amiga HAM

The Amiga HAM (Hold and Modify) format is a compressed form of Amiga IFF. It brings Macintosh PICT images into an Amiga computer. Photoshop can open Amiga images, but because the format compresses by using a pixel packing method (compressing approximately 12–bits into 6–bits), Photoshop must use an Export plug-in to save in this format. Choose Export from the File menu and Amiga HAM from the submenu.

The original Amiga HAM format had only two common sizes, 320 x 200 pixels or 320 by 400 pixels (Figure A–2). Some more current programs can read HAM images that do not conform to the above common sizes, but these applications use pixels that are not square. In order to prepare an image properly in Photoshop (so it maintains its proportions when exported), resize the file using the Image Size command under the Image menu. Uncheck the Proportions option. For a noninterlaced image, enter 120 percent in the Width text field and 83 percent in the Height text field. For an interlaced image, enter 60 percent in the Width text field and 166 percent in the Height text field. The image will be distorted in Photoshop, but will have the correct proportions on the Amiga.

Anti-Aliased PICT

The PICT format on the Macintosh is sometimes used to store vector images created by basic drawing programs. The Anti-Aliased PICT Acquire module rasterizes a PICT graphic into a soft-edged anti-aliased file. Because the entire PICT image must be in memory for rasterization to take place, you are limited by the memory (RAM) of your computer as to how large an image you can import.

To import a PICT image on the Macintosh, choose Acquire under the File menu, then select Anti-Aliased PICT. You can choose the image dimensions, opening it as Grayscale or RGB. This module is not available for Windows (Figure A–3).

Figure A–2
When exporting in the Amiga HAM format, make sure that the application you use can accept a non standard IFF file size.

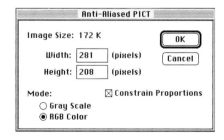

Figure A–3
The Anti-Aliased PICT dialog box

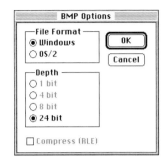

Figure A–4
The BMP Options Save
dialog box

BMP

BMP is the abbreviation for Microsoft Windows Bitmap. Developed by Microsoft Corporation, the BMP format is designed to be used under DOS, Windows, Windows for Workgroups, Windows NT, and OS/2. This format uses two methods of encoding: one for Windows and DOS and one for OS/2. It supports saving from Bitmap, Grayscale, Indexed, and RGB modes. BMP files support 1-, 4-, 8-, or 24-bit depth.

When saving to this format, the BMP Options dialog box will appear. Select the appropriate operating system (Windows or OS2) and pixel bit depth (Figure A–4).

CompuServe GIF

CompuServe GIF (Graphics Interchange Format) is a raster file format that allows Indexed Color, Grayscale, or Bitmap images to be easily transported between computer platforms. It was developed by CompuServe Inc., a public online service, to allow its subscribers working on different platforms to store and exchange bitmapped and scanned artwork.

CompuServe GIF is probably the most widely used graphic format in the online world. A vast number of images, usually 16- or 256-color, are stored on bulletin boards and other online services. The GIF format is highly compressed to shorten download and upload times. It is supported on many platforms. Photoshop cannot open 24-bit GIF images (only Inexed Color, Grayscale, and Bitmap images).

EPS (Encapsulated PostScript)

EPS (Encapsulated PostScript) is one of the most useful formats for exporting grayscale and color images to page layout and illustration programs. Using this format you can place images into programs such as Adobe

PageMaker, QuarkXPress, Adobe Illustrator, and CorelDRAW!. The EPS format works particularly well for images being prepared for color comprehensives or color separations.

Photoshop can open and place EPS files created in Adobe Illustrator (see Adobe Illustrator above). This is the only EPS format (besides the EPS files that Photoshop itself writes) that Photoshop can open. Photoshop can also open the PICT or TIFF previews of other EPS files (see EPS PICT or TIFF Preview below).

TIP: Another good format to place into page layout and illustration programs is TIFF. See the discussion of whether to use EPS or TIFF in Chapter 11, "Output." Some Photoshop effects, notably clipping paths and duotones, must be saved in EPS format to be used in another program.

An EPS file is made up of two parts. The PostScript part consists of the commands written in the PostScript page description language to create the illustration, image or page. This is sent to a PostScript printer at output time. The second part is an optional preview that is used in the application into which you place the EPS. It provides a screen representation, which is used for placing, scaling or cropping the graphic. On the Macintosh, the preview is a PICT resource. In Windows, the preview is usually a TIFF appended to the file.

When you choose to save in the EPS format you are presented with the EPS Format dialog box (Figure A–5). The Preview option gives you choices for 1-bit (black-and-white) or 8-bit (color) previews on Macintosh, 1-bit or 8-bit TIFF for IBM PC-compatible computers, or JPEG. JPEG is a form of compression discussed in Compression in Chapter 3, "Configuring Photoshop." A JPEG preview will create a smaller file than an 8-bit preview; it places into another application somewhat slowly because it must be decompressed.

Figure A–5
The EPS Format
dialog box

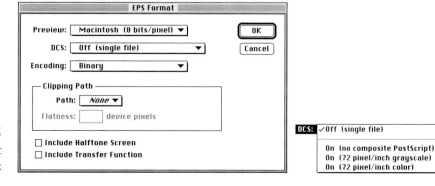

TIP: If you are printing color composites or color separations, always convert your images to CMYK before saving them. Photoshop will usually do a better job of converting colors than the default settings of most printers for color composites. You should save in CMYK for images to be color separated by illustration applications, page layout programs, or utilities like Adobe Separator which work with these programs. Avoid using JPEG compression.

For CMYK images, you will get a pop-up menu called DCS (Figure A–5). DCS, an abbreviation for Desktop Color Separation, is a special version of the EPS format originated by Quark Incorporated that has become widely adopted as a method of making color separations. You have two choices:

- If you are printing four-color separations, choose the option labeled "On (72 pixel/inch color)," creating a DCS 1.0 file version of EPS of five separate documents. This option pre–separates the high-resolution image data so that color separations can be printed more efficiently by illustration and page layout programs. Import the low-resolution color "master" file (which can be color, grayscale, or none) into your illustration or page layout program. The other four files contain the high-resolution information to be sent to the imagesetter when the color separation is printed.

- If you want a higher quality digital color print of your image placed into another application, select "Off (Single file)." The high-resolution image information can then be used to produce the color print. This choice produces a single file, instead of five files.

The Encoding option refers to how the image data is saved in the EPS file and sent to your printer. In most cases, Binary is the best choice, but if your setup can't handle it, choose ASCII. Another option is JPEG with four different levels of compression: low, medium, high, and maximum. Currently, you can use this option for printing a composite proof to a Postscript Level 2 color printer (not PostScript Level 1 printers). Avoid the JPEG option for printing separations because few applications can currently read and separate JPEG-encoded EPS files.

If you have an image incorporating pen tool paths, the Clipping Path option will appear with the option of choosing which path to save as a clipping path. You can also specify a flatness value. A clipping path is a path which is used for creating silhouetted images, which will knock out smoothly in another application. Chapter 6 describes how to create paths and save clipping paths.

When saving a Bitmap document in EPS format, the Save dialog box contains a Transparent Whites button. This button makes whites either transparent or opaque white when placed in a page layout program.

TIP: To prevent PostScript errors ("limitcheck") on high-resolution image-setters, save clipping paths with a higher flatness value. Flatness refers to how accurately the curves will be rendered. A value of 6 to 8 will print smoothly at high resolution on an imagesetter even though it looks rough on a lower-resolution printer.

If you select Include Halftone Screens, the choices you make in Screens in Photoshop will be saved with the EPS file; otherwise the image will print with the screen frequencies and angles that are set in the application that is printing the color separations. If you select Include Halftone Screens and do *not* set the screens in Photoshop, they will print at 53 lpi on any device, regardless of the desired screen frequency set in the other applications.

Any adjustments made in the Transfer Functions dialog will be saved with the EPS file, if Include Transfer Functions is checked.

Check with the service bureau or printer that will output your file as to whether you should save this information with your file. It is usually safer *not* to save with either Halftone Screens or Transfer Functions.

EPS PICT *or* EPS TIFF *Preview*

Photoshop 3 can open EPS preview images directly. On the Macintosh previews are saved as PICT files. On the PC, they are saved as TIFF files. You can use this feature to open previews from EPS files created in applications whose files Photoshop cannot itself open, such as QuarkXPress or PageMaker. The preview opens at 72 ppi and can then be edited like any other image. To open a PICT or TIFF Preview, click on the Show All Types button in the Open dialog box, select the desired EPS file, choose EPS PICT Preview or EPS TIFF Preview from the Format pop–up menu, and then Click on the Open button.

Filmstrip

QuickTime movies on the Macintosh or Windows platform exported from Adobe Premiere in the Filmstrip format can be opened and edited in Photoshop. Only the Mac version can save in the Filmstrip format. Photoshop can be used for *rotoscoping* (the traditional animation technique of tracing or drawing on individual frames of a film), special effects, and adding elements to movies. Individual frames or entire filmstrips can be manipulated (Figure A–6). No audio associated with that movie will be transferred, but as long as the number of frames in the filmstrip has not been changed, you can link the filmstrip back up with the sound in Adobe Premiere. See Chapter 12, "Multimedia," for more information on filmstrips.

JPEG

JPEG (Joint Photographic Expert Group) is a method for compressing color bitmapped images. JPEG is also the name of the committee that developed the method, and the file format for storing the compressed images. The format is based on the Discrete Cosine Transform (DCT) algorithm, which analyzes 8 x 8 or 16 x 16 pixel areas of an image (independent of resolution), and performs a sophisticated "averaging" of the values in the cell, dramatically decreasing image size.

JPEG is known as a *lossy* compression system. This is to contrast it from *lossless* compression schemes. Lossy compression sacrifices a level of detail and reproduction quality. The JPEG compression method allows you to specify the compression ratio. The higher the compression factor, the more data that is stripped out of the image, resulting in increasingly poorer quality in the final image. (Compression and JPEG are discussed in more detail in Chapter 3 "Configuring Photoshop.")

Photoshop automatically decompresses a JPEG file as it is opened. When you choose Save from the File menu, JPEG is one of the format choices. A dialog box (Figure A–7) allows you to choose a quality level: Low, Medium, High, and Maximum. "Maximum" will produce a larger file of higher quality; "Low" will produce a smaller of file of poorer quality.

TIP: Even with a good JPEG implementation, it is wise to minimize the number of times you compress an image. Save your final version on disk in JPEG once you have completed all the desired manipulation. Every time you resave an image in the JPEG format, the image quality is decreased.

MacPaint

MacPaint is the original Macintosh bitmapped format. Black-and-white images in 72 pixels per inch can be saved from the Bitmap display mode as MacPaint files. The size of this image is limited to 8 × 10 inches, which is 576 × 720 pixels. You can specify that the image appear either in the center or top-left corner of the MacPaint document (Figure A–8).

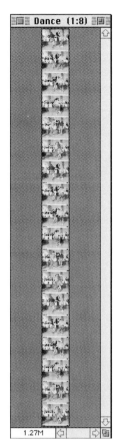

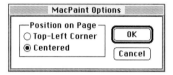

Figure A–7
The options when saving a JPEG file,
The higher the quality, the less
compression.

Figure A–6
A filmstrip document
window in Photoshop

Figure A–8
The MacPaint Options
dialog box

MacPaint is supported by most Macintosh programs and a few Windows programs, including Photoshop. Use this format with an old ImageWriter, for importing files into HyperCard, and when you absolutely want that crude neomodern digital look. (You can also save files in the Bitmap mode in the TIFF format for a similar digital look, but with more options for size and resolution.)

PCX

The PCX format was originally a proprietary raster file format developed in the early 1980s by ZSoft Corporation to support PC Paintbrush. ZSoft set up an OEM agreement with Microsoft which allowed Paintbrush to be distributed with various products including all copies of Windows. Because of the large

Figure A–9
The Photo CD Acquire plug-in
dialog box

Figure A–10
The Photo CD Open dialog box

number of images that were created with ZSoft products, PCX has become a widely supported format, particular for DOS and Windows applications.

The PCX format supports 1-, 4-, 8-, or 24-bit depth and can be saved from the RGB Color, Indexed Color, Grayscale, and Bitmap display modes. It has a relatively inefficient compression scheme which makes it a poor format for storing large images.

Photo CD

 Kodak Photo CDs use CD-ROMs to store and display images that originate by conventional photographic methods. Photo CDs can be opened either with an Acquire module available for both Macintosh and Windows (from Kodak), or the Open command. Choose Acquire from the File menu and Kodak Photo CD from the submenu (Figure A–9). The Open dialog box opens a Photo CD image using Kodak's Color Management System (KCMS) (Figure A–10). Photo CD files can be opened into Lab Color, RGB Color, and Grayscale modes at a variety of resolution choices. See Chapter 4, "Input," for a complete discussion of Photo CD technology.

Kodak Photo CDs can be opened directly into Photoshop, but Photoshop cannot save into the Photo CD format. Once a Photo CD file is opened it must then be saved into another format, usually the native Photoshop format.

The Photoshop Acquire module must be purchased from Kodak.

PICS

At first glance the PICS format seems inaccessible. A type of PICT Resource file, the PICS format is a common file format designed to exchange animation sequences between programs on the Macintosh. PICS files from supporting 3-D programs can be opened just like another other PICT Resources such as Scrapbook and Startup Screen files.

To open PICS files in Photoshop, use the Acquire submenu under the File menu and choose PICT Resource. Select a PICS file (or scrapbook) and Open. All frames of the PICS file (or scrapbook) are now available for editing one at a time in Photoshop (Figure A–13). After clicking the Preview button in the dialog box, click the arrow buttons to view each of the pictures in the file. Stop at the picture to be edited and click OK. Each image will open as an independent file. After editing, save each image into any format except the PICS format (Photoshop cannot save in the PICS format).

As previously mentioned, this process is identical for opening scrapbook files. To return images to the scrapbook, they must be copied and pasted one at a time back into the scrapbook.

PICT

PICT is a general-purpose file format for graphics on the Macintosh. There are two different types of PICT files: Version 1 and Version 2. Version 1 was the original format for object-oriented (vector) graphics programs (such as MacDraw) and for black-and-white bitmaps. Version 2, introduced simultaneously with the Macintosh II added support for complex vector files and color bitmapped (raster) images (of up to 24 bits of color depth). Virtually all applications on the Macintosh support the PICT format.

Although the PICT format can be saved, opened, or imported by most Macintosh programs and some Windows applications, including Photoshop, it is not recommended for use in programs where the final output will be printed to PostScript printers or for color separations. The TIFF or EPS formats are best for these uses (see the EPS and TIFF discussions). On the Mac, PICT files are good for on-screen presentations, movies, and animations created in applications such as Adobe Premier, Macromedia Director, Adobe Persuasion, Microsoft PowerPoint, and Vividus Cinemation. (See Chapter 12, "Multimedia.")

TIP: A bitmapped PICT file be can opened in Photoshop and saved in TIFF or EPS for output. If you have an object-oriented PICT file, you should use the Acquire plug-in on the Macintosh to open it. See Anti-Aliased PICT above.

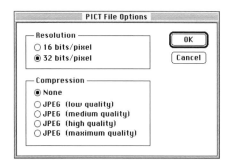

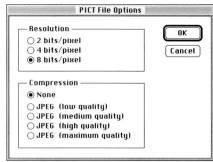

Figure A–11
The PICT File Options dialog box for saving from RGB Color mode

Figure A–12
The PICT File Options dialog box for saving from Grayscale mode

When saving from RGB Color mode you can choose between 16 and 32 bits per pixel. At 32 bits per pixel JPEG compression options become available (Figure A–11). When saving from Grayscale mode, you have your choice of 2, 4, or 8 bits per pixel. At 8 bits per pixel JPEG Compression options become available (Figure A–12).

When saving to the PICT format from the Indexed Color mode there is no choice as to the pixel depth or palette. These settings are determined by the palette in use, which was established at the time of conversion to the Indexed Color mode.

TIP: To save a document as an indexed color file with a custom color palette, you must convert the image to the Indexed Color mode at 8 bits per pixel, with the Adaptive Palette selected before saving. For the best results in saving an image with the System Palette, use the diffusion dither option with the System Palette selected when converting the image from RGB to the Indexed Color mode.

When saving a PICT file from Bitmapped mode there is no choice for pixel depth. The image will always be one bit per pixel, or black and white with no gray tones. Also, PICT files cannot be created from Lab Color, CMYK Color, Duotone, or Multichannel modes.

PICT Resource

On the Macintosh, the PICT Resource Acquire module imports PICT resources from files. Applications often store PICT images in their resource fork. The Scrapbook is an excellent example of this. To open a PICT resource, choose Acquire under the File menu, then select PICT Resource.

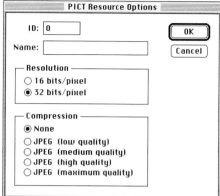

Figure A–13
The PICT Resource Acquire dialog box for opening Scrapbook images

Figure A–14
The PICT Resource Options dialog box

The PICT Resource dialog box lets you choose which resource to open (Figure A–13). With the Preview button you can scroll to the left and right through the PICT resources in the file. Clicking OK opens the displayed resource. This module is not available for Windows.

Photoshop allows you to save in Bitmap, Grayscale, Indexed Color, and RGB modes to create custom startup screens and to create PICT resources for inclusion in a Macintosh application (only programmers or computer nerds need apply).

When you save a file as a PICT resource, you can specify the resource ID (0 for startup screens), resource name, and resolution. The resolution and compression options are the same as the PICT format options (Figure A–14).

PIXAR

The PIXAR format is designed to transfer files to and from the high-end PIXAR computer workstations. These workstations are used for animation and photorealistic 3-D rendering. Only the RGB Color and Grayscale modes can be saved in the PIXAR format.

PixelPaint

You can save images in the PixelPaint format from Photoshop on both Mac and Windows versions in order to open the file in PixelPaint and PixelPaint Professional on the Macintosh. Later versions of PixelPaint

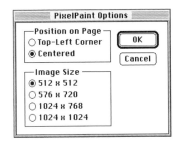

Figure A–15
The PixelPaint Options
dialog box

Professional no longer save to this format. Choose the document size (in pixels) and the position of the image on the page (Figure A–15). The PixelPaint format does not recognize 24-bit color, so make sure to convert color images to the Indexed Color mode before saving. PixelPaint will recognize and use a custom palette created by using the Adaptive Palette option when converting to Indexed Color mode. Only the Indexed Color, Grayscale, and Bitmapped modes can be saved in the PixelPaint format.

Quick Edit

This is not really a file format, but a method. The Quick Edit module allows you to open a portion of a large image, work on it, and then seamlessly insert it back into the main file. This is a good approach to working with large high resolution files that only need manipulations in certain sections of the file. The module works with uncompressed TIFF images and files stored in the Scitex CT file format. QuickEdit Acquire opens Photoshop 2.0 files, but not Photoshop 3 files.

TIP: Use Quick Edit to test a Photoshop effect on a small part of an image before taking the time to apply it to the whole picture.

To use this module, choose Acquire under the File menu and select Quick Edit. Select the file to be opened, and the Quick Edit dialog box will appear (Figure A–16). Drag with the cursor to select the portion of the image to be opened. The pixel dimensions of your selection and the file size are displayed. You may also check the Grid check box, in which you define a grid of *x* by *y* rectangles and then select one of the grid rectangles to be opened for editing. Click OK to open the selected portion of the image as a new Photoshop document. After all work is completed, choose Quick Edit Save in the Export submenu under the File menu to place it back into the original file in perfect registration.

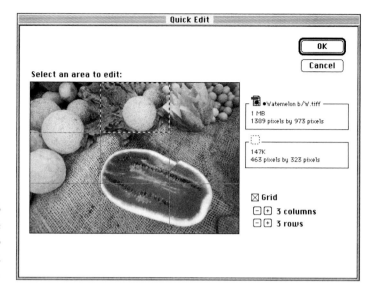

Figure A–16
The Quick Edit Acquire module allows you to open and edit a section of a document.

Raw

Raw format is a generic raster format, primarily for importing and exporting images to specialized applications that use other file formats or computer platforms. Binary code is used to describe pixels. All colors and channels are retained. The file type, file creator, and header can be indicated, as well as whether the color order is to be interleaved. You can save to the Raw format from any mode except the Bitmapped mode. Refer to the Photoshop manual for more information on how to open or save images in the Raw format (Figure A–17).

Figure A–17
The Raw Options dialog box

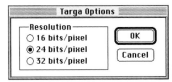

Figure A–18
The Targa Options
dialog box

Scitex CT

Scitex CT (Continuous Tone) is a raster file format developed to represent scanned images for placement and color separation in a Scitex prepress system. Images can be saved in Scitex CT format from the Grayscale, RGB, or CMYK Color display modes and then be transported to a Scitex workstation for high-end color separation and incorporation into page layouts.

The Scitex CT format can handle high-resolution images but it does not save Channels or Paths. When imported into Photoshop, a Scitex CT image automatically opens into the CMYK Color mode. Furthermore, Scitex CT file format requires special software for transfer to a Scitex system. Photoshop can save in the format, but not transfer.

Targa

Targa (TGA) is the most common format found in higher-end PC-based paint systems. TrueVision Company developed this proprietary raster file format for its high-end DOS TrueVision video boards and color applications. Long before Photoshop existed on either platform, people were creating images in TGA.

TGA files support 16, 24, or 32 bits depth (Figure A–18). The 32 bit images open in Photoshop with an extra Channel (Number 4) in RGB mode that can be used as an overlay layer or mask. Some programs expect the 24-bit RGB file to include an alpha channel, even though the alpha channel isn't recognized, hence the 32-bits per pixel option. Targa files can be saved from the RGB Color Indexed Color mode and Grayscale modes.

TIFF

TIFF (Tag Image File Format) was developed by the Aldus Corporation (now united with Adobe Systems) to allow page layout programs to import and print continuous tone images (scanned grayscale graphics) as screened halftone images. Aldus originally developed the format for its own PageMaker software, and then made the format specifications available for other software companies to incorporate into their software. In doing so,

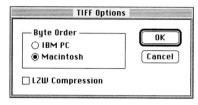

Figure A–19
The TIFF Options
dialog box

Aldus established a format that continues to be the standard for transferring scanned images among various programs and between multiple computers. The TIFF format is readily supported by Macintosh, PC/Windows, and many other platforms.

TIFF is designed specifically for scanned images, which are always raster (bitmap). It does not support vector (object-oriented) graphics, so it is not an efficient format for line art. TIFF files can be saved from all of Photoshop's modes (with channels and color properties included) except from the Multichannel and Duotone modes. While most people think that there is only one type of TIFF file format, there are actually a variety of TIFF subformats and variations. Most are supported by current software. For example, one variant of the TIFF format involves a built-in level of lossless file compression (LZW encoding), which some scanner software can output but some older page-layout programs do not support. Photoshop can import some types of LZW-compressed scanned images, and can save images with LZW compression (Figure A–19). If you want to export LZW TIFF images from Photoshop, make sure that your page-layout program will support compressed TIFF files.

When saving a TIFF file you have the option of including the Channels. There is no reason to save the Channels if you are saving the image in the TIFF format to import and print in another program. Some programs will not allow you to import the file if it contains Channels. You cannot save in the TIFF format if there are any Layers in the document; you must flatten the image prior to saving it.

TIP: Be sure to save the original version of your document with the Channels and Layers in place in case you want to use them again later.

The TIFF format exists on both Mac and PC platforms. When saving a file from Photoshop, you have the option to select for IBM PC or Macintosh formats (Figure A–19). The order in which the data is stored is different on the two platforms. Another file format that works well on both platforms is EPS. TIFF and EPS are the best choices for moving files between platforms, for printing to PostScript printers, and for outputting color separations. See the discussion in Chapter 11, "Output," on how to decide whether to use TIFF or EPS formats.

TWAIN

TWAIN is not a file format, but a method of acquiring images. Some scanners, particularly those with software for the Windows platform, use the TWAIN interface, which can be accessed as an Acquire plug-in. To use the scanner, choose Acquire under the File menu and then choose TWAIN Acquire (TWAIN for Windows users). See Chapter 4, "Input," for details on installation and use.

Appendix B: Contributors to This Book

Mark Siprut

School of Design, Art, and Art History
San Diego State University
San Diego, CA 92182
(619) 594-5446
PShandbook@aol.com

Contributing Writers

Anna Stump

744 G St., Suite 205B
San Diego, CA 92101
astump@aol.com

Steve Schubitz

Published Perfection!
7486 La Jolla Blvd. #552
La Jolla, CA 92037
(619) 546-9309
72047,3402 CompuServe

Steve Werner

Summit Communications
189 Duncan St.
San Francisco, CA 94110
(415) 550-7515

Andrew Rodney

Photographer
30 Gavilan Road
Santa Fe, NM 87505-8840
(505) 466-1993
71512,3205 CompuServe

Chris Swetlin

Mediaweave
39111 Paseo Padre Pkwy., Suite 207
Fremont, CA 94538
(510) 794-7553
mediaweave@aol.com

Matt Brown

Adaptive Solutions
140 Meadowood Dr.
Portola Valley, CA 94028
(415) 851-7460
powershop@aol.com

Sandra Alves

1912 Rowan St.
San Diego, CA 92105
(619) 262-5617
(619) 554-8233

Contributing Artists

Raquel Aceves

12642-14-16 Poway Road #146
Poway, CA 92064
(619) 788-0366
rockace@aol.com

Joseph Bellacera

100 Archer Place
Dixon, CA 95620
(916) 678-0163

Eric Benson

811 Vera Avenue
Redwood City, CA 94061
(415) 367-9124

Alan Brown

Photonics Graphics Inc.
700 W. Pete Rose Way
Cincinnati, OH 45203
(513) 723-4440
AlanBrown@pol.com

Dan Burkholder

7003 Forest Meadow
San Antonio, TX 78240
(210) 523-9913
Danphoto@aol.com

Craig Carlson

Photographer
266 J Street
Chula Vista, CA 91910
(619) 422-4937
(619) 420-7390 fax

Nino Cocchiarella

Cocchiarella Design
22 East Powell Avenue
Evansville, IN 47713
(812) 422-6250

Adam Cohen

252 West 17 St. #5B
New York, NY 10011
(212) 691-4074

Hagit Cohen

2 Aztec Street
San Francisco, CA 94110
(415) 821-6515

Tom Cross

278 Harvey Square Rd.
Whitney Point, NY 13862
(607) 692-4636
608 N. Casey Key Rd.
Osprey, FL 34229
(813) 966-3843
Tjcwiz@aol.com

Margaret Evans

44 Birch Crescent
Rochester, NY 14607
(716) 271-6072

Nick Fain

Electronic Images
300 Broadway, Ste 32
San Francisco, CA 94133
(415) 398-3434

Diane Fenster

140 Berendos Avenue
Pacifica, CA 94044
(415) 338-1409
fenster@sfsu.eduFoster

Ed Foster

Ed Foster Group
222 Newbury Street
Boston, MA 02116
(617) 262-5899

Charly Franklin

Charly Franklin Photography
3352 20th Street
San Francisco, CA 94110
(415) 824-4000

Craig Freeman

Department of Art/College of Fine Art
University of Florida
302 FAC
PO Box 115801
Gainesville, FL 32611

Wendy Grossman

355 West 51st Street
New York, NY 10019
(212) 262-4497

Francois Guerin

7545 Charmant Dr. #1322
San Diego, CA 92122
(619) 457-1546

Dennis Haradyn

Red Cloud Communications
71 Garfield Ave. South
Hamilton, ON, Canada, L8M 253
(905) 312-1657
Dennis_Haradyn@magic.ca

David Herrold

110 Art Center
Depauw University
Greencastle, IN 46135
(317) 653-3306
Dherrold@depauw.edu

Emil Ihrig

VersaTech Associates
2166B Elkhorn Drive
Prescott, AZ 86301-5303
(520) 776-4531
sybilihrig@aol.com
72730,1153 CompuServe

Stephen Johnson

P.O. Box 1626
Pacifica, CA 94044
(415) 355-7507
Sjphoto@aol.com

Sanjay Kothari

130 West 25th Street
New York, NY 10001
(212) 647-9743
(212) 242-4401 fax
Skothari@aol.com

Dorothy Simpson Krause

32 Nathaniel Way
P.O. Box 421
Marshfield Hills, MA 02051
(617) 837-1682
DotKrause@aol.com

Ellen Land-Weber

Art Department
Humboldt State University
Arcata, CA 95521
Landwebere@axe.humboldt.edu

John Lund

Photodigital Imaging
860 Second Street
San Francisco, CA 94107
(415) 957-1775

Gary McDaniel

Mediaweave
39111 Paseo Padre Parkway, Suite 207
Fremont, CA 94538

Hiroshi Miyazaki

P.O. Box 16904
San Diego, CA 92176
(619) 283-4063

Bert Monroy

11 Latham Lane
Berkeley, CA 94708
(510) 524-9412

Rick Nease

Editorial Art Director
The Blade
541 N. Superior
Toledo, OH 43660
(419) 245-6148

Bill Niffenegger

Niffenegger Studios
The Green Tree Lodge
1007 Grand Blvd.
Cloudcroft, NM 88317
(505) 682-2776
(505) 682-3311 fax
afc bill@aol.com

Greg Notzelman

37 Hall Ave.
W. Somerville, MA 02144
(617) 776-5340
gnotzelman@delphi.com

Jean-Francois Podevin and Larry Scher

Design and Computer Manipulation
5812 Newlin Ave.
Whittier, CA 90601
(310) 945-9613

Guy Powers

130 West 25th Street
New York, NY 10001
(212) 647-9743
(212) 242-4401 fax

Bruce Powell

Synergy, Macintosh Multimedia Consultants
1398 Bathurst Place
El Cajon, CA 92020
(619) 447-9424
synergymac@aol.com

Philip Rostron

Instil Productions
489 Wellington St. West
Toronto, Ontario
Canada, M5V1E9
(416) 596-6587

Jeff Schewe

Schewe Photography
624 West Willow
Chicago, IL 60614
(312) 951-6334
Schewe@aol.com

Sharon Steuer

Valley Road
Bethany, CT 06524
(203) 393-3981
ssteuer@aol.com

Rob Sturtz

Rob Sturtz Marketing Support
16 Idlewood Rd.
White Plains, NY 10605
(914) 682-0114
RobArtS@aol.com

Cher Threinen-Pendarvis

475 San Gorgonio St.
San Diego, CA 92106
(619) 226-6050
ctpendarvs@aol.com

Terry Toyama

60 Parkridge Dr. #7
San Francisco, CA 94131
(415) 824-2698

Ellen Van Going

1144 Cambridge Rd.
Burlingame, CA 94010
(415) 579-2532
(415) 579-2532 *0 fax
Goingoing@aol.com

Greg Vander Houwen

Interact
P.O. Box 498
Issaquah, WA 98027
(206) 999-2584

Lanny Webb

190 Skyline Parkway
Athens, GA 30606
(706) 548-1768

Appendix C: Vendors

This appendix lists some of the products and their manufacturers that can be used with Adobe Photoshop. Many are discussed in this book. Check with the manufacturers to confirm the latest models and compatibility for your system and software.

Accelerator Cards

Lightning Effects ME

Spectral Innovations, Inc.
1885 Lundy Ave., Ste. 208
San Jose, CA 95131
(408) 955-0366
(408) 955-0370 fax

Newer Technology Image Magic

Newer Technology
7803 E. Osie, Ste. 105
Wichita, KS 67207
(316) 685-4904 or (800) 678-3726
(316) 685-9368 fax

PhotoDSP 400 (PC)

Storm Technology
1861 Landings Drive
Mountain View, CA 94043
(800) 275-5734 or (415) 691-9825

Power Pro Processor Upgrade, Charger, Turbo 040 Processor Upgrade, FastCache Quadra

DayStar Digital, Inc.
5556 Atlanta Hwy.
Flowery Branch, GA 30542
(404) 967-2077 or (800) 962-2077
(404) 967-3018 fax

PowerShop 64 Photoshop Image Processing Card

Adaptive Solutions
1400 NW Compton Dr., Suite 340
Beaverton, OR 97006
(503) 690-1236, (408) 749-8721 or (800) 48CNAPS

Radius Rocket, PhotoEngine, and Thunder IIII

Radius Inc.
215 Moffett Park Drive
Sunnyvale, CA 94089
(408) 541-6100
(408) 541-6150 fax

RasterOps PhotoPro

RasterOps Corp.
2500 Walsh Ave.
Santa Clara, CA 95051
(408) 562-4200
(408) 562-4065 fax

Calibration, Color Management Systems, and Scanning

Agfa FotoFlow

Agfa
100 Challenger Rd.
Ridgefield Park, NJ 07660-2199
(201) 440-2500 or (800) 227-2780
(201) 342-4742 fax

Cachet and EfiColor Works

Electronics for Imaging
2855 Campus Dr.
San Mateo, CA 94403
(415) 286-8600 or (800) 285-4565
(415) 286-8686 fax

Color Encore

Southwest Software, Inc.
3435 Greystone
Austin, TX 78731
(512) 345-2493

Colorimeter 24 and ColorMatch

DayStar Digital, Inc.
5556 Atlanta Hwy.
Flowery Branch, GA 30542
(404) 967-2077 or (800) 962-2077
(404) 967-3018 fax

Kodak Color Management System

Eastman Kodak Inc.
164 Lexington Rd.
Billerica, MA 01821
(508) 670-6523, (508) 670-6538, or (508) 670-6550

Ofoto and Colortron

LightSource Inc.
17 East Sir Francis Drake Blvd.
Larkspur, CA 94939
(415) 461-8000 or (800) 231-7226
(415) 461-8011 fax

Precision

KEPS
Eastman Kodak Co.
164 Lexington Rd.
Billerica, MA 01821-3984
(508) 667-5550

ScanMatch

Savitar, Inc.
139 Townsend St., Ste M100
San Francisco, CA 94107
(415) 243-3030
(415) 243-3080 fax

Other Hardware

DrawingSlate

CalComp, Digitizer Products Group
14555 N. 82nd St.
Scottsdale, AZ 85260
(714) 821-2000 or (800) 932-1212
(714) 821-2832 fax

Kurta IS, XGT and XLC /ADB Drawing Tablets

Kurta Corp.
3007 E. Chambers St.
Phoenix, AZ 85040
(602) 276-5533
(602) 276-7823 fax

Leaf Lumina digital camera and Leafscan scanner

Leaf Systems Inc.
250 Turnpike Road
Southboro, MA 01772
(508) 460-8300 or (508) 460-8304

PC/Windows SCSI CARDS

Adaptec Inc.
691 Milpitas Blvd.
Milpitas, CA 95035
(800) 959-7274

PC/Windows SCSI CARDS

Future Domain
2901 McGraw Ave.
Irvine, CA 92714
(714)-253-0400

Radius PressView 21T Monitor

Radius Inc.
215 Moffett Park Dr.
Sunnyvale, CA 94089
(408) 541-6100
(408) 541-6150 fax

ScanMaker film and flatbed scanners

Microtek Lab, Inc.
3715 Doolittle Dr.
Redondo Beach, CA 90278-1226
(310) 297-5000
(310) 297-5050 fax

Wacom Drawing Tablets

Wacom Technology Corp.
501 SE Columbia Shores Blvd., Ste. 300
Vancouver, WA 98661
(206) 750-8882 or (800) 922-6613
(206) 750-8924 fax

Color Matching Systems

ANPA-COLOR (NAA Color)

Newspaper Association of America
11600 Sunrise Valley Drive
Reston, VA 22091
(703) 648-1367

Focoltone Ltd.

Focoltone Ltd.
Springwater House
Taff's Well
Cardiff CFF4 7QR
United Kingdom
(44) 0222-81094

Pantone Matching System

Pantone, Inc.
55 Knickerbocker Rd.
Moonachie, NJ 07074
(201) 935-5500

Toyo Ink Co.

Toyo/Dupont Internation Ink Co.
P.O. Box 6099
Newark, DE 19714
(800) 227-8696

Trumatch Colorfinder

Trumatch, Inc.
25 West 43rd St., Ste. 802
New York, NY 10036
(212) 302-9100

Compression

Compact Pro

Cyclos
P.O. Box 31417
San Francisco, CA 94131-0417

Disk Doubler

Symantec Corp.
10201 Torre Ave.
Cupertino, CA 95014
(800) 441-7234 or (800) 626-8847 (in CA)

PicturePress

Storm Technology
1861 Landings Dr.
Mountain View, CA 94043
(415) 691-6600 or (800) 275-5734
(415) 691-9825 fax

Stuffit Deluxe

Aladdin Systems, Inc.
165 Westridge Dr.
Watsonville, CA 95076
(408) 761-6200
(408) 761-6206 fax

ZipIt (PC)

ZIPIT.SIT
Shareware
Data Library 5, DTP Forum on CompuServe

Filters and Plug-ins

Aldus Gallery Effects

Adobe Systems, Inc.
1585 Charleston Rd.
P.O. Box 7900
Mountain View CA 94039
(415) 961-4400 or (800) 833-6687
(415) 961-3769 fax

Andromeda Photography Series 1, 2, and 3

Andromeda Software Inc.
849 Old Farm Road
Thousand Oaks, CA 91360
(800) 547-0055

AutoMask, CD-Q, and Select

Human Software Company
P.O. Box 2280
Saratoga, CA 95070-0280
(408) 741-5101 or (408) 741-5102

Black Box

Alien Skin Software
2522 Clark Ave.
Raleigh, NC 27607-7215
(919) 832-4124 or (919) 832-4065

ChromaPoint, Photospot, Cromassage, PaintThinner, and ScanTastic

Second Glance Software
25381-G Alicia Parkway, Ste. 357
Laguna Hills, CA 92653
(714) 855-2331
(714) 586-0930 fax

Chris Cox Filters

Chris Cox
110 Oakland Circle
Madison, AL 35758
cc4b@andrew.cmv.edu
chriscox@aol.com

CyberMesh

Knoll Software
P.O. Box 6887
San Raphael, CA 94903

DQ-Animaq

Diaquest, Inc.
1440 San Pablo Ave.
Berkeley, CA 94702
(510) 526-7167
(510) 526-7073 fax

Epilogue PS

Total Integrations, Inc.
334 E. Colfax Road, Suite A-1
Palatine, IL 60067
(708) 776-2377 or (708) 776-2378

FASTedit/DCS
FASTedit/TIFF

Total Integration, Inc.
334 E. Colfax St., Ste. A1
Palatine, IL 60067
(708) 776-2377
(708) 776-2378 fax

FotoMagic

Silicon Wizards Inc.
5-34-4, J-Haus, Jingunae, Shibuya-ku
Tokyo, 150, Japan
(81) 3-5485-5985
(81) 3-5485-5987 fax
AppleLink: Tengu.dv

HSC Convolver
Kai's Power Tools

HSC Software
6303 Carpinteria Ave.
Carpinteria, CA 93013
(805) 566-6200
(805) 566-6385 fax

Intellihance

DPA Software
P.O.Box 940710
Plano,TX 75094
(214) 517-6876 or (214) 517-2354

Kodak Photo CD Acquire

Eastman Kodak Co.; CD Imaging
343 State St.
Rochester, NY 14650
(716) 724-4000 or (800) 242-2424

LaserSeps

Second Glance Software
25381-G Alicia Parkway, Ste. 357
Laguna Hills, CA 92653
(714) 855-2331
(714) 586-0930 fax

LineWorker
PlateMaker

InSoftware
2403 Conway Dr.
Escondido, CA 92026
(619) 743-7502
(619) 743-7503 fax

Paint Alchemy

Xaos Tools, Inc.
600 Townsend St., Ste. 270 East
San Francisco, CA 94103
(415) 487-7000
(415) 558-9886 fax

Pattern Workshop

3401 101st St., Ste E
Des Moines, IA 05322
(515) 270-8109
(515) 278 6828 fax
@Product 3:MicroFrontier

Paul Badger Filters

Paul Badger
2626 Deming Avenue
Columbus, OH 43202

PhotoFusion

Ultimatte Corp.
20554 Plummer St.
Chatsworth, CA 91311
(818) 993-8007 or (818) 993-3762

Photomatic

DayStar Digital
5556 Atlanta Highway
Flowery Branch, GA 30542
(404) 967-2077 ex 243
(404) 967-3018

ScanPrep Pro

ImageXpress
1121 Casanova Ct.
Lawrenceville, GA 30244
(404) 564-9924 or (404) 564-1632

SpectrePlug-in Color Correction
SpectrePlug-In Unsharp Masking

Pre-Press Technology
2443 Impala Dr.
Carlsbad, CA 92008
(619) 931-2695 or (619) 931-2698

Terrazzo

Xaos Tools
600 Townsend, Suite 270E
San Francisco, CA 91403
(415) 487-7078 or (415) 558-9886

Watermark

John Dykstra Photography
4788 Anderson Lane
Saint Paul, MN 55126
jdykstra@aol.com

Illustration/Paint Software

Adobe Illustrator

Adobe Systems, Inc.
1585 Charleston Rd.
P.O. Box 7900
Mountain View, CA 94039
(415) 961-4400 or (800) 833-6687
(415) 961-3769 fax

Canvas

Deneba Software
7400 SW 87th Ave.
Miami, FL 33173
(305) 596-5644
(305) 273-9069 fax

Color It! and Enhance

MicroFrontier
3401 101st St., Ste E
Des Moines, IA 05322
(515) 270-8109
(515) 278-6828 fax

Fractal Design Painter

Fractal Design Corp.
335 Spreckels Dr.
Aptos, CA 95003
(408) 688-8800
(408) 688-8836 fax

Live Picture

HSC Software
6303 Carpinteria Ave.
Carpinteria, CA 93013
(805) 566-6200
(805) 566-6385 fax

Macromedia FreeHand

Macromedia
600 Townsend St.
San Francisco, CA 94103
(415) 252-2000
(415) 626-0554 fax

Monet

Delta Tao Software, Inc.
760 Harvard Ave.
Sunnyvale, CA 94087
(408) 730-9336

PhotoEdge

Eastman Kodak Co.
343 State St.
Rochester, NY 14650-0405
(716) 724-1021 or (800) 245-6325

PhotoFlash

Apple Computer, Inc.
20525 Mariani Ave.
Cupertino, CA 95014-6299
(408) 996-1010

Specular Collage

Specular International
479 West St.
Amherst, MA 01002
(413) 253-3100 or (800) 433-7732
(413) 253-0540 fax

Image Databases and Managers

Adobe Fetch

Adobe Systems Inc.
1585 Charleston Rd.
P.O. Box 7900
Mountain View, CA 94039-7900
(415) 961-4400 or (800) 833-6687
(415) 961-3769 fax

Kudo Image Browser

Imspace Systems Corp.
2665 Ariane Dr., Ste. 207
San Diego, CA 92117
(619) 272-2600
(619) 272-4292 (fax)

Shoebox

Eastman Kodak Co.
343 State St.
Rochester, NY 14650-0405
(716) 724-1021 or (800) 245-6325

SmartScrap

Solutions, Inc.
30 Commerce St.
Williston, VT 05495
(802) 865-9220

Multimedia and Animation

Adobe Premiere, After Effects, and AfterImage

Adobe Systems Inc.
1585 Charleston Rd.
P.O. Box 7900
Mountain View, CA 94039-7900
(415) 961-4400 or (800) 833-6687
(415) 961-3769 fax

Arrange It and Create It

Eastman Kodak Co.
343 State St.
Rochester, NY 14650
(716) 724-4000 or (800) 242-2424

Avid VideoShop

Avid Technology, Inc.
Metropolita Technology Park
One Park West
Tewksbury, MA 01876
(508) 640-6789 or (800) 949-2843
(508) 640-1366 fax

CameraMan

Motion Works
524 2nd St.
San Francisco, CA 94107
(415) 541-9333

Cinemation

Vividus Corp.
651 Kendall Ave.
Palo Alto, CA 04306
(415) 494-2111
(415) 494 2221 fax

DeBabelizer

Equilibrium
475 Gate Five Road, Ste. 225
Sausalito, CA 94965
(415) 332-4343 or (800) 524-8651
(415) 332-4433 fax

Infini-D
LogoMotion

Specular International
479 West St.
Amherst, MA 01002
(413) 253-3100 or (800) 433-7732
(413) 253-0540 fax

Macromedia Director

Macromedia
600 Townsend St.
San Francisco, CA 94103
(415) 252-2000
(415) 626-0554 fax

Morph

Gryphon Software Corp.
7220 Trade St., Ste. 120
San Diego, CA 92121
(619) 536-8815 or (800) 795-0981
(619) 536-8932 fax

QuickFlix! and VideoFusion

VideoFusion
1722 Indian Wood Circle, Suite H
Maumee, OH 43537
(419) 891-1090 or (800) 638-5253
(419) 891-9673 fax

Page Layout

Kodak Renaissance

Eastman Kodak Co.
343 State St.
Rochester, NY 14650
(716) 724-4000 or (800) 242-2424

PageMaker

Adobe Systems, Inc.
1585 Charleston Rd.
P.O. Box 7900
Mountain View CA 94039
(415) 961-4400 or (800) 833-6687
(415) 961-3769 fax

PosterWorks

S. H. Pierce and Co.
Suite 323, Bld. 600
One Kendall Square
Cambridge, MA 02139
(617) 338-2222
(617) 338-2223 fax

QuarkXPress

Quark, Inc.
1800 Grant Street
Denver, CO 80203
(303) 894-8888 or (800) 788-7835
(303) 894-3399 fax

Pattern and Automated Imagery

KPT Bryce

HSC Software
6303 Carpinteria Ave.
Carpinteria, CA 93013
(805) 566-6200
(805) 566-6385 fax

TextureMaker

Adobe Systems, Inc.
1585 Charleston Rd.
P.O. Box 7900
Mountain View CA 94039
(415) 961-4400 or (800) 833-6687
(415) 961-3769 fax

TextureScape

Specular International
479 West St.
Amherst, MA 01002
(413) 253-3100
(413) 253-0540 (fax)

Photo CD

Kodak Photo CD Access
Kodak Photo CD Acquire
Kodak PhotoEdge
Photo CD Player
and related Photo CD products

Eastman Kodak Co.
343 State St.
Rochester, NY 14650
(716) 724-1021 or (800) 235-6325

Stock Imagery

ArtBeats

ArtBeats
P.O. Box 1287
Myrtle Creek, OR 97457
(503) 863-4429 or (800) 444-9392
(612) 699-1858 (voice/fax) or (800) 598-9884 (orders)
(503) 863-4547 fax

CD Folios

CD Folios
6754 Eton Ave.
Canoga Park, CA 91303
(818) 887-2003 or (800) 688-3686
(818) 887-6950 fax

Classic Textures

Pixar
1001 West Cutting Blvd.
Richmond, CA 94804
(510) 236-4000
(510) 236-0388 fax

Cloud Gallery

Mary and Michael
555 Bryant St., #356
Palo Alto, CA 94301
(415) 326-9567
(415) 326 6247 (fax)

CMCD Stock Photos

CMCD, Inc.
600 Townsend St., Penthouse
San Francisco, CA 94103
(800) 664-CMCD
(415) 730-0711 fax

Comstock Stock Photography

Comstock, Inc.
30 Irving Pl.
New York, NY 10003
(800) 225-2727 or (212) 353-8600
(212) 353-3383 fax

Corel Professional Photos CD-ROM

Stock Photography
Corel Corporation
The Corel Building
1600 Carling Avenue
Ottawa, Ontario, Canada K1Z 8R7
(800) 772-6753

D'pix Folio

D'pix, Inc.
929 Harrison Ave., Ste. 205
Columbus, OH 43215
(614) 299-7192 or (800) 238-3749
(614) 294-0002 fax

Digital Photographics CD-Rom

Husom & Rose Photographics
1988 Stanford Ave.
St. Paul, MN 55105
(612) 699-1858 (phone/fax) or (800) 598-9884
(orders)

Digital Stock

Digital Stock
7163 Construction Court
San Diego, CA 92121
(619) 794-4040 or (800) 545-4514
(619) 794-4041 fax

Fresco

Xaos Tools, Inc.
600 Townsend St., Ste. 270 East
San Francisco, CA 94103
(415) 487-7000
(415) 558-9886 fax

Image Bank

The Image Bank
Williams Square, Suite 700
5221 N. O'Connor Blvd.
Irving, TX 75039
(214) 432-3900
(214) 432-3960 fax

Letraset Nature Images CD

Letraset USA
40 Eisenhower Dr.
Paramus, NJ 07653
(201) 845-7370 or (800) 343-8973
(201) 845-5047 fax

PhotoDisc

PhotoDisc Inc.
2013 4th Ave.
Seattle, WA 98121
(206) 441-9355 or (800) 528-3472
(206) 441-9379 fax

PhotoSphere

PhotoSphere
Dept. 8110, Suite 413
250 H St.
Blaine, WA 98230
(800) 665-1496
(800) 757-5553 fax

Three-D Programs

Adobe Dimensions

Adobe Systems, Inc.
1585 Charleston Rd.
P.O. Box 7900
Mountain View, CA 94039
(415) 961-4400 or (800) 833-6687
(415) 961-3769 fax

Alias Sketch!

Alias Research, Inc.
110 Richmond St. E
Toronto, Ontario, Canada M5C1P1
(416) 362-9181 or (800) 447-2542
(416) 362-4696 fax

Infini-D

Specular International
479 West St.
Amherst, MA 01002
(413) 253-3100 or (800) 433-7732
(413) 253-0540 fax

MacroModel

Macromedia
600 Townsend St.
San Francisco, CA 95103
(415) 252-2000
(415) 626-0554 fax

Pixar Typestry 2

Pixar
1001 West Cutting Blvd.
Richmond, CA 94804
(510) 236-4000
(510) 236-0388 fax

Ray Dream Designer addDepth

Ray Dream Inc.
1804 N. Shoreline Blvd.
Mountain View, CA 94043
(415) 960-0768
(415) 960-1198 fax

Strata Vision Strata StudioPro

Strata Inc.
2 W. Saint George Blvd., Ste. 2100
St. George, UT. 84770
(801) 628-5218 or (800) 869-6855
(801) 628-9756 fax

TrueSpace

Caligari Corporation
1955 Landings Drive
Mountain View, CA 94043
(800) 351-7620 or (415) 390-9600
(415) 390-9755 fax

Utilities

Access PC

Insignia Solutions, Inc.
1300 Charleston Rd.
Mountain View, CA 94043
(415) 694-7600 or (800) 848-7677
(415) 694-3705 fax

Acrobat

Adobe Systems, Inc.
1585 Charleston Rd.
P.O. Box 7900
Mountain View CA 94039
(415) 961-4400 or (800) 833-6687
(415) 961-3769 fax

Ares FontMinder (PC)

Ares Software Corporation
565 Pilgrim Drive, Suite A
Foster City, CA 94404
(415) 578-9090

Capture

Mainstay
591-A Constitution Ave.
Camarillo, CA 93012
(805) 484-9400
(805) 484-9428 fax

Click Paste

Mainstay
591-A Constitution Ave.
Camarillo, CA 93012
(805) 484-9400
(805) 484-9428 fax

CorelSCSI for Windows (PC)

Corel Corporation
The Corel Building
1600 Carling Avenue
Ottawa, Ontario, Canada KIZ 8R7
(800) 836-7274

ColorSwitch

Ambrosia
P.O. Box 23140
Rochester, NY 14692

DOS Mounter Plus

Dayna Communications
Sorenson Research Park
849 W. Levoy Dr.
Salt Lake City, UT 84123
(801) 269-7200
(801) 269-7363 fax

Jag II

Ray Dream Inc.
1804 N. Shoreline Blvd.
Mountain View, CA 94043
(415) 960-0768
(415) 960-1198 fax

MAC-IN-DOS For Windows

Pacific Micro
201 San Antonio Circle, Suite C-250
Mountain View, CA 94040
(415) 948-6200

Macintosh PC Exchange

Apple Computer, Inc.
20525 Mariani Ave.
Cupertino, CA 95014-6299
(408) 996-1010

MacLink Plus/PC Connect

Data Viz, Inc.
55 Corporate Drive
Trumbull, CT, USA
(203) 268-0030

WinCapture (PC)

Professional Capture System, Shareware
JASC, Inc.
10901 Red Circle Drive, Suite 340
Minnetonka, MN 55343

WinZip (PC)

Shareware
Nico Mak Computing, Inc.,
P.O. Box 919
Bristol, CT 06011-0919

On Line Services

America Online

America Online, Inc.
8619 Westwood Center Dr.
Vienna, VA 22182
(703) 448-8700, (800) 827-6364, or (703) 883-1509

CompuServe

CompuServe Information Service
CompuServe, Inc.
5000 Arlington Center Blvd.
Columbus, OH 43220
(800) 848-8199

Delphi

Delphi Internet Services Corp.
1030 Massachusetts Ave.
Cambridge, MA 02138
(617) 491-3342 or (800) 695-4005
(617) 491-6642 fax

eWorld

Apple Computer, Inc.
20525 Mariani Ave.
Cupertino, CA 95014-6299
(408) 996-1010

GEnie

General Electronic Information Services
401 N. Washington St.
Rockville, MD 20850
(301) 340-4000 or (800) 638-9636
(301) 340-4488 fax

Internet resources for Electronic Publishers
Anonymous ftp sites with some paths listed:

Adobe
ftp.adobe.com
Apple
ftp.apple.com
CorelDRAW related files for PC/Windows
elvis.sccc.ac.uk

Hewlett Packard
ftp-boi.external.hp.com
Kai's Power Tips & Tricks
ftp.netcom.com
/pub/HSC/Kais_Power_Tips
Kai's Power Tips & Tricks, shareware, plug-ins,
demos, etc.
export.acs.cmu.edu
/pub/PSarch
Microsoft
ftp.microsoft.com
Misc. shareware plug-ins, demos, etc.
uxa.ecn.bgu.edu
/pub/archive/photoshop
/Photoshop-Files

World Wide Web Sites

Adobe
http://www.adobe.com/
Adaptive Solutions
http://www.best.com/~mbrown/asi/asi.html
PC Week
http://www.ziff.com/~pcweek/
CorelDRAW
http://brother.cc.monash.edu.au/alst4/csc3170/nbai1
/WWW/corel.html

Art-related lists:

Adobe Photoshop
Send: sub photshop <Your real name>
To: listproc@bgu.edu
Adobe Illustrator:
Send: subscribe illstrtr-l
To: listserv@netcom.com
National Press Photographers Association:
Send: subscribe NPPA-L <Your Realname>
To: listserv@cmuvm
Desktop Publishing:
Send: subscribe DTP-L <Your Realname>
To listserv@antigone.com
Quark Express:
Send: subscribe QuarkXPR <Your Realname>
To: listserv@iubvm.ucs.indiana.edu
PageMaker:
Send: subscribe Pagemakr<Your Realname>
To: listserv@indycms.iupui.edu

Glossary

32-Bit Addressing A Microsoft Windows technology for communicating directly with your hard disk using 32-bit disk access. This technique improves the performance of Windows.

acquire A command for importing images into Photoshop. Acquire commands are installed into Photoshop as plug-in modules, which provide direct access to scanners, digital cameras, video sources and other file formats.

additive primary colors The three additive primary colors, red, green, and blue, create all other colors when working with transmitted light (such as on a computer monitor). Pure red, green, and blue projected on top of one another create white light.

alpha channel A grayscale (8-bit) component image. RGB images are composed of three channels, red, green, and blue. The other channels can be used for masking. See *channel*.

ambient light Light illuminating an environment; indirect light

analogous colors Colors that are next to each other on the color wheel

anti-aliasing A function that smoothes edges of selections, type, and painting tool strokes to eliminate the jaggies, or stairsteps, caused by pixels

arbitrary map An option in the Curves dialog box to precisely define a curve by drawing with a Pencil tool

ASCII A standard format for text that has a binary number for each keyboard character and function. ASCII (American Standard Code for Information Interchange) is the most common and versatile format for transferring text between applications and platforms. Photoshop cannot open an ASCII file. ASCII is a method of encoding images when saving in the EPS format.

aspect ratio   The height-to-width ratio of a document or selection (image or type)

ATM   Adobe Type Manager (ATM) is software from Adobe that you install on your Macintosh or PC/Windows system. It creates an accurate screen display of your PostScript fonts and allows Photoshop to create smooth anti-aliased type at any size. Without ATM installed, type in Photoshop appears with crude jagged edges.

banding   stair-stepping effect when there are insufficient tones to reproduce a blend.

Bézier curve   A mathematical curve that describes a vector path. In Photoshop, Bezier curves are created by plotting anchor points with the Pen tool.

binary encoding   Digital coding based on digits "1" and "0," represented in an electronic circuit by "on" and "off." Binary is the most efficient method of encoding when saving in the EPS format.

bitmap image   A black and white image with no gray tones or colors defined by a grid of pixels. A bitmapped image has one bit of color information for each pixel.

black generation   When converting an RGB image to CMYK color mode, black generation refers to the values that are generated for the black plate.

bleed   Printing that extends beyond the edge of a page so that the ink meets the edge after the page is trimmed

BMP   See Appendix A, "File Formats."

brightness   The intensity of light reflected from or transmitted through an image. A method of describing color when combined with hue and saturation.

burn   See *dodge and burn.*

cache   RAM set aside to store data temporarily

calibration   The process of adjusting equipment to a standard measure to produce reliable, predictable, repeatable output.

calibration bars   An 11-step grayscale in 10% increments from 0% to 100% that prints along the edge of a page. When outputting color separations a progressive color bar is also printed. Calibration bars can be read with a densitometer to ensure accurate output and printing.

caption   Text next to a printed image providing information such as who, what, why, when, and where. Photo credits can also appear in a caption. You can save captions with an image in Photoshop 3 in the File Info dialog box.

CCD   Charged coupled device. A small, light-sensitive electronic sensor found in scanners and digital cameras that sends signals to a computer to digitize an image. The array of CCDs determines the optical resolution of the scanner to its camera.

CD-ROM   A technology that uses compact disc to store digital information in a "read only" format.

channel   An 8-bit grayscale (256 tones) component of a Photoshop document. An RGB image is composed of three channels, red, green, and blue, each with 256 values which combine to create over 16 million possible colors. A CMYK Color image is composed of four channels, cyan, magenta, yellow, and black. The remaining channels (sometimes referred to as alpha channels), up to a total of 24 channels, can be used for masking and special effects.

CIE color   A three-dimensional color space similar to the Lab Color mode in Photoshop that describes color with lightness values (grayscale tones independent of color) as one axis and two color axes, *a* (magenta/green) and *b* (yellow/blue). CIE Color was developed by Commission Internationale de l'Eclairage, an international organization that defined a color model, in 1931, as the basis for all colormetric measurements of color.

clipping path   A path that functions like a cookie cutter, masking everything outside the path and displaying or printing what is inside the path. Clipping paths are useful for creating silhouettes. To use a clipping path with a Photoshop image that will be placed in another program, the path must be saved with the file in the EPS format.

CMYK color   Cyan, magenta, yellow, and black are the four process inks used in offset color printing. Cyan, magenta, and yellow are referred to as the Subtractive primary colors. An image in CMYK color mode has four channels, one for each of the process colors, each of which print to a separate plate when output as color separations.

coated stock   Paper with a coating of clay that prevents ink from being absorbed, reducing the amount of halftone dot gain. A coated paper usually appears shinier than an uncoated paper. Because coated papers have less dot gain, colors appear more brilliant on a coated paper stock.

color cast   An undesirable, pervasive tint or wash of color in an image.

color correction   Changing colors in an image to correct for unwanted color casts or to create different color moods or effects

Color Keys   See *overlay proof*.

Color Management System   Software utility programs that translate between color spaces to ensure predictable matching colors on various output devices.

color separation   An image printed with each of its channels as a separate plate. Each separate plate can then be printed with a different ink color. A process color separation is printed as four plates, one for each process color: cyan, magenta, yellow, and black.

color wheel   The circular relationship of all colors, based on light frequency. Each hue appears on the color wheel at a unique angle, starting with red at 0° in a counterclockwise direction, then yellow at 60°, green at 120°, cyan at 180°, blue at 240°, and magenta at 300°.

comp   A comp (comprehensive) is a simulation of a printed piece prior to actually printing the project on the printing press. The comp is usually shown to a client for approval prior to printing.

complimentary colors   Colors directly across each other on the color wheel; adding a color's complement makes the original color grayer.

Compuserve GIF   See Appendix A, "File Formats."

constrain   To restrict the movement of a tool or selection by holding the Shift key. For example, you constrain when scaling a selection to maintain its aspect ratio or when drawing line to draw keep it horizontal or vertical.

continuous-tone image   An image with a gradated range of tones. A continuous-tone image must be converted to a halftone in order to print on a printing press.

contrast   The relationship of tones between the light and dark areas of an image. A high contrast image has bright highlights and dark shadows with few middle grays. A low contrast image has many middle gray tones with no whites or blacks.

crop   A rectangular selection in an image that remains after the crop while the unselected portions is deleted.

crop marks   Short lines printed at the corners near the edges of an image indicating where to trim the image after printing. If an image is to bleed, it should extend slightly beyond the crop marks.

custom color   See *spot color*.

DCS Desktop Color Separation. A file format defined by Quark and used by many vendors for the separation of color images on a PostScript printer. Photoshop saves five EPS files; four files contain high resolution CMYK separation data, one for each process color (cyan, magenta, yellow, and black); the fifth "master file" is placed in a page layout program (for example, QuarkXPress). The "master" EPS file contains a preview of the image and a low resolution PostScript version for proofing. When output to an imagesetter as separations, the high-resolution CMYK files are linked and printed to each color plate. A later specification of DCS 2.0 allows more than four separations, facilitating spot color separations.

default The standard settings that already exist in a program

defloat To duplicate a floating selection in its exact position without deselecting it

defringe Blends the pixels along the edge of a selection to seamlessly merge it with a new background.

densitometer An instrument that measures the density of any tone: printed halftones, continuous tone, film, or paper.

density The measurement indicating how much an area will block or absorb light. Darker or more opaque areas will have higher density values.

density range The difference between the density of the lightest (highlights) and the darkest (shadows) parts of an image.

digital Computer data in the form of discrete 0 or 1 digits (on or off), as opposed to continuous analog data.

digital camera A camera with CCDs in place of film that reads light digitally, bypassing the need for photographic film.

digital print A page output from digital data directly to a printer attached to a computer. A color printer can print a composite image for comprehensives or presentations. If calibrated, some digital printers can be used to make digital proofs prior to making actual color separations to film.

direction lines The lines that control a Bézier curve on a vector path. Direction lines are tangent to the curve at the anchor point.

dithering To simulate additional grays or colors by turning adjacent pixels into different colors or values, such as scattering yellow and red pixels together to represent orange. This technique can be used on both computer monitors and output devices to represent more grays or colors than the devices can actually produce. In the case of a 1-bit Bitmap image, dithering simulates gray tones by scattering black or white pixels. Dithering can be used on a printer as a way to render continuous tone images.

dodge and burn   Dodging an area lightens the tones and burning darkens the tones. Photoshop goes beyond conventional darkroom printing by allowing dodging and burning to selectively affect highlights, midtones, or shadows.

dot gain   Due to absorption, halftone dots usually swell when printed on paper, causing images to print darker.

dpi   Dots per inch, number of pixels measuring resolution on output devices such as monitors and printers.

drum scanner   A high-resolution digitizing device that can scan reflective or transparent art

DSP   digital signal processor installed on a computer's acceleration board, which speeds up certain operations in Photoshop

duotone   An offset printed image created with two different colors of ink

emulsion   The photosensitive layer on photographic film, paper, or printing plates.

EPS   Encapsulated PostScript. A popular and flexible graphic format for storing object-oriented graphics and bit-mapped, grayscale and RGB images, used on most computer platforms. The EPS file usually consists of two parts: the PostScript description for printing resolution-independent graphics on a PostScript printer, and a low-resolution bit-mapped preview. On a Macintosh the preview image for cropping and scaling in a page layout program is stored as PICT; on a PC it is stored as TIFF.

fade-out rate   The rate at which the mark of the paint brush or airbrush fades out, or runs out of ink, as in the actual stroke of a brush or fountain pen.

feathered edge   The graduated area along the edge of a selection that, in part, changes when manipulating the selection, giving the area a softened edge

fill   To alter a selected area, covering or combining it with a gray shade, a color, or a pattern

film recorder   A device for outputting digital images to continuous-tone photographic film

Filmstrip   A file format developed by Adobe, which allows sequential images from a movie to be transferred between Premiere and Photoshop

filter In photography a filter is placed in front of the lens on a camera to distort or modify the light rays. The filters in Photoshop simulate these effects by mathematically moving, altering, combining, and replacing pixels in an image.

flatten To combine all visible layers in a Photoshop document into a single layer.

floating selection A moveable selection that is active and above a layer. A floating selection can be manipulated without affecting the pixel data underneath it.

Focoltone A trademarked color matching system that uses *process color inks*. The standard attempts to guarantee that a color chosen during the design process will match the ink used to produce the final product.

font The name of a typeface

fringe The pixels along the border of a selection that contain a combination of the selection and background colors.

fuzziness The amount of anti-aliasing along the edges of a selection

gamma The amount of change between input and output values represented by the slope of a line, which usually has a greater change at the midtone. Gamma is used to describe a monitor's contrast and brightness.

gamut The available range of colors for a particular input, display or output device or process. For example, color monitors have a different gamut than do CMYK inks.

gradient fill A fill that creates a gradual transition from one color to another

gray balance The amount of cyan, magenta, and yellow combined to make a neutral gray—important in the proofing and printing process

gray-component replacement (GCR) The removal of a mixture of cyan, magenta, and yellow, replacing it with black. GCR affects larger areas of the image and uses more black than UCR.

grayscale image A single channel, 8-bit image with up to 256 levels of gray per pixel.

halftone The reproduction of a continuous-tone image made by breaking up the tones into variously sized evenly spaced dots. Halftones are made photographically by exposing the photograph through a screen or digitally by creating halftone cells from smaller device pixels.

halftone cell   The pattern of device pixels that is repeated in a digital halftone screen. The shape of the pattern may be round, elliptical, linear, or other.

high-key image   Light, possibly overexposed image, with few dark tones, such as a polar bear in the snow

highlight   The lightest part of an image. In a halftone a highlight has the smallest dots, or no dots.

histogram   A graph showing the number of pixels in a color or gray value in a selection, layer, or image

HSB Color Model   A color model in which colors are represented by hue, saturation, and brightness. The Apple and Windows Color Pickers use the HSB model to describe colors.

hue   Color measured by its wavelength of light. Hue is represented by a position on the color wheel.

imagesetter   A device used to output computer-generated pages or images at high resolution onto photographic film or paper

indexed color image   An 8 bit color image with a limited palette of up to 256 colors

input device   Hardware that digitizes analog data to enter it into the computer

interlaced   The method of displaying images on television monitors using two fields of even and odd lines that oscillate back and forth.

interpolation   A method in which Photoshop creates pixel data from existing neighboring pixels when an image is resampled, resized, rotated, or transformed.

inverse   To select everything in an image except the original selection

invert   Converts an image to its negative

JPEG   See Appendix A, "File Formats."

kern   To manually adjust the spacing between characters in type

Lab color   The Lab Color mode is based on a model of visual color perception using a standard created in 1931 by the Commission Internationale de L' Éclairage (CIE). Color values are defined mathematically to exist independent of any device.

labels   A printing option to place the document and channel names next to the image.

laminated proof   A proof created from process color separation negatives in which four process color pigment layers are laminated to a sheet of white paper to create the color image. Examples are Cromalin (DuPont), MatchPrint (3M), and PressMatch (Hoechst).

layer   A plane of an image, similar to a transparent overlay. Photoshop can have up to 99 layers in addition to the background which facilitate the compositing images.

leading   The measurement of lines of text from baseline to baseline

lightness   The brightness component of an image without regard to hue or saturation. In the Lab color mode, lightness is represented by a grayscale channel.

line art   High-contrast black and white artwork that has no gray tones

linear fill   A graduated fill projected from one point to another in a straight line.

low key image   A dark, possibly under-exposed, image with few light tones.

lossy compression   When compressing a file, a loss of data

lossless compression   Data compression without any loss of data

lpi   Lines per inch, a measure of halftone resolution or screen frequency

luminance   The grayscale component of an image, independent of the color aspects

MacPaint   A graphic file format on the Macintosh for storing 1-bit bitmapped images that originated with the program of the same name. See Appendix A, "File Formats."

midtone   The tonal value located halfway between the highlight value and the shadow value.

moiré pattern   An undesirable pattern produced by overlaying or combining two or more patterns. Moiré patterns can occur when printing more than one halftone screen over each other on a printing press, when outputting a halftone screen on a digital printer, or when scanning an image printed with halftone screen. This problem can be minimized with the use of proper screen angles and screen frequencies.

multichannel image   A mode in Photoshop representing an image that has more than one channel, up to 24 in Photoshop 3

neutral color Gray without a color cast. In RGB Color mode, equal amounts of red, green, and blue make a neutral color

newsprint A cheap, extremely porous type of paper with high dot gain

noise A random grainy texture applied to an image. In subtle amounts noise simulates the natural grain in film.

NTSC National Television Standard Committee, which defines television signal standards in the Americas

object-oriented graphic A graphic made up of distinct objects that can be individually edited, layered, scaled, and transformed. When printed with the PostScript language, these objects are imaged at a finer quality on high-resolution printers and imagesetters.

on-line services Electronic, interactive communications services for accessing information, software, electronic mail, and bulletin boards

opacity The amount of transparency when combining a fill color, painted color, pattern, floating selection, or layer with another layer or background.

output device Hardware that converts digital information into viewable, readable, or aural form, such as a printer, a monitor, film recorder, video recorder, etc.

overlay proof A proof created from color separation negatives, which use sheets of acetate placed on top of each other to create the color image. Each film layer represents one of the colors. Examples are Color Keys (3M) and Chromacheck (DuPont).

palette A floating, interactive control panel in Photoshop

path A vector line described by Bézier curves

pattern An image that repeats in tiles to form a regular design.

PCI The Peripheral Component Interconnect bus. A high-speed slot in PC/Windows systems that can be used for video cards and hard disks.

PCX See Appendix A, "File Formats."

phosphors Tiny red, green, and blue lamps that light up each pixel in a computer monitor.

PICS The PICS format, a type of PICT Resource file, is a common file format designed for the exchange of animation sequences between programs.

PICT See Appendix A, "File Formats."

pixel Acronym for picture element, a single dot on a computer display or in a digital image. A *pixel device* is the smallest dot that can be made by an output device like a laser printer.

plug-in module Software that can be added to Photoshop (often developed by third-party vendors) that adds functions not normally available in the standard Adobe Photoshop application. Place plug-in modules in the specified plug-ins folder.

PMS Pantone Matching System is a trademarked standard for specifying and producing *spot colors* using proprietary ink mixes. It attempts to guarantee that a color chosen during the design process will match the ink used to produce the final product.

PMT photomultiplier tube; a light sensitive tube used in drum scanners

posterization Graduated tones or colors converted into a specific number of steps. Photographically, a posterization is made with a series of high contrast line shots (threshold).

PostScript A device-independent computer language developed by Adobe Systems and specifically designed to describe text, object-oriented graphics, and bit-mapped, grayscale, and color images. Using this language, the same page can be printed on output devices of different resolutions and color capabilities.

ppi Pixels per inch, the standard measurement for scanning and image resolution (sometimes referred to as samples per inch)

primary colors When mixing paint or pigments the primary colors are red, yellow, and blue. When mixing colors with light, the additive primary colors are red, green, and blue, and the subtractive primary colors are cyan, magenta, and yellow. See *additive primary colors* and *subtractive primary colors*.

process color separation An image that has been separated into the four process colors—cyan, magenta, yellow, and black (CMYK). When a computer application produces this separation, it prints a separate plate for each of these colors.

progressive color bar A bar printed on process color separations, showing all possible combinations of cyan, magenta, yellow, and sometimes black, which are used to ensure proper ink coverage and color.

quadtone An offset printed image created with four different colors of ink

quarter (1/4) tone The tonal value located approximately halfway between highlight and midtone

QuickEdit   A plug-in module that allows Photoshop to open and edit a section of another Photoshop file without having to open the entire document

QuickTime   An extension used to play back video or movies with sound on a Mac or PC

radial fill   A fill projected from a central point outward in all directions

random access memory (RAM)   Computer memory that stores information temporarily while working on a computer

raster   An image that exists bit by bit, as pixels in a graph, and is synonymous with bit-mapped image. Scanned images are always rasterized.

rasterize   To convert digital information, or object-oriented Bézier curves, into a grid of pixels for an output device or to be processed in a raster program like Photoshop

RAW   See Appendix A, "File Formats."

registration marks   Marks that appear on a printed image, generally for color separations, to help align the various printed plates

remap colors   The computer's attempt to match the original colors in a document with similar colors in the new palette

repeat rate   The rate at which paint is deposited on an image by the painting and editing tools when the mouse is stationary

resample   To change the resolution of an image. Resampling down discards pixel information; resampling up adds pixel information through interpolation.

resize   To change the size of an image while maintaining its resolution

resolution   The number of pixels per inch or centimeters in an image; total pixels in a document; or the number of dots per inch or centimeter used by an output device

RGB image   A three-channel image produced by projected red, green, and blue light

RIP   Raster Image Processor. The processor on an output device that rasterizes the PostScript description of a page so that it may be imaged by the output device

rosette   The tight cluster of halftone cells created when two or more halftone screens are properly oriented when printed over each other

saturation   Color purity. More gray in a color results in lower saturation, less gray results in higher saturation. Colors at the edge of the color wheel are more saturated, with saturation decreasing towards the center.

scanner   An electronic input device that digitizes images or objects into the computer

scratch disk   A virtual memory scheme used by Photoshop to temporarily use hard disk space to substitute for RAM (see *virtual memory*).

screen angles   The angles at which halftone screens are placed

screen frequency   The number of dots on the halftone screen, commonly measured in lines per inch

screen tint   A screened percentage of a solid color producing a lighter shade

selection   The active area of a document, identified by marching ants on its borders. Manipulations affect only inside the selection area.

shadow   The darkest areas in an image, represented in a halftone by the largest dots

sharpen   To enhance the contrast at edges of light and dark shapes to make an image appear more in focus

spacing   The distance between the pixels that are affected by each painting and editing tool

specular highlight   A perfectly white highlight (no halftone dots)

spot color   A method of color reproduction where the printer uses a custom ink on the printing press for each of the colors used on the page. Photoshop can print spot colors from the Duotone Color mode or from additional channels.

subtractive primary colors   Cyan, magenta, and yellow inks or other colorants used in process or digital color printing to render different colors. When cyan, magenta, and yellow are combined they produce black.

swap file   Microsoft Windows terminology for virtual memory. A contiguous area of a hard disk that Windows and most applications, including Photoshop, use to store or swap parts of themselves when more memory is needed or when these applications are not being used.

System Resources   A small 64Kb segment or heap of memory that Windows and all Windows applications use. Each window, icon, dialog box, and palette also consumes these resources.

Targa   See Appendix A, "File Formats."

three-quarter (3/4) tone   The tonal value located approximately halfway between the midtone and shadow.

TIFF   Tag Image File Format. A raster graphic file format widely used as an interchange format for images on most computer platforms. One of the most flexible and reliable formats, it has subtypes capable of storing 1-bit, 8-bit gray-scale, RGB, and CMYK images. The TIFF format is well supported by page layout, illustration, and color separation programs. See Appendix A, "File Formats."

tolerance   A variable setting for the Magic Wand and Paint Bucket tools, it controls the range of colors to be selected and filled.

toolbox   The floating palette of tools in Photoshop for selecting, painting, and editing images.

total ink limit   The maximum amount of ink a printing press can handle, measured as a percentage and representing the sum of percentages of the process color inks. It will vary according to the paper stock used.

Toyo   A system of custom color inks developed in Japan

trap   An slight overlap, either a choke or spread, of one color next to another color to prevent gaps from appearing along the edges of shapes due to misregistration on the printing press

tritone   An offset printed image created with three different colors of ink

TrueType   A font technology built into System 7 on the Macintosh and Windows 3.1

uncoated stock   Paper that is not coated with a layer of clay and which absorbs ink more readily. Dot gain is greater on uncoated paper than on coated paper.

undercolor removal (UCR)   Reducing the cyan, magenta, and yellow inks from the darkest neutral shadow areas in an image, replacing them with black ink

unsharp mask   A method of enhacing the perceived sharpness of an image by increasing the contrast at the edges of shapes in an image.

value   The relative lightness and darkness of a color or tone

vector graphics   See *object-oriented graphics*

VESA   The Video Electronics Standards Association bus. A high speed slot in PC/Windows systems which can be used for video cards and hard disks

virtual memory   The memory space separate from the main memory (physical RAM), such as hard disk space. Virtual memory allows you to work on large documents without requiring large amounts of RAM. (In Windows, this is referred do as a permanent *swap file*.)

Windows 95   The next version of Microsoft Windows, which is scheduled for release in 1995

zoom   To magnify or reduce your view of the current document

Index

Notes